# *Advance Blurbs for* Journey into Europe: Islam, Immigration, and Identity

Akbar Ahmed's profound and careful inquiries have greatly enriched our understanding of Islam in the modern world. His latest study, based on direct research with a group of young scholars, explores the complex interfaith reality of Europe, both in history and today, from an Eastern perspective, reversing the familiar paradigm. It is sure to be yet another influential contribution, one greatly needed in a world riven by conflicts and misunderstanding.

> Noam Chomsky, *Institute Professor and Professor of Linguistics (Emeritus), Massachusetts Institute of Technology*

Akbar Ahmed and his globe-trotting team of young scholars have done it again! Adding to a vital and urgently needed body of exemplary work, *Journey into Europe* provides an antidote to the fear and ignorance that is too prevalent in contemporary discourse. Ahmed delivers empowering knowledge combined with heartfelt compassion. Read it and share it.

> John Milewski, *Director of Digital Programming and Moderator and Managing Editor of Wilson Center NOW, Woodrow Wilson International Center for Scholars*

A deeply engaged and brilliantly executed book by one of our most distinguished anthropologists and public intellectuals. I know no other that throws as much light on the subject as it does. Read widely as it should be, it will make the world a less agonizing place.

> Baron Bhikhu Parekh, *former Professor of Political Theory at the University of Hull, Vice Chairman of the U.K. Commission for Racial Equality, Chairman of the Commission on the Future of Multi-Ethnic Britain, and Centennial Professor in the Study of Global Governance at the London School of Economics*

This book is essential reading to all who want to understand our world. As a South Asian Christian I can say with pride South Asia has produced two Akbars—Akbar the Great, the emperor who united India, and Akbar Ahmed, who brings peace and harmony among the nations through research and knowledge. Akbar who I have known for decades is my brother and my hero. He belongs to all of humanity. Long live the passion of Akbar to see one harmonious world with animosity and hatred for none.

> COUNCILLOR DR JAMES SHERA, *MBE, S.Pk., Former Mayor of Rugby, England, Freeman of the Borough of Rugby, and Distinguished Formanite*

Ambassador Akbar Ahmed is a treasure. His voice, insights, wisdom, and experience are desperately needed right now when so much U.S. and European policy toward the Muslim world is guided by fear, ignorance, and greed. We applaud Akbar Ahmed, perhaps the best-known scholar of Islam today, for continuing to enlighten us through his quartet of studies. *Journey into Europe: Islam, Immigration, and Identity*, the fourth in the series, is indispensable reading given the state of affairs today.

> OLIVER STONE AND PETER KUZNICK, *filmmakers and authors of* The Untold History of the United States

Akbar Ahmed has rightly acquired a reputation as one of the foremost scholars on Islam and Muslims in the modern world. His latest project, *Journey into Europe*, demonstrates yet again his unique talent for conveying complex ideas through accessible language, combining rigorous scholarship with compelling personal anecdotes based in intensive fieldwork, and relating today's problems to their oft-forgotten historical context. I strongly recommend this outstanding study to anyone interested in the ongoing discussion about Muslims and their contribution to European society.

> MASOOD AHMED, *President of the Center for Global Development*

Ambassador Akbar's exploration and insight into issues affecting European Muslims are needed now more than ever. Extremism fosters an environment of suspicion, and suspicion is born from ignorance; therefore Professor Akbar's detailed analysis will undoubtedly help governments, policymakers, and civic society to better tackle radicalisation in Europe.

> HUMZA YOUSAF, *Minister for Transport and the Islands, former Minister for Europe and International Development, and Member of the Scottish Parliament*

The Muslim world faces the most critical challenge in modern history with Islam under siege both from within and by the West, where Islamophobia is now widespread. Amid the unconscionable silence of Muslim political leadership and the faint voices of Islamic scholars, the inhumanity of radicals has come to represent Islam. Akbar Ahmed, whom I have had the pleasure of knowing since we trained together at the Civil Service Academy in Lahore half a century ago, has emerged to offer a rare voice of exceptional force, clarity, and dare I say sanity. His landmark study in four volumes representing outstanding scholarship should have a lasting historical impact in improving relations between Islam and the West and is indispensable reading.

> TOUQIR HUSSAIN, *Adjunct Professor at Georgetown University, senior Pakistan visiting fellow at the School of Advanced International Studies at Johns Hopkins University, and former Pakistani Ambassador and diplomatic adviser to the Prime Minister of Pakistan*

Akbar Ahmed cuts across disciplines with geographical breadth and historical vision, allowing him to illustrate that understanding Islam today means understanding ourselves. "Us" and "Them" are intimately connected. As anthropologist, ambassador, and humanitarian, Dr. Ahmed pursues policies of sanity, replacing fear with co-existence, and ignorance with documentation using film and the written word. All are issues of national security, both here and elsewhere.

> LAURA NADER, *Professor of Anthropology, University of California, Berkeley*

Of all the scholars I have studied, the work of none is quite so uniquely characterized as that of Akbar Ahmed by what traditional Islamic scholars called looking at the world through "two eyes," or Dhul Aynan—the capacity to see the exterior and the interior, the spiritual and the physical, the emotional and the scientific—which enables the accurate and fair understanding of different perspectives. He brings the same quality to his project on Muslims in Europe, and he makes me especially proud as a Muslim European.

MIRNES KOVAC, *editor,* Preporod Islamic Magazine, *and author,* The Siege of Islam

Ambassador Akbar Ahmed's tireless quest for coexistence and peace is essential for the planet's future. Either we explore the path to coexistence, or we shall be condemned to perish. Akbar Ahmed shows us the right path in this book. It is a treasure of understanding and wisdom. We are grateful to him for pursuing his admirable and noble quest.

FADELA MOHATAR, *President of the Institute of Cultures and Minister of Culture and Festivities, Melilla, Spain*

This project should be required in the classrooms of Europe and the world. Understanding that every continent is a collection of civilizations, not a clash of them, can only help the next generation overcome the shortcomings of this one.

NATHAN KING, *correspondent, CCTV America*

Akbar Ahmed continues his lifetime's work of building bridges of understanding between the Muslim and non-Muslim worlds. Against simplistic views of a "clash of civilizations," his combination of historical rigor and deep humanity reminds us of the long history of Muslims in Europe. *Journey into Europe* is an important and timely reminder that what binds us together is more important than what separates us. Where before this work was important, I would venture to say that now it is a matter of survival. Take courage, my dear friend; as Shelley said, "Ye are many, they are few."

PETER MOREY, *former Professor of English and Postcolonial Studies, University of East London, Leadership Fellow for Muslims, Trust and Cultural Dialogue project, coauthor of* Framing Muslims: Stereotyping and Representation after 9/11, *and Chair in English Literature, University of Birmingham*

Akbar Ahmed follows his earlier *Journey into Islam* and *Journey into America* with this brilliant new book. Along with his team of researchers, he has crisscrossed the continent to meet with a wide range of political figures and religious leaders of all faiths to help us understand social, political, and religious dynamics within Europe today. His deep empirical knowledge and engaging writing style will ensure this book is of interest to scholars, policymakers, and general readers.

JAMES GOLDGEIER, *former Dean of the School of International Service, American University*

Dr. Ahmed and his team explored the length and breadth of the continent as part of the project to examine the place of Islam and Muslims in European history and civilization. . . . It goes without saying all this is aimed at what the don calls "building bridges in an uncomfortable time" between the followers of the great Abrahamic faiths who form nearly half of the world. And given the yawning gulf that currently exists between them, this is nothing short of a Herculean task. A true jihad, if you will — the great jihad that all of us need to fight. This may be why the Prophet, peace be upon him, said, as often quoted by Prof. Ahmed in his lectures, that "the ink of the scholar is more sacred than the blood of the martyr."

AIJAZ ZAKA SYED, *columnist,* The News

In a time fraught with suspicions and uncertainties between faiths, some individuals continue to challenge the notion that the twains will never meet. One of them is Ambassador Akbar Ahmed, a world-renowned anthropologist, Islamic scholar and a filmmaker. He has been credited by many with contributing to the forging of better communication protocols and improving relations between the Muslim and the Western worlds. This is precisely the message that must resonate loud and clear: Christians, Muslims, Jews, and people of other beliefs must join hands and promote peace. We cannot just nod our heads and not be proactive. We must within our sphere of influence try to eliminate sowing discord and suspicion against those whose beliefs may differ from ours.

TARIQ A. AL-MAEENA, *columnist,* Saudi Gazette

Dr. Ahmed's *Journey into Europe* is about Europe. It is about how Europe should be more cohesive, more coherent, and more integrative. His captivating and gripping odyssey takes us from Andalusia to Sicily to the Balkans to Britain to France to Germany to Denmark—all places jolted periodically by the tremors of simmering religious discord. He gives us hope.

    MASOOD KHAN, *President of Azad Jammu and Kashmir*

Set against the background of increasing nativism and religious prejudice, *Journey into Europe* gives us deep insights into the current mood in Europe with respect to Islam. Professor Ahmed's thought-provoking and meticulously researched book based on extensive fieldwork throughout Europe points to the urgent need to find constructive strategies for overcoming these pervasive divisions.

    ANTHONY QUAINTON, *former U.S. Ambassador and Distinguished Diplomat in Residence, American University*

Akbar Ahmed has that rare combination of brilliance, enthusiasm, and empathy. He bridges communities by tearing down mythologies. As Islam continues to be vilified, his latest project shows how Islam has shaped the European experience and how Muslims have enriched life on the continent. This is an extraordinary and welcome intervention.

    ARJUN SINGH SETHI, *Adjunct Professor of Law at Georgetown University Law Center, former adviser with the ACLU, and Co-Chair of the American Bar Association's Committee on Homeland Security, Terrorism, and Treatment of Enemy Combatants*

Akbar Ahmed's historically deep, anthropologically rich work is an incredibly important contribution to building understanding between peoples in this dangerous time of growing intolerance in Europe and worldwide. "A way has to be found," Dr. Ahmed believes, discussing *Journey into Europe*, "where different peoples can live together in peace irrespective of their race and religion." Dr. Ahmed deserves tremendous thanks and credit for the many ways he is helping to forge that way toward peace.

    DAVID VINE, *Associate Professor of Anthropology, American University, and author of* Base Nation: How U.S. Military Bases Abroad Harm America and the World

In these times of rising fear and uncertainty, xenophobia, and re-emerging tribalism in the continent of Europe, Ambassador Akbar Ahmed's *Journey into Europe* is essential reading. As a Dutch native and global citizen, I—as so many but by no means all of my fellow Europeans do—strongly reject the recent rise of intolerance in my region of origin. Akbar Ahmed's work combines his anthropological knowledge, historical insights, and his considerable wisdom into a cohesive message to us, Europeans—guidance we most certainly need in building a more inclusive Europe for the 21st century. Akbar's monumental four-year study gracefully offers us the tools: now Europe, the choice to hear his message is ours.

> BRAM GROEN, *Senior Professorial Lecturer, School of International Service, American University*

The final element of his quartet, *Journey into Europe* provides an insightful and moving analysis of Islam and Muslims in Europe, the roles of culture and identity, and how they interact with the frayed modern democratic ideal. Akbar Ahmed delivers his argument with clarity and care. Combining theories and insights from anthropology, sociology, political science, history, philosophy, and theology, this study challenges many misconceptions about Europe and Islam, while giving us all hope for the future.

> TODD LANDMAN, *Professor of Political Science and Pro-Vice-Chancellor of the Faculty of Social Sciences, University of Nottingham*

*Journey into Europe* travels across the continent narrating stories of Islam that are inspiring, heartbreaking, and sensitive to the region they are a part of. Akbar Ahmed's measured insights are a much-needed intervention in a polarized debate on Islam in Europe and give us an original and compassionate understanding of the histories of Muslim communities and their integration in Europe. With a passionate commitment to scholarship, interfaith dialogue, and bridge building, this path-breaking study shows us how and why the story of Islam is an essential component of European life.

> AMINA YAQIN, *Senior Lecturer in Urdu and Postcolonial Studies, University of London*

*Journey into Europe* is a timeless and valuable contribution to the understanding of the diverse Muslim communities in Europe that helps the reader to overcome stereotypes and fears.

ANGELIKI ZIAKA, *Associate Professor of Religion, Aristotle University of Thessaloniki, Greece*

I don't exaggerate when I say that today Akbar Ahmed is the most knowledgeable scholar writing on Islam and the way the religion is affecting global affairs. In his extensive coverage of the subject he has brought new insights policymakers in the West would do well to understand. In my own work what I have found most helpful is Professor Ahmed's finding that Islam's appeal to some of the extremist elements in Muslim societies should be understood in the context of the survival of tribalism in the structure and value systems of some of the societies that are contributing recruits to Islamist causes. In dealing with these dissidents, the use of force is not the preferred solution. What would work ultimately is the development and modernization of these societies.

SHAHID JAVED BURKI, *former Vice President of the World Bank, former Finance Minister of Pakistan, and author of* Rising Powers and Global Governance

In the midst of a world burning down fast in the fires of xenophobia and hatred, where suspicion against Islam in particular is widening the divide between Muslims and the West, Akbar Ahmed offers invaluable insights by drawing our attention not only to his lived experience as a South Asian in postcolonial Europe but also to the "missing millennium," a transformative chapter of European history when Europe's Muslims initiated a legacy of convivencia or "peaceful coexistence," enabling Western civilization to be lifted out of "the dark ages." This book demonstrates why the West's omissions and distortions of Islam are damaging not only to Muslims, who are increasingly being made targets of Islamophobia, but are symptomatic of a diminishing civilization, one that perpetuates falsehoods that are ultimately self-destructive. The greatest gift of this work is that it teaches us the art of bridge building across differences as it reinvigorates the historical ties that have been mutually beneficial to Muslims and the West in the past.

SHADAB ZEEST HASHMI, *poet and author of* Baker of Tarifa *and* Kohl & Chalk, *and former Visiting Professor at San Diego State University*

# Journey into
# Europe

# Journey into Europe

## ISLAM, IMMIGRATION, AND IDENTITY

AKBAR AHMED

BROOKINGS INSTITUTION PRESS
*Washington, D.C.*

The Brookings Institution is a private nonprofit organization devoted to research, education, and publication on important issues of domestic and foreign policy. Its principal purpose is to bring the highest quality independent research and analysis to bear on current and emerging policy problems. Interpretations or conclusions in Brookings publications should be understood to be solely those of the authors.

*Library of Congress Cataloging-in-Publication data are available.*

ISBN 978-0-8157-2758-3 (cloth : alk. paper)
ISBN 978-0-8157-2759-0 (ebook)

9 8 7 6 5 4 3 2 1

Typeset in Adobe Caslon

Composition by Westchester Publishing Services

*Dedicated with love to*
*Gabriel Akbar Ahmed,*
*Zeenat Ahmed,*
*and Frankie Martin*

# CONTENTS

# Journey into
# Europe

# PART ONE

*European Dialectic*

# Europe: Turbulent and Mighty Continent

GREECE WAS DYING in the summer of 2013, and the drama around the event was as poignant as anything Sophocles has written. I was in Athens to deliver some lectures, but I was witnessing, if press reports were to be believed, what appeared to be the imminent downfall of the cradle of Western civilization and the disturbing inertia toward its plight displayed by the rest of the European family of nations. The pillars of a functioning state were shaking: inflation, unemployment, and the national debt were out of control, and law and order on the verge of collapse. The dying process was confirmed when one day state TV was abruptly and indefinitely suspended as employees could no longer receive their salaries.

The last straw was the steady trickle of desperate refugees arriving from North Africa, the Middle East, and South Asia swelling the ranks of those impoverished migrants already present. Squeezed by the economic crisis, the traditionally hospitable Greeks vented their frustrations at the unending numbers of refugees and immigrants as they sought aid and refuge; and the greater the economic woes, the greater the popularity of the Far Right parties and the more extreme their rhetoric of hate. Groups like the Golden Dawn, with their swastika-like emblem, were parading about dressed up as faux-Nazis, giving Nazi salutes, and even displaying pictures of Adolf Hitler. Their target this time around was the mainly Muslim refugee and immigrant community. Their message was simple and effective, and it was influencing how people thought about the subject: Muslims were not part of European identity, nor had they contributed anything to Western civilization. In short, Muslims had no right to be in Europe. Clearly, the cherished European ideals of humanism and multiculturalism that allowed for

3

the accommodation and integration of immigrant communities were being challenged.

It was with this foreboding sense of being on the cusp of history that I found myself that hot summer in a crowded basement with members of the Muslim community. It was Friday, and I had been invited by the Muslim leaders of Athens to join the prayers and address the congregation after the formal sermon. Appreciating the downtrodden state of the community, I was determined to make an appearance, as I thought my visit would be a small gesture of support.

As I collected my thoughts to address the congregation, some 400 in number, I was strangely unsettled to contemplate that in Athens, a major European capital that has a Muslim population of several hundred thousand, there was not a single actual mosque. The "mosque" I found myself in was a large, dark, and dank parking garage of a particularly sinister aspect. The low ceiling with ugly aluminum air ducts, the absence of any cooling facilities, and the sickly smell of the sweat and desperation of the worshippers packed tightly into its confined space created a claustrophobic atmosphere. I have never been a fan of underground parking lots, having seen too many scenes in movies of ravening, crazy, blood-thirsty men wielding machetes or chainsaws running amok there. And this was as menacing a basement as any good Hollywood director of a B movie could imagine. My instincts were not wrong. Members of the congregation described incidents in which neo-Nazi thugs had blocked the entrances to similar makeshift mosques in Athens; some had even been firebombed. The community lived in terror, as one young male Egyptian migrant confirmed: "The neo-Nazis placed notices outside of our mosque, threatening to slaughter us like chickens and burn down the mosque if we did not leave the country." With a shiver of anxiety, he added, "We are living like dogs here."

The congregants were mostly men from the Middle East and South Asia—Syrians, Iraqis, Afghans, and Pakistanis. I could see the beads of perspiration on the drawn and unshaven faces looking up at me. Their impoverishment hung over them like a dark cloud. I felt empathy for the immigrants whose only crime was their frantic need to seek refuge abroad for their families and themselves from the chaos and persecution at home. They had undertaken a hazardous journey to Europe in leaky boats and overcrowded vehicles, determined to find safety. The Syrians among them were escaping Bashar al-Assad's chemical and mustard-gas attacks, the use of cluster bombs, the destruction of their homes, and the real danger of the slaughter of their families. They had come to Europe hoping to salvage their lives. But here, it was a congregation of broken dreams.

My speech that day was one of the most difficult I have delivered in my life. But it was not the stifling heat, the audience, or the venue that made it so; it was the brutal realization of the plight of my community of Muslims—the *ummah.* Throughout their lives, Muslims evoke the two greatest names of God in Islam—the Compassionate and the Merciful—and dream of a world of peace and justice for which they must strive. Here, as I stood up to speak, I saw little evidence of these noble ideals. I could not help but wonder if the condition of this community was indeed a metaphor for the global ummah.

I felt a mild sense of unease at the free-floating anger and desperation that permeated the community and hinted at menace. These men had nothing to lose, and I could imagine the most desperate among them prepared to lash out in an unpredictable and even murderous manner. Their predicament needed to be handled with urgency, sympathy, and resolute common sense. This, I felt, was Europe's ticking time bomb.

In my sermon I could not just say that their lives would improve overnight in their present situation or that they would find peace if they were sent home; on the other hand, if I offered them empty words of optimism, they would sense the hollowness of my message. Yet if I did not give them some hope, I would be failing my fellow Muslims by not comforting them. It took all my optimism and faith, therefore, to deliver a message of hope. I asked them to take inspiration from the example of the Prophet of Islam, who had faced enormous challenges throughout his life, including assassination attempts, with patience, compassion, and courage. As for their mosque, I told them that a mosque is defined by the power and beauty of the faith in the hearts of its worshippers, not by the calligraphy and tiles of its building. This basement, I said, is as beautiful a mosque as any in the world.

Afterward we sat on the floor in a corner and the congregants gathered around me. They were bursting to tell their stories. Many told me of their ordeal as refugees and immigrants; they wanted to share the utter misery of their lives with me. Several of them remarked that they felt abandoned by their own communities and that I was, in fact, the first Muslim of any note who had bothered to visit them. They had never even seen an embassy official joining them. The young Pakistani men told us in hushed voices of being chased, kicked, and beaten by mobs while the public looked on or joined in. The police had stood by watching and in fact appeared to collude with the mobs. Some who had been in Greece longer than the more recent migrants spoke with sorrow of what once seemed a pleasant and welcoming land but had recently turned hostile against immigrants, especially Muslims. One of these early migrants, who said he had once belonged to the defense services in Pakistan, confessed that staying in Athens was too dangerous a risk. He was preparing to uproot himself after a successful two decades: his European dream had evaporated. They all noted the hostile role of the media in projecting an image of Muslims that conflated three words—Islam, terrorism, and migrants—and thereby created problems for them.

But even here in Europe as destitute refugees who had lost everything, Muslims were not learning lessons. They had brought their sectarian and ethnic rivalries with them. As we sat down to talk, several Arabs said to me earnestly, as you are an Islamic scholar, could you tell us whether as Sunnis we should consider the Shia to be Muslims? If not, asked a Syrian man, were they then liable to be punished by death? They had clearly been wrestling with the question, and it could be understood only in the context of the savagery inflicted on them by Assad in Syria and his Iranian supporters. I replied by asking whether the Shia believed in the Quran and accepted the Sunna and the example of the Prophet. They replied, yes. Then, I said, they are Muslim, and we must respect that fact. In Islam, only God decides who is a good or bad Muslim, I reminded them. They slinked back in apparent acquiescence.

Present were some leaders of the community including Naim Elghandour, an Egyptian businessman and president of the Muslim Association of Greece, and his Greek wife, Anna Stamou, a convert to Islam and the first candidate who wore a hijab to stand for a seat in the European Parliament. We had met at a lecture I gave soon after my arrival in Athens to a high-level interfaith gathering and at a well-attended public talk hosted by the prestigious Onassis Cultural Center. Both events were moderated by the renowned Greek scholar Sotiris Roussos, a fellow alumnus of the School of Oriental and African Studies (SOAS) in London. Later Anna, who is active in the Muslim Association, kindly assisted me in arranging excellent contacts with the local Muslim population of Xanthi in northern Greece near the Bulgarian border.

The Muslim community quickly became aware that I had been warmly received not only by Professor Roussos but in their respective offices by Bishop Gabriel of Diavleia, the chief secretary of the Holy Synod of the Church of Greece and the second-highest-ranking member of the Greek Orthodox Church, and George Kalantzis, the Greek government's secretary general for religious affairs. Roussos called the failure to build the

*Author and his team in Athens with Bishop Gabriel, the second-highest-ranking figure in the Greek Orthodox Church*

Athens mosque Greece's "shame." Bishop Gabriel, a prominent supporter of the mosque idea and of the Muslim community, described his work in the streets feeding migrants and said that he was "obliged to act as a true member of the Church" to see the migrants as people created in the image of God. The American ambassador received me at the U.S. embassy, and the British ambassador invited me to call on him at his residence, where, as an admirer of the Romantic Poets, I was delighted to read a letter by Lord Byron on display at the entrance. The Pakistan ambassador hosted a dinner in my honor. The leaders of the Muslim community were following my progress with a certain amount of pride and satisfaction. My arrival at the mosque thus had the effect of raising morale.

Present with me was Frankie Martin, my former student and a trusty assistant on all my major research projects for more than a decade, who was completing his master's degree in anthropology at Cambridge University. "Although I've worked with Professor Ahmed for many years and visited many mosques around the world, I was shocked and unprepared for what I encountered in Athens," he observed. "It was so saddening to think of the Syrians, Pakistanis, and others desperate to reach a better and safer life in Europe only to find a reality in Athens where they are stalked and brutalized simply because of who they are." Harrison Akins, my assistant at the time, had accompanied me from Washington, D.C., and described what he saw: "I couldn't help but be saddened by the fact that this claustrophobic space was where they went to find any measure of peace and solace from what I can only imagine to be an intolerable situation as immigrants in Athens." Also present was Ibrahim Khan Hoti, my teenage grandson, who had flown in from Islamabad, Pakistan, and was the advance guard for his mother, Amineh Hoti, who was to meet us later in London. He was astonished: "I was surprised and greatly disappointed to see that in one of the most famous and renowned cities in the world, one that has such a grand history and one that was the birthplace of democracy, a system that, ideally, should represent all walks of life, there was no legal mosque. It is still ironic when you see that Greece was once in the Ottoman Empire."

The refugees in that basement in Athens were like the first heavy drops of rain that precede the monsoons. The rains came shortly afterward and became a flood as hundreds of thousands of refugees arrived in Greece hoping to travel north to safety. Their arrival affected the way people saw Islam and their own national leaders. For a short while, Angela Merkel of Germany was elevated to cultural sainthood for her magnanimous response, and Viktor Orbán of Hungary was vilified in the media for his pusillanimous and hostile reception. Reputations were being made and destroyed and saints and villains were being created in the public mind by forces outside the political arena of Europe. Muslims had once again arrived on the continent and were directly affecting its internal balance and structure.

To some Europeans the presence of Muslim immigrants represented a third invasion—after the Arab and Ottoman invasions of centuries past. Yet the contrast between this latest Muslim invasion of Europe and the first one could not be greater. Islam first came to Europe when General Tariq ibn Ziyad, representing the Arab Umayyad dynasty in Damascus, landed in Spain in 711 and battled the Visigoths. His victory would eventually result in one of Europe's most celebrated civilizations—al-Andalus. There were moments in the turbulent sweep of Iberian history when different societies lived, worked, and prospered together. Muslims were then associated with art, architecture, literature, and philosophy. Their culture promoted libraries, colleges, and baths. They were also known for tolerance and acceptance of other cultures and religions. Their learning, confidence, prosperity, and power stand in stark contrast to the Muslims of Europe today. In another cruel contrast, the Muslims of al-Andalus reflected the glow of a powerful Arab superpower whose territory was larger than even the Roman Empire, whereas today they come from fragmented and violent societies in the throes of genocidal convulsions.

From this uprooted and broken Muslim community in Europe have emerged those who have repeatedly committed sickening acts of violence, killing themselves and others, regardless of religion, age, or gender, with the utmost heartlessness. After our visit to Athens, instances of Muslim terrorism exploded across Europe. Nothing was sacrosanct nor off limits—airports, editorial offices, cafés, nightclubs, sports stadiums, passenger trains, a promenade in a coastal city. The murder of an eighty-five-year-old priest in a church in Normandy by two Muslim teenagers in July 2016 prompted Pope Francis to declare, in an uncharacteristically somber mood, that "the world is at war"—while hastening to add that "it is not a war of religions." Pope Francis was not succumbing to the idea that the West and Islam were involved in a long-term "clash of civilizations," as propounded by scholars like Bernard Lewis and Samuel Huntington and publicly invoked and supported by prominent politicians like François Hollande and Manuel Valls.

One thing was abundantly clear: it was a matter of life and death to understand the European Muslims. From the presidents and prime ministers of Europe down to ordinary journalists, the question on people's minds was how to convert Jihadi John to Malleable Mustafa and Jihadi Jane to Loyal Leila. The problem was that this question could not be answered without proper understanding and knowledge of the Muslim community—its definition of its own identity, its leadership patterns, its religious and political players, the role of the imams, the position of mothers and women in the family, and relations with government and the broader public. While few people had the answers, these were precisely the questions that needed to be addressed.

The current dynamic agitating Europe is Islam; the long-drawn-out wars between Catholics and Protestants, the struggle against the Ottomans, the steady and large-scale migrations to America, the world wars, and the confrontation between the West and the Soviet Union are no longer center stage. On philosophic, political, and cultural levels, Islam is central to the discussion about Europe. Islam affects a wide range of people, from young Muslims unsure of what to make of their faith and its place in Europe to the leaders of the Far Right who project their political philosophy and strategy as a war against it.

In that encounter in the gloomy basement in Athens, I witnessed the problems of Europe today. I saw the need to conduct a detailed study of

Europe based on fieldwork to look at precisely these issues. I saw the desperate need to discover a paradigm or method for the future that would allow Europe's different cultures and peoples to understand one another better in order to live together in peace and harmony. To do so, we needed to locate an effective conceptual frame for our study in the context of the social sciences. I thus consulted the scholars who could best guide us.

## *Max Weber, Ibn Khaldun, and European Identity*

The ideas of Max Weber, a German sociologist living in the university towns of Bismarckian Germany, and Ibn Khaldun, a sociologist of tribal societies born almost half a millennium earlier on the edge of the Sahara desert in North Africa but with experience of working in Europe, help us explore ways to understand modern Europe. Weber and Ibn Khaldun have interesting similarities and differences that are reflected in their lives and work. Their ideas continue to fascinate contemporary scholars and commentators. There is a constant stream of new books and articles about them. *Weber's Rationalism and Modern Society: New Translations on Politics, Bureaucracy, and Social Stratification* was published in 2015 by the husband-wife team of Tony and Dagmar Waters; and the historian Stephen Frederic Dale published *The Orange Trees of Marrakesh: Ibn Khaldun and Science of Man* the same year.

The new material on Ibn Khaldun continues to be adulatory, with Dale echoing the renowned British historian Arnold Toynbee, who called Ibn Khaldun's historical writing "undoubtedly the greatest work of its kind that has ever yet been created by any mind in any time or place." Tony Waters, on the other hand, conscious that he is living in a celebrity culture dominated by entertainers, has felt the need to liven up Weber's image and advertises his own book with a blog post declaring that "Max Weber was a funny guy!" It begins, "That's right, Max Weber, the dour looking social theorist on the cover of your social theory text made jokes." But those looking for the satire and bite of Jon Stewart or Bill Maher will be disappointed. Weber is cited making mildly critical, but distinctly unfunny, comments on academics and politicians.[1]

Weber and Ibn Khaldun both lived in societies that were undergoing dramatic change. The German people had been traumatized as never before by the invasion and occupation of their lands by Napoleon Bonaparte early in the century in which Weber was born. By the end of the century, Bismarck, the Iron Chancellor, reversed the national humiliation that France had inflicted on the Germans by not only defeating the French but also crowning Wilhelm I the emperor of a newly united Germany in the Palace of Versailles, outside Paris. Thus Weber witnessed the birth of the mighty German nation as well as its subsequent defeat in the First World War and the collapse of the German monarchy.

Ibn Khaldun's tribal world was also crumbling around him. He saw the rapid rise and fall of tribal dynasties. The Arab world itself was fading away from the world stage. There would be vast and powerful Muslim empires after Ibn Khaldun—the Ottomans, the Safavids, and the Mughals—but they would not be Arab.

Weber placed his work in the context of modernity. He saw himself as an economist and used economic arguments to explain social and religious behavior. The title of his magnum opus, *Economy and Society*, published posthumously in 1922, makes explicit the connection between economics and sociology, and perhaps his best known work, *The Protestant Ethic and the Spirit of Capitalism* (1905), explains the growth of Northern European capitalism as the result of the Calvinist—that is, Protestant—work ethic. Weber's modernity was based on the twin pillars of rationality and reason: society chose to do things the way it did because they were the most logical and rational way of doing them. In contrast, Ibn Khaldun's tribal society organized and conducted life on the basis of tribal tradition and codes because of the assumption that this was the tried and tested way of previous generations and would be perpetuated in the succeeding ones.

Citizenship for Weber's modern man in the ideal thus presupposed a democratic order and equality for all. In contrast, Ibn Khaldun's tribesmen idealized group cohesion and, when they became the rulers of dynasties and empires, Islamic law, which does not favor one tribal or racial group over another and provides rights for religious minorities. In both cases, however, the assumptions and worldview of society, often unwritten and unstated, were normatively interpreted to reflect the dominant group. Thus minority groups in both political environments, whatever the theoretical arguments about equality, were dependent in some profound and often not-so-subtle ways on the goodwill of the majority population. The minority was therefore disadvantaged and constantly vulnerable to prejudice and even violence. Here was the chink in the armor of both modern and tribal societies, whatever the protestations of equality in the eyes of the state and the law, in the case of Weber, and Islamic compassion or the tribal code of hospitality, in the case of Ibn Khaldun.

It is important to note when discussing theorists like Weber and Ibn Khaldun in the social sciences that their theoretical interests need to be understood not as descriptive realities but as imagined constructions or ideal types, to use a Weberian concept. The categories and models, for example, those concerning the modern state or tribal society, are neither watertight nor permanent in nature. Otherwise such exercises would run the genuine risk of reductive reasoning and essentialism, which easily transform into broad stereotypes. They are merely useful starting points for taxonomic exercises.

There is an assumption in the writings of the sociologists of modernity like Max Weber that the modern nation-state, whatever its flaws, is the most advanced and therefore most desirable stage of human political evolution. Modern European societies, including, by extension, those influenced by them, as in North America, are analyzed and viewed in terms of modernity—that is, that they are essentially democratic, that their leaders are accountable and will uphold the principles of human rights, justice, and liberty, and that the electorate is the best judge of the nation's destiny. In the ideal, neither blood, nor caste, nor class will sway decisions for employment and advancement. Such societies are deemed modern and progressive. In contrast, societies like tribal ones in other continents are cast by Western commentators as backward and primitive. There is clearly an assumption, more openly stated perhaps until a half century ago, that advanced societies were innately distinct from tribal ones and were therefore superior. In time, it was hoped by the more optimistic and generous commentators of modernity that those tribal societies would become more like Western ones.

For Ibn Khaldun, the pressing question was to discover the principle that held tribal societies together and could prevent the disintegration of societies that he observed around him. At the heart of Ibn Khaldun's analysis was the nature of tribal society, which is defined through shared bloodlines and held together by what he called *asabiyyah,* or social cohesion. Simply put, when asabiyyah was high tribal groups were strong, and when it was low they were weak. In his cyclical model of history, tribal groups with strong asabiyyah came down from their mountains and out of their deserts to cities to dominate city folk, whom he described as having become effete. In time, the new tribal settlers, too, became soft and after three or four generations were vulnerable to fresher and more united tribes from the mountains and deserts. Ibn Khaldun idealized tribal societies in being just and noble. They provided honor and dignity to their members. He presents a plausible theory of the principles that hold small-scale tribal societies together and allows us to see the processes over time that weaken these ties, thereby transforming communities.

We see the process of the disintegration of asabiyyah in the very act of migration as tribal groups today from, for example, the Berber areas of North Africa arrive to create new lives in Europe. Families disintegrate over time, and the new generation in particular is left with only bits and pieces of asabiyyah. This loss of asabiyyah means that individuals are no longer rooted in their past tribal identity, and if they have not acquired a strong European identity, will be in a state of confusion about which norms and values to follow. Without guidance, the individual will be vulnerable to being misled, even into committing acts of violence.

There were fundamental differences in the approach to power and politics of Weber's modern man as distinct from Ibn Khaldun's tribal one. The former gained power to reinforce the law, the latter to provide patronage to the community and clan. To the former, not upholding the law was a perversion of normative values, to the latter not assisting kin was betraying the essence of social order. To both, these processes appeared natural and the only possible normative way of doing things. However, Weber was intellectually ambiguous about modernity. He was fearful of the dangers of people having to live in "bureaucratic iron cages" and becoming mere "cogs in the machine." He was aware that the pursuit of rationality and bureaucracy could lead to the curtailing of freedoms. His ethnic background would place him squarely as Germanic in terms of his identity, yet his thinking was not consistent with that of the National Socialists.

There are other differences between the two scholars beyond the obvious ones of two men living half a millennium apart and belonging to different cultural and religious traditions. Ibn Khaldun came from a self-consciously tribal background. He could trace his ancestry to one of the oldest tribes of the Hadramaut in Yemen, which was then and still remains a profoundly tribal society. Weber, on the other hand, was from a solid Protestant upper-middle-class family that provided him a comfortable life at home and, eventually, an established career as an academic. His father was a wealthy and senior civil servant with excellent contacts in government and academe. His mother was an orthodox Calvinist whose Puritan morality remained with Weber to the end, although diminishing in later life. In the life of Ibn Khaldun there is migration, danger, and disaster; he lost both his parents when still a teenager, and at one point he lost his wife, his family, and his entire library in a shipwreck. Weber's life was relatively sedentary and free of adventure, although he did suffer what is generally known as a mental breakdown, not unheard of in the lives of highly intelligent and sensitive people.

There is also a difference in their approach to knowledge itself. Ibn Khaldun lived at a time when Muslim civilization encouraged individuals to develop their skills in the whole array of human learning. A philosopher could grapple with issues raised by Plato and Aristotle in the morning, dabble in theological enquiries arising from a study of the Quran in the afternoon, and write love verses in the evening. In addition he could travel vast distances over many years to investigate the world, seek a fortune, or perform pilgrimage and still be recognized in lands distant from his birthplace. Ibn Khaldun was a polymath, in keeping with the norms of his civilization—apart from dabbling in politics he was a prominent jurist, poet, philosopher, historian, sociologist, and anthropologist. In many ways, he was a classic exemplar of what would come to be known as the Renaissance man.

In contrast, Weber lived at a time when modern Western societies were promoting the idea of specialization or concentrating one's time and effort in developing skills in a particular subject or profession. In the drive to specialize, professionals were urged to focus on their profession and not defuse their talents and interests. Those who dabbled perhaps led more interesting lives but invariably lost out on promotions and consolidation of their careers. A man of his times, Weber concentrated in his general area of academic work. While he saw himself as an economist, his great contribution is in the sociology of religions. There is no record of his indulging in either philosophy or love poetry, though he earned a law doctorate. Weber's work needs to be seen in the context of his life: he was a turn-of-the-century German scholar who was born when Europe dominated the world and Germany dominated Europe. Implicit in Weber's worldview is the classification of a static and otherworldly Orient in comparison with a rational, dynamic, progressive, and constantly improving Occident. The ancient societies of India and China were dominated by mysticism, asceticism, and otherworldly ideas, while European ones—which were in the process of intermeshing the two systems of capitalist enterprise and bureaucratic state apparatus—were essentially different.

As we know, these fundamental assumptions of Weberian modernity are being challenged today as events unfold on the world stage. Take China and India, both once dominated by Europeans. Both have surged ahead in economic terms, outpacing European societies and even posing a threat to the preeminent position of the United States. Confucian and Hindu work ethics have done very well for their societies. India in particular has shown that a traditional society can allow its ancient religion and culture to flourish while at the same time being part of a thriving process of globalization. Besides, even a cursory reading of the literature available on ancient Chinese and Indian societies would confirm that Weber misread the nature of those societies as otherworldly. Descriptions in the celebrated *Kama Sutra*, a text that titillates pleasure seekers even today, confirm a society fully appreciative of the sensual life, and the *Arthashastra* describes political machinations, intrigues, and skullduggery on a scale that would bring a blush to the cheeks of Machiavelli. Similarly, early Chinese history confirms the importance of military power and wealth in informing political and social life. It is significant that Confucius emphasized stability, order, and the good life, not withdrawal from and rejection of the world.

As for Weberian modernity, the European state had too easily compromised the essential features of Weber's definition of a rationally and neutrally administered bureaucratic state. The reality was that Weber's modern state could be unjust, unfair, and irrational in violating the basic norms of human society both during Weber's lifetime and after his passing. Germany, Italy, and other European countries in the 1930s and 1940s, with the rise of the Nazis, provide examples of compromised Weberian modernity. Just as modern European states are failing to deal with their Muslim minority fairly and justly today, thus failing the test of modernity, they failed then to treat their Jewish and other minorities fairly and justly, leading directly to the horrors of the concentration camps and the decimation of the Jewish people in the Holocaust.

The core principles of modernity in both Europe and the Muslim world were challenged after the terrorist attacks on New York and Washington on September 11, 2001. In Europe, the challenge came as local economies faltered, unemployment rose, and disillusionment grew following the arrival of asylum seekers. People began to fall back swiftly and unambiguously to their imagined core identities. It was not long before people became aggressive in promoting their own identity. With that, some of the fundamental precepts of modernity—in particular, the core beliefs that all are equal before the law regardless of race and religion and that human rights are to be upheld at all costs—were challenged. There was even talk of mass deportation and worse as far as the minorities were concerned.

In the Muslim world, not long after gaining independence in the decades following the Second World War, Muslim rulers inexorably moved to becoming dictators. They fell back on tribal support to prop up their regimes. Under Saddam Hussein in Iraq, the Assads in Syria, or Muammar Qaddafi in Libya, the pattern was the same: brutal regimes depending on their tribal base and promoting the cult of the dictator using torture and repression. In spite of the blatant violations of human rights, the regimes continued to project themselves as progressive and modern. But no one was being fooled, least of all their own people.

The compromises and challenges to modernity were more complex in Europe, the birthplace of modernity, than in the Muslim world, which, steeped in tribal culture, was still struggling with the concept. But the end result was the same. A new form of analysis had to be located. Modernity in Europe was also struggling, as we found during our fieldwork, to maintain its Weberian character. Consequently, we see the reassertion of traditional European identity with its emphasis on blood, lineage, and the group cohesion of the "native" people. Weber had pointed out the nature of traditional and charismatic authority—what we call "tribal"—that defined pre-modern societies. As was common at the time, he saw a linear progression in the trajectory of societies moving toward modernity. There were clearly demarcated stages of evolution in discrete categories as societies moved from "primitive" communities to modern ones based in large cities that reflected their industrial and economic development. It was widely agreed that modern societies had left primitive societies behind in economic, political, military, and intellectual ways. Yet today, as the European state begins to compromise on Weberian notions of modernity, we see the reemergence of older forms of identity. This is where we move from Weberian to Khaldunian territory.

Weber may have been hard put to explain the Muslims running amok in the heart of Paris and the million migrants turning up in his homeland, but to Ibn Khaldun it would have been clear in the context of his theories: the movement of communities in search of better lives from one part of the world to another, which was often accompanied by violence and dislocation. The Islamic State of Iraq and Syria (ISIS), for Ibn Khaldun, would be nothing more than a product of the disintegration of asabiyyah and thus a collapse of tribal leadership and tribal law. The results were the worst excesses of human behavior. The absence of justice and compassion, for Ibn Khaldun, would indicate a return to the age of *jahiliyyah,* or ignorance. The tribal societies in which ISIS operated were thus in the throes of a bitter and violent battle to re-create asabiyyah. Without understanding what was going on in those societies, it became difficult to effectively vanquish ISIS, as we saw in spite of so many different countries, Muslim and non-Muslim, joining together to combat it. The Weberian take on ISIS would be that modernity, with its emphasis on rationalism, genuine democracy, accountability, human rights, and the rule of law, had come to a juddering halt in the Middle East.

For Weber, the emphasis on racial identity in German society represents an abandonment of modernity and a reversal of the forward trajectory of progress. Society is thus moving backward away from rational bureaucratic forms toward those of traditional and tribal ones. The Germanic notions of the *Volk* or the people, the fatherland, purity of the bloodline, and the idea of the nation itself all fed into an extreme form of ethnic identity that drove Germany into two world wars and the horrors of the Holocaust. Today, many Germans are reacting to the sudden arrival of a million migrants from distant lands as a threat to their cultural and social mores—that is, to the internal cohesion of asabiyyah. Once again, blood and culture are acting as discrete factors to separate the natives from the migrants. Similar developments are taking place in other European countries.

For the purposes of our study, I do not see the discussion in terms of Ibn Khaldun versus Max Weber but rather Ibn Khaldun and Max Weber. We maintain that we cannot understand European society today without putting the two together. While Ibn Khaldun gives us a tribal frame to look at societies, Weber places them in the context of modern states. There is more use to Ibn Khaldun in European society than the advocates of Weber would care to admit, and we explore the reemergence of an earlier identity in Europe with its emphasis on blood and lineage keeping that in mind. This method will resolve the issue of how best to frame our study of European societies.

### *Tacitus, the First Anthropologist of Germanic Society*

While Weber and Ibn Khaldun provide, in their separate ways, a convincing frame and context in which to understand European society, we need to turn to a man who lived long before either Weber or Ibn Khaldun and left behind a masterly ethnographic foundation for the study of Europe. Tacitus, the Roman historian and statesman, who wrote his famous book *Germania* in the first century AD, provides a baseline, an extant text, and a credible conceptual frame to examine the Germans who have dominated Europe through their military and economic power.

If we define an anthropologist as one who studies a community objectively over a period of time to examine its history, leadership, organization, and values with a degree of empathy, allowing for a depth of understanding with the purpose of writing about it, then Tacitus is perhaps Europe's first true anthropologist of Germanic peoples. Tacitus's seminal ethnographic survey of the Germans, whom he described as living in tribal groups, most likely based on face-to-face encounters with people who had first-hand knowledge of the region, perhaps Germans themselves, and access to official Roman sources, was brief, dispassionate, and objective. It explained the geography and customs of the German tribes, which in time came to be the standard against which German peoples, wherever they lived, measured themselves. It is noteworthy that Tacitus attempted to preserve his objectivity even while arguing that the German tribes posed the most serious threat to Rome itself.

Tacitus's description of German tribes mirrors what British anthropologists have called the "segmentary lineage system" among African tribes. The concept of the segmentary lineage system, which I discuss in my book *The Thistle and the Drone* (2013), describes social groups that live according to defined codes of honor, emphasize hospitality, courage, warrior prowess, and revenge, and dwell in generally remote and economically deprived territories marked by tribal boundaries. They are egalitarian and exhibit "nesting attributes" of clans and sub-clans that form a neat geometric pattern as part of a larger lineage system that traces descent from an eponymous ancestor. According to Tacitus, Germanic peoples shared all these characteristics and even traced their descent from a single common ancestor, Mannus, whose three sons were the progenitors of the main German tribal divisions. Mannus himself was the son of the Earth-born Germanic god Tuisto.

The Germans were also governed by councils of male elders who resolved conflicts. Simplicity and austerity marked their societies, which were generally egalitarian because no one man could accumulate enough resources to actually dominate the group, and leaders were primus inter pares. Tribal identity gave pride to the members of the community. Tacitus additionally found purity in tribal bloodlines: "all have the same bodily appearance, as far as is possible in so large a number of men: fiery blue eyes, red hair, large bodies which are strong only for violent exertion."[2] There was another similarity between Tacitus and the British authors who wrote of such tribal societies: Both depicted these societies in a somewhat idealized and even romantic manner.

In spite of the turbulent changes of fortune over the millennia, the Germans, wherever they lived in Europe, but especially in their heartlands, clung to three features of their identity that would bind them together—the German language and pride in its achievements; the lands and territories on which they lived, which always at their core remained German in spite of political shifts; and finally the idea of belonging to a common Germanic people with a shared culture that comprised legendary gods and iconic leaders, writers, and artists who generate pride and reinforce German identity.

While many would probably be reluctant to associate the word with a modern Western nation, especially one as prosperous and powerful as Germany, I would suggest we could with fair confidence recognize among the German peoples attributes of what Tacitus called a tribe. Tacitus's description of the German people as tribal was shared by none other than Julius Caesar, who is widely credited with giving the name "German" to them. To my mind, the characteristics enumerated above are sufficient to apply the term tribal to the German people.

While modern Northern European nations like England, the Netherlands, and the Scandinavian countries are indisputably Germanic in origin, other countries, too, claim links: for example, French identity incorporates Clovis and Charlemagne, both mighty Germanic warriors of the Frankish tribal confederation that gave France its name; Italy claimed an *Aryan* identity under Mussolini based on the invasion and rule of Germanic tribes around the time of the fall of Rome; and the Spanish aristocracy long claimed descent from the Germanic Visigoths, which they used to define a Spanish identity based on blood lineage. While the Germans were fortunate in being "discovered" by Tacitus early in recorded history, there were, and are, communities throughout Eastern Europe with their own distinct tribal identity. These include the Slavs, such as the Poles, Czechs, and Serbs, the Hungarians, and the Baltic peoples.

## Tribal Europe

However tribal in origin, European societies like the Germanic peoples have been influenced over the centuries by Christianity, feudalism, monarchy, foreign invasions, long-drawn-out religious wars, imperialism and overseas colonization, and finally the advent of modernity and the modern state. These developments have tempered tribal identity, but they have not removed it altogether. Neither did the growth of state power, including the expansion of centralization, industrialization, education, and transportation, as well as immigration. What did happen, though, was that tribal identity in its raw and purest expressions evolved and developed to adjust to changing social and political situations.

*The Thistle and the Drone* identifies the tribal base of modern states such as Saudi Arabia and Afghanistan—both named after tribes. This is also the case in Europe. In the context of the modern European state, particularly in Northern and Eastern Europe, because the state is dominated by a majority ethnic group, the minority is not treated either equally or fairly. Try as it might, the minority will invariably find itself on the outside, especially when the majority revives the idea of defining identity on the basis of blood, culture, or land, the key concepts of tribal identity.

Tacitus noted the essential difference between a world-dominating military civilization with multiple varieties of people such as the Roman Empire, based in the city of Rome, and the German tribes who were seen as uncivilized, uncouth, and monolithic communities living on the periphery. Yet what he saw as tribal when writing of German society, modern European commentators such as Max Weber failed to recognize. Even anthropologists whose primary professional focus is the different types of societies could not quite acknowledge what stared them in the face: the tribal base and nature of European society.

### European Primordial and Predator Identity

To better understand and analyze European society we present three categories of European identity. The first two are *primordial identity*, which defines those societies that value their own unique traditions and culture, and *predator identity*, which defines those that promote their identity through chauvinistic, aggressive, and militaristic expressions, often targeting societies that differ from them in ethnic or religious terms. The third, *pluralist identity*, will be discussed below.

Predator identity is activated in a variety of situations, including the desire to aggressively defend the "purity" and identity of the tribe, especially when faced with an external threat. In this context, when we use the term "Far Right," as we have in this study, to describe a political movement or position, we are referring to predator identity. We may sum up the relationship between the two identities thus: primordial tribal man yearns for peace but is prepared for battle if necessary; predatory tribal man looks to battle and considers peace a sign of weakness. We suggest that tribal societies are dimorphic—that is, different varieties of the same species. Thus primordial identity and predator identity as we are using them are illustrations of this dimorphism.

Primordial identity is tribal in essence and memory, if not in form, structure, and substance. It is a re-creation of an already imagined construction—that is, the tribe. Primordial identity allows the community to feel a sense of association with some features from the past and reinforces its desire for group pride in its special status. Primordial identity in Germanic society, for example, has evolved into various overlapping codes of behavior that stress one or other aspect of the original tribal identity. These codes include *Heimat*, meaning homeland, with mystical, rural, and anti-modern connotations; *Volk,* or the particular spirit of the people based in blood, soil, and the culture and traditions of the ancestors; *Aryan,* a supposedly scientifically determined original and pure racial identity going back thousands of years and typified by blonde hair and blue eyes; *deutsche Tugenden,* or German virtues, commonly associated with Prussia, which include efficiency, austerity, discipline, and self-denial; *Leitkultur,* meaning the leading or dominant culture in society typically juxtaposed with the foreign culture of outsiders; *hygge,* or a state of warmth, good feeling, and coziness one experiences with others of the community, especially in the frigid Scandinavian winters; and *janteloven,* the law of Jante, which is used in Scandinavia to describe unspoken rules that govern society, especially the idea that one should not think oneself greater than or above anyone else and that no outsider should ever presume to be above the native group as a whole or to be a part of it. Janteloven underlines the egalitarian nature of tribal identity and remains a desirable ideal in primordial identity today.

While original tribal identity can accommodate outsiders through the social mechanism of what anthropologists call "affiliated lineages" in which their protection becomes a matter of honor for the tribe, primordial and particularly predator identity deny space to anyone not related by blood. The proponents of Aryan and Volk forms of identity such as the Nazis, for example, never accepted the existence of affiliated lineages, insisting on purity of blood. This was despite evidence to the contrary, such as in the descriptions of the Norse tribes provided by Ibn Fadlan, the Abbasid envoy who lived among them and wrote about their customs in the tenth century. Ibn Fadlan was allowed to live with the tribes even though he was not of their bloodline. The Nazis, of course, had a specific and sinister agenda. They promoted and personified predator identity, justifying it on the basis of the purity of the original tribal lineage, which denied a place for those who were not part of the tribe. The target for the Nazis was the minorities, especially the Jews. In their desire to reclaim the purity of the original German tribes, the Nazis attempted to manufacture a society that never existed.

Given the central importance of identity in Europe, it is clear that the traditional definitions of left and right in Western democracies can no longer accurately explain the growing reality of politics on the ground nor carry the theoretical burden of concepts that reflect such a range of political belief as to render taxonomy almost meaningless. The Right today attempts to convey the views of those who have traditionally conservative and benign positions regarding family and country to those who, at the extreme, talk of "concentration camps" and "making soap" with reference to the persecution of ethnic and religious minorities. The confusion is not abated when terms such as extreme Right, right wing, Far Right, and alt-right are used interchangeably. A similar problem confronts the current analyst explaining the movements on both the left and the right, both of whom may have regard for their traditional culture, as "populism," another term currently in vogue to describe the political movements surging across Western societies (see, for example, the 2016 book *The Populist Explosion* by John Judis). It is for this reason that we look at European societies through the categories proposed in this study, which are informed by the discipline of anthropology.

### European Pluralist Identity

Europe also has another historic identity besides the one derived from tribe and blood, which we are calling pluralist identity. This identity emphasizes learning, literature, and art and above all, promotes the idea of coexistence among Jews, Christians, and Muslims—or, to use the recently coined Spanish term to describe it, *la convivencia*. Several examples present themselves: Andalusia, Sicily, and parts of the Balkans, especially Bosnia. Andalusia, a region in modern Spain, is also the name of the central part of al-Andalus, the Muslim name for the Iberian Peninsula, which Muslims ruled from Cordoba more than 1,000 years ago. Whatever the controversies and debates about the past, the reality is that there were periods in Andalusian history when people felt that if they had not yet attained a state of philosophic and civilizational harmony they were well on their way to doing so. Therefore, in this study, we refer to the Andalusian model to suggest a pluralist society from the past that, suitably adjusted to our times, provides an alternative European identity to the one based in notions of tribe and race found especially in the northern and eastern parts of the continent. Indeed, Andalusia acts as a valid alternative or antithesis to the thesis that Europe is essentially formed of societies with a highly developed notion of primordial identity that can develop in dangerous predatory directions targeting minorities.

The Andalusian model was directly shaped by Muslim thought and culture and had a profound impact on Europe, influencing the development of the Renaissance, the Scientific Revolution, and the Enlightenment. Even when Muslims lost power, as in Sicily, the Andalusian model was maintained, most notably, in the case of Sicily, by King Roger II and the Holy Roman Emperor Frederick II. We find scattered evidence of the Andalusian model remaining today, especially in Southern Europe.

The idea was compelling enough to attract the attention of scholars across the Atlantic; Tamara Sonn of Georgetown University has spoken of the United States before 9/11 as a "New Andalusia."

A theme that runs through our study is the belief that the idea and practice of successful modernity that subsumes human rights, civil rights, and democracy is under threat. Today, the arrival of more than a million refugees and the rising controversy surrounding them feeds into the propaganda of Far Right groups challenging the very foundations of modern Europe. These groups have had the cumulative effect of reviving an exclusionary European identity based in blood and lineage. The rising Islamophobia and anti-Semitism must be curbed if Europe is to put its house in order. Acts of violence are adding up and are beginning to shake confidence in Europe's postwar project. There cannot be a stable and successful modern Europe without equality and justice for all.

The answer to the violence and tensions between religions in Europe today and the sense of alienation and confusion in Muslim youth is to revive and strengthen the Andalusian model as an alternative to that of a monolithic tribal society. It allows us to appreciate the rich variety of religions and cultures on the continent today even far beyond what our ancestors could imagine—for example, the Andalusia of a thousand years ago did not have the Hindu, Sikh, and Chinese communities that are thriving in today's Europe.

Yet because the Andalusian model is dated, impractical, and has little legitimacy, considering the chaos in the Muslim world, we need to think of a synthesis of our thesis and antithesis. If the thesis represents tribalism and ethnic exclusivity and the antithesis, the Andalusian model, is no longer possible, a synthesis needs to aim for a Europe that is genuinely pluralist and universal and thus living up to its greatest ideals, while recognizing and respecting indigenous culture and identity in the form of a New Andalusia. It must take into account the desperate need for a strong moral leadership reflecting both wisdom and compassion while transcending religious, cultural, and national boundaries.

### The Deep Structures of European Society

Europe presents a complex array of societies and a bewildering range of political entities with different and rich histories that explain the relationship with their varied Muslim populations. Countries like the United Kingdom and France have an imperial past that at one stage colonized vast swathes of overseas lands, including Muslim ones. Countries like

Germany and Denmark have a limited history of colonization but none-theless encouraged Muslims to immigrate as guest workers after the Second World War. European states like Spain, Italy, and Greece share the Mediterranean Sea with Muslim populations from across the waters and have a history of social, political, and economic interaction with them. There are also states with majority native Muslim populations, such as Bosnia, Albania, and Kosovo.

Considering the diversity of European societies, we attempt clarity by looking closely at European social structures and aim to penetrate them to excavate what lies beneath. The celebrated linguist Noam Chomsky has posited that all sentences have two structures: a phonetic or surface structure and a semantic or deep structure. The surface structure determines how a sentence sounds; the deep structure determines the nuance in how a sentence is understood. This terminology has been borrowed by anthropologists such as Clifford Geertz and Claude Lévi-Strauss and applied to their anthropological studies. "One can become conscious of one's grammatical categories by reading linguistic treatises just as one can become conscious of one's cultural categories by reading ethnological ones," argues Geertz. Deep structures, he maintains, can only be observed by analyzing the aggregate of a society's surface structures, or the society's ideas, habits, patterns, and institutions, and by "reconstructing the conceptual systems that, from deep beneath" the surface of society, animate and give it form. Ultimately, Geertz explains, "The job of the ethnologist is to describe the surface patterns as best he can, to reconstitute the deeper structures out of which they are built, and to classify those structures, once reconstituted, into an analytical scheme."[3]

By looking at the layers beneath the surface and seeing and locating the symbolic forms of society, we are able to reconstruct the foundations even though they may not exist in their original form. By that understanding we can draw conclusions as to how a certain people arrived at where they are today, why they arrived in the way they did, and what was saved and what was lost on the journey. This exercise is vital when dealing with societies that have undergone fundamental transformations as European ones have in the past few centuries—the revolutions of the eighteenth and nineteenth centuries, the world wars of the twentieth, and the globalization of the late twentieth and twenty-first centuries. In the case of the Germans, for example, we know the story begins 2,000 years ago. We would be presenting an incomplete picture if we simply took contemporary society and assumed that is how it is, without an understanding of its deep structures.

The question arises, how much can those from outside the culture really penetrate the deep structures? The answer is provided in the work of European scholars who have made lasting contributions to the study of tribal societies. Some of the most significant work in European anthropology—from that of Bronislaw Malinowski to Meyer Fortes and E. E. Evans-Pritchard and later Lévi-Strauss, Edmund Leach, Ernest Gellner, and Fredrik Barth—is based in fieldwork in Africa, Asia, and, in the case of Lévi-Strauss, South America. It can be argued that anthropology as we know it would be in danger of ceasing to exist if this corpus of material were to be removed from it.

I believe it is not only possible but time that we accept that anthropologists of any origin or background can penetrate the deep structures of any society they choose to examine if they do so through a correct use of the anthropological method. Anthropology must show signs of self-confidence and maturity by assessing the work of its practitioners on the basis of the rigor of their theoretical frame and quality of their fieldwork research and set aside considerations of ethnicity, nationality, or religion to judge the quality or excellence of anthropological work.

### *The Contentious Term* Tribe

In using the word *tribe* in this study I am conscious of the controversy around it. Perhaps it is such a difficult concept because it obstinately challenges the fundamental principles of evolution as they have been understood in the West. Tribal groups, seen particularly through a Darwinist, Marxist, imperialist, or secularist lens from the nineteenth century on, were either overlooked or relegated to mere social curiosities that should have evolved into the next stage of human development. Tribal members, if they were recognized at all, were seen through the haze of anthropological studies as primitive people who were faced with the evolutionary reality of extinction or radical adaptation. It was acknowledged—and various respectable studies confirmed the fact—that though tribes had survived into our times, they lived in the remote areas of the world. The citizens of modern society lived in glittering cities with lively centers of learning, libraries, theatres, museums, and cafés, or on ordered farmlands.

Tribalism in Western anthropology and culture thus came to define exotic groups with strange customs and codes living in distant lands. After the Second World War, anthropologists like Edmund Leach tended to shy away from the word *tribe* itself, while some American anthropologists, most notably Morton Fried, abjured the term. Bowing to fashion, the generation that followed Leach rejected the term altogether as toxic racial and ideological abuse. But their rejection of a definition that the local group itself used was merely another sign of outsiders imposing their own understanding on another culture. If the tribe calls itself a tribe, then the rejection of the term by outsiders, responding more to debates within their own societies than the self-perception of the group under study, rests on shaky methodological ground.

Rather than rehash old arguments in the dispute, suffice it to say that the term *tribe*, while eschewed, is still alive and well in mainstream anthropology. Raymond Scupin's authoritative *Cultural Anthropology: A Global Perspective* (2016) has no fewer than four references to the classic anthropologists of tribal societies, including E. E. Evans-Pritchard and Fredrik Barth. Prominent contemporary scholars such as Marshall Sahlins, Steve Caton, and the late Walter Dostal used tribe as a central concept in their work, especially in African and Middle Eastern societies.

I argue that the understanding of tribalism as a concept exclusively applicable to "developing" societies in places like Africa and Asia is an incorrect one. Tribalism is far more enduring and prevalent than thought of by social scientists. The classic attributes of tribes are present in modern European societies, however heavily they are buried or disguised, in cultural norms, language, rhetoric, symbolism, and assumptions of who "we" are. History, I argue, is not linear. Just over half a century ago we were shocked to discover the horrors that modern Europe had inflicted on itself—dragging the planet into its essentially tribal wars that cost almost 100 million human lives and giving the world an example of what extreme tribalism can lead to in the mad frenzy of bloodlust that was the Holocaust. While Germany grapples to redefine its character, we hear of Far Right groups across the continent rejecting the implicit humanism of the cry "Never Again." While the majority of Europeans have not abandoned the slogan "Never Again," there are loud and insistent voices shouting "Again."

If Germany in the 1930s reflects predatory tribalism out of control in its obsession with blood and purity, then its remarkable generosity in 2015 in welcoming the flood of asylum seekers also reflects hospitality—another classic characteristic of traditional tribal society. Yet the aggressive promotion of German tribalism is far from finished. The emergence of Far Right political movements such as Pegida (Patriotic Europeans against the Islamization of the West) and Alternative for Germany (AfD), the attacks on foreigners and Muslims, refugee shelters, and mosques, and the disturbing reemergence of anti-Semitism reflect a deep-seated hostility to all that is "impure."

What happens then when Muslim tribal groups with their own notions of ethnic purity find their way to Europe? The answer may be found in *The Thistle and the Drone*. To these tribes, the Prophet of Islam embodied their faith, and in addition they saw in him the ideal tribal chief. As tribal custom and tradition prevailed in these communities, Islamic law was only imperfectly understood and applied. Honor killings and female genital mutilation, two common practices in tribal societies, including Muslim ones, were not sanctioned by Islam but were and are widely assumed to be "Islamic." Even revenge, central to the tribal code of honor, was categorically rejected in Islam. Economic pressures or persecution in their ancestral lands have forced hundreds of thousands of tribal peoples from Morocco to Central Asia to migrate to Europe. Once in Europe, their old tribal identity did not disappear. On the contrary, in the new environment they clung to their tribal identity with tenacity. However, Europeans who were unfamiliar with Muslim tribes tended to look at them as part of the nation in the Muslim world from where they have migrated. For example, the Kurds who arrived in Germany from Turkey, against which they had been fighting for autonomy for decades, were seen simply as Turks. To a degree, this was understandable: Kurds entered Germany carrying Turkish passports. The same was true for the Berbers from Algeria who have been in conflict with the central state since before Algeria's independence. Once in France, Berbers found their tribal ethnicity subsumed into the general category of Algerian.

After 9/11, Europe once again gave these tribal groups another identity; this time they were all seen as Muslim. So the Turk in Germany, whether Kurd or Turk, or the Algerian in France, whether Berber or Arab, would now be called a Muslim. Europeans were interested in Islam because they associated it with Muslims, who were responsible for acts of violence. It was understandable that, for most Europeans, considering the nuances of Muslim society, especially where that involved taxonomic exercises, was a waste of time. To them, the matter was quite simple: Islam was on a collision course with Europe, and anyone from the Muslim world might be a Muslim terrorist or sympathizer. But however many identities were grafted onto the tribal groups and semantic changes made in describing them, their identity rooted in lineage and code could not be so easily obliterated. Even those born in Europe were finding that while their Islamic identity was always shaky at best, their tribal identity gave them a sense of community and kinship. It is no coincidence that so many of the

Muslim acts of terror can be explained by the code of revenge, which is discussed in greater detail in chapter 8.

Although all these groups are Muslim, there is a distinct difference between populations from the center, such as the Turks in Turkey, Arabs in Morocco and Algeria, or Punjabis in Pakistan, for example, and the Kurds, Berbers, or Pukhtun, respectively, who live on the periphery. The groups representing the center and those tribal societies on the periphery have different histories, cultures, social organizations, and leadership. Those from the periphery are also famous as hardened fighters and men of their word. Properly handled, with respect and dignity, they can be a great asset to the European societies they are now part of. The problem is that mishandling them can just as easily provoke the code of revenge and set them on a collision course with the authorities. Europe thus faces two problems: The urgent need to understand Islam and the need to understand tribal Islam. This line of inquiry is uncharted territory with anthropological, theological, and policy implications. It is an area that needs to be more fully investigated in the future for European governments to better understand their own immigrant populations, especially those with a tribal background, and thereby improve their counterterrorism efforts. It will also help authorities in the Muslim world deal with their minorities in a more effective and harmonious manner. In this study of Europe, however, the focus is on the broader Muslim community on the continent and its relationship with Europe both in the past and the present.

## Fieldwork Methodology

This volume is part of a quartet of studies that I conceived in the days following the terrorist attacks of September 11, 2001, to explore and examine the relationship between Islam and the West from four different perspectives. The first, *Journey into Islam: The Crisis of Globalization*, published in 2007, was based on fieldwork in nine countries and examined how people in the Muslim world viewed the West and what was occurring in their societies after 9/11. The second study, *Journey into America: The Challenge of Islam*, published in 2010, was concerned with how people in the United States saw Muslims and the place of Islam in American identity, and involved visits to a hundred mosques in seventy-five U.S. cities. The third volume in the quartet, published in 2013, was *The Thistle and the Drone: How America's War on Terror Became a Global War on Tribal Islam*. *The Thistle and the Drone* was concerned with the perspective of tribal peoples living in the interstices between states where the U.S.-led war on

terror was being conducted. This present book—the fourth and concluding volume of the quartet—is concerned with the European interaction
with Islam and involves an in-depth examination of both its historical
roots and the current situation, based in fieldwork conducted across the
continent.

Accompanying me for this project was a core team of two male and two
female field assistants—Frankie Martin, Harrison Akins, Amineh Hoti,
and Zeenat Ahmed. In addition, individuals joined us for short periods of
time to contribute to the study. I owe gratitude to all of them and a number
of other people without whom the study would not have been possible, and
I would like to thank them all most warmly. As the list is long, I have
acknowledged them at the end of the book.

The three previous studies in the quartet inform the current project on
Muslims in Europe. Muslim immigrants in the West, both the first and
the succeeding generations, could be broadly identified as falling into
three overlapping but essentially opposed categories, as discussed in *Journey into Islam* and *Journey into America*: literalist Muslims, modernist
Muslims, and mystic Muslims. With the caveat that these categories are
neither watertight nor permanent, we identified and interviewed individuals in each category. Our categorization of the three identities that we
found in the majority population in *Journey into America* helped us understand identity in European society, which was different and yet reflected
American society in some aspects. As in the study of America, we also
divided Muslims in Europe into three categories—immigrants, indigenous Muslims, and converts. The first generation of immigrants in Europe
faced great hardships in low-paying jobs in factories or driving buses—
unlike those doctors and advanced students from middle-class families
who arrived in the United States and very quickly became part of the
American dream. It would take two generations before the immigrants in
Europe stabilized their position in society.

Whatever their persuasion—literalist, modernist, or mystic—Muslims
faced racial and religious prejudice. They were seen in terms of stereotypes
as immigrants. There is also a significant difference between American
and European Muslims in terms of the composition of the community:
In the United States, there is a significant number of African American
Muslims whose Islam, they repeatedly told us, went back to the time their
ancestors were forcibly brought as slaves from West Africa, while Europe
has indigenous Muslim populations, largely in the Balkans.

It is important to point out that the terms *Islam* and *Muslim* are often
used interchangeably in the media and by commentators. In fact, the

behavior of some Muslims, especially in acts of violence, has little or nothing to do with Islam itself. The discussion in our study is not so much about theology, text, and the sacred as it is about society, leadership, and interpretations of how to live as a practicing member of the faith in our current times.

Even a cursory glance at the large numbers, some 5,000 or so, of European Muslims who left Europe to fight with ISIS in the Middle East, raises concerns about the extent of the integration and adjustment of Muslims into European society. Not that the commentators and experts on Islam and counterterrorism who should be providing clarity and direction have helped much. Many who have emerged almost overnight, smelling resources, international conferences, and a heady if brief recognition, with their own theories and terminology, have only succeeded in creating further obfuscation. Their rhetoric and jargon—Islamism, Islamic radicalism, jihadism, Salafi-jihadism—in the way they are used, are so far removed from their sociological and theological moorings as to have little real meaning. We therefore avoid such words and rest our taxonomic exercises instead on neutral ethnography based in observable behavior and detailed interviews conducted in the field. Our categories are therefore led by our fieldwork findings. The reader is thus able to use the same data and is free to interpret it in different ways if necessary.

## Exploring Europe

Early European anthropologists set sail for distant lands to study exotic tribal rituals and erotic mating habits of the "savages," a term they used freely in the titles of their subsequent studies, for example, Bronislaw Malinowski's *Sex and Repression in Savage Society* (1927) and Claude Lévi-Strauss's *The Savage Mind* (1966). Decked out in khaki shorts, knee socks, and solar topees, clutching binoculars, notebooks, and tape recorders, and suitably inoculated against deadly tropical diseases, they disembarked on the Pacific Islands or headed into the Amazon rainforest or the African hinterland. We, too, ventured forth to do our fieldwork; only our destination was Europe itself.

The nineteenth-century explorer Henry Stanley is thought to have coined the term *dark continent* to describe the lack of sources and data that plagued European understanding of Africa. Because Europe has been studied and written about for literally thousands of years, our problem was quite the opposite—not a dearth of data, personal accounts, and histories but a surfeit of them. Yet in another sense—one that is emphasized by the critics of

*Author and his team in front of the British Parliament*

Europe—Europe is indeed a dark continent. These critics cite the wars, the genocides, and the massacres of the twentieth century (for example, Mark Mazower's *Dark Continent: Europe's Twentieth Century*, 1998). For them, the idea of learning from or imitating European ways was "an obscene caricature," as the Caribbean-born anti-imperialist Frantz Fanon wrote in *The Wretched of the Earth* in 1961. Critics of Europe's imperial past listed the atrocities committed by colonialists in Africa, Asia, and elsewhere.

There is another Europe, however—the Europe of Shakespeare, Goethe, Mozart, Da Vinci, and Cervantes. This Europe in its art and humanistic thought reflects not only Western civilization in its finest expression but also because it derives from the Renaissance and the Enlightenment, points to the historic links with the Muslims in places like Andalusia and the Greeks.

The idea of Western civilization deriving from European thought and experience is a dominant "grand narrative" that is seen variously as an extension of imperialism or globalization today. The founding fathers of the United States, on one side of the globe, and the founding fathers of India and Pakistan on the other, drew inspiration from Enlightenment thinkers and the parliamentary practices of Europe. In the case of the United States, Europe is in its very DNA. From the ideas of the Enlightenment that shaped the founding fathers, to the Declaration of Independence and the U.S. Constitution, which define the meaning of America, to the language of the United States, to America's widespread fascination with Shakespeare and Homer, Europe has contributed to the idea of America and shaped its dominant Christian white culture and identity. In the most profound way, Europe truly is the definer and shaper of the modern world. If Africa can claim to be the continent where the history of man began and Asia where the great religions originated, then Europe can justifiably argue that it gave birth to modernity; for the modern world, Europe is thus the mother continent.

Some of the ideas most influential in shaping global history have been European, and their impact is still with us: ideas we can trace back to the Greeks—discussions of the city-state, democracy, and philosophy; ideas developed from the Abrahamic religions coming from the Middle East—one invisible, omnipotent God in heaven and commandments that must be obeyed; ideas of feudalism with its strict social divisions; ideas of religious crusades that sent hundreds of thousands of young Christian warriors to conquer the Holy Land in the Middle East; ideas of empires that took Europe beyond its own shores and boundaries to other continents; ideas of Darwinism and the selection of species; of Marxism and the ideal of each according to his need; of fascism and society based in a hierarchy determined by bloodlines; of socialism, secularism, and atheism; and the development of liberal social, political, and economic ideas that shaped the modern world.

We saw evidence that despite immense economic and social pressures, European humanism has survived, and we will present examples in this book. We noted how certain societies, for example, the Greeks, already struggling, faced the full brunt of the refugee crisis with a heroic humanity reminiscent of their ancestor Hercules and his myriad labors, while other more prosperous northern societies, Germany being the exception, locked their doors and closed their hearts to the suffering of the refugees.

European humanity, I suspect, was behind the affectionate concern for my welfare expressed by my distinguished Dutch colleague and friend, Professor Bram Groen. He was concerned that my study would evoke European "pride," as Europeans may not appreciate an outsider writing about them. However, and precisely for the same reason, when I informed the great Noam Chomsky about our study, he noted that it was reversing the traditional paradigm in the social sciences: In this case, it was not Europeans studying African and Asian societies but an Asian author examining Europe.

Although this study focuses on Europe, and we maintain methodological rigor, it provides lessons for other major areas of the world in which majority populations are finding it difficult to deal with their minorities, especially if they are Muslim. Countries like the United States, China, India, Russia, and Israel, all have Muslim minority populations, and there is a simmering tension between Muslims and non-Muslims. The study of Europe is therefore beneficial for those seeking answers to their own problems elsewhere in dealing with their minority communities.

### European Connections

I personally have much to appreciate in European culture and owe a great deal to those Europeans who over the course of a lifetime have befriended me and from whom I have learned so much. My team was equally beholden to Europe in different ways, either through ancestry—Frankie had links with the Italians and Harrison with the Scots—or, in the case of Zeenat, Amineh, and myself, having lived in Europe for long periods. My own studies were largely based in Europe and culminated in a Ph.D. in anthropology from the University of London. Zeenat not only worked with me during fieldwork, doing valuable research with the women, but also helped finish the writing of the thesis. Amineh was educated at the London School of Economics and received her Ph.D. from the University of Cambridge in anthropology. Both Frankie and Harrison obtained master's degrees from English universities—Frankie from Cambridge and Harrison from the London School of Economics.

My connection with Europe predates my studies, and in fact began at birth. I was born in British India, a subject of the king of England, who was also emperor of India. My grandfather, Sir Hashmatullah Khan, was honored with a knighthood for his services, and my father was a senior member of the British administration and contributed to the war effort as an honorary colonel along with 2.5 million South Asians who fought for the king against the Nazis. Another relative in an earlier century, Sir Syed Ahmad Khan, created the historic Aligarh University patterned on Cambridge University and wrote *An Account of The Loyal Muhammadans of India* (1860). Sir Syed almost single-handedly created a modernist version of Islam, which has contributed immensely in shaping Muslim discourse and politics.

Even after the British left in 1947, and my father opted for the independent nation of Pakistan, European priests at Burn Hall, the boarding school I attended, taught us to read, write, and think in English. Reading in English opened vast, new, and fascinating worlds to my young imagination. I snatched every opportunity between classes to escape into the mountains and deserts of Africa with Allan Quatermain; to enjoy the adventures of Bertie Wooster, dreading bad-tempered aunts with strong vocal chords and young females determined to marry him; and to read the tales of Lord Emsworth and his beloved Empress of Blandings Castle in a timeless England with its blue skies, scented gardens, and eccentric aristocrats. I was fascinated by the stories of the brilliant Sherlock Holmes using scientific methods and deductive reasoning to track down dangerous criminals. In our history lessons, we learned about the Tudors and Stuarts in England; in literature, we memorized the soliloquies of Shakespeare and the verses of Keats and Tennyson; and in geography, we mapped the rivers and mountains of England. We learned to play the English games of cricket and tennis with a passion. Indeed, my first trip to Europe to attend university in the early 1960s was exciting precisely because so much was familiar from my schooling, even though so much was new. One of the first things I did in London was to visit Baker Street to pay homage to my boyhood hero.

My education was both my predicament and my salvation; while it relegated my own culture and history to the background, it also gave me the reason and the capacity to reclaim it. It laid the intellectual foundations for me to remain the eternal student, constantly asking questions and looking for answers. From my early years at school I explored the philosophic conundrum contained in the eternal question, "Who am I?" The search for answers provided me a heuristic process and led me to unexpected places and peoples; I have been on a journey of discovery ever since.

## Anthropological Present and the Universe

While our fieldwork was not standard textbook anthropology, we made use of the anthropological method: we took part in participant observation, gathered fine-grained ethnography, recorded case studies, employed history to understand contemporary society, distributed questionnaires, and combined these with personal intimate interviews. We made cross-cultural comparisons and studied the present. We examined the relevant literature and history and consulted the experts in the field. Each member of the team was able to draw on his or her personal experience living, studying, teaching, and traveling in Europe. We therefore felt qualified to conduct an insider-outsider study of the continent.

As someone who has been writing about and practicing anthropology, and admires the discipline, it is with some regret that I need to place on record the observation that anthropology has never been able to fully move out of the shadow of the hard sciences and develop its own independent character. It therefore still carries a metaphorical chip on its shoulder—

"hey, physicists and astronomers, we're scientists too, kin you may say!"—and in the public mind it is still associated with the stereotypical work of earlier generations describing fieldwork stories of an outlandish nature of "savage" or "tribal" peoples in remote parts of the world. So while the scientists are valued in society for their discoveries and journeys into space and the marvels they observe there, anthropologists are seen as little more than surveyors attempting to explain the exotic sexual and dietary practices of primitive societies. Had more anthropologists held onto what made their discipline special—that is, unraveling the mysteries of human societies and thus laying the very basis of intercultural understanding that, in turn, engenders compassion and empathy for the "other"—they may have been recognized as being uniquely qualified to seek a solution to the dangerous ethnic and religious conflicts raging in the world today. In this study we build on previous research based in the field to illustrate both the scientific nature of the discipline and its capacity to see humanity with objective compassion across the boundaries of culture and religion; indeed, there is an entire subsection in the last chapter, called "Witness to European Humanity," which confirms that the discipline can carry the moral weight of the concept while remaining in the ranks of the scientists.

When I was taught the subject as part of my doctoral studies by its orthodox priests at the University of London, standard fieldwork methodology in anthropology rested on two shaky assumptions: that there was an anthropological present and that the fieldwork area constituted a discrete universe. The discipline had thus created for itself the problem of imposing artificial boundaries of time and space. Yet the strength of anthropology, like that of poetry, is that it attempts to capture the ongoing and unfinished business of life itself. Boundaries merely attempt to freeze and halt a process that can be neither frozen nor stopped. We look for beginnings and middles and ends, forever searching for neat boxes to divide and categorize the knowledge we possess. For purposes of tradition we mention both our anthropological present and our anthropological universe. Our fieldwork present stretches over several years between 2013 and 2017. Our anthropological universe is not a village but the entire continent of Europe.

### The Nuts and Bolts of the Study

*Journey into Europe* is not a chronological or encyclopedic account of European history, although we draw extensively on history. Neither is it a country-by-country compendium of facts and figures, a catalogue of flora and fauna, nor a detailed, research-based description of every Muslim community in every country in Europe. It is a research project based on extensive fieldwork conducted by a team of trained scholars with varying degrees of links with Europe. The conclusions in the end will rest on the research and interviews. In that way our own predilections and prejudices are kept in check and evened out to arrive at conclusions that are as transparent and neutral as is possible in the social sciences. What we present as a result is the picture of a dynamic, complex, and changing continent. We have suggested certain ways to look at this overstudied part of the world. As with my previous projects in the quartet, *Journey into Europe* is part-autobiography, part-anthropology, and part-travelogue.

Of all my previous field projects, this one perhaps was the most difficult. The money was uncertain and arrived only at the last moment. Having a relatively large team made rich ethnography possible but also created a nightmare of logistics. The travel was relentless and complicated and always with pressure to make important interviews and meetings in time. There was high tension around the Muslim community in most parts of the continent—in a sign of the times, we were forced to "retreat" from at least two mosques. There was the problem of the different languages that we had to negotiate from one end of Europe to another. There was the constant pressure of time as we wished to conduct fieldwork during the university's summer and winter breaks. Finally, our determination to achieve the high ambitions we had set out for the project created tension as we encountered delays and hurdles.

My team and I conducted hundreds of interviews, shot hours of footage, spoke to the media, and gave public lectures. We crisscrossed Europe to ensure a good representation of the different categories for purposes of our study: the United Kingdom, France, Spain, and Italy for countries with an imperial past; Germany and Denmark for societies with deep tribal roots that had welcomed Muslims as guest workers; and Bosnia-Herzegovina and Greece for European countries with an indigenous Muslim population. We visited Scotland and Ireland to gain a sense of tribal societies that were part of a larger empire. The northernmost city we visited was Edinburgh, the southernmost Melilla, the westernmost Cordoba, and the easternmost Xanthi in northern Greece. There was also the matter of selecting areas of Europe to visit that would be essential for the project while keeping in mind the limited time and resources. For example, to understand the migrants coming to Europe and interview migrants and local officials, we visited the three main entry points into Europe from the Middle East and North Africa—Greece, Italy, and Spain.

In the end we visited some fifty cities and towns and fifty mosques and spoke to about the same number of imams. We aimed for the standard cross section of society—men and women, old and young, rich and poor, powerful and ordinary. We interviewed scholars, students, politicians, and community and religious leaders. We also interviewed presidents, prime ministers, members of Parliament, chief rabbis, grand muftis, and a former archbishop of Canterbury. We sought out and spoke with leading members of Far Right parties that have targeted the Muslim community; in so doing we have recorded the reasons for their discontent and the real dangers their future plans contain. By the end of our journey, we had a veritable ethnographic treasure chest of interviews and transcripts, but owing to limitations of space we could use only a small portion of the material.

The pressure during fieldwork was unrelenting and could build suddenly and from unexpected quarters, as my daughter Amineh, who had come from Pakistan for the fieldwork, records:

As a daughter, I was always conscious of wanting to do more but it was also very challenging being a mother. I had a four-year old, Anah, in my care who I could not leave behind in Pakistan. We had some very positive moments—people in general relaxed more with a child around, women opened up, especially those with children, and the airlines always let our team go first to get our choice of seats in the plane. On the other hand, it was also a great responsibility to travel from place to place and hotel to hotel with baggage and a little child. At one point in Bradford, after I had conducted five interviews, one after the other, and dropped on the bed with exhaustion, Anah slipped from a ledge and fell onto a glass table in the hotel room. She became unconscious, and blood gushed out forcefully from her forehead, covering her entire face and eyes. Meanwhile, I had thrown her onto the bed in panic and held my pajama onto her cut, pressing tightly. My thoughts rushed to the recent tragedy in Pakistan when my niece, who was Anah's age, walked into a glass door and was cut in the neck, resulting in her death. Anah cried to God to help her and her older sister, Mina, who was particularly close to her and who would join us later. The ambulance arrived in several minutes. Along with my father we rushed her to hospital and spent a sleepless night making sure she was well.

The incident was another one of those that took us to a point of deepest reflection, that human life was most valuable, and at one point my father thought of packing me up with Anah and sending

*Fieldwork travel—Amineh and Anah Hoti*

me back home. But time helped heal the wound. Anah soon forgot the cut and my father got many chances to spoil Anah by buying her children's magazines, shifting the focus in our spare time onto the great value of close family ties.

Clearly, those who set out to seek knowledge must be prepared to cross many hurdles with patience and perseverance. In the end, the study yielded a film, a book and numerous articles, interviews, and public lectures. It was our small contribution to the continent that had given so much to each one of us.

*Journey into Europe* is divided into three parts, with each part containing three chapters, each further sub-divided into three sections. The first part explores two contending interpretations of European identity based in European history and culture. Chapter 2 examines the proposition that Europe may be understood in terms of a model of tribal identity based in blood, lineage, and land—what we call primordial identity. We focus on European tribal societies, including the Germanic and Eastern European peoples, to provide evidence of this interpretation. We discuss European tribalism in the context of history and society, noting its strengths, weaknesses, and dangers, especially when it is pushed to its extreme exclusivist form—what we are calling predator identity.

We then present in chapter 3 an opposing model of European identity exemplified by Andalusia, Spain, which was pluralistic in nature, attracting Jews, Christians, and Muslims, and emphasized humanism and the pursuit of knowledge. Andalusia saw the flowering of art, architecture, and science. At the heart of this civilization was the idea, known as la convivencia, that the three great religious traditions could coexist. This identity was also present in Sicily and parts of the Balkans and had an impact on Europe beyond these regions.

Part 2 consists of ethnography and presents our findings from the field. Its three chapters reflect the three different types of Muslim societies— immigrant (chapter 4), native or indigenous (chapter 5), and convert (chapter 6). The third part of the study draws in the major strands in the discussions around Islam and contemporary European society. Chapter 7 examines anti-Semitism, the Jewish population of Europe, the relationship between Jews and Muslims over history, and their difficult relationship today. Chapter 8 explores the issues of refugees, terrorism, immigration, identity, multiculturalism, and the rise of Far Right movements and their impact on rapidly transforming European societies.

Winston Churchill called Europe a "turbulent and mighty continent" shortly after the Second World War. After decades of peace, Europe is once again facing turbulence. In the final chapter we examine the predatory rhetoric of ethnic hate that is now sweeping across Europe and, given Europe's history, suggest the way forward, on the basis of our fieldwork findings, to avoid catastrophe. We suggest how Europe can forge a new identity out of its two main identities—exclusionary tribal and Andalusian— to create a synthesis for the Europe of the twenty-first century. This vision of a New Andalusia could be a beacon of moral and intellectual leadership to inspire the world.

# TWO

# Primordial Tribal Identity in Europe

IN THE SUMMER of 2014 the world's eyes were focused on the German national football team as Germany won the World Cup, in Rio de Janeiro, for the first time as a united country. But the world also saw the team's Muslim players, including the Turkish-German superstar Mesut Özil, staring stone-faced straight ahead in their moment of triumph and refusing to join the white players in singing the "Deutschlandlied" ("Song of Germany"), the German national anthem. Their refusal to participate left Germans scratching their heads in puzzlement. Our fieldwork in Germany, during which we watched the match in a crowd of hundreds of thousands at Berlin's Brandenburg Gate, allowed us to look into the mystery of the non-singing Muslim footballers and to ask what it revealed about German society and identity.

A national anthem is usually the product of patriots and poets conjuring an ideal society. In the case of the original German anthem, of which only the third stanza is today in official use, central features of German tribal identity are praised, German territorial boundaries are delineated, and the land is glorified. The anthem repeats the adjective *deutsch*, or German, to drive home the notion of tribal exclusivity and pride, beginning with the rousing cry of "Deutschland, Deutschland, über alles" ("Germany, Germany, above all"). One by one, the features of tribal society are listed: "German women, German loyalty, German wine, and German song," all of which "inspire us to noble deeds." The ideals of "unity and justice and freedom" are emphasized. Through the prism of the modern German national anthem, those very features that Tacitus described two millennia ago can be seen as forming the central part of tribal identity.

Perhaps immigrants with a tribal background, like the Turks, also see the anthem in tribal terms. They might find that singing the praises of a "tribe" to which they do not belong compromises their own tribal integrity. They might also be protesting the increasingly widespread prejudice and hatred they face. We know of the racist slurs—the grunting gorilla-like noises and bananas thrown at them—that non-German players have faced during football matches. Yet I wondered whether these Muslims appreciated the significance of rejecting this key symbol of German identity and whether they fully understood that it could be construed as a rejection of Germanness itself.

The rousing patriotic verses of the German anthem were written in the middle of the nineteenth century, when nationalist chauvinism was widespread in Europe as people campaigned for the new nation-states that were forming. The German peoples, who had yet to be joined into a unified modern state, believed that all ethnic Germans—regardless of where they lived—should be incorporated into a single nation. The anthem was not universally admired, however; one notable detractor was the German philosopher Friedrich Nietzsche, who called its opening line, "Deutschland, Deutschland, über alles," "the most idiotic slogan in the world." The fiercely patriotic anthem, however, suited the Nazis, and they used it with blaring martial music to stir emotions during their mass rallies.

After the Second World War, the first two stanzas of the anthem were considered inappropriate and fell out of use. Not only were they seen as too closely associated with the Nazis, but the generations that followed thought of themselves as much in terms of being part of larger European society as of German society. Riem Spielhaus, a prominent German authority on Islam who has an Egyptian father and a German mother, discussing the refusal of the players to sing the national anthem, surprised us by saying that she would not sing it either. She explained the problems associated with the anthem: the rivers mentioned in it that are not part of the German state, and a general sense of German "guilt" after the horrors of the Nazi regime and the Holocaust resulted in a revulsion against anything that evoked overt German national pride. In the postwar decades, Germany's focus was on rebuilding an economy that could stand as a bulwark to the Soviet threat while working to implement European integration. It was an unspoken article of faith that German ethnic pride must be discouraged. If it were to reemerge, no one was certain where it would lead.

As we were staying in the heart of Berlin during the World Cup finals, we were able to catch a glimpse of how modern German identity was changing. I saw hundreds of national flags fluttering on cars and bikes and even on human heads. There were flags painted on faces, backs, stomachs, and buttocks. One man walked about with great confidence completely naked except for the German flag around his loins and the flag he waved in his hands. People laughed with him and hugged him as he walked.

It was Germany's victory over Argentina in the World Cup final that in the end burst the dam that had held back expressions of German pride. When the game was won, Germany exploded with jubilation, and people flooded the streets. The triumphant German team had played a superior, unsparing game against its rivals. After returning to Germany, the team appeared in a celebration rally at the Brandenburg Gate, a stone's throw from our hotel, where they were greeted by hundreds of thousands of rapturous fans. It seemed the entire city had gathered to welcome the conquering heroes. Six of the white players, arms around one another, danced onto the stage, hunched over with their arms hanging down, in a way that appeared apelike, and mocked the Argentinians, chanting, "This is how the gauchos walk, the gauchos walk like this." They then stood erect and, strutting in an arrogant, exaggerated walk, chanted, "This is how the Germans walk, the Germans walk like this." These young Germans instantly lost some goodwill, but they also showed the world that German pride was back. This was a straightforward racist taunt based in ideas of physical superiority. They had thrown off the air of humility and rejection that had been cultivated as part of German identity for over half a century. They stood there—tall, triumphant, and golden—and for a split second nakedly proud of their Germanic tribal predator identity, like Vikings who had just returned with treasure from an overseas raid after defeating mighty warriors.

The world press quickly dubbed the incident "Gauchogate." The *Frankfurter Allgemeine Zeitung,* not missing the significance of the incident, called it "a gigantic own-goal," and declared that "the German world champions are squandering the image of an open-minded, tolerant nation."

The idea of tribal pride—the gut feeling that "we" are simply the best and, by inference, "they" are not as good as us—permeates the worldview of Germanic Europeans. "We have the best football team in the world," volunteered a white German taxi driver in Berlin, even before the Germans devastated and humiliated the Brazilian team on their home turf in what looked like a surgical operation in the World Cup semifinal. "We Germans make the best cars," another driver told me. Like the other taxi drivers we had seen in Berlin, he was driving a Mercedes. Warming up to his theme, he then gave a list of other fields in which Germans excelled: "We have the best food, the best climate, the best writers and artists, the best culture." To this he added the best education system and the greatest capacity for individuals to work in a disciplined and orderly manner. Everything German was being described in superlatives.

He was not alone. Whether in Berlin, Cologne, or Munich, we heard the same refrain—everything German was the best. Nor was this perception of Germany restricted to taxi drivers. The senior-most officials I met in Berlin, as well as the professors, artists, and students elsewhere in Germany, also pointed out that Germany was the best. Germans, I discovered, recognize the severe toll of the two world wars but also believe that Germany had the best chances for success of any modern nation leading up to the First World War. Hastily brushing aside the events that developed in the first half of the twentieth century, they believed Germany was once again emerging as a world leader.

The notion of superiority was not only expressed to us by local Germans but also by non-Germans who lived in the country. The Pakistani ambassador to Ireland, G. R. Malik, whom we met at a dinner given by Pakistani friends in Dublin, had been posted to Frankfurt as Pakistan's consul general for several years. When I told him we were heading to Germany and asked how he would best describe the country, he had a one-word reply—"perfect." The word was so strong that it left little room for discussion, and he repeated it several times: "Perfect, perfect, perfect." When I asked him what he meant, he said *everything* was perfect—social services, education, transport, the justice system, and so on. In a meeting at the Pakistan embassy in Berlin, the Pakistan defense attaché, when asked about Germans, said, "excellence dominates whatever they do."

## Primordial Tribal Identity and Germanic Society

The influence of the Germanic peoples, which include the Austrians, Scandinavians, Dutch, and the English, has extended far beyond their central areas and is crucial to understanding European identity and history. The Spanish, French, and Italian identities all have important Germanic elements going back to the presence of Germanic tribes in their regions. Quintessential "English" tribes like the Angles and Saxons were Germanic, and the Visigoths, another Germanic tribe, dominated the Iberian Peninsula before the arrival of the Arabs. Large German populations had lived for centuries in Transylvania, which is now part of Romania; the current president of Romania, Klaus Iohannis, is an ethnic German from this community. The Germans had a large impact in the Baltic states, dominating the politics and government of Estonia and Latvia for more than seven centuries until those nations achieved independence in 1918. Major European countries such as Germany, Belgium, Denmark, England, France, and Sweden are named after Germanic tribes or tribal confederations, as are such regions and cities as Birmingham, Essex, and Sussex in England; Gotaland, one of three main regions of Sweden; Saxony and Swabia in Germany; the Friesland province in the Netherlands; and Lombardy in Italy.

The place of Germany in defining Europe and European civilization has been undeniable. Not only did the Germans play a key role in bringing down the Roman Empire itself, but they were also the first to succeed in openly challenging the power of the Catholic Church in Rome. German troops played a vital role against the Turks at the Battle of Vienna in 1683, and at the Battle of Waterloo Prussian troops handed victory to the Duke of Wellington. In two world wars in the twentieth century the Germans again played a central role, although this time in a self-destructive way. Quintessential political and social systems and ideologies that we think of as European also have Germanic origins, from medieval feudalism to nineteenth-century nationalism; and two of the most prominent ideologies of the twentieth century—fascism and Marxism—are intimately connected with Germany. Today, Germany dominates the European Union, and its chancellor, Angela Merkel, towers above any other leader on the continent. It is no wonder that an entire range of commentators see Germany at the heart of Europe, from the social scientist Ulrich Beck writing of a *German Europe* (2013) to Steven Ozment's history of Germany titled *A Mighty Fortress* (2004).

In any modern examination of German history, culture, and society, Adolf Hitler is the proverbial elephant in the room. His life raises a puzzling and apparently unanswerable question: How could a nation as sophisticated, advanced, and progressive as Germany—not only in its own eyes but in the eyes of so many others—fall under the spell of a man so clearly limited and destructive as Hitler and follow him blindly to such unprecedented acts of genocidal cruelty as the Holocaust and the catastrophic wars that he inflicted on his nation? We will explore the answer below.

## Germany as Center and Periphery

Germans have been historically fascinated by *Hamlet* and its prince. The *New Statesman*, in a November 2015 article, wondered whether Germany is Hamlet—a country "plagued by indecision and inaction."

Nietzsche was so fascinated by Hamlet that he even coined a phrase, "the Hamlet Doctrine." Freud believed that Shakespeare had written the play for him as a classic case study of the Oedipus complex. Even to the layperson the comparison has some merit: there is the same vacillation between precipitous action and inaction, best exemplified in the famous "to be or not to be" soliloquy, the agonized philosophizing over the meaning of life, and the juxtaposed acts of cruelty and kindness. It would not be difficult to argue that Chancellor Merkel has shown Hamlet-like tendencies in her dealing with the refugee influx as she wavers between moments of doubt and dramatic action; coldly indifferent on television to a young Arab refugee girl, telling her abruptly she had to leave the country, and then opening her arms to warmly welcome a million migrants even at great political cost to herself.

But it is another aspect of Hamlet's behavior that interests the anthropologist in me. Hamlet is both the prince representing and upholding central authority and the rebel wishing to tear it down. The duality reflects an ongoing discussion about central authority and its relationship with the periphery in anthropological literature. *The Thistle and the Drone* illustrated the troubled relationship between central authority and the tribes that traditionally live on the margins of the state along inaccessible international borders, a relationship often marked by violence. The center and the periphery are seen as a binary representing opposed political, social, and economic systems. The center possesses the political and economic power, the administrative machinery, and the defense forces, while the periphery is relegated literally to the edge or margins of the state. The center sees itself as sophisticated and self-important, while tending to look down on the people living on the periphery as uncouth and uncivilized.

In the case of the Germans, we have an example of a people that are simultaneously center and periphery. We are thus presented with an example of a society that needs to be viewed not in terms of center *versus* periphery but center *and* periphery. This definition of Germany helps us understand the ambiguity that is part of its identity; it is the German internal contradiction à la Hamlet—the great German conundrum.

The idea of German identity as both central and peripheral is clearly illustrated through the historical relationship between the Germans as the periphery and Rome as the classic center. The German fascination with the Romans, as well as the Greeks, is detectable everywhere in German statues, literature, mythology, and politics. Yet there is a contradiction between the ideals of ancient tribal Germanic society, which emphasized egalitarianism, lack of hierarchy, tribal unity, and communal spirit, and the highly centralized, authoritarian political structures of the Romans, with an all-powerful emperor at the top ruling over vast territories comprising many different peoples. This conceptual problem has never been resolved.

After the fall of the Roman Empire, Rome was no longer the political center of Europe but remained the spiritual center of a Christian Europe as the home of the Catholic Church and the pope. Although the political center passed into the hands of the emperor, the pope maintained the primacy of the papacy. However, beginning with Otto I, the emperor was first crowned at Aachen, Charlemagne's "New Rome," clearly indicating an independence from Rome, before being crowned by the pope. Charlemagne had established the template for the Holy Roman emperor, who, in an example of German tribal egalitarianism, was elected. Charlemagne took as his model the biblical King David, who was also a tribal ruler, and his divine-right approach to monarchy. It was inevitable that tension would develop between the spiritual center and the periphery, and it is no coincidence in European history that it was the Germans who consistently challenged the pope. From Emperor Frederick II to Martin Luther, they refused to subordinate their ethnic identity for their religious identity. Emperor Frederick I Barbarossa, who added the designation "Holy" to the title of Roman Emperor in the twelfth century, is an example of this refusal to cede religious legitimacy to the pope.

When Luther finally broke from the Catholic Church in the sixteenth century, Germans reinforced Khaldunian asabiyyah in their creation of a German Christianity. It was at this time that Germans also rediscovered Tacitus's *Germania*, which became fundamental to German identity and self-perception in the centuries ahead.[1]

The question of German identity has been of greatest concern not only to the German people themselves but also to the rest of Europe. It is precisely the ambiguity of defining the Germans as either the periphery or the center that confuses both friend and foe. Traditionally, if a center is threatened it will negotiate, build up international alliances, and shore up its defenses. The behavior of a tribe, however, will be different. A tribe will launch a preemptory strike. This is because the code of honor underlines notions of courage and the taking of revenge as defining characteristics. Indeed, tribal themes of honor and revenge can be read in the actions of the modern state of Germany. The defeat of the French in the Franco-Prussian War, which enabled the unification of Germany in 1871, was seen as revenge for Napoleon's defeat of the Prussians some six decades earlier. Revenge was also a motivation behind the German genocide of the Herero people in their South West Africa colony (present-day Namibia), beginning in 1904. Here, Germany felt it had to take revenge to maintain German honor and prestige after the Herero launched a rebellion that humiliated Germany.[2]

When Germany lost the First World War, the European powers met at Versailles to inflict harsh terms—including the loss of territory—designed to humiliate the Germans. For two decades, Germany waited to take revenge. When Germany finally defeated France in 1940, it forced the French to sign their surrender terms in the exact same railway carriage and on the exact same spot as Germany had signed the armistice twenty-two years earlier. German national humiliation and shame at its defeat and its treatment afterwards, including reparations and the occupation of foreign powers, were indeed prime causes for the Second World War, which was seen by Germans as an imperative to restore German honor and dominance.

It is noteworthy that within Germany itself, because there is no center as distinct from and opposed to the periphery, we do not see the customary debilitating center-periphery conflicts. This again makes Germany different from other European countries. Thus in Germany there is no situation comparable to the English relationship with the Scots, Welsh, and Irish; the Spanish with the Basques and Catalans; and the Italians with the Tyroleans and Sicilians. There is nothing comparable in Germany to the situation in France, in which Paris treats all other cities, including Marseille—with a Muslim population of at least 30 percent, mostly from the former colonies of North Africa—as the periphery. The regional distinctions in Germany confirm rather than debunk the tribal theory, being nothing more than tribal groups asserting their independence and their spirit of egalitarianism. In engineering the unification of Germany in 1871, Otto von Bismarck made clear that he did not want a centralized model like the one in France or England and opposed the imposition of his own Prussian culture on the rest of Germany. Instead, he preferred, as he put it, to "absorb all German individualities without nullifying them," a position shared by Kaiser Wilhelm I.[3]

This decentralized model is reflected today in Germany's strong federal system, which is akin to segmentary-lineage tribal societies around the world. Among the Pukhtun, Somalis, Kurds, or Yemenis, people have a sense of being part of the whole and sharing a common language and lineage but at the same time remaining fiercely proud of their own families, clans, and territories. These societies behave in the manner of the Germans, as described by a writer in Saxony in the late 1950s: "Outwardly as unified as necessary, inwardly as diversified as possible."[4] Additionally, no overbearing and dominant capital city or center of gravity emerged in

Germany comparable to London, Paris, or Rome. Germany is alone in Europe in having a diffusion of centers, reflecting the background of the Holy Roman Empire with its multitude of duchies. An outsider finds it baffling to easily pinpoint the "capital" city of Germany: Is it Bonn, Berlin, Munich, or even Frankfurt? Each one of these cities could have a legitimate claim to the title.

### *The Code of Honor and Behavior*

The original word *Germani* was used by Julius Caesar, and Germans have self-identified as *Deutsche*, from a Germanic root word meaning "of the people," a term constituting language, people, and land, one fusing into the other. As the Germanic peoples live both within the modern German state and outside it, there is invariably some ambiguity about the definition and usage of Deutsche. The people of the Netherlands, for example, are called Dutch, which derives from the same root word as Deutsche. The current national anthem of the Netherlands, considered to be the world's oldest, begins with the lines, "William of Nassau, I am of German [Duytschen] blood, True to the Fatherland I remain until my death."

Primordial tribal identity among Germanic peoples is defined by several related codes of behavior, including *Volk, Heimat, Aryan, Wertesystem* (value system), *Gemeinde* (community), and *deutsche Tugenden*. In Scandinavian countries like Denmark, identity is expressed in terms such as *janteloven* and *hygge*. There is a great deal of overlap and similarity between these terms, and the distinctions are not watertight. The ideas of blood, homeland, and belonging to the "soil" are at the heart of these concepts, and they inform normative social behavior. There are also more recently coined terms such as *Leitkultur* (the leading culture) in Germany and the opposed but related concepts of *autochtoon* (from the soil) and *allochtoon* (from foreign soil) in the Netherlands, which are a response to the new social realities created by the immigrants and are discussed in later chapters.

Ibn Khaldun's notion of asabiyyah explains how these different but overlapping codes provide a kind of glue to keep societies together and thus maintain social cohesion. It is this asabiyyah that provides German society its resilience and has allowed it to reemerge with its major social features more or less intact in spite of the devastation it suffered after two world wars. I got a firsthand view of the code at work during our fieldwork in Germanic societies. When we traveled from Cologne to Aachen by train, for example, I was curious to note that there were no ticket collectors on board. When I inquired of the other passengers why this was so, they were surprised that I would be asking about something so obvious; it was assumed that passengers would have bought their tickets before boarding. Similarly, no one checks tickets before boarding the underground trains in Berlin. I also noted on an early morning walk on a Sunday in Copenhagen, when there was virtually no pedestrian or vehicle traffic about, that when pedestrians and cars did appear they invariably waited for the traffic light to turn green before proceeding. Although the road was deserted and it was extremely cold, I wondered whether anyone would actually break the code, so I stopped to observe. All the occasional pedestrians and cars observed the traffic rules impeccably. The point of a universally accepted code is that individuals uphold it even without the presence of the coercive agencies of the state. Their observance of the code illustrated the fact that members of society considered themselves equal and that no one was above the law. Rigid adherence to the law, reduced to a caricature at the time when the Nazis were in power, would become a staple of Hollywood films depicting Germans.

I wondered how recently arrived immigrants would have behaved, especially if they were walking on a road without a single car in sight. I do not doubt that many of them would have been tempted to violate the rules because "no one was looking." Yet if a minor infraction of the code, such as walking against the traffic light, elicits disapproval and even anger from the local population, I could only imagine what they would make of an immigrant failing to learn the language, making noisy public demands to build mosques, or, in extreme cases, engaging in crime, sexual assaults, or acts of terrorism.

There are indeed aspects of the Germanic codes that prevent the immigrant from being accepted by the local community because Germans perceive them as "not like us." Margret Spohn, a sympathetic Munich government official who deals with the integration of immigrants, admitted that Turks were half as likely as Germans to get a job they had applied for simply because of their Turkish identity. In Copenhagen, a man of Pakistani descent told us that he showed up for an interview for an IT job and was encouraged to leave before it even began because the firm did not wish to hire someone who was not an ethnic Dane.

Below we will briefly look at some of the more important concepts that reflect primordial tribal identity among Germanic peoples including Volk, Heimat, Aryan, janteloven, and hygge. It is precisely these concepts, we will point out, that in times of economic and political stress and conflict in society assume dangerous predatory forms and target minorities.

### Herder Defines the Volk

If Tacitus is the anthropologist of the Germanic peoples, Johann Gottfried von Herder (1744–1803) is their poet-philosopher. While the former depicted an overarching view of society, the latter focused on the concept of Volk. Of all the terms relating to the Germanic primordial tribal identity, the notion of the Volk is perhaps the most fundamental and important. At the core of Herder's articulation of Volk is primordial tribal identity and its organic link with the modern nation. The ideas of Herder, known as the father of nationalism, would be of utmost importance in shaping the nationalist movements of the Germans and indeed other peoples across the European continent.

One of the seminal European philosophers who would influence other major figures such as G. W. F. Hegel, Herder originated the concept of the *Volksgeist*, the unique spirit of a people rooted in their primeval character, which soon became synonymous with Volk itself. While the concept of the Volk, meaning "people" and linked to the terrain, history, culture, and lineage of the community, had been with the Germanic peoples for centuries, it was only around the eighteenth and early nineteenth centuries, as the Holy Roman Empire was approaching its demise, that the term was further refined and began to acquire its modern connotations of being aggressively linked to blood, soil, music, art, literature, culture, and ultimately ethnic nationalism. Characteristics of Volk and other overlapping definitions of identity were encapsulated by the phrase *Blut und Boden*, "Blood and Soil," later appropriated by the Nazis for their malevolent purposes.

Herder, a pupil of Immanuel Kant, believed that every ethnic nation of the world had its own unique spirit, its own Volk. Each nation was seen as a plant, with its roots stretching back into history. That each distinct national plant should develop separately was part of God's plan. For Herder, the world was likened to a garden of *Völker*, with each plant having its own particular fragrance. When taken as a whole, each nation in its distinctiveness contributed to a beautiful world, a sweet-smelling garden. Like other Germanic scholars, Herder emphasized soil and a link with ethnicity and blood as defining factors in determining both the spirit and identity of the Volk.

Herder believed that the essence of the Volk could be seen in its purest form in folk music, literature, and poetry. From these, Herder wrote, "one can learn the mode of thought of a nationality and its language of feeling."

These poems and songs, often known by the peasantry or people in rural areas, were for Herder "the archives" and "living voice" of each nationality and the "imprints" of its soul.[5] "A poet," Herder wrote in 1773, "is the creator of the nation around him, he gives them a world to see and has their souls in his hand to lead them to that world."[6] In keeping with this notion, to discover the spirit of one's authentic Volk one must eschew reason for emotion. The past, Herder said, can be understood "by feeling one's way" into it.[7]

Herder's philosophy of the Volk overlapped with Ibn Khaldun's concept of asabiyyah in conceptualizing the tribes and people living in rural areas as being more authentic in their Volk than people in the cities, whose society has been diluted and compromised. Herder also praised the code of honor and hospitality of the rural tribes as being preferable to the vague Enlightenment notion of the unity of man, which had currency in the cosmopolitan cities.[8] Herder believed that a natural, God-sanctioned state was one with a single nationality and a single Volk. As the historian Pierre James explained, "for [Herder], *nation, state,* and *Volk* were virtually synonymous."[9]

The thought of a pluralistic nation-state with different kinds of people living together was intolerable and horrifying. The nation, Herder wrote, is a family: "A kingdom consisting of a single nationality is a family, a well-regulated household . . . founded by nature." "An empire formed by forcing together a hundred nationalities, and a hundred and fifty provinces," he said, "is no body politic, but a monstrosity." Herder was concerned that Germany had been harmed by the influence of foreign ideas and customs and that it had been subjected to "an imposed foreign civilization." Herder was especially disparaging of the German tendency to speak foreign languages, particularly Latin and French. The dishonorable desire in a Volk to construct a culture based on foreign influences was an indication, as Herder put it, of "disease, flatulence, abnormal surfeit and approaching death."

The native language, Herder wrote, "is filled with the life and blood of our forefathers." Herder appealed to the honor of the Germans, arguing, "He that despises the language of his nationality dishonors its most noble public; he becomes the most dangerous murderer of her spirit, of her honor at home and abroad, of her sentiments, of her finer morality and activity."[10] In the poem "An die Deutschen" (To the Germans), Herder put his sentiments in verse:

> And you German alone, returning from abroad,
> Wouldst greet your mother in French?
> O spew it out, before your door
> Spew out the ugly slime of the Seine
> Speak German, O you German!"[11]

Herder believed that Christianity, in its attacks on "the tales, songs, customs, temples and monuments of paganism among the Germans," was also implicated in the loss of the German character. He lamented that the Germans did not seem to know their own folk literature. Herder desired a national literature that would be specifically and characteristically German and attempted to shame the German nation for not having come up with one: "You have no Shakespeare; have you also no songs of your forbears of which you can boast? . . . Without doubt they have been and still exist; but they are lying under the slime, are unappreciated and despised."

The honoring of ancestors was also fundamental to the exercise of rediscovering and reviving the spirit of the Volk. The Fatherland, as explained by Herder, "has descended from our fathers; it arouses the remembrance of all the meritorious who went before us, and of all the worthy ones whose fathers we shall be."[12] Herder believed that the key to the German rediscovery of the authentic Volk and the spirit of the German ancestors lay in the study of Tacitus's *Germania*: "Look about you in Germany for the character of the nation, for their particular sound of thought, for the true mood of their language; where are they? Read Tacitus; there you will find their character."[13] Herder celebrated the bodies of the tribal Germans, describing "their big, strong and beautiful figure, their terribly blue eyes . . . filled with the spirit of moderation and loyalty."[14] The Germans, Herder wrote, were "a living wall against which the mad fury of Huns, Hungarians, Mongols, and Turks dashed itself to pieces."[15]

## Volk, Primordial Identity, and German Nationalism

Herder's theories that so intimately associated German ethnicity with nationalism and statehood had an electrifying effect on the German people during Napoleon's occupation of the land in the early nineteenth century and led to the unification of Germany in 1871. Yet this was not considered sufficient for many Germans, as parts of the Volk, for example, in the empire of Austria-Hungary as well as the Germanic peoples of Northern Europe—the Scandinavians, Dutch, and English—still remained outside the Reich, or German Empire. These voices would continue to agitate and promote their vision of the unity of the Volk, leading to the rise of Hitler and the Second World War. During the nineteenth and the first half of the twentieth centuries, Germany's leading figures, including its most prominent politicians, philosophers, artists, and composers, wrote passionately about the concept of Volk and the necessity of incorporating it into a single state and simultaneously ridding it of foreign influences.

Prominent among the early advocates was Johann Gottlieb Fichte, the noted German philosopher in the Kantian tradition. In the aftermath of Napoleon's victory at Jena in 1806, which led to the French defeat of Prussia, Fichte attempted to rally Germans to the cause of nationalism in his *Addresses to the German Nation* (1807–08). Echoing Herder, he declared, "Our most urgent present problem is to preserve the existence and continuity of all that is German."[16] Fichte celebrated the Germans for their purity, declaring that they were an *Urvolk* (original Volk) of a "race" that was not mixed and therefore distinct to others like the Italians and French.[17] Only the Germans, wrote Fichte, "remained in the original dwelling places of the ancestral stock."[18] He went on to state that "only the German—the original . . . truly has a *Volk*, a *Volk* upon which they can count, and only the German is capable of having a wholly rational love of their nation."

Fichte additionally believed that it was Germany's duty to save Europe and the world: "if the Germans do not save humanity's level of civilization, then no other European nation will do so." Fichte at this early date was already pushing Herder's notions of primordial tribal identity toward predator identity in asserting the inherent superiority of the Germans. Whereas what is German is vital and alive, he argued, "'the foreign' was a 'belief in death.'"[19] We see the dangerous directions in which the arguments about identity are moving.

Also writing during the Napoleonic period was the German author and poet Ernst Moritz Arndt, who motivated German soldiers by invoking Tacitus, "one of the greatest men who ever lived." The Germans, Arndt wrote, "are not bastardized by alien peoples . . . they have remained more than many other peoples in their original purity."[20] He boasted, "the lucky Germans are an original [*ursprüngliches*] *Volk*."[21]

Another important nationalist in the early nineteenth century was the Prussian Friedrich Ludwig Jahn, also known as Turnvater ("father of gymnastics") Jahn. Jahn pioneered the use of gymnastics in Germany and had a lasting impact on the sport; memorials to him exist in places as far away as St. Louis, Missouri. Like Fichte and Arndt, Jahn was incensed by Napoleon's occupation and sought to improve the physical fitness of Germans in order to revive their spirit and fight for independence. Echoing Herder's comparison of the Volk to a plant, Jahn wrote of Prussia as "the stem of the German plant. . . . When Germany is united under Prussian leadership, she will become the founder of eternal peace in Europe, the protecting angel of mankind!" Jahn was a member of the Berlin Society for German Speech, where he promoted research to cleanse the German language of "foreign words."[22] "The purer a people," he said, "the better."[23]

Jahn wrote that "a state without a *Volk* is nothing, a soulless artifice, a *Volk* without a state is nothing, a bodiless, airy phantom, like the gypsies and the Jews. Only state and *Volk* together can form a Reich."[24] The Germans had lost the vigor of their ancestors and had become effeminate and soft under French influence, he argued, and if they used traditional Swedish exercises, they could rebuild both their physiques and their national spirit and morale.

The Brothers Grimm, who were inspired by Herder to discover and promote the folk tales of the Germans, were also strong advocates of German primordial identity. They regarded folk tales to be the true expression of the Volk and linked to the divine. As Wilhelm Grimm wrote, "only folk poetry is perfect. God Himself wrote it as He did the Ten Commandments."[25] The Grimms collected folk tales "from the lips of peasant women, shepherds, waggoners, vagrants, old grannies, and children."[26] There was an important link between the soil and the folk tales, Jacob Grimm observed: "All my works relate to the Fatherland, from whose soil they derive their strength."[27]

The Brothers Grimm inspired the life's work of the composer Richard Wagner. Wagner wrote in his autobiography that he was awakened in his mission to fight for the German spirit by the book *German Mythology* (1835) by Jacob Grimm. Wagner explained that he was at a spa reading the book when his life was forever changed:

> Even the most fragmentary legends spoke to me in a profoundly familiar tongue, and soon my entire sensibility was possessed by images suggesting ever more clearly the recapture of a long lost yet eagerly sought consciousness. . . . The effect they produced upon my innermost being I can only describe as a complete rebirth, and just as we feel a tender joy at a child's first sudden flash of recognition, so my own eyes now flashed with rapture at a world I saw revealed for the first time, as if by a miracle, in which I had previously moved blindly though presentient, like a child in its mother's womb.[28]

Wagner's mission, as he saw it, was to connect Germans with the spirit of their Volk by reminding them of the ancient tales. The "German spirit," he wrote, "does not require a new birth, but really only re birth," a "fantastic rise out of the past."[29] Wagner mined German history for inspiration and frequently featured themes and characters from German mythology. Wagner believed the German Volk to be under serious threat from foreigners and foreign influences and voiced scathing criticism of the influence of the Jews and the threat they posed to the Volk (see chapter 7).

The Volkisch nationalists who so glorified and venerated Wagner greeted the founding of the German state in 1871 ecstatically. During this period, "Wagnerian music and prose were hailed by the prophets of German nationalism as a kind of religio-mythological justification for German hegemony."[30] The center of Wagner's opera festivals was at Bayreuth, where his operas have been performed annually from 1876. Ever since, Bayreuth has been an important symbol of German nationalism and a center of pilgrimage for those fascinated by Wagner.

Yet there remained work to be done to integrate the remaining Germans into the new country. The Volkisch movement would continue and even intensify in the German-speaking areas. As the historian Christopher B. Krebs describes it,

> Numerous voluntary political associations formed a "secondary system of social power" wherein *völkisch* men—the majority were middle-class and highly educated—played a loud and oftentimes loutish role. Agitating with "beer-emphasis" (to borrow Thomas Mann's expression), they rallied behind national symbols for the sake of national causes, real and imagined. They joined major organizations like the Alldeutscher Verband (Pan-German League), founded in 1891, the Germanenorden (Germanic order), founded in 1912, and countless other associations, gymnastic societies, shooting clubs, student corporations, and youth groups.[31]

This was the social and cultural milieu from which Hitler emerged. Hitler saw himself, as did his followers, as the predestined Wagnerian hero who personified the Volk, linked as it was with nation and state. The Nazi slogan "Ein Volk, ein Reich, ein Führer" (One people, one empire, one leader) captured this association. Nazi racial theories, such as the Aryan thesis discussed below, led to further conceptualizations of the Germans as the *Herrenvolk*, the master race, and constituting the *Volksgemeinschaft*, the Germanic ethnic community.

After the fall of the Nazis, terms such as Volk and Aryan were discouraged. The concept of Volk emerged once again in the popular East German rallies against Communist rule in 1989 and 1990 immediately preceding German reunification, in which crowds chanted "Wir sind das Volk!" (We are the Volk). This same slogan is now used by anti-immigration Pegida activists in their demonstrations against Muslims (see chapters 8 and 9).

During our fieldwork we noted the enduring popularity of Wagner and the controversy he still provokes in Germany. When we asked—naively, as it turned out—if it would be possible to secure tickets to the annual Bayreuth Festival dedicated to Wagner's music, we were told that the waiting period is between five and ten years. Our casual queries about Bayreuth made people uncomfortable. Even our German host in Munich, the honorary Pakistan consul general, Pantelis Christian Poetis, grew visibly uneasy and advised us not to go there. He said, "We don't feel this is Germany."

Having failed to experience Wagner in his homeland, Frankie, Zeenat, and I were, ironically, able to join an enraptured American audience at the Chautauqua Institution in rural western New York State in the summer of 2017 to hear a full-blown symphony orchestra playing some of Wagner's most powerful selections. These included "Ride of the Valkyries" from his opera *Die Walküre*, "Forest Murmurs" from *Siegfried*, and "Entry of the Gods into Valhalla" from *Das Rheingold*.

In Germany, we found that contemporary concepts of the Volk were contested and controversial, especially in discussions of the place of minorities, as confirmed for us in our conversation with Rabbi Steven Langnas of Munich:

> German identity is connected with the land, it's connected with the idea of das Volk, the nation. But that means much more in German than the word "nation" in English. It is the very soul of the German nation and what it means to be German. . . . Language, culture, it's all a part of it, and Jewish people identify with it quite thoroughly. They did before the war. The third generation is beginning once again to feel that this is our home and to feel comfortable. A little bit different, with the language, with the mentality, but not necessarily with the nationalism, although many Jewish people that I know cheered for Germany with the football match.

## Volk in Nordic Societies

Herder's ideas spread rapidly from Germany to Germanic Scandinavia and the Nordic region, as Norwegians, Swedes, Danes, and Finns took up the task of finding their authentic Volk, known as *folk* in Scandinavia. In all these countries, poets, artists, and scholars followed Herder in going to the countryside. Their aim was to seek out the peasantry and locate the sources for a new nationalism rooted in primordial tribal identity, which was of crucial importance in shaping the character of their respective modern states.

In Finland, the poet, explorer, and linguist Elias Lönnrot was inspired by Herder to compile the epic poem *The Kalevala, or Old Karelian Poems about the Ancient Times of the Finnish Folk* (1835), from interviews with peasants. The poem became the national epic of Finland and had such a profound impact on Finnish culture and identity that the question is frequently asked, "Would Finland exist as a nation state without Lönnrot's Kalevala?"[32] Kalevala, the mythic name for Finland, is the land of the Kaleva tribe and of Kaleva, considered the common ancestor of the Finns.

In Norway, Peter Christen Asbjørnsen and Jørgen Moe followed Herder and the Brothers Grimm in collecting and publishing folk tales gathered from peasants and villagers, which helped establish Norwegian identity with characters and stories that "have become an important part of Norwegian literature, language, and culture."[33] Similarly, composers sought inspiration among the peasants: Edvard Grieg spoke of a person or a people's unchanging *folkesjæl,* or folk soul, and declared that "the folk song reflects musically the inner life of the people."[34] The playwright Henrik Ibsen, said to be the most performed dramatist in the world after Shakespeare, worked as a folklore collector and celebrated the Germanic past in works such as *The Vikings at Helgeland* (1858).

In Denmark, N. F. S. Grundtvig, the bishop, teacher, philosopher, poet, and Danish national hero, extensively studied Norse myths and was "the founder of the study of folklore in Denmark."[35] Attempting to avert what he called the "folk-death" of the Danes at the hands of foreign influences, he was inspired by Herder to develop and widely promote the idea of *folkelighed,* the communal egalitarian spirit of the people. Grundtvig believed that "the new democratic system would work only if every Dane was able to participate in political life," and the "Grundtvigian model . . . could be seen as the raising of village culture to a national level."[36] Grundtvig's *folkehøjskoler* (folk high schools), which offered subsidized education to Danes across the country, helped to achieve this objective, and they remain popular. Notably, Grundtvig believed that Denmark's Jewish community was outside the Danish folk and folkelighed (see chapter 7).

Hans Christian Andersen, the nineteenth-century writer, is a product of the Danish cultural milieu that produced a wealth of folk literature suffused with Herder's ideas of the importance of oral stories emanating from peasant sources. His fairy tales "The Emperor's New Clothes," "The Ugly Duckling," "The Little Mermaid," and "Thumbelina" are known around the world and are particularly popular in the United States.

The Danish poet and playwright Adam Oehlenschläger, the author of the Danish national anthem and widely considered the country's greatest poet, was heavily influenced by Herder and wrote frequently of Germanic themes. Oehlenschläger's poem "The Golden Horns," about two famous ancient Germanic artifacts, is one of the best-known works in Danish literature and "was the direct result of his introduction to Herder's philosophy."[37]

In Denmark, the idea of the folk continues to be fundamental to culture and identity: the Danish Parliament is Folketinget, the People's House; the Danish national church is Folkekirken, the People's Church; and democracy is called *Folkestyret*, rule of the people. *Folkelig* is a commonly used term meaning something popular, simple, unassuming, or for the people, and one of the leading political parties in the nation is the far-right Dansk Folkeparti, the Danish People's Party.[38]

In Sweden, Herder's call was taken up by the Gothic League and its journal, *Iduna*, named after the Germanic goddess of youth and apples and published by Erik Gustaf Geijer, who was "Sweden's most influential historian and one of its most admired poets." Geijer's poems about the Vikings "became seen as classic expressions of true 'Viking spirit,' and were often recited or sung at patriotic gatherings and later in many Swedish schools." The Gothic League drank from horns and performed "Viking rituals in the optimistic hope that such activities would rejuvenate and strengthen their country in future conflicts with Russia."[39]

The egalitarian philosophy of *Folkhemmet*, the people's home, has been Sweden's dominant social philosophy since the 1930s and was key to the development of the welfare state. Folkhemmet was institutionalized by Per Albin Hansson, Sweden's longtime prime minister, who articulated it as the governing philosophy of his Social Democratic Party in 1928: "The basis of the home is community and togetherness. The good home does not recognize any privileged or neglected members, nor any favorite or stepchildren. In the good home there is equality, consideration, co-operation, and helpfulness."[40] In this, Hansson evoked Herder, who, as noted above, defined the nation as a "family, a well-regulated household."

## Heimat

Another fundamentally important concept in German identity—one that overlaps with Volk—is Heimat. The term, broadly meaning home or homeland and carrying an often mystical, emotional, provincial, nostalgic, folkloric, rural, and anti-modern connotation, is notoriously difficult to translate into English. Heimat has been defined as "where one feels at home, where one's language is spoken, where one has absorbed the climate so much that it is part of oneself without one's being aware of it."[41] Like Volk, which Herder wrote could best be understood through the "language of feeling," Heimat was frequently identified as something that could not be taught, shared with others, or even communicated at all. It was instead something that Germans instinctively felt, in keeping with the spirit of the Romantic movement of the nineteenth century that coincided and overlapped with German nationalism and the promotion of primordial tribal identity. Germanic intellectuals used phrases like "deeply religious" and "impalpably magical" to describe the experience of Heimat.[42] The opposite of Heimat is *Fremde*, or foreign.[43]

For the German philosopher Martin Heidegger, Heimat was the locale where a person was able to live their most authentic life while speaking their own authentic dialect, an essential prerequisite for pursuing truth.[44] Nietzsche also incorporated Heimat into his philosophy, writing that Germans had lived with a "long humiliation under which the German genius, alienated from house and Heimat, lived in the service of treacherous dwarfs." Nietzsche sought to bring back the "long lost Heimat" by reviving traditional German culture, which he initially believed could be achieved through the music of Wagner.[45]

The word Heimat has roots in ancient German and has been present since the fifteenth century in various dialects.[46] Heimat traditionally denoted one's own homestead, such as "fields, house, livestock, extended family with hierarchical role and labor divisions"; those without Heimat who spent their lives traveling—such as laborers, farmhands, and musicians—were "treated with suspicion and associated with uncertainty, poverty, dishonesty, or worse."[47] Like Volk, Heimat in its modern sense became part of the mainstream debate and discussion about German identity only upon Napoleon's invasion and occupation of Germany.[48] In Friedrich Schiller's play *William Tell* (1804), about the famous Swiss freedom fighter against Hapsburg oppression, interpreted and celebrated by Germans in the context of resistance to French occupation, Heimat is seen as something to be protected and preserved against foreigners. Lines reflecting this theme include, "Sadly, your Heimat became a foreign land to you!"; "And when I came into the valley of my Heimat, when I found my father, blind and robbed, I didn't cry"; "Whether the lake or the mountains separate us, we still are one people of one blood, and it is *one* Heimat out of which we came"; and "I will find my happiness in my Heimat." We already see an overlap between Heimat and "blood" that will in turn mirror Volk.

In the nineteenth century, a movement emerged to celebrate and protect the Heimat against the corrupting influences of modernity, featuring poetry, publications, hiking programs, school curriculums, conservation initiatives—the natural environment, particularly the forest, was an essential part of Heimat—and the formation of various associations. This Heimat movement strove to build a feeling in Germans for their local villages, customs, costumes, and history through the promotion of literature, the exploration of nature, and the building of museums. Between 1890 and 1918, nearly 400 Heimat museums were founded across the nation. Local communities attempted to evoke Heimat by reviving traditional dress styles that had gone out of fashion with modernization and urbanization.

In the Nazi period, Heimat was associated with blood, Volk, and nation. When Hitler returned to Austria in 1938 upon the annexation of that country by Germany, he addressed the Austrians at the North Train Station in Vienna: "Can anyone wonder, then, that there remained in me that longing to enclose my own Heimat [that is, Austria] into this dearest *Reich?*" Hitler had invoked Heimat as early as 1920 in a speech about minorities in Germany: "It is impossible that those who are at home everywhere [that is, mobile populations, but here, especially, Jews and Sinti and Roma] can know what Heimat is, because they do not have one."[49]

Heimat has been a mainstay of German popular culture for many years, with an entire genre of film, the *Heimatfilme*, addressing Heimat themes. Heimatfilme date back to the beginning of German cinema: In 1910, the film *Heimatliche Scholle* (Heimat soil) told the story of a village boy who goes to the city, becomes a criminal, and then returns home. By the beginning of the 1920s there was market saturation, with one reviewer of a film released in 1921 remarking, "one can't bear to see any more Tyrolean farms, peasants' huts, open-air dance floors, and village inns."[50] Heimatfilme continued to be produced under the Nazis—for example, the 1942 film *Die goldene Stadt* (The golden city) was a massive hit. It tells the story of a young woman who moves from her rural town (representing Heimat) to Prague, the golden city, where she is impregnated by a Czech. She then returns home to the Heimat, where she is rejected by her family and the community for her impurity. The film ends with her suicide.

In the 1950s, 300 Heimatfilme were made, some of which achieved massive success: at least 20 million people saw the classic *Grün ist die Heide* (The heath is green).[51] Among the most successful German films of the 1950s was the Heimatfilme *Die Trapp-Familie* (The Von Trapp Family) in 1956, which was followed by a sequel in 1958. The story of the family was adapted for Broadway as *The Sound of Music* in 1959 and by Hollywood in 1965.

*The Sound of Music*, starring a young Julie Andrews and Christopher Plummer, provides one of the most famous international illustrations of Heimat. The film depicts the life of the dashing Austrian officer Captain von Trapp and his beautiful family of seven children in a rural community on the eve of the Second World War. The family, with their freshly scrubbed, rosy-cheeked faces and glowing white complexions shining with Alpine wholesomeness, is matched by the idyllic mountain vistas, lush green fields and forests, crystal-clear lakes and rivers, and picturesque churches: this is the perfect and quintessential vision of Heimat. Heimat here illustrates dramatically that while it is the ideal vehicle for the Germanic peoples, there is really no place for anyone not ethnically German and therefore outside Germanic tribal boundaries.

Despite German discomfort with the idea of Heimat following the Second World War, *Heimat* was the title of the most watched series in the history of German television. The series, which began airing in 1984, concerned twentieth-century German history as experienced from the perspective of a single village in the Rhineland. Made as a German response to the 1978 American television film *Holocaust,* starring Meryl Streep and James Woods, *Heimat* was criticized for glossing over anti-Semitism and the Holocaust as well as for its "negative image of the American liberators."[52] The historian Kenneth Barkin notes that Americans are depicted in *Heimat* as "shallow, rootless, money-grabbing materialists." America was thus "the antithesis to Heimat: a consumerist and soulless society."[53]

By the 1990s, and especially following the collapse of the Berlin Wall and the unification of East and West Germany, Heimat had come to "have more legitimacy and more power of evocation than such terms as *Fatherland* or even *nation*."[54] In the second half of the 1990s, more than 400 books with Heimat in their title were published in Germany.[55] There were many debates about Heimat, particularly in respect to the presence of immigrants and whether they would ever be able, or should ever be able, to call Germany their Heimat.

It was this question that concerned Heinrich Kreft, a German scholar and diplomat, who defined Heimat to me in the traditional manner while at the same time saying that he believed that Germany is now the Heimat for Turks and Muslims who live there. For Kreft, Turks and Muslims should be allowed full rights of identity in Germany. "If this is your home," he said, "you want to have it as a Heimat, a home. And this includes religious symbols, mosques. Frankly, when I was going to school in the 1960s, I didn't know where the Muslims were going to pray, because there were no mosques visible, they just used big halls for their prayers. But this of course changed when this became their Heimat."

For Naika Foroutan, a prominent German scholar of Islam in Germany at Berlin's Humboldt University, Heimat should be an inclusive concept. Her extensive research project on how young German Muslims define their identity is called Hybrid European-Muslim Identities (HEYMAT). Because Heimat means something akin to "home country," Foroutan explained, she wanted her project to be known as Heymat with a *y*—the *y* standing for hybridity—to indicate that "our project was dedicated to work on hybrid identities in Germany, focusing especially on hybrid German-Muslim identity." Foroutan, who is of Iranian and German parentage and has been heavily involved in the media debate about Islam in Germany, thus sends a signal to German Muslims and the public at large that Heimat need not be an exclusive concept only for white Germans but should reflect the complex reality of identity in the twenty-first century.

## HEIMAT AMONG OTHER GERMANIC PEOPLES

The concept of Heimat, it should be noted, extended beyond the borders of Germany. In Switzerland, the German word *Heimatort,* the place of origin determined by line of male descent, is the most important marker of identity. It is the Heimatort that is on Swiss citizens' passports, not their actual place of birth, even though the family may not have lived in their Heimatort for generations.

In Sweden, the equivalent term is *hembygd*, which "is often used with an emotional ring to it, and connotes a feeling of belonging to a place."[56] Hembygd overlapped with the Swedish concept of the folk, as expressed in the Swedish National Romantic movement of the nineteenth century, which in such fields as art and literature "promoted the love of one's childhood home and its landscape, as well as a respect for indigenous architecture, costume, and handicrafts. These emphases were rooted in a folkish ideology that stressed the interconnectedness of beings with their natural surroundings."[57] In Sweden, the hembygd "became a unifying symbol of the local community and whole nation."[58]

The hembygd movement, which coincided with the Heimat movement in Germany, reflected a similar anxiety about urbanization and industrialization and led to the "founding of regional and local associations dedicated to an interest in folk cultures . . . with both open-air museums and other related activities."[59] Today in Sweden there are 1,400 hembygd museums of local folk culture, customs, art, and history across the nation, most offering free entrance and some providing lodging for visitors.[60]

## HEIMAT, VOLK, AND CONTEMPORARY GERMANIC MUSIC

The enduring and current importance of Heimat and Volk can be seen in the popular music and culture of Germanic countries. After the Second World War, foreign music, especially that coming from the United Kingdom and the United States, dominated the German scene. In direct opposition to rock and roll and artists like Elvis Presley, music rooted firmly in German traditions of Heimat and Volk—such as *Volksmusik*, the music of the Volk, and *Schlager*, "hit" music, which was also popular outside Germany and impacted the pan-European Eurovision song competition established in the 1950s—grew in popularity. Schlager was the accompanying music of the Heimatfilme genre, and in the 1960s and 1970s acts such as Heino, one of the most successful German artists of all time, with his distinctive light blonde hairdo and sunglasses, became phenomenally popular by reviving German folk songs. Heino described himself as "the singer of the silent majority," claimed the considerable feat of outselling the Beatles in Germany, and believed his popularity was downplayed by journalists amid concerns about German nationalism.[61] Heino's recordings included the German national anthem, containing the verses that were dropped after Nazi rule, the famous nineteenth-century anti-French anthem "Die Wacht am Rhein" ("The guard on the Rhine"), which Nazi soldiers are depicted singing in the film *Casablanca* (1942), and "Schwarzbraun ist die Haselnuss" ("Black-brown is the hazelnut"), a folk song made popular by the Hitler Youth and the Nazi armed forces. His album covers showed the singer wearing traditional dress and also feature the classic depictions of Heimat and Volk, including forests, mountains, and wolflike German Shepherd dogs, as on *Seine großen Erfolge 6* (Greatest hits, volume 6) from 1978. We shall discuss the significance of such symbols in German culture below.

In recent years controversy has continued to follow Heino, who sports a skull ring and boasts a logo featuring a skull with blonde, Heino-style hair wearing sunglasses with lightning bolts in the eyes. When asked in 2013 about his health, Heino replied that he was "still as hard as steel, as tough as leather and as nimble as a greyhound," a clear paraphrase of a 1935 Hitler speech. He also compared himself to an "old oak."[62]

Despite being ignored by the many Germans who hoped that Schlager and Volksmusik would disappear—most radio and television networks ignore the colossal sales of Schlager, for example, in favor of their own Schlager-free music charts—the genres remain enormously popular.

Helene Fischer, the singer who in 2013 recorded "Atemlos durch die Nacht" ("Breathless through the night"), one of the most successful singles in German history, is a Schlager artist who has won multiple Krone der Volksmusik (Crown of Volksmusik) awards. "Turn on public network ARD at 8:15 p.m. on a Saturday evening," a 2013 report in *Der Spiegel* noted, "and you'll see an array of Schlager and folk music performers, often wearing dirndls and lederhosen, singing about the beautiful Alps or Heidi's deep blue eyes to the rhythmic clapping of an enchanted audience. The shows haven't changed since the 1970s."

### The Aryan Race

Another key concept articulating Germanic primordial identity—and overlapping with Volk and Heimat—is Aryan. The concept, developed by scholars and scientists to describe a particular racial type, became increasingly influential in Germany in the nineteenth century. The concept of the Aryan race exploded from the halls of academia and scientific conferences to become fundamental to German identity, statecraft, and foreign policy under Hitler.

The idea of the Aryan race was based on a theory first proposed by the eighteenth-century English scholar Sir William Jones, whose research in India had posited a relationship between Sanskrit and the languages of Europe, including Greek and Latin. Jones argued only that there was a relationship between Sanskrit and the European languages and did not speculate on a common source or common language. These languages became known as "Indo-European," a term coined by an English writer, although in Germany many preferred to call them "Indo-German."[63]

The prominent German philologist Karl Wilhelm Friedrich Schlegel drew on these ideas to move from asserting a lingual to a blood relationship between Indo-Europeans, arguing that the "famous nations sprang from one stock" and that, in the words of the historian George L. Mosse, "Germans, ancients, and Indians formed a true organic community; others did not."[64] Schlegel coined the term *Aryan peoples* to describe this community.[65] By the mid-nineteenth century, the Aryan racial thesis had become widespread and was adopted by thinkers inside and outside Germany. Hegel, for example, "pronounced as fact the phenomenon of the migration of an Aryan people to the west," which ran concurrent with the migration from East to West of the *Weltgeist*, or world spirit.[66] Hegel declared, "Europe is the absolute end of history and Asia the beginning."[67]

Integral to the Aryan thesis was the concept of race as a way of classifying humans, an idea first introduced by Kant, the "inventor of race."[68] Adopting the term "from the English language and from the animal kingdom," Kant theorized that there was an "original" white race from which four distinct races developed. He reserved special praise for the Germans, whom he described as the "tallest and most beautiful people" in the world.[69] German philosophers and scientists went on to posit the existence of an original, superior, Germanic white race—a race that became interchangeable with the Aryan—from which humanity then descended and degenerated. Among these philosophers was Christoph Meiners, who, writing in the late eighteenth century, first used the term *Caucasian* to describe the white race, which he believed lived originally in the Caucasus region. While the Caucasians had degenerated from their original state, leading to the development of different races, the Germans were closest to the original, and their "purity of blood" ensured their superiority in physique, intellect, and morality over all peoples in the world.[70] But it was the eminent German scientist Johann Friedrich Blumenbach, known as the father of physical anthropology and a court physician to Britain's King George III, who widely popularized the idea of an original, superior, beautiful, and white Caucasian race, of whom the Germans were the exemplars.

### Janteloven

In Scandinavian society, notions of Volk, Heimat, and Aryan were influential, but other quintessentially Scandinavian concepts overlapped with them. These terms reflected and promoted the same Germanic notion of primordial identity and highlighted the difficulty that outsiders faced in becoming part of that identity. One such concept is janteloven, first introduced by the Danish-Norwegian author Aksel Sandemose in a 1933 novel set in the fictional Danish town of Jante. Sandemose captured the social mores and culture of the village in such an authentic fashion that it resonated across the Scandinavian region. During our fieldwork in Denmark, Danes cited it to us constantly, and sometimes in a self-conscious manner, when we asked them about Danish identity. Janteloven, which is defined by ten "laws," is framed in the context of the relationships within a community and with outsiders; it emphasizes egalitarianism, humility, the identity of the collective, and the inability of a foreigner to become part of it.

Each person we interviewed, local or immigrant, emphasized that the traditional code discouraged individuals from "standing out" in relation to

*Author interviewing Flemming Rose, who published cartoons of
the Prophet of Islam in Copenhagen in 2005*

the community; difference was not tolerated. Sanila Rana, a successful
IBM executive of Pakistani descent, defined janteloven as "a law that tells
you that you shouldn't show yourself off, you shouldn't be different from
other people, otherwise we will take you down. So this is really inside
every Dane, as I've seen it, and that reflects in their minds, in their behavior, but also in their business behavior." Like immigrants in Germany,
Sanila spoke of the great difficulty of trying to become part of this tribal
society as an outsider. Rana Athar Javed, the director general of the Pakistan House, a think tank in Copenhagen, and of Pakistani background,
described Danish identity in similar terms: "I think fundamentally Danishness means—what they themselves, the Danes, would tell you—is that
they're like tribes. You know, the tribal mentality."

   Flemming Rose, the foreign affairs editor at the newspaper *Jyllands-
Posten,* who published the controversial cartoons of the Prophet of Islam
in 2005, also described Denmark as "tribal," which, he told us in his office in Copenhagen, was the secret to the famous welfare state found
across Scandinavia. The welfare state, Rose explained, works because of
the tribal status of the Danes and their ability to share and provide for
one another within the ethnic community. "Denmark in many ways is a
tribal society. . . . Within Danish culture," he explained, "we have a very
thick cultural code. Danish identity is many layered, but is very thick in
the sense that it is very difficult for outsiders to penetrate . . . and become
a member or insider in Danish society." Rose said that even his wife, who
is Russian by birth but has lived for decades in Denmark, would not be

considered a Dane and has, as a result, experienced difficulty finding employment.

Søren Espersen, the deputy chairman of the far-right Danish People's Party, also spoke of Danish identity in terms of the community and the virtual inability of outsiders to join it. Espersen discussed the difficulties that his British-born wife has also faced in being accepted as Danish.

## Hygge

Like janteloven, Volk, and Heimat, hygge (pronounced "hoo-ga") emphasizes the local community and sets up boundaries between it and outsiders. In the past few years, hygge has hit the international media as people around the world searched for those elusive factors that contributed to Denmark consistently being named the happiest country on earth. We have, it seems, entered a period of global hyggemania. Hygge was identified as the possible secret to Danish happiness, and there was a flow of articles, books, and commentary amid a global quest to understand hygge and to achieve it in one's own country. At least twenty English-language books on hygge were published in 2016.

As with the other terms articulating Germanic primordial identity, hygge has counterparts in other Germanic countries. Hygge itself is also a Norwegian word, for example, although *koselig* is the equivalent concept, and in the Netherlands the equivalent is *gezelligheid*. Germanic societies noting global hyggemania felt compelled to remind the world of their own versions which were central to their national identities, for example in this March 2017 headline from the Dutch English-language news outlet *Dutch News*: "Forget hygge, here's 11 essential steps to Dutch gezelligheid."

Hygge, which is a noun, a verb, and, when slightly modified, an adjective, was explained to our team by Michael, a waiter in the Café Petersborg in Copenhagen. The restaurant, he told us, opened in 1746 and was so named because the Russian consulate used to be located above it. Café Petersborg was homely and warm, with simple tables, huge wooden beams in the ceilings, and wooden floors, which contrasted with the bitter cold of a Copenhagen December night. Over a dinner of meatballs and potatoes, Michael defined Danish identity in one word—hygge. Michael said the word was difficult to translate, but he rendered it into English as "coziness" or "togetherness." "We Danes like to be together," he said, as Denmark's winters are cold and dark. Unlike in America, he said, where people who want to see one another meet in restaurants, in Denmark people like to spend time together in their homes—which is hygge. "We are inside our homes with candles eating this food," he said, referring to what was served in the restaurant. Hygge, Michael said, goes back to the time of the Vikings.

Hygge is an essential component in any effort to understand the Danes. The journalist and author Patrick Kingsley describes hygge as "the warm state of relaxation in which Danes find themselves when they're sitting around a fire with friends, or having a beer in their beach house (another Danish mainstay) on the North Sea in the summer."[71] The Danish anthropologist Jeppe Trolle Linnet ties hygge to egalitarianism, writing that it is the opposite of luxury and also the opposite of "traveling to exotic destinations far from home." Those who act in a pretentious manner, writes Linnet, are excluded "from the *hygge* of ordinary people." Furthermore, upper-class families are considered to have "lost *hygge*."[72]

The exclusionary nature of hygge for those who are not part of the community is a reality that has been noted by anthropologists in their ethnographies of the Danes. Comparing hygge to janteloven, the British anthropologist Richard Jenkins writes that hygge can be "normative to the point of being close to coercive" and "is necessarily exclusionary, because there are always boundaries to a magic circle. . . . Intolerance, actual or potential, is never too far away."[73] Linnet notes, hygge "acts as a vehicle for social control, establishes its own hierarchy of attitudes, and implies a negative stereotyping of social groups who are perceived as unable to create *hygge*."[74] In short, hygge is yet another manifestation and articulation of Germanic primordial tribal identity.

## Symbols of German Primordial Identity

From social concepts of society let us move to universally recognized symbols of identity in Germanic culture. Symbols are a key source of identity. Tribes on the periphery in anthropological literature—such as the Pukhtun Wazirs and Mahsuds in Waziristan, the Berber Ait Waryaghar of the Rif mountains of Morocco, and the Tuareg Berbers in the deserts of North Africa—saw their physical environment as a feature of their identity, as discussed in *The Thistle and the Drone*. The terrain provided shelter from their enemies, a permanent place to live, and a stable and secure home that belonged to them; above all, it allowed them to maintain independence. The Pukhtun adapted their style of living and strategy for war to their mountain environment. The Bedouin living in the Middle East and North Africa derived their worldview from their terrain, in their case from the feeling that they roamed the deserts freely like a sailor on an ocean. Even today the natural environment defines tribal communities and gives them a real idea of freedom and identity. The often-inaccessible locations where tribes traditionally dwell helps explain why they have remained largely independent and will fight to maintain their freedom against invading forces.

## FORESTS

It is the dense and dark forests that define Germanic peoples, whether in Germany, Austria, or Scandinavia. Tacitus noted that the relationship between Germans and the forest is akin to that between a nurse and an infant—the German nation is given life, is nurtured, and develops in the forest. Members in the main Heimat organization in the German Palatinate region, for example, greeted one another with the phrase "Wald-Heil" (Forest salvation, or Long live the forest).[75] Germans have long seen the forest as an essential component of German identity. The poet Ernst Moritz Arndt wrote in 1815 that "the German person must nowhere lack trees."[76] The ethnographer and senior adviser to the king of Bavaria, Wilhelm Heinrich Riehl, similarly noted in 1852, "We must preserve the forests . . . in order that Germany remains German."[77]

It was in the forest that Germans came closest to their authentic identity in the Heimat as well as the divine, associated as it was with the forest among the Germanic pagans. The mystical and religious aspects of the forest were captured in the Austrian film *Sissi* (1955), one of the most successful German-language films of all time, in which Empress Elisabeth of Austria tells Emperor Franz Joseph, "Should your life ever bring trouble or sorrow, then go through the woods with open eyes. In every tree and bush, in every flower and every animal you will observe the omnipotence of God, which will give you solace and strength."[78]

The German identification with the forest goes back to the start of recorded German history and the battles between the Germanic tribes and Rome. Chief among these, of course, was the Battle of the Teutoburg Forest in AD 9, "Rome's greatest defeat."[79] For Arminius, the battle's victor who is also known as Hermann, the forest was a strategic asset but it also provided his very identity as a free man. The Teutoburg Forest is situated sixty miles northeast of Cologne and is dense with beeches, conifers, and oaks. In the nineteenth century, when the Germans were in the process of forming a united nation, they built a colossal statue of Arminius, brandishing a gigantic sword, near Detmold to honor him. The statue stands over 175 feet including the pedestal, similar to the scale of the Lincoln Memorial in Washington, D.C. The Nazis, of course, appropriated Arminius and projected him as the archetypical German warrior, the prototype

*Arminius, 1875, located in the Teutoburg Forest*
*(photo credit: Dierk Schaefer/Flickr.com)*

Aryan Nazi and associated him with Hitler. The German backlash against the Nazis after the Second World War included a sidelining of Arminius and his role in history. In spite of the official chill, however, the 2,000-year anniversary of the battle, in 2009, was celebrated with great fanfare that included a reenactment and an exhibition on Germanic tribes at the battle site opened by Chancellor Angela Merkel.

However celebrated the forest is by Germans, for outsiders it can seem dark and forbidding. German forests are not a collection of gardens, ponds, pathways, and picnic spots for the family. Tacitus noted the Germans' "attachment to their *silvis horrida*, their horrid forest."[80] They frighten people with their wild animals and the risk of disorientation within—you could wander around for days and never find your way out. Julius Caesar, writing before Tacitus, pointed to the vastness of the German forest and its unchartered nature as well as the dangers that may lurk within it: "There is no man in the Germany we know who can say that he has reached the edge of that forest, though he may have gone forward a sixty days' journey, or who has learnt in what place it begins. It is known that many kinds of wild beasts not seen in any other places breed therein."[81]

Terrifying for their enemies, the Germans have felt profoundly attached to the forest. In the 1980s, concern about what was known as *Waldsterben*—German forests dying as a result of air pollution—created a panic in Germany. It was this issue that galvanized the environmental movement, which broke through to the mainstream of German society and contributed to the electoral success of the Green Party under its leader, Joschka Fischer. The cause for Waldsterben was believed to be sulfur dioxide from burning fossil fuels, and great pressure was put on politicians and German industry to reduce emissions.

Visiting Germany for our fieldwork, I was impressed to discover that about a third of Germany is forested today, as is more than half of Sweden. We were staying in Berlin, next to the Brandenburg Gate, yet we were only a minute away from the Tiergarten and its densely forested areas spread over 520 acres. The Tiergarten has real forests within it, not the kind of manicured "nature" often found in city parks. The Tiergarten, like much of Berlin, was destroyed during the war—West Berlin's mayor described its destruction as "the most painful wound that Berlin had suffered from the war"—but you would not know it walking through the Tiergarten today.[82]

## THE FOREST IN GERMANIC CULTURE

The Brothers Grimm also set many of their best-known fairy tales in the forest. One of the most popular stories, "Hansel and Gretel," begins with the immortal line, "Once upon a time, on the edge of a great forest, there lived a very poor woodcutter with his wife and his two children, Hansel and Gretel." The story remains popular in our own contemporary times as seen in the film *Hansel and Gretel: Witch Hunters* (2013). In *Snow White and the Huntsman* (2012), based on another Brothers Grimm story, a father warns his son not to go into the forbidding forests in search of Snow White: "You don't know the dark forest." He is right. Tree trunks suddenly rise to devour humans, branches assume the shape of large snakes, and unimaginable monsters lurk in the darkness. *The Brothers Grimm*, a 2005 film, is set in dark, thick, and dangerous German forests with people terrified of and disappearing in them. Trees, ravens, and wolves attack humans, and the invading French are shown as buffoons whose comical general sets out to burn the forests in vain. Yet in the end, within the mystical, nurturing aspects of the forest, evil will perish and good will triumph. It was a common allegory that Germans equated with their own destiny.

The German forests were a staple for generations of German composers, writers, and painters. Richard Wagner's four opera *Ring Cycle* is set in the forests and mountains along the Rhine. In its third part, *Siegfried*, based on Sigurd of Norse mythology, the hero encounters strange creatures including a dragon in the forest and the opera features pieces such as "Forest Murmurs." Goethe wrote one of the most famous poems in the German language, the second "Wanderer's Nightsong," on the wall of a cabin on a mountain in the Thuringian Forest, and Martin Heidegger lived and wrote in the mountains of the Black Forest in a small cabin, famous as "the hut." The forest was also prominently featured in films during the Nazi era, such as *Ewiger Wald* (The eternal forest) of 1936. A statement issued at the film's release by the Nazi government explained its significance: "Our ancestors were a forest people. . . . Germany in its new awakening has returned to the woods. All the laws of our existence make reference to the wood. The film *Ewiger Wald* sings this exalted song of the unity that exists between people and the forest from traditional times to the present." The film provides a history lesson of Germany through the forest. We see Germanic pagans dancing and at one with the forest. We see Arminius defeating the Romans. There is great destruction during times like the Thirty Years' War but, as the narrator announces, "under Frederick the Great all is restored. The King wants new forests to stand up like soldiers."[83] There would be more destruction later, for example, after the First World War, when occupying French forces with their African colonial soldiers cut down trees. The narrator asks, "How can you bear this suffering, my folk, my forests?"[84] Then we see the arrival of the Nazis and Aryan peasants dancing in pagan rituals just as they did at the start of the film. The film declares, "The people, like the forest, will stand for ever!"[85]

The forest in both its nurturing and dangerous aspects has been an essential component in Germanic filmmaking, as in the Heimatfilme genre. In the television film series *Heimat*, a nude corpse is found in the forest near a picturesque, tranquil village, and no explanation is ever given concerning it. In the Danish filmmaker Lars von Trier's work, forests are similarly presented both as nurturing and terrifying: The female lead in *Nymphomaniac* (2013) identifies with trees that are associated with Odin and Norse mythology and seeks solace in her memories of walking in the forest as a child with her father, who declares his "soul tree" is the oak. The couple in *Antichrist* (2009)—which was filmed outside Cologne—move to a cabin in a primeval forest called Eden and unwittingly unleash the dark forces of the forest, which are so ferociously primal they cannot be contained.

Knight, Death and the Devil, *by Albrecht
Dürer, 1513 (Wikimedia.org)*

## THE FOREST IN GERMAN ART

The significance of trees and the forest can also be seen clearly in generations of German paintings and artwork. In Albrecht Altdorfer's famous
painting *Saint George and the Dragon* (1510), the trees rise like a wall over Saint
George and are so dense and thick that little sunlight penetrates them, although we see a distant mountain peak through a parting. Because St. George
and the dragon are tiny in comparison to the trees and placed toward the
bottom of the painting they appear almost lost in the gigantic forest, an after-
thought. Saint George's lance is down and he appears somnolent while his horse
gazes curiously at the miniature dragon, which looks like an ill-tempered
lizard whose tail has been painted in bright colors by a group of high-spirited
schoolgirls who got bored with their subject and let him wander into the
forest. It is the forest that provides the drama and the color in this painting,
which effortlessly expresses its strength and subtly hints at menace. Ignoring
the painter's title, the forest has made itself the subject of the painting.

Great German artists such as Albrecht Dürer and Caspar David Friedrich also seem obsessed with forests, highlighting, in particular, the oak. *Knight, Death, and the Devil* (1513), perhaps Dürer's most famous work, is a striking portrayal of a melancholic but noble and courageous knight, with echoes again of Hamlet. The knight is aware of the dark and looming dangers in the sinister forest around him with its threatening, bleak winter oaks; but neither death, with snakes coiled around his head, nor the devil, who has an animal's head with large horns protruding from it, will deter him. The knight ignores death, who holds an hourglass to remind him that the sands of time are running out.

Friedrich's *The Chasseur in the Forest* (1814) deals with the Napoleonic period. It is significant that the only human figure in the painting is the solitary figure of the chasseur, a member of Napoleon's elite light cavalry. The soldier is painted at the bottom of the frame and is looking at the forest with uncertainty and anxiety. In front of the soldier there is a small opening covered in snow that leads directly into the dark woods. All around and towering over him are tall, dark, menacing trees; behind them, like unending battalions, are more trees. To complete the picture of unrelieved hopelessness, there is one more symbol of doom: a solitary raven sits on the stump of a tree, looking ominously at the soldier. Here, the forest is a malevolent force of nature. We see the forest as an active ally of the Germans against the French invader. Trees also feature heavily in other Friedrich paintings, such as *The Abbey in the Oakwood* (1810), depicting solitary oaks in bleak landscapes that appear as if blasted by nuclear apocalypse.

## Oak

While the thick forest acts as an important symbol of identity for the Germans, the oak tree embodies the very essence of German character. German identification with the oak goes back to the time of the Germanic tribes who, according to the nineteenth-century Austrian cultural historian Friedrich von Hellwald, "held their religious assemblies and war councils under them, and decorated their heroes with oak garlands and buried their princes and military leaders under their protection."[86] Oaks were seen as holy places, and it was at the oak where sacrifices to the supreme god Odin took place. The oak, known as the "thunder tree," was particularly associated with Thor, the thunder god: temples to Thor were built of oak, and Thor was said to ride in an oak chariot and shelter under oaks during storms. Germans kept oak branches as protection from lightning.

The significance of the oak is demonstrated in Friedrich Gottlieb Klopstock's epic poem *Hermann's Battle* (1769), one of the many works dealing with Arminius and the Teutoburg Forest, in which he relates the German nation itself to the oak:

O Fatherland! O Fatherland!
You are like the greatest,
All-encompassing oak,
In the deepest grove of the forest,
The tallest, oldest, most sacred oak,
O Fatherland![87]

When Charlemagne wanted to destroy German paganism, he destroyed a sacred Saxon oak, and in 723 the English missionary St. Boniface cut down an oak in southern Germany, known as Donar's (Thor's) Oak, to demonstrate the primacy of Christianity. The oak features on the Iron Cross military decoration instituted in 1813 as well as on generations of German coins right up to today's euro. On the occasion of Kaiser Wilhelm I's seventy-fourth birthday, on March 22, 1871, oaks were planted in towns across the country in commemoration of the emperor, the creation of the new nation, and the victory over France.[88] Even advertisements for Black Forest smoked ham today, which boast that it is prepared using German wood from the Black Forest, feature a prominent image of dark oak on the packaging.

The oak also features on one of the most recognized symbols of Germany—the chariot statue or quadriga atop the Brandenburg Gate in Berlin. A triumphant Napoleon, passing through the gate to occupy the city, ordered the statue transported back to Paris; eight years later, the Prussians, on their conquest of that city, brought the statue back to Berlin and placed it once again atop the gate. But this time the Prussian king ordered an addition. Henceforth, the goddess would hoist an oak wreath around an Iron Cross crowned by a Prussian eagle—representing victory, strength, and primordial tribal identity.

The Nazis drew heavily on the oak in their iconography. The emblem of the Nazi Party was the German imperial eagle holding an oak wreath. The signature bookplate that Hitler put in the books in his collection "comprised an eagle, swastika and oak leaves," and on his birthday, in the manner of Kaiser Wilhelm, several hundred tiny oaks were taken from a plantation near Hitler's birthplace in Austria to be planted throughout the German Reich. Nazi awards and distinctions also featured the oak, like the *Totenkopfring* (skull ring), bestowed personally by Heinrich Himmler to members of the notorious SS or Schutzstaffel (Protection Squadrons), as well as the Knight's Cross, of which only twenty-seven were given, including one to Field Marshal Erwin Rommel. The Hitler Youth badge of honor depicted the oak. The Nazis even incorporated Goethe's oak, under which he was said to sit and write poetry, into the Buchenwald concentration camp, and some of the 56,000 people who were killed there were hung from it.[89]

## THE THISTLE AS A SYMBOL OF PRIMORDIAL IDENTITY

In *The Thistle and the Drone*, I use the prickly thistle flower as symbolic of tribal societies. The reference comes from Tolstoy, who related the thistle in his novel *Hadji Murad* to the tribes of the Caucasus Mountains then fighting to preserve their independence from Imperial Russia. It would not be easy, Tolstoy wrote, for the Russians to pluck the tribal thistle from its soil lest they themselves be pricked in the process. As I note in my book, other tribal societies, such as the Scots, also associated themselves with the thistle. It was a perfect symbol for egalitarian tribal peoples with a warrior ethos who tenaciously fought for their freedom against the modern, centralizing, and hierarchal state. While preparing this study, I wondered whether the Germans also identified with the thistle. A visit that Frankie, Zeenat, and I paid to Berlin's Kaiser Wilhelm Memorial Church in the summer of 2016 would yield the answer.

Upon entering the ruins of the old church we found a rich harvest—no pun intended—of forest and plant themes, including oaks, acorns, sheaves of wheat, and yes, thistles. Framing and guarding the entrance to the old cathedral were two statues hewn from Carrara marble, dated 1906. One of them depicted a man with a large sword, described in the display as a "youthful warrior." But what excited us were the distinctly shaped thistles that flanked the warrior on both sides and their description in the official accompanying explanation. The warrior, the description read, was "framed by stylized thistle shoots." Here were Germans identifying with the thistle as the flower representing them and their warrior identity. Tolstoy would have been pleased.

The warrior's left hand rested on the hilt of his sword, in the pose of countless alert cowboys in Hollywood Westerns ready to draw. With his right hand, he was holding a laurel oak wreath. The warrior, in short, was asserting his tribal identity through the thistle and clasping his sword to indicate his willingness to defend its honor. On the other side of the entrance, our German warrior was paired with another statue, this one of a woman representing home and hearth. She was described thus: "With grain sheaf, surrounded by stylised cornflowers symbolizing peace." The cornflower was known as the favorite flower of Kaiser Wilhelm as well as Bismarck—who was also depicted in statue form in the cathedral—and it was the symbol of the Volkisch nationalist movement in the nineteenth century. This female statue represented wife and mother, hearth and home, family and community; in short, the essence of primordial tribal society that the warrior defended and fought for—the very essence of Heimat and Volk.

When the artisans of Wilhelm's cathedral included the thistle in their representation of the Germanic warrior, they were drawing on a long tradition of Germanic identification with a plant associated with warrior identity. The thistle was viewed as sacred to Thor, the god associated with Germanic warriors, and was a so-called lightning plant because, according to legend, the blossom of the thistle derived its color from lightning. The thistle, seen as a symbol of Thor, was believed to offer protection from evil.

## WOLVES

The German identification with and love of the forest also extended to animals that dwell within it, particularly the wolf, one of the most prominent and frightening figures of the German forest. The wolf was one of the animals most respected by Germanic tribes, and warriors wore wolf skins in battle, enabling them to adopt the characteristics of the wolf and even become wolves themselves.[90] In Germanic mythology, the warrior clan of the Volsungs was associated with the wolf, and Sigmund of the Volsungs, who was celebrated by Wagner, was raised by wolves and wore a wolf pelt that enabled him to become a werewolf while attacking enemies.[91] The wolf was associated with Odin, who kept two enormous and ferocious wolves, Freki and Geri, both names that meant "ravenous" and "greedy." The wolf even influenced German names, including Adolf ("noble wolf"), Wolfgang ("path of the wolf"), Rudolf (a combination of "fame" and "wolf"), and Ralph ("counsel" or "advice of the wolf").

The hooked Wolfsangel, a pagan symbol based on a historical wolf trap and thought to resemble the fang of a werewolf, features in the coat of arms of many German families and towns, such as Wolfstein, in Rhineland-Palatinate. The symbol was adopted by fifteenth-century German peasants during their revolt against princes and became a German symbol of independence and liberty.[92] During the Thirty Years' War in the seventeenth century, bands of Germans waged guerrilla war against foreign forces under the German name "Wehrwolf." They chose the Wolfsangel as their emblem, and the symbol was reportedly carved on trees from which foreign combatants were hanged.[93]

In the era of German nationalism, the wolf was identified with Germans themselves. In Hermann Löns's 1910 novel about the Thirty Years'

War, *Der Wehrwolf* (The Warwolf), a peasant named Harm Wulf leads the defense of his community against foreign forces, who are described repeatedly as "vermin" and likened to "lice." It became one of the most widely read books in Germany.[94] Bismarck also likened the Germans to the wolf when he declared, while speaking about the Poles before the Prussian Diet of 1886, "Beat the Poles until they lose all desire to live. . . . if we want to exist we must exterminate them. It is not the wolf's fault that God created him the way he is."[95]

Even the famous German Shepherd dog reflects the German love for the wolf. The German Shepherd was specifically bred by the Germans to create "the primeval Germanic dog," which would be as close to the wolf as possible. The German Shepherd was known as "wolf dog," and admired for its similarity to the wolf.

Hitler and the Nazi Party held the symbol of the wolf in high regard. Nazi units such as the Waffen-SS Panzer Division *Das Reich* and the Waffen-SS Division Landstorm Nederland used the Wolfsangel symbol. The Nazi admiral Karl Dönitz developed the *Rudeltaktik* (Wolfpack) method of U-boat warfare, in which multiple U-boats, like a pack of wolves, preyed on "weak" ships lacking sufficient protection. In 1934, one year after the Nazis took power, Germany became the first modern nation to officially declare the wolf a protected animal.[96] Hitler's military headquarters were named after wolves: his Eastern Front headquarters was called the "Wolf's Lair"; his headquarters on the Franco-Belgian border was called "Wolf's Gorge"; and his headquarters in Ukraine was called "Wehrwolf." Hitler's favorite German Shepherd dog, Blondi, slept in his bed with him and gave birth to a puppy that was named "Wulf," after Hitler's own nickname.

## The Clash between the Norse Gods and Christianity

The argument thus far has outlined various aspects of Germanic primordial tribal identity, including the symbols that articulate and promote it. Another important aspect of primordial identity is the pagan religion of the Germanic tribes, with its pantheon of gods. These include the chief god Odin; his son Thor, the god of thunder, lightning, and strength, known for his hammer weapon; and another son Tiw, once identified as a powerful, even principal, sky god and subsequently associated with war. Tacitus reports that the Germans believed they were descended from the god Tuisco, whom scholars identify with Tiw. The memory of ancient tribal identity is kept alive through such mythical figures, and these legendary heroes are celebrated through songs, stories, and more recently films and documentaries. They thus provide a legitimate base for identity and through the repetition of the tales perpetuate it from generation to generation.

Regarding deities, there has been a duality for the Germans, à la Hamlet, as they were always conflicted about their acceptance of Christianity and the subsequent surrender of both their ancient gods and sovereignty in the religious realm to non-Germanic foreigners. Following their conversion, Germanic peoples kept tales of their gods, mythology, and great heroes alive in works such as the twelfth-century *Gesta Danorum* (Deeds of the Danes) in Denmark, the twelfth-century *Nibelungenlied* (The song of the Nibelungs) in Germany, and the thirteenth-century *Prose Edda* and *Poetic Edda* in Iceland.

The adoption of Christianity presented an insoluble theological and historic problem for the Germans: the reconciliation between Jesus, whose origin lay in Asia, and the "indigenous" European Nordic gods. Herder, as noted above, believed Christianity was to a great extent responsible for the loss of German character, which needed to be revived. Hegel captured the German dilemma perfectly when he wrote of the devastating impact Christianity had on German identity and, evoking Herder, lamented that the Germans do not have "a religious imagery which is homegrown or linked with our history." Hegel then asked sarcastically, "Is Judea then the Teutons' fatherland?" This was a reframing of a similar question asked by the poet Klopstock in his complaint that the Germans seemed to revere the Greeks and their gods over their own: "Is Achaia [an area in Greece], then, the Teutons' fatherland?"[97]

Similarly, the writings of Nietzsche exhibit the inability of Christianity to fully challenge and subsume tribal identity. "I can't make out how a German could ever feel *Christian*," he wrote.[98] Nietzsche launched a full-fledged assault on Christianity in *Thus Spoke Zarathustra* (1883–91), in which he took the story of Zarathustra arriving back from the mountains after his long retreat and made the pronouncement about God being dead to declare that man must surpass God and create something new. For Nietzsche man thus becomes superman. He specified the instrument with which it was necessary to philosophize—"a hammer," in what might have been an unconscious nod to Thor. His target was the "idols," the false gods that would now be revealed to be empty and hollow after encountering the hammer. For Nietzsche, this could be accomplished in one blow, and he distilled his thinking into just one page in his book *Twilight of the Idols, or, How to Philosophize with a Hammer* (1889).

Other prominent Germanic voices shared this belief that Germans and Christianity were inherently incompatible, including Carl Jung, the

Germanic Swiss psychiatrist and scholar who founded the field of analytical psychology and spoke of "German Christians" as "a contradiction in terms."[99] Instead, he thought, the Germans would have to reach much deeper back in history for an authentic religious identity based in their own Volk traditions. Jung wrote that he had dreams about "gloomy" forests where he saw Odin, whom he described as "the Wild Huntsman" and "the god of my Alemannic forefathers."[100]

## THOR

While the Germanic peoples identified broadly with a pantheon of gods, there was a particular identification with Thor as embodying primordial tribal identity. Thor was depicted as a racial type with red hair and red beard. He represented a hard-fighting, hard-drinking, and hard-partying Viking warrior. His power rested famously in his hammer, and his ancient devotees carried a small hammer with them in order to be granted Thor's strength and protection. For them, the sign of the hammer functioned in a similar way to the thistle discussed above.

The swastika was also long associated with Thor, and for ancient Germanic warriors the swastika and Thor's hammer were one and the same. The association between Thor and the swastika can be seen in nineteenth-century works of art such as *Thor's Battle against the Jötnar* (1872) by the Swedish painter Mårten Eskil Winge. The painting shows a ferocious looking Thor, wearing a swastika on his belt, towering over anguished giants as he smashes them, his hammer sparking and attracting lightning bolts. To Volkisch activists, Thor and the swastika were desirable symbols; for example, Thor was evoked in the journal *The Hammer*, launched by the journalist and publisher Theodor Fritsch in 1902 to advocate anti-Semitism. A decade later, Fritsch formed the *Reichshammerbund* (Reich Hammer League), a symbol of which was the swastika, to coordinate anti-Semitic activities. In 1920 Hitler chose the swastika to represent the Nazi Party.

During fieldwork, we found widespread affectionate respect for Thor among the Germanic peoples, who still take the name with pride. On a flight from Copenhagen to Iceland, I met a fellow passenger whose name meant "the hammer of Thor," and a producer I met at the main state television studio in Copenhagen said his name meant "the flying weapon of Thor." The producer said that both Thor and Sif, the wife of Thor, are popular names for men and women in Denmark and that there are common sayings in Denmark about Thor, such as "the law must abide for Thor and for Loki."

The continuing influence of Thor and the Germanic gods is evident in the interview given by Søren Espersen, a leading Danish politician and

Thor's Battle against the Jötnar, *by Mårten Eskil Winge, 1872 (Wikimedia.org). Note swastika in Thor's belt buckle (inset)*

deputy chairman of the Danish People's Party. When asked if Danes have a connection to or identification with their Viking past, Espersen drew a seamless line from the Germanic tribes to present times. Not only do "lots" of Danes still worship Thor and Odin, he told us, Danish women have retained their "strong" character from the days of the tribes:

> We had Christianity in Denmark relatively late, 980s or something, when it was already Christian in many of the other countries. There are lots of people who still do that, the Nordic faith, the Asa faith, as their religion. We have, even out in Afghanistan, some of our troops there that I visited, they believe in Odin and Thor. It's true. We had a young candidate who wants to run for Parliament—I'm in the group of persons that do the interviews with those that want to run—and she's an Asa believer.

The Norse gods were also being evoked by Norwegian soldiers in Afghanistan. In 2010 a Norwegian serving in Norway's Telemark Battalion, the insignia for which is a Viking longboat, was killed by a Taliban roadside bomb in Afghanistan. Shortly afterward, a video surfaced of the battalion's commander rousing a large number of troops while standing on a tank and hoisting his rifle in the air. In his cry he invoked Valhalla, the final, desired destination for warriors in Norse mythology located in Asgard: "You are the predator. Taliban is the prey. To Valhalla!" The men then responded and continued to chant "To Valhalla! To Valhalla!"

If there is any doubt left as to the influence of ancient Nordic culture in Northern Europe today, we turn to Iceland, where worshippers of the Norse gods constitute the second-largest religious community after Christianity. Membership of the Norse religious group known as Asatru has tripled in the past decade, and the construction of a new Norse temple, the first in nearly a thousand years, was announced in early 2015 on a tree-covered hill in Reykjavík.

Thor and Norse mythology have even crossed into mainstream Western popular culture through blockbuster Hollywood films, with the strapping young Australian Chris Hemsworth playing Thor. In the hit American TV comedy *The Big Bang Theory*, Penny exclaims, "Thor! He's hot," when she glimpses the big, blonde, muscular god on the cover of a comic book. The fact that it is Penny—herself blonde and "hot" as well as the arbiter of popular culture among the group of friends—who makes the remark underlines the significance of her choice: Thor is someone Penny can admire and could date.

There is, however, a dark aspect to the cult of Thor and the ancient gods. European intellectuals as early as the nineteenth century were expressing their concern at the revival of the Germanic gods and the decline of Christianity. The nineteenth-century Jewish poet and essayist Heinrich Heine, foretelling the mass violence of the Nazis, wrote in 1834,

> Christianity—and this is its fairest merit—subdued to a certain extent the brutal warrior ardour of the Germans, but it could not entirely quench it; and when the cross, that restraining talisman, falls to pieces, then will break forth again the ferocity of the old combatants, the frantic Berserker rage whereof Northern poets have said and sung. . . . The old stone gods will then arise from the forgotten ruins and wipe from their eyes the dust of centuries, and Thor with his giant hammer will arise again, and he will shatter the Gothic cathedrals.[101]

Decades after the defeat of the Nazis, Thor was again being associated with mass violence against European minorities. Thor's influence on the thinking of Norwegian mass murderer Anders Breivik was profound. Breivik, who killed seventy-seven innocent people because he believed they were facilitating Muslim immigration, named his Glock pistol "Mjölnir" after the hammer of Thor and, using ancient Germanic runic script, carved this name into the pistol. Breivik named his rifle "Gungnir" after the spear of Odin, and he called the Fiat Doblò van that he used to drive from Oslo to the island of Utøya, where the vast majority of victims were killed, "Sleipnir," the eight-legged horse of Odin.

There is also Thor Steinar, a sleekly advertised neo-Nazi fashion line manufactured by Thor Steinar Mediatex GmbH, a German subsidiary of a Dubai company that has stores in Germany. In 2014 Thor Steinar opened an outlet in London called the Viking Thor Shop. Their logos feature Germanic runic script, including one that represents the god Tiw. In 2012 Thor Steinar opened a new store in Germany called Brevik. While it claimed this was in honor of the Norwegian town of the same name, the association with Anders Breivik was unmistakable.

## Thor versus Jesus

The central theological dilemma for Germanic peoples is this: Thor and Jesus cannot coexist within one spiritual frame. While Thor would urge his followers to wreak havoc on the enemy, including raping the women and killing the men, Jesus would tell his followers to turn the other cheek and love the enemy. While Thor would spend his evenings in bawdy, drunken orgies that often ended in violence, Jesus would spend his in the company of his disciples in prayer and contemplation. One stands for unbridled force, the other for unqualified love; one worships strength and represents power, the other advocates humility and commands people to love one another. The symbol of Thor is the hammer, which subdues enemies through brute strength; the symbol of Jesus is the cross, which represents the agony and torture he suffered for mankind. Thor triumphs by vanquishing his enemies, Jesus through embracing them. In spite of this clear-cut difference between the two, Germans are loath to choose one over the other.

Culture contains mechanisms that enable society to reconcile seemingly incompatible positions and thus provide continuity while preserving its essential integrity. Even in a religion as disparate from Christianity as Hinduism, Jesus was accommodated in the pantheon of Hindu gods and thus conflict was minimized between the two religious traditions when

Christianity arrived in South Asia. In the case of Germanic culture, Thor and Jesus, two irreconcilable entities at opposite ends of the theological spectrum, have been artificially fused. This process accelerated in the nineteenth-century era of Volkisch activism and the consolidation of the modern German state.

For Wagner, his hero Siegfried is merely another name for Christ, both being sons of God and of Germanic lineage.[102] Indeed, Wagner's opera *Parsifal* (1882) concerns his vision of the "Aryan Christ."[103] In the next century, the notion of the Aryan Jesus became common in Germany. By the 1930s, Jesus was fully recast as Thor in Germany and was now seen as a "heroic, aggressive, manly warrior whose life was the focus, not his death. Artistic representations of Jesus increasingly aryanized his appearance and portrayed him in heroic poses."[104] The fusing of Thor and Jesus was part of a larger German attempt to practice what Friedrich Ludwig Jahn called *Urchristenthum*—that is, the "original" or "pure Christianity," of which Germans, as the Urvolk, were the first adherents.[105] To define and promote a Germanic, "original," and "pure" Christianity, the supposed "Jewish influence" on Christianity would have to be excised, a task many German intellectuals would pursue with sinister enthusiasm (see chapter 7).

With the Marvel Comics superheroes now big business—and the public demanding newer and bigger budget films—there is a tendency to square off one superhero against another, for example, *Batman v Superman: Dawn of Justice* (2016). Taking this line of argument to its logical conclusion, one wonders when we might see *Thor v Jesus* and how Jesus would fare. I did not doubt that in the minds of many of Thor's fans, Jesus, with his gentle ways, frail constitution, and lack of martial skills or weapons, would not last very long against the might of Thor's hammer. And if Jesus looked to his father in heaven to come to his aid, so would Thor to his father, Odin, the mighty Norse god. It is precisely for this reason that society finds a cultural mechanism for accommodation, as in this case where it combines Thor and Jesus to the point that they become indistinguishable.

### Frederick the Great and Goethe as Champion and Opponent of German Primordial Identity

So far we have presented an almost deterministic picture of Germanic primordial tribal identity. Yet it is important to note that there are also prominent voices in German history who rejected it in favor of a universalist identity. Juxtapose, for example, Frederick the Great of Prussia, among the greatest proponents of primordial tribal identity, and Goethe, who opposed it. The two were contemporaries and lived during a crucial period in German history, in the early years of the nationalist movement that would result in the unification of Germans into a nation state. As such, they represent contrasting models of how Germans might respond to the modern age.

As a successful ruler and military commander, Frederick's vision was of aggressive nationalism, raw military power, state building, art and culture, and the promotion of the national code of honor; Goethe's ideal was universal humanism and the cultivation of the human being in art and culture. While Frederick, the enlightened monarch, symbolized German primordial values, Goethe opened the German heart and mind to embrace the world's cultures and religions, especially those from the East.

Among Frederick's admirers were Napoleon and Hitler. Napoleon visited Frederick's tomb to pay homage; Hitler, in the last days of his life, as he began to lose his mind, reportedly talked to Frederick's portrait in his bunker in Berlin. Nazi propaganda chief Joseph Goebbels had already declared that Frederick was a National Socialist. The adulation of the Nazis resulted in Frederick's being sidelined after the Second World War, and his beloved Prussia was erased from the map by the Allies.

Goethe's vision for Germany, on the other hand, is captured in the lines he wrote with the like-minded poet Friedrich Schiller, another iconic German literary figure:

> Forget, O Germans, your hopes of becoming a nation
> Educate yourselves instead . . . to be human beings.[106]

The thought of Germany being united by Prussia filled Goethe with a sense of "dismay."[107] There is a quote attributed to Goethe, possibly apocryphal, which has him declaring, "The Prussian is cruel by birth. Civilization will make him ferocious."

But even Goethe could not have imagined what lay ahead. His gentle soul would have been deeply disturbed to learn that in the future his universal vision of harmony between different peoples would be cruelly brushed aside by someone who would give predatory identity its fullest and most deadly expression. That man was Adolf Hitler.

## Rampant Predatory Identity and the Dangers
*of Distorting Tribal Identity*

"How did Adolf Hitler—described by one eminent magazine editor in 1930 as a 'half-insane rascal,' a 'pathetic dunderhead,' a 'nowhere fool,' a 'big mouth'—rise to power in the land of Goethe and Beethoven?" opens Michiko Kakutani's *New York Times* review of the book *Hitler: Ascent, 1889–1939* (2016) by the German historian Volker Ullrich. At 998 pages, the book is yet another mighty attempt to explain what seems the inexplicable. "What persuaded millions of ordinary Germans," the review continues, "to embrace him and his doctrine of hatred? How did this 'most unlikely pretender to high state office' achieve absolute power in a once democratic country and set it on a course of monstrous horror?"

Seven decades after Hitler's death, the Nazi leader remains an enigma, and the public still searches for answers. Various theories continue to be presented, as in another 2016 piece, this time by the British tabloid *The Sun*, which typically gives its readers a daily staple of buxom models in various stages of undress. *The Sun*'s headline sums up the article's main arguments: It informs us that Hitler had a "deformed micro-penis," which it offers as an explanation for his "rage." Not satisfied with introducing us to Hitler's genitalia, it goes on to offer us insights into the psyche of the Nazi leadership as captured in the popular wartime ditty sung to the tune of the "Colonel Bogey March": "Hitler has only got one ball, Goring has two but very small, Himmler has something similar, but poor old Goebbels has no balls at all." After reading the article, however, there is little doubt in our minds that more is needed to explain Hitler and the Nazis than references to their testicles.

### The Nazis and German Tribal Identity

The acts of Hitler and the Nazis were so vile that they leave us bewildered and puzzled as to how they could have happened, and there is an understandable revulsion in examining anything associated with them. Arminius, Barbarossa, Wagner, Nietzsche, Frederick the Great, and even Tacitus, who was not German but wrote about Germans, were names that the Nazis promoted to build an idea of what it meant to be German. Nazi propaganda made much of the fact that Arminius was a big, blue-eyed, muscular man— the name of Arminius's brother, Flavus, is Latin for "the blonde." After the Second World War these names were put aside as scholars wondered how much influence they had in the thinking of and propaganda put out by the Nazis. Contemporary admirers of the great Germanic philosophers, musicians, rulers, and artists shied away from them as if they were tainted simply because the Nazis had exploited their creative work and ideas. It still left scholars and commentators searching for explanations about the emergence and nature of the Nazis.

To the vast majority of people looking for answers after the Second World War, Hitler and the Nazis were explained in either theological terms as being "pure evil," the opposite of good, or, in the psychological sense of being "completely mad," the opposite of normal. While I do not for a moment exonerate or condone their actions, these terms reduce the Nazis to one-dimensional characters and fail to raise and explain several key questions: How can we explain the mass adulation Hitler generated among his followers? How did an entire modern nation appear to support the Nazi leaders despite information leaking to the public about the genocide being conducted at the concentration camps? And what cultural and social factors within society were activated to help the Nazis consolidate power and carry out their demented and sadistic objectives?

We need to look for answers not only in theology and psychology but in anthropology. Hitler and the Nazis focused with extraordinary intensity on the idea of German tribal identity as an antidote to problems that Germany faced after the First World War. By attempting to recreate tribal identity and reviving the notion of purity of German blood and spirit, the Nazis believed, all the major challenges facing Germany could be resolved; these included the loss of territory and the humiliation of the army, high levels of unemployment, political resentment at the lack of leadership, widespread fears that there was a conspiracy to destroy German identity by enemies inside and outside the nation, and anxiety that Germany was no longer viewed as a great nation and had lost honor and gained shame. It would also provide the opportunity, as desired by the Volkisch activists, of which Hitler was one, to finally unite all the Germanic peoples into a single state. Hitler, in his own words, "would make Germany great again."

By the early 1930s, Hitler had become the embodiment of German identity to his followers. Rejecting Hitler was thus tantamount to being a traitor to the German nation. And because the Nazis defined the German people in strictly tribal—that is, ethnic—terms, all those living within German territories who did not conform to the stereotype of what a true German looked like or did not have the correct ancestors were thoroughly investigated and persecuted. The Holocaust, the concentration camps, and the poisonous anti-Semitism of the Nazis during the time of Hitler reflected the dangerously high level of prejudice against and hatred for the

Jewish community that had fomented over the previous centuries (see chapter 7).

Hitler gathered together diverse ideas of tribal identity, lifted bits and pieces that suited him, and then reconstituted these into an ugly and dangerous ideology. His argument was simple: For "our" tribe to flourish, all others must perish. This was not part of the classic tribal codes of the Pukhtuns or Kurds, in which a noble character is noble precisely because he shows generosity and hospitality to others and protects the weak and vulnerable. Hitler's Germanic tribalism was instead a mutated and distorted version of primordial identity; it was the ultimate expression of predator identity, and the Holocaust was its direct result.

### *The Nazification of German History and Identity*

Hitler and the Nazis set about appropriating every prominent name and place associated with German identity. They were able to create links, however tenuous, with names and concepts from history through their own drive to identify with original Germanic tribal identity. Their aim was to equate the very name Hitler with the true meaning of being German. From Arminius to Wagner and Nietzsche, a process of Nazification of the past was launched. Those who could not fit into this pattern were simply targeted for destruction.

The misuse of Herder's conception of the Volk and Volksgeist is an example of how Hitler could take what is essentially a descriptive concept of tribal identity and twist it into a perverse form. Herder envisaged different Volk living in an environment of harmony, each cherishing its own special identity and each living on its own territory. Here is Hitler fusing the idea of Volk with his own Nazi Party: "To the same degree as the basic ideas of the National Socialist movement are *folkish* [völkisch], the *folkish* ideas are *National Socialist*."[108] The Nazis also co-opted artistic achievements and philosophical ideas associated with Dürer, Kant, Wagner, and Nietzsche: Those who identified with or were searching for German tribal identity were clearly ex post facto Nazi in their sympathy.

Hitler boasted that he carried the works of the philosopher Arthur Schopenhauer with him throughout the First World War and completely agreed with Schopenhauer's glorification of "will" over "reason." In his philosophic search for an ideal society, Schopenhauer was led to the idea of eugenics. Schopenhauer cited Plato in suggesting that all "scoundrels" should be "castrated" and that we should "give men of noble character a whole harem." If this were to happen, Schopenhauer predicted, then "a generation would soon arise which would produce a better age than that of Pericles."[109] Schopenhauer, for whom "the white races" represented "the highest civilization and culture," thus laid the philosophic foundations of an imaginary Utopia built on misogyny, racism, and eugenics.[110]

The Nazis also co-opted Nietzsche's philosophic concept of the superman and cast it in terms of the Aryan ideal of strength, power, and physical might. To the Nazis, the superman was the tall, blonde, blue-eyed, athletic young soldier who would obey orders and go on to dominate the world. To illustrate what an Aryan looked like, Nazi state sculptor Arno Breker created two gigantic menacing models of grim-faced warriors standing naked on either side of the entrance to the Reich Chancellery, Hitler's office in Berlin, one brandishing a sword, the other holding a torch. Hitler dubbed them "the Army" and "the Party." The Nazis combined the racial ideas of philosophers like Schopenhauer with their own understanding of Germanic primordial identity and all its components, such as Volk and Heimat, to justify their predatory genocidal actions. After Hitler became chancellor, German scientists, philosophers, and intellectuals enthusiastically bent to his way of thinking.

### "Purity" and Tribal Identity under the Nazis

Hitler, Himmler, and the Nazis set out an extensive project for themselves: to turn back the clock and reclaim the imagined "purity" of the original German tribes. Yet in their predatory zeal to enforce Germanic purity, they made themselves more tribal than Arminius himself. Tacitus's account of a "pure" tribal society in *Germania* gave the Nazis a model to aspire to. Himmler declared the book a "wonderful portrait of how high, pure and capable our ancestors were. This is how we will become again, or at least part of us."[111] Indeed, the extent of the Nazi devotion to Tacitus led the scholar Christopher B. Krebs to describe Tacitus's book as "dangerous" in his *A Most Dangerous Book: Tacitus's* Germania *from the Roman Empire to the Third Reich* (2011). The very title of Krebs's book suggests that Tacitus was somehow responsible for the emergence of Hitler and the Nazis; on the contrary, it was Hitler and his coterie of senior figures like Himmler who misused the scholarly historical account for their own nefarious purposes and illustrated the dangers of twisting knowledge and learning for ideological objectives.

In keeping with their goal of tribal purity, the Nazis promoted a policy of *Volkstum*, or "consciousness of the Volk," to prevent Germans from seeking to "shame" and "defile" their race. German schoolchildren memorized poems such as the following:

Keep your Blood pure,
it is not yours alone,
it comes from far away,
it flows into the distance
laden with thousands of ancestors
and it holds the entire future!
It is your eternal life.[112]

Countless German women accused of *Rassenschande*, or "race shame," were subjected to public punishment and humiliation, often by having their heads shaved and paraded through the streets.[113]

All those not considered to be of the Germanic lineage, race, Volk, or Heimat, who did not make up the "original" Germanic tribes, were marked for extermination. These included the Jews, of whom 6 million were killed; the Slavs (Hitler vowed to "annihilate the Polish people"); and homosexuals, who were given a death sentence because Himmler and the Nazis believed the Germanic tribes had executed homosexuals by drowning them in bogs.[114]

The Nazis also targeted the most historically marginalized ethnic minority in Europe, the Roma, murdering half a million of them—one quarter of the Roma population of Europe—in an event the Roma refer to as the *Porajmos*, or destruction. We visited the Documentation and Cultural Center of German Sinti and Roma in Heidelberg, considered the leading museum in the world on the Nazi genocide of the Roma. The museum explained that the Roma's many centuries of living in Europe meant nothing to the Nazis, who identified them as "subhuman" and their "alien" blood as contaminating the Germanic community. In 1936, the museum explained, the Research Center for Racial Hygiene was set up in Berlin, and in 1938 Himmler ordered the classification of all Roma. Racial reports were compiled for each person, including the measurement of heads and pictures of hands, eyes, and noses, which the museum characterized as a death sentence. Our guide at the museum, a teenager named Aaron Gärtner, pointed to a large photo on display and said it was his grandfather's family. He then explained that many of the people in the photo, including his grandfather's two brothers and eleven sisters, were all killed in Auschwitz.

## Himmler, Nazi Scholarship, and the Germanic Gods

Hitler and the Nazis had created the elite SS to directly implement their official ideology, and it possessed unchecked authority to ensure that orders were obeyed. Himmler was put in charge of this organization. To join the SS, one had to pass strict requirements: "pure Aryan descent back to the year 1750 for SS officers and 1800 for enlisted men, minimum height, and proper bone structure, no Slavic or Mongolian characteristics."[115] The SS, which ran the concentration camps, rapidly expanded to become a power unto itself; historians would describe it as a "state within a state." Himmler co-opted German universities and put SS officers in key academic positions. This ensured that "the Nazi version of history, prehistory, literature, genetics, and biology would replace authentic scholarship."[116]

The view that intelligence was a function solely of race led to a host of pseudoscientific theories advanced by scholars that only make sense in this context. As an example, one of Himmler's expert advisers was an SS Brigadier General, Karl Weisthor, who claimed to be descended from Thor and headed the Department for Pre- and Early History within the SS Race and Settlement Main Office.

Himmler announced that Germanic tribal law would be reinstated and incorporated into German national policy and law. His protective attitude toward animals demonstrated this obsession.[117] Himmler saw no contradiction in speaking passionately about the rights of animals while murdering millions of people as the architect of the Final Solution. German animals, for him, were considered essential symbols of German identity going back to the Germanic tribes and were far more important than those humans of minority groups whose very presence and existence were seen as a threat to German identity. Himmler's opinion of such outsiders can be seen in an anecdote told of his mistress, Hedwig Potthast, whom he called "Little Bunny" and who lived "in considerable luxury . . . not far from Hitler's mansion." "On one occasion, when her friend Gerda Bormann and her children dropped by for a visit, [Potthast] offered to show them something 'very interesting.' . . . Then she picked up a copy of *Mein Kampf*, explaining 'clinically and medically' that its cover was made from human skin."

Himmler believed that the Germanic gods were real. For him, "Aesir, the old gods of Norse legend—such as Odin, Thor, and Loki—were in fact beings of pure, undiluted Nordic essence, the earliest Aryans." Himmler declared, "After the war . . . the old Germanic gods will be restored." Thor's hammer, because of its association with lightning, especially fascinated

Himmler, who believed it "was in fact a sophisticated piece of electrical engineering developed by Aryans to vanquish their enemies." If Nazi scientists could discover how Thor's hammer worked, they would be able to develop a superweapon to use against the Allies. The Nazi version of Thor's hammer would be "a mammoth electrical weapon capable of shutting down all the electrical systems of Allied troops, from their radio communications and radar to the ignitions of their tanks."

Believing he was on the verge of making a world-changing discovery, Himmler instructed his scientists to discover the secret of Thor's hammer. A proposal to build it was submitted by Elemag, an "obscure" German company, in November 1944. As Himmler waited for the project to materialize, "he could not refrain from boasting to associates such as Adolf Eichmann and others about a new weapon that would render the Allies literally powerless."[118] By then, however, time had run out for the Nazis.

### Lebensraum *and the Germanic Settlement of the Eastern Territories*

A central pillar of Nazi policy was to facilitate what they viewed as the natural development and expansion of the German people. The Germans' need to expand had been used as a justification for colonization in South West Africa, and the genocide of the local population there was part of this effort. As the genocide scholar Benjamin Madley explains, "Like Nazi mass murder, the Namibian genocides were premised upon ideas like *Lebensraum* [living space], annihilation war [*Vernichtungskrieg*], and German racial supremacy."[119]

When the Nazis took power, they sought to implement a policy of Lebensraum that focused on Poland and the areas east of Germany. Hitler justified this by describing it as a revival of the eastern expansion of the Teutonic Knights, who conducted crusading wars of conversion against the Slavs, Lithuanians, and other Baltic tribes in the medieval period. The Germans for Hitler were "the advance guard of the West" fighting the "numberless hordes of Asia," and he called for the extension of Europe to the Ural Mountains and the creation of a Germanic "living wall" to protect "against the mid-Asian masses."[120]

The Nazi policy toward the east included a transformation of the landscape to one compatible with "Germanic man," who, as Himmler put it, "can only live in a climate suited to his needs and in a country adapted to his character, where he will feel at home and not be tormented by homesickness." Thus the landscape was to be engineered to replicate what Germany looked like at the time of the Germanic tribes. For example, "Himmler intended to plant hundreds of thousands of oak and beech trees to reproduce the ancient forests of northern Germany." Along with the revival of the ancient forest would come a *Jurassic Park*–like revival of animals understood to live at the time of the Germanic tribes. One of these programs concerned the extinct auroch cattle, with which the Nazis planned to populate the eastern territories.

To implement this vision, the people who lived in the eastern areas, such as the Slavs, Jews, and Roma, would have to be exterminated. In the early weeks following the invasion of Poland, Himmler's roving killing units, the *Einsatzgruppen*, murdered an estimated 60,000 Poles.[121] The planned settlement of large numbers of Germanic settlers in the East aimed to fortify and protect Europe, which the Nazis viewed as synonymous with the Germanic peoples, against the threat of non-Germanic, non-Europeans from Asia. Himmler announced that the eastern areas "must really be a Germanic blood wall" that "must restore Europe's position in the struggle with Asia."[122] To populate the blood wall, Himmler declared, he would "call on the Germanic race in all countries, the Norwegians and the Swedes, the Dutch and the Danes." To these groups he also added Germanic Americans and the English, which would "create security for the Germanic race, even if the English refuse to realize this."[123]

In an address to rally German troops facing the Soviet army, Himmler described the enemy as "animals." The stakes were high in the war against the Soviets, who for him represented a continuation of the Asian war on Europe that had been raging since time immemorial and who constituted "a mixture of races, whose very names are unpronounceable, and whose physique is such that one can shoot them down without pity and compassion."[124]

### *The Durability and Dangers of German Predator Identity*

The Nazis did not implode or collapse by themselves; their demise was brought about by a world war. In the end, nothing but the utter devastation of Germany and the complete annihilation of its military and economic structures would defeat Germanic tribal identity with its predatory impulses. When the horrors of the Holocaust were discovered, confirming what tribalism run amok was capable of, the world rightly said, "Never Again!"

But as any anthropologist will confirm, tribal identity is resilient and rarely disappears, even after a devastating defeat such as the Germans suffered. Within a few decades there were glimpses of different and extreme elements of tribalism—graffiti in public toilets and underground stations and the desecration of Jewish cemeteries and synagogues. Soon, the swastika was seen again, with youth quite brazenly displaying it and giving the Nazi salute. The sight of large groups of young, white, blue-eyed, blonde men lifting their right arms in a salute and shouting "Sieg Heil" should make Europeans pause and think about where this could lead (see chapters 7, 8, and 9).

## Asserting Primordial Identity on the Periphery

Had Tacitus written about the peoples of Eastern Europe, those considered by Western Europeans to be on the political periphery, he would surely have noted many characteristics that were to a large extent present in Germanic society: a code of honor and a distinct culture that glorified a warrior ethic, clans descended from common ancestors and inhabiting defined territories, and a pantheon of gods and goddesses. Yet of the three main tribal nations of Europe—the Germanic peoples, the Slavs, and the Hungarians—only the Germanic peoples were largely able to maintain their independence and territorial and cultural integrity over the centuries. The Slavs and the Hungarians, as well as smaller nations like the Lithuanians, Latvians, Estonians, and Finns, in contrast, endured long periods under foreign rule, retaining memory of their tribal identity as best they could and striving to rebuild it as soon as they were able to achieve independence.

To understand the identity of the nations of Eastern Europe, we must look again to Herder, whose theories of the Volk provided the peoples of Eastern Europe with a blueprint for how to conceive of themselves as independent nations. The list of Eastern European peoples so influenced by Herder includes the Czechs, Poles, Finns, Romanians, Bulgarians, Latvians, Estonians, Lithuanians, Slovenes, Ukrainians, and Russians. Herder addressed the Slavs directly with his hope that "you will at last awake refreshed from your long listless slumber and, having shaken off the chains of slavery, will enjoy again the possession of your fair lands . . . and celebrate on them your ancient festivals in peace together with the prosperity of your industry and trade."[125]

Founding fathers of Slavic countries expressed their admiration for Herder, including František Palacký, the Czech "Father of the Nation" and leader of the Czech National Revival movement, who called Herder the *"Apostle of Humanity."*[126] Herder's ideas are present in the Czech national anthem, which the writer and playwright Josef Kajetán Tyl, known as the father of Czech theater, wrote in 1834. In it, the phrase "Among the Czechs, my home!" is repeated several times. The land is described as a garden "glorious with spring blossom." It is "Paradise on earth."

In Slavic languages such as Czech, Polish, Serbo-Croatian, Slovenian, Bulgarian, and Russian, the concept of *narod* was equivalent to the German Volk. In nineteenth-century Russia, *narodnost*, the authentic spirit of the Russian people, adopted from German discussions of the Volk, became a focus of literary debate and soon crossed into politics. In the 1830s, narodnost, often translated as "nationality," became the official ruling ideology of Czar Nicholas I as part of a triad, along with orthodoxy and autocracy. The name of the modern Russian political party Rodina is the equivalent of Heimat.

The nineteenth-century pan-Slavic movement, which sought ethnic unification under Russian leadership, "derived its inspiration largely from Herder."[127] One visible impact of this movement is the clear influence of Russia's red, white, and blue flag on the design of many other flags, as adopted by the Slavs at the 1848 Pan-Slavic Congress in Prague. These include the countries of Croatia, the Czech Republic, Serbia, Slovakia, and Slovenia; former countries, including the Kingdom of Yugoslavia, the Socialist Federal Republic of Yugoslavia, and the Federal Republic of Yugoslavia; and entities within states, such as the Republika Srpska in Bosnia and Herzegovina and the Republic of Crimea.

Herder also had a particularly strong impact on the Hungarians, causing in them an existential dread of the death of the very identity that drove their nationalist struggle. Herder's assertion that the Hungarians, widely identified as Magyars, a name believed to belong to the most prominent tribe among them over a millennium ago, would lose their language by living among non-Hungarian peoples like the Slavs and Germans caused a panic among Hungarian intellectuals and led to a vigorous and rapid effort to preserve and promote Hungarian language, culture, and identity. The famous nineteenth-century statesman and modernizer, István Széchenyi, known as "the Greatest Hungarian," wrote, "Every day I am more convinced that Herder is right; the Hungarian nation will soon cease to exist."[128] Herder's dire prediction for the Hungarians, known in Hungary as *nemzet-halál*, or "national death," "became an enduring theme in the Hungarian national imagination" and a "recurring nightmare."[129] The fear of nemzet-halál is expressed in poems such as "Himnusz" (1823), by Ferenc Kölcsey, which became the Hungarian national anthem, and "Szózat" (Appeal) (1836), by Mihály Vörösmarty, known as the second national anthem, in which the Hungarian nation becomes a mass grave.

*Preserving Primordial Identity*

In this context we need to return to the opening image of this chapter, of the Turkish football players refusing to sing the German national anthem. Based on this example, we can predict with confidence that it would be virtually impossible for any player with a Turkish background in Hungary to sing that country's national anthem. Before the reader asks what is it with Turks and national anthems, we need to learn more about the Hungarian anthem. Written in the first half of the nineteenth century, like the German anthem, the Hungarian anthem also reflects the chauvinistic and xenophobic passions of the time. In the case of Hungary these are directed at outside invaders like the "plundering" Mongols and the Turks; the latter are explicitly singled out as villains. Full of gory images of blood, fire, torture, and slavery, the anthem depicts the "wild Turks" as an excrescence, a "barbarian nation." It glorifies tribal heroes such as the ninth-century chieftain Árpád, considered the founder of the Hungarian people and the namesake of the first royal dynasty; Bendegúz, the father of Attila the Hun; and Matthias, the most famous Hungarian king, who fought the Ottomans and Hapsburgs. The Hungarian anthem is a moving and powerful *cri de coeur* of suffering, tears, and misery that ends with a passionate appeal to God for salvation.

Hungary, like other Eastern European peoples, from the Poles in the north to the Bulgarians and Greeks in the south, was once under the sway in varying degrees and lengths of time of the Ottoman Empire. This interaction with the Ottomans has both shaped national identity and kept alive rampant Islamophobia. The national heroes of these countries often spoke in scathing terms about the Turks. The Bulgarian writer and revolutionary hero Lyuben Karavelov, an important figure in the Bulgarian National Revival, described the Turks thus: "'of raw Asiatic character,' 'a half-barbarous, half-rotten, half-dead people,' 'fanatics,' 'idiots,' 'with sodomic greed,' 'of wild cruelty,' or simply 'perverts.'"[130]

This background helps us understand why Eastern Europeans have been so unrelentingly hostile to Muslim refugees, however desperate their plight. For them, all refugees are associated with the hated Turks. This categorization lumps many peoples together even those who are, like many Arab peoples, former subjects of the Ottomans or from lands such as Gambia or Cameroon that were never part of the Ottoman Empire. The presidents and prime ministers of Eastern European countries have made inflammatory remarks about Islam and the Muslim refugees, and several have said they would allow in only Christian immigrants (see chapter 9).

The urge to preserve and promote primordial identity among Eastern European peoples facing larger hostile nations has historically often been accompanied by an intolerable living situation for minorities among them including Jews and Roma (see chapters 5, 7, and 9).

The swath of ethnic peoples who now form the nations of Eastern Europe have not only been subject to Muslim invaders, they have also often been under pressure from two giant predatory neighbors on their doorsteps—the Germans to the west and the Russians to the east. They have lost territory to the Germans and the Russians and are constantly pulled into their respective spheres of influence. The intense primordial identity of Eastern Europeans helps them resist these geopolitical maneuvers. Poland, for example, has reason to be nervous about its bigger neighbors. Germany's predecessor, Prussia, and Russia, along with the Hapsburgs, partitioned Poland out of existence in the late eighteenth century. The bitterness remains, as evidenced by the covers of popular Polish current affairs magazines. A January 2016 issue of *wSieci* featured Frederick the Great of Prussia and Catherine the Great of Russia alongside Angela Merkel salivating over various parts of Poland. Another popular weekly newsmagazine, *Wprost*, the same month depicted German chancellor Angela Merkel as Hitler, with the leaders of the European Union cast as senior Nazi advisers.

The compulsion of the Eastern European Slavs to preserve their primordial identity against their larger neighbors, in this case, the Germans, can be seen as far back as the thirteenth century in the document "Manifesto to the Poles" issued by the court of the Czech King and addressed to the Poles: "If the Roman King [German Emperor] will destroy us, then the insatiable mouths of the Germans will open even more freely, and their insatiable greediness will stretch out its shameless hands toward your country. We are your solid wall, and if this wall will not hold, a great danger will threaten you. . . . O, what kind of oppression will your numerous nation, which is so much hated by the Germans, have to suffer? Oh, how hard will be the yoke of slavery which free Poland will have to bear."[131]

Combining their distrust of their bigger neighbors with the intense revival of their primordial tribal identity, the Czech Republic, Slovakia, Hungary, and Poland formed an alliance after the fall of the Soviet Union. They called themselves the Visegrad Group, after the town in Hungary where regional leaders assembled in the fourteenth century to form a trade alliance against the Hapsburgs. The countries' initial aim was to assist one another in joining the European Union. Today, the Visegrad countries are presenting a united front in seeking to shut down the flow of refugees into Europe. Focusing its rhetoric on the idea that waves of Muslim migrants are a threat to Europe's Christian identity, the organization issued an ultimatum that if Merkel's plan to provide a solution to the refugee problem did not succeed, they would partner with Macedonia and Bulgaria to "shore up Europe's defences on their own" and to assist with building a wall on the Macedonian border "as tough as the Israelis have built in the occupied West Bank."[132]

### *The Loss of Tribal "Purity" among the Slavs and Hungarians*

Whether at the hands of the Mongol, Holy Roman, Hapsburg, or Ottoman Empires, the long periods of occupation aroused Slavic and Hungarian anger and fears that their tribal "purity" had been compromised. They cited, among other things, the infiltration of foreign words and expressions into their languages and the imposition of negative stereotypes. The American scholar George Fenwick Jones, for example, explains the German attitude toward the Slavs even before Charlemagne's push into their territories:

> After the Germans began their drive toward the East, most prisoners were Slavs, particularly Wends [the German designation for Slavs living in their territories]; and, as a result, the Wends and their descendants remained stigmatized, even after they had become legally free, just as the American Negroes continued to suffer the handicaps of slavery long after their emancipation. According to Wilhelm Raabe, "down into the eighteenth century no German guild accepted a Wend. The members of that despised race were dishonorable like the executioner and other infamous people. No one received them as guests under his roof, no one sat at table with them. In the thirteenth century 'Wendish dog' was the worst reproach that one Germanic Christian could offer another."[133]

As for imported foreign words, the language and dialects spoken by Serbs, Croats, Bosniaks, and Montenegrins today are considerably indebted to Turkish. The Serbian linguist Vuk Karadžić listed several thousand Turkish words that had become part of his people's Slavic language in his nineteenth-century dictionary, the first Serbian dictionary ever published.[134] While over the years Serbian scholars would work to identify—and often attempt to purge—Turkish references and expressions in their language in pursuit of their primordial identity, Slovenian scholars such as Jernej Kopitar, described as the "Slav Herder," did the same with their language with respect to German.[135]

History itself becomes a contest between different narratives. Through the centuries of foreign domination tribal peoples have retained and perpetuated an enduring historical mythology, celebrating a halcyon time when they had independence and strong leadership. This can be seen among the Serbs in their feelings toward Kosovo, considered the heartland of their medieval kingdom before Ottoman domination. Prince Lazar Hrebeljanović, the Serb ruler who lost his life battling the Turks in Kosovo in 1389, was subsequently enshrined as a saint and mythological figure. This mythology was invoked by President Slobodan Milošević when he addressed a million Serbs at the site of the battle in 1989, and it was promoted in Serbian films like *The Battle of Kosovo* (1989).

For the Hungarians, Matthias I, the greatest ruler of the independent Kingdom of Hungary who lived in the fifteenth century, dominates the national mythology even today. Matthias was the ideal hero in that he battled both the empires that sought to absorb the Hungarians, the Holy Roman Empire, led by the Hapsburgs, and the Ottomans. Matthias was even able to capture Vienna, the seat of the Hapsburgs. Legends of Matthias's feats have lasted into the present day, including tales of his battles with the Turks and the rescue of his wife from the Ottoman sultan, as well as an especially popular story featuring the just and humble king visiting his subjects in disguise. Hungarian history after Matthias was considered a tale of unremitting misery which is captured in the common Hungarian phrase, "King Matthias is dead, and with him Justice."[136]

King Matthias was such a towering figure that he looms not only over Hungarian mythology but also over that of the Romanians and Slavic peoples such as the Serbs, Czechs, Slovenians, Croatians, and even Ukrainians, who, like the Hungarians, battled the Turkic and Germanic empires. It is said that Matthias still sleeps under the mountains in Slovenia with his army and will emerge when the people need him most.

### *Primordial Identity and Islam in Postcommunist Eastern Europe*

When the Cold War ended and the peoples of Eastern Europe and the Balkans were freed from Communist rule, the newly independent peoples had an opportunity to freely forge their own national identities. Yet their pursuit of primordial identity too easily converted into predator identity. These peoples, who saw themselves as living through centuries of tyranny, were determined never to allow the specter of foreign empires to dominate them again, in particular, the Turks who were associated with their own Muslim minorities.

Instead of extending hospitality to their Muslim minorities from a position of confidence and goodwill, they instead sought nationalistic revenge for the past. The bloody twentieth century, with its two world wars, had already reduced the diversity of Eastern European countries; turmoil, violence, population exchanges, and outright ethnic cleansing beginning in the nineteenth century removed much of the Muslim population from former Ottoman lands in Europe. With its rich multicultural and multireligious diversity, Yugoslavia was an exception. But when the nation began to fracture along ethnic and religious lines in the early 1990s, the Serbs, using all the resources of the state, immediately set out to eradicate the Bosnians, whom they saw as Turks—despite the fact that they were of Slavic and Illyrian background—in a genocidal campaign that was only halted by American intervention.

For other Eastern European nations with a history of opposing the Ottomans, the reality of a Muslim presence hit home only with the refugee crisis, when Syrians and many others from mostly Muslim countries arrived in the hundreds of thousands seeking safety and shelter. Hungarian prime minister Viktor Orbán cast the refugees—whom Orbán said "look like an army"—as Turks, to be kept out of the country at all costs. In a March 2015 speech commemorating Hungary's 1848 anti-Hapsburg rebellion, Orbán praised King Matthias as one of seven "great forebears" of the Hungarian nation and described the empires of the Germans, Russians, and "the People of the Crescent in their multitudes, the wasp nest's unrelenting hum and ferment" who threatened Hungary. Orbán was confirming that the concept of the Volk, or *nép*, as it is known in Hungary, was alive and well. "The name of Hungary," he promised, "will be great again. . . . Honor to the brave!"

### *The Continuing Importance of Primordial Identity*

The lesson from European history is that the path from the Teutoburg Forest leads to Dürer, Goethe, Wagner, and Nietzsche—but also to Hitler's concentration camps. Here we see the core conundrum of primordial tribal identity: how to remain strong in your own identity without transgressing onto that of others—in effect, how to win the World Cup without expressing overtly racist contempt for the defeated. It is a delicate balance to maintain. After the catastrophe of the Nazi atrocities and their use of "original" and "authentic" Germanic culture and its symbols to justify and reinforce their position, the Allies wisely discouraged and dampened any idea of overt German identity.

However, the Allies may have thrown the baby out with the bathwater, leaving the next generation of Germans with a dangerous vacuum where their identity should have been. In view of the discussion above, it is important to place the concept of identity in a historical and cultural context. While there is little doubt of the dangers of predatory identity, we need to emphasize that primordial tribal identity provides stability, continuity, and a sense of belonging, especially in changing times. It is the current generation that now grapples with questions of identity. They do this amid the cacophony of confusing and conflicted voices of predatory far-right movements that threaten violence while promoting their ideas of "pure" tribal identity. The discussion of identity is thus no longer of merely academic interest; it is at the center of European social and political life.

Whether among modern Germanic peoples or Eastern European ones, outsiders face an inability to be incorporated into the "tribe." It is clear that immigrants confront serious challenges in being accepted. This is especially true of Muslims, who in addition to not belonging to the Volk are also identified with what is considered an alien and violent religion that once dominated large parts of Europe.

In the end, the Europeans we met who were sure and smug about the centrality of their primordial tribal identity and those immigrants who were disturbed by it were both right in pointing to its significance. Without this understanding, we cannot fully appreciate European attitudes toward terrorism, immigration, integration, multiculturalism, and the emergence of the Far Right. The story of tribal identity that began 2,000 years ago cannot so easily be set aside; but there is another parallel European story that is its very antithesis and though equally compelling is less well known. It is to that we now turn.

# THREE

# European Pluralist Identity

"THEIR FIRST AIM was how to acquire more knowledge and wisdom." We were in the Grand Mosque in Cordoba, and Imma Fernandez, our Spanish guide, was waxing lyrical about Muslim Andalusia a thousand years ago and seemed transported back to that time. Again and again she returned to the high regard Andalusians had for knowledge and learning: "The best present you could give to a caliph was a book, not material presents or gold or silver." Andalusia, she said, was defined by the "respect of religious minorities, harmony, and peace. There were no big wars at that time, it was a very peaceful century, the tenth century." "I have always been attracted," she mused, "by these aesthetics in Islam, by the beautiful harmony in Islam, like art, architecture." "Unfortunately," she sighed with a hint of sorrow, "we are far away from that, and I am considered a dreamer."

Imma, who was told by her father that their ancestors were Moors, pointed to the respect given to women at that time and cited the schools set up for them by philosophers like Averroes. She contrasted this attitude with that of societies in the "north of Europe," where it was "questioned if women had a soul." An avowed modern European feminist of Catholic background and a doctoral student of anthropology, Imma then made a comment that had us wondering if we heard her correctly:

Maybe at that time I would have liked to be a concubine because you could go to school, there were schools for women, which was a privilege. So you would know how to read, you would maybe

*Author and Amineh in Cordoba, Spain*

study medicine. There were women who were doctors, poets, musicians, dancers. There were very good poets at that time such as Wallada. . . . They were like Virginia Woolf, but at the end of the tenth century.

Like the Grand Mosque of Cordoba, now officially called the Cathedral of Our Lady of the Assumption, it was difficult to know in Imma's case where Islam ended and Christianity began; the border between them had ceased to exist. In that suspended state between the past and the present, Imma was able to claim both her identities—one that had not completely faded with time and one that had failed to possess her completely. In that state, Imma was the living embodiment of the pluralist and inclusive culture of Andalusia, what the Spanish call *la convivencia*, or coexistence. As we discovered during our fieldwork, she was not alone. Perhaps that hybridity, synthesis, the inclusiveness, the meeting point, was the copacetic allure of Andalusia, where ideas of primordial tribal identity, so glorified and cherished in one part of Europe, would have seemed strangely alien and uncouth in another.

## La Convivencia in al-Andalus

The story of the origin of the greatest of the Andalusian dynasties is as fantastic as if it were taken from the pages of *The Thousand and One Nights*. Abdur Rahman, a dashing young Arab prince, barely escapes with his life from Damascus following a palace coup and massacre, survives hair-raising adventures with a band of soldiers hard on his heels with orders to kill him, and after crossing many lands establishes his rule on another continent, in Cordoba, Spain. These events took place over a thousand years ago and throw light on the encounters between Islam and Christianity and between Europe, Africa, and Asia. There is courage, heartache, pain, defeat, and triumph here, and even in the darkest hours there are characters from all faiths who inspire us today.

When the youthful Abdur Rahman, the lone survivor of the royal family following the overthrow of the Umayyad dynasty by the Abbasids in AD 750, arrived in al-Andalus, he would have recognized the tribal identity of the groups who dominated it. Indeed, the name al-Andalus—the Arabic name for Iberia—is traditionally thought to be derived from the name of the Germanic tribe, the Vandals, who occupied the region before the Visigoths. These groups of different religions were tribal in the traditionally understood sense: their members believed in a shared lineage and culture and practiced a defined code of behavior. Abdur Rahman, a grandson of the caliph of the Umayyad dynasty, which ruled an empire larger than the Roman Empire, himself came from a tribal background; the very identity of his ruling family, the Umayyads, rested on its lineage links with the Prophet of Islam. His mother was a Berber, a fact that would stand him in good stead when he arrived in the lands dominated by the Berber tribes in the Maghreb in North Africa and southern Spain. He arrived in al-Andalus to find a reservoir of goodwill for his Umayyad dynasty; within a year of his arrival, Abdur Rahman would declare himself the emir of Cordoba and be recognized as such.

In Spain, Abdur Rahman was smart enough to understand that in the alien environment, with its large Christian and Jewish populations, he would need more than tribal loyalties to ensure the success of his rule. The Umayyads had consistently shown a tendency to reach out to other faiths. The wife of the founding caliph of the Umayyads, for example, was Christian. As a result, the Christian population could be counted on to remain loyal. Their loyalty did not waver even in campaigns fought against fellow Christians during the wars against the Byzantine Empire. Besides, Abdur

Rahman had grown up in a culture that valued learning, knowledge, and literature. He was thus bringing with him ideas of pluralist societies successfully living together and the appreciation of learning.

Abdur Rahman's dynasty would give Europe one of its most glorious periods of history, culminating in the reign of an illustrious successor, Abdur Rahman III, whose Jewish confidant, for all practical purposes, was his chief minister or vizier and whose ambassador to European courts was a Catholic bishop. Perhaps there is nothing more symbolic of that period and its fate than the ruins of Madinat al-Zahra on the outskirts of the city of Cordoba. Built by Abdur Rahman III, it was a glittering town that dazzled visitors. The architecture and town planning were breathtaking, and evidence of it can still be seen today.

The Almoravid Berber tribes who arrived from North Africa in the eleventh century, like a powerful storm, to overthrow the Umayyad dynasty were in turn displaced in the next century by another Berber dynasty, the Almohads. These tribal movements illustrated Ibn Khaldun's principle of conquering tribes coming from deserts and mountains to take over cities and agricultural lands. They were united by asabiyyah and practiced a simple tribal version of Islam. Members of these tribes saw the multi-religious societies of Andalusia, living in their cultured cities and on their prosperous farms, as decadent and effete. This is an instance of what I term "tribal Islam" meeting "settled Islam." The former was the irresistible force, while the latter, alas for them, was not an immovable object. It is this back and forth of history that explains Islam in the Iberian Peninsula—tolerance and intolerance, acceptance and rejection, ignorance and knowledge.

Although Madinat al-Zahra, which symbolized the glory of Andalusian civilization, was destroyed decades before the Almoravids captured power in Spain, the dynasty is widely blamed for its destruction. Even today commentators conflate events to provide a simplistic version of history and blame the "fundamentalist" Almoravid fanatics for its downfall, thus using history to fit into our current understanding of the dynamics of "radical Islam." Although Berber tribes were involved in the destruction of the town, the Almoravids were not the culprits: the Almoravids did not arrive in Spain until 1086, almost eight decades after Madinat al-Zahra was destroyed.

Despite this important distinction, it should be noted that aspects of settled Islam were also important for the Berber dynasties like the Almoravids. Contrary to their image as barbaric destroyers of culture, the

Almoravids had already built up a vast and powerful empire in northwestern Africa, which encouraged scholarship and learning. The legendary al-Karaouine University in Fez, which was founded by Fatima al-Fihri, taught science, mathematics, and astronomy and gave degrees centuries before Oxford and Cambridge, flourished within the Almoravid empire and counted among its alumni the great Jewish scholar Maimonides and a future pope, Sylvester II. Although the dynasty promoted a more orthodox form of Islam than that found in Cordoba, it was nonetheless the internal fighting that had weakened the Umayyad caliphate and brought it to its ultimate collapse. The emerging threat of aggressive Christian kings also prompted Muslims to appeal to the Almoravids for support, which aided them in gaining power in Spain.

Buildings are not difficult to destroy, but ideas are more resilient. The Andalusian model of convivencia, a pluralist society encouraging acceptance of others and the pursuit of knowledge, art, and literature—the polar opposite of primordial tribal identity—persisted for centuries after Cordoba had changed hands. It was evident in different ways and in different kingdoms on the Iberian Peninsula. It was even visible in kingdoms with Christian kings elsewhere in Europe, as in Sicily, where we were told the equivalent term in Italian is *convivenza*. Later, the same idea would be evident in the Balkans during the Ottoman Empire. As we shall see, it also had an impact far beyond these areas to shape the very civilization of Europe itself. Let us look then more closely at Abdur Rahman, the man whose dynasty more than any other came to represent that pluralist idea of society in Europe.

### The Falcon of the Quraish

Perhaps there is no greater recognition than that given by a sworn enemy. Al-Mansur, the Abbasid caliph of Baghdad, once asked his fawning courtiers who might best fit the title, Saqr Quraish or "the Falcon of the Quraish." Surely, the courtiers argued, the caliph himself deserved the title of the bird that is the swiftest and fiercest predator of the skies. The caliph pondered a while and then replied that the title belonged to his rival Abdur Rahman.

Abdur Rahman's reign lasted thirty-two years, during which he established a dynasty that would be the pride of Europe. It laid the foundations for the Umayyad caliphate of Cordoba that rivaled the other established caliphate in Baghdad, the Abbasids. Its capital, Cordoba, the jewel of al-Andalus, was the most populous and resplendent capital of Europe with parks, palaces, baths, and libraries. Abdur Rahman's personal story, in addition to his skills as an administrator, created wide sympathy for the man who was known as al-Dakhil—the immigrant. People were moved by his nostalgic yearning for the home of his youth. He never forgot his days in his Syrian birthplace of Rusafa and would do everything possible to remind himself of it. His greatest architectural triumph, the Grand Mosque of Cordoba, contained a thousand marble columns reaching up in arches to the high ceiling in a shape suggestive of palm fronds. Matching them, just outside, was a grove of actual date palms, a tree Abdur Rahman is thought to have introduced to al-Andalus. Worshippers in the mosque looking around and above would be forgiven for feeling they were sitting in a forest of palm trees. Abdur Rahman's poem of exile and longing, inspired by the sight of a palm tree in his Spanish palace named Rusafa after his home in Syria, captures the sensitivity of the man:

> A palm tree stands in the middle of Rusafa,
> Born in the West, far from the land of palms.
> I said to it: How like me you are, far away and in exile,
> In long separation from family and friends.
> You have sprung from soil in which you are a stranger;
> And I, like you, am far from home.

This was a man who in his time was a match for the other two titans of the age—Charlemagne, the most powerful Christian ruler in Europe, and Harun al-Rashid, the caliph of the mighty Abbasid empire. Yet today Abdur Rahman's name is hardly known in Europe, and few Muslims remember him with any clarity.

Abdur Rahman and his successors attempted to live up to the model of the just and compassionate Islamic ruler established by the Prophet of Islam. Abdur Rahman's grandson al-Hakam I, for example, faced an uprising of Cordoba theological students—the Taliban of their day—who deemed the ruler insufficiently Islamic. When, following several violent and bloody rebellions, one of the leading theological student rebels was brought before the ruler, the young man, expecting he would be put to death, declared that he was obeying the voice of God. Al-Hakam replied, "He who commanded thee, as thou dost pretend, to hate me, commands me to pardon thee. Go and live, in God's protection!"[1] And for all his power and wealth, even the caliph could be chastised when he failed to attend Friday prayer, as Abdur Rahman III was by the senior cleric at the Grand Mosque after he had missed three Friday prayers while building Madinat al-Zahra.

## *The Ilm Ethos and Convivencia*

Perhaps Abdur Rahman's greatest contribution would be in laying the foundations of learning and knowledge so that society would reflect one of Islam's core tenets, the instruction to seek knowledge, or *ilm*. The ilm ethos in time came to characterize the culture of Andalusia. It is easily forgotten how important ilm is in Islam. The first word spoken by the angel Gabriel to the Prophet when delivering the Quran, in the mountain cave outside Mecca, was "to read." The second most used word in the Quran after the name of God is ilm. The Prophet's saying about ilm sums up the essence of Islam itself: "The ink of the scholar is more sacred than the blood of the martyr."

There is a direct causal relationship between the ilm ethos and convivencia; one could not exist without the other. The former creates the spiritual, intellectual, and cultural conditions for the emergence and establishment of the latter. The urge to reach out to God through knowledge, which is embedded in the ilm ethos, is thus translated into an embrace of God's creation irrespective of racial, religious, or class differences, which may be defined as convivencia. This embrace, however, is not possible without compassion and love. The ability to seek knowledge about another's religious and scholarly traditions and collaborate in the pursuit of common goals was an important reason why convivencia worked. Everything—architecture, philosophy, and poetry—would grow from the ilm ethos, which was accepted by Muslim and non-Muslim alike.

What is apparent to even the casual visitor who contemplates Andalusia's architecture, calligraphy, or poetry is the intelligence, symmetry, balance, and beauty in each of these different expressions of human genius. Everything is infused with an idea that is bigger than the work itself and carries a universal appeal. This is perhaps most dramatically expressed in the Grand Mosque in Cordoba and the Alhambra, the palace and fortress that housed the Muslim rulers of Granada. Here we clearly see the balance between the symmetry of the architecture on the one hand and the expression of the idea of unity on the other. Every angle and every vista reiterates this balance. In the Alhambra we are reminded of the human predicament in the Islamic calligraphy that repeatedly proclaims, "There is no victor but God." It echoes the ineffable Abrahamic message that "this, too, shall pass" and reflects the Biblical warning, "The whole world, earth and sky, will be destroyed, but my words will last forever" (Matt. 24:35).

By promoting scholarship, Abdur Rahman established an ilm ethos in his kingdom. The Grand Mosque of Cordoba, which was a place not only of worship but also of learning, exemplified the ethos. Scholars from different parts of Europe and the Muslim world gathered here to talk to and teach eager young students before and after prayer. The ruler himself was known to participate in these gatherings to encourage scholars to attend. The Grand Mosque thus became the greatest house of worship and also the greatest center of learning in Andalusia. Yet Abdur Rahman also made sure that the Islamic spirit of ilm did not stop at the doors of the mosque. The main library of Cordoba was said to have 600,000 books and manuscripts at a time when the biggest library in Christian Europe, housed in Switzerland, had some 400. There were seventy libraries in Cordoba alone.[2]

The products of the ilm ethos in Andalusia were people of wide-ranging talents and interests whose creativity, curiosity, and passion for learning would profoundly impact European, Islamic, and world history. Ibn Firnas, who lived in the ninth century, is a good example: he wrote poetry, taught music, designed a water clock, manufactured colorless glass, and made magnifying corrective lenses, which he called "reading stones." But his main interest was to study the stars and work on plans for man's first flight. Ibn Firnas was able to achieve his dream of flight after strapping a contraption around himself and leaping off a mountaintop near Cordoba. He is commemorated in Cordoba by a bridge with striking giant winglike arches over it, and a crater of the moon is named after him.

The impact of the work of Ibn Tufail, an Andalusian philosopher, physician, and astronomer who was a key adviser to the Almohad caliph, was similarly far-reaching. The theme and structure of Tufail's twelfth-century novel *Hayy ibn Yaqdhan,* translated in English as *The Improvement of Human Reason: Exhibited in the Life of Hai Ebn Yokdhan,* about a man stranded on a desert island with a companion and engaged in raising philosophic questions about the nature of knowledge, the individual, and society, foreshadowed Daniel Defoe's *Robinson Crusoe* (1719).

In the field of astronomy, Nur ad-Din al-Bitruji, also of Andalusia and a student of Ibn Tufail, challenged Ptolemy's accepted model of the cosmos. Al-Bitruji's work on planetary orbits and his theory of planetary motion "will surge through Europe in the 13th century and will be studied, adapted, and even plagiarized repeatedly."[3] Copernicus, another critic of Ptolemy, would cite al-Bitruji on the position of Mercury and Venus relative to the sun in his discussion of famous scholars who had debated the position of the planets. Today, there is a crater on the moon named after al-Bitruji, using his Latin name, Alpetragius.

Other giants of Andalusian scholarship include al-Zahrawi, or Abulcasis, of Cordoba, who is considered the father of surgery. Al-Zahrawi's thirty-volume encyclopedia of medicine and surgery, *Kitab al-Tasrif* (The method of medicine), was the main surgical textbook in Europe for five centuries.[4] He was a pioneer of surgical techniques, and he invented many surgical instruments. Al-Zahrawi removed tumors, used stitches, and was the first to discover that hemophilia is hereditary. Many of his instruments and techniques are still in use.

## Philosophy and Faith in Andalusia

The question of how to balance logic, science, and reason with faith was a common quest of Jews, Christians, and Muslims in Andalusia. The three European giants of philosophy in the Middle Ages—Averroes in Islam, Maimonides in Judaism, and Thomas Aquinas in Christianity—were all engaged in this philosophic exercise, and each one of them was a product of convivencia and the ilm ethos. The very start of Europe's progress toward societies based in reason and logic can be traced to this time and the interaction of Muslim philosophers with the Greeks. One of the first to introduce the Greeks to Muslim thought was al-Kindi, a ninth-century scholar in Baghdad's famous House of Wisdom, who wrote, "We ought not to be ashamed of appreciating the truth and of acquiring it wherever it comes from, even if it comes from races distant and nations different from us."

The distinct intellectual traditions of Plato and Aristotle predisposed Muslims to respond to them in different ways. Because Plato dealt with shadows, forms, and ideals, and Aristotle was concerned with categorization and study of observable phenomena, the latter appeared more relevant to Muslims. Islamic civilization dominated vast regions of the earth, and its concerns were more practical and quotidian. Muslims were thus less inclined toward abstract philosophy compared with more practical subjects such as medicine and astronomy. In contrast, Plato made a far greater impact on early Christianity, as Christians, persecuted for centuries, waited for the promised better times while living in the dark corners of society. It was only centuries later, after Christianity was well established in Europe, that the work of Averroes, who was an unabashed Aristotelian, would introduce Aristotle to Christian figures like Aquinas and bring the Greeks into mainstream European thought.

## AVERROES, EUROPE'S PHILOSOPHER

Ibn Rushd, or Averroes as he is known in the European tradition, was born in 1126 in Cordoba and inherited a rich Islamic legacy from thinkers who argued for the compatibility of faith and reason. Trained in philosophy, Islamic jurisprudence, and medicine, Averroes's many notable works included his magisterial three-part *Commentary on Plato's Republic,* in which he examined the virtuous or ideal state and dealt with such topics as the education of the young and the supreme role of the philosopher-king. Averroes believed with Aristotle that effective political action requires both political and theoretical knowledge.

Averroes's patron, Ibn Tufail, introduced him to Caliph Abu Yaqub Yusuf, the Almohad ruler, who appointed Averroes chief judge of Cordoba and later court physician. The ruler was fascinated by Greek thought and asked Averroes to write a series of explanations of the essential ideas of Aristotle for non-specialists. Averroes continued to be influenced by Aristotle even in his interpretation of the Quran. For example, common Muslim belief holds that the universe has a beginning, but Averroes followed Aristotle in arguing that the universe has always existed and pointed out that nothing in the Quran contradicts this argument.

For Averroes, Aristotle was of primary importance because of his reliance on conceptual analysis and syllogistic demonstration and because he covered every aspect of what could be known. Averroes therefore set out to purge Aristotle's text of neo-Platonic material that he felt did not hold up to empirical scrutiny. He also attempted to complete the Aristotelian oeuvre by enhancing it with knowledge on questions of law and social organization gained up to Islamic times.[5] Averroes composed three different types of commentaries on Aristotle that aimed at reaching different groups of readers: "short synopsis," "intermediate commentaries," and "great commentaries." No work this developed on any Greek philosopher had been done until then. Averroes's genius lay in producing perhaps the most sophisticated understanding of Aristotle in Europe.

Averroes came to believe that while the Quran is true in its essence, it represents a "poetic truth," which only philosophers can "interpret."[6] Without critical and philosophic engagement, he argued, it was not possible to fully understand religion. The *shariah,* Islamic law, according to Averroes, allows everyone to have access to happiness, which made it a universal blessing— but it is philosophy alone that gives complete understanding of religion. The philosophers thus had a duty to interpret and educate.

Not all Muslims were pleased with Averroes's comments on Islamic thought, and there was pressure from his critics to silence him. Suffering the fate of many Muslim scholars, Averroes found himself exiled and his books banned in 1195. (The Jewish philosopher Maimonides, too, was exiled from al-Andalus and died a hugely respected figure in Cairo.) Averroes died in Morocco in 1198, and his body was returned to his beloved Cordoba. His funeral, as described by his contemporary Ibn Arabi, was a sad sight. Witnessing the great philosopher's coffin balanced with some of his books on a miserable donkey, Ibn Arabi noted wryly the futility of writing. It was a lonely death for one of the greatest philosophers of Europe.

It was in Christian Europe, however, where Averroes's writings made the most impact. He was known in Europe simply as the Commentator by Aquinas and others as they believed he needed no further introduction. A school of Averroists, in which Christian scholars used Averroes's models to reconcile Christianity with reason and philosophy, spread across the continent, despite the condemnation at various points of the Catholic Church. Even Raphael, the great Renaissance painter, included Averroes in his celebrated painting, "The School of Athens," which also depicted Plato and Socrates. Averroes's lasting impact on Western thought is summed up in the words of the American philosopher Robert Pasnau: he is the "Islamic scholar who gave us modern philosophy."

### Ibn Arabi, the Mystic Master of Andalusia

Ibn Arabi, who followed Averroes in Andalusia, was also a poet, philosopher, and religious scholar. His mystical writings earned him the titles *muhyiddin,* which means "reviver of religion," and *Sheikh al-Akbar,* the "greatest master." Ibn Arabi was an authority on Quranic learning and wrote more than 350 works, including some of the finest poetry in the Arabic language. He traveled to North Africa and the great centers of Islam in Mecca, Damascus, and Baghdad. In everything he wrote, in his philosophy and poetry, he expressed the "unity of existence" and the "oneness of being," which could be said to embody the spirit of convivencia, as reflected in these verses:

My heart can take on any form:
A meadow for gazelles,
A cloister for monks,
For the idols, sacred ground,

Ka'ba for the circling pilgrim,
The tables of the Torah,
The scrolls of the Quran.

My creed is Love;
Wherever its caravan turns along the way,
That is my belief,
My faith.

## *Jews and Convivencia*

The position of the Jewish community of Andalusia demonstrates to us convivencia in practice. The mighty caliph Abdur Rahman III had a Jewish chief minister, Hasdai ibn Shaprut, who held the most important position in the land at the height of Muslim power on the Iberian Peninsula. Jews also served in senior positions in the Muslim kingdoms of Almeria, Albar‑racin, Zaragoza, and Seville.[7] While the Jews spoke Arabic, in Andalusia Hebrew became a language of poetry and philosophy "for the first time in a thousand years" as Jews emulated what Muslims were doing in Arabic.[8]

The Jewish community lived throughout al-Andalus and had their own judges and their own governor of the community.[9] The ruler of Granada attracted the Cordoba-born Samuel ibn Naghrillah, a poet who had "stud‑ied Hebrew, Aramaic, Arabic, Berber and Latin as well as Biblical and Koranic literature," to be his vizier.[10] Samuel, a battlefield hero who is "considered the father of epic war poetry in Hebrew literature," was confi‑dent enough to call himself "the David of my age!"[11]

Charity, which is a central feature of Judaism, was interpreted in Anda‑lusia to include non-Jewish people like Muslims and was accepted as such by Muslim religious leaders. We have an example of a fatwa issued in the eleventh century that "discusses a Jew who established a charitable en‑dowment that would benefit poor Muslims, and the ruling considers it acceptable."[12]

The Muslim impact on Jewish culture, philosophy, and religious inter‑pretation during the period of convivencia was captured by Rabbi Lord Jonathan Sacks, the former chief rabbi of the United Kingdom, in his comments in an interview with me on Maimonides, who wrote in Arabic and is such a towering figure in Judaism that he is commonly referred to as "the Second Moses": "Moses Maimonides, the greatest rabbi of the Middle Ages . . . not only his philosophy, but almost every aspect of his work was influenced by and stimulated by Islam. His creation of this magnificent legal code was inspired by shariah codes. His formulation of the principles of Jewish faith was inspired by the fact that Muslim thinkers had done this wonderful presentation of Islamic faith."

Edward Kessler, the Jewish scholar who founded the Woolf Institute at Cambridge to study relations between Muslims, Christians, and Jews, emphasized the same point in his interview with Amineh for this project: "The growth of the sciences, of the arts, of poetry, are heavily influenced by Muslims. In fact, I'd say the whole of medieval Jewish philosophy could not have come into existence without Islamic philosophy. The rules of literature and grammar are basically taken from Muslim grammarians."

When facing expulsion from Spain in 1492, Isaac Abravanel, a Jewish senior adviser to the triumphant monarchs Ferdinand and Isabella, was able to renegotiate the final date of expulsion from July 31 to August 2, 1492, to match the date that the Temple of Jerusalem was destroyed in the Jewish calendar. For centuries, the Jews would lament this expulsion, adopting the identity "Sephardic," meaning Spanish, and keeping the Castilian vernacular language, Ladino, alive in their communities (see chapter 7).

### *Christians, Convivencia, and Alfonso X, "the Last Almohad Caliph"*

Like the Jews, the Christians of Andalusia spoke Arabic and used it as the liturgical language of church services. It was reported by a Christian writer in ninth-century Cordoba that "The Christians love to read the poems and romances of the Arabs. . . . All talented young Christians read and study with enthusiasm the Arab books; they gather immense libraries at great expense." Christian and Muslim rulers alike attracted notable and talented figures from different religious backgrounds to their courts, from soldiers such as El Cid to scholars like Ibn Khaldun. In Ibn Khaldun's case, Peter, the Christian king of Castile, asked him to serve as his vizier, although Ibn Khaldun declined. Peter's palace at the Alcazar in Seville was built by craftsmen from Granada and looked very much like the Alhambra, even proclaiming repeatedly the Arabic message emblazoned across the walls of the Alhambra about the ephemeral nature of human life and God's permanence.[13]

A remarkable example of the ideals of the ilm ethos and convivencia comes to us from Toledo, the former capital of the Visigoths and thus of significance for Spanish Christians. When King Alfonso VI of León and Castile, known as the "Emperor of the Three Religions," took Toledo in

1085, he mandated freedom of religion and all rights for the city's Muslim population, who were permitted to keep their properties and would pay a tax as the Christians had under Muslim rule. Muslims were also to retain control of the main mosque of Toledo.

But it was another Alfonso who best exemplifies the ideals of the ilm ethos and convivencia: Alfonso X, the ruler of Castile, known in history as Alfonso the Learned or the Wise for his commitment to knowledge and scholarship. Alfonso X—the son of Ferdinand III, who conquered Cordoba for Christianity in 1236 and was later elevated to Saint Ferdinand—was German through his mother, a cousin of the Holy Roman Emperor Frederick II. Alfonso X had a lifelong ambition to ascend to the position of Holy Roman emperor like his illustrious relative, but he was never able to accomplish this task. Nevertheless, Alfonso's advances in science and scholarship, law, and music had a lasting impact on Spain, Europe, and even the United States and Latin America, where his legal code remained in effect until the nineteenth century. Alfonso's portrait can be found today in the U.S. House of Representatives for being the "Originator of the Seven Parts, the code used as a basis for Spanish jurisprudence."

Alfonso's attitude toward Islam can be seen in the moving words he wrote while still a prince about the minaret of the main mosque of Seville, which would become the main cathedral of Seville after his father conquered the city: "With such mastery was it made . . . with such great nobility, that in the whole world there cannot be any so noble, or any equal." It is said that Alfonso so valued the minaret that he threatened with death anyone who would destroy even one brick.[14] When his father died, Alfonso had a tomb built for him of gold and silver and placed in the cathedral with an epitaph in Latin, Castilian, Hebrew, and Arabic.

Upon ascending to the throne, Alfonso found himself with large numbers of Muslim and Jewish subjects, and he laid down clear laws to enforce the rights of minorities. Disbelievers, he said, are of the same flesh and blood as us. On the subject of Muslims, Alfonso declared that "the Moors who are in all our realms are ours and we have to guard and protect them and to have our rights from them in whatever place they may live." Muslims, as well as Jews, Alfonso's law maintained, had the right to "live peacefully among Christians, 'observing their religion and not insulting ours.'" Alfonso bestowed knighthoods on Muslim rulers, including the king of Granada in 1273. Alfonso was also honored by Muslim rulers like the sultan of Egypt, who sent Alfonso gifts including "a giraffe, a zebra, and the skeleton of a crocodile" as well as "many precious cloths of many kinds, and many very noble and rare jewels."[15]

Under Alfonso's rule, Jews, Muslims, and Christians lived under their own laws. Where members of these groups were in litigation against one another, Alfonso ordered them to swear in a particular manner with reference to their own faith. Alfonso's court was a haven for scholars of all religions, including those from faraway lands. In 1254 Alfonso established in Seville what he called "general schools of Latin and Arabic" where, as a historian notes, the "cultures would share equally." Alfonso also guaranteed "the safety and security of the masters and scholars who came there" and "exempted them, their books and their goods from any tolls."[16] Alfonso's attitude could be further seen in the city of Murcia, where he built a madrassa-college especially for the eminent Muslim scholar Muhammad al-Riquti for the joint instruction of Jews, Christians, and Muslims. In Toledo, Alfonso sponsored the famous School of Translators, where members of the three faiths jointly translated Arabic, Hebrew, and Greek works. Toledo was critical to the dissemination of Arabic knowledge into the European Christian world and attracted eager scholars and students from across the continent. Alfonso also translated the religious texts of the different faiths, commissioning Castilian versions of the Bible, Quran, and Talmud.

Because Alfonso believed the population of his kingdom should be educated and that knowledge needed to be "easy to understand," he had the preferred language of translation changed from Latin to the local Castilian vernacular that the three faiths shared. Early standard Spanish was "arguably the result of the work of one man, Alfonso X," whose role in creating and establishing the Spanish language was similar to the role played by Frederick II in creating the Italian language, as discussed below.[17] While still a prince, Alfonso had ordered the Castilian translation of the Arabic book *Kalila wa Dimna*, produced in Baghdad by the Abbasids around 750. This Castilian version became the first work of literary prose in the Spanish language. It is a book of tales that refers to two lynxes, who appear in the first set of stories. They are described as "anthropomorphized animal characters" and are seen to represent "human characteristics" with their "half-comic tales" serving as lessons. The tales originally come from the ancient Hindu *Panchatantra* and were subsequently translated into Persian and Syriac.

Among the best-known works to be produced at Alfonso's court, in which trilingual Jews played a prominent role as translators, was the astronomical collection named after him, the *Alfonsine Tables*, "a set of data that made it possible to calculate the relative positions of the sun, moon, and stars." The *Alfonsine Tables* examined and revised the work of the eleventh-century Muslim scholar al-Zarkali of Cordoba "on the basis of observations painstakingly taken in Toledo between 1263 and 1272."[18] As part of the project, scientists at Alfonso's court also "translated over a dozen crucial treatises from the heritage of Spanish Islam."[19] The *Alfonsine Tables* would become the most popular astronomical tables in Europe for centuries: "Copernicus relied on the *Tables* in the 1490s as a student at the University of Cracow, and his personal copy still survives."[20]

Alfonso's legal reforms—which attempted to centralize state rule under the authority of the monarch, who guarantees God's justice for all citizens—were similar to reforms promoted by rulers before him, such as Roger II and Frederick II, who also drew upon Roman and Islamic law. This legal system, which had a powerful moral component that compelled the king to seek and codify encyclopedic knowledge and also surround himself with wise and incorruptible men, was heavily indebted to Islamic law. Alfonso's *Siete Partidas* (Seven Parts), written in Spanish, was "a direct adaptation of Muslim law" and "became the basis for the laws of modern Spain."[21] The multitude of straightforward copies from Islamic law and the Quran in the *Siete Partidas*, too numerous to list here, are described in Marcel A. Boisard's "On the Probable Influence of Islam on Western Public and International Law."[22]

All this was too much for Alfonso's nobles, who had been in a state of agitation and eventually rebelled against him. This forced the embattled king to seek the help of the sultan of Morocco, and the two kings together besieged cities like Cordoba. For his embrace of Islamic influences, Alfonso has been called, "the last Almohad Caliph."[23] For his contribution to knowledge, Alfonso has a crater on the moon named after him.

## The Limitations of Convivencia and the Tenacity of Germanic Tribal Identity

The concept and practice of convivencia had structural and philosophic limitations in Spanish society. While the pluralist identity of Andalusia was a reality, the older sociological and cultural base of society established by the Germanic Visigoths, who ruled Spain from early in the fifth century, did not entirely disappear. In Spanish primordial tribal identity, Christianity and blood descent from the Visigoths were fused and represented by the aristocracy. Christianity itself was thus made synonymous with Germanic lineage. While ensuring exclusivity for them, it also created an insurmountable barrier for the Muslim and Jewish populations, which conceptually could not, by definition, be fully Spanish even if its members converted to Christianity. Blood—not faith—defined the Spanish Christian.

These deep structures of Germanic tribalism thus became part and parcel of Spanish culture, folklore, and identity, but they created contradictions in the articulation of Spanish primordial identity. Neither Jesus nor his disciples, like Paul, would have been accepted as Christians according to this definition. The idea of a ruling aristocracy also contradicts tribal identity and society, which are egalitarian and do not encourage hierarchies. That Germanic tribalism has endured outside the northern Germanic heartland demonstrates its resilience in the identity of European societies.

The emphasis on blood descent in Spanish society can be seen in the ubiquity of words associated with lineage and purity in the Spanish, or Castilian, language. The Castilians, in the words of one scholar, had an "obsession with blood and genealogy," which "was manifested in the pervasiveness of a language of blood constituted by terms such as *sangre* (blood), *casta* (breeding), *generación* (lineage), *raíz* (root), *tronco* (trunk), and *rama* (branch)." To achieve maximum "purity" in Spanish society, one had to *descender de los godos,* or "descend from the Goths," as the expression went.[24] The idea of the nobility was synonymous with *Godo*, or Goth. Over the years following the coming of Islam to the Iberian Peninsula, popular songs and stories reminded the people of their Gothic heritage and its link with Christianity, such as the twelfth-century *Chronicle of Alfonso the Emperor*, about the Castilian ruler Alfonso VII. In it, the legendary ancestor Pelagius (or Pelayo), the son of the final Visigothic king who is said to have begun the Reconquista in 722 with a battle against the Muslims, "appears as a chivalric champion itching to restore not only the 'well-being of Spain and the army of the Gothic people' but also the 'church of God.'"[25]

The union of Christianity and the blood of the Goths had been established in the seventh century by Isidore, the archbishop of Seville, who declared that the Goths ruling Spain were God's chosen people. Isidore described Visigothic Spain as the "glory and ornament of the world."[26] Even the continuing existence of the last Muslim kingdom of Granada was widely seen as intolerable not only because it was Muslim but also because it was believed that only the blood of the Goths had legitimacy to rule in the Iberian Peninsula. "The total restoration of the empire of the Goths," wrote the Spanish historian Ramón Menéndez Pidal, was "the great historical preoccupation of Castilian thinkers."[27]

The task of enforcing blood purity in Spanish society fell to the Spanish Inquisition. In the *Estatutos de limpieza de sangre* (Statutes of the purity of blood), enacted by Grand Inquisitor Tomás de Torquemada in 1483 and the law of Spain until the nineteenth century, anyone not proved to be an "Old Christian," meaning one of pure blood descended from the Goths, was denied religious or secular office.[28]

Notable figures promoting the union between Christianity and blood also included Pero Sarmiento, the governor of Toledo, who in 1449 led a riot against the converted Jewish population in which many were killed and issued a proclamation that only Old Christians whose blood was not "tainted" were eligible to hold public office. Detailing what was to be Iberia's first "purity of blood" statute, Sarmiento addressed a large gathering in front of city hall and "catalogued all the evil deeds that the Jews were said to have committed. The first was that the Jews of Toledo had opened the gates of the city to Tariq's Moors in 711, thereby ensuring centuries of Muslim domination; and their descendants, the 'New Christians,' were continuing their 'intrigues' against true Christians."[29]

Many genealogies traced descent from Pelagius, who founded the Kingdom of Asturias in the mountainous northern region, the first Christian kingdom to be established following the institution of Muslim rule on the Iberian Peninsula.[30] In fact, anyone from the northern Asturias region "tended to claim automatic noble status."[31] Similarly, anyone able to prove Basque parentage was also granted automatic nobility on the basis of "purity of blood." The significance of Asturias in Spanish identity is reflected today in the title given to the heir to the Spanish throne, the Prince or Princess of Asturias, and the highest honor that Spain can bestow is the Prince or Princess of Asturias Award.

Commentators over the years have noted the absurdity inherent in the Spanish engineering and structuring of society on the basis of Germanic blood descent. By the sixteenth century, Spanish claims to "Gothic" blood were so frequent that they were "the subject of standing jokes in the *comedias* of the period."[32] The absurdity is perhaps captured best in the figure of Torquemada himself, whose grandmother was Jewish. In the twentieth century, Spanish primordial tribal identity shaped the regime of General Francisco Franco, which rested on the twin pillars of the Spanish monarchy and the Catholic Church. The Visigoths, said Franco in his 1969 decree establishing the Museum of Visigothic Councils and Culture in Toledo, gave the Spanish their "national love of law and order."[33] José Antonio Primo de Rivera, the founder of Franco's fascist Falange Party, traced the roots of the Spanish Civil War to the Reconquista and described leftists as "conquered Berbers who will not pardon the fact that the conquerors— Catholic, Germanic—bore the message of Europe."[34]

The Reconquista, with its emphasis on Germanic blood purity and Christian faith, provided several things to its supporters in history. First, as a religious cause it united the warring Christian kingdoms and feudal estates into the larger idea of Christian Europe battling an alien and heathen religion. Second, it promised material benefits in the substantial lands and properties that were seized from the defeated Muslims. Third, it played into the idea of taking revenge from the invading Muslims who had arrived as conquering warriors centuries ago. In short, the Reconquista was more than a simple military engagement. But to succeed, it had to be supported by an ideological structure that projected the idea of Islam as the eternal enemy and Muslims as heretics. Along with the Muslims, the Jewish community was also a target of the Reconquista. The Inquisition was thus created as an instrument to uphold the ideals of the Reconquista.

In Cordoba we saw reminders of the Inquisition—instruments of torture displayed in museums and in shops, tiny statues of men wearing pointed hoods and white sheets with large crosses on their chest. We also visited the Alcázar in Cordoba, once the palace of the Muslim rulers and the site where the famous library of Cordoba was housed. When the Christian rulers occupied it, the dreaded Inquisition was located here. The rooms in which they performed their terrible deeds had a cold ghoulish atmosphere that sent a chill down our spines.

It is well to recall that in the heyday of the Inquisition the litmus test of faith for Jews and Muslims after they converted was their ability to eat pig flesh. An example of the leftover zeal from that time can be seen at the spotless and sparkling new Madrid airport. Walking along the rows of shops, we saw several of them selling huge pig legs with hooves wrapped tightly in bright cellophane. The Food Society delicatessen displayed colorfully wrapped pork along with beautifully wrapped chocolates. Indeed, the sight of enormous pig legs hanging from the ceiling is common in Spanish shops and restaurants.

## *The Grand Mosque of Cordoba*

Of all the world's most celebrated heritage buildings, perhaps the Grand Mosque in Cordoba, which is now the Catholic cathedral of the Diocese of Cordoba, has the most pronounced problem of identity. Few buildings can lend themselves to interpreting the past as this one does. Every time I visit this great house of worship I also drift into a mood of melancholia at the thought of its predicament: not quite dead as a mosque, nor fully alive as a cathedral. The graphic and visual depictions of the triumph of one faith over another in the mosque-cathedral include saints with swords in one hand and bibles in the other. Santiago Matamoros, or St. James the Moorslayer, is depicted waving a deadly sword astride a mighty horse whose front hooves are planted firmly on the turbaned head of a panic-stricken Moor while another Moor lies trampled underneath. This statue is placed by the altar and reminds worshippers of how the clash between Christianity and Islam ended in history.

I found one figure especially disturbing—the image of Mary with a golden-hilted Spanish sword jabbed into her heart—because in Islam Mary is such a revered and loved figure as the mother of one of the most revered and loved figures, Jesus. There is an entire chapter in the Quran dedicated to Mary. Zeenat and Amineh, who had been educated at the Jesus and Mary Convent in Pakistan by Catholic nuns, found the images of a tormented Mary particularly upsetting: "I did not like to see the figures I adored and grew up with—Jesus and Mary—in blood and wounded by swords," Amineh noted. The Mary she knew and loved from her school in Pakistan "had a light smile on her luminous face with flowers in her hands and wore flowing blue robes that covered her from head to toe. But the statue of Mary in the Cordoba cathedral had a sword inserted in her left breast. This image of violence imposed upon such a special gentle figure was disturbing."

The predicament of the mosque-cathedral in Cordoba was captured by the Andalusian Spanish aristocrat Hashim Ibrahim Cabrera, who had converted to Islam: "Yes, they want to erase the name of the mosque. They have now a campaign to destroy the memory of the Islamic mosque. They say in the beginning it was a church and now there is a church—there was always a church but no mosque." He asked in anger and sorrow, "Where is the middle time of 800 years of Muslim rule?" He then laughed at the irony of what he was about to say: "But it's strange, because the 24,000 square meters of the mosque are not hidden." Cabrera said he had been trying to meet the priests at the diocese and present a petition on behalf of the mosque, but with no success.

Even the Hapsburg Holy Roman emperor and king of Spain, Charles V, who had authorized renovations inside the mosque to give it more the appearance of a cathedral, was shocked to see how his officials had mutilated it by building a full-scale cathedral inside it. When he first saw the renovations of the mosque he expressed regret: "You have built here what you, or anyone else, might have built anywhere; to do so you have destroyed what was unique in the world."[35] It had not prevented Charles from attempting a similar, though less intrusive, exercise in constructing a palace for himself inside the Alhambra complex. He was aware, however, of the failure to create anything approaching the standard of the Alhambra and lamented the fact that walking from the Alhambra to his own palace was like entering a stable.

In my visits over the decades, I have seen the attitude of the priests and local people toward the Grand Mosque change markedly. On my first visit in the early 1960s, Spain had yet to join up politically and economically with France, Germany, and Britain. It felt like a land that had been left behind by the rest of Western Europe. When I finally made my way to Cordoba by a really slow train with tiny carriages from Madrid, I found the local Spanish warm and welcoming. In the evening, when they served me wine, and I said politely that I did not drink because I was a Muslim, they smiled indulgently and said, "Well, the Muslims in Andalusia were great drinkers." To the best of my knowledge there were very few Muslims around, and Islam as a subject did not excite anyone's imagination. In Cordoba at that time, the Grand Mosque was referred to as *la mezquita*—the mosque. I was even able to pray in the arch of the *mehrab*, the designated place in the wall of a mosque that points toward Mecca, and no one seemed to care. I recalled that Allama Muhammad Iqbal, the celebrated Muslim poet-philosopher, had bowed in prayer at precisely this spot and in one of his most popular poems, "The Mosque of Cordoba," declared, "You have elevated Andalusia to the eminence of the Haram (in Mecca)."

Prince Turki al-Faisal, the son of King Faisal of Saudi Arabia who served as the Saudi ambassador to the United States and United Kingdom in the early years of this century, told me in Oxford in 2015 he had prayed on the very same spot in the 1980s. Because a ban on Muslim prayer was then in effect, he had to seek special permission from his official hosts to pray there. "You cannot help yourself," he said softly, as if to himself. He also recounted the story of his famous father visiting Spain as a guest of General Franco. When Franco asked King Faisal how he could accommodate his royal guest, Faisal replied that he would pay for the construction of the most magnificent cathedral in Europe if the general would give him the Grand Mosque of Cordoba. Franco said the building meant nothing to him and he had no objection—he could hand it over the next morning—but if he did so he would be lynched by the people of Spain. As an alternative, Prince Turki said, Franco offered the king the best piece of land in Madrid itself, atop a hill overlooking the city. King Faisal accepted the land and built what is now the Islamic Center there.

The period following Franco's death in 1975 was a heady time for Spain. The nation was in the process of creating a new all-European identity under the leadership of King Juan Carlos I. In the following years, Juan Carlos would lead a conscious effort to revive the Andalusian history of his land to promote harmony between the Abrahamic faiths. In 1991 I was a guest at a conference in Granada hosted by the king and the Aga Khan.[36] At the reception, the king took me aside so that we would not be overheard and urged me to ask Muslims to respond to his overtures of friendship, using Andalusia as a common cultural bridge. I sensed a hint of exasperation at the lack of Muslim response. Perhaps the Muslims did not realize the breathtaking boldness of the king's gesture in wanting to challenge the structures of Spanish identity based in Christianity, and beneath it, concepts of Visigothic blood descent, by reaching out to the very people that had been expelled half a millennium ago and whose history had been erased.

I returned to Cordoba with a BBC crew shortly afterward to film the television series *Living Islam*. In the Grand Mosque I noted that a thick silken rope had appeared which acted as a partition to block off entrance to the mehrab. Our English producers, however, managed to convince the guards, with that mixture of bravado and arrogance they reserve for the continent, to allow me to pray in the mehrab, and it was filmed for the segment on Andalusia. I was inspired by the idea that Abdur Rahman and Iqbal had worshipped on this very spot. Sitting lost in prayer I felt as if the present world, with its din, fever, and conflict, had faded away and a deep sense of spiritual calm descended on me. I prayed that the people of this beautiful land would live in harmony, peace, and prosperity.

My visit in the summer of 2014 for our fieldwork was markedly different. Security guards swarmed around the visitors, and there were wild rumors and newspaper stories about Muslims determined to recapture the mosque. The attacks of September 11 and the train bombings in Madrid combined with a fear of the Muslim immigrants from North Africa to create a general atmosphere of hostility toward Islam—and it found its focus on the biggest Islamic mosque in Spain. The building was now the center of intense religious and political controversy.

Writing of the facility in the late nineteenth century, scholars like Stanley Lane-Poole were unambiguous in referring to it as a mosque. But today the Catholic Church, which runs the property, has clamped down on any notion that the building ever had anything to do with Islam. During the lavish but solemn pageantry to mark the festival of Corpus Christi which seemed to take in the entire population of Cordoba, the bishop made loud and explicit statements about the Christian identity of the mosque and of Andalusia itself. The mosque's brochures and notice boards now proclaimed that it was a church before "the Muslim intervention" and had been a cathedral ever since, although leading specialists on the building, such as the art historian Susana Calvo Capilla of the Complutense University of Madrid, have argued that there is no clear evidence of a preexisting church on the site.[37]

For all the attempts to erase the Islamic identity of the mosque-cathedral, the mehrab, the masterpiece of this masterpiece of a building, remained untouched. The panel on top of the dazzling arch, which cited a Quranic verse, had survived intact, and I wondered why it had not been defaced. However, since the time of my last visit, in the 1990s, an ugly iron grating about five feet high had been constructed some twenty feet from the mehrab to seal it off from visitors. Now, no one could come near the mehrab, let alone pray there, as I had been able to do several times in the past.

Amineh described the emotions she felt after her visit: "The mosque-cathedral of Cordoba brought out in me a well of emotions: I cried for the loss of a glorious period, I prayed hard connecting with Him at the deepest level; another place I had felt this depth was in Mecca. I was horrified at the statue of St. James, whose horse's hooves were seen crushing the head of a Moor-Muslim. In a world where there was increasingly less tolerance, the symbols in the mosque of Cordoba brought to the fore all my hidden emotions. I made it a point to visit every day while I was in Cordoba."

Amineh was not the only Muslim who was affected in this manner. One evening Amineh returned from the mosque to the hotel where we were staying and met a young Arab-American woman she had encountered earlier in the day. The young woman had a Syrian background and wore a hijab. When Amineh asked her what she thought of the mosque, the woman burst into tears. This immediately triggered pent-up emotions in Amineh, and the two embraced and began to cry together. The guests in the hotel lobby were not sure what to make of this spectacle.

Even members of my team who were not Muslim, like Frankie and Harrison, were affected: "Visiting the mosque-cathedral was a sublime as well as a sad and depressing experience," Frankie reflected. A sensitive man, Frankie could not help but feel for the plight of the mosque: "Walking through the 'mosque' part of the structure, you feel a sense of awe and calm amid the incredible 'forest' of row upon row of columns. But passing into the towering and ornate 'church' at the center is disorienting and jarring." Harrison felt similar emotions and reacted negatively to what he saw inside the mosque: "The inside was dark and foreboding. There was organ music playing in the background throughout our visit with harsh Christian iconography popping up in different parts of the interior. The atmosphere made me feel uneasy, made worse by the constant hovering of the Spanish guards inside. It was a clear visual and theological clash."

### A Visit to the Bishopric of Cordoba

Given the tense environment around the mosque-cathedral, I felt it was important to speak with the senior priests of Cordoba. Javier Rosón Lorenté, who studies and writes about Islam in Europe at Casa Árabe, a Spanish government initiative to foster a better understanding of Andalusia and facilitate diplomacy with the Arab and Muslim world, told us that the Catholic council of bishops in Spain is extremely conservative and that the bishop of Cordoba is probably the most orthodox. Ambassador Eduardo López Busquets also thought the church was very conservative, but said he would try to get us an interview. Fortunately, he succeeded.

Considering the tense atmosphere around the mosque and the rumors of militant Muslims wanting to reclaim it, I was not surprised to find the bishopric prickly and defensive about the mosque or even meeting Muslims. The closed doors and shut windows of the bishopric reinforced the sense of being under siege. The windows of the room where we held our meeting faced the towering wall of the Grand Mosque but were shut by wooden planks. The priests presented us with an official lecture: There was no such thing as a Grand Mosque on this site; there had been a church, there was an "intervention," which referred to the mosque, there is a church now, and there will always be a church. We were also given a copy of the official history of Andalusia in Spanish, *History of the Christians in al-Andalus: Relations of Convivencia or of Antagonism and Fighting?* (2013), by Rafael Jiménez Pedrajas, which focuses on the conflict between Christians and Muslims.[38] There were several color illustrations in the book of Christian martyrs depicted as "superior" people while showing Muslims as "inferior." The cover itself depicts a confrontation between Christians and Muslims. This was the official version of history as far as the church was concerned. The Muslim period was a mere blip in the history of Christian Spain.

When I asked these senior-most priests to define Spanish identity, Father Fernando Cruz-Conde, the vicar general of the Diocese of Cordoba, replied without a second's hesitation: "Catholicism!" While they were cognizant of the negative aspects of Islam when it was projected as a religion of terrorism, the priests also realized the need to create some kind of dialogue with it. Amineh felt that the priests became friendlier once they learned of our educational background. But ironically the priest in charge of interfaith dialogue remained unwelcoming and sat in the corner as if not sure how to perceive us and how much to let go of his own perspective on Cordoba and Islam. Father Cruz-Conde added that the time of convivencia "was not peaceful, as we had a lot of martyrs." According to the priests, "al-Andalus gave rise later to Islamic fundamentalism."

Father Cruz-Conde was clearly the natural leader in the room and assumed the role of spokesman. He was descended from Spanish aristocracy and thus combined the authority of the church and blood. At the end of the interview, Father Cruz-Conde said he had to rush off because the Cordoba football team had just won a match that put them in the top Spanish league, and they were having a service at the church. A football enthusiast, he was in charge of honoring the team.

Concluding our meeting, Father Cruz-Conde said a beautiful prayer for the success of our project that invoked the patron saint of Cordoba and of travelers: "Let's pray then to the archangel St. Raphael, who is always together with the people who are traveling, so he might protect you and defend you against all evils, and that he might grant you success in your task, so that we all come to the truth and live in peace. We ask this through the intercession of the archangel St. Raphael through our God." When I put out my hand for a handshake as we rose to depart, he reached out and embraced me. On our way out, I noticed two large paintings hanging on the wall, just by the staircase. They were four feet by two feet in size and had been presented by President Pervez Musharraf of Pakistan. One declared the glory of Allah and the other of Muhammad, the Prophet of Islam. It appeared that in spite of the attempts to conceal the symbols of Islam, they kept bubbling up in unexpected places.

At our meeting there was a lay person who was tense and unfriendly. Amineh and Harrison ran into him in the courtyard of the mosque-cathedral the following morning. "As we were entering the mosque to film," Harrison recounted, "he didn't say hello or anything after we said 'Hola, it was nice to meet you yesterday.' He just kept pointing at his watch and saying the cathedral closes at 9:30."

## La Convivencia in Sicily

Like the story of Abdur Rahman, the stories of Christian rulers in Sicily sound as if they came from the *Arabian Nights*—Roger II, the powerful twelfth-century king of Sicily, was so much in love with his wife Elvira, the daughter of the Muslim Andalusian Zaida and King Alfonso VI, that when she died he was inconsolable; and he was known to rise from his throne to show respect to Muhammad al-Idrisi, his Muslim adviser, and the two would then sit together. Roger's grandson, Frederick II, as Holy Roman emperor, celebrated the *hijra*, the Prophet of Islam's journey from Mecca to Medina, with "a brilliant banquet, attended by German princes and bishops" and with such cultural initiatives created enough goodwill among Muslims to be able to take Jerusalem during the Crusades without the use of force or violence.³⁹ To further confound their critics, both men spoke Arabic, were protected by Muslim bodyguards, and had Arabic inscriptions on their royal mantle, which became part of the coronation ceremony for the Holy Roman emperors until modern times. Little wonder that fellow Christians dubbed them the "baptized sultans."

It is clear from these examples that ideas of convivencia were not restricted to Andalusia alone. Sicily provides another pole of Islamic influence in Europe. What is so significant about the case of Sicily is not only that Muslims ruled this major European region but that after conquering it in the late eleventh-century Christian rulers did not adopt the practice of the Spanish under the Inquisition and attempt to exterminate all traces of Islam. Instead, the Norman conquerors saw Islam as a worthy civilization and permitted Islamic influences to remain. In this, both Muslim Spain and Christian Sicily in the Middle Ages, though appearing quite different to modern eyes owing to the religion of those who ruled at the time, were actually quite similar. As the twelfth-century Andalusian geographer and traveler Ibn Jubayr noted of Sicily, "The prosperity of the island surpasses description. It is enough to say that it is the daughter of Spain (*ibnat al-Andalus*) in the extent of its cultivation, in the luxuriance of its harvests, and in its well-being."⁴⁰ He compared Palermo, which used to be the Muslim Sicilian capital and was now the Christian capital, with Cordoba: "It is a city full of marvels, with buildings similar to those of Cordoba, built of limestone. A permanent stream of water from four springs runs through the city. There are so many mosques that they are impossible to count. Most of them also serve as schools. The eye is dazzled by all this splendor."⁴¹ Indeed, Norman Palermo was "arguably the most populous city in Europe, and almost certainly its richest at the height of the

High Middle Ages."[42] For al-Idrisi, Sicily was "the pearl of this century. . . . it brings together the best aspects from every other country."[43]

There was in Christian Sicily, as in Muslim Andalusia, the constant urge to acquire knowledge and, while understanding the world as it is through reason and philosophy, to recognize and embrace the diversity of human life, religion, and culture. It was the opposite of the exclusivist European primordial tribal identity explored in the previous chapter. That two of the central players explored in this section, Roger II and Frederick II, were of Germanic descent makes their achievements even more significant.

## Roger II and the Normans in Sicily

The conquest of Sicily transformed the Normans, descendants of Vikings who had settled in northern France, from adventurers and upstarts on the Italian Peninsula to major European leaders. They had accomplished a historic feat for Christian Europe, the "retaking" of Sicily from the forces of Islam. While the pope initially had serious differences with the Normans, he was now fully behind the Norman project in Sicily. Roger I, the count of Sicily, was recognized overnight as one of the most respected rulers in Europe, with European kings asking to marry his daughters.

### Convivencia and the Age of Roger II

While Roger I was count of Sicily, his son, Roger II, the child of a Norman father and a Lombard mother, was recognized by the pope as king. It was under Roger II that Norman Sicily experienced its apex, extending its rule into North Africa, across Tunisia to Tripoli, and over the entirety of the southern half of the Italian Peninsula. Roger was born in Sicily and grew up exposed to Islamic culture and the Arabic language. His tolerance for Muslims and interfaith relations would deeply influence his grandson, Frederick II.

The antipathy of European leaders to Roger II stemmed in part from the fact that Roger's army was mostly Arab, enlisted by Muslim commanders who "formed a native aristocracy" in the Norman kingdom. Arab engineers were also highly valued in war, as it was the Arabs who worked the Norman movable towers and catapults used during sieges.[44] In campaigns in southern Italy, Roger's Muslim archers spread terror among the local people.[45]

Roger II drew on Islamic tradition, as well as that of the Romans and Greeks, to lay a new foundation for the Norman state. These included a new legal code, a formal civil bureaucracy and administrative structure, and extensive reforms that were similar to those of Christian rulers that came after Roger, including Frederick II and Alfonso X. One of the dominant languages of the land was Arabic, and "many key figures among the kingdom's ruling elite and administration were either Muslims, converts from Islam or Arabic-speaking Christians."[46] The elegant script of the Arab scribes was "probably derived from the chancery of the Fatimid caliphs of Egypt, with whom Roger enjoyed good relations." On one side of the gold coins of Roger's kingdom was an inscription in Arabic, "King Roger, powerful through the grace of Allah," and on the other side, in Greek, "Jesus Christ conquers." Other Norman coins featured the Arabic words, "There is no God except Allah."[47]

Roger's *Assizes of Ariano* has been described as "the first modern code of royal law in the history of the West."[48] Roger's laws stated that each religious community could enact and preserve its own legal codes and customs. An important aspect of royal authority was mediating between the communities and considering legal cases. The twelfth-century scholar Ibn al-Athir of Mosul wrote that Roger "founded a Court of Complaints, *dīwān al-mazālim*, to which those [Muslims] who had been unjustly treated brought their grievances, and [the king] would give them justice, even against his own son. He treated the Muslims with respect, took them as his companions, and kept the Franks [Norman or Latin Christians] off them, so that they loved him."[49] Any of Roger's subjects who felt that justice was not given by the local judges of the area could appeal directly to the king.[50] Oversight of judges is clearly spelled out in the legal code, such as the stipulation that judges who take bribes be subject to penalties as severe as death.

Roger II's tolerance of Islam continued under his Norman successors, including his grandson King William II, who reigned from 1166 to 1189. We have a detailed account of convivencia during William's time from the Andalusian traveler Ibn Jubayr, who recounts that after a difficult journey in the Mediterranean in a battered boat, he and his desperate crew arrived in Sicily but did not have the funds to pay the landing fee. William II personally intervened on their behalf and "ordered that their landing fee be paid with one hundred gold coins from his mint." Ibn Jubayr was impressed with the king's closeness to Muslims, who held very important positions in the palace: "He places much trust in Muslims and relies on them in his affairs and the most important matters of his work."[51]

Ibn Jubayr also noted the influence of Muslim culture on Sicily's Christians: "The Christian women's dress in this city [Palermo] is the dress of Muslims; they are eloquent speakers of Arabic (*faṣīḥāt al-alsan*) and cover themselves with veils. They go out at this aforementioned festival [Christmas] clothed in golden silk, covered in shining wraps, colourful veils and with light gilded sandals. They appear at their churches bearing all the finery of Muslim women in their attire, henna and perfume."[52]

## AL-IDRISI AND THE CULTURE OF ILM UNDER ROGER II

Roger II is famous in history for seeking knowledge and encouraging cultural and scholarly exchanges between the Arab, Latin, and Greek traditions. He commissioned major translations of texts, as the twelfth-century archbishop and diplomat Romuald of Salerno recounted, and attracted to his court "men of wisdom of different sorts from the various parts of the earth." Of all the learned men assembled in Roger's court, one stands above the rest. Roger specially invited the scientist and geographer al-Idrisi, who was born in Ceuta and educated in Cordoba, to come to Sicily and work for him. When al-Idrisi first arrived, Roger gave him silver weighing over 1,000 pounds with which to build a device depicting "spheres like those in the heavens."[53] When Roger found that al-Idrisi had used only slightly more than a third of the silver provided for this contraption, he let him keep the rest. The American scholar Samuel Parsons Scott describes the "mechanical genius" of al-Idrisi with reference to this invention.[54]

After completing this invention, Roger invited al-Idrisi to remain with him, and al-Idrisi accepted. Roger granted the scholar a princely income and showed him great respect. Al-Idrisi grew very close to Roger, as Ibn al-Athir attested, writing that Roger "respected and revered him, and depended upon his counsel, and preferred him to the priests and monks about him, and so the inhabitants of his realm said that [Roger] was a Muslim."[55] Al-Athir recorded an instance where al-Idrisi, after making a statement, was publicly mocked by Normans in front of Roger, who responded: "By God, don't laugh at him! This man always speaks the truth!"

Having read the available literature, Roger commissioned al-Idrisi to conduct a comprehensive study of different peoples and lands. Al-Idrisi completed a magisterial work that is known to us simply as the *Book of Roger*. This work, wrote al-Idrisi, stemmed from Roger's desire to gain knowledge of the entire world. In it, al-Idrisi praised Roger and wrote that the king was intimately involved in the compilation of the book and its research: "His knowledge of mathematics and applied science was boundless."[56] In addition to producing intricate maps showing the world as a sphere and meticulously compiling information about Roger's domains, al-

Idrisi wrote on a number of other topics, including England's poor weather and how the lack of sun in Norway affected the local harvest.

On the basis of interviews and reports of sailors and navigators, al-Idrisi described people living as far away as China and India. He noted the presence of concepts similar to convivencia and the ilm ethos among them. He even described the mysteries of what lay on the other side of the Atlantic Ocean. On this subject al-Idrisi wrote of the presence of "people with red skin" across the Atlantic. "There was not much hair on their bodies and their hair was straight," he wrote. "They were of tall stature."[57]

Samuel Parsons Scott, writing in the early twentieth century, sums up the importance of al-Idrisi's study: "Its descriptions of many parts of the earth are still authoritative. For three centuries geographers copied his maps without alteration. The relative position of the lakes which form the Nile, as delineated in his work, does not differ greatly from that established by Baker and Stanley more than seven hundred years afterwards, and their number is the same."[58]

## The Palatine Chapel, The Glory of Sicily

Roger II is most renowned for the Palatine Chapel in Palermo contained within the Norman Palace. It is a glorious monument to convivencia. Here, Kufic Arabic, Islamic, Jewish, and Christian influences intermingle, fuse, and overlap in luminescent colors and exquisite designs. Sicilians today are justifiably proud of the chapel. In Palermo, for example, we met Antonio Daniel Costantino, the owner of a bookshop next to our hotel, who is an author and historian in his own right. "For me," he expressed with joyful satisfaction, the Palatine is "the symbol of Sicilian culture, because in this church all cultures in this island are represented."

The audio guide provided at the Palatine declared with pride that the Palatine embodied "a cultural syncretism that to this day represents an extraordinary instance of peaceful and industrious cohabitation between peoples who were always at war." Thus the chapel is "the living testimony of how four confessions—the Catholic, Orthodox, Islamic, and Jewish—could and still may live together and produce such marvels." As the symbol of Roger's kingdom, vision, and authority, the church was used as a place of official reception for the king and his family. Instructions to guests in how to behave in front of the king were given in "stone plaques bearing inscriptions in Arabic, inviting visitors to greet the sovereign using rituals modeled on those practised during Islamic pilgrimages to Mecca." The chapel featured symbols that were shared by the different religions and traditions, such as the lion, eagle, and palm tree.

### The Muslim Ceiling of the Palatine Chapel

Observers over the years have run out of superlatives to describe the majesty and splendor of the ceiling of the Palatine Chapel, which was constructed by Muslim craftsmen. Today's audio guide says, "There is no way words can successfully convey the incredible intricacy of the ceiling's patterning, which in certain parts is as much as one and a half meters deep."

A recent book on the Palatine published in Italy, *The Palatine Chapel in Palermo* by Alessandro Vicenzi, similarly states, "There is nothing like the painted wooden ceiling over the Palatine Chapel's central nave anywhere else in the world." The chapel's wooden ceiling, which is in the Islamic design, evokes stalactites hanging down from above and consists of "twenty panels in the shape of eight-point stars, with twenty-two other panels containing small domes running outside them, and nine rhomboid panels running down the middle." Woven through and around the images on the ceiling are Kufic Arabic inscriptions that form greetings of good health, victory, and joy. Among the numerous images depicted on the roof panels, which reflect Muslim influences, is Roger II, sitting in the manner of an Islamic ruler; scenes of court life, including drinking companions of the ruler and poets; depictions of music, musicians, and typically Arab musical instruments; examples of Muslim mythology such as the *anna*, a bird with the head of a woman; scenes from Muslim lore such as the famous tragic love story "Diwan Majnun Layla," as seen in a panel depicting the final meeting between the two doomed lovers, each on a camel; images of mermaids, which entered Europe from Islamic legends and are "perhaps inspired by one of the many stories about mermaids, some of which are related in the *One Thousand and One Nights*"; and a depiction of two turbaned men playing chess, the earliest known image in the world of the game of chess, which was also brought to Europe by Muslims.[59]

### Monreale Cathedral

While the Palatine Chapel is undoubtedly the height of the Norman achievement and splendor in Sicily, capturing a moment in time in which convivencia was perhaps strongest in the Christian kingdom, Roger's heirs would attempt similar feats to define their kingdom and its vision, demonstrate their piety, and make their mark on history. Roger's grandson, William II, built his own spectacular, much larger, version of the Palatine Chapel in Monreale, a small hill town not far from Palermo. In one of Monreale Cathedral's mosaics, William is seen accepting the crown di-

*Catholic nuns pointing out Muslim
contributions to Monreale Cathedral*

rectly from Christ, in the same manner as Roger II is depicted in Palermo's Martorana Church, which too has significant Muslim influences and
which we also visited.

In Monreale Cathedral, which frames the central square of the town
of Monreale, Amineh initiated a conversation with two young nuns,
Sisters Francisca from Argentina and Maria Jose from Chile, both of the
Order of Our Lady of Loreto, with a cheerful "Good morning, sisters."
The nuns shared their deep knowledge of the cathedral, its history, and
the different artistic and cultural traditions reflected in it. In their gentle-
ness, kindness, and commitment to interfaith relations, they embodied
the best of Christianity.

The sisters told us that "the Arabs built Monreale," and in a street in
the "Arab" quarter they paused to give us a blessing as we continued our
journey. With their heads bowed in prayer, Sister Maria Jose, capturing
the spirit of convivencia, said, "We ask God to bless your journey and to
give you the fruits of the well-being of mankind. We pray that you find

more people who go through the same journey because it is something we all need, especially in the world of today."

## Frederick II, Stupor Mundi

With the arrival of the Germans in Sicily and the absorption of the kingdom into the Holy Roman Empire in 1194, five years after the death of William II, the Norman era came to an end. Yet the legacy of the Normans and Roger II, with their emphasis on ilm and convivencia, would live on through Roger's grandson Frederick II, known as *stupor mundi*, or the wonder of the world. A true son of Sicilian convivencia, "Frederick was said to be able to express himself orally in nine languages and to write in seven."[60] One of these was Arabic. As Holy Roman emperor and head of the House of Hohenstaufen, which originated in the German duchy of Swabia, Frederick II ruled an area that encompassed all or part of "Germany, the Netherlands, Austria, Poland, Czechoslovakia, France (southern Burgundy and Provence), Italy, Malta, Cyprus, Israel and Lebanon . . . [and] even won influence on the coasts of Tunisia."[61] Like his grandfather Roger II, Frederick proved that pluralism and the pursuit of knowledge—particularly the attempt to balance reason and faith—were as compatible with Christianity as with Islam. Frederick's Germanic background on his father's side—he was the grandson of the Holy Roman Emperor Frederick I Barbarossa—gave him an immediate base in Swabia and endeared him to the German people.

### THE ILM ETHOS IN THE AGE OF FREDERICK II

By the time Frederick became emperor, he had a passion for the Islamic emphasis on education, culture, and learning—in short, the ilm ethos. While Spain was the most important place for translations from Arabic into Latin, Sicily became a key conduit of Islamic thought into mainland Italy and thus Europe. Frederick's court philosopher, the Toledo-trained Scotsman Michael Scot, translated Averroes's commentaries into Latin, the first translation of his work.[62] Frederick considered them so important he sent them to the professors and students of the universities of Bologna and Paris. It was from the University of Paris—then the leading university in Europe and where Thomas Aquinas taught—that Averroes's thought was disseminated, creating widespread debates about his ideas and what they meant for Christianity. At the University of Naples, which Frederick created and which today bears his name, Frederick assembled the "great Arab, Jewish, Greek and Saracenic teachers" of the time.[63] Thomas Aquinas is one of the institution's renowned alumni.

Perhaps Frederick's view of knowledge can best be seen in the letter he sent to the universities of Bologna and Paris to accompany the translations of Averroes. In the opening of the letter, Frederick explains that from the time he was a youth he had esteemed and sought knowledge—"inhaling tirelessly its sweet perfumes," as he put it. The importance Frederick placed on knowledge, reason, and scientific inquiry is apparent in his recorded statement: "One should accept as truth only that which is proved by the force of reason and by nature." Frederick's emphasis on logic and the scientific method led him to challenge even Aristotle on the basis of his own book on falconry; Aristotle, as Frederick noted, had himself quite likely never hunted with birds and "was ignorant of the practice of falconry."[64] Indeed, the importance of observation can be seen in the way Frederick's book illustrates birds, which are drawn "down to the tiniest details."[65] Hundreds of species of birds are depicted, and the drawings are distinguished by their "incomparable accuracy."[66]

Frederick did not restrict his philosophical inquiries to the scholars who surrounded him in his own court, or even to European ones. The emperor opened up his questions to the rulers and scholars of the Muslim world, asking for their responses on the deep questions of existence—inquiring, for example, about Aristotle's belief that the world is eternal and was not created.[67] Frederick's questions additionally concerned optics: In one case he asked the Egyptian sultan why a straight object in water appears bent and also why a particular star in the constellation Carina "appears larger to the eye when rising than at its perigee." Frederick asked the scholars of Syria "to square a circular segment," and they, unable to solve the problem, passed it on to the scholars of Mosul.[68] Of the Arab scholar Shahabuddin, Frederick asked why people with cataracts saw black spots and streaks.

In another noteworthy episode, Frederick wrote to the Almohad caliph in Morocco to ask him questions such as how Aristotle demonstrated the eternity of matter and "What is the proof of the immortality of the soul, and is her existence eternal?"[69] Frederick received replies from Ibn Sabin, a prominent Andalusia-born scholar who lived in Ceuta, as the sultan felt Ibn Sabin was best suited to answer the emperor's questions. Frederick sent him money and numerous gifts, but Ibn Sabin refused them. Ibn Sabin dealt with Frederick's questions on matters such as the "necessary preconditions of theology" and the nature of the soul.[70] Ibn Sabin wrote separate dissertations on the various types of soul and discussed Plato, Moses, Avicenna, and the Hindu Brahmins before invoking the truth of Islam.[71]

The Egyptian sultan presented Frederick with the Arabic work of astrology, the *Book of the Nine Judges,* and dispatched the astronomer and mathematician al-Hanifi to Frederick's court after Frederick asked to speak with someone learned in astronomy.[72] Frederick additionally exchanged animals with the Egyptian sultan: the sultan sent Frederick an elephant, and Frederick returned the favor with a white bear, which "to the amazement of the Arabs eats nothing but fish."[73] The sultan also sent Frederick a giraffe, said to be the first in Europe since Roman times. From al-Ashraf, the emir of Damascus, Frederick received "a planetarium, constructed with admirable skill, on which were figures of the sun and moon indicating the hours of the day and night in the course of their determined movements," as a contemporary noted.[74] Frederick was "said to have described it as the most valuable thing in his possession, aside from his son Conrad."[75] In the capitals of the Muslim world, "it was well understood that the emperor valued a book, a rare bird, or a cunning piece of workmanship more highly than mere objects of luxury."[76]

In 1231 Frederick signed a commercial treaty with Abu Zakaria, who ruled Tunis, Tripoli, and part of Morocco and appointed his own Sicilian consuls to Tunis. This marked "the first time in history that a Western monarchy maintained a permanent representative overseas." Frederick's first consul to Tunis was a Muslim, Henricus Abbas. From Tunis Frederick received horses, leopards, and camels; he also received soldiers who supplemented his Muslim bodyguard. On occasion, Frederick's ships carried Tunisian envoys to Spain on behalf of the sultan.[77]

As with Alfonso X, Frederick's pursuit of knowledge also included language and an appreciation of the vernacular.[78] In Germany, his Proclamation of Mainz (1235) "was the first time that German had been utilised for a proclamation, and the importance of the fact that it was thus recognised as on an equality with Latin for an edict of the Roman Emperor needs no emphasis."[79] Frederick founded the Sicilian school of poetry, which produced the first love poetry in Italian, drawing from Arabic as well as European troubadour poetry traditions, and helped create the Italian language. It was here that the sonnet was invented.[80] According to Dante, the role of Sicilians in the formation of the Italian language is such that "whatever Italians write is called Sicilian" and he acknowledged the patronage of "The illustrious heroes, King Frederick and his good son Manfredi." The Arabic roots of Italian poetry are understudied, as the Romance language scholar Karla Mallette notes: "Literary historians did not look beyond *le origini* to seek an indigenous Sicilian source or indigenous inspiration for the Romance movement for a simple reason: that would entail tracing the Romance poetry to an Arabic origin."[81]

## THE TAKING OF JERUSALEM, FREDERICK II'S
## DIPLOMATIC MASTERSTROKE

Frederick's greatest diplomatic triumph—which should be taught in schools of foreign affairs, diplomacy, and geopolitical strategy today—occurred when he succeeded in taking Jerusalem for Christianity peacefully during the Crusades. Frederick did this through negotiation, not through military conquest. What makes the story even more compelling is that Frederick accomplished his objective, the dream of every Christian ruler of Europe since Saladin had recaptured the city decades earlier, while under excommunication by the pope. The story is worth retelling.

As word reached Sultan al-Kamil of Egypt, the nephew of Saladin, that a new Crusade was heading his way, he heard rumors about the emperor who was leading it. Al-Kamil sent his vizier, the Egyptian emir Fakhr ad-Din, to visit Frederick and assess the situation. It should be noted that a decade earlier, during a cease-fire between the forces of the crusaders and the sultan in Egypt, the same Sultan al-Kamil had met with St. Francis, who had tried his own, very different tactic to win the Crusades by converting the sultan to Christianity. While al-Kamil was not persuaded to convert, he did give Francis a hearing, provided him a military escort, and even "privately asked him to pray to the Lord for him, so that he might be inspired by God to adhere to that religion which most pleased God."[82]

A close friendship developed between Fakhr ad-Din and Frederick, which was enriched by the exchange of ideas and gifts. Frederick even knighted Fakhr ad-Din, enabling the emir to carry the coat of arms of the emperor on his banner. In an exchange between the two, Fakhr ad-Din explained to Frederick that the Abbasid caliph was descended from Abbas, the uncle of the Prophet. Thus the caliphate remained in the family of the Prophet. "That is excellent," Frederick responded, adding that it was superior to the practice among the Christians, who "choose as their spiritual head any fellow they will without the smallest relationship to the Messiah, and they make him the Messiah's representative. That Pope there has no claim to such a position, whereas your Khalif is the descendant of Muhammad's uncle."[83]

Apparently the negotiations over Jerusalem were at a stalemate when, as the fifteenth-century Egyptian historian al-Maqrizi recounted, "Frederick sent several difficult questions pertaining to the science of mathematics to the Sultan, who gave them to men of great learning for appropriate answers. This scholarly exchange appears to have succeeded where other methods failed."

Through the exchanges with Fakhr ad-Din, Frederick and al-Kamil negotiated a deal, known as the Treaty of Jaffa (1229), whereby Frederick would get Jerusalem but the Muslims would control al-Aqsa and the Dome of the Rock on the site of Solomon's Temple, which Christians could access for prayer. Jews would be permitted entrance to the city to pray at the Western Wall on the Temple Mount, Muslims would retain a *qadi* (judge) in Jerusalem, and nonresident Muslim pilgrims in Jerusalem were to be protected. Muslims were also to be allowed access to Bethlehem, which passed to Frederick's control. Nazareth, Sidon, Tibnin (Turon), Jaffa, and Acre were also handed over to Frederick.[84] The parties agreed to a ten-year true.

Escorted by his Muslim bodyguard and accompanied by his tutor in Arabic logic, a Sicilian Muslim, Frederick arrived in Jerusalem to be received with honor by Shams ad-Din, the eminent qadi of Nablus, who was assigned by the sultan to host Frederick. In his enthusiasm to honor his guest and not to disturb his rest, Shams ad-Din asked the local muezzins to forgo the call to prayer. But the next day Frederick was not pleased and complained to the qadi, "O qadi, why did the muezzins not give the call to prayer in the normal way last night?" Shams ad-Din replied, "This humble slave prevented them, out of regard and respect for Your Majesty." That did not please Frederick either. "My chief aim in passing the night in Jerusalem was to hear the call to prayer given by the muezzins, and their cries of praise to God during the night."[85] Frederick then reprimanded the qadi: "You have done wrong; why do you deprive yourself because of me of your normal obligation, of your law, of your religion?"[86]

Shams ad-Din accompanied Frederick to the al-Aqsa mosque, and the emperor expressed his delight at its beauty, especially the magnificence of the mehrab. Affectionately holding Shams ad-Din's hand, the emperor stepped out of the mosque to be confronted by Christian protesters led by a priest holding the gospels and attempting to force entry into the mosque. Frederick was furious and shouted, "What's that you've brought here? By God, if one of you tries to get in here without my leave, I'll have his eyes out. We're the vassals and slaves of this Sultan al-Malik al-Kāmil. He has granted these churches to me and to you as an act of grace. Don't any of you step out of line." The abashed priest beat a hasty retreat.[87]

Frederick had accomplished the seemingly impossible task of retaking Jerusalem for Christianity without bloodshed. In a letter to King Henry III of England, Frederick stressed the significance of what he had achieved: "In these few days, by a miracle, rather than by valour, that undertaking has been achieved which for a long time numerous princes and various rulers of the world . . . have not been able to accomplish by force."[88]

Paradoxically, Frederick faced an onslaught from Pope Gregory IX, including dastardly plots by the Knights Templar to do him harm. In 1229 Frederick returned to Italy from the Middle East to confront a serious challenge by the pope, who had invaded the Sicilian kingdom to seize it. From Italy, Frederick wrote a letter, preserved by Arab sources, in Arabic to his friend Fakhr ad-Din: "In the name of God, the merciful, the forgiving. . . . We departed, and left behind us our heart, which stayed (with you) detached from our body, our race and our tribe. And it swore that its love for you would never change, eternally, and escaped, fleeing from its obedience to me." Frederick then informed Fakhr ad-Din of the current news, telling him that the pope was acting "treacherously and deceitfully" in his actions and referring to his papal opponents as "a rabble of louts and criminals."[89]

After Frederick returned from the Middle East, he continued to speak effusively of the Egyptian sultan, telling distinguished visitors that his friend was dearer to him than any person alive save for his own son. When the sultan died in 1238, Frederick mourned. The situation in the Middle East now changed. Christian forces were defeated in battle in 1240, and shortly thereafter the emir of Kerak took back Jerusalem. In a letter to the king of England, Frederick lamented the sultan's passing, "Many things would have been very different in the Holy Land if only my friend al Kamil had been still alive."

### The Minorities under Frederick II and the Lucera Controversy

A key component of Frederick's administrative system was the protection of religious minorities like the Muslims and Jews, which were under the direct protection of the emperor. In his landmark legal code, Constitutions of Melfi (1231), which has been called "The Birth Certificate of Modern Bureaucracy," for example, Frederick twice states that both Muslims and Jews are too severely treated.[90]

In Germany, Frederick was faced with perhaps his greatest test and crisis concerning the Jews. In Fulda, thirty-four Jews were executed on the accusation of "blood libel," the belief that Jews had killed Christian children to drink their blood and use it for ritual purposes. Frederick, who had never heard of such a thing before, launched an in-depth investigation of the blood libel in which he enlisted the kings of Europe. In 1236, following the investigation, Frederick stated that the blood libel was fictitious and announced the Jews "absolved" of this crime. Frederick in his proclamation declared, "for the proper management of justice, it is required that we rule the non-believers properly and protect them justly, as a special group committed to our care . . . the common bond of the human species in which they also join Christians."[91] As the historian David Abulafia writes, the idea of shared humanity of Christians and Jews was noteworthy "at a time when Christians were denigrating Jews and other non-Christians as less than human, or incompletely human."[92] Frederick was "the first Christian prince to define succinctly the legal status of the Jews," and though later European rulers would not live up to Frederick's standards of justice and pluralism, his 1236 proclamation served "as a model for many later privileges, and vitally to affect the legal status of Jews in most central and eastern European Jewish communities to the eighteenth century."[93]

The epic contest and confrontation for continental supremacy between Frederick and the pope was, in an important sense, also about how Jews and Muslims were to be treated in Europe. The contrast could be seen, for example, when Frederick cited the Talmud as evidence to exonerate the Jews from blood libel, while just four years later the Vatican ordered the public burning of all copies of the Talmud.

There is controversy and debate, however, surrounding Frederick, this most sympathetic of European rulers to Islam, as he is held responsible for driving the Muslim community off the island of Sicily after four long centuries. Frederick had inherited a volatile situation in Sicily regarding the Muslim population that had been worsening for decades following the convivencia of Roger II's time half a century earlier. In the decade following Roger II's death, Lombard settlers living in eastern Sicily and originally from the north launched anti-Muslim pogroms, forcing the Muslims to flee west. Contributing to the growing deterioration was the steady emigration of leading Muslims for years following the Norman takeover. A Muslim revolt against the crown began around the time Frederick was born. The catalyst seemed to have occurred earlier when Muslims were put under the control of the archbishops of Monreale, ending the semi-autonomous status of the community. It was in Monreale that "pressure to convert, pressure of taxation, [and] long-boiling resentment at Christian rule exploded."[94]

In the mountainous interior, Sicilian Muslims waged a guerilla war against the government, which Frederick could not tolerate. In 1224 Frederick moved decisively against the Muslim community. He relocated between 15,000 and 20,000 Muslims to Lucera, a city on the Italian Peninsula that was located 150 miles from Rome. This largely ended the insurgency against Frederick. The novelty and audacity of building a Muslim city so close to Rome was not lost on the people of the day and factored heavily in the papal propaganda against Frederick. The city's Muslim residents remained loyal to Frederick, whom they called their "Sultan."[95] Frederick drew many of his soldiers from Lucera, which served as a royal retreat, and he kept a harem there. Muslims associated with Lucera rose to become some of the most important figures in Frederick's empire. The judge-administrator of Lucera, a Muslim named Johannes Maurus or John the Moor, who served as grand chamberlain, is one example.

## THE DEATH OF FREDERICK II AND THE END OF THE ERA OF CONVIVENCIA

The historian James Bryce sums up Frederick's relationship with the pope, who had declared a crusade against the emperor: "Excommunicated by Gregory IX for not going to Palestine, he went, and was excommunicated for going: having concluded an advantageous peace, he sailed for Italy, and was a third time excommunicated for returning."[96] When Frederick died in 1250, the church celebrated. Pope Innocent IV proclaimed, "Let heaven exult and the earth rejoice."[97] Immediately upon Frederick's death, the pope and his allies invaded Sicily.[98] The pope's crusade against Frederick was transferred to his son Manfred, the king of Sicily.

In 1266 Charles, the French count of Anjou and champion of the pope, defeated and killed Manfred in battle. Frederick's sixteen-year-old grandson Conradin was beheaded in Naples two years later on the orders of Charles. In 1300 Pope Boniface VIII and Charles's son finally overran Lucera, destroying it and either killing its inhabitants or selling them into slavery. With Frederick's death, strong centralized rule collapsed in Sicily and southern Italy, and the region became prey to the pope's interference and the emergence of local lords establishing their own authority on their estates and openly persecuting minorities.

After Frederick's death an entire culture developed that depicted Frederick as the Antichrist and ultimate personification of evil. Monks wrote about witnessing Frederick's disappearance into the sea off the coast of Sicily near Mount Etna, the supposed seat of Satan's empire, with thousands of horsemen and the waters making a hissing sound because of the devil's heat that Frederick's body presumably carried within it.[99] At the other extreme, Frederick was so beloved by the Germans that they refused to accept he had actually died. Many believed that Frederick was waiting to be resurrected, that he would soon reemerge to resume his unfinished mission of challenging the oppressive forces of the Catholic Church and the pope on behalf of the poor and common people. Frederick was seen as the "last emperor," who would reign for a thousand years of peace and prosperity. For generations, whenever Germans faced a crisis they would expect their legendary emperor to return and champion them. With Frederick II, the clash between the Germans and the papacy noted in the last chapter reached a climax that would not be surpassed until Luther emerged to make a clean break with Rome.

In time the Germans would fuse Frederick II and his grandfather Frederick I Barbarossa into a Marvel comic–like superhero. This mythical Frederick was said to be sleeping in a cave under the Kyffhäuser mountains in Thuringia, with his beard growing through the table he was leaning on, waiting to be resurrected. The story became part of German culture, appearing in tales by the Brothers Grimm and adopted by Washington Irving in his popular story "Rip Van Winkle."

When we visited the tomb of Frederick II in Palermo Cathedral, we found bouquets of flowers laid there. On one, a distinctly devoted visitor had scrawled in Italian, "On the occasion of the 820th year of the birth of the grand Emperor Frederick II, loved by me and my family, I am happy to offer this modest floral homage." The cathedral was once the site of the Grand Mosque of Palermo, and the inclusive nature of Frederick II and his equally illustrious grandfather Roger II, who is buried alongside him, is reflected in the Arabic engravings that still adorn the cathedral. We learned that Frederick's body had been laid to rest by his Muslim guard. To honor Frederick II and Roger II, the team paused for a moment of reflection and to offer Jewish, Christian, and Islamic prayers at their tombs. They would have appreciated the interfaith moment.

It is a curiosity of history that these truly remarkable rulers are barely remembered outside academic tomes. Frederick II and Roger II have met the fate of the American Roger Williams, a man whose enlightened thinking on race and religion was well ahead of his time and who can arguably be considered one of the founding fathers of American pluralist identity, but he is little known in comparison with the other more celebrated founding fathers of early America.[100] Frederick II is frequently confused with Frederick the Great, while Roger II is hardly known. They deserve to be fully recognized today in books, articles, films, and statues. Both are key figures with universal appeal who embody the ideals of convivencia and serve as authentic models for European society today.

## Andalusian Muslims as "Greek Half-Gods" or Forerunners of ISIS Terrorists?

A heated debate among scholars about the Andalusian, and by extension the Sicilian, past and the realities of convivencia has cast a shadow over the present debate around Islam itself. There are those who believe that Andalusia was once ruled by Muslims who resembled "Greek half-gods" and that the land was a mixture of Camelot and Shangri-La, a garden of bliss and a cornucopia of delights, in which the Abrahamic faiths could live and thrive together. But there are others who believe that this society did not really exist and the Muslim period was a prelude to al-Qaeda and ISIS terrorists seeking to destroy Western civilization. There are also those scholars who offer a point of view that quite self-consciously attempts to balance the two opposed views.

### The Idea of Andalusia as Camelot

The debate about Andalusia among scholars is usually projected somewhat simplistically as one between two major twentieth-century Spanish historians who held opposing views on Andalusia, Spanish identity, and convivencia, Américo Castro and Claudio Sánchez-Albornoz. Castro, who moved to the United States and taught at Princeton University, published his ground-breaking book, *España en su historia: Christianos, moros y judíos*, in 1948 (the English edition appeared in 1954). In it he puts forward the argument that Andalusia's tolerant and harmonious culture in the past accommodated different faiths, for which he coined the concept *la convivencia*. In seeking the origins of the Spanish people, Castro challenges the proponents of Germanic primordial identity in Spain by explicitly rejecting the notion that the Visigoths formed the essential part of Spanish identity. For Castro, the hybrid culture of Spain, with its strong Muslim influences, was evidence that "Spain is different."

Other writers also provide a rich and evocative picture of Andalusia, including the nineteenth-century American Washington Irving in the essays and stories on Granada collected in *Tales of the Alhambra* (1832) and the British scholars Stanley Lane-Poole, in *The Story of the Moors in Spain* (1887), and John J. Pool, in *Studies in Mohammedanism* (1892). Stanley Lane-Poole reaches heights of ecstasy with his extravagant praise of Muslim Spain and its civilized society, wise rulers, wealth, and powerful armies. John J. Pool "respectfully" dedicated his book to "Islam in England and to all seekers after Truth." José Antonio Conde, a Spanish scholar of Muslim

Spain who lived in the eighteenth and nineteenth centuries, describes Muslims as "brave, intelligent and enlightened people . . . whose genius, progress and study . . . invokes the magical ages of Homer and . . . presents them to us in the garb of Greek half-gods."[101]

It was left to María Rosa Menocal, the Cuban-born professor of humanities at Yale University, to popularize the idea of Andalusia as a time of interfaith harmony in her elegantly written study, *The Ornament of the World: How Muslims, Jews, and Christians Created a Culture of Tolerance in Medieval Spain* (2002). The book was published as the United States was reeling from the effects of 9/11 and touched a nerve. At her passing in 2012, Roger Boase of the University of London, a British Muslim and himself an authoritative scholar of late medieval Spain, remarked to the *Yale News* that her book "reads like a novel and has made al-Andalus relevant and accessible to a vast readership. She was dynamic, rebellious, generous and young in spirit, and it is hard to believe that she has died."

### *The Ornament of the World*, Menocal's Evocative Title

The matter of Menocal's title, *The Ornament of the World*, is a story within a story relating to the scholarship of Andalusia. For Menocal, Andalusia represents a glittering and optimistic example of human society, when people "transcended differences of religion," that attracts the reader to turn the pages. She describes the "deserved celebrity" of Cordoba under the Caliph Abdur Rahman III: it is "an astonishing place" of "astounding wealth," with "nine hundred baths and tens of thousands of shops, then the hundreds or perhaps thousands of mosques, then the running water from aqueducts, and the paved and well-lit streets." She cites Edward Gibbon's approving description of the "book worship" of Muslims and the example he presents: the catalogues of the Cordoba library alone ran to forty-four volumes that contained information on the 600,000 volumes in the collection.

Menocal's first chapter, "Beginnings," acknowledges the medieval German nun Hroswitha as the source of the phrase "the ornament of the world" and mentions in passing that the nun "perceived the exceptional qualities and the centrality of the Cordoban caliphate."[102] David Levering Lewis, like other modern authors writing about Andalusia, also accepts Hroswitha's phrase as unequivocal praise of Andalusia and its caliph.[103] "Tellingly," Menocal breezily proceeds, "Hroswitha coined the expression even as she wrote an account of a Mozarab Christian martyr of the tenth century." Hroswitha recounts the story of young Pelagius, who refused the caliph's lustful advances and was put to the sword. Perhaps Menocal and others like Lewis failed to note that Hroswitha saw blemishes and faults in the Andalusia of her time and that her description of Andalusia as "the ornament of the world" referred to the time when Spain was under Visigothic rulers and not when it was ruled by Muslims.[104] Indeed, Hroswitha might well have adopted the phrase "ornament of the world" from Isidore of Seville, who, as noted above, wrote during the time of the Visigoths and had used the phrase to celebrate the might and majesty of Visigoth rule.

Hroswitha's story of Pelagius, derived from the widely circulated Christian tract the *Passion of Pelagius*, also had a strong propaganda value, even if taken on a symbolic level—the evil Muslim with more than a hint of his homosexual predilection wishing to corrupt the young innocent Christian. The story was used during the Reconquista to great effect to establish the depravity of Muslim character. Hroswitha's account, however, raises several questions: the idea that one of the most powerful rulers of his time, known to have a well-stocked harem, would so publicly humiliate himself in court surrounded by his courtiers does not fit with the reality of that time. Abdur Rahman III was acutely aware of the dignity of his office, which also had a moral character. (Recall the reprimand administered to him by the head cleric at the Grand Mosque when the caliph missed Friday prayers.) Such a scandal may well have triggered an uprising and cost him his throne. Besides, there is some doubt as to which Muslim king was involved in the story, as there are so many accounts of it.

Menocal's idealistic enthusiasm for Andalusia appears to have overwhelmed her scholarly exactitude. We get glimpses of it throughout her book, which is dedicated to her father, "who has lived in lifelong exile from his own land of the palm trees." The reference to palm trees is a sly but romantic reminder of one of the main characters in her book, Abdur Rahman, the exile from the land of Syria and founder of Andalusia's greatest dynasty, who pined for his homeland and associated it with the palm tree. In returning to the nun's evocative phrase throughout the book, Menocal is perhaps guilty of intellectual lassitude but is innocent of dissimulation.

## The Andalusian Syndrome, Andalusia as "Perfection"

Menocal was not alone in falling victim to the seductive charms of Andalusia. We saw how Imma Fernandez, whom we met at the opening of this chapter, gently drifted in and out of an oneiric state that transported her to her beloved Andalusia. For her, Andalusia was "perfection" and "paradise": "I think Islam in some civilizations, as in Andalusia, in Persia, and in other countries, has probably reached the highest peak of wisdom that man can reach." Indeed, she told us that other tour guides in the mosque-cathedral did not share her views and had called her "Moorito," or Little Moor, when they heard her speak Arabic with a Moroccan tourist. I could only imagine the conniptions of the good priests at the bishopric to her musings about the beauties of Islam:

> I always imagined Islam . . . to be such a civilization with so much progress in all the sciences and such perfection and beauty in art. This society had to be of course, very refined, very subtle, very much a society of poets, of musicians, very close to God, to Allah, to the spirit . . . close to the breath of the universe, it's a description that we can make of Allah, and that was, for me . . . I'm maybe a dreamer . . . but deep inside me I believe in that.

Imma was affected by what I have called the "Andalusian syndrome"— that bittersweet sense of wonder at what was achieved and the scale of what was lost, the magnificence of the heights and the tragedy of the destruction.[105] It is a nostalgia felt too deep for words about a beloved civilization in the past that haunts the imagination. The Andalusian syndrome is a phenomenon that ranges from the writing of Shadab Hashmi, the Pakistani-American poet in San Diego (*Baker of Tarifa*, 2010), to the work of Karachi author Muneeza Shamsie in her 2016 article, "Introduction: The Enduring Legacy of al-Andalus," to Kristiane Backer, the German author, celebrity, and convert to Islam who calls on Europe to look to Andalusia and its Islamic golden age as a model for relations between cultures and religions in Europe today. In Islamabad, Ejaz Rahim, a distinguished author and poet writing in English, captures perfectly the Andalusian syndrome in his long and evocative poem, "Let the Andalusian Rivers Speak" (in *Toledo to Toledo*, forthcoming) from which I present these lines:

> Together they defined
> A new spirit, another age
> Giving shape
> To an Andalusian legacy
> Of universality
> And tolerance
> Still fragrant in the corridors
> Of memory

"The loss of Andalusia is like losing part of my body," Prince Turki of Saudi Arabia told me when I asked him what the loss of Andalusia meant to him as an Arab, a question that clearly struck a nerve. "The emptiness remains," the prince said. "Andalusia transcends space and time." "I have a passion for Andalusia," he continued, "because it contributed not only to Muslims but to humanity and human understanding. It contributed to the well-being of society, to its social harmony. This is missing nowadays." For the prince, "Andalusia was the exact opposite of Europe at that time—a dark, savage land of bigotry and hatred."

The lure of Andalusia makes for the strangest of bedfellows. To the example of Prince Turki, let us add those of Tariq Ali, an inveterate Marxist communist activist, and Salman Rushdie, a secular humanist with a fatwa hanging over his head for writing *The Satanic Verses* (1988). Ali and Rushdie, both constantly mired in polemics and controversy, have written several novels in their twilight years that evoke Andalusia with tenderness. Tariq Ali hovers around Andalusia in his Islam quintet, starting with *Shadows of the Pomegranate Tree* (1993). In his more recent novel, *A Sultan in Palermo: A Novel* (2006), Ali casts the legendary al-Idrisi, the Muslim scholar and adviser to Roger II, as the central figure in the Norman court.

Salman Rushdie's novel *The Moor's Last Sigh*, whose title refers to the sorrow of Boabdil, the final king of Granada, as he looks back for the last time at the Alhambra palace that he has been forced to leave, was published two decades ago, in 1995. In 2015 Rushdie returned to Andalusian themes in *Two Years Eight Months and Twenty-Eight Nights*. The novel portrays Ibn Rushd, or Averroes, as the model for the idealistic, open-minded, and scientific intellectual who stands in opposition to al-Ghazali, who in a disingenuous and misleading binary is projected as a close-minded fanatical precursor of the Taliban. In his positioning of the cosmic clash between good and evil, light and darkness, reason and unreason, Rushdie has chosen Ibn Rushd as the champion of all that is good and positive. In a semantic legerdemain, Rushdie shortens the name of Ibn Rushd to just Rushd, making the name look and sound similar to Rushdie, thus melding himself with Averroes as the great warrior in Islam for reason, logic, and scholarship who is persecuted for his position. The identification is crude and heavy handed: The "'reason,' 'logic' and 'science'" of Rushd gets him into trouble with the "Berber fanatics who were spreading like a pestilence across Arab Spain." They "disgraced" him "on account of his liberal ideas" and "burned" his writings. Rushd and Rushdie have become one in this evocation. The surprise is not that it is an act of some ego, as his critics may expect of Rushdie, but that by positioning himself within the firmament of Islamic intellectuals alongside one of Islam's most illustrious scholars, he may be indicating that he too seeks to be part of the Islamic tent.

Tamara Sonn, a renowned American professor of history at George-town University, has also written extensively about Andalusia with great affection and admiration. In her most recent book, Sonn—like Menocal—highlights the importance of knowledge in classic Muslim civilization, which includes Andalusia: its second chapter is titled "The Pursuit of Knowledge in the Service of God and Humanity: The Golden Age." Sonn describes this Muslim civilization as a "highly sophisticated culture," one "marked by openness and creativity."[106] In interviews for this project, Jean-Luc Marret, the French authority on Islam, thought, like the French Islamic scholar Gilles Kepel, France was ideally situated to be the "New Andalusia," and Rabbi Lord Jonathan Sacks argued for the need to appreciate the Andalusian model, which could teach Europe, indeed our world, lessons for the problems we face today.

### Critical Reassessment of Andalusia

Let us now turn to those scholars who oppose the romanticized idea of Andalusia and believe that convivencia was more myth than reality. A prominent voice taking this position is the eminent historian Claudio Sánchez-Albornoz, who rejects the idealistic picture of Andalusia as, in essence, little more than puerile fiction. Sánchez-Albornoz issues a direct response to Castro in his *España: Una enigma histórico* (Spain: A historical enigma, 1956). Despite his status as a prominent exile during the Franco regime (he was head of the Spanish Republican government in exile from 1962 to 1971), Sánchez-Albornoz firmly adopted the interpretation of Spain based in Germanic primordial identity. It was the Visigoths, Sánchez-Albornoz argues, who laid the foundations of Spanish culture, legal institutions, and the monarchy. Sánchez-Albornoz even challenges previous academic thinking about the continuity of Roman influences in medieval Iberia by putting forward the argument that the Visigoths gave birth to Hispanic civilization and to the Spanish "character," which was unique in itself and went on to define Spanish history and identity.

For Sánchez-Albornoz, the subsequent arrival of the Muslims and their presence together with the Jews on the Iberian Peninsula made little difference to Spanish culture. While he does not deny their presence, he argues that the basic culture of Spain had already been formed. Sánchez-Albornoz develops this thesis further in the three volume *El Reino de Asturias: orígenes de la nación española* (The Kingdom of Asturias: Origins of the Spanish nation, 1972–75), which was the result of decades of research. He argues that specifically the history of Spanish "blood" originated in the Asturias mountains with the Visigothic hero Pelagius, another mainstay of Spanish Germanic primordial identity, as noted above.[107]

Sánchez-Albornoz's ideas about an essential national Spanish "character" that drove history before and after the Muslim period have generated a passionate debate that continues to this day. Scholars making similar arguments as Sánchez-Albornoz's include Évariste Lévi-Provençal, a French historian with a Jewish family background in colonial Algeria who has been called "arguably the most important twentieth-century historian of al-Andalus."[108] The Spanish historian Eduardo Manzano Moreno more recently criticized the idea of convivencia as used by people like Castro and Menocal as a "political concept" rather than a "historical" concept. Convivencia, he wrote, has been promoted and defined at an international, and especially American, level in the interests of multiculturalism "with little or no input from Spanish historians." Indeed, Moreno concluded, "the data we possess on Jewish and Christian communities from the epoch of the Caliphate of Cordoba is very scant," and therefore the use of a term like *convivencia* is not based on sufficient evidence.[109] Maya Soifer Irish, a professor of Iberian history at Rice University, had a similar argument in her article on convivencia. For her, the juxtaposition of a tolerant multicultural Iberia and a persecuting northern Christian Europe is a "distorted picture," as "kingdoms of medieval Spain were . . . part of a Christendom that for most of the Middle Ages tolerated the coexistence of distinct groups."[110]

The American scholar Kenneth Baxter Wolf is also critical of convivencia; the title of his *Christian Martyrs in Muslim Spain* (1988) hints at his view of Andalusian history.[111] Like Moreno, Wolf argues against taking the example of "moments in Andalusian history that fit so nicely under a 'culture of tolerance' rubric, moments that have been extracted from their more ambiguous and nuanced historical contexts." Thus we must pay attention to the fact that "many of the highly regarded examples of positive *convivencia* came with a 'dark side.'" For example, Wolf writes that "while Muslim authorities allowed subject Christian and Jewish communities a remarkable degree of autonomy as far as their own internal affairs were concerned, they did this primarily because they were concerned about the contamination of their own religious community through excessive contact with Christians and Jews."

To reject Menocal's idealized version of convivencia and Andalusia, Wolf uses the tale recounted by the nun Hroswitha derived from the *Passion of Pelagius*. Considering the propaganda value of the tale, it is curious that Wolf would draw on it to examine the question of convivencia.

Indeed, the British historian Ann Christys writes that in spite of the story's setting in Cordoba, "details within the *Passion of Pelagius* . . . link the text very firmly with the north," and it "should be read through northern Christian eyes."[112] Nevertheless, Wolf argues that "from Hroswitha's perspective, the kind of acculturation that characterized Christian-Muslim relations in tenth-century Córdoba was tantamount to an act of cultural sodomy: an unnatural union." "So much for *convivencia*," he concludes.

Wolf cites another, similar story in his argument against Menocal that is equally shaky. He quotes from the *Life of John of Görz,* written by the priest John of St-Arnulf, which describes his subject's visit to the court of the caliph as an emissary carrying a letter from the Emperor Otto I. One glimpses Wolf's loyalty to these characters in the way he describes the interaction between caliph and priest when they meet. The caliph's conversation is nothing but "boasting" and "pumping John for information." In contrast, "John listened politely." In the end, concludes Wolf with an extravagant literary flourish, the caliph and the priest were reduced to "a pissing contest." Wolf does not question the authenticity of the opinion of a nun and a priest whose very job was to defend their church against what it saw as a heretical Muslim presence in Europe that directly challenged its supremacy.[113]

Other scholars, such as Richard Fletcher and David Nirenberg, have also contributed to the debate about Andalusia and convivencia taking a self-consciously more balanced middle ground. Fletcher's *Moorish Spain* (1992) points out that earlier authors, including Stanley Lane-Poole in his celebrated *The Story of the Moors in Spain,* create a highly romanticized picture of Andalusia. While agreeing that there were times of learning, harmony, and prosperity—Fletcher describes the interaction between Islamic and Christian civilization in Europe as "extremely fruitful"—there were also injustices and cruelty committed by Christians and Muslims against each other and against the Jews. Fletcher concludes, "Moorish Spain was not a tolerant and enlightened society even in its most cultivated epoch."[114] David Nirenberg opens his book, *Communities of Violence: Persecution of Minorities in the Middle Ages* (1996), by stating the usual positive and negative perspectives regarding Andalusia and declaring that the book argues "against both these positions, against a rose-tinted haven of tolerance and a darkening valley of tears, but it also borrows from both."[115] He argues that there was as much violence in Andalusia as elsewhere in Europe and that the Muslim rulers were as brutal as the other rulers of the continent.

Yet another strand looks at Andalusia through what Nirenberg calls "post-Holocaust eyes," which includes anti-Semitism and the Israeli-

Palestinian confrontation.[116] This approach questions the common belief of a Jewish "Golden Age" in Andalusia, and examples include Jonathan Ray's 2011 article, "Whose Golden Age?" and Michael Brenner's segment on Andalusia, "A 'Golden Age'?" in his 2010 book *A Short History of the Jews* (see chapter 7 of this book). In *Under Crescent and Cross: The Jews in the Middle Ages* (1994), the historian Mark R. Cohen of Princeton University analyzes how Jewish narratives about Andalusia and the position of Jews in Islamic societies have changed over the years. The "myth of the interfaith utopia" that focused on Andalusia, Cohen writes, was "invented" by nineteenth-century Jewish scholars such as Heinrich Graetz in Germany who were "frustrated by the tortuous progress of their own integration into gentile society" and were "seeking a historical precedent for a more tolerant attitude toward Jews." This narrative was then followed by what Cohen calls the "countermyth of Islamic persecution of Jews" that gained prominence following the Six-Day War in 1967.[117]

Scholars like Ray, Brenner, and Cohen were writing in the context of the work of the German-Israeli historian Yitzhak Baer, described by Ray as "perhaps the most influential historian of Spanish Jewry of the twentieth century." Baer, who also questioned the idea of a Golden Age, wrote that the heights of Jewish achievement in Andalusia involved those Jews of the "upper classes" who stood apart from the mass of the Jewish population and "enjoyed their life, tasted the pleasures of wine, women, palaces and gardens, and pursued the literary arts and the sciences."[118] This essentially represented a compromise of Judaism in favor of the dominant culture by the elite, keeping in mind that, as Aaron W. Hughes notes in his discussion of Baer, it was the masses, not the elite, who achieved the State of Israel.[119] The "cultural activity" of these Jews, writes Baer, flourished not because of a "definite policy of tolerance and individual freedom" but instead "through the neglect and the religious and moral laxity of the rulers."[120] Rather than interpret Muslim Spain as the Jewish Golden Age, he "regarded it as tantamount to the disappearance of traditional Jewish life that had sustained Jews for centuries."[121]

## ANDALUSIA AS A PRELUDE TO AL-QAEDA AND ISIS IN EUROPE?

After 9/11, arguments about Andalusia and convivencia were colored by Islamophobic sentiment that debunked the idea that Muslims had created societies that could be admired while linking all matters Islamic, however tenuously, to "Islamic terrorism." Such thinking about Andalusia emphasized Spanish identity with its roots in Germanic Visigoths. Onto this old narrative, according to which the Christians exclusively gave

Spain its culture and identity, was grafted the "security" language of terrorism.

No less a figure than the former prime minister of Spain, José María Aznar, addressing an audience at Georgetown University in September 2004, cast the Reconquista as the counterterrorist operation par excellence:

> If you take the trouble to focus on what bin Laden has written and stated in recent years . . . you will realize that the problem Spain has with al-Qaeda and Islamic terrorism did not begin with the Iraq crisis. . . . You must go back . . . to the early eighth century when a Spain recently invaded by the Moors refused to become just another piece in the Islamic world and began a long battle to recover its identity. . . . Every gesture of tolerance signifies the encouragement for them to commit further crimes.

Two years later, in September 2006, Aznar, who had recently joined the board of directors of Rupert Murdoch's News Corporation, gave a speech at the Hudson Institute, a think tank in Washington, D.C. Aznar again associated the Reconquista with the war on terror, declaring himself a "supporter of Fernando and Isabella," the monarchs who conquered Granada and expelled Jews and Christians from Spain in 1492. He also decried the "stupidity" of the UN-backed Alliance of Civilizations initiative, which his Socialist successor as prime minister had embraced.[122]

Aznar's words are not surprising considering his background: His grandfather was a personal friend of Franco's, held senior diplomatic posts in Franco's regime, and was one of Spain's best-known journalists, while Aznar's father was an officer in Franco's army and the head of propaganda for the fascist Falange Party. Indeed, in 2003, during Aznar's tenure as prime minister, while preparing for their deployment, "the Spanish military produced a new badge for the soldiers emblazoned with the emblem of Santiago Matamoros, St. James the Moor-Killer."[123]

When Aznar proclaimed that the Spanish had been fighting al-Qaeda since the eighth century, he did three things: First, he plugged into the Bush-Cheney narrative regarding their war on terror that involved "us" against "them," a binary that introduced the Islamophobic narrative into events after 9/11. Aznar, like British prime minister Tony Blair, was thus establishing himself under the captaincy of the United States as a loyal American ally in the war on terror. Second, he reduced Spanish history to a travesty by suggesting the eight centuries of Muslim presence in Iberia were nothing more than a reign of Muslim terror and sustained clash between Muslims and Christians. Third, he made it clear where he stood on the debate regarding the concept of convivencia: it was worthless.

The Aznar perspective has arrived on campus: the chapters in the table of contents of *The Myth of the Andalusian Paradise: Muslims, Christians, and Jews under Islamic Rule in Medieval Spain* (2016), by the Northwestern University scholar Darío Fernández-Morera, are the standard checklist of Islamophobic stereotypes—"Jihad," "Beheadings," "Female Circumcision," "Stoning," and "Sexual Slavery." Fernández-Morera seamlessly moves from the past to the present in his arguments, creating the single narrative of an inherently violent and monolithic Islam so crucial to Islamophobic discourse. Assessing what he calls the "terrifying" tactics of Muslims against Christians in the eighth century, he writes, "One is tempted to compare these terror tactics and their quick results with the ruthless tactics and similarly swift conquests of the Islamic State in Iraq and Syria during the twenty-first century."[124]

It is the Visigoths, Fernández-Morera argues, who have been unfairly maligned by historians, their kingdom being called "socially unjust." Visigoth "art and culture," he writes, have been dismissed, while "the art and culture of Muslim Spain have been correspondingly exalted."[125] In reality, Fernández-Morera argues, the heights of civilization that Muslims achieved in Andalusia were a product of Christianity and Visigothic heritage. Fernández-Morera gives the example of one of the most famous poets of Andalusia, Ibn Quzman, whose "admirers overlook that he was blond and blue-eyed, and that these facts, together with a name like Ibn Quzman (Guzmán or Guttman), mean that he was of Hispanic (indeed Visigothic, that is, Germanic) origin."[126] Resting analysis on racial grounds is shaky methodology: the caliph Abdur Rahman III had fair skin, blond hair, and blue eyes.

Even the regular Islamophobes have got into the Andalusian act: Hugh Fitzgerald, the vice president and co-creator of the Islamophobic *Jihad Watch* website, relates Menocal's position in *Ornament of the World* to Osama bin Laden himself in a November 2005 post titled, "The Persistent Myth of Andalusia." Not satisfied with mentioning a renowned Yale professor with one of the world's most notorious terrorists in the same breath, Fitzgerald proceeds to mock Menocal's scholarship and the notion of a tolerant Andalusian society with his own brand of literary elegance: "blah-blah-blah a lesson and hope for our age blah-blah-blah Maimonides blah-blah-blah."

### FREDERICK II AS ENLIGHTENED MONARCH
### OR MEDIEVAL TYRANT?

A similarly animated and contentious debate to that concerning Andalusia, though much less well known, has been taking place around Frederick II. Once serious historical scholarship began to emerge in Europe that challenged long-standing negative Catholic narratives about Frederick, scholars began to see him as forerunner of the Renaissance and the Enlightenment. The nineteenth-century Swiss historian Jacob Burckhardt, for example, called Frederick "the first ruler of the modern type who sat upon a throne," and his classic study of the Renaissance, *The Civilization of the Renaissance in Italy* (1860), begins with a discussion of Frederick II.[127] The nineteenth-century Oxford historian E. A. Freeman was similarly impressed: "It is probable there never lived a human being with greater natural gifts, or whose natural gifts were, according to the means afforded him by the age, more sedulously cultivated."[128]

This adulation continued into the twentieth century. In his 1949 study, David G. Einstein wrote that Frederick "is truly first among the enlightened despots of history."[129] In 1972 the American historian Thomas Curtis Van Cleve wrote of Frederick's court, "In contemplating the varied interests of the Sicilian court circle, in philosophy, in the sciences and mathematics, in literature and the fine arts, it is difficult to avoid the conclusion that, humanistically speaking, the Renaissance had already begun. . . . Frederick II has no counterpart or near counterpart in history."[130]

The debate about Frederick has been shaped currently by two studies: an enthusiastic labor of love written by Professor Ernst Kantorowicz in the 1920s simply titled *Frederick II: 1194–1250,* which runs to some 700 pages depending on the edition; and David Abulafia's less-enthusiastic biography published in the late 1980s, *Frederick II: A Medieval Emperor.* The contrast between the two authors, both Jewish, may well spring from the fact that Kantorowicz was writing before the rise of Hitler. While downplaying his own religious background, Kantorowicz nevertheless identified strongly with one of the great pluralist figures of German history. Abulafia, writing after the full horrors of Hitler's actions were widely known and documented, reflected the widespread revulsion and even suspicion of promoting anything that played up German identity.

Kantorowicz, who was from Prussia, wrote with awe about Frederick, seeing him as the German leader par excellence. Kantorowicz noted with perceptible delight Frederick's extraordinary encounters with the Islamic world and his quest for knowledge, which Kantorowicz considered to be out of step with the times and certainly the opposite of the position of the pope, whom he viewed negatively as the enemy of Frederick's mission. Kantorowicz too associated Frederick with the Renaissance and described his court as "Renaissance-like."[131]

Abulafia, in contrast, systematically challenged every one of the common perceptions of Frederick being a modern or enlightened ruler. One such perception that Abulafia dismantles is of Frederick as a promoter of interfaith coexistence. In fact, Abulafia writes, "The reign of Frederick II marks the end, not the revival, of *convivencia* in his southern kingdom."[132] Additionally, Abulafia downplays Frederick's religious tolerance, writing in a later article that Frederick's "approach to Judaism and Islam was in fact quite conservative, part of an established western tradition of toleration (rather than tolerance)."[133]

Frederick's rule was not one of great cultural mixing, according to Abulafia, and contrary to common perceptions, Frederick did not learn much from the Muslims he met. His Muslim bodyguard were comprised of "soldiers not scholars" and "the Arabs of Palestine who he met on crusade were not the standard-bearers of Muslim culture; what he learned from them was the art of seeing the eyes of falcons." Abulafia even cautions against "enthusing naïvely at Frederick's tolerance" for his extraordinary 1236 proclamation of protection for the Jews and exoneration of the charge of blood libel, writing that Frederick was merely demonstrating "the practice of impartial justice . . . to those who, as chamber serfs, were entirely at the mercy of his will." Rather than being out of step with his times, Frederick was instead a reflection of his age, as seen in the subtitle of Abulafia's book, *A Medieval Emperor*. Frederick's rule could be characterized and interpreted as "arch-conservatism, not of precocious enlightened despotism." Abulafia strips away the romance and wonder from Frederick in favor of interpreting him as concerned primarily with the perpetuation and succession of his own dynasty and family, a "concern that all medieval rulers, all secular lords, shared." For Abulafia, Frederick's "brainwave" of moving the Muslims to Lucera was one of opportunism, as they would be at his "beck and call" as he relied on the community for military purposes. Frederick "bonded to himself the most troublesome of his subjects, by a policy extremely tough in the short term—the misery of deportation—but almost generous in the long term," Abulafia wrote. "This does not mean he was especially tolerant towards Muslims. He used them for practical purposes."[134]

The debate over Frederick illustrates that even some eight centuries after his death the emperor remains controversial and little understood; people are still not sure what to make of him, the nature of his relationship with Jews and Muslims, and how to interpret his rule and its significance for Europe.

## How Convivencia Is Seen in Andalusia Today

Our fieldwork in Andalusia allowed us to speak with a wide variety of Spaniards about Andalusia and convivencia. Andalusians discuss the past with a tinge of nostalgic, almost romantic yearning. They graciously recognize the Muslim contribution to their history, many of them even believing that they are descended from Muslims or Jews. The past thus shapes their present identity. To them, convivencia is a way of living, a philosophy of life, an acceptance of others, an appreciation of shared art and culture. In their very ambiguity of identity, they have moved away from monolithic and exclusivist primordial identity such as that fashioned by the aristocracy and the Church in Spain.

### THE MAYOR OF CORDOBA

José Antonio Nieto Ballesteros, the mayor of Cordoba when he received us in his office, and subsequently appointed secretary of state for security in Madrid, gave himself enthusiastically to the lure of a pluralist Andalusia: "The first message I would like to give to the Muslim world is 'thank you,' because we owe them a culture, much of our character, we owe them the effort they put into Cordoba. They left their living footprint here in Cordoba." Expanding on his statement, he said: "Cordoba saw the development of a very prosperous caliphate. In the tenth century Cordoba was the great city of the world. We had Averroes, Maimonides, the best poets, the best writers, the best musicians, philosophers, physicians. This was all thanks to an expansive vision which was not restricted." The mayor also issued an invitation to Muslims: "You should know that Cordoba is a home for Muslims as well. We don't perceive you as a threat and are ready to receive you, and that you should feel comfortable in this city."

### PROFESSOR EMILIO FERRÍN, SCHOLAR OF ISLAM

One of the most prominent academic voices in Spain, Emilio González Ferrín, argues that convivencia was a reality and that Islam played an essential role in shaping Spain itself. A professor at the University of Seville, Ferrín is the author of several influential books, including *General History of Al-Andalus: Europe between East and West* (2006) and his novel *Bikes Are Not for Cairo*—part of his *Cairo Trilogy*—about the Arab Spring.

*Author and his team with the mayor of Cordoba*

Ferrín met us in Cordoba at a conference on Islam in Spain organized for us by Casa Árabe. Ferrín is the classic European intellectual forever viewing the predicament of the human condition through the lens of history and philosophy. He has empathy for the Muslim past in Spain but is also aware of the "serious problems" the religion faces today. With his background in Melilla—along with Ceuta one of the two Spanish city enclaves in North Africa—Ferrín is familiar with Muslim society. He has also traveled in several Muslim countries.

The focus of Andalusia, Ferrín said, was "universal" and was "not limited to a single community." In terms of identity, it was not a question of "us" versus "them"; everyone "in the Mediterranean basin" at that time was "us." Ferrín gave the example of King Alfonso X, who encouraged his title as the King of the Three Religions. A legacy of that period, Ferrín claimed, can be seen today in Malta, where people speak a language derived from the same Arabic spoken in Sicily and even today the ultra-Catholic use "Allah" for God.

Linking Andalusia directly to the Renaissance and Enlightenment in Europe, Ferrín discussed the marvelous achievements of the first man to attempt flight, Ibn Firnas, whom he called the "Andalusian da Vinci." On Averroes, Ferrín made a comparison with Jules Verne and said that Averroes predicted laser technology. Finally, speaking about Ibn Tufail, Ferrín explained that he drew upon Indo-Iranian philosophy in his book *Hayy ibn Yaqdhan*, considered the "first novel." *Hayy ibn Yaqdhan*, which Ferrín claimed influenced *Robinson Crusoe*, was the first to use the device of the desert island on which the protagonist finds himself alone and is forced to explore philosophical questions. This, concluded Ferrín, is the start of European anthropocentrism in focusing on the human being; it was "the start of the European Renaissance."

Sounding desperate, like a prophet who is not being heeded in his own homeland, Ferrín was pessimistic about the current situation and the future of relations between the faiths. He said he faced a struggle to depict Islam in a positive light and has been attacked because of his strong support of the idea of convivencia and the important contributions of Islam to Spanish and European history. People want to "overwhelm" you with their arguments and seek to remove 800 years of history, he lamented. Ferrín thought the situation was serious enough that we needed to "save Islam" in Europe, otherwise, he felt, it would not survive the current era and will end up again being expelled.

Ferrín related the negative image of Islam to the fact that there is no teaching of the Islamic period in Spanish schools. He gave the example of Ibn Firnas and said that outside of Cordoba no one knows him. Instead, the image of Islam is shaped by the media through hit TV series such as *El Príncipe* (The prince), which he compared to the American series *24*. The series, which is set in Ceuta and is about the sister of a Muslim drug trafficker and her love affair with a Spanish Catholic policeman from the mainland, portrays many of the common Spanish stereotypes about Muslims and North Africans. Although it takes place in Ceuta, a city with a population that is 50 percent Muslim, Ferrín noted that Muslims are not hired even for small roles.

Discussing the common myth that Islam is an inherently violent religion and is spread through violence, in a different manner from Judaism and Christianity, Ferrín argued that in reality there was "no distinction" in the way the religions spread. Islam expanded through a continual "transmission of knowledge, goods, and people." The myth that Islam promotes violence, Ferrín emphasized, is a lie, as all three religions use the same frame.

Ferrín was pessimistic about human nature and cited George Orwell's *1984* in describing how Spain deals with its Islamic history: If you manipulate the past, you control not only the past but the present and the future. Ferrín compared India and Spain, both of which, he said, deny that Islam has anything to do with their identity. India assumes Islam is not part of its culture and heritage, and Spain, through the projection of a Catholic identity and the concept of reconquest, "rejects in its historical DNA the presence of Islam." "We reject Islamic history in Europe," he said, "but it is an essential part of European history."

## Ambassador Eduardo López Busquets of Casa Árabe

Ambassador Eduardo López Busquets, who headed Casa Árabe and went on to be posted ambassador to Iran, was also appreciative of the Muslim era of Andalusia and Spain. When we met with him in Cordoba, he described the essence of convivencia that existed in the past: "This town of Cordoba has a tradition of convivencia, it has a tradition of dialogue. . . . The three different religions share a common culture. . . . So this can be a sort of model and paradigm, a link to the notion of Cordoba that pervades nowadays. . . . The idea is that those people, even though they were different, were able to cooperate and work together, and this is what convivencia is about."

López Busquets is himself the personification of the Spanish culture of hospitality. He became a patron of our project without reservation and even gave a lecture about Andalusia at American University in Washington, D.C., before we embarked on our fieldwork, as well as after it, at SOAS to discuss the project's preliminary findings. During our stay in Spain he was the most gracious of hosts, and the Casa Árabe in Cordoba was virtually our home. He invited a number of different Spanish experts on Islam to speak to us and answer our questions. He also took the entire team to one of the celebrated restaurants of Cordoba, which had enhanced its reputation among its clientele after a visit by Tony Blair, and as we studied the menu and discussed the celebrated Spanish dish of paella, López Busquets—who is from Valencia and, like all Spaniards, intensely proud of his native region—said under his breath that Andalusians did not know how to make real paella.

## A Spanish Virtuoso Guitarist

In Cordoba, we were fortunate to meet Fernando Pérez, a globally recognized virtuoso guitarist who specializes in many different styles of music. Originally from Zaragoza in Aragon, Spain, he has lived in places as diverse as Sudan, Egypt, the United States, Turkey, and India. He performs in concerts and music festivals across the world; he also teaches others through classes, films, books, and instructional DVDs—for example, *Guitar and Music Cultures* (2015) and *Greek Music for Guitar* (2015). He is as comfortable playing American Delta blues and country music as he is playing Japanese, Indian, Chinese, and Andalusian flamenco music, which was the topic of our discussion. Fernando was thus the perfect person with whom to discuss convivencia and the culture of Andalusia.

*Musicians Fernando Pérez and Mustapha Ghouzal in
Cordoba playing the guitar and the oud*

We spoke with Fernando alongside his Moroccan colleague, a fellow musician named Mustapha Ghouzal. While Fernando played the guitar, Mustafa played the oud, which Fernando described as the "mother of the guitar, the guitar came from the oud." They had performed together as part of a large ensemble at the joyous annual La Noche Blanca del Flamenco (The white night of flamenco) festival, when all of Cordoba comes out in the company of family and friends around midnight to enjoy the music, dancing, food, and drink. The night literally becomes white with the lights. The festival was recently instituted in Cordoba and attracts hundreds of thousands of people. What struck me was that in spite of the uncontrolled, jostling, joyous, and slightly inebriated mass of people, there was no rowdiness, no anger, and no fisticuffs. It was difficult to imagine a crowd of this size in Northern Europe drinking all night and behaving in this cordial manner.

Here, a day after their big performance, the two played for us during the course of our interview to illustrate their points. Fernando described eloquently and convincingly how much Spanish culture, especially music, owes to Islamic influences:

> In Spain, it's not only the music, it's part of the culture itself, it is in their blood, in their customs, in their habits. There are simple things like the famous "Olé!" in flamenco, where we always cry out, that comes from the "Allah," when you're playing Arabic music and you're

doing something really beautiful and people say "Oh, Allah, Allah." So really it's everywhere. At the same time it's a little sad, you see people sometimes even having negative perceptions about the Islamic world, especially nowadays with what's going on about the Islamic world, they don't realize that expressions they are using to condemn this culture they have taken them from them! All this science and knowledge that we got from the golden years of the Islamic civilization.

Fernando actually traced flamenco music back even further than Andalusia, and linked it to my part of the world in South Asia and the Mughal emperor Akbar the Great, who "supported the arts." "Flamenco has two main influences," Fernando said. "We have the Arabic influence coming from the south, coming from North Africa and coming into Spain. . . . At the same time we have another influence that was coming from India." Nomadic peoples living in what is today India and Pakistan, Fernando explained, found their way through the Persian, Arabic, and Ottoman lands to Greece and finally through Europe to Spain, bringing with them their music.

Fernando spoke passionately about the culture of coexistence in Andalusia as manifested through music especially:

> At that time they were living in harmony. When you listen to Sephardic music, that was Jewish music, it's based in the same musical system as the Arabic or Islamic music, which is called the *maqam.* So they were even following the same musical system, which was one of the richest ones. We see all these things happening and creating the treasure of the times of al-Andalus, getting along and being in harmony.

For Fernando, the tragedy today is that people are not able to connect the different cultures and religions as they did in Andalusia, which is why Andalusia worked and produced such a flourishing culture:

> Nowadays there is a lot of misunderstanding. Because really if one person understands Islam or understands the Bible or the Bhagavad Gita in India or the Dharma in Buddhism, you get to a point where they are all talking about the same thing, from different points of view, but people just don't realize it. . . . So Cordoba was a moment where we connected several people who were looking at the same thing. They were completing the picture; they were not fighting about it.

A Spanish Artist

In the countryside outside Cordoba near a historic castle, we interviewed Hashim Ibrahim Cabrera, a visual artist from an aristocratic Spanish family. Cabrera, who was born in Seville and grew up in Cordoba, was active as a young man on the political left and protested against the Franco regime. He converted to Islam in Granada in the late 1980s. We met him in his sprawling home set amid lush greenery and streams, which also serves as his art studio. He showed us some of his artwork, which has a strong Sufic element. The Islamic Andalusian tradition of symmetry, balance, and the concept of the unity of God is reflected in the pieces.

Like Fernando Pérez, Cabrera has worked in multiple styles and mediums, including painting, sculpture, performance, and photography. He has taught at universities and held major seminars hosted by the Spanish government, UNESCO, and other organizations on topics such as Ibn Arabi and "the Islamic cosmology in Andalusian art." He has also lived in and studied the art of other cultures, including Japan, where he exhibited his art, collaborated with Japanese artists, and studied Shintoism and Zen Buddhism. His work has been exhibited in Canada, Belgium, Italy, and Morocco. Cabrera is also the author of several essays and books, including *Nature and the Cultures* (1992) and *Disappearance of the Angels: Ibn Rusd and the Weakening of Creative Imagination* (1998), which analyses the anxiety of the current period in world history and includes a discussion of thinkers such as Aristotle, Plato, Averroes, Ibn Arabi, Wassily Kandinsky, Harold Bloom, Francis Fukuyama, Jean Lyotard, and Jean Baudrillard, and the rise and fall of civilizations.

Cabrera, who began painting in the early 1970s, said he converted to Islam after looking into his family's history and that of the region. As he put it, "In all the Andalusian families there is a Judaism element, an Arabic element, a Berber element, Germanic element, and a very rich mixture of things. . . . My father told me that God is merciful—that is an Islamic idea, a Quranic idea: *rahman, rahmatullah.* These ideas have the appearance of Christianity, but they are Islamic. Spanish history is very, very, very hard with Islam."

With this, he showed us a black-and-white photo of a young man who he described as the brother of his grandfather. The boy was wearing extravagant Middle East-looking garb. "Why were they wearing clothing like this?" Cabrera asked. I remarked that the man looked Moroccan. "He is a Christian!" he replied, "but why is he dressed like this? It is not a joke.

It's my grandfather's brother." He further noted that in his mother's family he had "discovered a strong line of Judaism." After Hashim converted, he said, his mother did not speak to him for eight years.

Discussing Spanish identity, Cabrera lamented that

> Spanish history is the history of our forgetting, a deep forgetting. Because of this there are problems like in the mosque in Cordoba, like with the Moriscos and the Sephardim, for example. Because while in other places in Europe, the modern state was constructed with agreements between people, in Spain modernity and the state were founded by destroying the diversity, the cultural diversity. The Catholic kings, they destroyed Jews, Christians, Unitarian Christians, Protestants, and Muslims-Moriscos. Because of this, Spain has many problems, the civil war, separatists now in Catalonia, the Basques, Galicia. And in all this history, Andalusia is the great forget, the great forget. Andalusia is nothing.

Cabrera summed up his vision of religion, which captures the spirit of convivencia voiced by Imma Fernandez, Fernando Pérez, and others in Andalusia:

> The objective of religion is love. This objective is the same for all the real religions, the authentic religions. I don't mean the New Age religions—that is syncretism. I think that a Muslim can believe like Muslim, a Christian like Christian, the Buddhist like Buddhist, and if we follow our own way, we will go to the same place as another, because it's like a circle that has spokes and we converge in the center.

Amineh, a painter herself, felt special empathy for Cabrera:

> He talked to us about how difficult it is to tread the path between the faiths. Cabrera is an intellectual and artist living in a beautiful home on the hill. While his children swam with mine outside and made friends and talked about the challenges they faced in school, Hashim told us inside about his experience of conversion to Islam which, he said, is seen as treason. He said, "They did not want to recognize the Islamic element" in him. I was surprised to learn that when he turned up at his own art exhibition and used his Spanish name Rafael, the visitors there were excited. But when he appeared using his own name, Hashim, people were frightened because of his Muslim name. I felt Hashim's lonely life isolated in his jungle-like

*Author and his team with Fadela Mohatar, second from left, Melilla*

surroundings had become a metaphor for his entire existence as he appeared to be cut off from both his own native community in spite of being part of the Spanish aristocracy and his adopted Muslim one.

### THE SPANISH MUSLIM MINISTER FOR WOMEN

In Melilla, one of the two enclaves on the north coast of Africa under Spanish administrative control, people told us again and again that they lived in an Andalusian environment with the concept of convivencia in mind. Fadela Mohatar, a Muslim Berber and senior government official who served as president of the Institute of Cultures and deputy minister for women before being appointed minister of culture, said that the ethos of convivencia is alive and well: "In Cordoba they may talk about convivencia; here we practice it," she asserted. "I was born in a city in which we had to share our lives as little children with the Christians and Muslims and Jews, so I was born in a city with mixtures, and we shared everything."

Mohatar drew a direct line between Muslim Andalusia in the past and Melilla today: "Precisely it is this model of al-Andalus, in a natural way, that has been transferred to Melilla. . . . We have been realizing that there is only one way, that we cannot turn our backs on one another, and that this common convivencia and togetherness is the most desirable and the best for everyone." Mohatar said that Melilla's Institute of Cultures is "working to nurture these relationships between the different communities. We are living in a little community here, which is just a little city, and we are only 70,000 people here living, and there's up to four communities here living together."

While a keen proponent of convivencia, Mohatar spoke of the pride she feels in her Berber identity, which she shares with a large proportion of the population of Melilla: "My ancestors were not only Muslim, but Amazigh or Berber, and Berber culture is even older than Islam itself. Even though my family is Muslim, their traditions and culture and even language are older and bigger and greater than the religion itself."

When asked the best way to improve relations between faiths, Mohatar replied: "The first thing is to know the other's beliefs and traditions. The second step is to fight against the stereotypes and manipulation of the media, because right now they are depicting Islam as the devil, and Islam is all love."

## SAIN BABA MANDIR

In Melilla we were invited to visit the Hindu temple which was the pride of Melilla and had been mentioned to us by several prominent officials, including the president of Melilla, as embodying the spirit of convivencia. The Hindu community leaders who accompanied us emphasized that convivencia was a reality in Melilla and also represented a tradition in their own culture, which they had brought with them from South Asia. Amid statues of Hindu gods and paintings of venerable gurus, we saw two pictures of Jesus and one of Mary, the Sikh holy book, and the Nuri Granth, which our Hindu hosts said was a Hindu sacred text written in the Arabic script because it came from the Sindh in Pakistan. The temple was called Sain Baba Mandir after the holy man revered by both Hindus and Muslims. The words "God is one love" were prominently written over the main altar. An elder said that Hindus believe one can bring any item of "good" into the temple, even if it relates to a religion different from Hinduism.

## THE LIVING LEGACY OF ANDALUSIA

During our fieldwork in Andalusia we also detected a pronounced north-south distinction in the comments of the Andalusians, who stressed to us that their culture, with its Arabic influences, is not shared with northerners. Hashim Cabrera noted that the pronunciation of Spanish words is different in Andalusia because it reflects an Arabic pronunciation, and a young woman working at the Cordoba Sephardic museum said that "everything is different" in Andalusia compared with the north: "The Arabic, Muslim influence still is very easy to find everywhere." Javier Rosón Lorente, our host at Casa Árabe and a native of Granada, said that the people also do not remember or consider Visigoth rule as part of their Andalusian heritage, which is noteworthy considering the mainstream articulation of Spanish primordial tribal identity. Therefore, the debate about Spanish identity can look very different in southern Spain than in other more northern parts of the country.

What is undeniable is that the remnants of Muslim civilization are everywhere in Spain. They include language, culture, and Spain's greatest tourist attractions—the Alhambra in Granada and the mosque-cathedral in Cordoba. Even our hotel in Granada, Casa del Capitel Nazari, was named after the last Arab dynasty and is situated in the Albayzín neighborhood renowned for its "Moorish" background. There was a statue of Boabdil, the last Nasrid king of Granada, outside our hotel. Names derived from Arabic—such as Alhambra (which means "red"), the Guadalquivir River that runs through Cordoba (the name comes from *al wadi al kabir,* or "the great valley"), and the Calahorra Tower (from *qala hurra,* or tower of freedom) in Cordoba—are common. Today there is also the physical presence of some 40,000 Muslims in Granada alone, and we came across an entire street in Granada dedicated to Muslim-run halal restaurants. Seeing the immigrant Muslims—mostly Moroccans and others from North Africa—Javier Rosón Lorente commented that some were saying, "the Muslim reconquest" has begun. It should also be noted that Portugal, much of which was under Islamic rule for five centuries, shares this same legacy—the Portuguese language, for example, contains over one thousand words of Arabic origin.

Scholars continue to investigate the richness of Andalusian culture as a mixture of different faiths and traditions working together to promote excellence in science, agriculture, philosophy, and literature (see, for example, *The Legacy of Muslim Spain,* edited by Salma Khadra Jayyusi, 1992, and *The Genius of Arab Civilization: Source of Renaissance,* edited by John R. Hayes, 1975). Roger Boase has illustrated the immense impact of Islamic culture on Spanish and European civilization in his scholarship—from his first book, *The Origin and Meaning of Courtly Love: A Critical Study Of European Scholarship* (1977), to his latest magnum opus, *Secrets of Pinar's Game: Court Ladies and Courtly Verse in Fifteenth-Century Spain* (2017). The demise of such a rich universal culture is a cause for lamentation.

## How Convivencia Is Seen in Sicily Today

In Sicily, we also found many people who were proud of their legacy of convivencia and, like those in Andalusia, felt it could be a model for the future. One of them was Sicily's most prominent elected official.

### THE MAYOR OF PALERMO

Leoluca Orlando, the mayor of Palermo, received us in his office, in the grand ten-acre Villa Niscemi palace, with its lush gardens and ponds, dat-

*In Catania, Sicily, with Mt. Etna, Europe's most active volcano, in background*

ing back to the sixteenth century. He spoke of his warmth for the Muslim community. As if to underscore his belief in convivencia, the mayor had invited two prominent Muslim men from Palermo, a Pakistani and a Palestinian, who work with him on intercultural projects. The mayor showed us a picture in which he is seen wearing Muslim clothing and praying with Muslims to mark the occasion of the festival of Eid al-Fitr. The Palestinian repeated excitedly, "He came and prayed with us!"

Mayor Orlando is no ordinary citizen of Sicily, and therefore his opinions and voice matter. A man of many talents, he has written a dozen books and legal treatises and even acted in films. He was first elected mayor in 1985, following which he launched a successful campaign to break the hold of the Sicilian Mafia over the city, a period known as the Palermo Spring. Orlando is also a major European statesman, having served in the Sicilian Regional Parliament, the Italian Parliament, and the European Parliament. He is currently the president of the association representing the mayors of Sicily and is perhaps the most respected of the mayors of southern Italy. His many awards and distinctions include the European Parliament's European Civic Prize, awarded in 2000, for "his struggle against organized crime and his engagement in favor of the civic renewal of his city."

"Please," said the mayor emphatically, "don't ask me the name of God. So, when I come inside a mosque, I pray to Allah, when I come inside a synagogue, I pray to Yahweh. At this moment I am Christian." This was as clear a reflection of the convivencia ethos that one could hear, and in

*Leoluca Orlando, the mayor of Palermo, presenting gifts in mayor's residence*

this statement he echoed the Andalusians we have cited above. Not surprisingly, the mayor also expressed his admiration for another historical figure who believed in convivencia—Frederick II. "Frederick II was very intelligent," he said. "Islamic culture was civilization, and he decided not to destroy but to use it."

The mayor proudly pointed out that the streets of Palermo today have signs in Arabic, Hebrew, and Latin script. He would even embrace the thousands of immigrants who arrive on their frail boats from North Africa and told us of his belief that people should be able to cross national borders without the need for residence permits. For the mayor, "immigration is a sufferance, mobility is a right," and he is promoting this idea to other officials in Europe. The mayor said he believed in "convivencia, not just tolerance." He defined Sicilian identity as "a mosaic made of different pieces of stones, of different colors and animation . . . a harmonious mosaic made by black and white pieces of stones, nice and bad, wonderful and not wonderful, and corrupted and not corrupted."

### THE ARAB MARKET IN PALERMO, THE SOUL OF SICILY

We also spoke with younger Sicilians who reflected Mayor Orlando's views on convivencia. Among them were Eugenio Vallone, a nuclear engineer whom we met on our flight from Marseille, and his friend Giulia Serio, a young woman from Palermo who was working with the United

Nations Development Programme. Eugenio spoke of *convivenza*, the Italian equivalent of convivencia, which he defined as people living and working together.

It is because of coexistence, he said, that Sicilian food is so good. He said a peculiarity of Sicily is that "this is normal for the different races to live together." "Everything is blended here." Out of all the cultures, Eugenio added, "Arabian influence is the strongest one." Eugenio said that to see the authentic Sicily, we had to see the markets, which were established by the Arabs, and the two offered to show them to us. While in the Ballaró market, which is also known as the Arabic market, Giulia said, "This district is called Il Cassaro, which comes from the Arabic word al-Qasr. It still remains the souk of Palermo. In this market you can find all kind of items from food to fish, and though it is in one of the poorest districts of the town, it remains alive."

Walking through the market, Giulia said that the method of bargaining in the market came from the way the Arabs used to sell their goods here. Looking at the multitude of foods being sold, Giulia spoke about further connections to the Muslim world. She said that not only do Sicilians have couscous, which they consider a Sicilian dish, but that "we also have sweets, the same kind of sweets as Middle East sweets, like those that are very sugary or with almonds for example, honey."

Sicilians believe, Giulia explained, that there are two types of Sicilians, Arabs and Normans: "We say in Sicily that you have the Norman type and the Arab type. I am definitely the Arab type, while we have very blond friends with blue eyes and they are descended from the Normans—that's what the legend says."

For Giulia and Eugenio, the market is the definition of Sicilian identity. Giulia said, "If you look at people, they're Indian, from Bangladesh, people from Middle East, North Africans, Sicilian, Arab Sicilian, Norman Sicilian." Eugenio agreed that the market represents Sicily: "Yes, if you come here, you can understand here the real soul of Sicily. All these kind of people, people coming from North Africa, India, and many other places. And I think it will survive despite the nationalism that has grown in the last period of crisis."

Giulia also said she was about to move to Tunisia to take a new job. In preparation, she began learning some Arabic, only to discover how similar the language was to Sicilian: "I started to learn some Arabic and I discovered that many Sicilian words have Arabic roots, like we say *mischina*, which is an entirely Sicilian word, it has nothing to do with Italian, which

*At Palermo Cathedral, Sicily*

comes from the Arabic *miskin*, which means poor. And in Sicilian *mis-china* is something you say to someone—like, it's an adjective you use 'oh poor him,' 'poor thing.'"

Much like Mayor Orlando, Giulia and Eugenio were proud of their history and tolerance toward immigrants. "Compared to the rest of Italy," Giulia said, "we're less racist in general because we're quite used to living with people from different cultures. . . . Here the hospitality is a very important part of our culture and the guest is kind of holy, you have to honor your guest."

## Discussion

We have heard the scholars argue both in favor of and against the idea that convivencia characterized Andalusia. Wherever you stand, with Castro or with Sánchez-Albornoz, you cannot understand any society outside its historical and cultural context. We have supplemented this information through our fieldwork findings. We have thus allowed readers to reach their own conclusion.

We note that the study of Andalusia presents a fundamental conundrum: How to acknowledge a society so clearly and heavily influenced by Muslims, when the same Muslims today are depicted as little more than tyrannical terrorists or feckless flibbertigibbets and belong to a reviled and marginalized community across the continent? To make matters worse, the Muslim period of Spanish history has been dropped into a deep black hole as if it never existed. We discovered in our field research that neither major European museums nor the standard history textbooks mention it except in the most fleeting of manner. The teaching of history in Spain begins after 1492, when Muslims were expelled from the Iberian Peninsula, as several Muslims in Andalusia reminded us. In Spain, officials presented us the book, *Spain: What Everyone Needs to Know* (2013), by William Chislett, which purports to explain who the Spanish are. In it, the author asks, "What was the legacy of the Muslim presence between 711 and 1492?" and in a book that runs to 226 pages answers the question in just over two pages (see the first chapter, "Historical Background, 711–1939"). In short, some 800 years of Muslim presence in Spain are reduced to less than one percent of a standard history book.

The history of Muslims in Spain came to an end in 1492 with the fall of Granada, the last Muslim kingdom of the Iberian Peninsula, and, in the same year, Christopher Columbus sailed for the Americas. The Muslims had lost Sicily centuries earlier. One chapter of European history was firmly closed shut and another vigorously opened. The two central ideas that had been in play—tribal identity and convivencia—had finally come to a head with the triumph of the former and the defeat of the latter. Over the next few centuries tribal identity would shape and inform European imperialism and nationalism; convivencia would be written out of official history so that Europe itself would forget its own past and the role that convivencia, ilm, and Islam played in shaping its culture and heritage.

Contrasting the events and contents in this chapter on Andalusia with the previous chapter on primordial tribal Europe illustrates the fundamental difference between the two European approaches. While German poets and philosophers found inspiration in the contemplation of the Volk and gods of German mythology, those in Andalusia found fulfillment in the idea of the unity of the universe suffused with the spirit of the divine. The zeal and ardor for the tribal nation in one case and the zeal and ardor for the divine encompassing all of humanity and creation in the other, in each case, however different the context, the object of adoration induced devotion in the worshipper.

The new European chapter shaped our world, and continues to do so, in far-reaching ways. From it would come, as we see in part 2, European imperialism, colonization, and, in their wake, immigration from the former colonies to Europe and the attendant tensions and problems.

# PART TWO

*Islam in Europe*

# FOUR

# Muslim Immigrants: The Ghosts of European Imperialism

"ALGERIA AND TUNISIA were under the colonization of France, and today they are still struggling," lamented Imam Haroun Derbal, who heads one of the main "mosques" of Marseille, which is located in a warehouse in a large market. "But you have Pakistan and India, who were under British sovereignty, who have today the nuclear bomb, and they are more and more advanced." With a bitter chuckle, he seemed to express his preference for British over French colonization. "There is no comparison between the Commonwealth and the Francophone countries."

The imam also felt that with all the contact France has had with Muslims, given over a century of colonial history, French society and government should have a better understanding of the Muslim community. "We have ayatollahs of *laïcité* here in France," he said, referring to the French tradition of secularism. "France is a really conservative country. You have the French language, for example, and you don't want to hear another language. It's not like the Anglo-Saxon system. The French don't see farther than their own nose."

The irony was that European imperial authorities, including the British and the French, projected their rule to their native subjects as the benevolent overseeing of parental guidance, not unlike a mother and father caring for their children. Indeed, British district officers in rural India liked to be considered *mai-baap* (which is colloquially understood in South Asia as meaning mother-father), and the French encouraged their subjects in Africa to see them as the "father," a conceit that was as much self-deception as an attempt to cozen native societies. The current generation of immigrants in Europe is experiencing the lingering effects of this complex relationship that promised care and compassion but provided brutality and exploitation.

The age of European imperialism, which could be traced to 1492 and the defeat of the last Muslim kingdom in Spain, initiated a new phase of the relationship between Europe and the Muslim world. Over the next centuries, the disparate kingdoms of Europe evolved into empires with overseas colonies. At this time we see a broad and clear correlation in the rise and fall of fortunes of the Muslim world and Western nations: as signs of political, military, economic, and social declivity developed in Muslim lands, there was, at the same time, evidence of corresponding acclivity in Western societies. The results were foregone: Muslim lands—a kingdom here, a region there—were colonized by Western powers or came under their sphere of influence. The centuries of colonialism checked and distorted Muslim thought which had already begun to lose vitality. That interaction continues to color the thinking and identity of the immigrant communities in Europe today.

In this chapter we consider the immigrant Muslims of Europe, who adhere to the literalist, modernist, or mystic models of Islamic interpretation identified earlier, in two broad categories. First we discuss the immigrants who came from the former colonies of Britain and France, the two nations that exemplified European imperialism in its latter phase. We then look at the guest workers who came to Europe after being contracted by Germanic European countries that desperately needed labor after the Second World War, through the examples of Germany and Denmark. For the immigrants in the imperial countries, there was already a relationship (albeit an asymmetrical one) that facilitated the growth of a pluralistic society. There was no such relationship for the Muslim guest workers in the Germanic countries. They were outside the Volk, the native ethnic community, and had no place in their new societies. The even-more-recent wave of immigrant Muslims in Europe—the refugees and asylum seekers coming from Africa and Asia—are discussed in later chapters.

All colonization is oppressive and in the ultimate analysis detrimental to the colonized; but colonization is neither homogeneous nor monolithic as we can see in the British and French examples. The British came to India as unctuous traders and slowly but inexorably converted their role to become masters of the land. In the great uprisings against the British in the middle of the nineteenth century, the Muslims, seen as the main culprits, lost an empire, an emperor, and their dominant cultural and political position. Once the upheaval and bloodletting had died down, British India saw a period of relative calm, with progress being made in certain regions like the Punjab, with its celebrated canal colonies and irrigation networks that made it "the granary of Asia." In contrast, there was the relentless malevolence of French colonization in North Africa. In each case the Europeans claimed they were bringing a superior civilization to their subjects.

The debate about the relationship between Western civilization and the ones they colonized continues into our times: Niall Ferguson, for example, is unabashedly triumphalist and creates a simplistic binary in his work about the merits of what he calls the "West" against the "Rest" (for example, *Civilization: The West and the Rest*, 2011), while other, more critical perspectives include Mike Davis's *Late Victorian Holocausts: El Niño Famines and the Making of the Third World* (2000), Pankaj Mishra's *From the Ruins of Empire: The Revolt against the West and the Remaking of Asia* (2012), Shashi Tharoor's *Inglorious Empire: What the British Did to India* (2017), Lawrence James's *Empires in the Sun: The Struggle for the Mastery of Africa* (2017), and Dierk Walter's *Colonial Violence: European Empires and the Use of Force* (2017).

When it was over, in the middle of the twentieth century, the Indians asked Lord Mountbatten, the last British viceroy, to stay on and become India's first head of state. In Pakistan, similar requests were made to senior British officers to serve the new state. Strangely, even the deaths and displacement of millions of Hindus, Muslims, and Sikhs during the partitioning of India in 1947 did not dampen the goodwill that had developed for the British. In Algeria the fight for independence was long, bloody, and unforgiving, and in the end the separation was bitter. There was little nostalgia on either side.

Let us take a closer look at what made the British and the French approaches different. After 1835, when Lord Macaulay issued his seminal "Minute on Indian Education," which expressed a wish to create in India "a class of persons Indian in blood and color, but English in tastes, in opinions, in morals and in intellect," other significant measures meant to integrate and placate the colonized were taken. Several decades after Macaulay's Minute appeared, major universities were established in Bombay, Calcutta, and Madras, which, in turn, created an influential and vocal literate class, soon to become the journalists, lawyers, and doctors of the subcontinent. Queen Victoria, in another example, issued a Royal Proclamation in 1858 that invited Indians to join the powerful and elite Indian Civil Service. The Indian Civil Service, the well-oiled administrative organization and structure of some 1,000 members of an elite corps educated in top English schools, was an example of British genius that enabled them to rule the vast Indian empire, known as "the jewel in the crown." The British military, while always a potent tool for the administration to use, was subordinated to the civil service.

The opportunities opening up in British India in the late nineteenth century resulted in the development of what we are calling modernist Islam—in which Muslims attempted to balance their faith with the modern world. This was, in a very real sense, a revival of the Andalusian project of philosophers like Averroes to balance faith and reason. Patterned on Cambridge University, the Mohammedan Anglo-Oriental College, later to become Aligarh University, was one of the key symbols of this Muslim renaissance. Sir Syed Ahmad Khan, the founder of Aligarh, declared that "Philosophy will be in our right hand and Natural Science in our left; and the crown of 'there is no God but Allah' will adorn our head." Many future leaders of India, Pakistan, and Bangladesh were products of the school. Leading figures of South Asia were also educated in Britain itself: Mahatma Gandhi and Muhammad Ali Jinnah, the founding fathers of present-day India and Pakistan, attended the law colleges of London; Allama Iqbal and Jawaharlal Nehru, the first prime minister of India, studied at Cambridge University.

In contrast to imperial Britain's attempts to include its subjects in its cultural and educational image while allowing them to retain their own identity with integrity, there was no such possibility of French colonial subjects being accepted as part of France. For Algerians to become French citizens, they had to renounce their cultural, religious, and tribal identities. That is why, after a hundred years of French colonization from the 1830s to 1930s, only 2,500 Algerians had obtained French nationality.

The British also instilled in their subjects a coherent if vague philosophy of service that drove many British administrators in the field. British ideals for these empire builders was best summed up in the ringing words of perhaps the most grandiloquent and learned viceroy of India, Lord George Nathaniel Curzon, who urged his administrators "to feel that somewhere among these millions you have left a little justice or happiness or prosperity."[1] The British believed they were promoting an irenic vision of justice, peace, and harmony; and for them London was the very omphalos of the universe.

The French, on the other hand, had no such idea of service and were themselves conscious of the differences between French and English imperial administration. The first French colonial official in charge of Morocco, for example, stated, "Before us rises the admirable English organisation: large, supple, commanding, directed from top to bottom by gentlemen or men who live and act like gentlemen, whatever their origins, who practise a humane code. . . . They have the personnel, we do not." Indeed, French administrators were often less than illustrious characters.

A 1911 pamphlet declared that "a barber, a peanut vendor, a navvy with the right connections, can be named an administrator of native affairs without the slightest concern for his abilities, his intelligence, his attitudes or his aptitudes." Between 1900 and 1914, less than half of the recruits for the French colonial administration had a secondary education.[2]

What the imam in Marseille, perhaps giving in to the adage that the grass is always greener on the other side, failed to mention was the devastation that colonization wrought to local culture and identity. Macaulay's Minute gave his estimate of "Oriental" learning thus: "A single shelf of a good European library was worth the whole native literature of India and Arabia." Winston Churchill, the "grand old man" of British imperialism in its most unrepentant form, made no secret of his racial opinions: gas the Kurds and starve the Bengalis appeared to be his broad approach to those peoples. He called the Hindus a "foul race." Perhaps few images convey the reversal of fortunes of former imperialists and their subjects than that of Churchill's infamously arrogant statement about wanting to have Mahatma Gandhi tied and brought to the main square of Delhi to have a heavy elephant placed on him juxtaposed with the image of David Cameron, another British prime minister, alongside Narendra Modi, the Indian prime minister, humbly strewing flowers at the feet of the statue of Gandhi in London.

British subjects in far-flung lands saw their colonial masters as coldly applying the policy of divide and rule, as between Hindus and Muslims in India, thereby creating deadly divisions and conflicts that are still in play long after the era of colonization. It was a sentiment echoed in the memorable quote of an Anglophilic Pakistani friend with a passion for cricket and the English language who has lived in London for half a century. At the end of a delicious Pakistani dinner and in the midst of one of those long and heated political discussions that South Asians so love, he summed it all up by saying, "Har shaitani yehan say shuro hoti hay"—"Every devilish plan originates from here." He was reflecting the belief that the former imperial masters run the world from London even today. Another conversation yielded another insight—this time from a senior Pakistani diplomat who had served in several Western posts. In the mind of the diplomat, as in those of so many in the Muslim world, the United States was the current imperial power and had taken over its imperial mission from the British. But there was a difference and it lay in their legacy: "Wherever Americans go, they leave behind three things—rubble, rubble, and rubble."

The British often put down rebellions with great brutality, including the 1817–18 Uva-Wellassa revolt in Sri Lanka, the 1857 Indian uprisings, and the Mau Mau rebellion in Kenya in the 1950s. In 1919 British troops fired into a crowd of peaceful pilgrims at Jallianwala Bagh in Amritsar near the holiest of Sikh shrines, killing and wounding an estimated 1,500 innocent civilians. There were also devastating famines, such as the 1899–1900 famine in large parts of India that left between 1 million and 6 million dead, and a famine in Bengal that was directly linked to colonial policy during the Second World War, in which more than 3 million died. The British philosophy of mai-baap collapsed swiftly in 1947 as the colonial masters of India abruptly abandoned their responsibilities and prepared to take what the American historian Stanley Wolpert in his 2009 study called *Shameful Flight*. Perhaps few events in history can match the scale of the bloodshed that summer which resulted in the death of more than 1 million people and the displacement of some 15 million.

A direct result of British colonization was the collapse of the local economy, as Shashi Tharoor reminded us in his Oxford Union address in 2015: "India's share of the world economy when Britain arrived on its shores was 23 per cent. By the time the British left it was down to below four per cent. Why? Simply because India had been governed for the benefit of Britain. Britain's rise for 200 years was financed by its depredations in India."

From the start, French colonial policies in Algeria, which was the first European colony in Africa in modern times, were unrelentingly brutal. French colonial officials in Algeria, especially at the lower levels, were violent and corrupt. They acquired vast lands for themselves and used the Algerians virtually as slave labor to grow cotton and become rich. The French were responsible for the deaths of some 2 million Algerians in the first four decades of French rule, out of a total population of 3 million.[3] Algeria was organized and run by a ruthless French military administration known as the *régime du sabre,* or "government of the sword." To organize the vineyards, which produced fine-quality wine for export, Algerians were forced off their lands, and many died from starvation. Leading French politicians openly advocated a "war of extermination." The mass killings, with entire communities herded into closed shelters and burnt alive, were not the only punishment inflicted on Algerian society: Widespread rape and destruction of property and infrastructure were common. The bloody climax was reached when, out of a population of 10 million, an estimated 1.5 million Algerians were killed in the struggle for independence, which was conceded in 1962. The French military lost about 25,000 dead and 65,000 wounded. Ten thousand French settlers lost their lives in the violence.

Other European colonial powers displayed similar levels of brutality: In Africa, the Germans wiped out 80 percent of the population of the Herero tribe and half that of the Nama in Namibia, killing 100,000 people, while as many as 300,000 people lost their lives in the Maji Maji uprising against German rule in Tanzania in the early twentieth century. The king of Belgium reputedly murdered and mutilated more than 10 million of his subjects in the Belgian Free State of Congo. Italian rule resulted in the deaths of between one-half to two-thirds of the population of Libya's vast Cyrenaica region, including as many as 70,000 people in concentration camps in the early 1930s. In Indonesia, more than 100,000 people in the kingdom of Aceh—nearly 20 percent of the population—were killed fighting Dutch colonizers in the late nineteenth and early twentieth centuries; and a further estimated 100,000 people died in Indonesia's war of independence in the second half of the 1940s. In the end, the brutal *Nacht und Nebel*, night and fog, strategy to deal with dissidence in the colonized and their cultural and economic suppression ensured a population suffering from stunted growth.

European imperialists promised much but delivered little. They left behind miserable and confused societies that are still ferociously debating their identity and are frequently beset by corruption, poverty, collapsing state structures, and savage civil wars that have led millions to seek opportunity and refuge in Europe over the decades. Haris Silajdžić, the former president and prime minister of Bosnia and Herzegovina, reprimanded Europeans for failing to connect the fraught relationship between colonialism and immigration and its attendant problems:

> If you pay a visit, you should expect a return visit. . . . So the Europeans went to the subcontinent, North Africa and so on, so these guys are now paying a return visit to them, and some of them don't seem to like it. . . . They don't even ask for their artifacts to be given back to them which were taken by the Europeans. So they are coming in peace, they want to work, and this is their right. You cannot go to the subcontinent and take what you want, come back, and say we have nothing to do with this. That is not how it works. That's not life.

## Children of the Raj—British Muslim Immigrants

Few monuments capture the spirit of an empire as the grand memorial to Prince Albert in Kensington, London. The gothic extravaganza of the late Victorian era represents the inclusive spirit of the British Empire in its depiction, at its base, of the four corners of the empire. There is a bull representing Europe, a camel Africa, an elephant Asia, and a buffalo America. Each animal is accompanied by appropriately dressed human figures of noble and grand bearing. On top of the monument, of course, is Albert, the prince consort and symbol of British royalty—although everyone in Britain seemed to know he was actually a German from Saxony. The marble ensemble projects an idea of one world, each part with its own special place and respected in its own character, united by the British. Immigrants arriving in the United Kingdom thus knew they were different, but they also knew that somewhere in this vast British Empire there was a place for them.

### From Lord Macaulay to Sadiq Khan

After the British left in 1947, their influence in the education, judicial, military, and civil service structures of South Asian countries still remained. South Asian countries had taken to the English game of cricket with religious zeal. The English language was spoken with varying degrees of mastery throughout the region from Karachi to Chittagong; and dozens of world-level literary prizes were garnered by South Asians. South Asians also carried this modernist tradition to other parts of the world.

It can be argued that there is a direct line, however tenuous, between Macaulay's Minute in the early nineteenth century and London mayor Sadiq Khan early in the twenty-first. A glance at Khan's family photographs confirms the impact of Macaulay. Dressed neatly in tie and clean shirt, his immigrant father Amanullah Khan appears the earnest workingman providing for his eight children. Amanullah may have never heard the name Macaulay, but he was carrying the Englishman's imperial design somewhere in his cultural inheritance. So when large numbers of immigrants like Amanullah from the former British colonies arrived in Britain to provide cheap labor, they had an idea of British culture, how to conduct themselves, and what to expect of local people. Amanullah labored for twenty-five years on the buses until the end. Sadiq Khan's victory therefore is greater than that of a single remarkable individual; it embodies a historic arc with its roots in imperial colonialism and its high point in successful immigration and integration.

In the United Kingdom, Sadiq Khan is not alone in being elected mayor. There are at least five other Muslims holding the job. In contrast, France has none, nor does Germany or Denmark. The Netherlands had a Muslim mayor in Rotterdam even before Sadiq Khan, though he had been nominated, not elected. There are also many other immigrant success stories in British politics, such as Baroness Sayeeda Warsi, Sajid Javid, Humza Yousaf, and the dozen or so Muslim members of the Houses of Commons and Lords; in sports, with the Olympic runner Sir Mo Farah, the boxer Amir Khan, and Moeen Ali who is a beloved cricket star in spite of a distinctly Islamic bushy beard; in literature, with Hanif Kureishi and Salman Rushdie; in journalism, with Mishal Husain and Adnan Nawaz of the BBC; in music, with Zayn Malik, the pop star, named "sexiest man in the world"; and in science, with the Nobel Prize–winning physicist Abdus Salam. The Pakistani-born teenager Malala Yousafzai, who attended school in Birmingham and joined Oxford University, was awarded the 2014 Nobel Peace Prize and has become a global peace icon.

What greater proof of the impact that British culture had on South Asians than to see, as we did, Pakistanis holding their own in international plays and films—Faran Tahir playing Othello, one of Shakespeare's most complex lead characters at the Shakespeare Theater Company in Washington, D.C., in 2016, and Riz Ahmed, who was on the cover of *Time* Magazine in 2017 as one of the 100 most influential people in the world, in the major role of the dashing pilot, Bodhi Rook, in *Rogue One: A Star Wars Story* (2016). Aziz Ansari, Aasif Mandvi, and Fareed Zakaria, who are all from Indian-Muslim families, are popular mainstream American television personalities. Hasan Minhaj hosted the 2017 White House Correspondents' Dinner in Washington, D.C., which the president decided not to attend.

On our journey I was reminded of the influence of Macaulay on South Asians in Melilla, Spain. At a lunch on the idyllic Mediterranean beach hosted by our interfaith friends, people talked animatedly with one another. At one point Rajkumar, a prominent Hindu leader whose family came from India, asked Harrison a question and, with his usual courtesy, Harrison began to expound with a fairly detailed answer. After a few minutes, Rajkumar interrupted him sweetly but firmly in his impeccable English accent and said that he had not understood a word Harrison had said because of the way he pronounced his words. We were taught, Rajkumar said proudly, to enunciate each word clearly and slowly, while you use three words at one time.

Upon their arrival, the first hard-laboring generation of Muslims in the United Kingdom, mainly from rural backgrounds in South Asia, had few expectations and tended to keep their heads down. They understood that though they were British citizens from the British Empire, they were not equal to white British citizens, and that life in England would never be a bed of roses for them. It is the second and third generations, born and growing up British and therefore not prepared to accept second-class citizenship, that find themselves on the horns of a dilemma: they are pleased to possess legal passports, but are aware they may not be fully accepted in society because of their religious and ethnic backgrounds.

This can lead the young generation to shun the society that their parents and grandparents had embraced; many of them have rejected Macaulay's legacy. Here is Amineh describing the scene when we rushed little Anah to the hospital in Bradford after she injured herself in their hotel room:

> Unfortunately, we had to wait in the emergency room for about three hours to see the doctor with about a dozen local women, all of them wearing the full black *niqab* and *abaya*. They were all young, spoke English with a Bradford accent, and were not friendly or social. When two white boys in grey tracksuits walked by, one of the women wearing a niqab opened a Quran and began to read it, as if to ward off evil.

### The British Definition of Identity

The fate of the minorities in European countries, as demonstrated in the discussion in the last two chapters, is tied intimately to the definition of national identity. In the case of the British, modern identity is multilayered and unresolved. With the empire long gone, the real possibility of Scottish independence looming on the horizon, and the unexpected separation from the European community represented by Brexit, a wide range of British society, including immigrants, fears a rise in primordial and predator identity. Modern Britain itself marks an incorporation of four ethnic groups: the English, the Scottish, the Welsh, and the Irish. The English—the base of British identity—are heavily indebted to their Germanic background. The foundation for the English legal system—the Magna Carta, signed in 1215—was the result of English barons reinforcing "Germanic customary law" and primordial identity that "upheld the supremacy of law over kings."[4] The Viking ancestry of the English, which links with one of the many Germanic groups that formed the English, is referred to by no less an authority than that unmatched observer of the human race, P. G. Wodehouse, who in one of his most popular novels, *The Code of the Woosters*, describes the mood of Jeeves, possibly his greatest literary creation, in the words of Bertie Wooster, his employer, as colored by his lineage: "That old Viking strain of yours has come out again. You yearn for the tang of the salt breezes. You see yourself walking the deck in a yachting cap. Possibly someone has been telling you about the Dancing Girls of Bali."

When I asked Sir Nicholas Barrington, over tea and scones by the Cam River in Cambridge, to define English identity, he named Shakespeare as well as an English "tradition of continuity" stretching over centuries, naming the "judicial systems" and England's status as the "father of democracy." All these, said Barrington, my friend for decades and a former British High Commissioner to Pakistan, "we can be proud of." Barrington also framed English identity in terms strikingly similar to the Germanic notion of Heimat. English identity was "the beautiful countryside," he said, and he gestured to the serenity around us as stately swans glided by within reach. Poets during the First World War like Rupert Brooke, who wrote so lovingly of Grantchester, a village not far from where we sat and one of my favorite spots in England, "were in the most awful conditions . . . but they were thinking of their fields at home, and the rivers at home."

Like many from the imperial past, Barrington, who was stationed at the British Embassy in Afghanistan in 1959 and arrived in Pakistan for his first tour in 1965, had a soft spot for the peoples he encountered. In his case he was "entranced" when he "first met Islam" in Spain and Morocco as a young man, and he chose to learn Persian when he was appointed to the Foreign Office. While in Pakistan, Barrington was involved in a project that would prove to be of critical importance in the story of Pakistani immigration to the United Kingdom: the construction of the Mangla Dam near Mirpur, the largest city of Pakistani Azad Kashmir. "When I was in Pakistan," he explained, "I went to visit the Mangla Dam, which was central to the operation of the Indus Valley water system and for the agricultural development of Pakistan. Many villages were flooded there, and it was a time when we needed labor in the Yorkshire mills, and many Pakistani Muslim workers came over and worked in Britain. That was the first influx." While their descendants "have found themselves lost" and are "between two cultures," he also noted with pride that Britain has "huge numbers of Pakistani Muslims as councilors in local British government. We have two British cabinet ministers who have been Muslims, not from any other non-Christian religion that I know of, except of course Jewish, which is rather remarkable when you think about it."

When discussing identity with Muslims and non-Muslims alike during our fieldwork, the distinction between "English" and "British" identity was consistently raised. For the English like Barrington, there was not much of a difference: "I'm English and British," he said. British citizens with non-English backgrounds, however, drew a sharper distinction. The celebrated Indian-born Hindu political theorist Lord Bhikhu Parekh, whom we interviewed in London and in his home in Hull, said, "Being English means a certain kind of color, being white. It also means, by and large, a particular kind of religion, not necessarily Christian, but Judeo-Christian. An Englishman can't be a Muslim or a Hindu. . . . But I will certainly call myself British, because Britain is a political entity, of which I'm a citizen."

In London, Jonathan Benthall, a prominent British anthropologist who is of Jewish background, similarly explained to us the impossibility of someone who is not of English blood being accepted as English. "There is a social anthropologist called Sir Raymond Firth, who is a New Zealander, who said to me once, 'I am British, I have a British passport, but I can never be English like you can be English.' I think that's what a lot of people whose parents or grandparents have come to this country from former colonies feel certainly. They can say they're 'British Muslims,' but can't say they're 'English Muslims.'" English, Benthall said, "has connotations of being white," and "I'd rather call myself British really."

Displaying the famous self-deprecating sense of humor of the English, Jon Snow, the main anchor for Channel 4 News, described the English to us as "unquestionably the dullest" of Britain's four ethnic nations, who "have very little to say for themselves," in contrast to the Scots and Welsh, who have a more visible and defined identity. "It's much easier," he said, "to call ourselves British, and we're defined in part by each other" as well as "the other," and he noted the "huge diaspora of different nations living here in London . . . a very culturally diverse society." Snow's description of his Zimbabwean wife confirmed the phenomenon of immigrants from the former colonies who identify closely with the mother country. "She's more English than I am," Snow said. "She's a Catholic, educated in a convent school, etc. And I would say she herself knows more about English literature than I know and is more English than I am."

Dr. Susan Fell, an accomplished medical doctor with a successful husband and outstanding children, defined her identity as English and Christian, explaining that "my Englishness, my religion, and my own immediate family are the essence of my identity." Dr. Fell, who lives in Cambridge, spoke about the "good things" that were "part of the whole myth of being British, if you like. We're supposed to be fair-minded, and stiff upper lip, and just and inclusive, and tolerant." Yet there are "other aspects," she added, "which are not too great. We do drink too much, we can be yobbish, we can be snobbish, we can be xenophobic." She says she has friends who express "ideas and perspectives that you wouldn't have expected" and "that's always a shock." "I don't know how many people hide these feelings," she confessed. "I reject all that. . . . If that is part of being British, I'd rather adhere to what I think is morally right."

In London, we interviewed Gerard Russell, whom I first met when he was Prime Minister Tony Blair's point man on Islam and later when he served as a key British official in Iraq. Author of *Heirs to Forgotten Kingdoms* (2014), he named William Blake as one of the figures who in-

*Anah Hoti with Lord Rowan Williams in Master's
Lodge, Magdalene College, Cambridge*

spired him: "Such a curious character, but inventive—in Islam he'd probably be a Sufi, in Christianity he was a free thinker you might say." Russell
defined English identity as "a willingness or desire not to take yourself
seriously, with everything that kind of goes along with that, it's a particular form of humor really. I would say a love of nature. I would say a willingness to obey the rules—that's much more of an obvious difference from
when I lived in Saudi Arabia and other countries." The challenge of reconciling tradition to modern national identity in the face of contemporary
economic pressures, Russell suggested, was fueling the rise of far-right
movements such as the U.K. Independence Party (UKIP): "It speaks to a
loss of communication between the people who run the country and the
rest of the people. If you look at UKIP—and of course it's the great irony
of UKIP that its leader Nigel Farage has a German wife—its supporters
include people who are second-generation immigrants."

In Cambridge, I asked Lord Rowan Williams, the former archbishop of
Canterbury, who is Welsh, to define Welsh identity. He maintained, in an
illustration of Welsh primordial identity, that the Welsh have long been
"very participatory" if "not quite egalitarian" and that the economic
hardship many have endured has fostered "a powerful sense of solidarity."
There is also, he added, "a very strong commitment to literary art," particularly poetry. "When I was at school," he said, "we were obliged to

study Welsh history as well as English. So it was like having binoculars, two things to look at." Williams also explained how, in the context of English resistance to immigration, "the English themselves are a wave of immigrants from the point of view of the Welsh, rather late on the scene."

For a Scottish perspective on identity, in Edinburgh I asked Alex Salmond, the first minister of Scotland, who led the Scottish independence movement that resulted in a 2014 referendum. When the Scots voted to remain in the United Kingdom, Salmond stepped down and went on to serve as a member of the British Parliament. Salmond defined Scottish identity in open, inclusive, and pluralistic terms but highlighted, like Rowan Williams, a primordial identity that differentiated his people from England, saying "we are a nation," "one of the oldest nations in Europe." When I asked him if Scotland faces any threat, he replied that it would be "to allow distinctive traditions and culture, our economy, and our vibrancy as a country to be submerged or to disappear, or not to be allowed expression. A country cannot express itself unless it has the instruments of expression."

It was this ambiguity and uncertainty in defining what it means to be British that encouraged the organizers of the London Summer Olympics opening ceremony in 2012 to fall back on fictional characters such as James Bond and Mr. Bean. The Queen was represented more as a character from pop culture than as a dignified monarch with gravitas. British celebrities like J. K. Rowling and Paul McCartney were on hand to lend cultural authenticity to this version of Englishness. It was this idea of "cool" Britain that partly explains why Tony Blair was swept into power earlier in 1997. The disasters of his policies—especially his enthusiastic commitment to the Iraq War—would later jolt Britain out of its infatuation.

### British Muslim Male Voices

Like the distinguished Hindu and Jewish commentators noted above, the Muslims we met during fieldwork chose to define themselves primarily as British rather than English. The first generation of Muslim families who immigrated to the United Kingdom was largely rural and conservative. Pakistani Kashmiris from the Mirpur district make up 70 percent of the Pakistani population of the United Kingdom, which, in turn, forms the vast majority of the Muslims in the country. These immigrants were insular, tended to congregate together on the basis of clan loyalties, and had rigidly defined gender roles. The young men today, like the women we meet below, are torn between the traditional, rural, and highly conservative culture of their parents and that of Britain. They face social problems and prejudice in their daily lives and have a variety of ideological and sectarian loyalties (as discussed by the British Muslim author Sadek Hamid in his *Sufis, Salafis, and Islamists: The Contested Ground of British Islamic Activism*, 2016). Recent developments such as the increasing English nationalism and xenophobic feelings aroused by Brexit, which seven in ten Muslims voted against, only puts them more on the defensive.

## The Lord Mayor of Bradford

In Bradford, Lord Mayor Khadim Hussain, a member of the Labour Party at the time of our fieldwork, hosted me in his office at city hall. Hussain stated that as lord mayor he was "the representative of the Queen" and he explained the difference between lord mayors and ordinary mayors, noting that there were "only 25 lord mayors in all of England, the rest are mayors." Hussain, who identified as "a British Muslim," came with his parents from Kashmir in the 1960s at the age of seven. He marveled at the distance he had traveled from the time his family had arrived to work in the mills to becoming lord mayor of a major British city with an illustrious history: "Bradford in 1910 was the richest city in Europe and third richest in the world, because it was the center of the woolen trade." Of the 530,000 population of Bradford today, he explained, about 100,000 are of Pakistani-Kashmiri origin who arrived mainly at the time of the construction of the Mangla Dam. But he also spoke of the diversity of the city and pointed out that it elected Marsha Singh, a Sikh, as its first Asian member of Parliament. He additionally talked with pride of the Brontë sisters who had lived nearby, though he regretted his community showed little interest in them.

Turning to the challenges faced by the young generation of Pakistanis, the lord mayor discussed drug use and the controversy around "grooming," the disgusting practice of men deliberately providing drugs and alcohol to vulnerable young girls to "groom" them for purposes of sex. He admitted "grooming" did unfortunately involve young Pakistanis. He added with some indignation that other communities were also involved in this practice but only Pakistanis were accused of targeting white girls, to underline a racist element in the sensationalist reporting. He was working closely with the police to defeat the scourge. "The people who are third and fourth generation," he said, "class themselves as British because they are born here, bred here, they are British. But if the society as a whole does not accept them just because they are Muslim, then despondency creeps in, frustration takes over, and then on top of that you're unemployed." He told us that "the Muslim population in the U.K. is probably approaching

5 percent, but the prison population is 15 to 20 percent Muslim." Making matters worse, he complained, were the actions of the Islamophobic far-right groups like Britain First, who even showed up at his house and intimidated his daughter (see chapter 8).

In March 2016, after concluding his tenure as lord mayor, Hussain was suspended by the Labour Party for anti-Semitism after sharing a post on Facebook "that complained that the deaths of millions of Africans are not taught in schools but 'your school education system only tells you about Anne Frank and the six million Zionists that were killed by Hitler.'"[5] The action came in the midst of an anti-Semitism controversy involving Labour that resulted in other politicians being suspended, including the Bradford MP Naz Shah, whom we also met during fieldwork. Hussain stated that the allegations of anti-Semitism were "unfounded" and resigned from the party, vowing to continue his political career as an independent candidate. These controversies surrounding senior Muslim figures who served as role models for the community only heightened the atmosphere of tension surrounding it.

### The BBC Commissioning Editor for Religion

At the BBC headquarters in London we met Aaqil Ahmed, the British-born son of Pakistani immigrant parents who arrived in Britain from Lahore in 1961 and was the first Muslim commissioning editor for religion and head of religion and ethics at the BBC. Discussing his identity, he said, "I probably feel more British than white English people." His father, he said, "has an understanding of the British Empire, of what it means to be British."

Ahmed, whose role models included Imran Khan, Muhammad Ali, and the British rock star Paul Weller, said he has had the opportunity to create a number of television programs relating to Islam that have made an impact on the larger British public. "Many people in the U.K., they won't know about me," he said, "but they'll know about my investigation into the corruption of the halal meat industry twenty or so years ago, which changed the whole nature of how we now consume and regulate halal meat. . . . I was in charge of the first season of programs on Islam, which included the first-ever documentary on the *hajj* [yearly pilgrimage to Mecca] on British TV."

Since the terrorist attacks in New York and Washington, D.C., on September 11, 2001, and in London on July 7, 2005, Ahmed said, "the mood has changed" among both Muslims and non-Muslims. "There's a breakdown in the relationship in what are British values, liberalism as well."

Ahmed believed it was critical to have normalized views of Islam. To illustrate this point, Ahmed highlighted Muslim football players. "We've got forty, over forty, forty-five Muslims playing in the Premier League. From Africa, from Asia, from Europe, Manchester City, just to use an example of Edin Džeko who's a Bosnian, Samir Nasri who is French Algerian, you've got Yaya Touré from Africa. We've got Demba Ba at Chelsea. . . . When Demba Ba scores a goal, he then goes down and prostrates on the ground. And you have football fans cheering his name. This normality is how we will build relationships."

## ONE OF THE LARGEST LANDLORDS IN ENGLAND

Mohsin Akhtar arrived in England in 1952 with only ten pounds in his pocket; today he owns Heydon Grange golf course and farm near Cambridge, with holdings of two and a half thousand acres. We visited Akhtar, a friend of mine from the time I was in Cambridge in the 1990s, and he showed us the golf course and the main hall, which is 650 years old, and explained that John Major, Benazir Bhutto, Nawaz Sharif, and Pervez Musharraf had all been frequent visitors. The convivial Akhtar was effusive in his praise of England, remarking, "It's a wonderful country, the people. . . . There is no color bar here." "I'm aware of the class system here," he admitted. "You're a gentry if you own land, if you're a professional you don't mix with ordinary working people, but I try to mix with everyone, they're human beings." Since opening the golf course, Akhtar explained, "I've been doing a lot for charities. Anybody who needs a voucher or a bit of money, I'm happy to make a donation. The local hospital, I've given so much per month as a standing order, and they come and want to play golf, I say it's all free, and I feel very privileged and honored to do it, really."

Akhtar also spoke of the turmoil in the Muslim community and observed many of the problems have to do with the lack of Muslim leadership. "I think it's the fighting within the community—Sunni, Shia, Wahhabi—and fighting for control of the mosque. They are fighting and they still haven't learned. I think they've got to reach out, there is some sort of barrier, Muslims have a very bad name."

## THE PRESIDENT OF THE BRADFORD COUNCIL OF MOSQUES

Mohammed Rafiq Sehgal is the president of the Bradford Council of Mosques, the city's most important Muslim organization. He also runs a halal meat plant, which he invited us to visit. Sehgal said that the Islamic method of slaughtering an animal, which has aroused controversy in

*With leaders of the Bradford Council of Mosques*

Europe and under which a certified person kills the animal with a single quick motion, was humane and noted that "the Jewish community is doing exactly the same." He said, "There's a huge chapter in the Holy Quran, which specifically defines the welfare of animals. When they kill animals for sport, we think that's inhumane." While he respected the concerns of animal rights activists who oppose the halal method, he said that Islamophobes use it as "extra ammunition." He described halal as "probably the fastest-growing industry. I was looking at some figures and it was in billions and trillions." It also benefits Britain, as "a lot of export happens from the U.K."

Discussing the Muslim community, he spoke of the older generation's "frustration" with the youth concerning "how the young ones behave at times with the culture they pick up." The first generation also "had a lot of problems with the language," but "the young ones are speaking English in the home. My kids, they all speak English. Punjabi would be their second language." "So I'm expecting," he said, "the younger graduates and younger people to communicate with people from other faiths and communities." For Muslims, he claimed, "You can be part of Britain and have the Britishness inside of you. And we do. We feel that this is where we belong." "We're proud to be British. We're proud to be Muslims. We're proud to be Bradfordians. We're proud to have a heritage in Pakistan."

### THE FORMER DIRECTOR OF THE MUSLIM COUNCIL OF BRITAIN

In London we interviewed Muhammad Bari, a leading British Muslim and former director of the Muslim Council of Britain (MCB), one of the most prominent organizations representing Muslims in the United Kingdom. Bari was born in a village in Bangladesh and served in the Bangladesh

Air Force before moving to London to pursue a Ph.D. at King's College in physics.

Bari, who named Newton, Einstein, and Rumi among his role models, said, "Muslims overall, they feel more British than other British." Despite this, Bari felt that "Muslims are seen through the monochromatic lens of security." He was frank about the challenges of the Muslim community. "Muslims are very good at giving money to mosques," which he described as the "hardware" of the community, but in terms of the "software," the people themselves, they "lack confidence, and their knowledge is shallow." There was also, he admitted, a lack of support for the MCB in the community.

He was also concerned about what he called "Muslim nutters" and was worried about the younger generation. "There is a level of despondence that can make them further introvert, insular, and make them more ghettoized, so that is the danger." He spoke of a disconnect between the old and the young and predicted that fifty years from now, because of the onslaught against them, Muslims will shy away from public life and either turn toward Salafism or will become totally "diluted" in their religion.

Expounding on the topic of Salafism, Bari said that some people don't consider wearing a tie or Western dress as "good" or "enough Muslim." People say, he continued, "We want a *khalifa*, by which they mean good governance," but he explained that these terms get "hijacked." Comparing his community in the United Kingdom with the United States, he said with some envy that America was fortunate in that it got "the cream of the cream of the Muslim world."

## The Media Director of the East London Mosque

In the majority Bangladeshi neighborhood of Tower Hamlets in London, we visited the East London Mosque, one of the largest and most prominent in Britain. Bari accompanied us and introduced us to his protégé, Salman Farsi, a young British native of Bangladeshi descent who is the media and communications officer for the mosque. Farsi echoed Bari in discussing the challenges facing the community. "I think since 9/11 and 7/7, there has been a hysteria in the press about Muslims and Muslim communities, and since then it's just been turned up against the Muslim communities living in here, in Europe, and now it's reached a stage where it's a bit intolerable. And it's affecting our communities, affecting our behavior."

"Every single part of our community is under scrutiny," Farsi complained. "From what we eat to the way we dress to the women in our community, to the schooling and education our children receive, everything is under scrutiny." Such pressure, he has found, "amplifies certain extremist elements within our own community." Farsi also criticized how many older British Muslims tend to exclude the youth from their worship practices. "That's not the way the Prophet would have treated young children, especially if you're trying to encourage them to be very good Muslims."

"I think only a handful of older Muslims understand" the importance for the older generations to reach out to the youth and make them feel included, he asserted. "This is the future generation. If there's no connection with them, then there'll be trouble to come."

## THE FIRST MUSLIM CHAPLAIN IN THE BRITISH ARMED FORCES

Imam Asim Hafiz, the first Muslim chaplain in the British armed forces, joined us for dinner at American University on his visit to Washington, D.C. in 2016. Hafiz is the Islamic religious adviser to the chief of the defense staff and service chiefs and was nominated to his present post in 2005. In 2014 he was given the Order of the British Empire in recognition of his work. Hafiz, who was born in East London to an Indian Gujarati family, admitted that initially the Muslim community was suspicious of him, asking how he could be Muslim and work in the armed forces, but now this has changed.

Before his appointment, Hafiz was an imam in the prisons. He painted a bleak picture of the state of Islam in Britain, saying that the prevailing mood among Muslims is "despair," having previously been "anger." He also described the mood as "hopeless." "British Muslims ask, 'Where do we go?' 'Who do we go to?' 'We can't see a way out of the situation.'" In terms of Muslim leadership, there is currently "nobody" at the steering wheel. Hafiz said that Muslims are being "demonized" and that Islamophobia is on the rise.

The Muslim community, Hafiz said, contributes billions to the British economy. They have produced the best thinkers, doctors, and other professions. They are proud to be British, and "they reject terrorism." But after the recent attacks in Paris and Brussels, Hafiz regretfully explained, kids were asking their parents, "Should we say we're Muslim?" Speaking about extremism in the Muslim community, Hafiz said we are at a "tipping point" and "if we don't grab our youth now, we're going to lose another generation. . . . But I'm worried it's going to get worse before it gets better."

## AN IMAM IN NORTH LONDON

In the Finsbury Park neighborhood in Islington, London, we interviewed Imam Toufik Kacimi, a prominent imam and leader in the Muslim community who is the co-president of the interfaith organization

Christian-Muslim Forum. He is also CEO of the Muslim Welfare House, where we met him, a prominent Muslim charity, mosque, and community center with a mixed population including North Africans and Somalis. Unlike the Muslim voices above, Kacimi is not part of the majority Pakistani and South Asian population but came to the United Kingdom from Algeria in 1996. Echoing the imam in Marseille we met earlier, Kacimi said, "We are so lucky to live in this country." "Britain is the best. France is worse. Germany is even worse." Muslims, he said, were the "best citizens for all European countries to dream of."

Despite his warm feelings toward Britain, Kacimi was extremely concerned about the current situation. The media, he said, "makes Islam look evil." He was frustrated that real Muslim leaders are ignored by the media in favor of people like Anjem Choudary, the British Islamic radical convicted of supporting ISIS, who speaks like he is in a "fantasy film saying things like we should kill white nations," and Abu Hamza, the notorious former imam of the nearby Finsbury Park Mosque convicted of terrorism, who is "not an Islamic scholar" and is a "nobody." He mentioned a mosque in Muswell Hill, three miles away, which was burned to the ground. Looking to the future, he was "not optimistic." If you have a different opinion from others, "people think you are a terrorist."

Kacimi's fears for his community were realized in June 2017 when a white man driving a van and screaming "I want to kill all Muslims" plowed into a crowd of worshippers, who were leaving Ramadan prayers near the Muslim Welfare House, killing one person and injuring ten. When a crowd wrestled the killer to the ground, the imam of the Muslim Welfare House, Mohammed Mahmoud, intervened to save the man's life, saying "No one touch him—no one! No one!" Mahmoud was hailed as the "hero imam" in the British press. Kacimi and Mahmoud welcomed Prince Charles to the mosque shortly after the attack and the prince said he was "deeply impressed" with the imam's actions and "Her Majesty's thoughts and prayers are with you all."

## A SUFI IMAM IN LONDON

Sheikh Babikir Ahmed Babikir was born and raised in Sudan, where he received his religious training and joined what he described as "one of the biggest schools of Sufism in Sudan," the Sammaniya Sufi Order. Babikir is the founder and director of both Rumi's Cave, a popular community center where we interviewed him, and Ulfa Aid, a global relief charity. He also served on the board of Prince Charles's Mosaic charity to help youth from disadvantaged backgrounds and was the imam of the

Islamia Primary School founded by Yusuf Islam or Cat Stevens. He initially came to Britain in 1977 to study business management and help his family. When he arrived, "it was a shocking experience that I had, because there were no mosques. The only mosque that was built as a proper mosque in London, beautifully built, was the Central Mosque or Baker Street Mosque. The rest were houses, and there were not many of them." "Today," he claimed, "there is no town or city around Britain where there is no mosque."

Despite how accepting Britain was, Sheikh Babikir noted, communities faced threats stemming from ignorance. Sheikh Babikir believed that Muslims should educate the world about Islam by example: "If non-Muslims want to come in, welcome. The mosque doesn't belong to the community; it belongs to God. Number two, Islam, it is not the ritual that we act upon, Islam is sharing your food and sharing greetings with those whom you know and those you don't. This is Islam."

### British Muslim Female Voices

We noted a new generation of dynamic Muslim women who had overcome considerable obstacles to succeed in British society, despite having grown up in a conservative domestic environment. Many of these women, whose fathers worked in the mills of northern England, had to first fight the highly patriarchal family structure, go through the traditional marriage, often to their cousins and frequently to men living in Pakistan, sometimes split from their husbands, and finally, triumphantly, discover their own individual voices and new expressions of their identity while maintaining their integrity. This new, confident generation of modern British Muslim women was being overlooked by the media in discussions of Muslim society in favor of the negative angry-Muslim-male stereotype.

### THE BARONESS WHO LED THE TORIES

In Bradford, we interviewed Baroness Sayeeda Warsi, whose life had followed the trajectory above. Warsi made her name on the national stage as a major political figure, an experience she describes in her autobiography *The Enemy Within: A Tale of Muslim Britain* (2017). She was, like us, in Bradford for the celebrated Bradford Literature Festival, run by two dynamic young Pakistani-British Muslim women, Irna Qureshi and Syima Aslam, whose lives had progressed in a similar fashion, including marriage at a young age and a subsequent divorce. Warsi, who was born in Yorkshire, was made a member of the House of Lords as Baroness in 2007.

*Author with Baroness Sayeeda Warsi at
the Zoya Pakistani restaurant in Bradford*

She took us for a magnificent breakfast at a Pakistani restaurant in Brad-ford, where, with a wry sense of humor, she recounted how she had found herself, at the age of thirty-six, as part of an institution in which the aver-age age of the members was sixty-nine. She told us that her father, who heroically brought up five girls, took pride in the fact that, in 2010, his daughter was the first Muslim in history to become co-chair of the Con-servative Party, but he took greater pride in the fact that she had the cour-age to resign from government on a matter of principle over British policy toward the war in Gaza in August 2014.

## A YOUNG SCHOLAR IN BRADFORD

In Bradford, Amineh interviewed a young Pakistani woman who was pursuing a Ph.D. and asked to remain anonymous, so we will call her Nadia. "When I'm around South Asian men, I feel claustrophobic," she confessed. "When I'm in the Western world—I mean in academia with all of the professors around—I'm a very confident person. But the moment I'm in my own community, confidence just drops. It's because I feel like my own community doesn't want to hear my voice." Nadia, who wore the hijab, said that people were overlooking the important roles that Aisha and Khadija, two of the Prophet's wives, played in the founding of Islam. "I think those examples are forgotten, because of culture. In South Asian culture, religion is kind of diluted with cultural values. . . . I deliver lectures to 500 students, but plant me in a room with ten imams and I'll find it very difficult."

She named her role models as her father, who she praised as "humble," and her aunt, who she said was the first person in her family to go to university. Nadia explained that her aunt had an arranged marriage at "a very young age" and that she was taken to Pakistan for the wedding. Her aunt told Nadia, "When my father took me to Pakistan to marry me, it wasn't a wedding. It was like my father took me to a room and said to another man, rape my daughter." Yet her aunt then got a divorce, which freed her to go to university. Her aunt, Nadia said, is once again married, and this time happily. Not only that, but her aunt "still has a positive relationship with her father. So she was not only able to build herself, but she was also able to kind of open her father's eyes. And that was fantastic, because that is one of the things that women who are suppressed forget. That there is light at the end of the tunnel, you just have to try."

Nadia also noted the "segregation" between communities in Bradford, which she attributed to the British class system: "There is this class divide, between South Asians too in fact. . . . White people who are in a hierarchy of white organizations will not allow the working class, whether Caucasian or South Asian, to progress."

## A British Islamic Scholar

In Edinburgh, we met Mona Siddiqui, professor of Islamic and Inter-religious Studies at the University of Edinburgh and a prominent British Islamic scholar who regularly appears in the British media. Siddiqui was born in Karachi, Pakistan. Her father, a psychiatrist, moved her family to Britain in the late 1960s, when Siddiqui was about four years old, and settled in West Yorkshire.

Siddiqui, who has had a contentious relationship with the Muslim community, admitted, "What I wanted to do was always to talk of Islam with a kind of self-critical approach. And especially when I first started appearing on radio and television, a lot of people were upset. I would always argue, 'Look, I'm a Muslim, but it's not in any of our interest to be talking about Islam in a way that makes no sense to the wider community.'" "Muslims are the ones who are least performing, less than Sikhs and Hindus," she confessed. "I'm not saying there aren't genuine problems with some communities," such as "economic deprivation." "I hate the word Islamophobia," she noted, "but there is Islamophobia everywhere." Ultimately, however, "you either live as a victim, or you go out and do something about it."

## A Social Activist in London

Humera Khan, a co-founder of the An-Nisa Society, which aids Muslim women, moved to the United Kingdom with her family from Pakistan when she was a year old. She named her role models as the Prophet of Islam, Malcolm X, Florence Nightingale, and Jane Austen. She saw British identity as "an amalgamation of a long history, of lots of different cultures and tribes and nations coming to Britain over the centuries, millennia."

Khan, who wore a colorful headscarf, finds that she is constantly challenged by the mainstream perception of Muslim women—particularly the head covering. "In the Western world," she asserted, "the choices women make for the way they dress are very varied, so why is it alright for white women to have variety and not for us?"

"I feel that to understand for myself as a woman, to understand what Islam is about, how it speaks to me, it's a really a deep spiritual journey, and it's not easy to explain to somebody who's not interested in that and just wants to attack me for the choices I make in my life." Khan, who has been an activist in the media for years, concluded with disappointment that "tackling Islamophobia has failed." As a result, she admitted, "I've stopped getting involved in so many things, I've stepped back from it, because there's absolutely no point in having a dead-end argument, getting angry about it, and nothing happens, nothing changes. It's just pointless. If the government and the media are serious for change, then they have to be serious in the way that they look at the issues themselves first."

### *The Muslims of Scotland*

In chapter 2, we outlined the primordial identity that lies at the base of European societies with a tribal background. Scotland presents us with another model of a primordial tribal society, one that has largely included immigrants. In our meeting, First Minister Alex Salmond perfectly summed up Scottish identity by referring to the tartan. Pointing to my

*Alex Salmond, the first minister of Scotland, gives
author gift of a tartan tie in Edinburgh*

tartan tie, he said, "I notice, my friend professor, that you are wearing a tartan tie. Well, I love tartan and I'm going to present you with another tartan so you'll have a choice of tartans."

Salmond went on, without pause or hesitation and with an extraordinary eloquence that any statesman would envy, to describe what he meant: "Tartan is a very special cloth which is woven in a very particular way of many different colors and shades and designs, and it comes together, each tartan distinctive in itself with a combination of all of these colors and threads within it. And I like to think of Scotland like a great tartan with all the distinctive threads and communities woven to make that very special cloth."

"Your project," he continued, "I'm going to describe as the 'tartan project'—because your project is going to explain to people on a worldwide canvas of the particular contribution that Muslims have made throughout history." It is thus no surprise that Muslim after Muslim in Scotland told us that they felt Scottish, while frequently comparing themselves with Muslims in England who did not identify as English. Many Muslims we met supported Scottish independence. Thus Scottish "tartan tribalism" is a form of tribalism that is flexible enough to accept immigrants with different religious and racial backgrounds. This is an important example of convivencia in the Northern European context and the equivalent of Palermo mayor Leoluca Orlando's definition of Sicilian identity as a "mosaic."

While shooting *Living Islam* for the BBC in the early 1990s, I saw firsthand the striking identification local Muslims had with Scottish identity. At that time, I came across a small Muslim community of Pakistani origin, about fifty in number, on the remote island of Stornoway in the Outer Hebrides (hence the subtitle of the BBC book that accompanies the series, *From Samarkand to Stornoway*). The Muslims of Stornoway spoke with a broad local Gaelic accent that was at times difficult for me to understand. They reiterated, "We are real Scots," adding "but also Muslims." When I visited, the senior member of the community owned the biggest car and the biggest store on the island and employed more than a dozen local Scots. He had maintained the original name of the store, James Mackenzie. These Muslims even showed me the small plot they had purchased in the local Christian cemetery.

It is important to note that today while Muslim immigrants in Scotland repeatedly spoke of their feelings of pride in their Scottish identity, they have not been free from the Islamophobia targeting Muslims across Europe, including attacks on women wearing the hijab and on Muslim establishments. Muslim leaders repeatedly stressed to us, however, the support, trust, and close relations they enjoyed with the Scottish authorities, which they again compared favorably with the situation in England. (For a recent account of the community in Scotland, see Stefano Bonino's *Muslims in Scotland: The Making of Community in a Post-9/11 World*, 2016.)

## THE FIRST MUSLIM ELECTED OFFICIAL IN THE UNITED KINGDOM

In his home in Glasgow, we met Bashir Maan, an old friend and distinguished public figure. The first elected Muslim politician in the United Kingdom, Maan is also the author of the 2008 book *The Thistle and the Crescent*, which chronicles the history of the interactions between Scotland and Islam. Discussing Scottish identity, he noted, "I wrote the history in my first book, *The New Scots*." "From the dawn of history, people have been coming to Scotland. There is nobody who can say 'I am the real Scot.' So, when we the Asians came, naturally they were the New Scots."

South Asian Muslims began arriving in Scotland in the 1920s, Maan explained, and became peddlers, as there was a lack of factory jobs. They traveled from place to place, selling their goods in a trade that they learned from the local Jewish community. Maan left his home in Punjab in Pakistan in 1953 and came to Britain as a student. He soon became involved in the Scottish Pakistani community, which consisted of about 200 people at the time. Wanting to make a difference in the community, he joined the Labour Party in 1964 and, in 1968, was appointed justice of the peace—the first person of a non-Scottish ethnicity to be appointed in Scottish history. In 1970 he stood in the elections for councilor in Glasgow against four Scottish candidates and won, which he described as a "miracle." "That shows you," he exclaimed, that "the best people here . . . take you as you are. If you're a good man, they follow you."

Maan explained why Muslims entered political life in Scotland before England: "It didn't happen in England because the two cultures, the behaviors of the two people, are totally different. Scottish people, they sympathize with oppressed people because they have been oppressed by the English all their life, and when in India, during the colonial days, they were more sympathetic to their subjects, the Indians, than the English, and the English hated them for that. They didn't want them too friendly with the local people because the English didn't ever make a friend of the local people." Maan, who advocated Scotland's staying as part of the United Kingdom, was full of praise for Britain, the country in which he was able to do so well: "I had a wonderful life in this country. . . . The Queen made me the Commander of the British Empire. . . . I have done very well, I think, more than I had expected."

## A Scottish Cabinet Minister

When I met with Alex Salmond at his office in the Scottish Parliament in Edinburgh, he made a point of inviting two young Muslim stars from his Scottish National Party. One was Humza Yousaf and the other was Tasmina Ahmed-Sheikh, who would go on to run successfully for the British Parliament and we will meet her below. Yousaf, the Scottish minister for transport and the islands and a Scottish MP, was, when we interviewed him in 2014, serving as the first-ever Scottish minister for Europe and international development. He was also involved in the independence movement on behalf of his Scottish National Party led by Alex Salmond. Yousaf's father came to the United Kingdom in 1964 from Pakistan to work in Glasgow; his mother was from a South Asian Kenyan family who immigrated to Britain in 1968. His father has had his own business for thirty-five years.

Yousaf spoke about the impact of the first generation of immigrants on Scotland: "The reason why the Pakistani community, when they came here in the sixties, particularly in the sixties, were so well thought of was that they opened up shops, takeaways, restaurants, and they employed local people. The reason things are so much better is because people saw that contribution that was being made and it led to dialogue."

Yousaf, who said his role models were Malcolm X and Nelson Mandela, explained that Scottish identity is characterized by what he called a "civic nationalism," which he described as "open and inclusive." Yousaf compared this with the "type of nationalism that you see across Europe." This includes, according to Yousaf, England: "I've never been asked once as a Scot, whether I'm Scottish first or Muslim first, or whether I'm Scottish or Pakistani, and 'which identity do you choose over the other.' . . . That's not necessarily the experience of my friends south of the border." But even the optimistic Yousaf voiced alarm at the emerging situation in Europe: "There seems to be a xenophobic tidal wave sweeping across Europe currently, with Islam as one of the main targets in the spotlight."

## A Member of the British Parliament

In an interview in Glasgow, Tasmina Ahmed-Sheikh, who was elected to the British Parliament in 2015, presented her vision of identity in terms as expansive as Yousaf's and with an equally distinct Scottish accent: "The biggest thing I would say it means to be Scottish is that you can be absolutely anything you want to be. We absolutely don't define people by where they come from. If people ask me what I am, I usually say I am a Scottish-Asian, and a proud one."

The multitalented Ahmed-Sheikh—a lawyer focusing on minority rights, an actress who starred in Pakistani dramas, and the founding chair of the Scottish Asian Women's Association—comes from a diverse background. Her father arrived from Pakistan in the 1960s, and her mother was of Welsh-Czechoslovakian background. She passionately believed that Muslims and Muslim women can contribute to European society. "We follow the teachings of the Quran. Beyond that, though, you have to abide by the laws of the country which you've chosen to call home. We are law-abiding citizens, wherever that may be, whether it's in France, Germany, Scotland, or England."

## A Muslim Leader in Scotland

At the Edinburgh Central Mosque, we met Zareen Taj, the chair of the Muslim Women's Association of Edinburgh and a prominent leader in the Muslim community. At a gathering in the mosque of young Muslim mothers who wore the hijab and were accompanied by their children, who were playing with great joy and energy, Amineh asked Taj why Muslims are stereotyped for not treating their women equally. She replied,

> Because we don't conform to Western ideas of how we should behave, we cover up, we cover our head, some women cover their face. That empowers us to go out, we take our covering with us so we can interact, and that's different. Now I grew up in this country in the

seventies and it was quite normal for a woman to go out with a scarf on her head not being a Muslim. The Queen does it, the Queen wears a scarf on her head. It's just a covering, we do it for a spiritual reason and probably Christian women used to do it for a spiritual reason and it became just what you do to cover your hair because you don't want your hair to get messy. . . . It's considered an oppression like we're being made to do it. I can honestly say that the people I mix with in this society in Edinburgh, in Scotland, cover up out of choice. . . . The first thing in Islam is there is no compulsion in religion.

## Muslims in Ireland

There is a small Muslim community in Ireland that is also part of the legacy of British imperialism, and we had an opportunity to meet its members during our fieldwork in Dublin.

### A Successful Immigrant Family

Mian Ghulam Bari, of Punjabi ethnicity from Pakistan and head of one of Ireland's most prominent Muslim families, was already established in the clothing business when, some four decades ago, I was his house guest in the countryside outside Dublin. Bari's family flourished, and two of his sons are now prominent figures in Ireland—Mazhar Bari, the founder and CEO of Biometric Technology Solutions, and Ashar Bari, who ran the clothing business, Barry & Sons—the Pakistani name Bari adapted to the Irish Barry. Like many evenings previously, I spent a pleasant evening at Mian Bari's comfortable home in Dublin during fieldwork, enjoying the best possible Pakistani food prepared by the family. The Pakistan ambassador to Ireland joined us for the evening.

### An Irish Imam

Imam Muhammad Umar al-Qadri is the imam of the Al-Mustafa Islamic Centre on the outskirts of Dublin and has a diverse congregation. We talked to his students and were his guests for lunch. Imam al-Qadri noted that as many Irish have emigrated to other countries such as America and Australia, "I think they understand better than anyone else how it is to be a minority." "When I arrived here in 2005 from Pakistan," he said, "I would walk down the shopping center, and some people would address me as doctor, thinking that I am a medical doctor, because I have a beard and most Muslims were medical doctors." There are, however, problems

*Amineh with Muslim women in Ireland*

within the Muslim communities in Europe: "Muslims have, as a community, decided to isolate themselves not only from the outside community but within the Muslim community. You have the Pakistanis who have their Pakistani mosque, you have the Africans who have their African mosque, you have the Turks who have their own mosques and there is no unity between these communities." Al-Qadri believed that the Muslim community's "biggest responsibility is that we try to eliminate those misconceptions and misunderstandings and challenge the narrative that is found in the media. Our code, conduct, and attitude should speak for itself." Given his positive experiences, Al-Qadri believed that Muslim immigrants in Ireland will ultimately be viewed as Irish, much like the Irish immigrants to the United States were ultimately seen as American. "The Muslims in Europe," he concluded, "they have their own identity, they're not just Muslims" from places like Pakistan or Turkey. "They are European Muslims, and a lot of Muslims do not realize this. . . . We are European Muslims, and this is a new identity."

### An Irish Sufi Leader

Mia Manan Hameed, another leader in Ireland's Muslim community, is a vivacious force for interfaith conviviality and goodwill in the city. While walking with him on the streets of Dublin, we were constantly greeted by people who came up to thank him for some favor he had done them or just to say hello. He owns a popular restaurant serving South Asian dishes and organizes a major mosque, both of which have strong Sufi themes.

Mia comes from the Punjab in Pakistan and a family with a strong Sufi tradition. While in Dublin he took me to the countryside to meet a leading Sufi master who was visiting from the Punjab, and we spent the afternoon performing the Sufi *zikr*, or recitation of the glorious names of God. Mia is proud of his passion for the Prophet, whom he blesses every time he mentions his name: "Well, personally, it's my life. It's my life from morning, noon, evening, when I go to sleep. I can't go to sleep without reading the salutations to the Prophet, giving a greeting, the salaam to the Prophet." He believes there is a mystical presence among the people of Ireland, which connects them to Sufism. He called Ireland "the land of saints," and St. Patrick, the patron saint of Ireland, "Sheikh Patrick."

> Last year, I climbed the Croagh Patrick, the important mountain site of pilgrimage where Sheikh Patrick is buried, and when I climbed it I did prayer, the zikr. An amazing thing happened at that time because a group of ladies, they joined with me spiritually. They were Christians. And they go, "What are you?" And we said, "We are Muslims, we walk on the path of Sufism." And they said, "Sufism? We love Rumi!" Yeah, they love Rumi! I said, "Rumi is my love, Rumi is in everyone, you know?"

## Les Misérables—the Muslim Immigrants of France

The first French imperial foray into the Muslim world would prove to be very different from subsequent ones. In one brilliant global strategic move, Napoleon Bonaparte captured Cairo, then as now one of the key centers of the Arab world, and by allying with Tipu Sultan in India against the British, aimed to prevent India from falling into British imperial hands. Upon his arrival with his armies in Cairo, Napoleon wore Arab robes, honored the scholars of al-Azhar, declared his admiration for the Quran and the Prophet, praised the social and civil clauses of shariah law, and promised to introduce them to France. In a scene reminiscent of Frederick II's celebration of the hijra of the Prophet, Napoleon hosted a grand reception in honor of the birthday of the Prophet of Islam. He was, by now, widely known as Ali Bonaparte, named after the son-in-law of the Prophet and one of the great caliphs of Islam. In the end, Napoleon's forays in the Muslim world ended in failure, and the monarchy was restored in France.

Napoleon's approach came from his own interpretation of the Enlightenment and the core themes of the French Revolution—liberty, equality, and fraternity. But when France next embarked on an adventure in the Muslim world, in 1830, it would take a very different approach. It was this operation in Algeria that would set the tone for the entirety of French colonial rule and influence the position of Muslim immigrants in France itself.

The consequences of the French approach to colonization are in evidence in the circumstances of the immigrant community in France today. In Britain, there are twenty-five Muslim members of the House of Commons and House of Lords. In contrast, in spite of having the largest Muslim population in Europe, about twice the size of Britain's, in mid-2016 there was only one person with a Muslim background in the entire 577-member National Assembly, France's directly elected lower house of Parliament. Following the 2017 election, however, the Muslim number had increased to fifteen. The first French Muslim to ascend to the position of presidential cabinet minister, Azouz Begag, who is of Algerian Kabyle Berber descent and the author of more than twenty books—including the autobiographical novel *Shantytown Kid* (1986), which was adapted into a film—observed in 2015 that "of the 36,000 municipalities in France, perhaps only 5 are directed by councilors of Maghreb origin." "Is this normal?" he asked.[6]

## French Identity and the Challenge of Islam

French identity is tied to the notion of French civilization, including the language, literature, food, music, art, and an intense patriotic love of the idea of "Frenchness." Perhaps it is best described by Edmond Rostand's Cyrano de Bergerac from the nineteenth-century play of the same name. Cyrano possesses biting wit, a poetic tongue, irrepressible courage, and a spirit that is fiercely independent and generous. He is romantic, vain, pompous, and intoxicated with the French language. Here is Cyrano defining himself and, through that definition, French culture:

> To sing, to laugh, to dream, to walk in my own way and be alone, free, with an eye to see things as they are, a voice that means manhood—to cock my hat where I choose—At a word, a *Yes*, a *No*, to fight—or write. To travel any road under the sun, under the stars, nor doubt if fame or fortune lie beyond the bourne—Never to make a line I have not heard in my own heart; yet, with all modesty to say:

"My soul, be satisfied with flowers, with fruit, with weeds even; but gather them in the one garden you may call your own."[7]

But that definition created problems for the immigrant. If an Algerian, a former subject of the French Empire, spoke perfect French and wished to be part of French culture, could he be accepted as French? We know from the discussion in the work of Frantz Fanon, who was in Algeria during the last days of the empire, of the dilemmas these definitions created for native Africans who aspired to be French. The problem comes with those who may wear the hijab, as in the case of Muslims, or a skullcap, as in the case of Jews. French identity, based in the imperial days, is one of centralization and cultural conformity. In a legacy of the French Revolution, it rejects visible displays of religion; it is quintessentially laic.

But there are deeper cultural issues at work: Take the *Song of Roland*, the oldest and most influential epic ballad in French literature. The first known *chanson de geste*, a literary genre that celebrated heroic deeds, the *Song of Roland* recounts the seven-year war of Charlemagne against the Muslims in Spain. The eponymous hero of the story had died defending Charlemagne against the treacherous Muslims who had broken their word by attacking the rear of the king's departing army. The actual historical account of Charlemagne's expedition tells a different story: he retreated from Spain a defeated man, sacked Pamplona, a Christian city, and was then attacked not by Muslims but by the Basques.

The *Song of Roland* was composed at the time of the First Crusade, centuries after the events were supposed to have taken place. It became a rallying cry against Muslims across France, which was leading the Crusades. This French national epic has predisposed generations into a distrust and dislike of Muslims as a people. That it is based in fiction merely makes it ironic and tragic. The vision of France that it represents, which is linked to the monarchy, the Catholic Church, and the white or ethnic French, and is associated with conservative forces in French history, is still very much a feature of French identity, as seen by the emergence of the National Front (see chapter 9).

Along with this medieval background, the French Revolution, and secularism, satire is another important component of French identity. French satire—of which the French are particularly proud—aims to draw blood. French satirists have been cruelly lampooning the mighty and the powerful, whether in the military, government, or the church, at least since the Enlightenment and the French Revolution. For example, Madame Bernadette, the wife of former president Jacques Chirac, was portrayed during her husband's presidency as masturbating with her handbag in the television show *Les Guignols*. The hateful and vindictive satire of *Charlie Hebdo*, the popular Parisian magazine, goes back to Voltaire, as do the attacks on Islam. Voltaire was making a point in the context of freedom of expression and his right to criticize the high and the mighty. People who saw his plays understood who the targets were. So while Voltaire appeared to be mocking Islam, in fact he was debunking the still-powerful Catholic Church. The situation for satirists like those working for *Charlie Hebdo* is fundamentally different. There are now some 5 million Muslims in France, and unlike Voltaire's hypothetical attacks on Islam, the current satirical depiction of Muslims acts to further oppress and isolate an already oppressed and isolated minority and creates an atmosphere that encourages attacks on them.

These Muslim immigrants were never accepted as French; nor did they wish to fully integrate into French society if that meant abandoning their culture and religion. Reflecting the hard-line attitude of the government, the French immigration minister launched what became known as the "great debate" in 2009 around the banning of the Muslim veil and questions over whether France's essential identity was under threat. Early in 2016, another French cabinet minister, this time ironically holding the portfolio for women's rights, equated women who wore the veil to "American negroes who were in favour of slavery" and criticized those firms marketing the hijab as "not 'socially responsible.'"[8]

The debate about the hijab in France first arose in September 1989, with what became known as the *affaire du foulard*, the headscarf affair. The national controversy began when, in the city of Creil, in northern France, three Muslim schoolgirls were expelled for refusing to remove their headscarves in the name of laïcité. The French education minister, however, ruled that the girls could not be forced to remove their headscarves and proceeded to overturn the school's expulsion decision, which led a group of five intellectuals to publish the manifesto "Profs, ne capitulons pas!" ("Teachers, let's not surrender!"), in which they stated that allowing the headscarf in schools was akin to appeasing the Nazis in 1938. The matter of the headscarf in schools was hotly debated in French society until an outright ban was implemented in 2004, which in turn foreshadowed the ban in 2016 of the "burkini," the Muslim female bathing suit. France, it appeared, was adamant in demanding such bans, and the women who covered were equally adamant in emphasizing their right to dress according to their faith. For the French, giving in would have meant compromising their concept of a laic and secular society. The prominent philosopher

André Glucksmann referred to the headscarf as a "terrorist emblem" that is "stained with blood." For the Muslims, many of whom do not promote covering, it was, as in the case of *Charlie Hebdo*, yet another deliberate affront to their faith and culture.

### French Identity and Muslims as Internal and External Enemy

The first chapter of the distinguished French scholar Jocelyne Cesari's 2013 book, *Why the West Fears Islam*, is called "Muslims as the Internal and External Enemy." As the internal enemy, they are accused of not wishing to integrate, are told that their religion is incompatible with Western values of freedom and democracy, and are said to oppose national values such as French customs, language, and history. As the external enemy, their religion is accused of being the main cause of terrorism and of threatening Western civilization.

In interviews for this project, Cesari told us that the French approach to immigration and integration is "to minimize difference in the public space." She was critical of this approach, asking how it was possible for Islam to be seen as something exotic and foreign to France in a French classroom full of Muslim students. For Cesari, feeling alienated by the teaching in French schools is a personal matter. Her father was an Italian who had traveled to Algeria, where he married her mother, an Algerian Jew. So when Cesari was told in school that her ancestors were the Gauls, a common refrain directed to the children of the empire, she reiterated, "My ancestors are not the Gauls!"

"Algerians," she noted, "blame the French" for the exploitation in the colonial era. Cesari said she saw this in interviews with Algerians in the early 1990s in Marseille. Algerian parents told their children, "I fought the French. You cannot be French." People from the elder generation, Cesari said, told her that they were going back to Algeria. But she knew that the children would not go back. The new generation reacted against their parents, Cesari observed, and adopted "the Martin Luther King model," a more accommodating approach that says, "we are both French and Algerian."

Ronit Lentin of Trinity College in Dublin, another European professor who studies France and is Jewish, was equally concerned about the situation regarding the minorities: "France is very much an assimilationist country. There if you assimilate and behave like the French, you're okay. If you wear the hijab to school or wear the skullcap to school, then you're seen as separate and non-assimilable. And I think that's part of the problem." Lentin elaborated that discriminatory government practices in France are not recent, noting that French governments "have been racist, have been anti-Semitic, anti-Muslim, colonialists. They behaved appallingly toward their natives or their subjects in Algeria, and they had created the image of the Muslim long before these right-wing parties have emerged. . . . So the right wing is really an elaboration of the state itself."

Leading French intellectuals let their imagination run free with hyperbolic purple prose, which built on the gloomy scenario described by Cesari and Lentin. In Michel Houellebecq's 2015 novel *Submission*, France wakes up in the near future as a Muslim country. All the stereotypical horrors imaginable are rehearsed—women in veils, men enjoying polygamy, the Sorbonne taken over and run by a Muslim-only faculty, mosques everywhere and—sacré bleu—no alcohol. The novel became an instant best seller and was endorsed by Marine Le Pen, the leader of the National Front party. The Algerian novelist Boualem Sansal's 2015 novel, *2084: The End of the World,* draws a scenario as bleak as Houellebecq's, when in the near future a totalitarian nightmarish caliphate is instituted in Europe, with a city resembling Paris as its capital. For Alain Finkielkraut, French civilization and identity, which he defines as "women, literature, and cuisine," is being threatened by Islam. Finkielkraut believes there is "a clash of civilizations" occurring amid a "re-Islamizing" European Muslim population. Bernard-Henri Lévy, in *Left in Dark Times: A Stand against the New Barbarism* (2008), warns of the threat posed by "Fascislamism" and the leftists who tolerate it. In a November 2015 interview with Israel's i24 News, he declared that "Islamism . . . is the third attack on civilization. First we had Nazism, then came communism, and now today we have Islamism, which attacks all the values which we stand for." In April 2016, Lévy responded to Muslim female students at Paris's elite Sciences Po university staging a "Hijab Day" by asking, "When will there be a shariah day? Stoning? Slavery?" Éric Zemmour, the author of the best seller *The French Suicide* (2014), argues that immigration is dooming France and that French Muslims should be deported to avoid a civil war. Zemmour warned that the "white proletariat" is "helpless before the 'ostentatious virility of their black and Arab competitors seducing numerous young white women.'"[9]

In contrast, Jean-Luc Marret, an expert on Islam and terrorism at the Foundation for Strategic Research in Paris, presented a more upbeat picture of Islam in France in an interview with me. Indeed, he included Islam in his definition of French identity: "I would call that a mixture of long-term tradition based on Latinity and Gallicity, Christianity, and a more recent characteristic including Islam. There is no question about that. Islam has been part of French culture, French civilization, for sure, exactly, it is a part like Christianity, atheism, and the French Jewish, too."

Marret, who named Voltaire as his number-one role model, followed by Charles de Gaulle and Victor Hugo, spoke of the problems France is currently facing with immigrants. He said there was a tension between the acknowledged French "republican revolutionary ideas" and the reality of immigration. He explained that "as a citizen, I'm assimilationist, which means I don't see the other French citizen through his ethnicity or religious belief. I see him as a citizen having equal rights and equal duties as I have." As to how the issues surrounding immigration and Islam will be resolved, Marret reflected, "I'm pretty much optimistic, although that's very demanding."

*French Muslim Male Voices*

Our fieldwork among French Muslims allowed us to hear firsthand the challenges the minority is facing. In Marseille, a city with a Muslim population of 300,000, we were surprised to discover that there is no official mosque. Instead, Muslims are forced into seventy or so irregular prayer spaces—half of which are believed to lack proper plumbing. This is not a problem unique to Marseille. Throughout all of France, there were only five purpose-built mosques in 2002, and while more have been built recently with great difficulty, for example, in Strasbourg in 2012, it is again illustrative to make a comparison with Britain, where there are around 200 purpose-built mosques.

The Muslim population of France is nearly synonymous with the impoverished *banlieues* or suburbs, which have routinely erupted in rioting. In 2005, for example, rioting in the Paris banlieues and other French cities following the deaths of two Muslim teens while evading police resulted in 10,000 cars and 300 buildings being set on fire. Many of the Muslim citizens of Marseille live in bleak housing projects where there is a persistent crisis of organized crime—with crime bosses running entire neighborhoods—and drug trafficking. Marseille has been described in the media as France's murder capital and "Europe's most dangerous place to be young." The situation in 2012 grew so dire that Samia Ghali, the mayor of two Marseille districts and a Muslim Algerian Berber, called for the French army to intervene. Rachida Tir, who headed the resident's association of the La Savine housing project in northern Marseille, said of the young men of the community, "There is a suicidal instinct, a desperation in some of these boys. . . . They see no future. They live for the present, in a world of easy money and, now, violence."[10] It was a theme we would hear again and again.

## The Imam of the "Great Mosque in Southern France"

The prayer room of Imam Haroun Derbal's Islah "mosque" in Marseille is a large rundown room with old worn-out carpets on the second floor of a warehouse in a bustling Muslim market. Derbal proudly described it as the "Great Mosque in Southern France." It is also the city's largest—attended by as many as 2,500 people every Friday. During the interview, the electricity failed, and we were plunged into darkness. It was one of the serious social issues facing the community, Derbal complained, along with "housing, work problems, unemployment, discrimination." The Muslim community, he continued, is divided: "Unfortunately, we have mosques which call themselves Algerian mosque, Tunisian mosque, Comorian mosque. In some districts, neighborhoods, you have two mosques, and people ask you, 'Which mosque do you go to? Do you go to the Algerian one, the Comorian one?'" Furthermore, Derbal explained, France lacks national Muslim leadership, noting that "we don't have here in France a personality like Tariq Ramadan. The first generation of immigrants came here to work, and they didn't think about being represented with their faith, and they didn't think they would have children here and grow in this country." The imam also explained that the reason Marseille lacks a central mosque is "a lack of political will to make it happen." His advice: "The Muslims have to take their destiny in two hands, they have to fight for their freedom and their rights. Freedom, you take it."

## A Muslim Official in the Marseille City Government

In the Marseille City Hall, we met Salah Bariki, of Algerian descent, who is the senior Muslim in the Marseille city government. He is a member of the mayor's cabinet and is in charge of relations between the mayor's office and the minority communities, especially the Muslim community. He also leads the mayor's interfaith initiatives.

Whereas Paris has the "intellectual elite" of France, Bariki explained, "in Marseille we have no intellectual elite, it's really just workers here. . . . Marseille is recognized as one of the poorest cities in France." Bariki also said there is no presence of France in Marseille and that French identity "does not exist" here. "We are first Marseillan, and after that we are Arabs, Jews, and after that we are French—the third time we are French!" he said, chuckling. He elaborated, "Marseille is a multiethnic town, and every group is considered a minority, so we are equal."

*Salah Bariki and Frankie Martin at the site of the proposed mosque in Marseille*

Bariki described the French Muslim community as "anarchy" and discussed the problem of the imams: "Everyone can proclaim himself to be imam." "Most of the imams do not speak French, but they don't speak real Arabic either," he observed. "They speak bad French and bad Arabic. When the imam speaks, for example, the Algerian dialects from the east, in front of him you have many people who are not from the east. They don't understand really what he said." Besides, the imams are "not very intellectual." People ask them questions like, "Imam, I take biscuits, but I read that there are some that are forbidden. Is it forbidden? Can I pray with my work clothes?" As a result, he noted, "Young people try to find the answers on the Internet. This is a problem also because on the Internet you can find all things."

As Bariki demonstrated to us, the community is working hard to build a central mosque, which would be a huge victory for the integration of the community. Bariki showed us the plans for the mosque and drove us to the proposed site—a dilapidated slaughterhouse marked for demolition. "Until 2005," he noted,

> the problem was that the authorities did not accept the mosque as a concept and did not accept the Muslim presence here in Marseille. Now, it's okay. In the last elections we didn't hear anything about the mosque. Until now, every election campaign was based on, should we have a mosque or not have a mosque—it was the flag for the National Front. Now the problem is really a Muslim problem, organization and financial.

Bariki had arranged a meeting at city hall with other senior officials in Marseille, including Clement Yana, the president of the regional Jewish Association of Provence-Alpes-Côte d'Azur (see chapter 7), and Aude Eisinger, the head of the mayor's cabinet. Eisinger claimed the issue of Islam in France has not been dealt with: "There are about 4 or 5 million people who have no place to pray and no place to preach and so they are in the streets and we can see them. Twenty years ago that was not the case. Today people can see them, so people are afraid because it's not dealt with by institutions who still don't want to give them some places."

### A Young Journalist and Interfaith Activist

In Marseille, we met Samir Akacha, an independent journalist and interfaith activist who works with Coexister, a national organization of more than twenty French groups. When we first met Samir, he served as the president of the Marseille chapter. In April 2016 he came to visit us in Washington, D.C., and we learned he had become the vice president of Coexister Europe and was conducting a ten-month tour of thirty-two countries to study "grassroots" interfaith dialogue as part of a team along with a French Jew, a Christian, and an atheist.

Samir summed up the goal of Coexister by saying that "it's possible to live together. We developed a theme called 'Coexistence Actif,' in Spanish it will be 'Convivencia,' to live together." He discussed some of the initiatives Coexister has taken in light of recent terrorist attacks. The head of Coexister started the "We are United" hashtag on Twitter, he said, an expression that was used by the French government and even put on the Eiffel Tower.

Reflecting on his own background and identity, Samir, who was born in Algeria and came to France in 1995 at the age of seven because of terrorism in Algeria, said he has "two mother tongues, two passports, and two identities." "For me," he admitted, "French culture is about the pursuit of freedom and knowledge." He spoke about some of the words in the French language that come from Arabic, such as *kif-kif,* meaning "the same," and told us that couscous is the most popular dish in France.

Samir has found, however, that the French are not living up to what he considered the French ideals. The concept of laïcité, he noted, has become a tool of oppression toward Muslims: "Today many young Muslim girls can't go to high school because they have the veil and they have to take it away." "People never think that Mary, the mother of Jesus, had the veil, even some Jewish women have the veil. But when it comes to Muslims, because of the remains of colonialism, people think 'they are in a state of submission' and 'they are inferior.'" "People said, 'Yes, but laïcité's really important, laïcité's in danger.' But they don't see that it is people who are in danger. It's a shame that we use it this way to justify oppression against people who believe." As a result, Samir explained, Muslim women have been attacked for merely wearing a veil. He recounted a story from Paris: "A pregnant woman had been attacked by extremists, and she lost her baby. Today Islamophobia, like anti-Semitism, can kill."

Considering the future of Muslims in France, Samir observed, "I'm really scared of people's stupidity and ignorance," and "I fear a civil war." Yet he was passionate about the impact that interfaith dialogue can have, and he vowed to keep pressing ahead. He said he wanted to name his son Jihad, noting that "it means to struggle and fight your own soul." He saw "young Muslims getting involved in politics, in the media, in medicine," who "are more and more a part of the society." Our generation, he noted, "recognizes their Muslim identity." Unlike the previous generation, "we want to settle and be part of French society. We are fully French and fully Muslim."

### French Muslim Female Voices

As in the United Kingdom, there is a young generation of women in France who are passionate and confident in their identities as French Muslims and are fighting fearlessly against immense obstacles for their equal rights as French citizens. They are concurrently challenging gender expectations stemming from the patriarchal and rural cultures from which many of their families originated. Examples include politicians such as the French-Senegalese Rama Yade, who served as secretary of state for foreign affairs and human rights; Rachida Dati, who is of Algerian and Moroccan descent and served as justice minister, member of the European Parliament, and mayor of the Seventh Arrondissement of Paris; and Najat Vallaud-Belkacem, a Berber born in the Rif mountains of Morocco, who in 2014 became the first female education minister in French history.

Fadela Amara, who was born to Algerian Kabyle Berber parents in a banlieue in the French city of Clermont-Ferrand, became known as the "ghetto warrior" for her activism on behalf of women from similar backgrounds. She became an activist when, at the age of fourteen, she saw her five-year-old brother killed by a drunk driver, and the police responded by siding with the driver and expressing racist sentiments to her parents. Amara, who was appointed French secretary of state for urban policies in 2007, headed the organization Ni putes ni soumises (Neither whores nor submissives), which described the challenges facing women in the Muslim community in its manifesto: "Socially oppressed by a society that shuts us up in ghettos that accumulate misery and exclusion. Suffocated by the machismo of men in our neighborhoods, who in the name of 'tradition,' deny our most basic rights."[11]

### A Young Social Activist in Marseille

Messaouda Akacha, like her brother Samir whom we met above, is a charismatic social activist in the Muslim community interacting with the media to improve relations between communities. Now in her mid-twenties, Messaouda, who wears the hijab, was born in Algeria and moved to France when she was six. She defined herself as being both French and Algerian. Messaouda's family, like other first-generation immigrants, faced many challenges when they arrived in France as laborers. "My grandfather passed away a few years ago," she explained, "and I remember that he said he was quite sad—because with everything that he did for France, France was not grateful."

When asked to define laïcité, Messaouda said, "When I was younger, in primary school or something, I had a teacher, and she asked me, 'What is laïcité to you?' I said, 'This is to accept all of the religions, all together.' She said, 'This is quite the contrary. It is not to have any religion at all.' . . . I would think, 'Why would you see something in a negative way rather than in a positive way?' . . . Laïcité shouldn't come to be something that is against freedom."

The French, Messaouda believed, are "very, very scared." People sometimes tell her to go back to her country or stare at her menacingly. "When they stare at me like that, what I do is just to smile at them. They're just surprised. . . . And then they smile back at me, so this is really nice. When they do that, you know, I feel like this is a small victory, this is something important. I'm not that bad, you know. I'm just like you." Messaouda was concerned that "the situation for Muslim people is getting worse. That's sad. People are more and more angry. And it's like they're keeping all of this anger. It will come out at one time or another."

### A Paris-Based Social Activist

Samia Hathroubi is a French social activist based in Paris with a particular focus on interfaith relations who frequently appears in European and international media such as CNN. Her father came from Tunisia in the late 1960s to work in a factory. She was born and raised in a small French town and went on to attend a prestigious college. A student of Greek,

Latin, and the humanities, her professors told her she was going to be part of the "elite." Wanting to give back to her community, she became a teacher and began teaching in what she called "a very disadvantaged area in the suburbs of Paris," close to the banlieues that rioted in 2005. Samia described the experience as "a turning point in my entire life, in the way that I was seeing friends, in the way that I was seeing the Republic, and in the way I was witnessing these issues that people like me were facing."

"France is blind to identities of its citizens," she believed. "They are not inclusive at all. This word inclusiveness is completely nonexistent in media discourse, and it's very complicated for us and for myself, at least, to bring those new topics and say 'wake up.'" Samia has observed the far-right narrative of Marine Le Pen emerge dominant, "not only in the extremist movement but in the Socialist Party and in the traditional Right party who are using the same narrative of Marine Le Pen and using the words '*Français de souche*,' originally French, as against immigrants with Northern African roots. And they have won: in the media, in the policy makers' discourse, and in the common belief of French people."

Samia explained that the clear differentiation between the French and the Muslims, despite the rhetoric that everyone is the same, is inherited from the colonial era. The French see Islam as fundamentally foreign and treat their Muslim citizens in the manner that "the French Empire used to treat Islam and the 'cult of Islam.'" France is "not willing to help in any way the Muslim community to build its own capacity. . . . They keep treating us as if we were citizens of foreign countries."

Expressing frustration, Samia complained that she is still not considered fully French, despite being born in France and attending elite schools: "Whatever I will say, they won't look at me as a French woman talking. But the first thing, whenever I am meeting a minister or the media, they will look at me only as a Muslim or someone of Northern African roots. And this is a failure, they should look at me as a French woman doing something or saying something interesting and not focusing only on the differences that I have, and coming only from an immigrant background."

Even though her grandfather fought against the Nazis on behalf of the French during the Second World War, Samia confessed, he has "no place" in France: "The French government has given not a penny to my grandfather for his remarkable sacrifice, until now he has a problem in his leg. So I could be very bitter against France, which I'm not." She also noted that "the first time I heard the name of Hitler it was from my grandfather, it wasn't at school. But the story of my grandfather wasn't taught in schools."

While Samia says she is not bitter, "a lot" of her friends have said they are leaving France. In fact, her mother had recently told her that she should consider leaving the country. This surprised Samia. "My mother has never said anything bad about the French or about the others. . . . But she was telling me, 'Leave this country. You will be better in the United Kingdom or the United States.'"

## A SENEGALESE-FRENCH STUDENT

In Marseille, we met Maty Seck, a student of urban studies born in Bayonne, near the Spanish border, whose background is Senegalese. She was so frustrated living in France that she considered moving back to Senegal, where she feels "accepted." She confessed that "every time" she met anyone in France she was treated badly. People talk to her as if she is "stupid," she said, even though she speaks perfect French and has a master's degree. The French are "afraid" of Muslims, she believed, and the media is hostile toward "our beautiful religion." Seck described an experience she had on a bus with a white mother and her child: "The child started to cry and she said, 'Mama, I don't want to stay here because she's black, I don't want to stay in the same bus.'" Mother and child promptly left the bus.

### "A Shrinking"

From Napoleon dressed in Arab robes hosting a dinner for the Islamic scholars of Egypt in Cairo to President François Hollande canceling an official lunch in honor of President Hassan Rouhani of Iran in early 2016 rather than accommodate his dietary preferences is a dramatic example of what Jocelyne Cesari calls "a shrinking." Hollande had chosen an expensive French restaurant for the occasion, and the Iranian president, who was also a prominent ayatollah, one of the most senior figures of Shia Islam, requested, as he was bound to do, a halal meal without wine. Yet compromising on French cuisine would essentially mean surrendering to the so-called "barbarians" threatening French civilization. The episode reflected French "defensiveness," another phrase of Cesari's. The vision of France had shrunk from an irresistible ideal that stirred and embraced the world to a set of single issues associated with one minority community—the Muslim immigrants. Jules Verne and Victor Hugo once explored universal themes that embraced human societies everywhere; now Bernard-Henri Lévy, Alain Finkielkraut, and Michel Houellebecq seemed to be obsessed with sadistically attacking the marginalized and impoverished Muslim community.

The cumulative impact of the quondam imperial experience and the repeated contemporary blows against the Muslim community combined with the current allure of the proponents of violence have created the terrorists and suicide bombers of France (see also chapter 8). The aim of the terrorists is not simply to kill: It is to cause the maximum of hurt. They are paying back in the only way they know how. Their actions have directly plunged France into a genuinely existentialist crisis with a fierce debate raging about French identity and Islam's place in it.

## Guest Workers and Immigrants among Germanic Peoples

The "miracle" of Germany's economic revival after the Second World War owes something to *Gastarbeiter*, or guest workers. Desperately needing able-bodied men willing to work long hours, West Germany entered into contracts with countries like Turkey, its ally in the First World War, to recruit workers for its factories. Starting in the early 1960s, they came in the hundreds of thousands. The nature of their contracts, which were temporary, and the fact that they came in numbers and could therefore live in their own communities meant that there was reluctance for them to lay down roots and become fully part of German society. That generation of immigrants found it difficult to speak or learn German and preferred to live in their own cultural cocoons.

It was the same in other Germanic areas such as the Scandinavian nations. For the first time in their history, Germanic populations had to deal with and accommodate millions of Muslim immigrants whose religious and ethnic backgrounds were completely different from theirs. Unlike immigrant labor in imperial Britain and France, where the vast majority came from their former colonies, the guest workers of Germanic Europe often came from societies that had no direct relationship with the European country in which they found themselves. The Dutch and the Belgians, for example, had no historical association with the thousands of Turks and Moroccans they recruited to work in their factories and mines.

The guest workers often came from rural places like Anatolia or the Rif mountains and had little if any schooling, which put the community at an added disadvantage. In an interview for this project, Ahmed Aboutaleb, a Moroccan Rif Berber who is the mayor of the Dutch port city of Rotterdam and the first immigrant mayor in the Netherlands, described the

Dutch preference for brawn over brains when handing out work permits: "They were not looking for the most intellectual people to bring them to Europe. They were looking for people, with all respect, also my father was part of them, with a good physical shape to do the hard labor." The result, he said, was a "lack of intellectual capacity" in the community.

Desiring equality and equal opportunity, the next generation is now confronting Germanic societies in which Islam and Muslim immigrants are often viewed with extra or even hostile scrutiny. They have also been subject to sustained incidents of shocking racial violence, which has left them feeling vulnerable and with little confidence in the capacity of the system to either understand or protect them.

## Germans on Islam and Immigration

During fieldwork in Germany, we had the opportunity to meet many distinguished and dedicated Germans who are working to integrate the Muslim population. They are sophisticated and compassionate and reflect the open and pluralistic German identity that developed after the Second World War. Yet they are also keenly aware of the often-exclusionary nature of their own society rooted as it is in notions of primordial identity and of the backlash that is taking place against Islam and immigrants.

### A German Diplomat-Scholar

Heinrich Kreft, the current German ambassador to Luxembourg, met me in his office when he was at the foreign ministry in Berlin. Kreft's previous job as ambassador for dialogue among civilizations was established in 2002 as part of the German government's response to 9/11. While initially the position dealt almost exclusively with establishing a dialogue with Islam, Kreft explained that this was changed in 2005 to a dialogue among civilizations.

Kreft is a passionate believer in the ideals of the European Union and the European idea, which fostered reconciliation and unity among nations with centuries of animosities. "If you talk to people who lost part of their memory, or who have Alzheimer's," he said, "what they forget last is the oldest memories. I keep telling people, if you want to work in cultural dialogue—that's my job—this is really something you have to plan for in the long term." This principle, he said, also applies to Europe's relationship with Islam.

In chapter 2, Kreft was quoted as saying that Germany has become the Heimat for its Muslims, and he is committed to making this a reality for the immigrants and their families. Muslim religious education in schools, he believed, needed to be more widespread, but the lack of organization and cohesion within the Muslim community made such work difficult. He discussed the major German government initiative to formulate a policy toward Islam and the Muslim minority, the German Islam Conference that was launched in 2006, stating that "those seven organizations which played a role in the German Islam Conference only represent about 30 percent of the Muslims living in Germany, so what about the other 70 percent?"

"During the Islam conference," Kreft said, giving an example of the community's diversity, "Germans found out that a substantial number of the Turks and the Kurds were not Sunnis, but were Alawites. So even the Turks within Germany are a diverse group." The number of Muslims in Germany may be inaccurate: "When we say 4.2 million Muslims, I am actually thinking much about this term, because I'm not doing justice to all of them. Because some might be quite nonreligious and I'm reducing their identity to their religion, which I think is totally wrong." For example, Kreft noted, "I remember in my hometown after 9/11, those who were referred to as the Turks, after 9/11 were referred to as the Muslims."

## A German Legal Scholar

Mathias Rohe is a former judge at the Higher Regional Court, Nuremberg, and founding director of the University of Erlangen-Nuremberg's Center for Islam and the Law in Europe in the cities of Erlangen and Nuremberg in Bavaria. His magisterial *Islamic Law in Past and Present*, a mighty tome that runs to 658 pages, was published in 2015. Rohe's definition of German identity strongly incorporates a cultural synthesis:

> I came across a sign in New York that said "Döner: German Specialty." Do you know what döner is? It's a Turkish fast food that the Turks brought, and the sign was "German Specialty." So if we talk about German identity, we have always been a mixture of cultures in Germany. My roots are from France and Sweden, some centuries ago. And many people are coming from all parts of Europe.

Rohe, an expert in the shariah, told us that "there is no necessary contradiction, there is virtually no difference between the German contract of law and the shariah contract in the modern sense. . . . A large part of shariah fits under the constitution." Because he is a scholar of Islam, Rohe said he has received death threats from far-right groups, and he noted that "the fear of Islam is an abstract one," "biggest among those who are most likely to never have met a Muslim in their life." Rohe believed that many of the problems that Germans attribute to Islam are actually "social issues" stemming from the community's guest-worker background: "They have high rates of unemployment. The dirty jobs they did because the Germans didn't want to do them. . . . I have public lectures, for example, on any kind of Islamic issue. After three questions, we are in language issues, cultural issues, labor market issues—nothing to do with Islam."

## A Government Integration Official in Munich

We met Margret Spohn, who worked for the Office for Intercultural Affairs of the Munich city government to facilitate integration, particularly concerning the Muslim community, and was responsible for the historic 2014 *iftar* dinner in Munich—the city's first official iftar—that we attended. In an interview, Spohn, who wrote her dissertation on Turkish male identity of first-generation immigrants to Germany, discussed the challenges that Muslims face in German society. "They do everything for integration, but there is a glass ceiling that they can't get through. . . . Migrants have double the unemployment rate of Germans. We have a lot of studies showing that if you would like to go to the work market with a Turkish name, your chance to go to work is 50 percent less than without a Turkish name, so we have racism, we have discrimination, and we have not equal opportunities." These institutional barriers are having a devastating impact on the young. "You have the youth, the young Muslims who say, 'Well, whatever I do, they don't accept me, they don't want me here, so one day, I will turn against them.'"

Spohn pointed to a poster on the wall of her office, which declared, "Munich says thank you," and was commissioned to mark the fiftieth anniversary of the guest worker agreement between Germany and Turkey:

> We decided just to use the colors of the city of Munich, which are black and yellow, and a pretzel, which is part of Bavarian identity, and chai, which is a part of Turkish identity. Germany had hundreds of officers in these countries to say to the people, "Come to Germany. We need you. Please work for us." But when the people came here, they didn't get the impression that they had been welcomed. And it took fifty years until our chancellor said, "Thank you for coming." And so we wanted to do this with Munich as well. So our mayor said thank you, for what you've given us, your parents and your grandparents, over fifty years.

## A Business Executive in Munich

Pantelis Christian Poetis is a successful business executive in Munich who also happens to be the city's honorary Pakistani consul general. Born in northern Germany to a German mother and a Greek Cypriot father, Poetis is the CEO of Powergroup, which develops marketing strategies and is active in more than fifty countries. Poetis and his charming family are proud representatives of Pakistan and fly its flag. Poetis has found several key points that have fostered common ground between Germans and Pakistanis: "I would always emphasize that Pakistanis are very hard working and very, very friendly, and they are willing to go for higher education, which are three very great characteristics. So I feel the two cultures actually have many similarities."

Once Germans have had the chance to better understand the people and culture of Pakistan, Poetis has found that they often rapidly warm to Pakistanis. "Most people are not aware how the Pakistani people are and what are the issues in Pakistan. They hear all the media stories about terrorism." "Pakistan is a brand," he said, "and this is what makes things even easier for me, because part of what I am doing for Pakistan is part of my day-to-day job and business. So there is nothing which really is too difficult for us to solve, as we feel it is a communication issue." He recounted the response the people of Munich gave to Pakistanis several years ago when he led a flood-relief fund-raising campaign. "They donated major amounts. Here at the consulate we received 1.5 million euros, which is quite a sum. Everybody donated and actually it made me cry."

### German Immigrant Muslim Voices

Our fieldwork in Germany allowed us to interview numerous Muslims with immigrant backgrounds. From the heads of major organizations to politicians, diplomats, academics, and taxi drivers, they are making a significant impact on the country in spite of the challenges they face.

## The Turkish Ambassador to Germany

Hüseyin Avni Karslıoğlu, the Turkish ambassador to Germany, is the classic outsider-insider. The ambassador's bold opinions, sturdy frame, and striking appearance—he wore an earring and had light silver hair that came down to his shoulders—made him stand out among the other Muslim diplomats in Berlin. I could visualize him as an Ottoman commander in a military expedition on its way to lay siege to a European city; someone

Richard Gere could play convincingly in a Hollywood epic. We were privileged to have three meetings with him and met him initially courtesy of Syed Hasan Javed, the Pakistan ambassador, who hosted an extraordinary dinner at his home in our honor and invited some two dozen leading Muslim ambassadors and diplomats.

Karslıoğlu was keenly aware of the xenophobic violence the German Turks had faced, and he spoke of "a collective trauma" in the community. The ambassador, we discovered, had a long history in the country. His parents had brought him to Germany when he was a child in the 1960s, and he had lived in Donaueschingen, a town in the Black Forest in southwestern Germany. Before finishing high school, Karslıoğlu returned to Turkey. The Germans—particularly "Grandma Frieda," his landlady in Donaueschingen—had a lasting impact on him. Frieda had lost her sons and husband in the Second World War, and she brought the ambassador up, he told us, as if she were his own grandmother. For him she embodied the German ideal—considerate, positive, clean, honest, and punctual. Her behavior reflected what the ambassador referred to as the German code of *deutsche Tugenden*, an example of German primordial identity (see chapter 2).

As an example of deutsche Tugenden, the ambassador cited Chancellor Angela Merkel, whom he admires. She is very modest when she travels and in the way she dresses, he said. Merkel lives a simple life, he explained. She wakes up at six every morning and has a simple breakfast. She travels with a modest entourage, carries her own luggage, and stays in simple hotels. He recalled that one of her assistants once showed up barely one and a half minutes late for a meeting, and she asked, "Why are you late?"

The ambassador believed that there was "institutionalized racism" against immigrants—especially Muslim immigrants—in Germany. The entire administrative structure of police, judges, and officials unite whenever there is a case involving Muslim immigrants, he believed. When a German meets you, the ambassador averred, he will try to dominate you and will not accept you as an equal. Everything was defined by "bloodline." In this, the ambassador's views would be publicly shared by his own president, who in 2017 compared German leaders—and then, for good measure, Dutch ones—with "Nazis."

## The Head of Germany's Largest Islamic Organization

As the largest Islamic organization in Germany, the Turkish-sponsored Turkish-Islamic Union for Religious Affairs (DITIB) administers an extensive network of mosques, schools, and programs throughout the country. In Berlin, the group runs the city's flagship Sehitlik Mosque, where we met with the head and assistant imams. In Cologne, we interviewed Bekir Alboğa, the secretary general of DITIB. Alboğa was born in Turkey to parents who moved to Germany as guest workers and went on to earn a Ph.D. in Islamic studies at the prestigious University of Heidelberg. His dissertation related the thinking of the eleventh-century Islamic scholar al-Mawardi to Thomas Hobbes and John Locke. Alboğa defined German identity as rooted in the German language and highlighted the diversity of influences in Germany, citing the role of Turkish food in German culture as an example of this multifaceted identity.

The DITIB organization, Alboğa explained, runs more than 920 mosques in Germany and has between 600,000 and 700,000 members. The imams, he noted, are trained in Turkey and serve tours in German mosques. He told us of the important role women are playing in Islamic education and said that about two-thirds of the people in DITIB's programs were women. Alboğa also discussed Goethe, whom he described as "like a brother to me," and "a great thinker with a great affinity for Islam." Goethe "wrote a wonderful poem about our Prophet," he stated, referring to "The Song of Mahomet." Alboğa believed that the Islamic dimension of Goethe's work is ignored, if not intentionally suppressed.

## THE DITIB SPOKESWOMAN

Ayşe Aydin, the media representative of DITIB in Cologne who directs public relations for the large new DITIB mosque in the city, visited my office when she came to Washington, D.C., before our fieldwork. Aydin is an intelligent, articulate, and sensitive woman who feels passionately for her Turkish community, and indeed for her German identity. She desperately yearned to join the two and wish away the differences, but the ugly facts of prejudice constantly overwhelmed her. When she described the ghastly murder, in 1993, of five Turkish women by four male neo-Nazis who surrounded their house and set it on fire, she could not control her tears.

In Cologne Aydin was a different person; she was now on home territory, and we were her guests. She organized visits to the central mosque, which was still under construction, the interview with Alboğa, and arranged for our attendance at an iftar dinner with the community that combined the hospitality of the Turks and the efficiency of the Germans. Aydin was born in Turkey but came to Germany at the age of three, when the guest workers first began arriving. She contrasted her generation with the first generation, who thought of going back home. When she went to Turkey, she recalled, "it was always, 'The German girl is coming.' I mean even my color was lighter than the others because we don't have so much sun here like they had in Turkey." She also proudly and dramatically recited verses from Goethe's *Faust* for us. She emphatically stated, "I am very German!"

Aydin described the new mosque with pride as "a Turkish mosque" but also as "a marriage between traditional and modernity." The main minaret towered high above at fifty-five meters. The mosque itself had rooms for conferences, seminars, and libraries and for conducting youth programs. She said that the main prayer hall could hold 12,000 people, a number limited by government safety codes. For Aydin, the mosque marked the "architectural point of no return" for the Muslim community in Germany.

Non-Muslim Germans in Cologne are also proud of the mosque, Aydin claimed, and want to show that it belongs in Germany. This could be seen when they demonstrated their opposition to anti-mosque protesters who called themselves Pro-Cologne and stood outside the mosque chanting, "We are the Volk!" Aydin said the mosque had received donations from non-Muslims, including from a church that had gathered 5,000 euros from the Sunday collection plate because "they said every religion should have the right to build their own house of God." She did note, however, that the archbishop of Cologne was "not amused" by the church's generosity.

## The DITIB Academic

At Cologne's new mosque we interviewed the chief of the DITIB Academy, Taner Yüksel. Born and raised in Göttingen, the son of Turkish guest workers, Yüksel described himself as having a hybrid German-Muslim identity. He spoke of the "earthquake" that shook the structure of the Turkish families that immigrated to Germany. "It's very interesting, when you look from outside, you think that's the system they have had for the last 3,000 years." In reality, however, "the role between the children and the parents has been turned around. Our parents have been like children in this society. They couldn't speak, they couldn't solve their problems here in this land. My mother needed her children to go get the doctor when she was sick."

Yüksel argued that mainstream Germany's view of Islamic history, as it is taught to German schoolchildren, is a major obstacle to better relations between Muslims and non-Muslims. "The history between Islam and Europe is very old—and it is full of lies." Europeans see Muslims as bringing "war and struggle and death and blood." Europeans are unaware, he believed, of the advanced state of Islamic societies in history and that the

Turks welcomed the Jews both when they were expelled from Spain in 1492 and when they were fleeing from Hitler.

> When you black out all of these positive things and only talk about the negative things, then you will never in this society accept the Muslims as they are. And we as Muslims, until now, because of our migration history, our parents have been workers, never have had the intellectual possibilities to tell our own stories, our own history, our own side of things. But now, we are prepared to talk about ourselves in the language that people understand.

### BERLIN'S LARGEST MOSQUE

In Berlin, we visited the city's largest mosque, the Sehitlik Mosque, which is run by DITIB, and spent the afternoon interviewing two of the mosque's imams, Imam Süleyman Kücük and Imam Müfit Sevinç. Kücük explained it is one of the few buildings in Europe that resembles seventeenth-century Ottoman architecture: "Everything, each stone, the marble, this chandelier, is brought from Turkey."

Kücük explained that this plot of land was a gift to the Ottoman sultan from Prussia, in exchange for a gift to the Prussian ambassador from the sultan of a plot with "a view of the Bosporus." The Sehitlik Mosque has faced a number of attacks over the years, as has the Muslim community, especially women who wear a headscarf, and families often report that their wives and daughters have been attacked that day. While the German Muslim community faces a number of challenges, Kücük outlined some concrete steps he believes the community can take to improve relations with the German majority. In particular, he has found that the good behavior of Muslims and education can play a major role in improving relations from the Muslim perspective. He stated, "Our behavior, Muslims' behavior—we have the best example from the life of the holy Prophet Muhammad, peace be upon him. He was a very good example to the people with his behavior."

As far as the operation of the mosque is concerned, Kücük explained that in DITIB mosques, "Our imams come from Turkey for five years. And then they go back." Imam Sevinç told us how he struggles to wrap his mind around both the phenomenon of Muslim terrorism and the rise of Islamophobia. Sevinç has also found that many in Germany are clearly starving for a spiritual path, and many have come to him just to gain some foundational spiritual guidance: "So many youngsters come to me and just cry. And why? Because this population has a hunger for spirituality, something is missing here that is nonmaterial. And they also need a lot of love."

*After interviewing immigrants in Berlin's Tiergarten*

### Young Muslim Women in Berlin's Tiergarten

In Berlin's Tiergarten, we interviewed three young Muslim women born in Germany who were students and professionals—Rafiqa Younes, a young Palestinian who wore the hijab; Nusrat Sheikh, whose family is from Pakistan; and Saboura Beutel, who is half-Muslim and half-Sikh. Their combined assessment made me aware of the enormity of the challenges ahead. Here are some of their sample opinions: "I am German, born and raised here . . . but people deny my German identity." "They feel they are better than you, they feel they are more civilized than you; they feel they have more feelings than you." "Career officials at school encourage us to take low-paid jobs after school and not proceed to university." "They once said Germany is a Christian land. Now they say it is a Judeo-Christian land. There is no place for Islam in this." "They celebrate Aryan ideals. We have no place in that." "People insult you. Hit you with stones. Spit on you." "Many Muslims have given up Islam." "For me it is an identity crisis." "It is hard for us to breathe."

They suggested that the Germans were acutely conscious of the terrible things they had done to the Jews and were set on making amends. The problem was that they could not transfer their sympathy from one minority to the other; that is, from the Jews to the Muslims. It meant that Muslims were suffering in broad daylight as it were and nothing was being done about their problems. Saboura spoke of her shock at some of the brutal and murderous attacks that had been carried out against the Muslim community: "All these things were a scandal, and they were talked about a little bit, but now nobody talks about them anymore."

As if to confirm what the girls were telling us, during the interview we became aware of individuals and groups of young men walking by us. My grandson Ibrahim, who was with us, quietly told me that some of them were making "monkey gestures" and "monkey noises." I then observed the next group of passersby more carefully and saw that he was indeed correct. Some of them not only made the gestures and grunting noises but also lifted up their shirts and, in simian fashion, scratched their stomachs.

## A Muslim Member of the Bundestag

When she was elected to the Bundestag, the German Parliament, in 2013, Cemile Giousouf became the first person of Muslim descent to represent the conservative Christian Democratic Union party in the Bundestag. We met her first at the iftar dinner she hosted in Berlin's Kreuzberg neighborhood, which has a large Turkish population, and we later interviewed her in her office in Berlin. At the iftar, Germany's interior minister, Thomas de Maizière, addressed the gathering and told me afterward of the debate about Germany's Leitkultur and that he wished to promote a version that valued "pluralism, tolerance, freedom, unity, to keep the people together."

Born in Germany to Turkish guest workers from Western Thrace, Greece, Giousouf was educated near Cologne and graduated from the University of Bonn. She said that in contrast to her parents' generation, there is now "a new young generation which says we are Muslim, we are Greek, we are black, and we are German, and we want to have a place in this society."

Giousouf spoke of the institutionalized barriers to integration that people from migrant families continue to face: "We really need to say everyone has to get the same chances." She noted that women who wear hijabs continue to face discrimination in the workplace and that the entire community is implicated in terrorist acts being perpetrated around the world. Giousouf hopes to become a role model for young German Muslims: "My parents weren't professors, they were really working in a factory, and when the children or the younger people talk to me, they say if you can be successful, maybe I can be successful too. And this is a little dream, I really want to show them that this really can be true." She shared her dream, "I think we really need a new vision of Germany. We are trying to build up a new German identity."

## AN INTEGRATION COMMISSIONER IN BERLIN

Gabriele Gün Tank, the integration commissioner for Berlin's diverse Tempelhof-Schöneberg borough, is a Berlin native born to a Turkish mother, Bundestag member Azize Tank of the Left Party, and a German father. In discussing German identity, Tank said that since the Second World War Germans have been "trying to hide themselves," while they simultaneously "want to have something that they can be proud of." She elaborated, "When they think about Germany, they think about white Germany. . . . They have a special picture of how a German is."

Tank was particularly concerned about the challenges faced by Muslims in German schools. There is "institutional racism," she believed. "We have in Germany a school system where you get segregated at an early age." Teachers often have a stereotypical attitude toward their Muslim students, which Tank described as "they're bad and we can't really handle them." "What can happen," she explained, "is that the kids would say, 'If you want me like that, I am like that.' People start to believe it."

This stereotyping also happens in the media, she claimed.

> When they talk about women's rights, they frame it as having something to do with Islam. . . . But you shouldn't put it in an ethnic-religious way because it has nothing to do with that. It is much more the power of men and woman. It is the macho society which we have in the white German society, too. . . . In our case, we are pretty good because we are doing a lot of good things for our women.

Turning to the attitude of the German mainstream toward Islam, Tank was apprehensive about the future:

> It's pretty, pretty scary, because, I mean, we have a history in Germany. . . . I think we have to be really careful in Germany when it comes up to racism because right now, I would say there's the right-wing parties. They're not that strong, but it's through all the parties, there's some kind of racism. I mean not everyone in all parties, but you will find in every party at least some people who have those stereotypes in their mind.

## A GERMAN PUBLIC INTELLECTUAL

In Berlin, we interviewed Naika Foroutan of Humboldt University, the vice director of the Berlin Institute for Integration and Migration Research and one of the leading scholars and media commentators on Islam in

Germany. She was born in Germany to an Iranian father, who once coached the Iranian national football team, and a German mother. Her family later returned to Iran with the intention of staying. Following the 1979 revolution, however, her parents sold their belongings to migrant smugglers to enable her father to flee to Germany via Pakistan and Turkey, and she and her mother later flew to Germany to join him.

Foroutan named her extensive academic project on German identity and the place of migrants in it HEYMAT, a variation of the German term Heimat, for homeland. To Foroutan, the *y* in the term emphasizes the hybridity of modern German identity (see chapter 2). Foroutan and her team surveyed 8,200 subjects and found that while many Germans say that identity has to do with citizenship, they feel that "a real German might still be connected to a religious, a cultural, an ethnic, or another form of identity." "Being Muslim is disconnected from being German," she explained, "and it's disconnected from being European. Empirically, we can show that by our data."

While she was collecting data for the project in 2010, a public debate and controversy arose over the book *Deutschland schafft sich ab* (Germany abolishes itself) by Thilo Sarrazin, a German economist and politician, in which he attributes the fact that Muslims in Germany have lower rates of employment and education to inferior genetics. Foroutan and her team countered the arguments in the book, which she described as the biggest best seller in Germany since the Second World War, with empirical data. Foroutan began appearing frequently in the media and became the public face of the opposition to the book. She described the backlash that resulted, including threats against her, her family, and the university, but said she believed the Muslim community "gained more power after this debate." Looking to the future, Foroutan is cautiously optimistic, "Already 35 percent of the German children have a so-called migration background, so classrooms of diversity are getting completely normal. Especially the second and third generations are developing a completely new way of perceiving their identity."

## A Sociologist Studying Islam in Europe

Schirin Amir-Moazami, a professor of Islam in Europe at the Institute for Islamic Studies at Berlin's Freie University, is another prominent scholar commenting in the media. The institute and Amir-Moazami's position there were established in 2008 as a result of the German government's commitment to funding universities to study Islam and Muslim communities. Amir-Moazami's father was an Iranian doctor, and she was born in Heidelberg and raised in the Frankfurt area.

Amir-Moazami explained in an interview in her office that she was in the midst of a "Foucauldian analysis of governmentalization of Islam in general, in the specific context of Germany." She is examining initiatives that purport to facilitate dialogue but are "problematic." For example, she was critical of the government's establishing Islamic theology chairs because "the main model that's behind it is actually Catholic or maybe Protestant theology" and the government is forcing Islam into this frame. "Who is involved in institutionalizing the curriculum?" she asked, "And who has a say in terms of what should be the Islamic tradition that has to be taught and instructed?"

On the subject of German identity, Amir-Moazami discussed the concept of the Leitkultur, explaining that the debate about how to define it and how immigrants fit into it emerged in the late 1990s. She said the discussion around Leitkultur, another expression of German primordial identity, was indicative of "the idea of the cultural and blood-based nation, which is very strong in Germany." She dated the rise of the Leitkultur discourse to the reform of German citizenship laws, implemented in 2000, which made it possible for many more Turks to become citizens. "I think this whole notion of integration is very problematic, because most of the people who ask Muslims or people who are not yet integrated, they don't know into what kind of entity they should integrate."

## A PROFESSOR OF ISLAMIC STUDIES

Riem Spielhaus, like Professors Foroutan and Amir-Moazami, is a prominent female academic involved in the debate about Islam in Germany and appears often in the media. Also like the other professors, she has a Muslim father, in her case from Egypt. We met Spielhaus, who was born in East Berlin and grew up under communism, in 2014, in Berlin, where she had been invited to chair my lecture organized by the British Council and the Aspen Institute. Upon meeting again in Berlin, in 2016, I learned she had been promoted to the post of professor of Islamic studies at the University of Göttingen and head of the Textbooks and Society Department at the Georg Eckert Institute for International Textbook Research.

Like Kreft, Spielhaus believed that the mainstream discourse has shifted from discussions of ethnic minorities to discussions of religious minorities. For example, she referred to the case of Aygül Özkan, "the first so-called Muslim minister in Germany," who served as the minister of social affairs, women, families, health, and integration in the German state of Lower Saxony from 2010 to 2013. Özkan was identified not as a

Turkish minister but as a Muslim minister. By comparison, Spielhaus noted that the first Turkish members of the Bundestag, Cem Özdemir, the current co-chair of the Green Party, and Leyla Onur, of the Social Democratic Party, were described as Turks rather than Muslims when they were elected in 1994.

Spielhaus also shared insights from her work on textbooks. "A lot of what is taught right now in school is fostering suspicion rather than coexistence," she believed. She gave an example of how Muslims are represented:

> When Islam or Muslims are pictured, it is a crowd. It's a mass of people, and it's mostly dark. When Christianity is pictured, it might be a picture of the Pope, but it's an individual and he is in white. . . . Or another example for migration, you know people come to Germany as migrants because they suffer in their own countries and they have war or poverty and they are fleeing from that, and we can help them. So this again, can you see, it's not about the many, many highly skilled workers that are coming. . . . A lot of doctors in our hospitals are of Muslim background. These people are not seen.

### *The Ahmadi Experience in Germany*

The Ahmadi community, originally from South Asia, is one of the oldest immigrant communities in Germany, having first established itself in the 1920s. Following waves of persecution in Pakistan, increasing numbers arrived in Germany and other places in Europe, including a community we visited during fieldwork outside Cordoba in Spain. Ahmadis are officially recognized by the German government alongside such religions as Lutheranism, Catholicism, and Judaism, while Sunni and Shia organizations have not been so recognized.

We had met Muhammad Asif Sadiq, representative for public relations and external affairs for the Ahmadiyya Muslim Community of Berlin, at the Berlin iftar hosted by Bundestag member Cemile Giousouf. He invited our team to visit his community, which in 2008 built what he described as "the only proper mosque with a dome and minaret" in former East Berlin, if not in the entirety of what was East Germany.

Taking up the invitation, Frankie set out in a cab, and as he rode past dilapidated and run-down buildings his Turkish cab driver expressed alarm, saying he never comes to this area because it is associated with Nazis. As they arrived, Frankie saw a police car parked outside the front gate.

Ahmadi teenagers lingering outside talked about the harassment they receive from small groups of neo-Nazis. Inside, Frankie interviewed Sadiq as well as Imam Said Ahmad Arif. Imam Arif, who was twenty-eight years old, had studied Islamic theology in Toronto and was assigned to the community in Berlin. He was born in Sargodha, a city in the Punjab province in Pakistan, and came to Germany when he was six. Sadiq was also twenty-eight years old and an engineer specializing in fluid mechanics and process engineering in addition to his duties directing public relations for the mosque. He said his great-grandfather was from Punjab and became an Ahmadi in 1905. Sadiq was born in Pakistan and came to Germany at the age of one.

When asked to define German identity, Imam Arif replied that "we consider ourselves as German Ahmadi Muslims. We speak this language, we have grown up here, we are—our second generation especially is not closer to any other nation than Germany. There is a saying of the Holy Prophet Isaiah, the love for your country is part of your faith, and we live that." Sadiq said the Ahmadiyya community in Germany consists of about 35,000 people "organized in around 225 local communities and in every significant city of Germany."

Sadiq told Frankie that "the Ahmadiyya Muslim community was founded in 1889 in India by Hazrat Mirza Ghulam Ahmad. The founder of the community actually claimed to be the promised messiah and Mahdi of Islam." The Ahmadiyya came to Germany, Sadiq explained, "when the second caliph of the Ahmadiyya Muslim community . . . sought to found a community in the heart of the Western World, and especially in Berlin, as the gateway to West and to East." After Pakistan enacted laws in 1974 that declared Ahmadis to be non-Muslim, Sadiq continued, "huge groups of Ahmadis flew from Pakistan owing to religious persecution in several waves."

Sadiq noted that where they were in East Berlin, compared with the western side of the city, "there are no foreigners," meaning immigrants like those in his community, and there was fierce opposition to the newcomers. However, the situation is now much calmer: "For the first time Germany has accepted a Muslim group as part of their living and forming their society, and this is something very unique."

## The Muslim Community in Denmark

In chapter 2 we met several leading white Danish voices in media and politics who defined Danish identity as essentially tribal and exclusivist. Here, we meet the Muslim immigrant community of Denmark. As in

Germany, the community began arriving in Denmark as guest workers in the 1960s and more recently as asylum-seekers looking for refuge. Unlike Germany, Denmark lacks a clearly dominant Muslim ethnic community, and there are many groups, including Pakistanis, Turks, Arabs, Bosnians, and Somalis.

## A Minority Rights Activist

Bashy Quraishy is an author, journalist, and social activist. Quraishy's organization, the European Muslim Initiative for Social Cohesion, works for the equality of the Muslim population on a European level. Quraishy is originally from Pakistan and has lived in Denmark since the early 1970s. He recounted a remarkable story involving the Queen of Denmark when he first arrived. He was estranged from his family at the time and was out of touch with them. To reach him, his mother wrote a letter to the Queen. "It said, 'Queen Margaret my son lives in your kingdom, please find him and ask him to write to me, I miss him.' The Queen herself sent a man to the chief of the police with a letter pad and a golden pen and asked the chief of the police to find me and make me write a letter to my mom." Quraishy was summoned to meet the chief of police and recalls he was "trembling in my boots. . . . He looked at me and said 'Mr. Quraishy, you're a very naughty man.' I said 'Sir, what did I do?' So he showed me my mom's letter and the Queen's letter. He asked me to sit down. I was crying. My letter was soaked but I wrote a beautiful letter to my mom and apologized. The letter was sent to the Queen and from the palace the letter was sent to my mom and she had it until the last day, hanging over her bed. When I wrote my book *From Punjab to Copenhagen*, I sent a copy to the Queen. After many years, she remembered this incident. So that was my beautiful introduction to this lovely land."

"Unfortunately," Quraishy added with a note of resigned sorrow, "that Denmark is gone. It has been replaced by extreme statements against ethnic minorities, refugees, and especially against Muslims." Quraishy spoke of his frustration that despite fulfilling every one of the criteria he felt was necessary to become "Danish," it is never enough for the Danes. He noted he has "lived here almost fifty years" and yet, "it's very strange. I never go to mosque. I do not keep any of those tenets of Islam. I'm actually more Dane than Danes are. So why am I put in the same box like anybody else? Why am I considered a terrorist or a fanatic or whatever they think Muslims are?"

Quraishy also lamented that it seems as though Danes want him to change his name and disown his South Asian heritage, which deeply offends him. "I don't want to change my name. I have a culture, very proud culture. I come from India and Pakistan, with a 7,000-year-old culture. Danes and Europeans are just starting. So why do they want me to throw my culture, my identity, out the window and take over an identity which is artificial?"

An anecdote from a conversation with an Iraqi refugee in Denmark allowed Quraishy to sum up the immigrant experience in Denmark: "He came from Iraq with a very high education. He was a doctor in Baghdad, and when I met him he was selling sausages. His education was not accepted; he was just a refugee. He said, 'In Saddam's Iraq, they will put you in front of a wall and shoot you and you are done; in Denmark, they strangle you slowly, slowly.'"

## An IBM Business Executive

Sanila Rana, a data sales executive at IBM Denmark, is a Pakistani-Danish woman who has made an impact in business, being responsible for a spurt in growth in the company. In her dark business suit and driving an expensive sports car, Rana exuded confidence and looked the picture of success. But her story belied her appearance. She faced many challenges both personal and professional. Her life's path has followed that of other successful Muslim women in Europe, particularly those in Britain—she had a bitter marital breakup from her bullying Pakistani husband, who was not prepared to adapt to life in Denmark.

Born in Denmark to guest workers who arrived in the country in the late 1960s, Rana received her bachelor's degree in Denmark and went on to work for IBM. In this, she proved wrong the university professor who told her, "You are a woman and multicultural. You will never get a job here in Denmark, so give up." In 2011 Rana established a nonprofit association called Multicultural Business Women to educate women of all backgrounds in what she described as the "unwritten rules" that exist in the business world. Today it has 417 members, and nearly fifty cultures are represented. She has worked hard to push back against patriarchal norms in the Pakistani community, while also stressing that much of what one sees in European Muslims is not true Islam.

Rana, who was quoted in chapter 2 discussing Janteloven, an important expression of Danish primordial tribal identity, explained that the Danes are "very loyal" to their own families. Outsiders face a difficult challenge to be allowed into this structure: "Even though you are born here, you are raised up here, they will never let you in." "Racism is in their blood," she said. In the business world, she demanded respect as a professional woman

on the basis of her work. She was aware that there were ample sexual overtones in the references to her attractive "dusky" looks. In the end, she felt
that she got the respect she demanded. Indeed, she is something of a poster
child for the firm, whose success depends more and more on understanding international markets and cultural trends.

Rana said the Prophet of Islam was her "biggest inspiration." She saw
him "as an inspiration in terms of he was a great leader but he had his
feet on the ground. And he was taking care of his neighbors." Rana,
who once wore the hijab, also spoke out against the idea that a Muslim
woman needs to wear it. "I believe that if someone wants to take on a
hijab, or a Jewish hat, or color their hair green, it's their choice," she
believed. "I would never judge them. However, if they say that a hijab
means being a complete and a good Muslim, a better Muslim than not
wearing a hijab, I would say speak up for yourself. Because hijab, for me,
it's an interpretation of what is written in Islam, about a woman covering
herself and a man covering himself." Modesty, she was sure, comes from
inside.

## An Arab Professor at the University of Copenhagen

Ehab Galal is a professor in the Department of Cross-Cultural and
Regional Studies at the University of Copenhagen, focusing on the Arab
world. Born in Cairo, in 1955, he immigrated to Denmark around 1980
after meeting a Danish girl in college during a trip to the country and
having a child with her. Because Denmark did not recognize foreign degrees,
he had to begin his studies all over again.

Galal, who speaks impeccable Danish and passable English, said there
were barely any immigrants in Denmark when he arrived. "You could only
find one shop, you could say, immigrant shop or two and no more. . . .
I had hardly any friends at that time." "I got this impression already, from
the beginning, that they don't like *fremmed*, strangers or foreigners, they
prefer to have a Dane. And my wife and I were separated. It was almost
impossible for me to have a room or flat with a Dane."

He even stopped going to parties, because people could only relate to
him as an outsider clouded with their own preconceived stereotypes.

I have been so tired of sitting with people who I don't know and they
cannot talk with me on another subject than the pyramids. Because
as soon as they ask, "Where do you come from?" "Ahh, Egypt? Oh!
The pyramids." I don't like to use my time talking about the pyramids
because I think that I can talk much better about the Queen in Den-

mark or what's going on in the daily life in Denmark or on my research.

These stereotypes and misunderstandings also find their way into the national discourse on Muslims and the Islamic faith. "I always say, we have 5 million Quran experts in Denmark. We have 5 million imams in Denmark. I have been reading the Quran over a lifetime, and I don't understand it. How could you understand it, especially in a foreign language? I read the original and many things I cannot understand in the Quran, how could you?"

The media, Galal stated with weary bitterness, will call many other white Dane professors on the Middle East before him. He is often seen as "one of them" and the "enemy," he noted, and people assume he cannot speak Danish properly, even though his Ph.D. is in the Danish language. Even in his own university, he said, "I think that it is the only Arabic department in the Western world which does not have an original Arab. I am working here, with a contract, for a few years. But if you look at my publications, they are much, much, much higher than many others."

"The Danish are right that many foreigners in Denmark don't learn Danish," Galal stated. "But I always say, who has the key? The owner of the flat, or a foreigner who comes from outside? So if you don't open the door in a good way, you will never get good feedback from your guest."

## A Lawyer in Copenhagen

Suraiya Kasim immigrated to Denmark from Pakistan at the beginning of this century and is now a top lawyer in Copenhagen. She praised many things about Denmark, including its health-care system and the Danish policy toward mothers and childcare, which "has been extremely helpful in me feeling very secure in this country." Kasim, who told us her children are growing up as Danes, praised the Danish for their honesty and gave us an example of the respect for order and integrity that lies at the heart of Danish primordial identity. She explained that she twice left her wallet in the park and both times a stranger found it and brought it home to her. "The amount of trust that they have, it's amazing." She said if you are ill, you can take off from work for up to fifteen days with no doctor's note and still be paid. The Danes think, "Why would you cheat the system?" "Unfortunately," she added "in Pakistan, I have experienced that people will go to I don't know what lengths to cheat."

Kasim discussed the challenges Muslims face in Denmark and related a story that saddened her about two young Muslim female members of

Danish political parties who were asked if they believed in shariah law. When they said yes, they were asked to leave the parties. This is not correct, Kasim argued, because "shariah law is very compatible with Danish law. I mean the way the social system is over here is exactly the way Muslims are supposed to take care of each other."

To facilitate integration, Kasim believed that the Muslim community in Denmark should refrain from making a fuss about certain things: "I don't have to go and ask the waiter, 'Is this burger halal?' Why do I need to make a fuss? I can just say I'm vegetarian." On Denmark's controversially restrictive policy on accepting asylum seekers, Muslims needed to think of the Danish position, especially concerning their social system. "You cannot just stand up and say that Denmark is against refugees or immigrants," she added. "There's a reason behind why they are. You have to answer questions of why people are like that rather than just saying, 'Yeah they are racist.'" She summed up her philosophy thus: "If you ask about what my struggle is, it would be as an ambassador for my country and an ambassador for my religion and to be as best as I can, so others can see this is what a Pakistani is and this is what a Muslim is."

## The Chairman of the National Party of Denmark

In Copenhagen, we met Kashif Ahmad, the chairman of the National Party in Denmark, at a community gathering to welcome us hosted by Bashy Quraishy. Members of the Muslim community, especially Pakistanis, surreptitiously informed me that he was an Ahmadi, although Ahmad consciously spoke up for the entire Muslim community. Ahmad said the National Party, which he founded in 2014 with his brothers Aamer and Asif and which uses the Danish flag as its symbol, wants "equal rights for everyone in Denmark" irrespective of ethnicity, religion, or color—what he described as "the real Danish values." He explained that in choosing the name they sought to ironically push back against the Far Right in Denmark: "Many years ago, there used to be a National Party of Denmark, and their main objective was that every immigrant and every Muslim was not meant to be in Denmark. So their main objective was that we only want white Denmark, and that's why we said, okay, let's use this name, and put it upside down."

Ahmad related one stark case of discrimination he had faced. His tickets for a Champions League football match in Copenhagen had once been suddenly canceled. In an email he was told it was because of "your foreign names." Ahmad was not alone in this case—as many as "700 people with a foreign, strange name had their tickets canceled owing to some security issues." Ahmad asked, "What is next—are we going to sit at the back of the bus, can we be on the plane?" They sued for discrimination, and won.

In a lunch discussion with Ahmad, his brothers Aamer and Asif, and their father, we learned that the parents came in the 1970s from Pakistan in a destitute state to Denmark, where Ahmad was born. It was a welcoming land even though they could not speak the language. However, Ahmad stated, "since then a lot of things changed in Denmark." They noted that Muslims have been described in Denmark as a "plague" and a "cancer," and it is said that Muslims have children like "rats." Their party has received death threats, Ahmad explained, and said that in a Facebook discussion about their party held by the Danish television network TV2, almost all of the comments were aggressively intolerant, such as "We should shoot them" and "Get out of Denmark and take your Islamic terrorism with you." There is a double standard here, Ahmad and his brothers claimed: "Whenever there is a death threat to a Danish personality by Muslims, there is blanket media coverage and people begin saying that Danish values are under attack. But when it is against us, nothing happens." Such threats, however, only "make me more determined," Ahmad proclaimed with gusto.

## A THEATER DIRECTOR

I met Sananda Solaris, a noted stage director and producer in Copenhagen, at the event hosted by Bashy Quraishy, and she invited our team to her home in Hvalsø, a small town in the Danish countryside several hours drive from Copenhagen. She sent her boyfriend and soon-to-be husband, Uffe Gavnholt, a tall, well-built, and bearded white Dane with long hair, who looked like a Viking, to pick up Amineh and Frankie and take them to her home for an interview. On the drive, Gavnholt, discussing Islam in Denmark, observed, "People are getting more and more scared, and the more scared they become the more dangerous they will become. I'm afraid to guess the outcome." The common perception of Muslims, he said, is that "if you meet them in a dark night, you're fucked."

Gavnholt, who had worked in a computer company, believed meeting Solaris had broadened his horizons and changed his life. She has an "ability to engage people around her from all backgrounds," he said, and "I'm kind of experiencing myself in a world I never imagined I would be in." Solaris, who runs her own theater company, was born in 1972 to an Iranian father, whom she never knew, and a Danish mother. She described her background: "I am one of the first born in Denmark who is half–Middle Eastern and half-Danish. Of course, there have been also Middle

Easterners in Denmark previously. Scientists have recently proved that there were a lot of Arabic people, actually, in the Viking times." She noted that her birth came before the waves of refugees who arrived in the 1980s and 1990s from places like Iran, Iraq, Pakistan, and Sri Lanka. She was, she told us, the only person with a Middle Eastern background to gain admittance to Denmark's elite National Theater School, formerly the Royal Theater School and now constituted as the Danish National School of Performing Arts, and she has directed operas for the Royal Danish Opera.

During her time in theater school, Solaris faced abuse on the basis of her ethnic background. "It was kind of a miracle that I came through the whole thing," she commented. "I almost died of it, I would say, because of sadness and grief and feeling like an outsider being pushed out." She lamented that "you have no Muslim women in Danish theatre, none," and said she is trying to change this through her own projects. Solaris's life experiences informed her later work as an advocate for refugees in Denmark. Shortly after our visit, she began hosting Syrian refugees in her home and engaging them in theater projects. "Ultimately," she argued, "I think Danish identity is broken up now. I think there is a big, big, crisis going on for Danish people."

## A Muslim Politician

In their home in a Copenhagen suburb, the Pakistani businessman Ashfaq Ahmed and his wife hosted a dinner for us with a group of successful middle-class immigrants, mainly Pakistani. Among them was Abbas Razvi, a city councilman of Pakistani background who was the first Muslim councilor in the region that includes Copenhagen. He explained that he is vice president of an official committee that deals with issues of traffic and the environment.

Razvi praised the Danish politicians and businessmen he has dealt with as having "a very pragmatic approach where they find solutions" but also had observed Danish chauvinism. He noted that, for example, at European Union meetings in Brussels, although Danes spoke English, they insisted on speaking their own language, and if English was used they demanded translators. Razvi cited a colleague: "She was a Dane, a highly educated woman, who said 'Danes have this master mentality that they are the masters. . . . So if you think that you will get even with Danes, or you come on the same level as Danes, maybe you will be disappointed.'" The overwhelming fear of the Danes, Razvi said, is of losing their identity, and the right-wing parties exploit this sentiment. The focus now, he warned, is on Muslims with the ominous themes "Muslims are coming" and "Muslims are taking over."

## THE IMAM OF MINHAJ-UL-QURAN

In Copenhagen, we visited the Minhaj-ul-Quran mosque complex. It is the first of several centers established in Denmark. Well-oiled, well-organized, and bustling, the center is headed by Allama Abdul Sattar Siraj, who reflects some of the articulate charisma of Maulana Tahir-ul-Qadri, the Pakistani founder of the global Minhaj-ul-Quran movement. In his neat, crisp shalwar-kameez, beard, and colorful cap, Imam Siraj oozed confidence. He said there were twenty-five Minhaj centers like this in Europe. He was proud of his Pakistani background, pointing out, "we have everything in Pakistan—mountains, rivers, fruits, and vegetables" and contrasted it with Denmark, "a country that cannot grow anything. Even the onions are imported from abroad." He found the people "cold" and "inhospitable" but admired the social and legal systems of the land.

The center has a Youth League and a Women's League. We saw the well-stocked library—with over a thousand books in Danish, Urdu, English, and Arabic—and talked to students in the different classes and the staff. Students recited the Quran, which they had memorized, and read out their essays in Urdu. The students were confident that they had absorbed the best of Islamic and Danish cultures. The staff and students at the center reminded me that Islamic values are universal and gave the example of the Prophet of Islam who faced hatred and anger with compassion and patience. Exhibiting Pakistani hospitality, the imam insisted we stay back for dinner, and we shared a pizza with his family. At the end of the meal, he served us delicious carrot halwa, a favorite sweet dish of Pakistanis. He said, "Our home is yours."

## THE GRAND MOSQUE OF COPENHAGEN

The Hamad Bin Khalifa Civilisation Center, or Grand Mosque of Copenhagen, is considered the largest mosque complex in Denmark and is named after its benefactor, the former ruler of Qatar. It is located in the city's working-class neighborhood of Nørrebro, with its diverse population of Muslim immigrants. The area is stereotyped in Denmark and associated with gangs, crime, and drugs. In early 2015, just weeks after our visit, Omar Abdel Hamid El-Hussein, a Nørrebro native of Palestinian background, killed two people in attacks on a synagogue and a "free speech" event featuring a Swedish cartoonist who had drawn the Prophet of Islam.

We were received warmly by the Grand Mosque's leadership and given a tour and a dinner. The recently constructed and squeaky-clean mosque still smelled of new carpets and furniture. The visitor could not fail to be impressed by the magnificent ceiling in the main prayer hall with the ninety-nine names of God and its chandelier, which weighed 350 kilograms, the smart new gym, library and conference rooms, and most important, the significant active participation of young Muslim women. We were told that some 350 worshippers came for Friday prayer, that it was always a full house, and that 300 children took Islamic lessons there over the weekend. The center housed the biggest Islamic library in Denmark, with some 5,000 books. The mosque had state of the art high-tech equipment which operated the doors closing and opening, screens coming down to divide halls into classrooms, and lights dimming with computers.

The center had arranged for some thirty to forty guests from the community to join us in an impromptu seminar. When we discussed building bridges with the larger Danish community, I asked them if they had attempted to meet the editors of the paper that had published the insulting cartoons of the Prophet of Islam. They had not. In the end one of the conducting Arab officials summed up the feeling of the others by saying, "The Danish society, they don't understand Muslims. And the Muslims, they don't understand the Danish people."

They showed me sayings of the Prophet neatly depicted on a large wall inside the mosque. They also pointed out, somewhat self-consciously, the unflattering quotations of Pia Kjærsgaard, which too were featured on the same wall to show the mosque's commitment to free speech. The significance of quoting Kjærsgaard was not lost on us. She is not only one of the leading critics of Islam and the Muslim community in Denmark, but also the co-founder of the far-right Danish People's Party and speaker of the Danish Parliament. The community in the mosque was living in an exquisite bubble, but it was aware of its vulnerability.

## The Head of Security at Copenhagen's Grand Mosque

After we met the Grand Mosque's head of security, Muhammad Nazir Din, during our visit, he came to have breakfast with us at our hotel, and we interviewed him at length. Originally from East Africa and of South Asian background, he came to Denmark in the 1970s and found "a kind and gentle people." In two meetings with us, he described the problems of the local Muslim community and his work to help Muslim youth. "They do a lot of drugs," he admitted, and talk about money. But where can the youth turn? The imams, he noted, will give them the wrong ideas. Din spoke about the tensions within immigrant families, explaining that the children "always have a conflict with the parents at home." The children have what he described as an "outside" and an "inside" life. The youth, Din believed, from places like Nigeria and Somalia do not know how to handle freedom. He was worried about the next generation. "My son asks me, 'Who am I?' What do I tell him?" He also noted that the controversy about the Danish cartoons is "underground" in the Muslim community and "is not finished yet." Din was "not comfortable with other Pakistanis," because of their bad habits. Yet he missed his roots. "Pakistan," he admitted, heaving a sigh not unlike that of a frustrated lover contemplating the beloved, "is number one with me, it is in my blood."

## Facing Radicalization in Copenhagen

Din's concern about radicalization in the Muslim community was shared by other Muslim leaders we met. At the Minhaj-ul-Quran mosque we attended a meeting of a youth group consisting of men and women, led by Hasan Bostan, a twenty-three-year-old law student whose grandparents came to Denmark from Punjab in Pakistan. Radicalization was a frequent topic of conversation, and Bostan noted of groups like ISIS, "You don't combat that by telling the young guy that democracy is the best way of living. You have to combat it by telling him what the true ideology of Islam is." For Bostan, "Islam propagates integration." Bostan said that one of the traits he most admired in the Prophet Muhammad was his ability to "integrate in any society."

On a visit to the Danish Islamic Center in Copenhagen, which has a modernist approach to Islam, Imam Naveed Baig, who is active in Jewish-Muslim dialogue, spoke of a "crisis of authority" in the Muslim community: "Everyone has their own Google imam." He explained that groups like Hizb ut-Tahrir and the Salafis, divided into militant and Saudi streams, appeal to the young on the Internet. Another member of the group, a Turk, said that one Copenhagen mosque was "100 percent behind ISIS."

Muslim leaders at the Grand Mosque in Nørrebro also discussed Hizb ut-Tahrir, which they said had about 500 members in Copenhagen. They characterized the group as against integration, whereas their mosque believes in "positive integration" and the ability of people to be both Danish and Muslim. The Hizb ut-Tahrir has criticized their mosque, they complained, spreading the falsehood that there was a Christian cross inside the mosque and Muslims prayed to it. One night, Hizb ut-Tahrir hoisted their black flag on one of the mosque's flagpoles.

## A HIZB UT-TAHRIR LEADER

After listening to the discussions about Hizb ut-Tahrir, we arranged an interview with Chadi Freigeh, who served as the spokesman for Hizb ut-Tahrir in Scandinavia. Freigeh, smartly dressed in jeans and a blazer and sporting a well-cropped short beard, works in computer graphics. He was born in Lebanon to Palestinian parents and came to Denmark when he was eleven years old. At that time, in the 1980s, he admitted, Danes were curious and open minded. Soon political debate started around Muslims and immigrants, the Danish People's Party formed, and Muslims became "taboo." In Denmark, he said, "they have made Islamic beliefs criminal."

Freigeh said he joined Hizb ut-Tahrir seventeen years ago because he felt it made the strongest arguments for an Islamic worldview. He dismissed the characterization that Hizb ut-Tahrir, which was formed in Jerusalem in 1953, is radical or terrorist, saying that the group rejects violence and attacks on civilians. However, "You can say that I'm a challenge to Western society in an intellectual sense or ideologically, and I will accept that. But are my ideas a security threat? I can't accept that." In Islam, he believed, there are fundamental values that are the opposite of the values of Western countries. Freigeh stated that the Prophet of Islam is his biggest role model, and it is not European secularism but the Prophet who delivered a frame that can secure pluralism.

"We want to have an Islamic state," Freigeh commented, summing up the ultimate goal of Hizb ut-Tahrir. But he was unsure when the caliphate will be established. A caliphate, he believed, would eliminate many of the problems the Western world faces, as Islam is "the best solution for mankind." A caliphate will also end Western military interventions in the Muslim world, and with no military interventions there would be "no reason for what the West refers to as terrorism." Freigeh described it as an "obligation to fight the occupier," saying he has a message of "jihad in Palestine," as well as places like Afghanistan. He noted there is a "weak understanding" of Islamic concepts and ideas among Muslims, which can lead to Muslims, for example, following movements like ISIS. Freigeh rejected the West's actions to challenge ISIS, saying that Muslims have to deal with ISIS "internally."

## AN ALTERNATIVE SCANDINAVIAN APPROACH TO IMMIGRANTS

In concluding the discussion on Denmark, I would like to mention my conversation in the summer of 2017 with Linda Zachrison, the cultural counselor at the Embassy of Sweden in Washington, D.C., regarding the current hostility toward immigrants in that country. Zachrison presented an alternative Scandinavian approach. Pointing out that the Swedes were different to the Danes in their approach to immigration, she talked enthusiastically of Sweden's long, complex, and proud tradition of accepting and integrating refugees with humanity. She pointed to the literature on the subject produced by the Swedish Institute and invited me to the embassy to discuss the subject. With the emergence of the Far Right, however, the situation regarding the immigrants throughout Scandinavia has been changing. The future promises uncertainty and tension in these Scandinavian countries as the debate about national identity and the place of the immigrants intensifies.

### Immigrants behind the Wheel

We talked to many taxi drivers who told us of the struggles in their daily lives. There was sadness in them as they attempted to cling to their identity through memories of home, aware that their larger community is dehumanized in the public mind, which often depicts them as monolithic and heartless brutes. In December 2014, after I had appeared on Danish television in Copenhagen discussing the terrible massacre at the Army Public School in Peshawar in which some 150 staff and students, mainly young boys, were slaughtered by the Taliban, our team took a taxi driven by a Pakistani who could not contain his joy at meeting us. When we arrived at our destination, he came out of the vehicle and wished to unburden himself. We contemplated the terrible tragedy, the loss of the young lives, the violence and corruption in Pakistan, yet we spoke of the country with affection. As we stood there shivering in the Danish winter, I noted that the cold did not prevent a tear or two trickling down his face. Another Pakistani taxi driver in Copenhagen swerved his vehicle in excitement when we spoke to him in Urdu. He admitted he had not heard the language for months and was hungry to hear its "sweet sound." That was, he said, beaming with pleasure, the happiest day for him in a long, long time.

Some would not let go of the problems of their homeland, such as the heavyset Palestinian with thick hair and beard who drove us on a cold and dark winter's evening to a remote suburb in Copenhagen. When we asked his name and where he was from, he became defensive. But we persisted. "Life is shit," he exclaimed, and seamlessly transferred his thoughts and woes from Europe to the Middle East. He had been in an Israeli prison for three months on a flimsy pretext along with 15,000 women and children. He called Israel a "cancer." For the Israelis, he said in a matter-of-fact tone, "the only good Palestinian is a dead Palestinian."

Others, like the Dari-speaking Afghan taxi drivers in Munich and Cologne, were content to be in Europe and wished to forget the violence at home. On both occasions I thought I heard the dulcet sounds of old Bollywood film songs from its "golden days" in the 1950s and 1960s on their radio. I asked for the volume to be raised as I recognized some of my favorite songs from films like *Awaara*. The man in Cologne said he did not attend the large new Turkish mosque in the city. Both men simply wanted education, healthcare, and jobs for their families. They did not say so, but they were ethnic minorities dominated by the Pashtuns, the largest tribal group in Afghanistan, and were victims of the Taliban.

Still others have obtained some distance in their assessment of Europe, such as the weather-beaten driver of the Pakistani ambassador in Copenhagen, who drove us home after a dinner hosted by his boss. He had come to Denmark from Pakistan decades ago and referred to the Danes several times as *dako*, dacoits, and *lotairey*, those who loot, because, he believed, their current behavior reflected the heritage of their pillaging ancestors, the Vikings. The passing of a law in Denmark in January 2016 that allows authorities to seize whatever paltry assets refugees have on them would undoubtedly have confirmed the driver's worst fears about the Danes. Nonetheless, he praised the Danish social services as the best in the world: "They provide everything—health, education, housing. It is perfect." That set him off comparing the care lavished on its people by the Danish government to the indifference to its people of his home country and the lack of facilities there, which had brought him to Europe in the first place.

# FIVE

# Indigenous Muslims: "We Are Europeans"

IN THE EARLY 1990s, I found myself in the middle of a particularly vicious war in the Balkans that gave us the term *ethnic cleansing*. I was in Bosnia to film a program for the BBC, seated with a large group of dazed women of every age and description in a college auditorium. They had one thing in common: They had been systematically defiled by drunken soldiers in "rape camps" and were petrified that their tormentors would come back. I was meeting the indigenous Muslims of Europe, and it was a distressing experience.

The women sobbed softly as they told me, hesitantly, mechanically, and with resignation, their harrowing stories of gang rape and forced pregnancies. They were finding it difficult to complete the telling of their tribulations; and by covering their faces with their hands they indicated the violation of their honor, leaving little to the imagination. A young woman, wearing a red sweater, her dark hair falling freely, spoke in a soft voice of hiding from the Serbs who slaughtered her neighbors and pillaged her community. She maintained a solemn, sober expression throughout her testimony. "For four days after the slaughter, we stayed in the house—nobody dared to go outside," she recounted. "Suddenly the Serbs were everywhere. We heard they were raping the young women." At this moment the pain and fear became too much and she took a tissue to her eyes, turned slightly away from the camera, and sobbed quietly. Then a middle-aged woman, wearing a flowing blue dress and a hijab, began to recount her torment: "We ran away to another village. I was in that village for maybe a month, at my sister-in-law's. After a month we had to run away to yet another village—Bišćani." At the mention of the name, her expression

249

changed abruptly and, like a dam bursting, her tears poured out uncontrollably, and she had to cover her face with a handkerchief as she muttered, "In Bišćani they killed . . . it's too horrible to repeat." All of us within hearing of these soft-spoken women could feel their pain and suffering, as if witnessing the events unfold before our very eyes.

I was staring into the abyss. It was becoming difficult to maintain the modicum of authority and control I needed as presenter of the BBC television series *Living Islam*. Even the senior producer, an Englishman and seasoned BBC TV executive, turned his face away from the crew, not wanting anyone to see the tears in his eyes.

We were based in Split, a small picturesque port on the Croatian coast, and would go into Bosnia early in the morning to film and conduct interviews and return late at night. During these interviews, there was a constant background noise of gunfire. Yet in spite of the human misery that was all about, I could not fail to be struck by the resilience and spirit of the people, and the beauty of the land, with its rolling grass fields, scenic wooded hills, and small, neat houses and villages.

In Split I also came across a group of young British Muslims of South Asian immigrant background who were there to provide aid to their Bosnian religious brethren. In private, they complained to me that the Bosnian Muslims knew little of Islam and could not even say their prayers properly. I was outraged. The Bosnians were facing genocide with courage and dignity, yet all these British Muslims could do was to carp about their lack of Islamic ritual. I reprimanded the group for showing lack of compassion and understanding and reminded them of the core values of Islam, which emphasize precisely these virtues. The encounter alerted me to the different strands of Islam that were in play on the continent and the consequences that would arise from their confrontation.

In the meantime, I was finding it difficult to reconcile the fact that here in Bosnia there were Europeans butchering and raping other Europeans. Most appalling of all, this was happening barely a half century after Europeans piously said "never again" when the horrors of the Holocaust were discovered. As the state of Yugoslavia weakened and then fell apart, the concealed primordial tribal identities came roaring to the surface, and Serbs, Croats, and Bosnians were at each other's throats. This was a war not of large tank divisions clashing with each other across continents but one of sneaking into the neighbor's home with hatchet and axe. This was the Balkans; the very name had the connotation of a dark and dangerous region in the minds of many Europeans. It was here, in Sarajevo, that a wild-eyed young man with a revolver started the First World War, which in turn triggered the Second World War. In the end, the two wars cost some 100 million lives.

The native Muslims of Europe—which include Bosnians, also known as Bosniaks, Pomaks, Turks, Albanians, Tatars, Roma, and Cham—live mainly in the Balkans and are often overlooked in discussions of Islam in the West. We meet them in this chapter and hear their voices. While these Muslims took pride in their Muslim identity, they were equally proud of their European identity. Because they are seen as existing between two cultures—one based in the West and the other in the Muslim world—they are often dismissed as too Muslim by Europeans and too European by Muslims. They have faced brutal persecution, and further research needs to be conducted of their extraordinary but little-known histories and cultures.

The Balkan region was on the front lines of the confrontation between Christian Europe and the Muslim Ottoman Empire. For centuries there was clash and conflict, but there were also times of peace and harmony between Jews, Christians, and Muslims characterized by convivencia and the ilm ethos. Indeed, the Balkans under Ottoman rule provided a refuge for the Jews fleeing Andalusia who went on to thrive in cities like Sarajevo and Thessaloniki, as discussed in chapter 7. Yet the centuries of military conflict in the region, in which large areas passed back and forth between the control of powers like the Hapsburgs and the Ottomans, created an idea in the minds of Europeans that Islam was threatening, predatory, alien, and uncivilized.

As communism collapsed, the former Ottoman Christian peoples of the Balkans charted a new course of nationalism and an aggressive promotion of primordial identity with strong predatory overtones that too often reverted to old hatreds and prejudices, as was seen in the horrific cases of genocide and ethnic cleansing in Bosnia. Serbian president Slobodan Milošević and his government cast the Bosnians and Albanians as Turks who needed to be removed from the Serb state and from Europe itself. Reviving the memory of their resistance to the Ottomans, the Serbs set out to finally and completely take revenge for hundreds of years of Ottoman rule. Between 1988 and 1989, the coffin of Prince Lazar, the Serb commander killed in the 1389 Battle of Kosovo against the Ottomans, was taken on a pilgrimage to towns and villages across Serbia, accompanied by sobbing mourners dressed in black. Milošević's 1989 address to a million Serbs on the 600th anniversary of the Battle of Kosovo immediately preceded the breakup of Yugoslavia and the Serb campaigns of genocide and ethnic cleansing.

The war in the Balkans was being conducted in the context of a changing world and the emergence of what was being called "global Islam," a discussion triggered after the Iranian Revolution. The crisis in Bosnia had come between the ignominious expulsion of the Soviet Union from Afghanistan in the late 1980s and the emergence of the Taliban and al-Qaeda in that country in the late 1990s. During this brief interval the sympathetic and undivided focus of the Muslim world was on Bosnia. I was active in the 1990s from my base at Cambridge University in speaking about the genocide in the Balkans. British society, including the government and royal family, were outraged at the horrors that were being carried out in Europe. I spoke, for example, at the invitation of Vanessa Redgrave along with her, the Bosnian ambassador to the United Kingdom, and two members of Parliament in Central Hall, Westminster, in July 1995. Prince Charles in March 1996 wrote a letter to me in which he said, referring to my experience in Bosnia, "You saw far more than I was ever able to see and I can well imagine how scarred you must have been. . . . It is a monstrous, criminal act that has been perpetuated on the Muslim population and especially on their most treasured religious and cultural monuments. It breaks my heart to think of what has been lost."

It was during this period that I had the privilege of first meeting Dr. Haris Silajdžić, who was then prime minister of Bosnia and Herzegovina, in London. I presented him my book *Living Islam*, which the BBC had published to accompany the television series of the same title. He accepted the book graciously, and we discussed the situation in the Balkans and in the Muslim world.

The meeting with Haris had reminded me that there was more to the Muslims in the Balkans than their suffering. This was an ancient community that had contributed to literature, architecture, and the creation of a pluralist society in which neither anti-Semitism nor hatred of any religion had any place. I was determined one day to explore the Muslim societies of the Balkans in greater detail.

## *The Bosnian Muslims of the Balkans*

Two decades later in 2014, as we conducted fieldwork for this project, I would meet Haris in Sarajevo. Not surprising for a European intellectual, he was sitting by himself, lost in thought, drinking coffee and smoking a Dunhill cigarette in a corner of the appropriately named Café Morocco situated next to Hotel Europe where we were staying, just yards from where Archduke Franz Ferdinand was assassinated, an act that still reverberates in our times. In our lengthy, free-wheeling conversations, I found that when he began to develop an idea he would not let it go until he had explored it to what he thought was its logical conclusion. Once, as we left the café, we stepped into a torrential downpour. As neither of us had umbrellas we were quickly soaked, but he stood there resolutely and continued talking, oblivious to the rain. Briefly he diverted the conversation to global warming and climate change, pointing to the "Malaysian-like" rain that was falling, before returning to the topic under discussion.

Like André Malraux, the French minister of cultural affairs under de Gaulle, and Václav Havel, the first president of the Czech Republic, Haris is the quintessential European public intellectual. Like them, he is both philosopher and national statesman; the former forever fascinated by and in despair at the human condition, and the latter embodying the hopes and aspirations of the people in spite of it. A Bosnian Muslim, Haris has held the offices of foreign minister, prime minister (twice) and president of Bosnia and Herzegovina, a nation he helped create in the 1990s. He is also a poet acutely aware of the world around him and the pain and joy and tears and laughter in it. Surprisingly, for a man who has held the highest offices in his country, is possibly the last surviving founding father of the nation, and is widely considered its most prominent living statesman, there was never any kind of security around him. Indeed his low-key appearance, usually in an open somewhat crumpled white shirt and grey trousers, confirmed the impression of an ordinary Bosnian going about his business. Perhaps it was his religious training—at one point he ran the office of the grand mufti—or perhaps it was the characteristic Bosnian down-to-earth attitude toward life.

We talked of our admiration for Goethe and Rumi and compared them, about the purpose of life and its meaning, of faith in an increasingly secular world, and of the fragility of human societies. He returned to Goethe again and again: "When I think of Europe in positive terms, what it aspires to be, I think of one word—Goethe." Haris kept raising the question: "Why do we exist?" He said with awe: "We are a miracle." The siege of Sarajevo, which he described as the longest in European history, taught him many lessons about the uncertainty of life as, he reminisced, he risked death every time he walked out into the street. People today are in such a hurry that they have little time to reflect on life.

During our conversation, Haris spoke at length about the Asian impact on Europe, especially the contribution of all of Asia's major religions, including Christianity. His view of contemporary Muslims was not complimentary, as he believed they were too obsessed with recreating the past. Muslims had still to answer the question Bernard Lewis famously raised, "What went wrong?" He agreed with the assessment of the renowned scholar of Islam that Muslims had fallen far behind the West and it would take some time before they caught up.

> Whatever is happening, the Muslims must turn to themselves. Not to look outside or blame racism or colonialism forever. . . . Yes they are there, sometimes they raise their ugly heads even today, but Muslims should look into themselves. What is around them will not change unless they change themselves and that is what their holy book, the Quran, says explicitly: God will not change whatever is around you until you change what's in you. So some of them are adapting, some of them are not, but it's a big crisis and again coming at the speed of change, it's happening very fast.

As for those Europeans who argue that Muslims are not part of Europe, Haris told me that the ethnic roots of the Bosniaks in Europe go back thousands of years. "We are here to stay," he asserted. "I'm a Muslim," he continued, "and my ethnic characteristics—my DNA, if you like, although I don't care about that—goes back at least to 2000 BC to the existence of the Illyrian tribe. There is a lot of Illyrian DNA here, and those are, by recognition of all people of science, the oldest European stock. So what are they talking about? Who is that person to say you are not of this? Does he own a monopoly of culture, of religion?" When I asked who his heroes were, he mentioned Croat and even Serb figures, but his main role model was the figure of the anonymous and idealized Palestinian woman. In the most difficult circumstances, he stated, she keeps the family together, her children clean, her posture dignified and she never abandons hope for the future. Clearly he saw an echo of what his Bosnians had suffered in the figure of the Palestinian woman.

Haris's pride in his European identity is matched by his anger and disappointment at Europe's indifference to the massive human rights violations in the Balkans in the 1990s. He recalled that French president François Mitterrand told him that "they," European leaders, would never allow a Muslim nation to exist in Europe. The European strategy was to place an embargo on weapons in the region in the hope that it would stop the fighting. In fact, all the embargo did was to allow the Serbs, who inherited the bulk of the military machinery of Yugoslavia, to carry out their sinister ethnic designs while tiny land-locked Bosnia was denied access to weapons even for self-defense. It was common knowledge that the Russians were providing full military support to the Serbs, whom they consider their ethnic Slavic kin. The Serbs also spread propaganda that the Bosnians were breeding "Islamic terrorists" and were therefore a threat to Europe.

Just when it seemed Sarajevo would fall in a matter of days and its inhabitants braced for the threatened genocide, a miracle happened. Desperately seeking assistance, Haris met the Pakistani prime minister Nawaz Sharif in Islamabad, who asked what he could do to help. Haris told him that without antitank missiles, Sarajevo would fall, and his people would be exterminated. The Serbs had dug their tanks into the hilltops surrounding Sarajevo, and their constant barrage of shells rained down death and destruction. The defenders—which included those Serbs who wished for a united and inclusive nation—were fighting with primitive hunting guns and farming tools. After listening to Haris for five minutes, the prime minister agreed to provide the antitank missiles.

With a quiet glee that two decades had not dimmed, Haris recalled the moment when the first antitank missiles were fired by the Bosnians. The missiles struck their target and in an instant destroyed the tanks. The Serbs literally had no idea what hit them. Baffled, they immediately pulled back all the tanks from the hilltops. It was a turning point in the war. The worst was over. "That changed the character of the war," he stated. Pakistanis are a noble people, he reflected. Perhaps the Pakistanis were sympathetic, he thought, because they too had suffered during the creation of their nation in 1947.

Haris suggested that Bosnia had developed its long history of cultural pluralism and acceptance—and its compassionate nature—as a result of being situated along civilizational fault lines. "Our region was caught between the East and West always. Going back to Roman times, it probably created an empathy for those who suffer." He noted in particular that Bosnian history has been largely shaped by inclusive, pluralist institutions. "We have had authentic pluralism here for hundreds of years, long periods of peace and stability in Bosnia here. There was a place for women, electing their own king, and things like that, so this is not exactly a savage place. But we live in Europe, which has invented two world wars—not by Bosnia, by the way, and not by Muslims."

Bosnians, Haris explained, have simply been living out their charter as Muslims in fostering pluralism. "That's why in the Quran it says that—and I'm paraphrasing—we have created you, peoples and tribes, so that you can know each other." He continued, "Today, we still can show or remind Europe of its great genius and its great ideas of pluralism—of *egalité, fraternité, liberté*. Small Bosnia can do that, but they don't want to hear it." In a letter written in late 2017, he was not sanguine about the future: "Bosnia is targeted, once again, by its neighbors. This time the pretext is 'potential terrorist safe haven.'"

*The BBC Book That Helped Shape a Nation*

When Haris accepted the gift of my book *Living Islam*, I had little idea of its fate. I was astounded when I heard that he had arranged to have the book translated and widely distributed—after all, it was the equivalent of George Washington or Thomas Jefferson in the thick of fighting for the creation of the United States taking time to supervise the translation, printing, and distribution of a book. I began to understand the magnitude of what occurred when I visited Bosnia and Herzegovina two decades later. As Bosnia's prime minister at the time and one of its leading intellectuals, Haris was well aware that over the last century the identity of his Muslim community had been systematically under attack and was in danger of being lost. He had to help re-create elements of Bosnia's religion, culture, and customs. Haris had undoubtedly asked himself, what would be the ideal philosophy for establishing the new nation's identity, how would it relate to Islam, and what kind of Islam would it be? How could Bosnia balance Islamic influences with Western ones while taking the best of both? Believing that *Living Islam* provided some of the answers, Haris passed the book to the urbane Professor Enes Karić, the Bosnian minister for education, science, culture, and sport at the time, who gave the book to the Bosnian professor Zulejha Ridanović to translate into Bosnian. "I would say the message of your book," Karić told us in Sarajevo, "is *Living Islam*, not Islam of the past, it is Islam from the very life, and that is why I myself and my colleagues are delighted with your book."

> We decided to publish it in Bosnia in almost the same layout and format as it was published in English. After that we heard that there is a program done by the BBC in collaboration with you under the same title. We as a government, as an independent state of Bosnia-Herzegovina, sent a letter to the BBC and the BBC offered it to us without paying any money, for free, and the official letter is still available. I remember now every year during the month of Ramadan, everyone sees the program on TV. It really is a wonderful program.

For me, meeting Professor Ridanović was a highlight of our visit. Now retired, the professor came to see us at our hotel in Sarajevo accompanied by her daughter, Lejla Ridanović, who works for the United Nations in Geneva. Together they recounted the story of the translation, which the team and I heard with fascination.

Professor Ridanović had written to me in April 1996. I received the letter at Cambridge and will always treasure it. It was typed on an ancient typewriter, and the paper was rough. Even now, reading the letter takes my breath away as it reflects an extraordinary story behind an already dramatic one. After introducing herself, she wrote,

> I must say that it was a tremendous pleasure translating your book. It is so close to the heart of every Muslim that I considered myself privileged to have the opportunity to do the translation. Both the book and the series were ready just before the month of Ramadan and were received with great satisfaction and admiration by the public. I was translating the book in the days of heavy shelling, knowing somehow, that I shall live to see it completed and published. And I did thank Allah, the Merciful.

She ended her letter with greetings for Zeenat, my wife, and Umar, my son. "I sincerely hope that some day, you will all be able to come and visit us here in Sarajevo. Please, give my best to Zeenat-hanum and Umar."

It is important to place the story of my book in the context of the siege of Sarajevo, which lasted from April 1992 to February 1996. Zulejha was working on the translation at the height of the attempt by the Serbs to break the spirit of the Bosnians and capture Sarajevo. Serbs, with tanks and heavy artillery, were firing incessantly and indiscriminately into the city, killing Muslims and non-Muslims alike. The Serbs had boasted that it was only a matter of days before Sarajevo fell. They had promised a blood bath—but they had not taken into account the resolve of the Bosnians.

Zulejha and Lejla slept in the corridor of their flat at that time, where they felt safer from the shelling. Lejla described coming home to the cold apartment, without water and electricity, the windows blown out, and finding her mother working on a particular sentence by candlelight and then reading it to her with pride. "Do you think I have got it right?" Zulejha would ask. "Have I captured the spirit of the author?"

When she left the apartment each day, Lejla said, her mother never knew if she would make it back alive. "We had some really serious days in that period, 1993 was really, really tough, up to 3,000 shells a day, so you never knew whether you would survive the day, you just go and do your work. And every morning when you say goodbye, that could be the last day you see each other." Lejla thought back to those days with a shudder. "It was very difficult to find firewood. We would burn newspapers, old tires, shoes, anything. She translated the book by hand, I was bringing the paper."

Lejla, so proud of her mother, recounted how her mother refused to leave the pages that she was translating behind in their flat when she left for the office. Clutching the manuscript, she would say, "What if a shell

*Author and Amineh with Haris Silajdžić,*
*Zulejha Riđanović, and Lejla Riđanović*

landed on my flat when I am away and destroyed them? I would therefore prefer to have the translation with me and safe." When it was finished, the translation was a triumph. "The interest for the book," Zulejha said with glee, "was tremendous, everybody, and it just disappeared because it was delivered all over the place. And it helped people to feel better and we're very proud of everything." *Living Islam* "gave us courage," recalled Zulejha. She said that the translated *Living Islam* "was really given as a present to our soldiers, generals, all the foreign guests. . . . They were all the people who meant something, I think it was like a sign of praise to all of those who were really important, soldiers, religious people, other people, artists, all those who were really active and very important for the morale." "It's really everywhere," she claimed, "It speaks to everybody."

Now, here we were, in Sarajevo, drinking tea with the translator of *Living Islam*. Lejla mentioned with some awe the role of Haris as the patron of the project. While Lejla was talking, I received an email from Haris, asking if I was free to meet for a cup of coffee. I suggested he come across and join us. Within a few minutes he arrived, much to the delight of the Ridanovićs. Serendipity indeed: As we laughed and talked, it seemed that time stood still, the past and the present, different cultures and continents conflated, and humanity became one.

We saw the widespread impact of *Living Islam* during our Bosnian fieldwork. Mustafa Jahić, the director of the historic Gazi Husrev-bey Library in Sarajevo, proudly showed copies of it to us in the library, as did the head librarian at Sarajevo's Bosniak Institute from its library. The grand mufti of Bosnia and Herzegovina, Husein Kavazović, stated when we

*Author and his team with the Grand Mufti of Bosnia and Herzegovina, Husein Kavazović*

called on him, "We are honored to have you visit us. Your book was an inspiration to our religious scholars, the *ulema* here."

The story of the translation and distribution of *Living Islam* has been presented as a case study to illustrate the commitment to the ilm ethos—learning, knowledge, and compassion—among the Bosnians. Perhaps there is no greater challenge than to preserve the pursuit of ilm under the most violent conditions; and the Bosnians had met it. The example also provides insights into Bosnian society and how individuals relate to one another to get things done even in the middle of a war. Finally, it is a story that tells us how ideas in a book written in one part of the world can find an echo in another and help a nation rediscover itself.

### *The Former Grand Mufti of Bosnia and Herzegovina*

In Sarajevo, we were privileged to interview both the present grand mufti and his predecessor, Mustafa Cerić, as he prepared to take part in elections for the presidency of the country. Cerić was educated in Sarajevo before going on to attend Al-Azhar University in Cairo and the University of Chicago, where he obtained a Ph.D., and went on to serve as grand mufti until 2012. He is a highly respected figure in the Muslim world. Cerić compared the approaches of both the famous universities he attended. "When I was at Al-Azhar I was told everything has been solved. Islam has solved all the problems. So I was very sad. I didn't know what to do, because everything has been solved. When I came to the University of Chicago, they told me nothing has been solved. Everything is waiting for you to research and to study and to give solutions."

It is for this reason, Cerić explained, that he was seeking the Bosnian presidency at the time of our visit. To explain his thinking on the matter, he mentioned the famous French statesman Cardinal Richelieu who, in a time of religious wars, "realized that the only solution was the state, and he built the French state. But he allied with the Ottoman emperor and asked that they help, and they helped him." Cerić was seeking, he explained, to reconcile religion and politics. He believed this will be a "major theme of the twenty-first century, and it is because Muslims are bringing these messages of religion, of morality. . . . I think that Muslims are the only people today who are caring about what is right and what is wrong. It is another thing whether they do it in a right way. . . . They are doing it very aggressively and so on."

Cerić discussed the importance of the Balkans as the European region with the most diversity and also the importance of the indigenous Muslims of Europe. "The history of the Balkans and Europe cannot be separated. . . . The Balkans was always a boiling pot, if you like. But my point is this: the Balkans remained the most dense in its multicultural, multilingual, multinational character, more than any other region in Europe." In this, Cerić believed, the Balkans is unlike the rest of Europe, which was, in places such as Spain, "ethnically cleansed a long time ago."

Liberal democracy, Cerić maintained, is not able to comprehend and live up to its ideals. He analyzed why it was failing, tracing the development of the philosophy of liberal democracy and international cooperation, which he associated with Kant:

We are now in the dilemma between the philosophy of Hegel and Kant. Hegel believed that war is the legitimacy of the establishment and the maintenance of the state. . . . Kant believed, on the other hand, that the only way humanity can survive is to adapt and accept international law based on morality. If Hitler had won in the Second World War, then Hegel's philosophy would have prevailed. But fortunately America intervened in Europe in the Second World War and Roosevelt adopted Kant's philosophy rather than Hegel's philosophy, and this is why we have the United Nations and we have international courts, and I as a Muslim in Bosnia now can say that despite what happened to my people, in the genocide and so on, I can say, thanks to Kant and to Roosevelt, that the International Court of Justice and the International Tribunal for the Crimes against Humanity in The Hague were established for the first time in history as a single court because of the genocide against my people.

Discussing the challenges Muslims were confronting, Cerić stated, "I think our teachers are not up to the challenge of the time. Too much religion in a wrong way is very dangerous." "Unfortunately," he lamented, the "so-called modernists," who obtained an education in the West before returning to Muslim countries, "are lost, they don't know what to do."

Speaking to Europeans, Cerić said, "I don't care whether you love me or you don't love me, but I do care whether you respect me or not." The question for Europe is clear: "can it have somebody there, whose identity is Islam and Muslim?"

I don't feel inferior to anyone. I feel equal and decent and happy, because I am Muslim. I don't need to tell you all the time, because I don't ask you what is your religion or what is your nationality, and so on. The problem is that somehow we accept that others are teaching us that somehow we are a problem. No, we are not a problem, we are a solution of this world.

### *The President of Bosnia's Islamic Constitutional Court*

In Sarajevo, we met Fikret Karčić, a professor of law and Islamic studies at the University of Sarajevo and the president of the Constitutional Court of the Islamic Community of Bosnia and Herzegovina. He is a native of Višegrad, a town in eastern Bosnia, which, he noted, was also home to Ivo Andrić, a Yugoslav novelist and Bosnia's only Nobel Prize–winning author, who wrote his famous book *The Bridge on the Drina* (1945) about the town and its historic Ottoman bridge.

Karčić defined Bosniak identity, as

Islamic ethnic origin, Slavic language with Arabic, Turkish, and Persian words, Bosnian language . . . and also belonging to Bosnia and Herzegovina. Bosnia was part of the Ottoman Empire for 500 years. In 1878 Austria-Hungary came and occupied Bosnia for 40 years, and during that period we experienced Western type of modernization, and then after that the Yugoslav kingdom for 20 years, the Second World War, and then communist government for 50 years. And now we are free.

Speaking as an eminent authority on the subject, Karčić addressed the important matter of interpreting shariah in a modern society, explaining that many Muslim states focused on criminal codes in seeking to apply shariah. In this, they displayed an incomplete understanding of the shariah: "We see a number of Muslim states from the 1970s onward proclaiming that they're going to apply shariah, and they started with criminal law. They did not start with human rights; with guarantees with constitutional law, etc. They started with the administration of penalties." "Some military regimes," Karčić continued, "were connected with projects of applying shariah. You know, by their nature military regimes are not democratic; therefore, non-Muslim public opinion was influenced by such developments in addition to prejudices toward Islam."

Turning to the role of the shariah in Bosnia, Karčić noted that "Muslims have opted for secular law in the field of marriage and family law." "Even during the Islamic revival, which we have witnessed in Bosnia since the 1970s," he noted, "there was not a single public call for the administration of shariah. What is important is to keep Muslim identity, and if Muslim identity can be safeguarded by secular laws, in that case we don't need to go for specific demands for special laws. And there is one proverb which says that those who are administered by special laws can be executed by special laws as well."

Karčić showed us several framed items on his walls, including one depicting the shariah as a tree with the branches representing the different legal schools of Islam; another showing Istanbul in Ottoman times, "to show the connection between Bosnia and the Ottoman state"; and a third displaying "the founding documents of the United States of America, representing the modern world." "Together," he stated, "they represent comparative legal history. It is a course that I teach here. . . . We take very important examples from the human past in terms of law and legal developments and we study them on a comparative basis."

I asked Karčić how he explained the Bosnian desire for justice rather than revenge, and he replied, "Yes, that is true. . . . After such terrible crimes and such terrible experience, we did not have any kind of terrorist attack or revenge by Bosnian Muslims." "Just to give you an illustration," Karčić said, "during wartime, I remember, I watched on Bosnian TV there was news that a particular child was killed by a Serbian sniper and his father said on camera, 'I would like to sit down with the killer to take coffee and ask him why did he kill my son?' You just imagine that kind of reaction."

## *The Director of Sarajevo's Gazi Husrev-bey Library*

In Sarajevo, Mustafa Jahić gave us a tour of the historic Gazi Husrev-bey Library, where he has served as director since 1987. Following the destruction of the old building during the war, the library's new and impressive building opened on January 15, 2014. Jahić told us that the library, founded in 1537, is "maybe the oldest institution in all of Bosnia and the Balkans." The library showcases the Islamic heritage of Bosnia, containing more than 100,000 books, manuscripts, and documents. Jahić said that after the destruction of Sarajevo's National Library in 1992 and its 2 million books, the Gazi Husrev-bey Library was left as the "library with the most books, documents, and historical articles."

The incredible and inspiring story of how the Gazi Husrev-bey Library's priceless books were preserved during the war was the subject of a 2011 documentary by the BBC (*The Love of Books: A Sarajevo Story*). As Jahić explained, "In April 1992, after we saw what is happening, we took the documents and manuscripts out of the library. We moved them eight times from place to place to save them. . . . Our biggest fear was that if we lost all these documents and manuscripts, we would lose ourselves, we would lose our identity." Jahić believed that while, from a certain perspective, human life can be replaced, books and heritage—once destroyed—cannot. "We lost 500,000 people but somehow we hope, inshallah, that we will gain again those people. But once you lose heritage, history, culture, represented through books, that is something you cannot return." He spoke about the horrific experience the Bosnians went through in the course of the siege of Sarajevo, during which he attempted to save the books:

> Almost every day, I came here to the library to try and save more books. Every day we were facing death. When we left our house, it could be the last time we saw our families. . . . Five-hundred meters from our house there was a division line, and we could hear the Serb soldiers. After they destroyed the mosque in our area, we heard them say how happy they were. . . . Today, in these modern times, let's call them modern, it's really hard to find time to show your family you love them. But in war, you use every moment because you know you can lose them any second, and you use every moment to show and to be with your family. And at the same time, war sometimes makes people closer to God. When you lose all hope, then you see that you have faith and that you have Allah, and that you are not alone.

Jahić said he wanted Bosnia to be remembered for more than war.

> We want to be famous for our books, for our heritage, for our library. . . . Sarajevo usually is known as a place where the First World War started, but we wanted to preserve the memory of Sarajevo having to do with our scholars, our library, showing that here is a meeting point of cultures, of civilizations. . . . We as Muslims should be proud of our heritage, our culture, and our tradition. We are Europeans and at the same time we have our Islamic civilization and culture.

## A Bosnian Intellectual

In Sarajevo, we interviewed Mirnes Kovač, editor of the *Preporod* newspaper, the oldest Islamic news magazine in the Balkans, and contributor to *Al Jazeera* and the *Huffington Post*, who recently edited *The Siege of Islam*, a volume of interviews with leading Muslim and non-Muslim intellectuals on relations between Islam and the West. Considering the situation in Bosnia, Kovač referred to the country's "three visions"—the parallel narratives and histories of the Serbs, Croats, and Bosniaks—concerning what occurred during the 1990s and who was to blame. "The problem of these three visions of Bosnia," he believed, "is that we didn't have processes that Germany had after Second World War. We did not have the process of de-Nazification. We still, twenty years later, we didn't find a way to resolve our conflicts in our heads." He is concerned about the future: "The whole world, and especially Europe, should learn the lesson of Srebrenica and commit itself again that it will not allow genocide to ever happen to anyone anywhere in the world. That is my hope."

Since Europe has problems that involve the Balkans, Kovač hoped that Europe, as well as the United States, remain engaged in the region. Yet he fears that Russia's 2014 annexation of Crimea could be a harbinger of things to come, noting that Crimea, like the Balkans, was part of the Turkish sphere of influence but is considered crucial by Russians to their interests and identity. He compared this with how the Serbs associate Bosnians with the Turks. In that context, Kovač believed, the slaughter of Muslim Bosniaks at Srebrenica was seen as "revenge" against the Ottomans. "According to some Serbian historians," Kovač noted, "the hatred of Islam and Turks was a defining feature in creating Serbian national identity, and still it is."

Kovač is not discouraged by his difficult surroundings and remains committed to interfaith initiatives: in the summer of 2017, I received a

*Zeenat, Amineh, and team at the historic Ottoman mosque and market in Sarajevo*

large, starkly produced volume published by him called *One,* which lays out, page by page, Biblical sayings with matching Quranic ones on the opposite page on subjects such as peace, compassion, and unity (published by the Interreligious Council of Bosnia and Herzegovina, undated, Sarajevo).

### Bosniak Librarians

At the Bosniak Institute in Sarajevo, which is dedicated to the history and culture of the Bosnian Muslims, we met two young Bosnian women, Narcisa Puljek-Bubrić, the Institute's head librarian, and her colleague Merima Memić, an art historian. The two women discussed the Serb nationalism that led to the genocide against the Bosnians and said it is still very much alive. The "meat" of this argument, said Puljek-Bubrić, "is that all of the Bosniaks are Ottomans, and they should kill them." She went on to describe the current environment. "They have their circles, and when they are born they are taught to hate, to take revenge, to hate everything. They have lists of people who they hate. . . . By law it's forbidden, but you can always see on national TV. They are publishing their books and nobody is forbidding that." They believe, claimed Memić, that Srebrenica was "nothing bad. They think it was right to do because we are in their country and they need to put us out."

Memić has no faith in the future: "I don't because really . . . it's just a matter of time before we go there," she said gloomily, pointing downward.

In Bosnian people, there is always a fear. We always live in fear, and that is a really horrible thing to live with, you know. When I am thinking about my family, I really want to have a family, to have children, but always when you are thinking about the future, you are always thinking somehow, what if, what if it is going to happen? Are we going to be killed? Are we going to be exiled? Are we going to have to find another country to live? And for the human part, it's really hard to live with that.

Capturing the dilemma of the Bosniaks, Memić remarked, "You go around and see people, they are really optimistic because they live here, they don't run away, they are trying, they are making their lives. But it's really not a normal life. You have to know that. Because the people who lived through the war experienced a great trauma."

Memić sent me a spirited letter from Bosnia after I returned to Washington, D.C.: "It is annoying to listen to all those so-called intellectuals who always speak in clichés and at the end of a story they say nothing at all. Everything you say makes sense—common sense which has become so rare. I also believe that in 'ilm' is hope, people need to become aware of themselves, they need to learn more and more. . . . But that is a main problem I think—knowledge is highly controlled by those who are in control unfortunately. That is the case here in Bosnia."

Puljek-Bubrić also wrote to me on my return:

Your questions about identity, war, and Bosnia and Herzegovina challenged me to rethink again about the past, and about the future of my country. I feel ignorant, worried, scared, little bit angry, and optimistic at the same time is the best explanation of my condition, and the condition of other people, too. Very rarely do we exchange these emotions with each other. Everyday, life is forcing us to focus on today's life, but deep down in our souls we feel that we cannot carry all of these emotions. To talk with you gave me new perspective, not to fight back but to rethink and to share feelings. Thank you for that. I forgot that I can do it.

## A Bosniak Social Worker and Refugee

In Penzberg, Germany, we visited a Muslim community that had many Bosnians, under the leadership of Imam Benjamin Idriz, a Macedonian who is a *hafiz,* someone who has memorized the Quran by heart. There we met the imam's Bosnian wife, Nermina Idriz, a social worker, whom Amineh interviewed. Later, in Sarajevo, we met the imam and his wife again, and Amineh spoke with her further.

Nermina, from Mostar, arrived in Germany as a refugee fleeing the war. On the subject of Islam and Europe, Nermina stated, "I'm from Bosnia, but I'm also a part of Europe, Sarajevo is the heart of Europe." Nermina said that she came from a Bosnian tradition of "very strong women." "My husband," she explained, "says all the time, that if you meet a Bosnian woman, the first thing she will say is 'I have rights.'"

Casting her mind to those terrible days in the 1990s, she sighed, "It was our friends who killed us. Our own friends. Our neighbors." She went back to an attack on her house, in which her younger brother was killed: "So, what happened with my family, we sat in one room, it was one grenade. I lost my brother. He was five years younger than me."

When her brother was killed, the trauma was so overwhelming that Nermina lost the will to live: "At this time, I think that my life also ended. And I don't like to live. I don't like to live." She was ready to die: "I wanted to go to my brother, you know, to be with him, and this *dunya,* this world, I wanted to forget it, it is nothing, actually." "My parents," she stated, "decided that I have to live, they wanted me to live. I had one aunt in Germany, she called us and we went there. I still did not like this life."

When she married and had children, she began to feel "different," saying, "I have two sons." At this point Nermina was overcome by emotion and began to cry. The interview came to an abrupt halt. Amineh reached out to embrace Nermina. When Nermina recovered, she went on to say that,

> We have to live and to make this part of earth something better for our children. So now, I want to live and to make Europe and Bosnia better. We have to live together, and also to drink coffee together. When I came to Germany, all the holidays, it was not new for me, because I have Christian friends. So, it is normal in Bosnia that we are living together, all our religions, and I like it.

To prevent such conflict in the future, she stated, "I take my children to Srebrenica, I want them to see it. And to vow that something like this

*With Imam Hisam Hafizović in Mostar, Bosnia and Herzegovina*

never happens again. We wish that no one ever has to experience what we did."

### *The Killing Fields of Srebrenica*

Srebrenica; the very word had come to mean ethnic cleansing and I was not looking forward to visiting the town. Steeling ourselves, as part of our fieldwork, we visited the Srebrenica Memorial Cemetery, site of the worst genocide in Europe since the Second World War. In July 1995 thousands of Muslim men and boys were slaughtered here while the UN peace-keeping forces looked on. The cemetery contains row upon row of thousands of white grave markers, and more remains continue to be found in the region and buried here every year. Visiting the cemetery is an emotional experience, and the sight of family members of the victims, particularly the wives and mothers, wandering about amid the tombstones like lost souls, is heartbreaking. The political tension that remains in Bosnia and Herzegovina, where many Muslims fear a return to ethnic war, is heightened in Srebrenica, which is located deep in the Serb-dominated part of the country known as Republika Srpska and near the international border with Serbia.

At the cemetery, we met Hatidža Mehmedović, the president of the Mothers of Srebrenica Association, and Hasan Hasanović, who works at the Srebrenica Genocide Memorial and serves as translator. Mehmedović's family members, including her two sons and her husband, were killed in the genocide. "In 1995 all of them were killed," she said. "The entire family of mine—my husband, my elder son Azmir, my younger son Almir. My brothers were killed also, two sons of my brother, and over fifty of my relatives. All of them were killed in the Srebrenica genocide." Mehmedović has never recovered. "This is not life that I live," she stated. "This is just a punishment to live without a complete family. Without a whole family, without anybody. To ask questions, every night, thousands of questions, and not have any answers. It's been twenty years since the Srebrenica genocide happened. For me, it's like twenty minutes. I've been longing for my children until now. I will never wish this kind of life even for those perpetrators."

"They kept killing everyone they could not trust," Mehmedović recalled, "regardless of age. We have boys who were as old as eight, children who were thirteen or fourteen, more than a thousand of them were minors. . . . The children didn't get to know any of life. They were not guilty of anything. If I had known that this would happen to me, probably I would never have decided to have children. We had healthy, smart children. We had not taught them to hate. We had not taught them to differentiate between people. We had not taught them to kill. And probably because of these things, we became victims. And many mothers now live alone. Many came here to live on the memories of their children here."

In addition to the torment experienced by the killing of so many family members during the war, Mehmedović said that many women in Srebrenica carry the psychological scars of having been raped by Serbs.

> These women who were raped, they never spoke. They are my siblings, my relatives, but they never talked about their personal tragedy, because they feel ashamed. There are women who are sick mentally, because of that experience, and someone has to be with them to take care of them. The women who have been raped, they never want to come back to Srebrenica, because they feel so insecure, knowing that those perpetrators are still at large—they are still here, they walk through the streets freely.

The atrocities perpetrated in Srebrenica were the "shame of the whole world," Mehmedović complained. "Those who could have prevented aggression against Bosnia, they just failed to do anything. This genocide happened after Srebrenica was declared a safe place. . . . The United Nations, they sympathized with Serbs. They gave them uniforms and some weapons and military equipment." The genocide, Mehmedović explained, was organized and conducted by people the Bosnians thought were their neighbors and friends.

> We thought we had friends, we are civilized people. We thought we wouldn't have any problems with our neighbors. . . . But we were wrong, we were very wrong, because our neighbors from Serbia came to take away our loved ones and kill them. . . . At the time, we were totally unarmed and we couldn't have escaped from here. Our loved ones were deprived of their right to live. Everything was as Serbia had planned—to get rid of one people, to get rid of one geographic area. It was not done by one or two men, not in one or two days. They had a strategy, they had a plan. And they kept working to ethnically cleanse one nation.

Mehmedović expressed alarm at the lessons Serb children are being taught today. "Those who are being acquitted for these crimes are teachers to youth. They are poison to youth. They tell children that they are heroes, that they have won a battle, that they took revenge against Turks. . . . They don't tell the children that those were unarmed civilians." Mehmedović's pain has been worsened, she explained, by the abuse hurled at her by Serb nationalists clad in black uniforms who "lined up" in Srebrenica. "I feel ashamed to repeat to you those words," she said. "Those were mostly kids, I mean teenagers, in those black uniforms. Some of them were not even born yet when the genocide happened. That's why I'm telling you that children need to know the truth."

Despite having suffered the loss of her closest family members, it was not revenge that Mehmedović desired but justice, which she explained derives from Islam.

> God knows how big of an injustice happened to us. May God judge those responsible. We just rely on God. Us returnees here, we never took revenge. We never took revenge. Allah left me to live, not just because I should live, it's because he wants me to tell the story to people who don't know. . . . If someone would give me the whole Serbian population to take revenge, I would never be able to take revenge on anyone. As Muslims, we should not take revenge.

"I never thought to hate anyone," she confessed. "I love all children. My faith keeps me going. I'm Muslim since I was born."

She described the Srebrenica Memorial Cemetery as "another Mecca for us." "Just one night in Srebrenica is a hajj." Mehmedović said that the grand mufti of Bosnia once asked her to go on the hajj, but she replied,

"No, I have done my hajj a long time ago. And in 2000 I did my hijra getting back to Srebrenica."

Hasanović, who translated for Mehmedović, was also in Srebrenica during the genocide and shared his own terrifying story. In describing his experience, he spoke in particularly scathing terms about the role of UN peacekeeping troops from the Netherlands who looked on as the genocide occurred. Hasanović said that he, his twin brother, and his father were among more than 10,000 men and boys who fled Srebrenica to the town of Tuzla, where they believed they would be safe. "We started to move," he explained, "to walk in a column one-by-one, marching from Srebrenica through the woods to Tuzla. We were literally afraid to come down here to the Dutch base. Because we knew the Dutch battalion would hand us over to the Serb Army."

During this march, when Serb forces opened fire on them,

> I lost the sight of my twin brother and my father. And I had never seen them again in my life. I just kept walking, pushing forward, to Tuzla, to safety. It took me six days and nearly six nights. I was almost captured and somehow I managed to escape. I saw them shooting at men and boys. And I was very lucky to sneak out and escape from those ambushes. Finally on the 16th of July 1995, I got to Tuzla, to the first Muslim village, a free village. At the same time, I was not very happy, because I was still thinking of my twin brother and my father, what happened to them. And of course, what happened to the rest of my family. When I got to Tuzla, I found my mother, my younger brother, and my grandfather at Tuzla airport, where all of the refugees from Srebrenica were placed. But still, my father and my twin brother were not there. And we were hoping that they will show up one day. And it took many years. Finally, in 2003, my father was buried here. And in 2005, my brother was buried here.

Hasanović went into further detail about the actions of the Dutch troops in Srebrenica. He told us there were about 5,000 Bosnian Muslims who had sought shelter inside the Dutch military base. Most of these were women and children, though 300 of them were adult men. Outside the base there were nearly 25,000 other refugees. After the refugees outside the base were shipped off to Tuzla by bus and truck, Hasanović recalled, the Dutch battalion expelled those refugees still inside the base. All of the men were later killed, he recounted, taking little consolation in the fact that a Dutch court had recently found the Dutch government responsible for the deaths of the 300 men.

Our visit to Srebrenica affected the entire team—especially the female members, who cried inconsolably as they heard the stories. "It shook my strong sense of optimism and faith in humanity when I walked through the sea of mass graves and heard the stories of an ethnic group savagely turning on innocent neighbors, babies as little as two days old murdered, and men as old as ninety-five, shot mercilessly," Amineh noted. "Pregnant mothers were beaten by drunken men in army boots till they bled and miscarried their babies. Fifty thousand women and girls between ten and sixty years of age were grouped together in a hundred concentration camps and repeatedly raped by the aggressor's army. These women were enslaved for more than three years."

"For Muslim women whose very identity is built on the concept of avoiding shame and maintaining physical honor," Amineh ruminated, "it was worse than death." She recalled a sketch by the artist Mevludin Ekmečić that vividly illustrated her point. On exhibit at the Bosniak Institute in Sarajevo, "Killed Souls" portrays a young teenage girl who is being heavily abused by soldiers in front of her parents and younger siblings. The caption reads, "I forgive you my life, but save my dignity."

Amineh captured well the entire team's impressions of the Bosnians, who had emerged from unspeakable tragedy with their sense of compassion intact: "The Bosniaks are one of the most dignified people I have met—they are intelligent, smart, noble, gentle, and forgiving—people who value knowledge, respect for the Other, and humanity. . . . At the risk of romanticizing them, the Bosniaks are a model for the rest of the Muslims, the world, and for humanity."

### The Mayor of Srebrenica

From the genocide memorial outside the city center we visited city hall to meet Ćamil Duraković, the mayor of Srebrenica. At thirty-five years old, he was serving his second year in office. Before turning to politics, Duraković worked for an international nongovernmental organization in Bosnia, aiding victims of the genocide. In October 2016, he lost his bid for reelection to a Serb candidate, Mladen Grujičić, marking the first time since the genocide that Srebrenica has had a Serb mayor. The vote ignited political turmoil and controversy, particularly as Grujičić denied that the killings in Srebrenica constituted genocide. Srebrenica had been the only municipality in Republika Srpska to have a Muslim mayor.

I had requested to meet Mayor Duraković at the Srebrenica memorial, but he wanted to meet in his own office to send "a message that there is a life outside of the memorial center." Duraković was born in Srebrenica in 1979 and was still a child during the war. Traveling along with 15,000 people through the mountains for seven days, he was able to flee Srebrenica and reach the safe area of Tuzla. He was fortunate, he said, but "15,000 of us started and only a few thousand survived. Everybody else was pretty much captured or killed. So all seven days were not a walk through the woods to get there. It was walking and fighting, ambushes and all this. . . . Yes, I was one of the lucky ones to survive." He said that he "lost two of my uncles, my mother's brothers, and three of their sons. . . . I lost seventeen male friends, boys from my class, prewar class. I am one of only two of us to live. One is a Serb and I am the only Bosniak that's living."

Duraković explained how the demographics of Srebrenica had changed following the genocide. Today, the Bosniaks are still a majority, but "before the war we were 80 percent, now we are close to 55 percent, maybe. We had 37,000 people living here before the war, now we have around 8,000 people living here. We had 11,000 pupils in school, students, and now we have 1,100, which is a huge demographic collapse."

The mayor spoke of the scale of the genocide of the Bosnians and the fact that it was part of a coordinated and organized system. "Kill 10,000 people, hide their bodies, you just hide them in the woods in mass graves and then, after a year, you dig them out and hide them in second and third and still, ten different places. So it's a system—you need politics, civil engineering, machinery, transport, and then you need police, you need army." Duraković said this system is still in place, particularly in the Republika Srpska, involving the police, army, and the Serb Democratic Party, which was established by the convicted war criminal and former president of Republika Srpska Radovan Karadžić. "They're still existing with their rhetoric of Greater Serbia, saying that Karadžić, General Ratko Mladić, they're heroes of the war, and you still have people living around us, neighbors, who still think the same way."

The Serbs are "collectively responsible for genocide in Srebrenica," the mayor claimed. "Who was driving the trucks, civilian trucks, who was washing these trucks after they got dirty, who was driving this machinery to dig the bodies up and hide them?" The mayor mentioned another mass grave that contained 800 bodies and was "fifty meters from a place where you have houses and a village, people living there. And now if you ask people, did you know about this, they all go 'No.' Well, nothing can happen in a small town that everybody doesn't know. I mean, we know everything."

While the communities live together today, and the Bosnians do not seek revenge, Duraković believed, the unwillingness of the Serbs to acknowledge what occurred is a serious problem inhibiting coexistence that jeopardizes future peace. "We still do not have consensus about the past. You have three people, three nations, three histories, and you cannot come up together to have one truth. Why? Because we have facts, they have stories." To ensure peace in the future, the mayor said, there needs to be less focus on "reconciliation" and more on "honesty" about what really happened. He explained, "I am afraid that in this case, I am raising my children and I'm teaching my children our history, and they're raising their children teaching them another history, and I am afraid that sometime in the future they will just collide and then we will have the same thing."

The mayor believed things would have been different in terms of the European response to the genocide if the Bosniaks were not Muslim. "Some of François Mitterrand's decisions were explicitly talking about Muslims in the middle of Europe," Duraković claimed. "I think Europe is afraid of European Muslims, because we are literate compared with Saudi Arabian Muslims. We have different traditions. We are educated, European, civilized Muslims. We practice our religion, we wear suits and ties, and we go to mosque and we go to politics. And I think that if we were Croats or Catholics, things would go differently, and I think we're still a problem because we're Muslims."

I asked Duraković why he believed that Europe was frightened of Muslims, and he replied, "The people of Europe are afraid because they don't know. They are being filled up with information that is false." As an example of what he meant, he told us about what happened on September 11, 2001, when he was sitting in a lecture hall at his college in New Hampshire in the United States. He said he was the only Muslim in a class of 300 people. His ethics teacher told the class that the attacks were in keeping with Islam—because the Quran says that when you kill a nonbeliever you go to paradise:

> I raised my hand, and I stood up and I said, "Okay, I'm Muslim." The students went, "You're a Muslim? We never knew." "Yes, I am," I said, "and I will give up my religion if you bring the Quran from the library and show me this verse that says 'If you kill a man of another religion, then you go to paradise.' I will convert to Catholicism." And the professor goes, like, "Well, it's just a paraphrase." I said, "No, no, please, we have the Quran in the library. I'll go to get it." So, I went and I got an English version and I found the verse

where it says, "If you kill a man without a reason, it is just like you killed all humanity."

## Religious Pluralism in Bosnia

From Bosnian Muslim voices let us now turn to some inspiring non-Muslims who will discuss the legacy and challenges of religious pluralism in Bosnia. We will meet the head of Sarajevo's Jewish community, Ambassador Jakob Finci, in chapter 7, but here we introduce several Christian figures. In the small town of Fojnica, several hours away from Sarajevo in the countryside, we met an agreeable young Croat priest, Father Nikica Vujica. He wore the cassock of a Franciscan monk and gave us a tour of the spectacular Franciscan Monastery of the Holy Spirit, which was built in the seventeenth century and is situated on a commanding site overlooking the town and the valley. Vujica proudly took us to see, in a portion of the monastery set aside as a museum, what he clearly considered to be the monastery's most-prized possession: the famed Ahd-Namah, the fifteenth-century order of protection given to the priests by Sultan Mehmed II that permitted them to freely practice their religion under Ottoman rule.

Vujica said that when Mehmed II issued the proclamation, he "took off his robe and said, 'Now you are under my cover,' and put it around the priest. This meant, symbolically, that he would protect him. It symbolized that Christianity and Islam could understand each other." To illustrate the meaning of the Ahd Namah, the priest held up one of the two ribbons that hung from the amice draped over his shoulders: "Islam," he said. He then held up the other ribbon and said, "Christianity." Tying the two ribbons together, he exclaimed triumphantly, "the Ahd-Namah brings them together."

Unfortunately, the father admitted, "at the moment we are really far off" in terms of harmony between Christianity and Islam. "There are a lot of people who do not understand the Ahd-Namah," Vujica stated with regret. But only "after we understand that we should be connected, will we have peace."

"For sure there is one God," the priest explained, echoing almost exactly the words and sentiments of the Spanish guitarist Fernando Perez talking about convivencia in chapter 3, "but we see God from different sides. We see one side, which is from here and somebody looks from the other side. The problem is when the opinion is absolute, when someone is looking at the front side, and he accepts only the front side, and he speaks only about what he knows, and another is looking from the other side, and they have absolute opinion, then there is a problem." In these situations, "God is laughing at us," the priest explained tongue in cheek. At the same time, he elaborated, "he loves us. And the world. We Christians believe that God is absolute love. And we just have pieces of that love. And it's not absolute. . . . Jesus Christ brought the attribute of love to us."

It was a remarkable testament to the enduring ethos of convivencia that the priest's optimistic view of relations between the religions had not been dimmed by the tumultuous history of the region. The monastery, however, was not immune to the violence and killing of the 1990s. Vujica showed us a plaque and a candle dedicated to the memory of two priests from the monastery who were killed by a Muslim during the conflict. Nevertheless, it was clear that Vujica strongly empathized with the plight of the Muslims. "If you want to talk about war," he declared, "we should talk more about Srebrenica."

We also met others in Bosnia who, like Vujica, are dedicated to religious coexistence and are working to make it a reality. In Sarajevo, we visited the Interreligious Council of Bosnia and Herzegovina, which brings together the leadership of the Orthodox Serb, Catholic Croat, Muslim Bosniak, and Jewish communities to work for peaceful coexistence. There we met Bozana Ivelić-Katava, a Catholic Croat and senior adviser to the council. Born in Sarajevo and raised in a nearby village, Ivelić-Katava went on to earn graduate degrees in Catholic theology and religious studies. In Bosnia, Ivelić-Katava proudly claimed, "We have meeting of civilizations, East and West, Islam and Christianity."

Ivelić-Katava said the council's work focuses primarily on women, youth, and religious leaders. "We have a lot of programs with youth. We educate youth. We have a lot of programs with women, women of faith, because youth, they have to be educated. . . . Women—as mothers, as teachers, as workers—have a strong influence on future generations. Then we work a lot with religious leaders, with priests and imams. . . . We establish such a good cooperation among priests and imams that they become friends." The council, she explained, organizes public dialogues that feature local Orthodox priests, Catholic priests, and muftis. Ivelić-Katava also elaborated that to build empathy for the suffering of other communities and to reinforce the idea that all communities have suffered in Bosnia, she guides Catholic, Orthodox, Muslim, and Jewish youth to visit sites of mass atrocities with differing perpetrators and victims. "We have family memories, that there was this period of history where 'they' were killing 'us,'" she said. "We remember only our victims. We do not remember that we were perpetrators at one point of history and that others also have history."

Although Ivelić-Katava works tirelessly at fostering understanding between Bosnia's different religious communities, she is realistic about the challenges to peaceful coexistence. In this tense environment, Ivelić-Katava said, there are continuing attacks on religious sites. "Regularly, in one year," she explained, "we have fifty attacks on religious sites" spread relatively evenly across the communities. She also told us of frequent acts of vandalism committed on houses of worship, including, "a lot of urination in the mosques. They just come to mosques, break a window, urinate on the carpet, and then leave. Or in the Catholic Church we have sometimes that they steal the *hostia*, the communion bread, you know, that is very holy for Catholics."

"We have to educate people about others," she stated. "That is most important. . . . When you are not familiar with something, it's very easy to hate it. . . . Wherever we live, we will always have others who are different, different nations, different religions living next door, and if we do not start respecting each other, probably we will be shooting each other."

## Non-Bosnian Indigenous Muslims in the Balkans

While the Bosnian Muslims have assumed great historical and contemporary importance in the context of Islam in Europe, there are also other notable Muslim populations in the Balkans who we met in our fieldwork. All are linked to the Ottoman Empire and its history in Europe and include Turks, Pomaks, and Albanians.

### The Turks of Greece and Bulgaria

There is a sizable Turkish population in Greece and Bulgaria remaining from the time of the Ottomans. In Bulgaria alone, there are around 600,000 Turks, and their political party, the Movement for Rights and Freedoms, is described as the kingmaker in Bulgarian politics. Members of this party—such as Ilhan Kyuchyuk, the youngest member of the liberal party in the European Parliament—have made an impact on European politics as a whole.

After the Second World War, the Turks of Bulgaria were subject, like the rest of Bulgarians, to one of the most repressive communist regimes under Todor Zhivkov, who ruled from 1954 to 1989. For Bulgaria's Turks, communism meant both forced secularization and forced assimilation to "Bulgarian" primordial identity, which increased in intensity as the years went on. In 1984 the government "officially declared the Bulgarian Turks to be Bulgarians . . . who had been forced to adopt Islam and Turkish as their mother tongue under the 'Ottoman Yoke.' . . . As a consequence, Turks had to 'renew' their Bulgarian names." The Turkish language was banned in public, "Turkish place names were changed, the observance of Muslim customs was strictly banned, Turkish tombstones were destroyed, and in some libraries even Turkish–Bulgarian dictionaries disappeared."[1] Zhivkov infamously declared, "There are no Turks in Bulgaria." This wave of repression resulted in the expulsion of over 350,000 Turks to Turkey, "with tales of being given just a few hours to pack."[2] It was only after 1989 that the official "process of national rebirth" for the Muslim population was ended and Turks who had been expelled were allowed to return.[3]

In several interviews for this project in Thessaloniki, the second largest city in Greece, Jamshaid Iftikhar, the Pakistani ambassador to Bulgaria, discussed the Muslim community in Bulgaria. He told us that Bulgarians have a close relationship with Russia because they feel grateful to the Russians for freeing them from the Ottoman Empire. The ambassador said that the Muslims of Bulgaria, despite their considerable numbers, are often not visible, that there is only one mosque in the capital city of Sofia, and he spoke of a "general pressure" against Turks in urban areas. Muslims hide themselves, he noted, and you will not see a woman, for example, wearing the hijab. Yet in the southern mountain region of the country, he said, there are many Turkish and Muslim villages, and you hear the call to prayer despite the fact that it is prohibited by law. The Muslims were "resilient and defiant." He also spoke of the influence of an "Erdoğan factor" on Bulgaria's Muslims, which has led to more women wearing the hijab. Turkey's revival, Iftikhar explained, has led to a revival in pride among Bulgaria's Turks and improved economic fortunes. The ambassador spoke of his affection for these people and their land; his sense of affinity was apparent to us.

In northern Greece, we also observed an upsurge in pride among the local Turks linked with the rise of Erdoğan's Turkey. During our visit to the Tsinar Mosque in Xanthi, Western Thrace, for example, which was built in 1775, we saw beautiful new tiles that had recently been sent from Turkey, and members of the community told us there had been a rediscovery of identity over the past decade. As Professor Angeliki Ziaka of the Aristotle University of Thessaloniki explained to us, the Turks are part of a larger population of 120,000 "Greek Muslims" located "mainly in the region of Western Thrace, where they have 111 mosques and smaller masjids."

This local Muslim community, as Ziaka and other Greeks were quick to point out, is distinct from the recent Muslim immigrants, who are seen as non-local and who congregate mainly in Athens. The Muslim population in Western Thrace was part of a much-reduced Muslim population that remained in Greece following the massive deportations and population transfers between Greece and Turkey that culminated in the 1923 Treaty of Lausanne. The treaty left a Greek Orthodox population in Istanbul, enabling the seat of the Orthodox Church to remain in the city, and a Muslim population in Western Thrace. The Turks of Greece, though largely able to practice their religion, were nevertheless subject to constant state surveillance and repression, which only began to lessen, people told us, after Greece was admitted to the European Union. The community has always been seen through the lens of the volatile and often-hostile relationship between Greece and Turkey, although the Turks we met in Greece were adamant that they wanted to be treated as equal Greek citizens just like everyone else.

## A Turkish Professor from Western Thrace, Greece

In Thessaloniki we met Ali Hüseyinoğlu, a member of the Turkish minority of Western Thrace, along with his wife fresh from their honeymoon. Hüseyinoğlu lives in Komotini, the capital of the Rhodope region of Western Thrace, but crosses the border into Turkey to lecture at Trakya University. Hüseyinoğlu discussed the challenges of being part of the Turkish minority in Greece. In Greece, he said, saying you are Muslim is acceptable but not saying you are a Turk, a word that has come to mean slavery, again reflecting the time the Ottomans ruled here. In terms of identity, Hüseyinoğlu noted that while he was serving in the Greek military, a friend of his told him that in Greece, identity is "a matter of black and white." No one, emphasized Hüseyinoğlu, ever says "I am Greek-Turkish." Hüseyinoğlu underlined the importance of the Turkish part of his identity, "Turkish is much heavier than Greekness." In some places, he claimed, if he orders Turkish coffee, he will not be served. Yet he was not concerned about Greece's far-right Golden Dawn party, whose members "can't come into our villages" lest they be beaten up. Outside of Western Thrace, Hüseyinoğlu admitted, it is "really difficult to keep your own ethnic and religious identity." There are no mosques, for example, and most Muslims do not like to pray in church.

Under the Treaty of Lausanne, Hüseyinoğlu explained, 500,000 Muslims left Greece for Turkey and 1.5 million Greeks left Turkey for Greece. Most people, Hüseyinoğlu believed, did not want to leave their homes during the population exchange. In terms of Greek identity, Hüseyinoğlu said, the massive population transfers occurred amid a "Hellenization" and "homogenization" in Greece, essentially a process of consolidating and promoting Greek primordial identity.

The Treaty of Lausanne initiated a "principle of reciprocity in Turkish-Greek relations," Hüseyinoğlu explained. If two Greeks are beaten up in Istanbul, he said to illustrate his point, then two Turks should get beaten up in Greece. Under the treaty, the Turks in Greece retained their right to religious expression and to carry out their religious duties. The Greek state, for example, did not curtail the Muslim prayers. But at the same time, many rights of Greece's Turkish Muslims were "violated." In the 1980s, he claimed, people "suffered because their name was Ali." He said that you might have to wait eight years to get a landline phone link to a Turkish village in Greece; you had to wait up to four years to get a driver's license; you could not renovate your home; and you could not go to court "because of your name." While the treaty gives the Turks the right to practice their religion, Hüseyinoğlu stated, there is tension over the government's appointment of muftis. For example, in the northeastern city of Xanthi, there are two muftis—an official one appointed by the government and an unofficial one elected by the Muslim community.

Hüseyinoğlu lamented the "destruction of the Ottoman heritage" in Western Thrace. During the Ottoman era, he reminded us, Thessaloniki was a thriving center of pluralism, with Muslims, Christians, and Jews living together. But the old multicultural Thessaloniki is finished, he noted. Turning to some of the other Muslim populations in Greece, Hüseyinoğlu said there were up to 6,000 Muslims on the Greek islands of Rhodes and Kos, which Italy ceded to Greece following the end of the Second World War. On Rhodes, he said, there are more than twenty mosques with proper minarets, and there are several mosques on Kos, but only one is open and the azan, the call to prayer, is forbidden. All mosques are in need of repair, and some have already collapsed. Hüseyinoğlu stressed that the Muslims of Rhodes and Kos are not subject to the Treaty of Lausanne, and thus they are "at the mercy of the Greek state."

### The Incoming Mayor of Myki, Western Thrace, Greece

We invited the incoming mayor of Myki, Cemil Kabza, to have lunch with us in Xanthi. He told us the name of his region, which is on the border with Bulgaria, is pronounced "like Mickey Mouse." Kabza attended journalism school in Turkey and then wrote for a local Turkish weekly newspaper. Kabza explained the position of the Muslim minority in the area.

Greece is an Orthodox Christian country, and we are Muslims. . . . We are the officially recognized religious minority of Greece. We live as Muslims here. Our ethnic background is from the Ottomans, from the Turks. . . . We have the Treaty of Lausanne, which gives us a kind of identity, a minority identity, and it also gives us some rights. We freely can go to our mosques. We can freely pray, fast, and even dress.

"I was born here," he said. "I was educated here. I joined the Greek army. I'm paying taxes. I have a house here. I have a car. My family is here. My grand family is here. We live here. We don't want to go anywhere else. We want to be here. But we want to live as Muslims.

The mayor-elect called the local community of Muslims "indigenous" to Europe. "Indigenous means that we are not immigrants," he explained, "we are a part of the Ottoman Empire left here. We have been living here for more than 500 years." Kabza spoke of the difficulties the community experienced under the Greek military junta from 1967 to 1974, which he called a bleak period. Then, in 1981, Greece joined the European Community, the forerunner of the European Union. When Greece adapted its laws to meet EU and international human rights norms in 1997, conditions began improving for the minority. Until 1997, Kabza stated, you had to have a special ID to get into any village in Myki. "Because you are a member of the Muslim community, you have a different name than a Christian, then you always face problems." In the 1990s Bosnian War, he said, "the Greeks helped the Serbs and we helped the Bosniaks."

Kabza confessed his community is a "closed community" to the outside world. He explained that although he has heard of rare cases, "there are no mixed marriages" in Western Thrace; and if there is a mixed marriage, the couple leaves and goes to Athens. Kabza named his role models as Turkish president Recep Tayyip Erdoğan and Greek prime minister George Papandreou. He described Europeans as "confused" and admitted, "I couldn't find a person to inspire me that much" from Europe. "Inspiration comes first from Turkey, then Greece, then Europe."

The mayor-elect discussed his concerns about the ascendant Far Right, describing it as "very dangerous for Europe, for all religions, especially for Muslims, Jews, and others. It is dangerous for democracy, and for the future of Europe. . . . It is very difficult to say what the future is for humanity." Speaking about the far-right Golden Dawn party, Kabza recounted that before an election, twenty to thirty people on motorbikes went to the Turkish villages to say "We are here," and they sang nationalist songs. The Far Right is "more dangerous than Kalashnikovs," he believed, and there is no dialogue with them. "They close all the doors. It's difficult to know how they think, what they can do to you." Yet Kabza explained that it was not easy for them to go into his area, noting, as Hüseyinoğlu did, "My community is strong. They know we also can fight with them." Instead, he said, Golden Dawn prefers to go to villages where the population is mixed.

"My message," Kabza stated, "would be for everyone: that we have to understand one thing—that life is really short."

> No one knows how long he is going to live, where and how, and when he is going to die. This world belongs to everyone, to this humanity. To protect this world is everyone's duty. To protect this atmosphere here is everyone's duty. Everyone should promote peace. When there is peace, there is understanding, there is success. . . . In Europe, everyone has to understand that Islam is one of the main and important religions of Europe. Islam will stay there, will remain there, and it's not a threat."

## GREECE'S ONLY MUSLIM POLITICAL PARTY

In Xanthi, Greece, we met with members of the Party of Friendship, Equality, and Peace, a political party created in the early 1990s to speak on behalf of the Muslim minority of Western Thrace. Nearly all members of the party are Muslim, making it Greece's first and only Muslim political party. Their bearing reflected the desperation and despondency of their situation. Ozan Ahmetoğlu, a journalist and the party's vice president, explained that the party was created for the Muslim minority to have its voice heard in Athens. Ozan said that the party has so far fallen short of the 3 percent threshold in national elections that would enable it to gain seats in the Greek Parliament.

They presented an unrelentingly pessimistic picture of their place in Greece. "Our national identity of being Turkish, it's not accepted," complained Ozan. "We can't elect our own religious leader, mufti," he explained.

> We don't accept the fact that the government can appoint someone and say this is your religious leader. And in the past two years the state has gone a step further. Now the state is saying it wants to appoint the teachers that teach our children the Quran. And also, in state schools, not minority schools, the state starts appointing teachers to give religious education in Greek. What the state executes is very anti-democratic.

He also spoke about the problem of the media and the way it depicts the Muslim community: "There's no media center or any sort of media that objectively puts across our views as the Muslim Turkish minority. For example, in the media, the headline is that Muslims in Greece don't want this law. They're against us. And therefore this negative image is continuing and there's no improvement."

## *The Pomak Muslims of Greece and Bulgaria*

A large number of the Muslims of Western Thrace are ethnic Pomaks, Muslims who speak a Slavic Bulgarian dialect and have a Slavic background. The Pomaks, who dwell mainly in the Rhodope Mountains on both sides of the Greek-Bulgarian border, have traditionally lived, and continue to live, an isolated village lifestyle characterized by self-sufficient agriculture. In Bulgaria, where they are referred to as Bulgarian Muslims, they number around 200,000. Prominent Pomaks in Bulgaria include the grand mufti of Bulgaria, Mustafa Hadzhi. According to the historian Ulf Brunnbauer, "Most scholars would agree on the definition of Pomaks as Bulgarian-speaking Muslims of South Slav ethnic background" but "various non-Bulgarian nationalists challenge this assumption (especially Turkish and Greek ones)."[4]

Indeed, how Pomaks are seen is firmly in keeping with the complexity of identity in the Balkans and the legacy of the Ottoman Empire in the region. The Pomaks have thus been seen as Bulgarian, Greek, or Turkish, depending on the nationalist position in question. Greek nationalists have seen Pomaks as Greeks connecting them, for example, with ancient Thracian tribes. In Bulgaria they are seen as Bulgarians who converted to the religion of the Turkish oppressors.

The renowned Bulgarian ethnographer Stoyu Shishkov, in keeping with the ideas and project of Herder, argued early in the twentieth century that the Pomaks speak "the most pure" Bulgarian and referred to their "memories of kinship relations with Christian Bulgarians." These were Bulgarians, he believed, who had been subjected to "forced Islamisation." In Bulgaria, therefore, there have been campaigns to convert and assimilate the Pomaks for decades, similar to the campaigns against the Turks described above. During the 1940s, the government used "violence and threats" to change the names of around 60,000 Pomaks to Bulgarian names.[5]

The Pomaks of Western Thrace, Greece, with a population of about 30,000, have been in the thick of the confrontations between Greece and Turkey and have been wooed by both countries. The Greeks have sought to study and promote Pomak culture, language, and identity in initiatives such as the state-supported presentation of new Pomak dictionaries in central Athens in 1996, which was "first of all motivated politically by a wish to prevent linguistic assimilation toward Turkish." Such identification between the Pomaks and the Turks is very common, however, and in Western Thrace, we found the Pomak population to be, as the historian Vemund Aarbakke puts it, "in all stages of transition from being 'pure' Pomaks living in their mountain villages to fully assimilated Turks of Pomak origin."[6] In the confusing ethnic patchwork of the Balkans, it is worth pointing out that in Macedonia there are some 100,000 Pomaks, known as Torbeshi, with a predilection for Sufism.

### A POMAK TEACHER IN XANTHI, WESTERN THRACE

Nuseybe Bosnak, a young teacher and a Pomak, was our guide in Xanthi. She was introduced to us by Anna Stamou, a prominent Greek Muslim convert and media spokeswoman for the Muslim Association of Greece, whom we met in Athens (see chapter 1). Nuseybe was born in Medina, Saudi Arabia, where her father, who is an imam, was studying. The family returned to Greece when Nuseybe was one. For primary school, she attended a special "minority school" for Muslim children in Komotini. She then went to school on the island of Kos with Greek Christians and was instructed exclusively in Greek, which she described as a "great experience." At the age of twelve, she moved to Turkey to study, and now she teaches English to local children.

Nuseybe explained that the Pomaks speak an unwritten language. "It's just a spoken language," she stated, "it's Slavic. There are Pomaks in Greece, in Bulgaria, in Turkey, and in Macedonia." Reflecting the discussion and debate concerning the origins of the Pomaks, Nuseybe commented, "I don't know where they come from exactly. There are many sayings about Pomaks, but who knows? In Pomak, there's a word, *pomaga*, which means 'help,' 'helping.' So Pomak means something like 'helper,' probably the original is from that." Nuseybe believed that her surname, however, could also indicate Bosnian roots. "We haven't found our roots yet. But probably we are from Bosnia, because when the Ottoman Empire brought people here, they brought them from everywhere, and I have Bosnian friends who I love a lot, so I think the blood is the same somehow."

In defining her identity, Nuseybe stated, "I see myself as European, Greek, Turkish, Pomak, Muslim. I'm all of it now, because I'm Greek, but I belong to the Turkish minority." Yet, Nuseybe said, "we are pessimistic here in Greece, the Muslims, because we are a minority." Before Greece joined the European Community, Nuseybe explained, the Muslim minority faced severe restrictions. "In the past, about thirty to fifty years ago, we couldn't build a house. They didn't give us the permission easily. That was not a rule, but they did it to us. They didn't give us driving licenses easily. We could not go to university. But now, everything is fine. We can drive, we can build houses, but the problem is economic now. . . . When Greece got into the European Union, things started changing here for us. . . . Now we are happier."

Nuseybe said education was the main problem faced by the Muslim minority today. "The standards are not the same" for the government's official minority schools, she claimed. "They are lower, low." The minority schools "don't want us to know a lot of things," she added. She said that students in minority schools are taught nothing about seminal figures such as Mustafa Kemal Atatürk, the founder of the modern Turkish state. Lack of education forces men into migrant labor, she argued, which puts pressure on families. "Kids don't get the proper education from minority schools, and somehow they find themselves like fish out of the sea. So they go to work, mostly boys, go to Germany, to Poland, to many other countries of Europe, they go there and have a good salary and come here, they get married, they go back, they work their whole lives, and their kids grow up without their dads. That's a big problem, you can understand, for a child growing up without a father. There are kids who don't see their dads for one year. You can imagine the mother's situation, raising a child without their dad's help, they have to look after the kids. . . . They are all alone, mothers."

Speaking of the older Pomaks, Nuseybe noted, "Most of them are tobacco farmers. . . . Of course there are some educated people who have been to Turkey or Saudi Arabia, or Egypt, they have studied there. But most of them are farmers or workers. . . . The Muslim men are the builders in Xanthi and Komotini." While the Pomaks and Muslims are the workers and farmers, she said, most shops are owned by Christians. "We're just workers in that shop. The Christians have more . . . properties, let's say."

Despite the economic and religious differences, Nuseybe said, "Most people who study here in Greece have lots of Christian friends." "For example, they share rooms in university now. They share, they go to the weddings of each other, they go to parties together, and of course, I'm sure if there is something, I think, like a war, good friends will help them, I hope." In terms of interfaith dialogue, she believed that imams who speak only Turkish and no Greek are at a big disadvantage.

Turning to the dangers of the Far Right in Greece, Nuseybe pointed out, "There are some political parties, racist political parties, who threaten us, who openly say they don't want other people in Greece, just Greeks. Last year, before the elections, two of my local people here in Xanthi were attacked by that group of people with the black t-shirts, you know, at night. So we were all afraid to go out at night. And they sometimes attack our mosques, they break windows, they leave pig heads in the mosques. . . . I mean, in your own country, you feel like you are not wanted." Nuseybe explained that in the last two to three years anti-Muslim pressures have gotten worse. Greek schoolchildren are being taught a version of history that is anti-Muslim, she said, and they are being told that "Greece belongs to the Greeks."

Nevertheless, Nuseybe believed, "we are lucky to be Europeans, you know. There are a lot of countries who are in worse conditions than us. A lot of Muslims who are in very worse conditions than us, so I think we are lucky here." Nuseybe spoke of her hopes for the future and for her children. "First of all," she elaborated, "I want a good education for my kids. That's my number-one problem. I hope to change the education here somehow for the minorities." She said she could have remained in Turkey but wanted to come back to Greece. "I want my kids to live in Greece. I love Greece, so I don't want my kids to go away. I want a good life for them. I want good jobs for them . . . and I want to be comfortable as a Muslim."

Nuseybe claimed that all the Muslims are asking for is their rights. "The Western Thrace minorities are not rude. They are very kind to Greek people. They're obedient. We obey the rules. We don't have high crime rates here. People trust Muslims. So we can ask for our rights, kindly, we ask for them kindly, and I hope Greece, the Greek government, will give them to us, so we can live all in peace all together."

## THE OFFICIAL MUFTI OF XANTHI

The importance of Pomaks can be gauged by the fact that both the grand muftis of Xanthi, the official and the unofficial one, are Pomaks. We met Mufti Mehmet Emin Şinikoğlu, the Greek government's officially appointed mufti, an elderly, frail-looking but energetic Pomak, in his disheveled and shabby office. Şinikoğlu self-consciously projected an air of dignity and gravitas; throughout the interview he strained to straighten himself for the camera as we filmed our visit and struggled to gather his black mufti's robes into some semblance of order as they clearly had a will of their own, lacking pins and buttons to hold matters together. It was painfully obvious that he knew that we knew that his office suffered from a lack of resources. Even his young female assistant was Christian and appointed by the Greek government. He had left Western Thrace to study in Istanbul in the late 1950s but was forced to leave after the Turkish government was overthrown in a coup in 1960 and the state's religious schools were closed. He went on to study in a madrassa in Komotini, Western Thrace, and at the University of Medina in Saudi Arabia. In 1991 he was appointed mufti of Xanthi by the Greek government. Şinikoğlu, who said his role models included prominent Saudi figures such as King Faisal and the grand muftis of Saudi Arabia, told us that there were 45,000 Muslims in Xanthi, who come from "three ethnic backgrounds: Muslim Pomaks, ethnic Turk Muslims, and Roma Muslims."

Western Thrace, Şinikoğlu explained, is one of the few areas in Europe that have implemented aspects of the shariah in religious matters. He said that the matters he can adjudicate under the shariah include "marriages, divorces, alimonies, inheritance problems, and custodies." He explained that "the decision of the mufti is recognized by the Greek state, by the prefecture, by everybody, by the Greek courts." As a member of the Muslim minority, a person has the right to choose whether they wish to be judged by the mufti or by a government court. The mufti believed this was a "great liberty" given to the Muslims. The mufti was right. That the government of Greece has allowed parts of the shariah to be implemented in this European nation is noteworthy and needs to be acknowledged.

The mufti admitted that when he was a child, there was a mentality in the Muslim community that hindered education. "When I was ten years old, my mother used to see me study English or Greek," and she would say, "No, these are not God's things." His mother believed that the Quran was the only book he should read. The community's girls had it even worse, the mufti recalled, rarely receiving formal schooling beyond middle school. Then, after the 1970s, things began to change. Today, he explained proudly, there are around 300 Muslim female lawyers in Western Thrace and around 150 Muslim female doctors. Current government policy requires that 0.5 percent of the seats in Greek universities be reserved for Muslims, both men and women. This, the mufti believed, "was a really favorable measure for the minority here, in order for them to be educated."

The mufti estimated that around 70 percent of Muslim women in Xanthi wear the hijab; in the villages outside the city, it is closer to 100 percent. The hijab began increasing in popularity fifty years ago, Şinikoğlu noted, after the fall of the Kemalists in Turkey. "When the Kemalists fell from power in Turkey, because the Kemalists were pro-openness in women, and the more conservative government took rule, there was a shift here as well. . . . Because the women watch Turkish television a lot, they are affected by the changes they see in Turkey." Despite the influence of neighboring Turkey, the mufti, now loudly tooting the Greek horn, stated that "the Muslim people want to stay here, they don't want to go to Turkey. Because the country here is more democratic than in Turkey. It's a European democracy, it's really different."

The mufti concluded with a rosy if idealistic picture of interfaith harmony. "Muslim people here have no problem with Christians or Jewish people. There is not a single problem. They say prayers from the minaret, and there is not a problem with the Christians, and the bell rings, and there is not a problem with the Muslim people."

### THE UNOFFICIAL MUFTI OF XANTHI

Nuseybe Bosnak took us to meet the unofficial mufti of Xanthi, Ahmet Mete, who was elected by the local Muslim community in defiance of the officially appointed mufti. Mete, a well-built Pomak oozing confidence, assumed the position of mufti for the community in 2006. His spacious office in Xanthi, complete with Turkish symbols and memorabilia openly suggesting affiliation with Turkey, the source of support for the unofficial mufti according to local people, contrasted with the run-down character of the official mufti's office. There were several well-dressed men and women in the bustling office. The mufti also introduced us to his assistant, an energetic woman named Fatima, and said that it was the "first time in Greece that a mufti's helper is a woman."

The mufti has a son and two daughters, both of whom have graduated from university, he told us with pride, with one attaining a degree in Islamic studies and another teaching the Turkish language. Mete began primary school in his village near Xanthi but finished in Istanbul before going on to complete secondary school in Istanbul and attending university in both Turkey and Medina. Mete said his role models are the Prophet, explaining, "In every situation that I face, I think how he would have reacted," and the four caliphs. He also praised Erdoğan, calling him a "great leader."

Mete spoke of the challenges of the Muslim minority in Greece. "It's difficult to get together, Muslims and non-Muslims, when we are a minority," the mufti claimed. "There was a deep hate by the Greeks for the Turkish people, they hate them." In response to hatred and provocations, Mete said he and other religious leaders "tell the Muslims to be positive, not to act like they act. We are trying to teach the young people peace. In every talk that I have in the media or in articles that I've written, I have tried to give the message that we are here forever and we want to live in peace."

The mufti criticized the Greek government's lack of assistance in addressing the problems of the Muslim community, particularly those most affecting Muslim youth. "The government, our government, should help us but they don't help at all." Young people, Mete explained, receive instruction in the Quran and Islam in primary school, but "afterwards families can't control them." Only 50 percent of the local Muslim youth go to mosques regularly, he worried, though during Ramadan attendance might reach 90 percent. He shared his strategy to reach the youth the rest of the year: "We are trying our best. We are having conversations with the young people. I do it every week, and in the villages there are groups who go and talk to young people." For the past four years, the mufti explained, he has been hosting a program on local Turkish radio in which he "takes questions and answers, every kind of question that young people ask me."

When asked about the position of women in the local community and the challenges they face, the mufti replied, "The women's problem is the same as all the women in all Islamic countries—that they don't know how important a woman's place is in Islam, and they don't accept it yet." At every wedding the mufti officiates, he speaks for ten to fifteen minutes about the equality of women and men in Islam. "I am advising and helping many families try to educate their daughters." Encouragingly, female education has come a long way in recent decades. In the past, only about 1 percent of the female population was educated; now it is around 30 percent. In the mosque courses that instruct young people in the Quran, Mete claimed, about half of the 2,700 children are girls. "We have female teachers, English teachers, doctors, and lawyers."

While Mete spoke of some of the problems of the community relating to the government and the majority society, he maintained that "this doesn't mean that we have great, deep problems between Christians and Muslims here. For example, when I am coming here in the morning, there are shopkeepers, Christian shopkeepers, who say hi to me, smile to me. . . . I go to the market after I go to work. People have spoken angrily to me sometimes, but nobody has ever used violence." "Our problems here are not with the Christians," Mete believed. "The problems are created because of the politicians. We live here, our children are going to live here." "The children of Adam," he explained, "of course they will have different conflicts between each other, but they should live in peace."

## TENSIONS IN WESTERN THRACE

We had a fruitful visit to Western Thrace and were received with hospitality by the local people there, including some of the senior officials of the region. We met the sitting mayor of Myki, Mustafa Aga, a Pomak, for example, who received us in his office with warmth, arranged a delicious lunch for us at a local restaurant in a scenic spot in the mountains, and drove us to the restaurant himself. Yet the political tensions and sensitivities surrounding the Muslim community in Western Thrace were always apparent to us. As the mayor drove us through the winding roads deep in the Rhodope Mountains near the Bulgarian border, it was always possible to see a car following us. When we asked the mayor about the car, he did not offer much of a response, and as we ate we could see the car parked at a distance, watching us. It was soon apparent that this was Greek intelligence, and later when we explored the town of Xanthi on foot, two men also followed us, stepping behind shrubbery or some other obstacle when we turned around.

The tense atmosphere was captured by Amineh, who noted,

> I was surprised and felt discomfort at being spied on and followed by two intelligence agents in Xanthi. It was obvious that they were following us clumsily wherever we went but always pretended that they weren't. My father joked that this was the Greek version of Inspector Clouseau. When they followed us into the lobby of the hotel, my father walked up to them and offered them cake and juice as it was a hot day and the portly senior agent was sweating profusely. My father asked why they were following us. They said to protect him as he was a VIP. It turned the uneasy clandestine relationship into a more open one. We left in our van the next morning with a sense of unease. . . . We were followed all the way out of Xanthi, but as we entered the motorway we noticed the car and motorbike that followed us on the ride turning back.

### The Albanian Muslims of the Balkans

Like other Muslims in the Balkans, the Albanians—a European segmentary lineage tribal society in Albania, Kosovo, and Macedonia—have been subjected to sustained campaigns of violence by surrounding larger ethnic groups, particularly the Serbs, over the past century, as discussed in *The Thistle and the Drone*. Not all Albanians, however, are Muslim. In Albania today, about 60 percent of the population is Muslim, 10 percent

Roman Catholic, and about 7 percent Greek Orthodox, although some estimates put the Orthodox as high as 20 percent. The percentage of Muslims is higher in Kosovo, where 96 percent of the Albanian population is Muslim, and 98 percent of Macedonian Albanians are Muslim. Many Muslim Albanians are influenced by the Bektashi Order of Sufis, which has a long history in the Balkans. During Ottoman rule, Albanians made a profound impact on the far-flung empire at large and "supplied a stream of Grand Viziers."[7]

At the root of the conflict between Albanians and Serbs has been the region of Kosovo, the heartland of the medieval Serbian kingdom where Albanian tribes also lived. In events that have become shrouded in mythology, the invading Ottoman Turks conquered the region from the Serbs in the late fourteenth century, and most of the local Albanian tribes subsequently converted to Islam.

Albanian identity has been bitterly contested in the post-Ottoman era, particularly with respect to the Albanian relationship with the Ottomans, Islam, and European Christian identity. After Albania's independence from the Ottoman Empire in 1912, as the historian Cecilie Endresen writes, "Albania's rulers were eager to detach the country from foreign influence, especially Turkish. Like the other religious communities, the Muslims came under considerable political pressure to pursue a secularist, Albanianist line."[8] The position was captured by the prominent Albanian Ottoman official, diplomat, writer, and poet Pashko Vasa, also known as Wassa Effendi, who famously declared that "the religion of Albanians is Albanianism."

Following the Second World War, Albania was subject to the extreme communist dictatorship of Enver Hoxha, and the nation was declared the first officially atheist state on earth. In post-communist Albania, discourse on identity has served to "legitimise the country's role in the Western political hemisphere," which can be seen in the recent Albanian embrace of Mother Teresa, a Catholic nun born to a Kosovar Albanian family in Skopje, Macedonia, then part of the Ottoman Empire, who was known globally for her charity work in India.[9] In an article about Albania's embrace of Mother Teresa as the "Mother of the Nation," Endresen argues that it "goes right to the heart of Albanian identity building and political re-orientation Westwards after the fall of the isolationist Communist regime." This fed into a discourse in Albania that Christianity was more deep-rooted and "authentic" than Islam among Albanians. The president of Albania, Alfred Moisiu, who is from a Greek Orthodox background, pointed in 2005 to the association of Islam with the "political abuse" of the Ottomans and claimed, "In any Albanian you will find a Christian core if you scratch."[10] Upon the visit of Pope Francis to Albania in September 2014, Albanian prime minister Edi Rama, a recently baptized Catholic, similarly declared that "Albania is not a Muslim country, but European" believing in religious coexistance. Pope Francis echoed this assessment in nearly verbatim terms, while commending Albania for essentially living up to his own ideal for Europe—a vision of convivencia: "Albania is a European country precisely because of its culture—the culture of coexistence, also its past culture."

The Muslim Albanians we met in the course of our fieldwork captured some of the nuances of Albanian identity, as well as a sense of pride in their European identity and the multifaith character of Albanian society. A good example is the senior-ranking Kosovar diplomat serving in Germany, whom we met in Berlin. She spoke of one small town in Kosovo that had a synagogue, a mosque, and an Orthodox church right next to each other, which for her demonstrated the "old Ottoman tradition" of religious tolerance. As a Kosovar, she said, she felt "very European."

## A Former Adviser to the Prime Minister

We interviewed Agri Verrija, a former adviser to the prime minister of Albania, in my office at American University in Washington, D.C. Verrija is a Muslim from a prominent family of landowners in Albania dating back to the time of the Ottomans. He explained that his grandfather on his mother's side was an Ottoman Bey and the deputy mayor of Tirana, and his father's family had close connections to the Albanian king Zog, who fled Albania when the Italians invaded the country in 1939. Albanians were unified under the Turks, Verrija said, but "suffered a lot" at the hands of the Serbs. Verrija spoke of the "historical injustice" of international borders separating the Albanians into different nations. He explained that Kosovo, which he described as the "cradle of Albanian nationalism," was split from Albania and that Albanians constituted the only non-Slavic population in Yugoslavia. There are also substantial populations of Albanians living in Macedonia, he stated, where they constitute 23 percent of the total population, and there are an additional 50,000 Albanians in Montenegro.

Albanians identify as "European and not Oriental," Verrija asserted, while also stressing that "Albania is a tribal society" and that the code of honor is at the core of identity. When someone gets a job, he noted, the first person they hire is a family member. Society is governed informally by tribal law known as *kanun*. Albanians also behave according to *besa*, the tribal code of honor, which Verrija described as an "institution" and a "set of things you do." In this, he observed, the Albanians are similar to the Pukhtun and Corsicans.

Important components of besa include honesty, loyalty, trust, and hospitality. A house in Albania is not seen to belong only to its owner; rather, "my house belongs to God, to the guest, and to me," and a guest is protected from all harm. It was on the basis of besa, Verrija explained, that Albanians protected Jews from the Germans during the Second World War. The Albanians gave the Jews a house, food, and their word of honor that they would not surrender them to the Germans. The Germans understood, he claimed, that if they went after the Jews they would be fighting the Albanians. Verrija was speaking from his own family experience as "my dad's family rescued two Jewish families." Yet revenge and the blood feud are also essential parts of besa according to Verrija, and taking revenge in response to a challenge to honor is described as "giving besa."

Verrija spoke about the oppression of communist rule, explaining that it was a time of gulags and rehabilitation camps. While Kosovo declared independence in 2008 and Albanians are now running their own affairs there, Verrija discussed the difficulties Albanians were facing in neighboring Macedonia, where they are not integrated into the rest of the country. They have rights on paper, Verrija told us, but these rights mean little in practice. He described Skopje, the capital, as "two separate cities" and "two separate realities," with Albanians and Macedonians living on two distinct sides of the city. The government builds monuments dedicated to Slavic Macedonia, he said, but not to Albanians, and Macedonians destroyed a centuries-old mosque and tomb of one of the first Muslim scholar-missionaries. They do not take care of Albanian monuments of cultural heritage, he complained, and no money is put into maintaining them.

## THE FORMER FINANCE MINISTER OF KOSOVO

Ambassador Ahmet Shala served as minister for economy and finance in the government of Kosovo following its 2008 declaration of independence from Serbia and was subsequently the country's ambassador to Japan. Despite losing many members of his family and seeing his home destroyed in the 1998–99 war, he calls for Albanians to "apologize and forgive. . . . I am proud of my people and my nation—the nation of Mother Teresa. Her spirit, soul, and heart are present—today and forever." Albanians, too, should apologize in recognition that "there are sufferings on the other side."[11] Shala told me in my office that the Kosovo War was not the first time he had lost family members to conflict; his grandfather was killed by the Serbs in 1922, when his father was only three days old.

Shala also spoke of besa and emphasized hospitality: "The guest is somebody God sent to you to test you," he noted, and "whoever comes, you must accept." Yet, as Shala admitted, Albanians faced a problem with the Serbs, who since the 1870s had followed a policy that Shala characterized as killing a third of the Albanians, expelling a third, and converting the remaining third. The Serbs wanted to change the population demographics, and Serbia and Turkey forged an agreement in 1912 in which 250,000 people were expelled from Kosovo to Turkey. Foreign fighters—the mujahideen—arrived in the 1990s to help the Albanians fight the Serbs, but Shala emphasized that the Albanian leaders rejected them. Ultimately, it was the United States that saved the Albanians of Kosovo. For Shala, if the United States had not intervened, "we would not exist."

Shala lamented the current image of Islam in Europe—"the picture of Islam is of killers, crazy people, very primitive"—and insisted it is important "to give the real picture of the Muslim heart." He confessed that some Albanian families reject "European values," which he believed was very dangerous and spoke of the dangers of "radical Islam." "Those people don't serve Islam, they just serve some crazy fundamentalist."

## Europe's Forgotten Muslims

In this section we meet several Muslim communities, nations unto themselves, which are almost invisible in the eyes of the world. They have faced persecution and genocide in Eastern Europe over the centuries, and their communities hover on the brink of extinction. The treatment of the Roma and the Cham, particularly in the Balkans, is nothing short of deplorable by any standards of humanity; following the 2014 Russian annexation of Crimea the Tatars too face a perilous future with echoes of Stalin's genocide against their people. While the existence of the Roma hangs by a thread, the Cham have ceased to exist in the official records of their ancestral lands in the Balkans. These were not the Rohingya, and this was not Myanmar, where the Nobel Peace Prize winner and leading political figure in the land, the Buddhist priests sworn to pacifism, and the civil service and army officials aspiring to Macaulay's ideas of a civilized society, all shared in various degrees the guilt for the genocide inflicted on the Rohingya; the Tatars, Roma and Cham were Europeans.

The desperate plight of these communities needs to be urgently brought to the attention of the world. Here is the dark abysm of Europe: At the bottom of the pit amidst the bones, skeletons, and what remains of the human flesh, lie the soiled and battered European ideas of compassion and humanity. The putrefaction is advanced, the stench overwhelming, and the triumph of predator identity complete. Europe's Enlightenment project has come to a juddering halt here; for modernists, the surprise is that we are not in the jungles and forests of either Asia or Africa but the mother continent of modernity.

## The Tatars

The Tatars, who first entered Europe centuries ago and once saw themselves as masters of the world, now exist as a tiny ethnic minority in Eastern Europe (also see chapter 6). In Poland, where they have been historically well adjusted and have found an honorable place for themselves as loyal warriors, their identity and small number—about 3,000—are under threat. Paradoxically, the threat comes from Muslims and non-Muslims alike: the recent arrival of 30,000 Muslim immigrants from Africa and the Middle East challenge their customs, and the far-right parties claim that Poland is only for the Poles. In Lithuania, their population is around 3,000,[12] and in Belarus, which was also part of the Polish-Lithuanian Commonwealth, the historical entity that encompassed these countries, they number about 10,000 today. Finnish diplomats in the United Kingdom also told us of Finland's Tatar population of around 1,000 in number, which they described as an "established indigenous community" of Muslims who relocated from the Russian Volga region as merchants beginning in the late nineteenth century, as Finland was then part of the Russian Empire. In Crimea, the Tatar population was decimated when Stalin forcibly moved them to a different part of the Soviet Union; after returning over the decades to their ancestral land in Crimea, they are now struggling to survive under Putin. While the Crimean Tatars retain their Tatar language, the Tatars in Poland, Lithuania, and Belarus have lost their language and struggle to preserve other aspects of their identity and traditions. Paradoxically, the Tatars' worst periods have been under the "secular" rule of Moscow and their best periods under the Catholic kings of Lithuania and Poland.

The Crimean Tatars emerged from Turkic populations that had earlier been incorporated into the Golden Horde, the Mongol armies that swept across Eurasia and into Europe in the thirteenth century. As the Golden Horde declined and disintegrated, the Kipchak Tatars, who had converted to Islam in the fourteenth century, formed their own kingdoms, or Khanates, stretching across Eurasia. These included the Kazan Khanate, the Astrakhan Khanate, and the Crimean Khanate, which were all ruled by descendants of Genghis Khan. While the Kazan and Astrakhan Khanates were conquered and absorbed by Ivan the Terrible of Russia in the sixteenth century, the Crimean Khanate, balancing precariously between the empires of Poland-Lithuania, Russia, and the Ottomans, was able to maintain its independence until the eighteenth century, when it was annexed into Russia by Catherine the Great.

The Crimean Tatars were the fountainhead of the European Tatar community, and the story of how they came to have such an impact on Europe, especially on the empire of Poland-Lithuania, at one point the largest country in Europe, is an extraordinary one. The Crimean Tatars gave vital assistance to Poland-Lithuania in the conduct of its wars, for example, against the German Teutonic Knights, who were pushing east in the medieval period as part of the Northern Crusades to kill or convert pagans. The Grand Duchy of Lithuania, which had expanded from the Baltic to the Black Sea in the fourteenth century and incorporated some Tatar communities, invited additional groups of Crimean Tatars from the fragmenting Golden Horde to settle in Lithuania as soldiers under Grand Duke Vytautas the Great, the most famous Lithuanian national hero. In return, Vytautas granted the Tatars fiefs, which gave them a status similar to that of the nobility. The Tatars who settled in Lithuania became known as Lipka Tatars, after the Crimean Tatar name for Lithuania.

The Tatars "participated in all significant battles and military campaigns of the Polish-Lithuanian armies" and "took part in all of the important events in the history of Poland."[13] Perhaps the most famous was the Polish-Lithuanian victory over the Teutonic Knights at the Battle of Grunwald in 1410, known in Germany as the Battle of Tannenberg, one of the most decisive battles of the Middle Ages and fundamental to both Polish and Lithuanian identity. The Tatars sang the praises of the Polish and Lithuanian rulers. For example, in a 1558 treatise on Polish Tatars written by a Polish Tatar for Sultan Suleyman the Magnificent, the author noted that the Tatars honored the memory of the great Vytautas: "The name of this monarch, who was like a pillar of Islam in the land of the unbelievers, is Vytautas. . . . Every year we celebrate a day dedicated exclusively to the memory of that king."[14]

In 1683 the Tatars defended Vienna from the Ottomans fighting alongside the Polish-Lithuanian king John III Sobieski. The Tatars also fought in the major uprisings against Russia beginning in the late eighteenth century, and, a year after Polish independence from Russia in 1918, they were given their own regiment in the Polish army, known as the Tatar Cavalry, officially called the Regiment of the Tatar Uhlans. The Tatars even provided a model and ideal for non-Muslim Polish soldiers. It has been said that *uhlan*, the Tatar word for "warrior" or "brave," "stands for Polishness itself."[15] In 1936 the Polish Parliament officially recognized Islam as a state religion. The Polish foreign ministry appointed Tatars as diplomats to foreign countries, and Tatars achieved senior positions in Polish society, for example, Olgierd Najman Mirza Kryczyński, who was the prosecutor of the Polish Supreme Court and vice president of the Appellate Court. Tatars also ascended to high-ranking military offices and received Poland's highest military honors. The Tatars defended Poland against the Nazi invasion of 1939 and "served in all units of the Polish Army on almost every front in the world" during the Second World War.[16]

The imposition of Soviet communist rule after the war was devastating for the Tatars. As the current grand mufti of Lithuania, Ramadan Yaqoob, explained, "The Soviet period was the worst. All the religious leaders and people of any knowledge were either killed or sent into exile into the farthest reaches of Siberia. Books and archives were burnt. Mosques were closed and destroyed. Communities were closed. Islam was forbidden."[17]

In recent years, the Catholic Church in Poland has undertaken remarkable steps toward interfaith understanding shaped by the history of Tatars in the country. In November 2003 the General Meeting of the Conference of Polish Bishops at the Jasna Góra Monastery in Częstochowa honored the six-century history of the Tatars in Poland by initiating the annual Day of Islam, a day of prayer dedicated to Islam, in the Catholic Church.

In 2006 the Polish newspaper *Rzeczpospolita* reprinted the cartoons of the Prophet of Islam, a decision that was condemned by the Polish prime minister. "The publication of the cartoons," the prime minister affirmed, "crosses the boundaries of the well-understood freedom to express one's opinions. . . . Poland was and still remains a country of tolerance. This fact is confirmed by the 600-year presence of the Muslim Tatar community in the territory of the Republic of Poland." *Rzeczpospolita* soon apologized, acknowledging that they had "hurt the feelings of a large group of people, Muslims, but also Christians and non-believers."[18]

Despite the deep historical ties between the Tatars and the Poles, the present immigration crisis and the rise of the Far Right in Poland has led to a feeling of insecurity among the Tatars. In 2013 a Tatar mosque was firebombed, and the following year, "anti-Muslim slogans, a pig and a red X" were painted on an eighteenth-century Tatar mosque in the northeastern city of Kruszyniany, near the border with Belarus. The mosque's cemetery was also vandalized, with assailants "painting wartime resistance symbols and covering Islamic religious script on Tatar tombstones."[19]

The Tatars of Lithuania voiced alarm at the new environment of escalating rhetoric, including a debate in 2015 about banning the burqa, which observers noted is nonexistent in Lithuania. Adas Jakubauskas, the chairman of the Lithuanian Tatar Union and a law instructor at a university in Vilnius, told *The Economist* in September of that year, "It hurts me as a Muslim and a believer when politicians engage in this [burqa-ban] publicity."

Yet the historically close relationship between Lithuanians and Tatars was on display in April 2016, when the president of Lithuania condemned Russia's persecution of Tatars in Crimea in a meeting in Vilnius with Crimean Tatar leaders and the chair of the Lithuanian Tatar Union. In 2015 the Crimean Tatar leader Mustafa Dzhemilev, a human rights activist, member of the Ukrainian Parliament, and former Soviet dissident, was awarded the Cross of the Knight of the Order for Merits to Lithuania for defending the rights of the Tatars of Crimea.

In our fieldwork for this project, we interviewed Tatars from different areas, in an effort to understand the community and its relationship to Europe. Liliya Karimova, a lecturer at George Washington University who is from Kazan in Tatarstan, Russia, told us that Tatars were Muslim as early as 922, as recorded by the Abbasid traveler Ibn Fadlan, who visited Volga-Bulgaria. Gulnaz Sharafutdinova, a senior lecturer at King's College London who is also from Russian Tatarstan, said that Tatars see themselves as "a bridge between Europe and Asia . . . which is even present in the thought and in the way . . . Tatar intellectuals have perceived their religion and their spiritual foundation."

### Meeting the Crimean Tatars

In my office at American University in April 2016, we met Nariman Celal and Ayder Bulatov, two of the leaders of the Crimean Tatar community, thanks to their untiring and compassionate supporter Walter Ruby, the Muslim-Jewish program director at the Foundation for Ethnic Understanding and coordinator of the U.S. Working Group for the Crimean Tatars. Celal and Bulatov were visiting the United States to raise awareness of the dire situation of their people, who number around 250,000, following Putin's seizure of their homeland from Ukraine in 2014. Celal, who is in his mid-thirties, serves as the first deputy chair of the Mejlis, the highest executive and representative body of the Crimean Tatars, and also worked as a journalist for *Avdet*, a Crimean Tatar newspaper. Bulatov, in his mid-sixties, is an Islamic scholar who since 1999 has worked in the Department of Crimea District Authority in positions dealing with interethnic and interfaith relations. Both Celal and Bulatov said that Stalin had deported their parents, along with the entire Crimean Tatar population, to Central Asia in 1944. They met us shortly after discussing this catastrophe, which killed nearly half of the entire Crimean Tatar population, at the United States Holocaust Memorial Museum in Washington, D.C. Celal's family returned to Crimea in 1989; Bulatov's in 1992.

Celal and Bulatov appeared weary and subdued when they arrived at the office. They came clutching the fading memories of a past they could not abandon and faced a future that promised little besides uncertainty. I looked carefully for the spark that once fired this martial race and made its name a byword for the warrior ethos across Asia and Eastern Europe; I glimpsed it in their bearing as they began to talk of their history and culture with increasing animation and show signs of pride in their identity.

The Crimean Tatars have a "friendly" and "tight" relationship with the Polish Tatars, they told us, who share the same roots in the larger Kipchak Tatar people, although they consider themselves distinct communities. Celal explained that in the mid-fifteenth century, the Tatar leader Hajji Giray, a descendant of Genghis Khan, sought to break away from the Golden Horde and create an independent khanate in Crimea. This was during the time of the "great Lithuanian king." With the support of the Lithuanians, Giray, who had been living in Lithuania, was able to take advantage of the weakness of the Golden Horde and create the Crimean Khanate.

The two men described the extraordinary culture of the Crimean Khanate, which put a high value on learning and knowledge. Celal discussed the madrassa known as Zincirli, which he described as the oldest in Europe. It is located in the city of Bakhchysarai, the capital of the Crimean Khanate, and was founded in 1500. "It wasn't a huge building," Bulatov noted, "but it was a huge, incredible idea and an architectural landmark." As you walk into the madrassa's entrance, he told us, there is a chain that causes you to bow your head, which historians believe symbolized that "in that way, we bow before knowledge." Along with the focus on knowledge came pluralism, and the Crimean Khanate was a place where Jews, Christians, and Muslims all lived together.

Celal recounted that the Crimean Khanate ended in 1783, when it was annexed by Russia. Crimean Tatars regard Putin's actions as a second annexation, Celal said, and publicly oppose his seizure of Crimea. "The whole community is being persecuted right now," he stated sorrowfully. "The biggest tragedy is that we are now in the middle of two countries,

Ukraine and Russia. We have a lot of our country mates living in Ukraine, especially in Kherson in southern Ukraine. About 9,000 Muslim Tatars have fled the country because of the possible threat or persecution. Very negative things are happening right now, which may make more leave."

Discussing the question of whether Islam and Europe are compatible, Celal observed, "Islam has become a European religion. It is understandable and normal that Europeans want to preserve their way of life, but we need to find alternatives to conflict." Celal believed that Crimea, with its multiethnic and multireligious population, provides Europe a model of how to proceed: "Crimea is an example for Europe. We have a rich experience of coexisting together with different nations and different religions. Some Tatars look more European, like me. Others have more 'Mongoloid' features. Despite the fact that we have Asian roots, the European values are very close to us and we honor them. We developed together with a young independent country of Ukraine, and we supported integration into Europe." Bulatov believed that there is a "mutual enrichment" in the interaction between Islam and Europe. "The Islamic religion enriches the European community with its values. A lot of European nations accept Islam, and there is a very powerful movement to accept Islam. At the same time, when Muslims accept those European values, they start to practice a softer version of Islam, a 'Euro Islam.'"

### The Roma

In the popular European imagination, the Roma, a traditionally nomadic people, are known as feckless and dangerous gypsies accused of stealing, kidnapping children, and even cannibalism. They have been the target of aggressive persecution and deportation, especially in the Balkans. The majority of the Roma of Europe live in the Balkans and include large populations in Romania, estimated at over 2 million; Bulgaria and Hungary, each with half a million or more; Serbia, 400,000; Greece, 300,000; and Macedonia, 200,000. It may come as a surprise to most to learn that half of the Roma in the Balkans are Muslim, meaning that the Roma are one of the larger Muslim nations of Europe.[20]

Some Roma are Christian and others Muslim, but they are not defined as part of the Volk as understood by Europe's tribal nationalists. For the advocates of primordial and predator identity in the Balkans, the Muslim Roma are enemies twice over, on both racial and religious counts. Cases of extreme violence and persecution against the Roma continue to occur with the rise of the Far Right. By all accounts, the Roma of the Balkans, both Muslims and Christians, inhabit the bottom rung on the socio-economic ladder. They often live in squalor and continue to be subject to profound discrimination, hatred, and oppression. In Europe, "more than 90 percent of Roma households live below the poverty lines of their respective countries. Only 15 percent have completed secondary education."[21]

The Roma, originally from northern India, arrived in the Balkans in the medieval period and found a place in the Ottoman Empire as "musicians, blacksmiths and ironworkers, leather workers, horse traders, and dancers," while others had jobs ranging from "seasonal agricultural labor to military functions and even petty official roles."[22] In the Ottoman Empire, "the basic legal rights of the Gypsies were the same as those of their fellow-Christians or fellow-Muslims." A 1604 Ottoman decree proclaimed of the Muslim and Christian Roma of southern Albania and northwestern Greece, "Let no one harass and oppress the race in question."[23] According to the scholar Zoltan Barany, "the Ottoman Empire . . . was a haven for the Roma," and their situation contrasted markedly with the Roma of Christian Europe. For the Roma of the Romanian lands of Moldavia and Wallachia, who until 1864 were enslaved—indeed "slave" and "Roma" were "synonymous terms"—"The Ottoman Empire became the promised land."[24] By "the nineteenth century there were between three and four times more Muslim Roma than Christian in the Balkans."[25]

The downfall of the Ottoman Empire dramatically reversed the fortunes of the Roma. The brutality and discrimination with which they were then treated reached a climax in Hitler's Germany, as discussed in chapter 2, and half a million Roma were killed by the Nazis and allied governments like Croatia and Hungary. After the war, governments continued with their plans to "assimilate" the Roma, a euphemism for cultural and physical genocide. In Bulgaria, the distinguished Muslim Roma activist, member of Parliament, and leader of the Roma organization Democratic Union Roma, Manush Romanov, who was forced to change his name from Mustafa Aliev, noted that while the world became aware that the Bulgarian Turks were forced to change their names in the 1980s, "The so-called 'revival process' was begun with the Gypsies" thirty years earlier.[26]

During the 1990s wars in the Balkans, the Roma were again subject to violence and massacres. In Kosovo, where around 150,000 Roma, the majority of whom were Muslim, lived before 1998, "Roma were killed, wounded, threatened, raped, and expelled by both ethnic Albanians and the Serbian police, and their property looted and burned by both sides."

There was a Roma refugee exodus, and a year later, the Roma population of Kosovo had been reduced to 30,000.[27] Many Roma from the Balkans, escaping the misery of their lives, attempted to move westward to places like Germany and France, but rising tensions surrounding the migration crisis have meant that their position in Western Europe is increasingly precarious, and they are subject to deportation. Their dilemma was captured by a November 2015 headline in *Deutsche Welle*: "No Way Out for Deported Balkan Roma."

## The Cham

Few have even heard of the Cham Muslims, whose very name, identity, and territory have been taken from them. The Cham are ethnic Albanians who speak their own dialect of Albanian and are indigenous to the area known as Chameria, which is on the Adriatic coast and mostly in the present-day northern Greek province of Epirus. During the Balkan Wars in 1912 and 1913, their region was annexed by Greece, and the Cham found themselves cut off from Albania by the international border. Killings were immediately carried out in villages like Paramythia, in which more than seventy Muslim notables were executed a few days after the entrance of the Greek army.[28] Thousands escaped, many dying of fatigue, starvation, and typhus, and a stream of Cham began to flee to places like the United States.

The Cham were seen in Greek discourse as Greeks who betrayed the Greek nation by converting to Islam under the Ottomans. Albanian language education was banned, and the speaking of the Albanian language was forbidden in both public and private.[29] A campaign to drive the Muslim Cham out of Greece and assimilate the Orthodox Cham was initiated, with paramilitary groups attacking villages and "terrorising the population, and hundreds of young men were deported to camps on the islands of the Aegean Sea. Large swathes of land were expropriated under the pretense of an agrarian reform."[30] The final push was made by the Greek military in 1944 and 1945, resulting in as many as 25,000 terror-stricken Cham crossing the border into Albania.[31] Massacres by Greeks in one village alone, Filat, killed 1,286 people.[32] A Cham woman who was twelve years old at the time recounted the horrors of what she witnessed in Filat,

> They ordered all of us—men, women, girls, and boys, a total of 3,500 persons—to assemble on the main square . . . separating the men on one side from the women on the other. They took the men off

somewhere and killed them, some with knives and other[s] with cleavers. . . . I saw the three boys who were all tied up. They sliced off their ears, gouged out their eyes, cut off their feet, skinned them alive and then left them quivering like hens in a sack. . . . The women and girls were stripped, raped, and murdered.[33]

The "cleansing" campaign was successful, and the Cham minority disappeared in Greece. Over a period of less than ten years, "nearly all mosques and especially minarets, visible symbols of Muslim presence, were demolished." The Cham were even purged from Greek documents and public registry rolls. The Cham population in Albania now numbers around 250,000 and they have a further population of 400,000 in other countries. The Cham continue to seek a right of return to their lands and properties in Greece, an acknowledgment of what was done to them, which they have commonly referred to as genocide, and the ability to gain back their Greek citizenship. Complicating matters is the fact that Albania and Greece have technically remained in a state of war since 1940. The Cham are referred to by Greek television anchors as "the pseudo-Chams" or "the self-so-called Chams."[34] The Greek government maintains, as its Foreign Ministry did as recently as September 2016, that "the Cham issue does not exist."

SIX

# Muslim Converts: Seeking God in an Age of Secularism

"PROPHET MUHAMMAD, PEACE be upon him, is our role model," murmured Kristiane Backer lovingly with a coy smile. Kristiane, a German convert to Islam and former star presenter on MTV Europe, did not fail to omit the blessings Muslims add when mentioning the Prophet. "He's our beloved, you know. We love Muhammad," she added with a shy spreading smile of someone who is allowing us to glimpse a secret. "All women would love to be married to Muhammad," Kristiane admitted with affection.

> We love him because the way he treated his wives. The way he . . . was so romantic with his wives, so caring, and gracious, and so full of love for everybody. He was a champion of women's rights, an environmentalist, a formidable statesman, and most importantly a Prophet of God who guided people to salvation. I could talk to you for an hour about Prophet Muhammad, peace be upon him. Prophet Muhammad, peace be upon him, means everything. He's my favorite man, and I would love to see him and be near him one day, inshallah.

Then her face clouded and without pause she complained: "So when he gets attacked, of course it feels like, you are hurt, you feel personally hurt and personally under attack."

Kristiane's love for the Prophet is, as is ultimately all love, a mystery and a miracle in itself. It is a sociological curiosity how a European TV presenter and author, working in the full blaze of the media, hobnobbing with the likes of Mick Jagger, Robbie Williams, and Annie Lennox, so passionately and voluntarily converts to Islam, and then, in spite of the malicious distortions around the Prophet of Islam, ends up seeing him, as do Muslims all over the world, as the ultimate *mahboob*, or beloved of God. Her faith in our age of secularism and cynicism reflects the nature of religion and our very human aspiration to seek something beyond ourselves to inspire and create love in us.

## Finding Refuge in Islam

Over the past few centuries, as Europe moved inexorably toward modernity and increasing secularism, its intellectuals and philosophers—Voltaire, Marx, George Bernard Shaw, and Nietzsche—used the battering ram of logic and reason to smash down the doors of the castle of faith. In addition to the more generalized attacks on religion, there is now the more recent Islamophobic assault that developed after 9/11 led by public figures like the Dutch politician Geert Wilders. With the toxic environment that has been created around Islam, even one conversion to the faith should be sufficient cause to send scholars of the sociology of religion scurrying to dust off their volumes of Émile Durkheim for explanation. But so far no satisfactory thesis has been fielded and defended that explains why, in the face of rampant Islamophobia, thousands of Europeans, especially women, are converting to Islam.

In this chapter, while I do not claim to have solved the puzzle, I will share the fascinating stories of why and how Europeans are converting to Islam. The stories are rich with human interest and provide us fertile sociological insights. We note the spirited attempts of the converts to reconcile their native primordial identity with the universalist and compassionate version of Islam that attracted them to it in the first place, and we recognize the same Islam from our discussions of convivencia in Andalusia. The unvarnished ethnography will thus allow the reader to draw their own conclusions.

On the face of it, Islam has proved as resistant to arguments of godless science as to racial and religious prejudice. It has survived centuries of attacks, and just as the Muslim world appears to be imploding in tribal and sectarian wars, fresh blood has come to its aid in the form of Europeans converting to Islam. In France, where the convert population has doubled in the past twenty-five years, there are an estimated 100,000 converts to Islam;[1] and there are perhaps another 100,000 converts in the United Kingdom. These new Muslims bring the zeal of the convert with them; even more important, they bring their European tradition of looking at the world in a pragmatic and scholarly manner. The continent that centuries ago launched the crusades against the Muslim world and later colonized it is now, ironically, providing Islam with a new lease of life.

For many Europeans, joining a religion that is widely perceived as violent makes little sense. As a result, they regard these conversions as acts of psychological disorder. They are horrified that European women who have struggled so long and hard for female rights should so easily surrender them. In the general environment of secularism, materialism, and consumerism, they wonder why Europeans would be willing to relinquish their personal freedoms for a religion that demands strict discipline and boundaries.

During our fieldwork, we discovered that Europeans approached the subject of conversion to Islam with intellectual seriousness and careful reasoning. They are in the tradition of the European philosophers in their quest for truth and meaning. They find comfort in what they see to be Islam's continuity from their previous faith traditions, with its Abrahamic values and prophets. They are particularly drawn to the attractive spiritual notion of *tauhid* or the unity of existence. Their conversion is invariably a mixture of head and heart. It should also be noted that European primordial identity—which has reservations regarding morally vacuous materialism, consumerism, and globalization and defines differentiated roles for men and women—finds an echo in the attraction many converts feel toward Islam today.

While Europe's far-right parties have responded to the current uncertain era by reviving ethnic chauvinism, targeting the other with violence and drawing borders around their own ethnic nations, several far-right politicians are among Europe's most notable converts to Islam. Daniel Streich was a member of the Swiss Party of the Volk, the Swiss People's Party, which successfully led the effort to ban minarets in the country. He had researched Islam in order to refute it—but ended up denouncing the party after his conversion. Of his embrace of Islam, Streich said, "Islam offers me logical answers to important life questions, which, in the end, I never found in Christianity." In France, Maxence Buttey, a young councilor with the National Front, also converted to Islam after discussions with an imam he met while campaigning against Islam. "I was Catholic, but when I reread the Bible I noticed all its inconsistencies," Buttey admitted. "When I read the Quran thoroughly, I understood that this religion is more open," he told the newspaper *Le Parisien*. Sacked from the National Front, Buttey called on party members to convert to Islam and join him in his mission to "unite all men and women."

Earlier, the English musician Cat Stevens converted to Islam in the late 1970s and took the name of Yusuf Islam. He became the face of the religion in the West. Like so many converts, he initially came to practice a more rigid, literalist form of the faith. Under the influence of orthodox Arab teachers, he consciously rejected his European identity and even gave up singing and playing the guitar. In recent years, however, he has returned to music and touring, once again using his talents in his own Western medium that he sees and understands as fully compatible with Islam.

Other European celebrities have expressed their attraction to Islam. After hearing the call to prayer while filming in Istanbul, the movie star Liam Neeson admitted, "It just gets into your spirit, and it's the most beautiful, beautiful thing. There are 4,000 mosques in the city. Some are just stunning, and it really makes me think about becoming a Muslim."

## *Muhammad Asad, the European Scholar of Islam*

There is one prominent European convert to whom Kristiane Backer and other Muslims turn to for inspiration and guidance—Muhammad Asad. The renowned Muslim scholar, diplomat, and writer was born Leopold Weiss in 1900 to an Orthodox Jewish family in Lemberg, Austria-Hungary (now Lviv, Ukraine). Upon converting in 1926, Weiss, who had also rejected Zionism, took the name Muhammad Asad. Asad's conversion was influenced by his visit to his uncle in Jerusalem and his travels throughout the Arab world working as a journalist. He yearned for the golden age of Andalusia in Europe, a time when Jews, Muslims, and Christians lived in harmony, all able to practice their faith and express their own identity.

Soon after his conversion, Asad went on his first hajj to Mecca. He had felt alienated in Europe, but here in Saudi Arabia, he wrote, "I am no longer a stranger." He decided to establish himself in Saudi Arabia, where he would serve as an adviser to the royal court. Ultimately, however, his relationship with the royal family soured, and after six years Asad traveled to India. After arriving in India in 1932, he met Allama Iqbal, who encouraged him to stay in India to assist in the development of an Islamic state and to serve as a scholarly bridge between Europe and the Muslim world. Asad agreed and, in 1934, he published his book *Islam at the Crossroads*, in which he addresses fellow Muslims and discusses his discovery of Islam. Asad continued his scholarly work even when he was interned for the duration of the Second World War under suspicion of anti-British agitation. Ironically, he lost close members of his family to the Holocaust. He remained

*Author and Amineh offer benediction at
Muhammad Asad's grave in Granada*

in India after the war and played an integral role in the establishment of
Pakistan following its partition from India. Asad first served as the head of
Pakistan's Department of Islamic Reconstruction, and in the early 1950s
he represented Pakistan at the United Nations. He went on to devote himself to Islamic scholarship and published his famous autobiography, *The Road
to Mecca*, in 1954.

Asad's life reflects the romance of Andalusia through his embrace of
European pluralist identity and his rejection of European primordial
identity. He wrote several well-received books as a Muslim traveler and
what remains, to my mind, one of the best translations of the Holy Quran
into English, *The Message of The Qur'an* (1980). Upon his death in 1992
in Andalusia, special permission was given for his burial in the Muslim
cemetery in Granada. It had been a remarkable journey for Asad—from
Austria to Andalusia, from Judaism to Islam, from a European exile to a
Pakistani diplomat, from a writer of travel books to a religious scholar and
translator. We took time from our fieldwork in Granada to visit his grave
under the shadow of the Sierra Nevada mountain range and pay homage
with a prayer and a blessing.

While Kristiane's role as media celebrity encouraged her to look to
the future as a spokesperson for Islam in Europe, Asad's scholarship
drew him to the past. There is irony in both cases in the sum of their lives:
Kristiane, the MTV star, becomes the well-known and well-respected
champion of Islam, even battling with the hosts of *Fox News* on its behalf,

while Asad, the scholarly descendant of rabbis, is revered by scores of Muslims for his contribution to Islam, which includes his peerless translation of the Quran. As an example of the respect Asad commands among Muslims, Mirnes Kovač, the Bosnian scholar we met in the last chapter, in his recently published book, *One,* acknowledges Asad's translation of the Quran as his main source.

## Female Converts

Studies on the subject confirm that the majority of Europeans converting to Islam are women. In the United Kingdom, for example, 75 percent of converts to Islam were women according to recent surveys.[2] Wherever we went in European Muslim communities we commonly met converts, particularly women. We also met several young women in places like Marseille and Copenhagen who were studying Islam and spending time with Muslim friends and who said they were close to converting.

In my 2010 book *Journey into America,* several American female converts explained that they were tired of objectification and superficiality in mainstream culture. Many of the female converts we met across Europe felt they needed to escape the same pressures. The women were keenly aware that Islam in its early history provided strong role models for females. Khadija, the Prophet's wife, for example, was a widow and a successful businesswoman who, though older than the Prophet, proposed marriage to him, explained his revelations when they came, and took him for further spiritual advice to her relative, a Christian priest. European female converts like Kristiane Backer commonly cited the example of Khadija and other women from early Islam.

### From MTV to Mecca

In *The Thistle and the Drone,* I argue that the role and status of the Prophet of Islam within the faith found an immediate analogy and therefore sympathy in the somewhat similar position of the popular tribal chief in tribal society who, while restricted to the role of primus inter pares, is nonetheless a pivotal figure in society. Germanic converts to Islam like Kristiane Backer find an echo of their own primordial tribal identity in their new faith, especially in the figure of the Prophet.

Born in 1965 and raised in a middle-class Protestant family in Hamburg, Kristiane looked on Christianity more as a formality than as a way of life. By the age of twenty-four, she was a top presenter on MTV Europe in London, but she soon found herself feeling empty and worn down by the pressures of the entertainment industry. This sense of emptiness came to the fore when her sister developed appendicitis on their family vacation in Morocco and returned to Hamburg near death. During this episode, Kristiane felt she could not take time off work to visit her sister, causing her to face head-on the overwhelming dominance of her career in her life.[3]

God really does move in mysterious ways, and in the case of Kristiane Backer, God's moves were more mysterious than usual. A freethinking, liberated modern German, Kristiane was introduced to Islam, Sufism, and Qawwali, or South Asian Sufi music, when she met the cricket star Imran Khan. In an interview for this project, she recalled,

> I was an MTV presenter interviewing rock stars for a living. . . . And I met a famous Muslim who had just won the World Cup for Pakistan. It was Imran Khan, former cricket captain, and he really became my Islam teacher. He was my introduction to Islam. So, you see, basically, I like to say, "I wasn't looking, I was found."

Kristiane explained that her first interactions with Khan caused her to begin questioning the way women sometimes carry themselves—particularly in terms of dress—in Western society:

> When I first joined him with a couple of friends to go out in London, I turned up in a miniskirt and he asked me if I wouldn't mind keeping on my coat all evening, even on the dance floor. . . . Even now, I wonder in business meetings, why do women have to wear miniskirts and show their cleavage, whereas men are fully dressed? I find it very degrading and exploitative that women have to always look sexy . . . to be recognized, to get somewhere in life.

"The first thing I changed was my sense of dress a little bit," she recalled, "I ditched the miniskirts. . . . I felt more feminine. . . . Who needs those whistles on the streets, just this energy you attract when you walk around?" She highlighted a Western double standard: "It's fine if you show your tummy, have a piercing in your tummy, and wear miniskirts, but it's not fine to wear long clothes and a headscarf? That's wrong."

Her frequent travels to Pakistan opened Kristiane's eyes to a different way of life; the warmth, the generosity, and the humanity of the Pakistanis she met touched her deeply. Believe in God and do good deeds was the essence of Islam, Imran explained. She was introduced to Qawwali and was deeply moved by its beauty, feeling that each lyric seemed connected to a higher form of spiritual love that could not be felt between humans.

Kristiane went on to learn more about the faith from books such as Asad's *Road to Mecca*, Gai Eaton's *Islam and the Destiny of Man*, Ali Shariati's *Man and Islam*, and my book, *Living Islam*. Her reading helped her to draw inspiration from and find her place in Islam:

> What I discovered was mind-blowing. It was like a whole new universe, and I was intrigued from the first book I read. I wanted to know more. . . . This idea of one God, worship of one God and our origin, our destiny and that we're self-responsible for our own deeds, and babies are born pure, not as sinners. . . . I also learned how verses from the Quran can help me in my daily life, and just help me make sense of my life.

Kristiane's interest in Islam endured its greatest test, however, when Imran Khan—who it was assumed would propose marriage—abruptly ended the relationship. One of Imran's "spiritual advisers" was against the match with the European woman. This was a feeble excuse, as shortly after breaking up with Kristiane, Imran courted and then married another European—this time Jemima Goldsmith, a woman of the Jewish faith. Both that marriage and Imran's subsequent marriage would end in divorce.

A perplexed Kristiane recalls in her autobiography, *From MTV to Mecca: How Islam Inspired My Life*, that Imran rang from Pakistan and accused her "of betraying him with another man" and ended the relationship.[4] In her defense, Kristiane cited the story of Aisha, the Prophet's wife. Aisha was inadvertently left behind when the Prophet's caravan moved on and a young soldier brought her to the camp. This gave the critics of the Prophet a chance to accuse his wife of infidelity. It created a great deal of soul searching for the Prophet, which included Quranic revelations, but ended in exoneration of Aisha. The lesson was that those who slander against the good name of others are committing grievous sin.

If Kristiane had reacted by recoiling against Imran's religion, it would have been understandable. Instead, she continued to explore Islam for herself and eventually converted to it in the mid 1990s, finding comfort in the London Muslim community. Though Kristiane's family members were not always happy with her conversion, they did eventually come at least to accept it, even if they wished not to speak much about it. In recent years, she has resumed her career in television and hosting galas and festivals while speaking out for the rights of Muslim women. "The beautiful values of Islam and the teachings of our noble Prophet are one of the best-kept secrets in the West," she said. "And it is time we lift that veil."

Kristiane has observed a "very big trend" of Europeans—particularly women—converting to Islam.

A thousand Westerners convert to Islam every year, most of them white, educated, middle-class women who convert not for marriage, for convenience, but out of conviction. They convert to Islam because obviously Islam has something to offer to all these well-educated modern women, and what could this be? It could be that Islam actually does appeal to the inner nature of the woman.

The Prophet, Kristiane said, "loved women" and honored them.

Women fall in love with the teachings of Muhammad, the teachings of Islam, and they like the fact that Islam recognizes the nature of a woman who wants to have children and to be able to look after the children. . . . In the West . . . women are expected to work. . . . In a traditional Muslim family, or in Islam, a woman can choose whether she works. That it's the man's duty to support the family does not exist in the West anymore at all. If you go out with a Western man you are expected to go Dutch.

She added, however, "Sadly, when you are a Muslim, you're confronted with the reality of Muslim men who really do not measure up to the Prophet. . . . If Muslim men were to follow the Prophet, Muslim women would be the happiest in the whole world."

On being a convert, Kristiane explained,

There are also a lot challenges that converts face here in Britain as well as in the rest of Europe, because it's a very lonely journey being a convert. We are a minority within the minority. Where do we pray? Which mosque do we go to? Do we go to the Pakistani mosque, to the Persian mosque, to the Turkish mosque? Islam is very divided by ethnicity, here in England and in Germany. We don't have a European mosque as yet. . . . Hopefully there will be in the next few generations. . . . . As a convert, you sometimes don't feel truly accepted.

Kristiane, however, noted hopeful signs in the community, "Alhamdulillah things really have changed over time. And I'm very lucky to have made a great number of Muslim friends."

Kristiane expressed pride in her German identity and said she felt it was compatible with Islam. "I wholeheartedly believe and know that Islamic values are compatible not only with German values but with all

European values. Islam is a religion for all times and all worlds and therefore also for Europeans in our day and age. I'm living proof." She defined being German in terms that would immediately be recognizable to us from our discussions of German primordial tribal identity: "It means to be reliable, it means to be honest, it means to be straightforward . . . very hard working . . . high standards, health care for everybody, concern for the environment, you have your rights, whether you are a poor person or a rich person, you get your rights. . . . All of these values are also Islamic values."

Not only was German identity compatible with Islam, Kristiane believed, but some of Germany's greatest literary figures were themselves influenced and shaped by Islam, particularly by Sufism.

> In the past, writers like Heidegger, Goethe, and even Schiller, a number of writers were inspired by Eastern literature, they loved Nasimi, Rumi, and Omar Khayyam, Hafez, a lot of the Persian poets in particular. . . . I think it was the love for this kind of literature that inspired the great Romantic movement in Germany. . . . Even heads of state like Frederick the Great were inspired by Muslims through trading and through diplomatic relationships.

Kristiane pointed out that Goethe in particular displayed this fondness for Islam.

> Goethe was so profoundly influenced by these writers that he wrote *West-Eastern Divan*, where he uses a lot of imagery from Hafez and from Rumi. He was the first one to bring the image of the butterfly extinguishing itself in the flame. You know the finale. The extinguishment of the mystical lover of God in God. . . . The way he describes Jesus in this very book is like a Muslim. And, he criticizes the Christian view of Jesus. He goes so far as to say, how can your leader, the savior, not even save himself? How can you believe in this sad figure there on the cross if he cannot even save himself? Some Muslims even claim for this reason Goethe must have been a Muslim. But this remains questionable. However, he knew Arabic, a little bit, and I have seen writings of his in Arabic, certain verses from the Quran.

Speaking of this rich history of towering German figures who reached out to Muslims and were influenced by Islam, Kristiane observed, "We do not see this Germany right now." She cited her own experience, in which, she told us, she lost her career in Germany after converting "and suddenly I was accused of being a supporter of terrorism." Some time later, however, Kristiane felt the situation improving: "Nowadays it is fine in Germany."

The problem in Germany today, Kristiane believed, is that Germans are not seeing the intellectual approach to Islam that attracted her and so many illustrious Germans like Goethe, but perceive the Muslim presence as a threat because of the problems associated with immigration and guest workers, primarily the Turks. "There is a bit of a problem" in Germany, Kristiane said,

> because the Turkish people don't really like to . . . befriend the Germans very much. . . . The problem is that a lot of the Turkish people bring their Anatolian culture to Germany and into German schools. You know, they bring knives to schools, and things have happened. There are honor killings and these kinds of things. This is all very shocking for the German people. So they're not really exposed to a highly intellectual and spiritual side of Islam through the Turkish people living in Germany. A lot of them know perhaps a very rudimentary version of Islam.

"Suddenly," Kristiane observed, "they want to build mosques, and German citizens are opposed to seeing so many mosques." Kristiane contrasted the situation in Germany regarding Islam to her current home in England, where British imperial history has meant a greater exposure to Islam and, she believed, a greater tolerance for difference. "We are respected here. There is a mix of Muslims who came for intellectual reasons to England, not everybody came as guest workers like in Germany. . . . They are in Parliament. They are in the economy. You can find even hijabi women working at L. K. Bennett clothing stores and even on TV."

European Muslims, Kristiane said, should look to Andalusia as a model for how cultures and religions can thrive together and ensure mutual respect. "Unfortunately, the Muslim world has decayed. Why is this? Have Muslims perhaps moved away from their faith? Why is it that so few Muslims are Nobel Prize winners? We really need to revive all of that. We need to get our own house in order and encourage education, make sure Muslims excel again in life." To those born Muslims who lost their faith and think Islam is backward, she says, "Islam is compatible with science. Islam is a religion for people who think."

She encourages young Muslims not to "blindly follow what people tell you, even what your parents tell you. The problem is that Islam here, in Europe, can be a bit fossilized and it is up to the young people to do their research to take things forward. They must really look into the sources of

Islam, study the religion well through contemporary and classical scholars, and then educate not only the mainstream society but even their own families." "And remember," she reminds Muslims, "whatever you do, that you are not only a servant of God but also an ambassador of Islam."

Kristiane believed that while a "fear and fascination with Islam" is part of "the DNA of the Europeans," people must challenge the negative stereotypes and deep-seated prejudices. There should be "documentaries on Muslim culture, and have Muslim characters featured on soap operas, but positive ones." Muslims need to be in the media themselves, she argued, and explained that the reason she wrote her autobiography, *From MTV to Mecca*, was to convey the realities of being a European Muslim. "I really wanted to make my contribution through this book to show people that Islam is a religion of all worlds and all times and I very much—as a modern woman—in London, in Europe, in the West, can live Islam very happily."

When the film accompanying this project, also called *Journey into Europe*, was completed and we exhibited it at film festivals and special events, the German Stiftung Mercator Foundation asked Kristiane to moderate a screening in Berlin in June 2016. We had a full house and a distinguished audience, and Kristiane handled the event masterfully. Kristiane had made the transition from one culture to another and in doing so had become a bridge between the two.

### Promoting the Music of Muslim Women

In Copenhagen, we interviewed another dynamic convert, Annette Bellaoui, the founder and director of Missing Voices, an organization that arranges and promotes musical performances by Muslim women. Annette, a white Dane in her mid-fifties, said she had been a Muslim for the past fifteen years. She described her family as "militant atheist" and "the atheist version of the Taliban."

"They think I'm a bit weird, but that's okay," chuckled Annette, who wore a colorful headscarf. "I can live with that." Her family accepts her, she said, "because they have no choice." From the time she was a girl, she knew what she wanted and could not be swayed by anyone, an attitude she retains. When her brother teases her about her headscarf, Annette replies, "Come on, you've known me for all these years, you know that when I was a year-and-a-half old, mother could not tell me what to wear. Do you seriously think that anybody can tell me what to wear now?" Her mother, she admitted, still asks her why she covers her "pretty hair."

Growing up, Annette was aware that she was uncomfortable with her family's atheism. "In my early teens, I think, I sort of started realizing that it just didn't feel right. I often compare it to shoes. You know if you have shoes that are one size too small, you can wear them, you can walk around, but there's something bothering you constantly." Annette began seeking to learn about various religions and belief systems.

The catalyst for her conversion came when she took a trip with her twelve-year-old daughter to Morocco, a destination she chose because she wanted to be in the sun and relax, and the travel agency offered a good deal to Morocco. She described what occurred on arrival:

> The very first morning I woke up really, really early, about half-past four maybe. Because I'm a chef, I have a highly developed sense of smell. Every place in the world I've ever been to has a different morning smell. . . . So I went out to the balcony to get that morning smell. And I can still remember it. . . . It smelled of a freshly baked croissant and of earth just sort of a warming up, because I could just see sort of a tiny sliver of sunrise. And then I heard, for the first time ever, I heard the *adhan*, the call to prayer, because there was a mosque a hundred meters down the street. And it sounded so wonderful, but I didn't even sort of take it all in. I just stood there like . . . I always describe it as a cartoon figure, you know one of these cartoon figures when somebody drops an anvil on their head, I just stood there like "what happened?" . . . In that moment I said to myself "one day, I will be Muslim." It took another three years, but the decision was made then and there. And until the end of my days I will swear I heard Allah call me.

Annette's role models are strong women, including the American TV star Oprah Winfrey, because "she's done great things for African American women, and I love the fact that a woman is in control of a media empire"; Malala Yousafzai, because "she stands up for education, which I think is the number-one priority for the whole of the Islamic *ummah*, and especially education for girls and women"; and the medieval Queen Margaret I of Denmark, who presided over a united Scandinavian kingdom, which was "almost like the beginning of the Common Market, you know, the European Union. At a time when women were not supposed to be in a position of power, the Queen was a brilliant strategist, she knew how to do the power play." Annette also cited her maternal grandmother, another strong woman who was a single parent who just had seven years of education but "taught herself by studying and reading in what little spare time she had."

She defined Danish identity as oscillating between having chauvinistic pride in being Danish and being aware of Denmark's small size and its tiny population on the world stage. The Danes also have a strong warrior identity, which Annette related to the Germanic god Thor and linked to their participation in modern wars led by the United States. "We actually really like the image of the Vikings traveling all over the world and pillaging everywhere, creating havoc where we go, because we don't like the idea that we are small and insignificant."

Like Kristiane, with her German primordial identity, Annette is proud of her Danish identity and does not see it as incompatible with being Muslim. For example, she noted that the Danes have an ethos of equality, egalitarianism, personal freedom, and free debate: "My Danish identity makes me a strong believer in 'I can do what I want if I put my mind to it.' I have complete freedom to make my own choices as long as I don't violate relevant laws." For Annette, this identity is summed up in the famous quote attributed to Voltaire: "We have this as a proverb, it's very strong in Danish culture.... Monsieur, I vehemently disagree with everything you're saying, but until the last drop of blood in my body, I will fight for your right to say it.'"

The sense of equality, including between men and women, she explained, comes from Viking culture:

> In the time of the Vikings, every small town had an assembly or Thing, which was like a place of justice, where people would meet and debate, male or female.... The lowliest farmer had the right to bring a case against the king.... Women had more or less equal rights with men. They could run businesses, they could marry or divorce at their own choices, they had the same rights of inheritance.

The "strong need for consensus achieved through debate," she believed, "is something extremely important in the Danish mentality. A person who is unwilling to debate or unwilling to compromise will be looked down on, they will be thought as a badly behaved person, or not well raised, even uncultured."

While Annette felt that there was no contradiction in being both Danish and Muslim, she admitted it can be a struggle to balance her compulsion to respond to personal challenges by others head-on and the Quranic imperative to be compassionate. "I have a general attitude of I take crap from no one. I generally consider myself patient, friendly, and tolerant and everything, but there is a limit. Don't dish up crap in my face, that I will not take. Women should not be averse to using violence in the right situation. And in my neighborhood, in my area of the city, where everyone knows me, I'm mostly known as a nice and friendly person, helpful and kind. But also one with a very hard right hook."

Annette said she has a "sense of revenge," which "I have taken with me, from the Viking culture." Although her example may sound negligible compared with the bloody accounts in the Viking sagas or *The Thistle and the Drone*, Annette perfectly summed up the dilemma of "tribal Islam." "I do not forgive or forget," she said, "and I can be very mean when taking revenge. Once, I didn't speak to my sister for three years, I literally did not speak to her. . . . I struggle with this, because I know the Quran says that Allah loves those who can forgive, even if you have been greatly wronged. But sometimes I can't, sometimes I can't forgive it. And then I do what I think I have to do, then I ask for Allah's forgiveness and I hope for the best."

Annette's status as both a Dane and a Muslim gave her insight into the Danish reaction to the furious response in the Muslim world, where Muslims burned Danish flags, to the publication of the Danish cartoons of the Prophet. She stated that Danes thought this was "stupid," as "our attitude would be more, if you're mad at me, why are you burning my flag? Why don't you come and try to punch me on the nose? Be more direct about it." Annette said that her position as a convert meant that she is at the same time respected by both Danes and Muslims and also seen as a "traitor" by both:

> I either win-win, on both sides, because as a convert to Islam I have a highly respected standing in the Muslim community, and in my Danish community, because of the things I do, because I make no bones about anything. But, at the same time I also encounter like accusations of "traitor" from both sides; where some Muslims, they think that because I'm not a born Muslim then I'm not a real Muslim.

Muslims asked her questions like why was she wearing the hijab. Danes, she said, "want to ask questions about Islam . . . but they don't dare." "Let's say if my mother sat next to an Arabic woman in hijab on the bus," Annette noted, "she wouldn't even dare to speak to her." With Annette, however, "they are not so afraid of asking me questions, and they can ask me all the difficult questions; things that they would never dare to ask an Arabic woman with hijab."

At the same time, Danes often "don't quite take me seriously because as a Muslim woman I cannot be well educated or intelligent or anything like this. I find sometimes people they would sort of go out of their way to be extra nice to me—almost like they pity me a little, because I'm a Muslim woman, I wear hijab, so I must be a little slow. I must be in need of help and support, and God forbid anybody should say anything harsh to me because for sure that would make me cry or make a scene. . . . I sometimes have felt inclined to bring all my diplomas, because I have quite a few, just to show that I am educated and I am intelligent. But I haven't done it yet. I usually prefer to let my work speak for itself."

Conscious of the image of Islam among Danes and alarmed at seeing the violence in the Muslim world, Annette spoke in scathing terms about Muslims committing violent acts while "proclaiming their Islamic identity."

> We have allowed a small minority to take the floor, to speak for all of us. And they scare the bejesus out of everybody, you know, that's the guys with the long beards and the ones that like to cut people's heads off. They make everyone afraid. . . . And really it's not for me to judge who is a Muslim or not, because only Allah knows what people have in their hearts, but I cannot relate to those people. I cannot.

In keeping with her Danish and European identity, Annette said the only thing that she can do in response to these violent "freaks of nature" is to "disagree with everything you say, from a European view" and challenge them in the manner of Voltaire. "I think even the idiots should have the right to talk, to say what they want, because also that's the only way we can challenge them and say, 'Come on, you're an idiot. Why are you spouting nonsense?'"

In the face of these challenges, Annette still retained her sense of humor and described two episodes where she responded to severe and threatening-looking men by blowing them kisses:

> Once I had visited Parliament to hear a debate. As I was walking out, I was coming down the main staircase, I met one of the leading politicians of the Danish People's Party, and I will never forget the way he looked at me, like he was seriously contemplating, does this woman have hand grenades in her pockets? I mean there was fear and anger and everything in his face. And, you know what I did? I smiled at him, my sweetest smile, and I know that's naughty, but I did like [she puckers her lips and gives an air kiss and giggles]. I also

did this in Iran once, I was there for a big conference and there was a whole group of mullahs and one of them, and he looked at me, and he was walking past me and looked very [she makes an angry face and grunts] and so I winked at him and [she makes another air kiss]. I think many others of our brothers, if they could sort of get into that mode, you know a bit of humor, don't take yourself too seriously, communication will be easier.

Annette said she has tried working with the media, but

they don't really want to hear. The angry story sells a lot more media time or space than the good one. . . . I think the media has a great responsibility. And I think that a lot of the media people, they should hang their heads in shame. . . . But also, as Muslims we have a great responsibility to again and again, no matter how, even if it takes the rest of our lives, we have to keep going and remind people of all of the good things in Islam.

Through her work with Missing Voices, Annette tries to challenge the "media-enhanced idea" of Muslim women as "poor benighted creatures who sit at home shrouded in black." "We're positive," she said. "Unfortunately, the negative sells better."

As evidence of music's ability to transcend language and cultural barriers, Annette recounted witnessing Danes crying at one of her Missing Voices shows.

I had one of the singers I've worked with for a long time, Sarah, she's born and raised in England but from Pakistani parents. She was singing a Bosnian song in a small town, in a small concert hall in the north of Jutland. And I'm willing to take a bet that nobody in the audience understood a word of the song. But, quite a few of them, they were actually listening with tears rolling down their faces because the show is so beautiful and so full of feeling. And I thought, if you can touch people's feelings that way with music . . . it's like a hand extended in friendship.

## A German College Student in Heidelberg

In Heidelberg, we met Miriam Maxeiner, an undergraduate student at the city's renowned university. A white German from Dusseldorf, Miriam had converted to Islam three and a half years earlier, after being introduced to the religion while doing volunteer work in Turkey. She said she hoped to become an English teacher in the future. When I asked why she converted, she replied, "I read the Quran and I believed that it was a script sent by God. So I believe that Muhammad was the Prophet of this book." Miriam, who wore the hijab, added she found "logic" in Islam. She also said that the Quran's emphasis on ilm was "actually one of the things I always liked about Islam." Miriam explained that she saw Islam as a "continuation" of the faith she already had:

> For me, I still believe in the same God that I believed in before that. So for me, God is God, there's just one God, Christians believe in the same God like Muslims do. . . . I didn't convert to Islam because I had the feeling that something was missing in my life, or because I had a feeling that Christianity was not the right religion for me. It was a continuum of the same thing that I already believed in. For me, the Trinity was never an important issue. I have been a Christian; this wasn't working for me. And now I find it much easier to have just one God, that I believe in, I trust in, and not the confusion of who exactly, what exactly is the role of Jesus, who is the Holy Spirit?

Miriam also said that she appreciated the fact that the Islamic religion "covers all aspects of life. Not just going to church on Sunday, but everything you do can be part of the religion. Going to a university campus can be part of the religion and not just a religious service. And I like this concept. . . . I think that's a very nice thing."

Before encountering Islam in Turkey and reading the Quran, Miriam admitted she had a negative impression of the religion. "People don't know what Islam is. For example, before I went to Turkey, I was under the impression that Islam must somehow be bad, because so many bad things happen in the name of Islam." Miriam said that she has not had negative experiences as a Muslim but is conscious of the special scrutiny she gets. Before she converted, as she returned from Turkey, she decided to try wearing the headscarf and immediately noted the difference in how she was treated. "When I went to Turkey without a headscarf, there was no problem. But when I came back with a headscarf, they checked my handbag I think three or four times and I had to remove, each time, each and every item from my bag and put them separately in a box."

Being a Muslim in a non-Muslim country, Miriam observed, is a good opportunity for Muslims to learn about Islam. She spoke of an experience she had in Ireland meeting Muslim women from Malaysia.

They said that they actually got to know their religion much better after coming to Ireland, because people question them. Because back in the Muslim country, everyone is the same, so you don't think about it. You don't think, why am I wearing a headscarf? Why am I praying? Why am I fasting? But in a non-Muslim country you can't, you have to explain yourself. And so you have to go out and find these answers for yourself to be able to explain.

## *The Convert Community of Granada*

When I first visited Spain in the early 1960s, Islam did not officially exist in the country. It was only after the death of Franco in 1975 and the more accommodating attitude toward Islam of King Juan Carlos I that a space was again made for the practice of Islam in Spain (see chapter 3). Toward the end of Franco's rule, however, a community of converts began to form in Andalusia. As Professor Sol Tarrés Chamorro of the University of Huelva told us in Cordoba, these conversions had to be seen in the context of the opposition to Franco's government. What, she asked, could be more anti-government than converting to Islam?

The new Spanish converts established a prominent community in Granada, where they were joined by converts from other parts of Europe. Granada soon became a hub for European Islam—especially for converts—a status it retains to the present day. Leaders like Shaykh Abdalqadir as-Sufi, or Ian Dallas, a Scotsman who converted to Islam in Morocco in 1967, emerged to guide the Granada community. In 2003 the convert community overcame local opposition and built the city's first mosque since the Muslim expulsion in 1492, the Grand Mosque of Granada. Situated in the historic Moorish neighborhood of Albayzin, the mosque is constructed on a hill with a spectacular view of the Alhambra and the Sierra Nevada behind it.

Munira Mendonça, an American from California who arrived in the 1970s and converted to Islam, is among the most notable members of the community. She is a successful businesswoman who runs a shop selling specialty leather goods in the center of Granada and is a leading figure in the city's Grand Mosque. Like the other converts we met in Granada, Munira was exceedingly proud of the mosque and the city's Muslim community. She also expressed great pride in her son, a hafiz of the Quran who had recently been named the imam of the Granada mosque. "I came traveling to Europe when I was twenty-three, very young," Munira told us when we interviewed her at her shop.

I met the father of my children and I stayed and then we discovered Islam and we became Muslim. And we were searching, we were all Catholics and none of us were fulfilled, and so we were investigating in those days, we were looking into Rumi, Idries Shah, Sufism, various things. I had a very tiny baby, six months old, and my parents had died in America, and I didn't want to go back being a single mother. . . . That was thirty years ago.

"When we first became Muslim," Munira observed, "there were no Muslims here." Not even the Moroccans and Syrians who would later come to study in Granada, a university town. At that early point, Munira recalled,

I didn't know how it was going to work, I thought my kids would marry my friends' kids. But then when they became of age it was like, well what about so and so's daughter, and he was like, mom, she's like a sister. So it was a way of expansion, our children in the university et cetera are meeting people then converting. . . . Really extraordinary, I don't have parents but many of the people in the community, their parents have become Muslims and now there's a big community of Moroccans and Syrians and Senegalese and immigrants and they're really helping with the population.

Munira spoke of the considerable opposition the Muslims once faced from the local community. "If we wore a scarf, they wouldn't rent us houses. I have had rocks thrown at me. . . . There is a very derogatory word which is called 'Moro' in Spanish, saying, like, 'Moros go home.' . . . They were terrified. They thought we were going to take over the Albayzin; they thought we were going to take over Granada." The non-Muslim community was particularly opposed to the converts' attempts to build their mosque. For Munira, it was a point of intense pride that not only did the Muslims ultimately succeed in building the mosque, which took twenty years, but also that they were able to do so entirely with their own funding. "There are mosques in Malaga, in Madrid, in many other places," Munira said, "but all built with money from Saudi Arabia. . . . We didn't want that."

Over time, as people have come to know the Granada Muslim community, they have begun to accept them as well as their mosque to the point that today, as Munira explained, "we've now become very ok and very well looked upon in that area which is wonderful." Yet Munira still feels pressure being a Muslim in Granada. "Especially nowadays," sighed

*Amineh interviewing female converts in Granada, with the Alhambra in the background*

Munira, "after 9/11 in America and the bombings in Madrid. . . . Always when something like that happens, everything gets very difficult. We get looked upon badly, and it's like back to square one." Munira experienced particular stress when it came to the hijab, keenly aware of how it appears to Europeans. "I wore a hijab for over twenty years. And it was a change, because I don't wear it, I don't always go covered. . . . When we wear the hijab, we are always making a political statement. And sometimes I don't feel strong enough to make that statement. Sometimes I just want to go across the street to buy some bread."

She had drawn strength from the strong female role models in Islam going back to the time of the Prophet, which she contrasted with the position of some women in the Muslim community today:

> I used to go to our teacher with complete frustration and say, "From what I've read, the women, the wives of the Prophet, are not like this." And he always said, "Go back to Medina, go back to the first community, go back to how the women were then." And that's what saved me. Because Khadija, the first wife of the Prophet, peace be upon her, was a businesswoman, Aisha was a woman of knowledge; women worked with leather, another worked perfumes. They were women who were very involved in the community. They were not women just sitting in their homes. They were women who were active, and that's very much our community. We are very much that way.

Munira felt particularly connected to the legacy of al-Andalus, especially the place of women in it, and lamented that people are not aware of the Andalusian past. "The whole history of al-Andalus was summed up in one paragraph in the history books." Munira described Andalusia under Muslim rule as "the splendor of Europe." "When the rest of Europe was in the Dark Ages, al-Andalus was full of light and full of knowledge. We had women who were poets, who were writers, who had very important roles."

To improve relations between communities, Munira advocated "love and forgiveness." In her shop in the main square of Granada, a city she described as "magical," Munira said she engages in dialogue and friendship with the many tourists who stop by on their way to see the Alhambra, Spain's most-visited tourist attraction. Munira said that she did demonstrations in the shop of her leather-working techniques. "I've also got the workshop upstairs," she stated proudly, "and when people come upstairs and they see us all, I have two young women working with us, and my son works in the shop, and he will be taking over the shop, inshallah. People see us and ask what we have, and that's where the conversation begins."

"I think it's very, very important to be open," Munira emphasized, "to reach out to other people. We do a lot of *dawa* [invitation to the faith] in the mosque. We have a lot of groups come, university groups, interfaith groups. . . . We offer the service of dawa and also *juma* [Friday prayers and other religious activities]. We serve couscous and we invite people—our friends that aren't Muslim— to come, or people that are interested." During the month of Ramadan, she said, "all the women take turns making soup, and all the neighbors that live nearby come with their pots and pans to get little servings of soup."

Munira showed us her intricate and high-quality leather products, some with calligraphy designs, including handbags and wallets, and she explained how she makes them. She talked about the different styles and methods as practiced in the different regions, for example the Cordoba method, where sheepskin is used, versus the Granada method, where cowhide is preferred. She showed us one product with the coat of arms of the Nasrid dynasty, the last Muslim rulers of Granada. Other styles on display in the store evoked the Alhambra. Munira's teacher was the last artisan practicing a particular Granada style, she explained, so she is able to continue the local artisanal traditions through her work.

We were introduced to Fauzia Benedetti, a young Muslim woman who works in her shop. Fauzia was born into a family of converts, to a Swiss mother and an American father. Munira beamed with pride: "Fauzia studies and now has learned Arabic, and translates, and is incredible. I'm very proud of her."

At this point, Munira began to cry as the enormity of how far the community has come in her lifetime hit her. "It's incredible what's going on here," she said through her tears, "It just moves me sometimes so much, and people like Fauzia are so young and raising their kids and it's just extraordinary. . . . I just love it and I love our lives and we're so blessed, and you want people to know it."

On our first visit to the main mosque of Granada, Amineh described the experience of meeting Munira and other female congregants:

> We entered the Granada mosque and on the first encounter I found the first two women—an American and an English woman, both converts to Islam—a little suspicious of us. I wasn't surprised as we were a group of Americans and Asians with a camera! But as soon as we made the purpose of our entrance clear, we were embraced with open arms. The ladies took me into the mosque for breaking the fast, they shared their home-cooked meals with me, as they did with each other, on the mat and after prayer at the mosque each one turned to the other on her right and kissed her on her cheeks and then on the left and kissed her on the cheeks. I had never seen this level of warmth before in a mosque. Was this Muslim community of female converts recreating itself and its notion of Muslimness? Here, I felt, the warm charm and compassion of al-Andalus had not left us even in our modern days.

The English woman was Hanna Whiteman, a young blonde from Cambridge who had moved to Spain with her small daughter some ten years earlier. Hanna, who belongs to a family of converts, said of her identity, "Well my mom's American, so I never felt very English either to tell the truth." Hanna noted that it was strange to see the Spanish negative reaction to Islam given that "they have more Muslim blood than me actually, because I'm a first generation convert." When Amineh asked Hanna to explain why the women kissed each other's cheeks in the mosque, she replied, "It's very Mediterranean!" Hanna explained that there were about 40,000 Muslims in Granada, with about 200 families of converts that attended their mosque regularly. "Normally," Hanna continued, "the parents are converts and the children are first generation."

Of Granada, Hanna felt,

It has a real pull. Because, you know, we're Muslims, it fosters a heritage that's not anything we can create nowadays. It's fantastic, it's beautiful, it's kind of the height of the Muslim reign in Europe. . . . It's enchanting, it has something about it, a lot of struggle here, a lot of great times and bad times. It has its highs and its lows. You know, it has its low rivers and its high mountains. But it's certainly a very attractive city to live in. It's also very international, it's like Cambridge, it's a university town. So there is an influx of students from all over the world, and that really contributes to a rich fabric of society. You know, anything goes. Especially in this area. Lots of different faces, lots of different nationalities.

When Amineh asked her about the hijab, which she was wearing at the mosque, Hanna laughed, "You just have to bring it up, it's like the token question. That's alright, we'll forgive you." Hanna told Amineh that she started wearing the hijab while in England, but she faced many challenges following her move to Spain.

> I started wearing the scarf when I was eighteen, nineteen, and I really felt it. And I felt empowered and strong. And I came to Spain and it all fell apart, it really did. I had some terrible comments from the older generation, the Spanish older generation in Cordoba. And I remember feeling so awful. . . . I don't wear a scarf on a daily basis. I only wear a scarf when I pray and at Muslim gatherings out of respect. I wear it inside. I have my hijab inside. My interior hijab. And when I feel like it's the right moment I may wear it daily.

Speaking about how the Spanish see her, Hanna said, "People get to know me thinking I'm some foreign student, or expat, a blonde expat living in Spain. And they can't imagine that you have a spiritual life and that you're a Muslim when you're born." When asked who her role models were, she first named the Prophet of Islam, "who taught us humanity, which we all lack nowadays" and then "entrepreneurs like Munira who are role models for the younger generation."

Hanna was effusive about her community: "I have had the most amazing empowering feeling, because I live among a bunch of Muslim women. And they have, they're mothers and they study and they travel and they work. . . . Those relations between women, it makes us stronger. I do have to say, these women in Granada who wear the scarf every day, they are all so glamorous, and they are all so well dressed."

The converts of the community felt very close to the legacy of al-Andalus and lamented the extent to which the Islamic history of the region and convivencia are not well understood. "I think a huge fear factor has been created here," Hanna said, "and it's still there. My brother grew up in Spain and the history books started in 1492." She believed we can learn much from the time of al-Andalus: "I think here in al-Andalus was the best example. We were one culture and now we're fractured. And we can't get on. In general, the Jewish community, they had a terrible treatment under the Visigoth rule. They were very happy when the Muslims arrived. . . . It was one culture in the end, the Christians and the Jews would speak Arabic. They would wear the same clothes. The baths, they were shared, the same Arab baths, they had a certain morning or afternoon."

Hanna dismissed those who say that Islam is not compatible with European identity, and advised them to "go jump in a lake." Hanna lamented the current negative image of Islam, saying of many non-Muslims,

> Probably what they think of Islam is quite wrong. It's a shame, but it's in the interest of the media to use this for whatever reason, it's ridiculous. We're bored of it now. They're not right. We are completely different from what they think we are. I think everyone should make a step toward getting to know a Muslim and getting to find the truth. Just like us, we've got to find the true Islam. And they should do the same thing as well.

Also present in the group was Iman Travieso, a middle-aged woman from Valladolid in northern Spain who converted around thirty years ago and has lived in Granada since then. At the time of her conversion, she said, "there were very few Muslims in Spain. I think it was like, something very strange. Many people, over many years, many people tell me I speak very good Spanish. I try to say, yeah I'm Spanish, I am from Valladolid, the place where they speak the best Spanish. The people don't understand." In terms of her own identity, Iman explained, "I feel mostly Spanish, but sometimes in Spain I feel like a foreigner because I am a Muslim." Iman discussed the Spanish view of the centuries of Muslim rule as something imposed from the outside, like an invasion, but said this view overlooks the extensive numbers of Spaniards who converted to Islam during this long period. The Muslims at the time of al-Andalus, she claimed, "were mostly converts. It was impossible, only with an invasion of people."

Over the past five to ten years, Iman believed, Spaniards are beginning to understand that there are Spanish Muslims. "But before that it was something impossible." Iman said that there are many new Spanish converts to Islam; "here in the mosque every week there are people who converted." The local people of Granada, who resisted the community initially, have also been more accepting recently, she stated. Like Hanna, Iman was happy to have found a community of convert families in Granada. "After thirty years you love the people around you."

Iman, who was wearing the hijab, explained how she saw it. "I think that the hijab came for the Muslim women to be respected. I think that is the mission of the hijab. It's not like you have to wear the hijab like chains." For Iman there was no contradiction between Islam and European identity,

> I think this is a misunderstanding about what Islam is. And it's not culture. People mix both things and especially in the Muslim countries, it has to be like this, like Turkey they take Islam and they keep things from their culture. But the culture of Islam of Europe is wonderful and beautiful, we have wonderful musicians and writers, and why forget them when we become Muslim? They make beautiful things for humanity, not the opposite of what Allah has commanded or provided.

### A Young Irish Woman in Dublin

In Dublin, Amineh met Claire Tomer, a twenty-seven-year-old white Irish woman who had converted to Islam the year before. Amineh was excited about her and insisted I meet her, too. She said that Claire reminded her of the statues of Mary in her convent school in Pakistan as Claire wore a blue hijab accentuating her alabaster complexion and radiant face. There was a certain spiritual glow about Claire.

Claire grew up a Catholic in Belfast, Northern Ireland, and had been living in Dublin for four months. She identified as a British Muslim. Her Irish identity was still very important, and Claire commented on the compatibility of Catholic and Islamic values. Like Miriam, the young German convert we met earlier, she saw a continuity from her Christian identity to her Muslim identity. "I still practice the Catholic faith and I am a Muslim. . . . My family's Irish, so kind of that culture I grew up in. . . . I think the Catholic background is very similar, the values of Muslims." "They are much more accepting of Muslims and people of different faiths in southern Ireland," she stated, referring to the Republic of Ireland, than in her native, majority-Protestant Northern Ireland.

Claire attributed her conversion to Islam to her reading the Quran and attending a class at a mosque in Belfast. "I was seeking knowledge. I actually bought a Quran and a Bible and I started to read." As part of her spiritual quest, Claire attended a Protestant church in Belfast led by the prominent pastor James McConnell, who would later make international news in 2014 when he called Islam "heathen," "satanic," and a "doctrine spawned in hell." Claire described her experience at McConnell's Whitewell Metropolitan Tabernacle in Belfast:

> There was a girl I know that attends that church, so I went with her one night and listened to one of the sermons he did. I would say it was a bit terrifying, a bit threatening. The sermon was about backsliding, and if you are a Christian and you fall off the path, it is called a backslide, with quite a lot of references of going to hell. I just found him very set in his ways and not respectful of others' faiths. I think for someone who has so much influence in Northern Ireland—like his church is a very big church, it is very well known, and he has a massive influence on people's views—he puts certain religions at fault with that kind of position.

Claire's experience at a Belfast mosque was much more positive. "I got halfway through the Quran and I started going to class in a mosque. For some reason, the Bible I was confused about and I could not get answers. . . . I got all the answers from the mosque. Any question that I had, they gave me an answer." Claire tactfully kept her studies of Islam to herself. "I sought knowledge in private. I did not tell my family and any of my friends. I did not want other people's views to come in."

About a year after her conversion, Claire married a Pakistani man from Bradford, England, whom she had met through a large mosque in the Republic of Ireland. At the time of her interview, they had been married a few months. Claire said that she found Muslim men more respectful of women than non-Muslim men, and said of her husband,

> I would say that he has a huge amount of respect and so much understanding to let me do what I want. I come from a Christian background, my sister is married to a Catholic person, and not that I compare the two, but I would say he's better. I think Muslim men

have more respect for women. I see how my husband is with other women. He is so respectful and, not shy, but in the right way. I do not see that in non-Muslim men.

Claire told us that she began wearing the hijab a few months before she was married. "I do think it is a big challenge. I think a lot of people's views are that women are forced to wear the hijab—that it's not a choice. And I think it is a mistake to have the stereotype that the women are not free to choose what to wear themselves." In terms of Islamophobia, Claire compared the experiences of the Muslim community in Belfast, which faces "a lot more" stereotyping, with those in the Republic of Ireland. "If they go for jobs," she explained, talking of the former, "someone cuts them off right away when they see them wearing the hijab."

The majority culture's impression of Islam was a challenge, Claire believed. "I think that we are kind of stuck in a stereotype. And I would say the biggest challenge is changing people's minds." In terms of how the Muslim community should behave vis-à-vis the majority, Claire advocated,

They should stick up for their beliefs and the way it is and help people to understand, but not in a harsh way. There needs to be a respect of all other faiths in the Islamic community, and to bring them all together, and if we do that, that would change local people's minds, and say, "This is us. We are coming into your culture, and this is how we want to be."

She gave us her advice on how to improve relations between people of different cultures and faiths: "I think the biggest thing is through communication and working with different communities. I think what I have learned is the biggest thing in Islam is how accepting we are of other faiths. Even in the words of the Quran, accept the People of the Book. I did not come across that in my Christian background."

Claire said she would like to help other women who are new to Islam, to give them guidance and to help them maintain continuity with their non-Muslim families:

I would love to help other sisters who, especially ones with my passion for seeking knowledge, who are not Muslim, and are coming into the faith. I mean, my own family is a perfect example. I still practice Catholic faith and I am a Muslim, and we respect each other, and it is kind of showing that you can do that, and you can live that life and still be part of one community. We are still a family.

### A German Convert in Penzberg, Bavaria

In the Penzberg Mosque at the foot of the Alps in the German state of Bavaria, headed by the prominent imam Benjamin Idriz, we met a middle-aged, white female convert named Veronica Aisha. It was Eid, and she was wearing a black dress but no head covering. A native German, Veronica told us she had previously been a Catholic and had converted to Islam in 1978, while living in Beirut. "I took a couple of years to find out about Islam. . . . I was Catholic before and now I am Muslim, and I'm proud to be a Muslim. I didn't know anything about Islam. It was during the war in Lebanon, in Beirut, and my friends had told me, it's better to convert because I was living in the Muslim area. So it was more safe."

Speaking about her experience as a Muslim woman and her understanding of the place of women in Islam, Veronica countered the stereotypes Europeans often have.

> In the Quran, it says, the woman, she has rights like men. But the men have got a bit more rights because he's responsible for you. But this is not like, people say, the woman she has no rights at all, she must go three meters behind her husband, no it's not true. She has the right to work. She has the right to go out. But she should tell her husband, like any other husband wants to know.

There was "of course" no contradiction, Veronica felt, between being a German European and being Muslim. "A Muslim believes in God, like the Catholic, the Orthodox, we believe in one God. So there should be the possibility to accept each other, and not to fight. We believe in one God, and we pray, and we try to do our best. Like any other religion."

Speaking forcefully against the terrorism that is so often associated with the Muslim community, Veronica stated, "A terrorist has nothing to do with Islam. Or Islamists—they have nothing to do with us. . . . Islam is peace. . . . Those people are sick. They are not normal. . . . It's not written in the Quran you should kill people or you should kill yourself. It's *haram*, forbidden."

Veronica extolled the virtues of the religious communities of Penzberg:

> Here in Penzberg, it's a great community. . . . The Muslim, the Catholic, the Evangelical, each time when there is a celebration, they are working together, they pray together, they are coming for iftar, the evening meal breaking the day's fast during the month of

Ramadan. . . . It's not like other countries, where Muslims are being killed, or Catholics are being killed. It's totally different in Penzberg, and it should be all over the world like this. Peace should be all over.

Veronica said her mosque is open and that Imam Idriz's sermons are accessible to anyone. "He is praying in German, so everybody can listen to what he is saying. He is not telling you to go and kill people outside in the street. He doesn't preach that you need to put the bomb out or whatever. It's an open door, it's an open house."

## Male Converts

Like European women, the men of the continent also convert to Islam for a variety of reasons that involve both head and heart; they too are seeking spiritual solace. Some lean toward modernist or mystic Islam, others prefer a more literalist interpretation (see, for example, the case of Hermann in chapter 8). Several Muslim converts to Islam have provided the community with celebrity names, such as the singer Yusuf Islam, once known as Cat Stevens. We begin our discussion of male converts with another well-known figure, that of the Cambridge scholar Tim Winter.

### The Dean of the Cambridge Muslim College

Tim Winter, or Shaykh Abdal Hakim Murad, presides over the Cambridge Muslim College, which opened in 2009. Winter studied at Cambridge University, Al-Azhar University in Cairo, and the University of London and is among the most highly regarded Islamic scholars of Europe. A native of London, Winter converted to Islam in the late 1970s, at the age of nineteen, when he was an undergraduate student at Cambridge. He noted that at the time many English people conceived of Islam as "something you'd encounter when you were serving with the colonial office or as a missionary, but otherwise it was not there on the English radar at all, for good or for ill." Yet he noted, "There were quite a lot of people also coming into Islam at that time."

Winter's decision to convert to Islam came after an exploration of some of the world's other great faiths during his teenage years, what he described as "the usual kind of teenage late-night soul searching." For him, Islam felt like the best fit for his spiritual needs. "My decision was rather cerebral, based in the library rather than coming about as a result of human interaction." He entered Cambridge as a "freelance monotheist," he explained, searching for the right spiritual path:

> I wanted to go through the major religious traditions, which were those cultural enterprises where humanity has most seriously and consistently tried to work out the big questions for life. The Far Eastern traditions seemed to me too culturally remote and also not leaving a sufficient space for prayer, I felt. The Jewish tradition certainly ticked all of the boxes in terms of a personal God, a monotheistic tradition, a moral tradition, but seemed to have a strong dimension that was focused on the story of a particular people, rather than something that aimed ultimately to embrace the whole world. Christian tradition had been essentially deactivated for me at school when our school chaplain failed, God bless him, to explain to our sneering, skeptical young minds the basic teachings of Christianity, the Incarnation and the Trinity, the blood atonement, and none of it made any sense, and he admitted that it was something that should just be accepted on faith, and didn't have any Biblical or rational basis.

While at Cambridge, "I decided to switch from the economics degree to the Arabic degree." He began to study Islam and "things started to snowball. After a year in Cambridge, I became a Muslim." He found Islam, as he put it, "ticks" the boxes that Christianity does not. One of them was bringing him closer to Jesus than he felt he was able to as a Christian.

Following his undergraduate career, Winter went on to live in the Middle East and North Africa for seven years to learn more about his newfound faith. "I was sitting at the feet of some of the great sheikhs of Cairo and Saudi Arabia, and also I spent a year in Turkey, so seven years altogether studying with traditional scholars, working in the libraries and acquainting myself with the facts of my religion."

Upon returning to Britain, Winter began his multifaceted career working with the British Muslim community, first "on the preaching circuit" in English mosques, then by beginning his own film production company, which produces lectures for "Islamic TV stations here and some other features as well." Now, in addition to his work at the Cambridge Muslim College, he is the director of the Anglo-Muslim Fellowship for Eastern Europe, which he described as facilitating "cultural and religious collaboration between Muslim communities in Western Europe and our opposite numbers in Albania, Kosovo, Macedonia, and also Tatarstan in Russia, where we have some good connections."

As role models for his own life and career, Winter discussed prominent early Muslim converts such as Lord Stanley, who in 1869 became the first Muslim member of the House of Lords, and Abdullah Quilliam, who founded England's first mosque in Liverpool in 1889. These pioneers, he explained, "really laid the foundations for Islam in Britain. Creating a British, faithful Muslim identity during the reign of Queen Victoria in the age of empire was a much harder thing than the challenges that are facing us today, and I think they did it with extraordinary elegance."

The concept of British identity, Winter argued, is a "political construct" that lacks a certain "recognizable figure," rendering moot the argument that Muslims in the United Kingdom should become more "British." In any case, he maintained, there has been a "post-imperial unraveling" of British identity, and "we no longer are clearly in touch with what it is to be British." Winter said he is troubled by the degree to which the British state reflects a Christian identity, while society itself is largely secular:

> I think there are deep philosophical problems. . . . Our traditional constitution is theocratic, the head of state is head of the church, we have speakers of prayers in the House of Commons, the bench of bishops is in the House of Lords. It's a Christian political unit, and the legislative assumption is that the Bible and Christianity are the ground rock of where the values come from. That's no longer the case for most people—because only 5 percent of British people go to church any longer. So one of the big conversations that has to happen over the next fifty years is where do the values come from if they're not from Christianity any longer?

Winter thought the increase in the number of converts in the United Kingdom was remarkable, considering that "public attitudes toward Islam have hardened." Converts come from all walks of life, are "preponderantly female it seems," and include "members of the aristocracy," "people from different ethnic backgrounds," "people who are post-men," "people in the armed forces," and "even churchmen. In this very room, at the Cambridge Muslim College, a few months ago we had an Anglican priest who converted to Islam."

Winter postulated that conversion to Islam could become a mass movement, though he explained that the community has many hurdles of perception to overcome before this could be a reality. Today, as dean of the Cambridge Muslim College, Winter works hard to ensure that top graduates of Britain's Islamic seminaries are fully engaged with British society and are able to bridge "Islamic traditionalism and Western postmodernity." Students are taught British classic literature beginning with Beowulf and including the works of Chaucer and Shakespeare. Winter explained that the program teaches students "how to relate religion to the modern world" and that interfaith engagement is a major pillar of the work of the college. Students make an annual visit to the Vatican, where they "stay in a monastery, and they meet the Pope, and they get to talk to Catholic experts. . . . It's a kind of fairly intensive but high-level immersion." He emphasized that the program is not designed to challenge students on what they have previously learned but rather "to help them to see how they can relate what they've learned to the reality of modern Britain. The British Muslim community is not quite what it ought to be, so our purpose is to give them a capacity to reach particularly the younger generation of people who have been exposed to contemporary education and want answers to contemporary questions which the traditional preacher simply can't do."

The Muslim College program additionally helps seminary students gain a sense of how to best work with troubled individuals in the community:

> We do a lot of counseling and pastoral issues as well, so how to deal with people who have problems with relationships, problems with families, problems with the law, problems with addiction, all the problems one gets in modern inner-city communities, perhaps in particular how to counsel them, how to know at which point to refer them to health care professionals, and to social workers, or to get the police involved.

Winter discussed the events that were shaking the confidence in the status quo in Britain, from the financial crisis to the huge burden of debt that ordinary people carry and the income inequality they face. "One percent of the British population," he argued,

> owned more assets than the poorest 55 percent of the British population. And there's something about wealth acquisition and maintenance now, which means the more you have the richer you get. And the gulf between rich and poor is a huge rift opening up in the heart of society now that, with the decline of the old socialist rhetoric, can't really be dealt with by any of the existing political formations.

Winter believed that such uncertainty creates a space for the Far Right in Europe to argue "that the indigenous is being eroded, and in such circumstances people look for an easy visible scapegoat." While Europe's identity is actually being eroded by globalization and Hollywood and McDonald's, Winter explained, the Far Right has focused on the visibly different Muslims. This is alarming because Europe has historically been less tolerant than other continents, and particularly Muslim societies:

> In the history of what's been one of the world's least tolerant conti-nents, certainly compared to Asia and Africa, in Europe the places where there's been a certain amount of what the Spanish call convivencia, sort of living together, they tended often to be Muslim places. So Muslim Sicily, Muslim Spain, and to some extent the Balkans under Ottoman rule, the Crimea, with its huge Jewish population, and the Tatar Republics further east in Europe and Russia. It's, I think, not a coincidence that the points of light in the dark continent historically have tended to be Muslim points of light. The Middle East was historically much more tolerant than traditional Europe. So is traditional China. So is traditional India. Europe always had this idea of you had to follow the religion of the king, or you could be hung, drawn and quartered, which was not what the Chinese and the Indians and the Muslims historically believed.

Speaking of the challenges facing the British Muslim community, Winter warned,

> The mosques are full, but the message in the mosques is not always ideal. And this is recognized by many preachers and traditional scholars—that their training is essentially shaped by the presumptions of eighteenth-century north India . . . very brilliant curricula, but not designed for . . . central Birmingham in the twenty-first century.

While emphatically pointing out that the mosque did not play a role in radicalization, and that the culprit was the Internet, Winter was also concerned about the manner in which the British state has interacted with and antagonized the Muslim community and how this has influenced the way Muslims interact with the state, religious scholarship, and wider society: "The Muslim masses are increasingly turning to religious scholarship, particularly as they see the mainstream culture as becoming more hostile, the state as becoming suspicious, coercive." Still, Winter believed, "The British Muslim community is a success story in many ways. The mosques are packed everywhere, which must mean we're doing something right. The community's growing very fast, establishing itself economically, creating an increasingly positive relationship with existing state and non-governmental agencies within society."

When asked how relations between Muslims and non-Muslims can be improved, Winter answered that Muslims need to stand up for themselves and look to the core values of Islam. In this way, they can help Europe address the many challenges it is facing:

> The moral resources in the Islamic tradition are limitless in terms of love for neighbor, love for the other, solid family values, respecting the old. All these things that Europe is starting to lose are present in the ethical teachings of Islam. . . . If we see ourselves as bearing gifts here, rather than just being a pack of troublemakers, which is what the media tend to assume, if we come here with therapeutic intentions, and make ourselves invaluable, which is already starting— I mean, the Spanish olive harvest would fail without Muslim workers, the National Health Service here in England would collapse but for the Muslim doctors and nurses. If we can move that forward so that we become the great harbingers of ethics and compassion and neighborliness, in an increasingly atomized and self-oriented, materialistic Europe, then I think we'll have justified our presence here.

### *The First Imam to Preach in Danish*

As the first imam in Danish history to conduct the Friday prayer in the Danish language, Abdul Wahid Pedersen has played an important role in the development of Islam in Denmark and Scandinavia. Copenhagen's Danish Islamic Center was established to fill the desire for a mosque that gave the sermon in Danish. "We realized we had a problem," Pedersen said of the reasons for starting the Danish Islamic Center in 1997, which we visited during fieldwork. Converts and young foreign Muslims including Pakistanis, Arabs, and Somalis, he explained, were all speaking in different languages. The Danish Islamic Center brought them together in the local language.

We met Pedersen in the headquarters of the global charity organization Danish Muslim Aid, which he co-founded and currently heads. He explained that while his organization helps Muslims around the world, such as those in war-torn Syria, he also has projects to help non-Muslims in the Muslim world, such as Christians and Hindus in Pakistan. In addition to his other duties, Pedersen translates and publishes books. He also runs a small shop that benefits the charity by selling a broad range of products, including books and texts in Danish and English on subjects including the Quran and Hadith, Islam, the Prophet of Islam, Islamic life, philosophy, politics, history, and architecture.

Pedersen described himself as "an ordinary hillbilly in Denmark" who went on "to become an imam in Copenhagen." He was born Reino Arild Pedersen in Denmark and raised as a Christian, often ringing bells as a child at the church where his grandfather served as a clerk. As he grew up, he began questioning his beliefs. At age sixteen, he set out on a journey to figure out what or in whom he wanted to believe. His search took him around the world in his early twenties, to Africa, the Middle East, and finally to India, where he bought a one-way ticket, settled down for two and a half years, and became a Hindu. He discarded all his material possessions for a simple life with self-made clothes and little money.

Pedersen first connected spiritually with Islam on a mountain in the holy temple town of Hampi, India, in the summer of 1977. Pedersen had climbed up a mountain toward a temple at the top, on a moonlit night, and as the chanting echoed above, he had stopped for a drink of water at a small stream along the way. The opening was so low that he had to bend down in order to catch the trickle. Lying on the ground, he had stretched his hand forward toward the water. At that moment, with the moon on the mountains, he realized that, "God wanted me to lie flat in front of him." When he did so, Pedersen had unintentionally completed a prostration before God, "Time seemed to stand still, and I was totally lost in that feeling for as long as it lasted. It would, nevertheless, take another few years before my brain and heart fully understood this message, and I surrendered to Allah."

When he returned home to Europe, he was barefoot. He renounced Hinduism, attracted by the notion of *tauhid*, or the monotheistic unity of God. When he heard the *shahada*, the Islamic declaration of faith of "There is no God but God and Muhammad is his messenger," Pedersen agreed without hesitation. He has considered himself a Muslim ever since. He continued to believe, however, that all religions come from the same source.

Like other converts presented in this chapter, Pedersen can be thought of as a living bridge between Islam and Europe. Like them, he remains proud of his own national identity and feels it is fully compatible with Islam. "Islam does express itself in different cultures and traditions in different ways," he stated, "and therefore for me, being a Dane and being a Muslim is just expressing Islam in a Danish way of living, which isn't incompatible with Islam in any way whatsoever."

*Art by Salma Pedersen, daughter of Imam Pedersen,*
*synthesizing Muslim and Danish identity*

When he converted, he said, "I did not become a Pakistani or a Turk." "Don't ever try to be what you're not," he emphasized. Pedersen explained that though he is often called "un-Danish" by fellow Danes, he completely rejects the slur. "I would say that the older I get, the more Danish I feel."

In terms of his Danish identity, Pedersen felt particularly connected to the Vikings:

> I'm from an old nation of seafarers. My ancestors, the Vikings, used to be well known for crossing the oceans, going abroad, knocking on doors everywhere. Now modern-day Muslims in Denmark have to become good sailors because we have a headwind coming on. We have to learn how to sail up against the wind, and that's actually not so bad because when you know how to navigate your little vessel in a strong wind, then you will become a skilled sailor.[5]

Pedersen showed us the artwork of his daughter, Salma Pedersen, who painted a calligraphy of the Arabic "Bismillah, ar-Rahman, ar-Rahim," or "In the name of Allah, the Beneficent, the Merciful," in the shape of a Viking ship. "My father was an artist, my daughter is an artist, and they have their different styles. She's doing this kind of calligraphy, and here, of course, putting it into the shape of a Viking ship. We've got the combination of the Danishness and Islam, because the Viking ship is very much Danish."

Speaking about the challenges facing the Muslim community, Pedersen criticized the reliance on a rigid textual interpretation that he did not find in places in the Muslim world. He gave the example of some of the questions he receives on social media like Facebook, where people can reach out to him for religious guidance. People ask questions such as, "Can I watch TV in Islam? Give me a textual reference." People then begin to follow "sheikh this or sheikh that," said Pedersen, which often amounts to "the one who shouts the loudest." Pedersen believed it was difficult as there are people whom he knows he has no way of reaching. He associated those with a "stiff" and "rigid" interpretation of Islam with the "Salafi path" and argued that we need to be presenting the classical tradition of Islam.

The lack of domestic schools to train imams, Pedersen explained, forces people to go abroad to study. He called imams who are imported into Denmark "useless"; they know the text, but they cannot contextualize the knowledge for Danish Muslims. Pedersen also cited a "lack of unity" as an additional challenge. "Muslims in Denmark are, by and large, made up of immigrant communities. Many of them try to consolidate within their own traditions of origin. Pakistanis have become more Pakistani, Moroccans becoming more Moroccan, Turkish becoming more Turkish." There are Muslim "people who are becoming frustrated, agitated, even opposed to Danish society." He spoke about some of the public initiatives taken by Danish authorities that have led Muslims to feel they are under siege:

> Recently, we have had a bill passed, or a policy stated in the Copenhagen city council, that they want to bring down the number of people who respect the shariah. . . . We all live according to shariah when we are Muslim, it doesn't mean we're going to impose it on anybody else, but we certainly do have the freedom and right to impose it on ourselves: what we eat, how we dress, when we pray, etc.

Pedersen criticized the way in which Muslims—particularly second-generation immigrants—are treated in Danish society. These people, he noted, feel like they are Danes, but the Danes say that they are not Danes and are second-generation immigrants. He mentioned that he has told the government many times that this group's sense of alienation is getting worse. "For the weak ones it's a very bad situation," he observed. "They don't share a dream," he noted of the Muslims living in ethnic and religious enclaves in Denmark, "they share a nightmare."

Yet Pedersen does not believe the situation of Muslims in Denmark is all that bleak when put in a global context: "By and large, we are living in a quiet society. I think mostly what we have are luxury problems. I travel to many parts of the world where there are real problems." A definite bright spot in the Danish Muslim community are the women, Pedersen noted. He himself has three daughters and two grandchildren, and he said that Muslim women, whom he called "brilliant," are "winning." He praised the Muslim female volunteers in their twenties who work at Danish Muslim Aid.

Pedersen believes that we are at a "unique moment in history" with Islam in Europe. When he was a child, he explained, there were no Muslims in Denmark; Islam has only come to Denmark in the past forty to fifty years. Christianity, in contrast, has had centuries to develop in Europe:

> I believe that when Christianity came into Europe, they had probably been shouting the same things at the Christians as they are shouting at the Muslims today. So there has always been a sort of right-wing traditional community or group of people in any community. And they will try to remain true to what they have known for generations, and whatever comes new, they will shun it and discard it and fight it.

### The Shia Afro-Caribbean Imam in London

In London, we met Sheikh Ahmed Haneef, an imam at the Islamic Centre of England in the Kilburn neighborhood, a Shia mosque. Before being converted into a mosque, the building once housed a dance hall and later a gambling hall called Mecca Bingo. Haneef was born in the British colony of Trinidad in the 1950s, immigrated to Canada, supported the black rights movement, and converted to Islam at the time of the 1979 Iranian Revolution, which he said inspired and spoke to him. He went on to spend nineteen years in Iran. When we interviewed him, he had been in the United Kingdom for the past two years. He had a *zebibah*—a black mark on his forehead from repeatedly lowering his head to the floor mat in prayer—and was wearing a red skullcap.

Haneef felt that as a non-Persian convert he fills a niche in the mosque. Referring to the mosque members, he said, "We're the cool ones." Some mosques are strict, he noted, and would not let the female members of our team in or would make them cover up. He described the Islamic Centre of England as a "feminist organization" that takes the side of the woman in marriage disputes all the time. Some of the men "are terrible," and he added with a big smile, "We are anti-man." In marriage agreements, he explained, the Islamic Centre always makes sure the woman has the right to an attorney for divorce. Sheikh Haneef also spoke about his wife and her talents as a poet. He used to be a poet, he admitted, but he stopped because she was so much better than him.

Speaking about his own identity, Haneef explained, "I'm Muslim, I love Islam. I'm black, I love Africa. But it is not a place I want to live. At the end of the day, I'm a Westerner," and he talked about his love for cities like London, New York, and Toronto. Islam is a set of principles, he explained, that are adaptable to the "environment of the times," and "British Muslim is not a contradiction of terms." There is a "Western Islam . . . and Islam has many beautiful things to offer to this society."

Turning to the problems of the Muslim community in the United Kingdom, Haneef discussed his concern for London's unemployed under class, particularly the Bengali youth who "fall through the cracks." There are "ghettos of Muslim culture who see the outside world as a threat." Many Muslims perceive themselves as "reluctant guests," Haneef explained, although they want to be part of society. Terrorism emerged as a serious problem only after 9/11, Haneef believed. "After 9/11, there is a preponderance of radical Muslim groups led by immature young people that are very angry with society." Shadowy groups are there to take advantage of these vulnerable youth. He emphasized that Muslim youth born in the United Kingdom and with British accents need to be engaged. They would not fit into Niger or Pakistan, but they also do not quite feel British. "We need to tell them, 'You belong here, you are British.'" These problems are not just problems in Islam, Haneef claimed, but exist in society in general. He gave examples of non-Muslim girls who join gangs and non-Muslim boys who stab people "for twenty pounds."

The largest threat to Britain, Haneef felt, is the "stupefaction of the common man through the media as a distraction." He discussed the tabloids, describing *The Metro* as "a piece of crap," and lamented that this is what people read. It allows them to be taken advantage of. He explained that Muslims are also being targeted by government and opportunist elements to destroy the image of Islam. There is a greater burden on the common man today, particularly as the gap between haves and have-nots is increasing and the middle class is dying. Education, he complained, is only for the rich now.

Haneef believed that, to improve relations between people, it was important "to know one another." There needs to be therefore an emphasis on knowledge, and Muslims should research Islam. "Ignorance," said Haneef, "leads to fear, especially if the media encourages it." It is a struggle for Muslims to win hearts and minds in the West, he stated. People "want to be friends, but don't know how."

Harrison greatly enjoyed his visit to the mosque and found Sheikh Haneef to be a very warm person. "He took us upstairs to the sitting room and was extremely friendly and hospitable, with a good sense of humor. He immediately offered us tea and would not allow any of us to assist him with it. At the end of our visit, he hugged me and kissed me on the cheek three times."

During the interview, one of Haneef's colleagues, an Iranian Sayyed, came into the room and told them that he had been arrested fifteen years ago after being picked up by the authorities at a mosque and imprisoned by the Americans. He said to Harrison, "Americans are wonderful—your government is awful." Then he turned and walked out.

### A German Photographer in Copenhagen

In Copenhagen, we met a photographer named Ahmed Eckhard Krausen, who grew up in Germany outside Cologne and Aachen but has lived in Denmark for the past thirty-six years. Krausen, a white German who converted to Islam, has undertaken an extensive project called *Islam in Europe,* in which he photographs European mosques to document the presence of Islam in Europe. His message is that there is a too-often overlooked compatibility between Islamic and European identity. "Islam is a part of Germany," Krausen said. "Islam has been in Europe for 1,400 years."

Krausen, who has a Somali wife and four children, first came to Denmark in 1978. "I came to Denmark, and I found I could stay here and I could realize myself here." Shortly afterward, Krausen decided to travel around the world. The first country he visited was Egypt, where on Christmas Day he met a Muslim Egyptian whose hospitality and kindness set Krausen on the path to converting. As Krausen explained, the Egyptian man came up to him and said, "Today's Christmas. If you want, I can bring you to the church." "He opened my mind," Krausen explained, "and I became interested in Islam. This idea, the tolerance and harmony to respect the other religion, it was the most important thing for me. If Islam could give me this, then I could become Muslim."

"But I'm not good at reading," Krausen continued, "so I had to travel to listen to people and observe, and my camera was the thing I had with me. . . . So I photographed a lot, I listened to people and to different views of Islam. And I was thinking, if an Egyptian, Indonesian, Pakistani, and so on, have a way to come to Allah, then I also can find a way, my own way to Allah. Allah guided me, and my heart guided me. And that is why it took me more than fourteen years to become Muslim."

The welcoming way Krausen was treated as a non-Muslim by Muslims, he believed, played an important part in his conversion.

> I always felt welcome by Muslims, even though I wasn't Muslim. They respected me, as the Egyptian man did. In Pakistan I found many, many Muslims who acted in this manner. I was in the mountains of Kashmir, and when I said I'm German, one person exclaimed, "Annemarie Schimmel!"—and he knew Annemarie Schimmel better than me, because Annemarie Schimmel was a German poet who translated a lot of poems by Muhammad Iqbal.

Krausen stressed to us that he did not belong to any particular sect or interpretation of Islam. Instead, he seeks "balance." In his travels across the Muslim world, including

> in the jungles of Malaysia, Indonesia, in the desert of Sudan, in East Africa, in Kenya, Tanzania, I met different Muslims . . . and I have learned from them. That is why I call myself today Muslim, and not Salafi, I don't call myself Sufi, I don't call myself anything. I'm just Muslim. . . . That's why for me it's so important to have a balance in Islam, and Islam is balance.

"I'm German," Krausen explained, "my wife's Somali, my children are born in Denmark, so even my family, my little family is a little multicultural society." At his wife's Islamic school in Somalia, he said, the children were struck if they did not answer correctly. "In this way, my wife became educated as Muslim."

> I wasn't. That makes a difference, you know. I'm a little bit more in Sufi Islam. My wife is a little bit more in Salafi Islam. So if I start to fly away, my wife brings me back home to the earth. That is important, this balance, to be "new Muslim" and to be "traditional Muslim." And it is not okay, if new Muslims like me become like Turks and like Arabs.

Krausen's philosophy of balance is evident in the names he has adopted. "Ahmed, my future. Eckhart is my past, but they have to be together, united." The name Ahmed, he explained, was given to him by the Muslim he met in Egypt.

Ahmed is one of the names of the Prophet. Meister Eckhart was a German mystic from the Middle Ages, and a Christian one, and my mother gave me this name, I don't know why, but later I found out that I can connect my tradition of Meister Eckhart and Islam in a beautiful way. I don't have a conflict. Many new Muslims, if they become Muslim, they feel they must change their Danish name and only take an Arabic name or a Muslim name. If your name is not in conflict with Islam, and my old German name brings my Islam to a higher level, because this is my background, I don't need to feel shame about it.

As a photographer, Krausen feels that Islamic art in all its forms is a very important part of his Islamic identity. "Islamic art is the soul of Islam, because Islamic art speaks to your feeling and to your body. . . . I mean the new, modern Islamic art. That means hip-hop, it means graffiti, and music. . . . It could be jazz, it could be rock music. Of course, you will find some Muslims protesting with expressions like 'astaghfirullah' and 'haram.'" To Krausen, art is "the right answer to all the Islamic States and bin Ladens. And this is the right answer, too, to all people on the right wing, the Nazis and Islam haters and so on. If they show the bad picture of Islam, you have to show the beauty of Islam."

This dedication to "showing the beauty of Islam" can be seen in Krausen's photographs of European mosques. "Photographing is my life, my message, my everything. . . . My work is to show how beautiful Islam is, how beautiful a mosque can be." Krausen believed that part of the message of his *Islam in Europe* project is to prompt people to ask,

What should a mosque be? Should a mosque be Turkish, or should a mosque be Arabic, or should a mosque be Danish, or German, or Italian, or something like that? The new Muslim generation doesn't have this background any more. They are born here, they have the traditions of Denmark, of Germany. They feel like foreigners, but they should feel like normal people as Muslims, so they should also change the mosque, to suit their identities as European Muslims.

One of the photographs Krausen showed us was of a Danish Muslim family on bicycles.

The bicycle is a tradition in Denmark, and the bicycle is not only for the poor people. Even ministers, politicians, and rich people ride bikes in Denmark. And that became very famous even in the United States, this photo. A bicycle is, it's also a symbol of environment protection, to keep the car at home, to take a bicycle, because Islam is green. And the Prophet Muhammad was also green, so we should protect our environment.

Krausen then showed us one of his photographs of a Danish student of Somali descent who had just passed her school examination wearing a hat. Krausen explained, "In Denmark, the tradition is to have a hat with a Christian symbol on it, because Denmark is Christian country. But the government allowed Muslims to have a Muslim symbol on her head. And this picture is what my idea was to show, this is Islam, this is a human being, and this is society. That means there should be a harmony between Muslim, Islam, and society."

Showing us his photograph of the Penzberg Mosque that we had also visited in Bavaria, Krausen said the Germans

> develop mosques in a very beautiful and new way. It's very special. Penzberg is a little town in South Germany, about one hour outside of Munich, near the Alps, and it has a lot of immigrants, especially from Bosnia. They built a mosque, and this Bosnian architect built a mosque in a German context, and he found out that adhan by voice is just not allowed in most of Germany, so he has written the adhan, the call to prayer, as Arabic calligraphy on the minaret, so this mosque makes adhan by light. That is what I mean, to develop new ideas.

We were then shown a photograph of a wooden mosque in Vilnius, Lithuania, which Krausen admitted was his favorite mosque.

> It is the most important mosque of the Lithuanian Tatars. In this mosque, the Tatars educated their imams. . . . It was the only mosque that was open in the Soviet time, by the way. . . . It is made of wood, and it's humble, it's modest. And Islam is for me humble and modest. I'm not so crazy for the big mosques like in Rome or like in other countries, because I feel like they are a little bit arrogant. And it's a very special atmosphere, this wooden mosque, and the smell is wooden, and if you're walking in a forest, and you come inside to the mosque, you are connected between your creator and nature.

This humble wooden mosque of the Lithuanian Tatars is, in fact, reflective of German primordial identity, at one with the divine and nature and located in the forest. Krausen said that when he saw the mosques of the Tatars, he knew that this was "my Islam." The Tatars, Krausen stressed, represented one of the "roots of Islam in Europe, the natural roots, where you find Islam, like a little plant, was growing up."

Krausen cited the Tatars' long history in Lithuania, where "they had their own Islamic schools, they had mosques, they had rights, by the king. There was a respect between the king and the Muslims, always." While Sarajevo and Granada are well known, Krausen explained, "the third pillar of Islam in Europe is Vilnius, but nobody knows about it, it's a secret part of Islam in Europe. It's beautiful." He said he has visited all the locales in Europe where the Tatars lived, including "Poland and Belarus. I have photographed all these mosques. I have met the mufti of Belarus."

Discussing how the Muslim community sees him, Krausen complained, "the Muslims don't accept me as Muslim. Most of the Arabic, Somalian Muslims . . . will never greet me *salaam a'alaykum* peace be upon you. They say, 'hi, hello,' in this way. And they're surprised if I answer salaam a'alaykum. . . . 'Are you a Muslim? Why are you a Muslim? Because Muslim's only for us, not for you.'" Krausen feels a similar rejection from non-Muslims in Germany and Denmark. "The Danes and the Germans, if they get angry, they say, 'Why will you run away from your own culture?' And some of them will say, 'It is nonsense to become Muslim, because Islam is an authority killing people,' and so on. Because many, many non-Muslims have some funny ideas about Islam."

The behavior of many Muslims, Krausen explained, contributes to this perception:

> It is also the fault of many Muslims, because they give the impression of a funny idea, of their own idea. That is not the life that the Prophet tells us. We should be normal like the other people. We should be friendly, help them, and so on. Then the Danes will accept us better. And the Germans too. But it is a conflict, and it is a conflict starting very much after September 11, I think. I think this day has changed the world, in my mind, even the Muslims had humor before, the Muslims had more tolerance, and all this is gone. Now every Muslim feels like a victim, and this is also wrong.

Krausen stressed that Muslims should respect European laws:

> For Muslims living here in Denmark and Germany, they have to respect the law and the country itself. And because I feel most of the European countries are tolerant, you can go to a mosque, to a synagogue, you have everything here. You are protected by the law, and

so on. Sometimes you can be a better Muslim here than in Saudi Arabia or in other countries that I have seen, I am sure.

Krausen commented on the eclectic and interconnected nature of our contemporary societies:

> Is Christianity American? No! It is from Middle East. We have to realize, Jesus Christ was not German, he was not Italian, or American. Jesus Christ was Arab. Like Prophet Muhammad, like Musa and so on. Many Europeans they say, this is our culture. . . . But every coffee you're drinking, this is not German, this is not Danish, this is Turkish. In England the drinking tea, they have from India.

The fate of Muslims in Europe concerned Krausen, given what he described as Europe's very poor record at dealing with minorities and religious difference. "In the thirties it was the Jews. Now the Muslims are the problem. Who is next? I'm afraid, because Europe never had traditions for tolerance and democracy. And if they are tolerant, it is because they have learned from two world wars. They had to kill 40 million people before they understood tolerance."

Krausen's ideas of how to proceed in the future are encapsulated in his love and devotion for the great writers Goethe and Allama Iqbal, whom he called his "icons." He discussed a work of his own that imagines a meeting between the two and features images and poems by Goethe and Iqbal juxtaposed. Krausen felt that while contemporary Germans admire Goethe, they "ignore that Goethe was very near to being Muslim" and that he had a deep understanding of the Quran. Krausen noted that Iqbal was directly responding to Goethe in his 1923 poetic work *Message from the East*.

"When I read Goethe and Iqbal," Krausen said, "I was so confused after, I didn't know anymore what Goethe said and what Iqbal said, because they complement each other in their opinions." Though Goethe died just over four decades before Iqbal's birth, Krausen told us he imagines them meeting and having a conversation, with Iqbal traveling to meet Goethe in Weimar from Heidelberg, where Iqbal lived. Goethe, as a non-Muslim, speaks about Islam, and Iqbal, as a Muslim, speaks about Europe. The work of Goethe and Iqbal, Krausen said, shows that "we have to be together. There is no difference between us. . . . We want to show in Germany, and to other people, that there are European poets that have written about Islam so beautifully. Now, today we have this conflict, the clash between worlds . . . it is important today to have these kinds of idols, because they are gone. You don't have any more."

*The Curator of Munich's Five Continents Museum*

In Munich, we spoke with the anthropologist Jürgen Wasim Frembgen, a German convert to Islam who has worked as the chief curator of the Oriental Department at Munich's Five Continents Museum, formerly the State Museum of Ethnology, for nearly three decades. Frembgen told us that about 22,000 objects in the museum's 160,000-piece collection are from the Muslim world; its collection of 2,000 objects from Pakistan is possibly the largest collection outside the Muslim world.

Frembgen was born and raised in Bonn but had a long-standing interest in the Islamic world because his godmother was married to an Afghan. He studied for a Ph.D. at the University of Heidelberg, where one of his mentors was Annemarie Schimmel. Frembgen soon developed a strong affinity for Pakistan. "I became invested, from 1980 onward, in the Sufi tradition of Pakistan, and the lowlands of Pakistan, Punjab. And then it became, I would say, a lifelong dedication, so I feel almost Pakistani at heart and I feel almost sometimes more at home there than in Germany."

Explaining how he came to convert to Islam, Frembgen recalled:

In the 1980s, I converted to Islam—well, Islam embraced me, actually. I was brought up in a Catholic context. . . . But I was drawn to a very crisp and clear faith and orientation of life, and then in Pakistan, after some initial skepticism, after meeting people in Punjab and visiting Sufi shrines, I experienced their experience of the tranquility of Sufi shrines . . . their love for children, their love of family, these kinds of values in Muslim families. . . . It has become my philosophy of life.

His conversion to Islam did not mean that Frembgen gave up his German identity, which he defined in the context of Germanic primordial identity and Heimat. "I think I have a very deeply ingrained love for books and to study and a sense of discipline, and orderliness, which helps us scholars. . . . There is an emotional attachment to the landscape, to the Rhineland, it's a bit like Kashmir also probably with the River Rhine, the lightheartedness which you don't find for instance in Bavaria."

Frembgen supported the idea of a "European Islam" and said that work toward this goal was already happening in Germany, but more must be done.

I think there has also a step to be taken from Muslim communities, that they should avoid the kind of ghetto you sometimes find in certain areas, in Berlin and elsewhere. I think there is also a German philosopher who talks about a kind of mutual respect for each other and a quest for learning from the other side, and this is not yet enough initiated by politicians and supported.

He gave as an example, "a center for European Islam which has been founded in Munich by esteemed personalities like Benjamin Idriz, for instance, and his supporters."

"Constant communication," Frembgen said, was key to improving relations between Muslims and non-Muslims.

> I think the only way is through dialogue and keeping up meeting people, talking to them, trying to open them up. . . . I think that most people who are a bit Islamophobic or are anti-Muslim, to put it that way, I ask these people, "Do you know Muslims? Do you have any Muslim friends?" . . . They don't actually meet Muslims and should open up in that way because Muslims are living among us and there are about 4.5 million Muslims in Germany right now.

### A Spanish Activist in Melilla

In Melilla, the tiny Spanish enclave on the north coast of Africa, we met Yasin Puertas, a journalist and political activist. Yasin showed us around the city and told us of his work on behalf of the local Muslim population. He was born a Catholic in Melilla, educated in a Catholic school, and attended college in Madrid, where he received a degree in communications as a journalist. He also lived in the United States. Shortly after college he began to learn about Islam, because "I was born and lived in a city with a 50 percent Muslim population, and I was really curious about what was going on in the Islamic community in my city to learn about my neighbors."

Yasin explained that he began to read many books on Islam. One of them was my own *Discovering Islam*, which Yasin said

> was such a different perspective of what Islam was. It was a shock for me because I didn't see a lot of these things in my own neighbors, so it was presenting Islam itself from the root, from the sources of Islam and of course it was easy for me to start thinking that I would be able to become a Muslim. . . . Then after this book I started to read more about Islam and the Quran and the life of the Prophet, peace be upon him. And after two to three years I accepted Islam and by the grace of God now I can say that I'm a proud Muslim.

"My first role model is, of course, Muhammad, peace be upon him," Yasin declared. "Not because I'm a Muslim, even before I became a Muslim I thought Muhammad, peace be upon him, was a very interesting person. Like Jesus, for example, that's another example of greatness. And, of course, you know, anyone that works toward peace in the world." Shortly after converting, Yasin married a local Muslim politician who he said became the first Member of Parliament in Europe to wear a hijab: "I am proud to say that I married her and she is the mother of my children."

For relations to be improved between different religions and cultures, Yasin recommended the following steps:

> First of all, I would say know each other. . . . To know each other is not only to know about the other but being able to live together and share things together. A second step would be sharing, if it can be in every single part like in government and media. For example, if you have a television channel and it's made by people of only one culture, what is going to happen is that they are only going to give one point of view, not a lot of different points of view. We're just so concentrated on the differences between us that we don't realize that we are human and we live in the same world.

As a journalist, Yasin said, he is trying to improve relations between the communities.

> I am happy to say I've been working toward telling the truth about Islam and trying to improve relationships between Muslims and non-Muslims for a better knowledge of each other, and not only tolerate each other but respect each other for what they are, and what their beliefs are and that we all have one thing in common—love. This is something that is in Islam and Christianity, in Judaism, even the atheists they have some kind of morality that tells them do not harm others and work toward a better world. And this is what I believe in and that's why I became a Muslim.

### The Irish Expert on Afghanistan

In Belfast, we met Michael Semple, an Irishman and research professor at the Institute for the Study of Conflict Transformation and Social Justice at Queen's University Belfast, where he focuses on Afghanistan. Our host in Belfast, Hastings Donnan, the Director of the Institute and himself a distinguished anthropologist, had specially urged us to talk to Semple. While the BBC described Semple, who speaks Pashto and Dari and was a fellow at Harvard University's Kennedy School of Government, as "one of the west's most respected experts on Afghanistan," he differs from other Western foreign policy experts in that he is also a Muslim. He first arrived in South Asia, he said, before attending university and "I lived and worked in Pakistan and Afghanistan on and off since 1985." Semple's status as a European Muslim in Afghanistan speaking the local languages and wearing local dress placed him firmly in the middle of the "Great Game" in the region.

While living in Pakistan, Semple told us, he made the decision to convert to Islam and he married a Pakistani women he had met at the University of Sussex: "I've been a Muslim longer than I wasn't a Muslim." Semple, who sported a long red beard and an Afghan vest when we met, spoke of his pride in his Irish identity and how it perfectly aligns with his Islamic identity. One point of "convergence" between Irish and Islamic identity, Semple explained, is that the Irish, like the Muslims, helped preserve ancient Greek texts during the Middle Ages:

> When you learn more about the Irish story of their global, cultural role, there's this image of the Irish as the sort of island of saints and scholars, who helped preserve many of the ancient texts. . . . You will find references to it, particularly the idea of the island of Iona and the role of St. Columba and the priests who studied, copied, preserved, the manuscripts under him. . . . What the Irish feel so proud of doing themselves, it's the same story that the Muslims tell of the role of the high point of Muslim civilization, transmitting the texts of the ancient world.

There is also a bond between the Irish and Muslims due to the history of colonization.

> Irish self-identity is complicated by different takes on the colonial experience. . . . One trend in Irish identity is of course this idea of having had a colonial past and therefore having been colonized. . . . So there is a certain sense of Muslims as being one of the groups amongst other colonized peoples.

The Irish also, Semple felt, know what it is like to be stereotyped as terrorists. Speaking of experiences he has had when his wife is stopped at airports, he said,

Often there has been a sense of people around us particularly expressing a sense of solidarity, saying this has all happened to us in an earlier era of conflict when all Irish came under suspicion, because the IRA were letting off bombs in Great Britain, therefore the Irish were to be suspected. So I think that there's actually been a sense of empathy between many Irish people and Muslims as part of this, the push back and increased prejudice that Muslims have faced post 9/11.

He recounted a remarkable story that involved a 1631 Barbary pirate raid on Baltimore in County Cork, Ireland, in which the pirates "basically carried off all of the townsfolk into servitude as is the pattern in the period." The story is told that the British crown's response to the Irish being taken in the raid was long in coming because "the British authority didn't prioritize anyone from Cork." When, the British authorities eventually tried to ransom and get the Irish back, the Irish in Algiers said "'We are far happier here. This is a more civilized, thriving place.' And so only a handful of them agreed to be ransomed and brought back. And so the genetic makeup of the people of Algeria, there are plenty of red heads popping up in the gene pool."

Exploring the links between Islam and Ireland has led Semple to some unexpected discoveries. In fact, one of the most famous symbols of Ireland could have a North African Islamic origin:

One of the stories, I'm not sure of the literal truth, but there are certainly several people who argue it, that the sort of Irish cultural symbol, the Claddagh brooch—as an American tourist in Ireland, you have to go and buy a Claddagh brooch, your aunt expects you to bring back a Claddagh brooch—it was actually designed in Algeria. The Claddagh brooch is an embodiment of the seventeenth-century interaction between Ireland and the great Muslim civilizations. And the Claddagh brooch was actually brought back by someone who started off as a slave in Algeria, worked their way up to be an independent jeweler and in later life came back to Ireland to continue his business and brought with him the Claddagh brooch.

In terms of identity within the Irish Muslim community, Semple felt that "fellow Muslims impose stereotypes on us and try to push us to conform to their ideas of what Muslims should look like." This is in contrast to the situation in the Muslim world, where, "we know that majority Muslim countries have multiple ways of looking like and behaving like a

Muslim, which is something that when you get to somewhere like Ireland is dropped along the way."

In order to improve relations between the communities, Semple spoke of a "rediscovery of al-Andalus," saying that he hoped it would be possible to "pull that off as a cultural project." "When you're talking in Europe," he said, "people slip into Huntington's idea of ah-ha, this is Judeo-Christian society which is juxtaposed to Islamic civilization as the 'other,' but I just don't buy it." The best way to build bridges between Muslims and non-Muslims in Europe, he argued, is for Europe not to see Islam as something new but instead to have a "reconnection with Islam, a rediscovering Islam, not as a stranger, but as a cousin. The most appropriate way to engage in the Islamic encounter and al-Andalus encounter in Ireland would be the return of a cousin rather than the arrival of a stranger."

PART THREE

*Lessons from Europe*

# SEVEN

# *Judaism, Islam, and European Primordial Identity*

DACHAU STILL SENDS chills down the spine of the visitor. The very name Dachau is redolent of malevolence and pathological sadism; its setting in the lush, green, bucolic Alpine countryside outside Munich, with its picture-postcard small farms and villages, evokes Hannah Arendt's phrase, "the banality of evil." My team—Jewish, Christian, and Muslim, young and old, male and female—was as affected as I was by the dark malignancy of the place and the memory of its victims. We walked about as if in a daze, each of us grappling with the enormity of what had happened here. We were speechless as the tour guides described the grisly acts of barbarity conducted with cold and clinical precision. The guide explained that the dreaded SS who ran the camp, usually in their late teens, uneducated, and poor, were taught that the prisoners in the camp were not human; they used the term "subhuman." We looked aghast at the gas chambers and the ovens. We were horrified at the rooms and instruments used for the "scientific experiments" on the prisoners. And we were ashamed at what the human race had done to itself. Tears glistened in every eye.

It was here that Adolf Hitler built his first odious concentration camp, and it was here that we glimpsed the deepest, darkest depths of man's inhumanity to man that was the Shoah, or Holocaust. It is well to keep in mind that Hitler's execrable concentration camps, Auschwitz and all the others, were patterned on Dachau. Hitler had set out to exterminate the entire Jewish population of Europe, and walking about here we understood why all of us, whatever our faith or race, all of us, must hold true to our pledge, "Never again," and repeat it—"Never again, never again, never again."

Even a cursory contemplation of Dachau forces us to become sociologists. We see the direct relationship between extreme expressions of predatory tribal identity in the pursuit of tribal "purity" and the consequences for those who are not part of the tribe. There are thus lessons in Dachau for human societies everywhere.

## Judaism, Islam, and European Primordial Identity

Jews and Muslims in Europe have a long and complicated history with each other. Theologically speaking, there are no two religions closer together; yet politically there are no two religions further apart. For large parts of a thousand years, the two religions were able to coexist with a remarkable degree of harmony. Jewish history records a golden age under Muslim rule in both Andalusia and the Ottoman Empire, particularly in Thessaloniki. Today few in either community know much about these periods and the extent of the interaction between the faiths. Jews and Muslims are thus not able to judge the significance of their shared history and its implications for the current troubled relationship. With relations between the communities at an all-time low, perhaps an acknowledgment and study of these periods could act as a catalyst to begin a dialogue and explore ways of building bridges in Europe and elsewhere.

### How Germanic Primordial Identity Affects Jews and Muslims

We can only understand the relationship between Jews and Muslims in Europe if we look at them in the context of Germanic primordial identity. For more than a millennium in the Germanic lands, and indeed in larger Christian Europe, Jews were seen as a small, alien, powerless, and marginal minority in society. They were Hebrew by language and ethnicity and originally from the distant lands that lay between Egypt and Syria. They were kept separate by their professions, often restricted to money lending, forced to live in ghettos, and were visibly different in culture and appearance from the majority. Their separateness was heightened by customs that appeared strange and foreign, such as strict dietary laws about not eating swine. They were also often compelled to wear distinctive dress or badges that identified them as Jews. They were always vulnerable to violence, and there were frequent pogroms and expulsions. Confiscation of Jewish money and property was a constant temptation for local tyrants. In addition to prejudice arising from their different ethnicity, the religious notion that somehow the Jews were responsible for the death of Jesus Christ earned them the label of "Christ killers." False stories circulated about Jews drinking the blood of Christian children and acting against the interests of the community. In the most profound sense, they were outsiders to the core notion of Germanic primordial identity of Volk and Heimat or "Blood and Soil," *Blut und Boden*, a slogan that was appropriated by the Nazis for their own malignant designs.

These attitudes resulted in sustained acrimony against the Jews in Europe over the centuries. In Germany, the Rhineland massacres in 1096 cost some 10,000 Jewish lives, and two centuries later, massacres led by Rintfleisch, reputed to be a knight, were carried out in around 150 communities in Bavaria and Austria in which as many as 100,000 Jews were killed, having been blamed for desecrating the Christian host, or communion bread. Six thousand Jews were killed in a single day in 1349 in the city of Mainz, the largest Jewish community in Europe at the time, after Jews were blamed for the bubonic plague. The belief that the Jews caused the Black Death would result in the total destruction of more than 300 European Jewish communities, particularly in Germany.[1] The initial Rhineland massacres occurred during the Crusades as German and Frankish warriors marched through Europe on their way to the Holy Land. In a twelfth-century text, a Jewish writer in Mainz described what the Crusaders told the Rhineland Jews to justify killing them: "You are the children of those who killed our object of veneration, hanging him on a tree; and he himself had said: 'There will yet come a day when my children will come and avenge my blood.' We are his children and it is therefore obligatory for us to avenge him since you are the ones who rebel and disbelieve in him." The writer, Solomon Bar Simson, described one instance where 800 Jews were stripped naked and slaughtered; "men, women, and infants, children and old people" were all killed.[2] In desperation, Jews killed one another rather than succumb to the attacking Christians.

In Eastern Europe, violence against the Jews came to be known as a "pogrom," from the Russian word *pogromit*, meaning "to wreak havoc." In 1648–49, Slavic Cossacks in Ukraine led by Bohdan Khmelnytsky rebelled against Polish-Lithuanian rule and killed between 100,000 and 200,000 Jews, and between 1917 and 1921, in the aftermath of the Russian Revolution, pogroms in Ukraine by mainly Ukrainian and White anti-Bolshevik forces killed an estimated 200,000 Jews.

Jews also routinely faced the confiscation of their properties and expulsion from European kingdoms. For example, 16,000 Jews were expelled from England in 1290, and 100,000 Jews were expelled from France in 1306. In 1420–21 Jews were expelled from Austria, except for 210 wealthy

Jews who were kept behind and burned, and expelled again in 1669–70.[3] Jews were also expelled from Hungary (1360), Croatia (1456), Bohemia (1542 and 1561), and Moldavia, one of the major regions of Romania (1579). In 1622, the diet of the thirteen cantons expelled the Jews from Switzerland. They were driven out of cities as well, including Cologne (1424), Berne (1408 and 1427), Speyer (1435), Zurich (1436), and Berlin (1348–49, 1446, 1510, and 1571), to name but a few. Jews were commonly expelled, readmitted, and then expelled again from the same location.

Fleeing often, with the memory of the expulsion from their ancestral lands after the destruction of Jerusalem never far from them, the negative stereotype of the "wandering Jew" formed around the community, feeding into the generalized anti-Semitism. Fictitious anti-Semitic literature such as the *Protocols of the Elders of Zion*, a creation of the Russian secret service, was distributed widely and kept hatred against the Jewish community at high levels. The Jews were often blamed and targeted for natural or economic calamities the nation faced. In Germany, even as Jews integrated into society socially, intellectually, and culturally from the eighteenth century onward, their separateness was never forgotten. Despite having produced some of the greatest German philosophers, scientists, musicians, and artists, anti-Semitism was always present—even those who converted to Christianity could not escape it. It was precisely this deep-rooted prejudice that Hitler exploited after Germany's defeat in the First World War, which he blamed on the Jews. The stage was being set for the unprecedented tragedy of the concentration camps and the Holocaust.

The Muslims, too, were seen as an alien minority among the Germanic peoples. But unlike the Jews, Germanic tribal society looked on Muslims not as a minority living within their society—that is, internal to it and therefore dependent on it—but as an outside "tribal" entity in its own right. More than a thousand years ago the Germanic peoples faced Muslim armies on the Iberian Peninsula, and it was a Frankish Germanic commander, Charles Martel, who at Tours turned the tide against the Arabs and prevented them from further advancing into Europe. Later, German forces clashed with Ottoman Turks on Europe's eastern flank. Twice in consecutive centuries Ottoman armies laid siege to Vienna, aiming to capture one of Europe's prized cities. No one among the German rulers underestimated the strength and power of Muslim armies and the civilization they represented. When not clashing with them, the Germans forged peace treaties with the Muslims that resulted in cultural, commercial, and economic exchanges.

For the Germans, and for Europeans generally, Muslims came to be equated with the Ottoman Empire, a mighty imperial power whose shadow stretched over large parts of Europe. In the Turks, the Germans recognized something of themselves. They, too, were warriors and empire builders and consisted of a tribal society with its own clans, territory, codes, and traditions of honor, courage, chivalry, and revenge and were thus worthy of a kind of grudging respect. Muslims, perceived in opposition to Christianity as heathen, were seen as an opponent—but nonetheless a worthy opponent.

The Ottomans' alliance with Germany in the First World War cost them their entire empire. After the devastation of the Second World War, Turkey—the successor to the Ottoman Empire—responded to Germany's request to send strong young men to work in its factories and industries as "guest workers." Initially there was goodwill toward them. As they extended their stay and made attempts to create roots by bringing families from Turkey, however, the mood in Germany began to change. Once welcome guests coming from a powerful and respected nation, they became an unwanted and unwelcome community dependent on the German state. Attacks against mosques, homes, and individuals increased in frequency. Between 2000 and 2007, for example, neo-Nazis targeted the Turkish community in a series of attacks—which the media dubbed the "döner [kebab] killings"—resulting in the deaths of ten people, and it was estimated that there were more than 3,500 attacks on refugees and refugee centers in 2016. In an ironic twist of history, the relationship of the Jewish and Muslim communities to Germanic society has been reversed. We discuss the reasons below.

### German Scholars Relate Primordial Tribal Identity to Jews and Muslims

In the modern era, the relationship between Germans and Jews and Muslims may be seen in the context of the work of Johann Gottfried von Herder. As discussed in chapter 2, Herder introduced the idea of the Volksgeist as the original and authentic spirit of a people bringing together blood, soil, and cultural traditions, a concept that became equated with Volk itself. Herder's work firmly adheres to the typical attitude of primordial identity toward Jews and Muslims explored in this chapter: Herder disparages the Jews for abandoning their own Volk and having a negative impact on the German Volk, while admiring the Arabs for their ability to retain theirs in their own homelands. Herder praised "The Arab of the desert," who, he wrote, "'belongs to it, as much as his noble horse and his patient indefatigable camel.' His simple clothing, his maxims of life, his manners and his character are in unison 'with his own region; and after a lapse of thousands of years, his tent still preserves the wisdom of his fore-fathers.'" Herder marveled at the preservation of Arab poetry, the essence of the Volk: "The poetry of the Arabians . . . sprouted from a peculiar root, and is the pure expression of the nationality which composed it, of its language, its mode of life, its religion and its mode of perception."[4]

Herder's respect for Muslims generally, however, did not extend to the Turks living in Europe, who were far from their authentic Volk. Herder asked, "For what should foreigners, who still after millennia want to be Asian barbarians, what should they be doing in Europe?"[5] Herder's views of the Jews were akin to this latter perception of an "Asian" Volk in Europe. The relocation of the Jews in Europe, he believed, rendered them unworthy of the respect that could be given to Muslims living in their own lands of origin. While Herder admired the ancient Hebrew culture, he noted that the Jews, because they were severed from their lands of origin, "never arrived at a maturity of political culture on their own soil, and consequently not to any true sentiment of liberty and honor."[6] Herder, in language relating to his view of the world as a beautiful garden of separate Völker, described the Jews as a "parasitic plant upon the stems of other nations." For Herder, there was thus the "problem" of what to do with the Jews of Europe and their foreign Asian Volk.

It is important to reiterate that Herder was a philosopher who defined and promoted primordial identity as distinct from predator identity. As such, he did not argue for aggressive state policies against the Jews; rather, he hoped that the state could benefit from their abilities. "A time will come," he wrote, "when in Europe no-one will [any] longer ask who is a Jew or Christian: for then the Jew will also live according to European laws, and contribute to the state's well-being."[7] However, others writing during and after Herder's time—especially after Napoleon's occupation of Germany—were unprepared to tolerate the existence of a "parasitic" minority on the German "stem." Thus what began as a philosophic articulation of primordial identity by Herder in the eighteenth century increasingly took the form of a call to aggressive predatory action.

The widespread advocacy and promotion of Germanic primordial identity had accelerated with the Reformation, which set the Germanic peoples on the path of attempting to identify a "pure" German Christianity unaffected or uncontaminated by either Catholic or Jewish influences.

Martin Luther had separated the virtuous ethnic "beloved" German nation from the Jews, "the devil's people" who were abandoned by God, boasting in works like *On the Jews and Their Lies* (1543) that Gentiles and Germans were descended from Noah's eldest son, and not his second son, Shem, the ancestor of the Jews from whom we get the name "Semitic."[8] Eventually, German scholars would be condemning Saint Paul as a Jew who corrupted Christianity and arguing that Jesus was not Jewish.[9] In the mid-nineteenth century, for example, "the annual meetings of the German Protestant Church (*Kirchentage*) . . . were filled with sermons that equated Christianity with the Volk. . . . Christian revelation must therefore have grown out of the history of the nation and not from some foreign, Semitic root."[10]

The field of "Oriental" studies was developed, in part, to discover what in Germanic religion and culture was of Jewish origin, with the goal of surgically separating it from what was Christian and German. The Germans dominated the field of orientalism and were profoundly influential beyond the core Germanic regions in countries like France.[11]

A key foundational figure in the German orientalist movement was Johann David Michaelis, the first chair of Oriental studies and biblical sciences at the University of Göttingen, whom historians widely consider "one of the fathers of modern biblical criticism."[12] In 1750 Michaelis published the first textbook in Germany that examined the New Testament through the critical lens of historical scholarship, and he also published a Hebrew grammar textbook. Michaelis believed that German biblical scholarship would greatly benefit from a scholarly expedition to the Arab world, and in 1756 he approached the Danish crown to fund such a trip. Michaelis wrote, "One will hardly find a people that has kept its customs the same for so long as the Arabs; which is a result of their never having been brought under the yoke of other peoples." He believed that by observing contemporary Arabs, German scientists could deduce the behavior of ancient Jews before the advent of the diaspora.[13]

The expedition, which Michaelis directed from Göttingen, departed from Copenhagen in 1761. Over the next six years it visited the Arabian Peninsula, Egypt, Syria, and present-day Iraq and Iran. The journey was difficult, and five of the expedition's six members died in the course of their travels. The lone survivor was Carsten Niebuhr, the expedition's cartographer, who wrote up his experiences in *Description of Arabia* (1772) and *Travel Description of Arabia and Other Surrounding Lands* (1774–78). Niebuhr, who was in correspondence with Herder, believed that studying the Arabs was an excellent way to learn about the ancient Jews. In the interior of Arabia, Niebuhr wrote with admiration, echoing Michaelis's praise, there were independent sheikhs and princes "who have never been subdued, but [who] continue to harass the Turks, and to drive them towards the coasts." "A nation of this character," he wrote, "cannot readily sink into a servile subjugation to arbitrary power." Niebuhr also saw a clear distinction between the Arabs in cities and the "genuine Arabs," the Bedouin.[14]

For Michaelis, the expedition provided material and increased authority to his scholarly work on Judaism. Michaelis's mission became anti-Semitic as he sought to portray the Jews, with their "Oriental" customs, as completely alien to Germany and aspects of Judaic law as anathema to Christianity. Between 1770 and 1775, Michaelis published his six-volume magnum opus, *Mosaic Law*, in which he sought to "grasp the 'foreign' and 'Asiatic' laws of Moses in order to then allow Europeans to *gain distance* from their Oriental heritage." This would enable aspects of Oriental Judaic law to be purged from the German judicial system.[15] Scientists like Johann Friedrich Blumenbach also studied the supposed "Oriental" nature of the Jews and wrote in 1775: "the Jewish race . . . can easily be recognized everywhere by their eyes alone, which breathe of the East."[16]

Once German intellectuals had established the inherently foreign and Oriental character of the Jews and Judaism, the question then became what to do with them in Germany. Luther had argued that the Jews, who he compared to gangrene and wrote of their "mixed, impure, watery, and wild" blood, "must be driven from our country. Let them think of their fatherland."[17] "If they could kill us all, they'd gladly do it," Luther observed, and he advocated forced labor, burning their synagogues, homes, and religious literature, and also pondered even more drastic measures, writing, "We are at fault in not slaying them."[18] Michaelis was an advocate of Jewish deportation and forced labor, writing that Germany should acquire Caribbean islands and dispatch Jews to work on them. The hot climate would be natural for the Jews given their Oriental origin, he believed, and they would be productive there.

In 1803 Carl Wilhelm Friedrich Grattenauer, the commissioner of justice at the Berlin superior court of justice, published the pamphlet, "Against the Jews," his first of three such treatises and a publishing sensation. In his pamphlets, Grattenauer argued that the Jews were an "Oriental foreign people" who sought to dominate Germany and the entire world. Grattenauer also rejected any relationship between Christianity and Judaism. Grattenauer additionally railed "against the Jews' characteristic 'odor,' their innate inability to feel compassion, and other physical deficiencies."[19]

For the philosopher Johann Gottlieb Fichte, one of the founders of the movement of German idealism, the Germans were an Urvolk, or original

Volk, of unmixed "race" and the Jews were a direct threat to the Volk.[20] "The only way I see by which civil rights can be conceded to them," he wrote, "is to cut off all their heads in one night and to set new ones on their shoulders, which should contain not a single Jewish idea."[21] The best option seemed to be deportation: "If we want to protect ourselves from them, I see no other way than conquering the holy land for them and sending them all there."[22]

Carl von Clausewitz, the well-known Prussian military theorist, also envisioned the destruction of the Jews, this time by fire, while on his way to Russia through Poland in 1812. "Dirty German Jews, swarming like vermin in the dirt and misery, are the patricians of this land," Clausewitz wrote. "A thousand times I thought if only fire would destroy this whole anthill [*Anbau*] so that this unending filth were changed by the clean flame into clean ashes."[23] For Ernst Moritz Arndt, the German author and poet, Jews should not be permitted to enter Germany "because they are a thoroughly foreign *Volk* and because I wish to preserve as much as possible the purity of the German tribes from alien-type elements."[24]

The composer Richard Wagner, who considered it his life's mission to bring about a "re-birth of the German *Volk*," saw in the Jews its greatest threat.[25] The Jews were "an utterly alien element," and Wagner laid out his arguments against them in his 1850 essay, "Judaism in Music."[26] Wagner argued that the Jews—whom he called a "ground-less *Volk* breed [*Volkstamm*]"—represented the "invasion of all totally foreign elements into the German being."[27] Wagner foretold a German "war of liberation" against Jews and wrote, "For the Jew to become human with us is tantamount to his ceasing to be a Jew."[28]

The journalist and writer Wilhelm Marr, known today as "the father of anti-Semitism," is credited with coining the term when he founded his Anti-Semites Party.[29] Marr, whose pamphlets included "The Victory of Judaism over the Germans" (1879), argued that the Jews had nearly triumphed in an "eighteen-thousand year war" they had been waging against Germans. It had become so bad, he wrote, that "we *Germanen* can barely distinguish ourselves from the Jews." Marr called the Germans "'Jew-eaters' *par excellence*" and predicted "the violence of the soaring vehemence of the *Volk*" and a "brutal anti-Jewish explosion." Marr felt that the Jews should be expelled, which would restore the "fatherland," calling on Germans to "*Redeem the mistakes of our forebears and pack the Jews off to their fatherland.*"[30]

The nineteenth-century orientalist and biblical scholar Paul de Lagarde, whom Thomas Mann described alongside Nietzsche and Wagner as one of "the giants of our people," wrote with alarm that the Jews had taken over the press and controlled German thought through "the Palestinization of the universities, of the law, of medicine and of the stage."[31] Lagarde's solution was to call for the Jews to be "exterminated root and branch."[32] He described the Jews as "usurious vermin" and compared them with "trichinae and bacilli" with whom "one does not negotiate . . . they are exterminated as quickly and as thoroughly as possible."[33] Lagarde wrote that it was the duty of the Prussians and the Germans to finish the Jewish threat and thus save Europe, "otherwise Europe will become a field of death."[34]

For the best-selling nineteenth-century art historian and philosopher Julius Langbehn, "the racial identity of the Volk was symbolized by the nature within which it lived. Thus, every race had its landscape: the Aryans were set in the German forest, and the Jews in the desert, which expressed their rootlessness and the barrenness of their souls."[35] The biggest threat to Germany, Langbehn wrote, were the Jews: "The Jews are the oppressors and the enemies of all German being."[36] Only when Germans removed this "poison" from their midst, Langbehn wrote, could they really be German and revive the spirit of the Volk. Leading the Germans against the Jews, Langbehn predicted, would be a "secret kaiser" who "stands in an intimate bond with the spirit of his *Volk*." Under this leader, the Germans would "return to their basic and original characteristic" and fulfill "their destiny in the 'domination of the world.'" Langbehn prayed, "May he come!"[37]

When Hitler—the "secret kaiser" that some Germans had been waiting for—did emerge, he focused his personal and political animus, backed by his security apparatus, on the Jewish community. Hitler likened "the Jew" to a "type of germ: 'a noxious bacillus [that] keeps spreading as soon as a favorable medium invites him. And the effect of his existence is also like that of spongers; wherever he appears, the host people dies out after a shorter or longer period.'"[38] For Heinrich Himmler, one of Hitler's key henchmen and known as the architect of the Nazi "Final Solution," the Jewish community was "Oriental." Himmler therefore objected to their presence in German society: "Do we germanize the Jews? No, but they turn us into Jews. . . . It disgusts me when I see a Jew strolling on the Bavarian mountains in *Lederhosen* (leather shorts). I don't go about in a caftan and ringlets. There, in terms of racial feeling, are two different worlds."[39]

### *Jewish Intellectuals Respond to Germanic Primordial Identity*

Over the nineteenth and early twentieth centuries, the Jewish community had watched the growth of anti-Semitism with increasing concern and wondered where it would lead. Despite heroic efforts to integrate into the Volk, they found themselves cast outside of it, creating a sense of anguish, anxiety, and foreboding. This can be seen in the exchange between the Danish bishop and national hero N. F. S. Grundtvig, and the Danish Jewish writer Meïr Aron Goldschmidt. Grundtvig, who was inspired by Herder to develop the idea of *folkelighed*, or the communal egalitarian spirit of the folk, or people, wrote that Goldschmidt, whose family had been in Denmark for almost two centuries and who has gone down in history "as the master of Danish language—the foremost developer of modern Danish literary prose," was merely a "guest" in Denmark.[40] Goldschmidt, wrote Grundtvig, did not belong to the Danish "people's congregation," although he had "the notion" he was "a thorough Dane."[41]

In 1848 Goldschmidt published his reply to Grundtvig in Goldschmidt's journal *Nord og Syd* (North and South):

> Who is originally Danish? . . . Are the rest of us, who love Denmark, and who speak and write its language fluently, who have given our lives to the service of the state—irretrievably placed outside the Danish nationality, that is without a homeland, because there is a foreign sch in our name, or because we have dark hair and dark eyes? . . . Lord, how merciless people can be in their patriotism.[42]

A century before the emergence of Hitler and the Nazis, the German-Jewish writer Saul Ascher, in his 1815 book *Die Germanomanie* (The German-mania), was alarmed at the anti-Jewish sentiment being expressed by the German nationalists: "According to the opinions of these enthusiastic idealists, Germanness [*Deutschheit*] und Christianity should be amalgamated to the extent that it is impossible for one to exclude the other, and to this a first-rate antithesis was found in the Jews." Ascher asked, "What is the final goal of these fanatics in their zealous German-mania [*Germanomanie*]? Where will this incitement for a crusade against everything un-German and foreign lead? . . . In order to maintain the fire of inspiration, fuel must be collected, and our German-manics want to lay the Jews as the first bundle of kindling to spread the flames of fanaticism through the masses."[43]

In October 1817, at the conclusion of a Volkisch festival at the Wartburg Castle overlooking the central German town of Eisenach, hundreds of Volkisch student activists burned Ascher's *Die Germanomanie* alongside other works, such as the Napoleonic Code, they considered "un-German." The burning was held on the fourth anniversary of the Battle of Leipzig, in which Prussia and other European powers had defeated Napoleon, and on the site where Luther had translated the Bible three centuries earlier.

Noting that the writings of the German nationalists were paving the way for terrifying action against the Jews, the prominent German-Jewish writer and poet Heinrich Heine appeared to predict the Holocaust and warned his fellow Germans not to take that path: "Smile not at the fantasy of one who foresees in the region of reality the same outburst of revolution that has taken place in the region of intellect. The thought precedes the deed as the lightning the thunder. . . . There will be played in Germany a drama compared to which the French Revolution will seem but an innocent idyl."[44] Not surprisingly, Heine's books were burned during the Nazi period. With chilling insight, Heine had commented on exactly such a contingency in an 1821 play about Andalusia, putting these words into the mouth of a Muslim referring to the Spanish burning of the Quran: "Where they burn books / In the end, they will burn people too."[45]

### The Holocaust, Indelible Blot on Human History

The Holocaust was one of the deadliest genocides in history, with some 6 million Jews and 5 million other minorities systematically killed by the Nazi regime in Germany and German-occupied Europe between 1941 and 1945. State-sponsored persecution of the Jewish minority began when the Nazi regime came to power in 1933, but systematic killing of the Jews accelerated in earnest in 1941. Throughout the war, a network of approximately 42,500 camps, including six extermination camps created for the sole purpose of killing, would serve to confine, coerce, force backbreaking labor from, and murder millions of Jews across the continent. Dachau, which began as a camp for so-called political prisoners in 1933 before interning Jews on the basis of their ethnicity in 1938, had the dubious distinction of being in operation for the entirety of the Third Reich. The most notorious of these camps, Auschwitz-Birkenau, an hour's drive from Krakow in southern Poland, killed around a million Jews.

An estimated 75 percent of all those brought to Auschwitz were gassed to death on arrival. They were given soap and towels and told they were going to take a shower. This was done so they would avoid panicking. They were stripped naked and led into the chamber. After those in the chamber had been gassed to death, the strongest, healthiest camp prisoners removed the bodies and extracted anything from them that could be of use, such as the teeth and hair, collections of which are on display today in large rooms in the camp. Then the bodies were burned. The purpose of this exercise in genocide is explained in a quote on display in the camp by Otto Thierack, the Third Reich's minister of justice: "We must free the German nation of Poles, Russians, Jews and Gypsies."

The Holocaust is an occurrence of such catastrophic proportions as to leave the imagination in distress and despair. It has a devastating impact on sensitive Germans today. While the event has shaped and informed modern German society—making it more aware of the other—Germans remain baffled as to how the Holocaust was possible. When I asked Ambassador Heinrich Kreft this question, he replied that he had been asked it a thousand times. In spite of pondering on the question, like most thinking Germans, he was still trying to understand how his people were capable of organizing and implementing an event as terrible as the Holocaust.

### Germanic Tribal Identity and Jewish Genocide in Iberia

Long before the Holocaust of the twentieth century, the dangers emanating from European predator identity's extreme tribalism and enforcement of purity based on blood had led to mass genocide in Iberia. As the Jewish-American historian David Levering Lewis describes, Jews faced a "final solution" in Spain in the seventh century. In 646 the Seventh Toledo Council, called by Germanic Visigothic rulers in their capital city Toledo, declared that "the King will tolerate no one in his kingdom who is not Catholic." The Visigothic Spanish state itself resembled a "prison," and Catholicism in the kingdom "was exceedingly mean-spirited and brutish." In 695 at the Sixteenth Toledo Council, a plan for the Jews was presented that involved "emigration; forced conversion; impoverishment; and worse." According to Lewis, the Muslim arrival in the Iberian Peninsula meant salvation for the Jews: "After so many years of living under the Damoclean sword of property expropriation, forced conversion, and expulsion, Jews throughout Hispania welcomed the Muslim invaders as deliverers."[46] The legal scholar Samuel Parsons Scott, who translated the seventh-century Visigothic legal code from Latin to English, argues in his preface, "The cruel and unrelenting pursuit of the Jews, commanded by the Visigothic Code, was the foundation of the Spanish Inquisition and its diabolical procedure."[47]

As we saw in chapter 3, the Spanish rulers and aristocrats enforced a definition of Spanish identity that fused Christianity and Germanic blood descent, and they were successful in exterminating the Jewish and Muslim populations of the Iberian Peninsula after the fall of Granada in 1492, with Portugal following in 1497. Hundreds of thousands of Muslims and Jews crossed the narrow Strait of Gibraltar and found their way to new homes in North Africa or in Ottoman lands.

The Sephardic Jewish Museum in Cordoba illustrated the dark days following the end of what the museum called the "neighborly coexistence between Christians, Muslims and Jews" and described the Inquisition's method of execution by public burning—the auto-da-fé or "act of faith." We were informed that the first auto-da-fé was held in 1483 in the Convent of the Holy Martyrs, where one woman was burned alive for "Judaizing and for living with the Cathedral's treasurer," although other sources give a slightly earlier date. The museum said that of all the people who were "relaxed," the euphemism the Spanish used for burning people alive or in effigy, from the start of the Inquisition to its dissolution in 1833, "95 percent were under accusation of Judaizing." The number of victims of the auto-da-fé was 5,565, the museum explained, and included ordinary people in society like merchants, weavers, seamstresses, bakers, and even priests. The museum also discussed one of the bloodiest autos-da-fé, conducted in Cordoba in 1504, where 107 people were burned alive in a single night. The Inquisition had its tentacles in all sections of society including the realm of thought, and even "the mere act of buying a book was seen as suspicious."

To illustrate the preoccupation with Germanic blood purity among the Spanish, the museum quoted from the popular seventeenth-century text *Sentinel against the Jews*. In it, the author argues that "to be an enemy of Christians, it is not necessary that both the mother and the father are Jews, one is sufficient. It is not important that it be the father, the mother is sufficient . . . and if not even that, a fourth is sufficient, or an eighth, and the sacred Inquisition has discovered in our times that even those with an ancestor twenty degrees removed can still be Judaizers."

Today, prominent Christian scholars look back on the doings of the church and find many troubling questions that do not have easy answers. When asked to comment on and explain the persistent anti-Semitism in European history, Rowan Williams, the former archbishop of Canterbury, brought together the varying strands of centuries of European anti-Semitic prejudice:

> To be honest, the Church has to take a very heavy share of responsibility. If you look at the beginnings of Christianity, you can see there a rhetoric, which comes from the time when Christians are a minority and Jewish authorities are making their lives difficult. So there's resentment against the powerful Jewish authorities of early Palestine, from a relatively powerless Christian community. And from at least the fourth Christian century onwards, the bitterness is now expressed toward the powerless, and that is a relentless theme, even in some of the greatest of Christian writers. . . . It comes out in

Spain in a set of legal enactments prohibiting people of Jewish birth from certain offices in the church. It's exactly like the laws of the Third Reich. And this is Christian Spain, in the sixteenth century. The Statutes of the purity of blood in sixteenth-century Spain was a terrible story, which not enough people know about. And that, of course in a context where a few hundred years earlier Jews and Christians had been living side by side. . . . Centuries before Hitler there is already that racial exclusivism elevated to a legal and religious degree. . . . The poison is still in the system, and even now, even today.

## The German Soft Spot Theory

The apparent contradiction of Kaiser Wilhelm's benign acceptance of Muslims on one hand and crude anti-Semitism on the other cannot be resolved without recourse to what I am calling the "soft spot" theory of German social behavior, which determines the relationship between Germans and Muslims and Jews in terms of Germanic primordial tribal identity. The theory elucidates both the sustained Germanic admiration for Islam and Muslims and the aversion to Jews discussed in the previous section. In one case, the minority is "over there," in its own homeland as a distinct tribe in its own right, and therefore deserving of respect; in the other case, the minority is "over here," and uneasily present among the Germanic population of which it cannot be part as it is separated by blood and lineage. This dynamic is not mutually exclusive: there are examples in German history of Germans reaching out to Muslims and Jews in equal measure, but these are the exception, not the rule. The soft spot theory also accounts for the reversal of the traditional German position in contemporary society, where Germans now appear to be showing hostility to Muslims and exhibiting appreciation for the Jews.

### THE HISTORICAL SOFT SPOT FOR ISLAM

After concluding his trip to Jerusalem, Kaiser Wilhelm wrote that his "personal feeling in leaving the holy city was that I felt profoundly ashamed before the Moslems and that if I had come there without any Religion at all I certainly would have turned Mahommetan!"[48] His admiration for the great Saladin, whose grave in Damascus he restored with his own funds, was unbounded. Speaking in Damascus, the Kaiser declared, "Let me assure His Majesty the Sultan and the three hundred millions of Moslems who, in whatever corner of the globe they may live, revere in him their Khalif, that the German Emperor will ever be their friend."[49] The Kaiser became known as Hajji Wilhelm in the Middle East, the title given to someone who has performed the hajj to Mecca.

In contrast, the Kaiser blamed the Jews for Germany's defeat in the First World War: "Let no German ever forget this, nor rest until these parasites have been destroyed and exterminated from German soil! This poisonous mushroom on the German oak-tree!" He advocated a "'regular international all-worlds pogrom à la Russe' as 'the best cure.'" He said that Jews, like mosquitos, were "a nuisance that humanity must get rid of in some way or other. . . . I believe the best would be gas!"[50] In the case of Muslims, Wilhelm is reaching out in the most positive and respectful way in what could best be termed, in today's parlance, the dialogue of civilizations; in the case of the Jews, he is the precursor of Hitler himself, even suggesting the use of gas.

In entering Jerusalem, the Kaiser was walking in the footsteps of another German emperor known for his soft spot for Islam, Frederick II, whom we have already met in chapter 3. The soft spot is detectable as far back as Charlemagne, who, during his reign as emperor, allied with the Muslim rulers of Barcelona, Saragossa, and Huesca against the Umayyad emir Abdur Rahman I of Cordoba in the late eighth century. Charlemagne also developed an unusually warm relationship with the Abbasid caliph Harun al-Rashid in Baghdad, who sent him an elephant as a token of appreciation along with other gifts such as a robe of honor with the inscription, "There is no God but God."[51] As a result of the friendship of the two rulers, Charlemagne was given control over Christian interests in Jerusalem. The historian F. W. Buckler characterized the relationship between Charlemagne and al-Rashid in the following way: "The status of Charles . . . would appear to be that of *amīr* of Spain and *walī* of Jerusalem."[52]

A century later, Charlemagne's great-great-granddaughter Bertha of Tuscany, who described herself as "queen of all the Franks," sent the Abbasid caliph a variety of gifts, proposed marriage, and wrote him a letter featuring the following lines: "In the name of Allah, the Compassionate, the Merciful. . . . My Lord, I invoke upon you profound peace in the [name] of Allah's love."[53]

The soft spot is also visible in the case of Wolfram von Eschenbach, a Bavarian knight regarded as the greatest German poet of the Middle Ages, who treated Muslims with humanity during the Crusades. In his early thirteenth-century poem *Willehalm*, a beautiful Muslim woman, Arabele, becomes a Christian and makes an appeal: "Is it not a sin to slaughter people who have never heard of Christianity as we slaughter cattle? I would even say that it is a great sin, for all men who speak the seventy-two languages are the creatures of God."[54]

In Eschenbach's *Parzival*, which Wagner adapted into an opera, the character Gahmuret of Anjou has a Christian European son named Parzival and a Muslim son named Feirefiz, who do not know each other. Gahmuret had traveled to Baghdad to serve the spiritual leader of Islam, the "Baruc," meaning mubarak or "blessed one" and had his Muslim son with a Saracen queen. When Gahmuret dies serving the Baruc, a grand tomb glittering with jewels is constructed for him in Baghdad funded by the Baruc and in accordance with Christian customs: "Baptized was he as a Christian tho' Saracens mourn him yet." A particularly dramatic moment comes when Gahmuret's sons, who are both knights, finally meet on the field of battle. The sword of Parzival, who has set out to seek the Holy Grail, breaks and Feirefiz, demonstrating his honor and magnanimity, refuses to kill an unarmed man. The two men then realize they are brothers, embrace each other, and depart to feast with King Arthur. Feirefiz, the Muslim, is accepted and honored as a knight of the Round Table.

Albrecht Dürer, widely considered to be Germany's greatest artist, appears to have been intrigued by Muslim society and drew on a range of Muslim subjects for his works, including "Oriental Rider," "Three Orientals," "A Turkish Family," and a portrait of Suleyman the Magnificent, the Ottoman Sultan. Suleyman had just ascended to the throne and would go on to take the Ottoman Empire to the zenith of its glory. Dürer's portrait is in black and white, and its simplicity only enhances the dignity of the subject. Suleyman is depicted as a strong and stately man with a certain compassion in the eyes, a hint of a smile on the lips, and strength in the chin. There are no robes or swords or medals or jewelry on him, yet he conveys a certain majesty. Except for the simple bulbous turban, there is no other hint of Suleyman's Islamic identity. Considering the extent and meanness of the caricatures and cartoons of Muslim figures in Europe today, one scrutinizes Dürer's Muslim subjects for signs of ridicule or caricature in vain.

Frederick the Great of Prussia, the "enlightened absolutist," forged strong ties with the Ottoman Empire, which provided the Prussians with camels during Prussia's campaign against Austria in the Seven Years' War.[55] Frederick—who appointed the first Prussian imam, Lieutenant Osman, in 1744—welcomed the Turks to Berlin, reportedly saying, "If Turks come to Berlin, mosques must be built for them."[56] Muslims in the Prussian army helped defeat Napoleon at the 1807 Battle of Eylau, in which Prussian troops arrived late in the fighting and put the Russian side over the top. There was also a Prussian craze for all things Turkish, which Frederick observed with some amusement: "It is now the fashion in Berlin to eat dates; and any moment now the *petits maîtres* will be wrapping turbans round their heads and those with enough money will set up harems. To be fashionable you have to have seen the Turk, everyone is telling stories which would make you fall asleep on your feet."[57] Indeed, when the first Turkish envoy arrived in Berlin in 1763, he and his extensive entourage were given such an enthusiastic reception by the cheering Berliners that the bemused envoy wrote to the Sultan, "The people of Berlin recognize the Prophet Muhammad and are not afraid to admit that they are prepared to embrace Islam."[58]

Wolfgang Amadeus Mozart, among history's greatest composers, was fascinated by the Turkish musical style, which involved the use of "cymbals, bass drum, triangles with the characteristic thrusting Turkish beat."[59] Turkish elements can be seen in his most popular works such as Violin Concerto no. 5, known as "The Turkish," and the Piano Sonata no. 11, which concludes with the grandeur and beauty of the "Turkish March." The clearest example of Mozart's fascination is his opera *The Abduction from the Seraglio* (1782), which tells the story of the Spaniard Belmonte who sails to rescue the woman he loves from an Ottoman pasha who has locked her away in his harem. In the end, the pasha releases the Europeans, declaring that, "it is a greater pleasure to repay with good deeds an injustice suffered, rather than punish evil with evil."[60] The opera's dramatic and joyous conclusion, depicted in the 1984 film *Amadeus*, features the Europeans singing the praises of the pasha.

Johann Wolfgang von Goethe, Germany's greatest literary figure, developed a particular fondness for Islam and the Muslim world, and his poetic collection *West-Eastern Divan* (1819), evokes the famous Persian poet Hafez, whom Goethe called "the true source of all poetic joys." Goethe included direct quotations of Quranic verses or variations of them in key passages of the *Divan*.[61] No Muslim can fail to be moved by Goethe's poem, "Mahomet's Song," dedicated to the Prophet of Islam, whom he calls "head of created beings." The poem compares the Prophet to a powerful river that slowly but surely gathers other streams as it flows to its destiny in the ocean where it meets the divine. The poem's message is the discovery of the essential unity of the universe realized in the search for the divine. Goethe's affinity for Islam lasted his entire life; while he wrote "Mahomet's Song" at the age of twenty-three, at the age of seventy he publicly declared he was considering "devoutly celebrating that holy night in which the Koran in its entirety was revealed to the prophet from on high."[62] Goethe's comments on Islam have led to speculation about the extent of his commitment to the faith, for example, in the following verse: "If 'Islam' signifies 'submitting to God' / In Islam, we all live and die." When announcing the publication of *West-Eastern Divan*, Goethe wrote that the author "does not reject the suspicion that he may himself be a Muslim."[63]

The soft spot is evident in the large, ornate mosque completed in 1795 by the Palatine Prince Elector Karl Theodor at Schwetzingen Palace, his summer residence, near Mannheim and Heidelberg. The mosque is lavishly decorated and features gold letters proclaiming "There is no God but God" in Arabic and German as well as a series of Quranic maxims. Karl Theodor spared no expense and the mosque, "reputed to be the finest and most expensive garden structure ever," symbolized Karl's tolerance for religious diversity.[64]

The composer Richard Wagner's view of Islam contrasted markedly with his opinions on Judaism. His unfinished opera *The Saracen Woman* depicts Frederick II, whom he called "the most intelligent of all the emperors," imbuing the world "with the heady perfumes of a fairytale," his son, King Manfred of Italy, and Muslims in heroic terms.[65] At first lazy and indulgent, Manfred's life changes when he meets a mysterious Muslim woman, Fatima, who appears in his court and tells him she has been sent to him by none other than his deceased father, Frederick II. Fatima tells a shocked Manfred that though in the West people may think that Frederick, "the greatest Kaiser," has died, in the East Frederick lives on, and "a thousand songs keep green his fame." Frederick, says Fatima, "was neither Mussulman nor Christian; a god was he, and reverenced as god he lives still in the morning-land"—or the world of Islam, which contrasts with Christian Europe, the "land-of-evening." For Fatima, the coexistence of Muslims and Christians in Italy depends on Manfred, and she envisions in the future "glorious days, the days when Christian brother is to Mussulman."[66]

Friedrich Nietzsche, whose work contributed to philosophic fields such as existentialism and postmodernism, blamed Christianity in his 1895 book *Der Antichrist* for the elimination of the advanced civilization of Muslim Spain: "Christianity destroyed for us the whole harvest of ancient civilization, and later it also destroyed for us the whole harvest of *Mohammedan* civilization. The wonderful culture of the Moors in Spain, which was fundamentally nearer to *us* and appealed more to our senses and tastes than that of Rome and Greece, was *trampled down*." Nietzsche went on to condemn the Crusades, noting that instead of the Europeans having "groveled in the dust" before Islamic civilization as they should have, they waged war against it. Challenging the notion of "progress" so common in his society, Nietzsche wrote that late nineteenth-century European civilization seemed "poor" and "senile" compared with Islamic civilization at the time of the Crusades. Nietzsche, like Wagner, also praised Frederick II, calling him a "genius" and celebrating the fact that he fought the papacy while seeking "peace and friendship with Islam."

Following the First World War, a wide range of Germans expressed their admiration for General Mustafa Kemal, or Atatürk, whom they saw as a heroic figure standing up to the Allied Entente forces who had occupied both their nations. As Atatürk fought his battles to create the modern state of Turkey, the German press took ownership of him, calling him "our Mustafa Kemal" and was "fascinated, if not obsessed, with Turkey." The idea that Turkey, known as the "light from the East," was a "model" for Germany became widespread. A 1921 article in the *Hamburger Nachrichten* proclaimed, "We Germans are watching the prudent actions, the brave deeds, and the successes of Mustafa Kemal and of his national warriors, because they provide us with a role model of how a stout band of national fighters led by a determined Führer can oppose the allied bandits and swindlers by fighting a guerrilla war and can prevail." In his 1935 biography of Atatürk, Hanns Froembgen wrote that as a child Atatürk could "feel the spirit of the 'grey wolf' . . . of eternal Turkendom, of his blood awakening within himself. He was 'inspired' by the 'difference in blood,' which he could feel vis-à-vis the 'lesser races' (referring to the Greeks, Armenians, and Levantines) who were controlling the Ottoman Empire." Froembgen called Atatürk "a thunderstorm turned man" and proclaimed that "Turkey is the most modern state of the twentieth century."[67]

The emerging Nazi Party would also seize on the example of Turkey, with the official Nazi newspaper *Völkischer Beobachter* running headlines like "Turkey—The Role Model" and "Heroic Turkey." In 1922 *Völkischer Beobachter* declared, "In these days of dishonor and infamy . . . there has shone for the past few years one name, which proves what a real man can do. Everyone who feels [truly] German has followed with great admiration the heroic struggle of Mustafa Kemal Pasha." Hitler called Atatürk a "star in the darkness" and "the greatest man of the century." On Hitler's birthday in 1938 he met a delegation of Turkish politicians and journalists and told them, "Atatürk was a teacher; Mussolini was his first and I his second student." The following year he said to the Turkish ambassador that he "'was copying Atatürk' . . . just as Atatürk had demolished the Treaty of Sévres, so he was now destroying the Versailles Treaty." Hitler was also impressed with Atatürk's handling of the Islamic clergy, declaring, "How fast Kemal Atatürk dealt with his priests is one of the most amazing chapters [of history]! . . . The Duce told me in 1934 in Venice: 'The Pope will one day leave Italy, there cannot be two masters!'"[68]

Hitler expressed high praise for Islam, describing it as a *Männerreligion* (a religion of men), and he "often praised the 'attitude' of the 'soldiers of Islam.'" When he contemplated his vision for a new European order following the war, Hitler "insisted that his New Europe would have engaged in 'a bold policy of friendship toward Islam.'"[69] Hitler also regretted that the Germans had not become Muslim themselves and lamented the defeat of the Muslims at Tours by Charles Martel in 732. If Martel had not been victorious, Hitler ruminated, the Germans may well have converted to Islam and "would have conquered the world."[70]

Hitler was not the only senior Nazi to regret the defeat of the Muslims in decisive European historical battles. Heinrich Himmler, the head of the SS, who himself had toyed with the idea of emigrating to Anatolia, lamented the role of the "German people" in defeating the Muslims both at Tours and at Vienna in 1683, "depriving Europe of the flourishing spiritual light and civilization of Islam."[71] General Gottlob Berger, the head of the SS main office, similarly declared, "Germany would be better off and the old Germanic Kultur would not have perished if at that time in Vienna God wouldn't have helped the Europeans, that is the Germans, but rather would have helped the Moslems or Mohammedans, because if they had been victorious in Vienna, then Jewish Christianity wouldn't have been able to spread all over Europe and we would really have a Germanic culture and not a Jewish one."

Himmler was "convinced that Muhammad was one of the greatest men in history" and "apparently collected various books on Islam and biographies of the Prophet."[72] Himmler's personal physician wrote that he once entered Himmler's bedroom to find him in bed with the Quran on his night table.[73] Himmler told his physician that he "wanted to visit the Islamic countries to continue his studies once the war was over." Himmler would "regularly contrast his idea of Islam with Christianity," which, unlike Islam, "made no promises to soldiers who died in battle." For Himmler, Islam was "a religion of people's soldiers."

Conscious that Nazi race policies might adversely impact the Semitic Arabs and other Muslims, the authorities took pains to demonstrate that their target was the Jews—and only the Jews. Turks, Iranians, and Arabs were explicitly excluded from the Nuremberg Laws and as early as 1935 the Propaganda Ministry "instructed the press to avoid the terms 'anti-Semitic' and 'anti-Semitism' and to use words like 'anti-Jewish' instead."[74] In 1936 the government began an investigation to decide the racial status of the Turks, and the Turkish press announced the results in the headline, "The Turks Are Aryans!"[75] In early 1942 the Propaganda Ministry's Anti-Semitic Action office was renamed Anti-Jewish Action. The Nazi physician Walter Groß, who headed the Office of Racial Policy, wrote, "National Socialist race theory in fact recognizes Arabs as members of a high-grade race, which looks back on a glorious and heroic history." In 1943 the Nazi Party stated explicitly that it accepted "followers of Islam" as members. Despite this, the Nazis were keen to avoid racial mixing—for example, between Germanic and Turkic peoples—and German officers were "instructed to explain to the 'Turkic peoples' that they were 'racially valuable' but that their 'bloodstream' was different from the Germans' and therefore mixing would have negative consequences for both sides."[76]

The Nazis launched a massive effort, as Kaiser Wilhelm had done previously, to rouse the Islamic world to the war effort. Nazi propaganda in North Africa and the Middle East during the war spoke of *"Hajj* Hitler," who would liberate the population from the English and the Jews, cast as "the common enemies of the Arab-Muslim world and of Germany."[77] Hitler counted among his allies Hajji Amin al-Husseini, the grand mufti of Jerusalem, and he presented the blonde and blue-eyed mufti with a certificate declaring him an "honorary Aryan."[78] Hitler's contempt for non-Aryan peoples, however, was difficult to contain: He is on record as referring to Arabs as "half-monkeys."[79]

The Nazis were clear that they sought to ally with Islam on an equal level and would not attempt to change or influence it in any way. As General Berger said, "It is not intended to find a synthesis of Islam and National Socialism or to impose National Socialism on the Muslims." Instead, "National Socialism was to be seen as the 'genuine *völkisch* German worldview,' while Islam was to be seen as 'the genuine *völkisch* Arabic worldview.'"

Nazi propaganda included Quranic quotes and celebrated Islamic anti-colonial fighters like 'Abd al-Karim in the Moroccan Rif, Imam Shamil in the Caucasus mountains, and Mirza Ali Khan, known as the Fakir of Ipi in the mountains of Waziristan, who the Germans were arming from their consulate in Kabul. The German public knew the Fakir as the "Freedom Hero of Waziristan." Even nonreligious terms were rendered in a religious context in Nazi propaganda—for example, "the German word for 'dive bomber,' 'Stuka' (*Sturzkampfflugzeug*), which was translated into Arabic as an 'aircraft that like the eagle of the Prophet flies down from heaven and destroys the enemy on the ground.'" The Nazi efforts often found a receptive audience: In Crimea, Tatars praised Hitler with the honorific, "Adolf Effendi," while in Cairo Anwar al-Sadat, then a young military officer, reported demonstrators in the streets chanting "Advance Rommel!"[80] Popular songs honoring "*Hajj* Hitler" were composed in both rural and urban areas in North Africa.[81]

Literature distributed to German soldiers serving in North Africa instructed them to respect Islam; if they did not, "every possibility for communication and sympathetic cooperation is at risk from the outset, and sometimes made impossible." Soldiers were told to "Never enter a mosque unless you are invited to visit it, or if the guard of the sanctuary shows you his approval to let you in. At any sign of rejection, refrain. . . . If you have to gather information at a Muslim house, ring or knock, then turn your back to the door, in order that you do not see the woman who might be answering." As the Germans entered Muslim areas they had seized from the Soviets in the Caucasus, the mosques and madrassas were reopened to great appreciation from the local populations, who were able to practice their religion once again and use their written script. Nazi officers celebrated Muslim holidays in lavish fashion, and Nazi-organized events included circumcision ceremonies involving as many as fifty Muslim children.[82]

The Nazis expressed sympathy for the suffering of the Muslims in the Balkans, a key theater of Nazi policy and strategy. General Artur Phleps of the SS, an ethnic German from Transylvania, described to General Berger "the terrible situation of the Mohammedan population in Croatia, Bosnia and the Herzegovina. They were oppressed, robbed and violated by partisans of every political colour." Berger, to "protect the Moslems who were suffering worst," proposed to Hitler that "a Croat and a Bosnia-Herzegovina division composed only of Mohammedans" be organized.[83] In 1943 the SS "declared the Muslims of the Balkans part of the 'racially valuable peoples of Europe.' . . . They were the first non-Germanic peoples allowed to enter the ranks of the Waffen-SS." The Nazis also launched a humanitarian relief campaign for suffering Balkans Muslims, collecting money at the festival of Eid in the autumn of 1943.[84]

Himmler declared he was reinstating the Austrian Hapsburg policy of religious freedom for Muslims and told Bosnian military commanders in January 1944 that Germans and Muslims worshipped the same God.[85] There were as many as 300,000 Muslims fighting for the Nazis in units with their own field imams, including Turkic Muslims, Crimean Tatars, Volga Tatars, and tens of thousands of Muslims from the North Caucasus and Azerbaijan. Of the non-Germans fighting for the Nazis in the East, Hitler said, "The only ones I consider to be reliable are the pure Mohammedans."

In his bunker in Berlin at the end of the war, Hitler lamented that more had not been done to mobilize the world's Muslims. He felt that his effort had been hampered by Germany's alliance with Italy, a colonial power in the Muslim world, which hindered what Hitler described as a "splendid policy with regard to Islam." Hitler had, however, "brought more Muslims to Germany than had ever lived there before." After the war, in Munich, these Muslims "formed the first Islamic community of postwar Germany," the Islamic Religious Society (*Religiöse Gemeinschaft Islam*), which was led by a former Nazi field imam.[86]

Prominent Nazi officials also converted to Islam. The professor and SS officer Johann von Leers, one of the Nazis' most important ideologues and propagandists who was close to Goebbels, for example, converted after the war and took the name Omar Amin von Leers. Louis Heiden or Luis al-Haj, a former SS official and Muslim convert, translated *Mein Kampf* into Arabic in the 1960s and worked, like Leers, for Nasser in Egypt. Aribert Ferdinand Heim or Tarek Hussein Farid, was an Austrian known as "Dr. Death" for his gruesome work in the Mauthausen Concentration Camp. Heim also moved to Egypt, and each day would walk fifteen miles to the Al-Azhar mosque, where he had converted to Islam. He died in 1992.

Perhaps the best-known Nazi Muslim convert was Ludwig Ferdinand Clauß, an anthropologist, lecturer at the University of Berlin, bestselling author, director of the Institute for the Study of the Aryan Race, and "one of the most influential race theorists in Nazi Germany."[87] Like Herder, Clauß argued that non-German peoples may be worthy of praise, but could not be German. Clauß's main theory concerned what he called the "Race Soul" as expressed in his 1926 book *Rasse und Seele* (Race and Soul), which was published in eighteen editions between 1926 and 1943. Clauß argued that a key component and determining factor in shaping the Race Soul of a people is the terrain in which they live. Searching for the Race Soul, Clauß traveled to the Middle East and converted to Islam, living among the Beni-Sachr tribe in Jordan, where he was known as "Muhamad al-Feri, Sheikh of the German Bedouins." The Bedouin, Clauß believed, were very close to the Nordic peoples of old. For Clauß, "the Nordic heroes as well as the Bedouin warriors served as antipoles of the decadent and civilised Western world."[88]

Clauß's ideas would live on through his students like Sigrid Hunke, a bestselling author in Germany who joined the Nazi party in 1937, contributed to the SS journal *Germanien*, and whose books include *Allahs Sonne über dem Abendland. Unser arabisches Erbe* (Allah's Sun Over the Occident. Our Arab Heritage, 1960) and *Europas andere Religion* (Europe's Other Religion, 1969). A television feature based on "Allah's Sun Over the Occident" was shown in every Arab country. Hunke argued that while Judaism and Christianity are incompatible with Europe, the same cannot be said for the Arabs and Islam. Hunke called for a revival of Germanic paganism and "a spiritual elite to fight against the tyranny of the American way of life and to rejuvenate a decrepit Europe."[89] She believed the "path is clear for a European religion that acknowledges its debt to medieval Arabic scholars but is irreconcilably opposed to the Judeo-Christian tradition."[90] For Hunke, the Arab impact on Europe was "a step in Western history on its way to gain independence from Christianity." She glorified the rule of Frederick II, under which the German Reich stretched across Europe, a fact she attributed in part to "the relationship with Arab culture and goods."[91] In 1974, Hunke was named an honorary member of the Supreme Council for Islamic Affairs in Cairo, the highest Islamic council, becoming the only woman and only European given the honor. In 1988, President Hosni Mubarak bestowed on Hunke Egypt's highest award for science and art.

Given the poisonous racial ideology and horrific genocidal actions of Hitler and the Nazis, any association with them is a black mark. The willingness of Muslims to fight alongside the Nazis raises questions in the minds of many. It is important therefore to point out that in spite of the German attempts to win over Muslims, millions of Muslim soldiers, especially from the British Indian Army, fought alongside the Allies against the Germans. The British Indian Army raised a combined total of about 4 million soldiers to fight its two wars against Germany and its allies; of these, it is estimated that more than a third were Muslims. Many of the Muslims won awards from the British Empire, bestowed for gallantry against the enemy, including the Victoria Cross, Britain's highest military honor. Both Winston Churchill and General Bernard Montgomery, fighting against General Erwin Rommel in North Africa, acknowledged the capabilities of the Indian soldiers. In a letter to Franklin Roosevelt in 1942, Churchill wrote, "We must not on any account break with the Moslems, who represent a hundred million people, and the main army elements on which we must rely for the immediate fighting."[92] Regarding his victory in the North Africa campaign in 1943, Montgomery remarked, "I sent the First Army my best . . . 7th Armoured and 4th Indian."[93]

In concluding the discussion of the German soft spot for Islam, let us mention some contemporary names. In the late 1980s, when I was commissioner in charge of the Sibi division in Sibi, Pakistan, I welcomed Annemarie Schimmel to my home for lunch. Nothing about the speaker was ordinary, and neither was what she told me. "I am here to search for a final resting place for myself among the Sufis of the Sindh," she murmured softly, a faraway look in her eyes, as if she was already viewing a potential cemetery for herself. Schimmel, who was encouraged to study the Muslim mystic Rumi by her Nazi professor in 1939 in Germany, served as the first woman and first non-Muslim to teach at the University of Ankara in the 1950s before going on to teach at Harvard University. She was widely revered in Pakistan, particularly for her studies of Allama Iqbal, the national poet of Pakistan, and spoke Urdu, Arabic, Turkish, Farsi, and Punjabi. With her numerous books, articles, and lectures on Islam, Schimmel, who passed away in 2003, is renowned as one of Germany's most prolific and loved scholars of the subject.

Perhaps few today embody the soft spot theory more than German chancellor Angela Merkel. The spirit of Emperor Frederick II, which slumbers deep in the German psyche, was awakened in Merkel by a young Palestinian girl seeking asylum who pleaded with the Chancellor on television and began to cry, and she has been transformed into a full-fledged warrior ready to do battle for humanity, peace, and understanding. In 2015 Merkel made the controversial decision to admit around a million asylum seekers and almost single-handedly helped to change the mood toward refugees. Stating "Islam belongs to Germany," the typically cautious and subdued Merkel participated in an anti-Pegida rally organized by Muslims in Berlin in January 2015 and joined Muslims at an official iftar dinner in Berlin held by the government to break the fast in the month of Ramadan. Muslim asylum seekers were naming their children "Angela Merkel," and those stranded in Hungary chanted "Germany, Germany, Germany."

## THE EMERGING SOFT SPOT FOR JUDAISM

Had the Jewish minority controlled territory in their original homeland and possessed both arms to defend itself and wealth to be able to live comfortably and with dignity, then surely relations with the Germans, with their emphasis on the Volk, would have been different. The Jews would have then been another flower, to use Herder's metaphor, in the garden of the world's peoples. And this is precisely what happened after the creation of Israel in 1948: The Jews now had territory, powerful armies, and commercial and economic wealth. Their status demanded respect. This, added to the heavy weight of guilt that the Germans felt for the Holocaust, ensured the changed attitude of Germans toward the Jewish community, both in Germany and in the Middle East.

West Germany provided considerable aid and construction resources after the war, paying billions of deutsche marks to Israel to build the nation, including quadrupling the state's electricity-generating capacity, constructing a new railroad, improving telephone and telegraph systems, and expanding the port of Haifa. It also paid millions of deutsche marks in reparations to the Conference on Jewish Material Claims against Germany for the Holocaust.[94] In 1960 German chancellor Konrad Adenauer and Israeli prime minister David Ben-Gurion held their historic first meeting, and full diplomatic relations between the two nations were established in 1965. On a visit to Israel in May 1966, Adenauer declared, "The Israeli Volk has a long past, and it is almost a miracle that they are now called again as a Volk to raise their voices in the circle of Völker. . . . It is a stroke of fate that the Israeli Volk could rise anew so strong and so powerful, as the visitor to your country sees with amazement and admiration."

The Germans constructed The Memorial to the Murdered Jews of Europe, a striking memorial to the Holocaust, in the heart of Berlin adjacent to the Brandenburg Gate as another act of *Vergangenheitsbewältigung*, or struggle to overcome negative things in the past. The memorial was inaugurated in 2005 and is built in the form of large, solid blocks of concrete without decoration. It symbolizes with sobriety the enormity of what was done to the Jews and the German expression of contrition.

Speaking in the Knesset on the sixtieth anniversary of the founding of Israel in 2008, Chancellor Merkel declared, "The Shoah fills us Germans with shame. I bow my head before the victims. I bow before the survivors and before all those who helped them so they could survive. . . . For me as German chancellor, therefore, Israel's security will never be open to negotiation." At the end of her speech, Merkel firmly indicated that Germany views Israel as an equal: "Our relations are special, indeed unique, marked by enduring responsibility for the past, shared values, mutual trust, abiding solidarity for one another, and shared confidence."

The same year, the two countries held their first annual joint cabinet meeting in Jerusalem. It was the first time Germany had held such a meeting with a non-European partner. During the meeting, the countries signed a bilateral agreement for closer military, cultural, political, and economic cooperation. In 2016 Israeli prime minister Benjamin Netanyahu lauded the relationship between the countries as a "unique partnership." The Germans were finally seeing Jewish people as another tribe worthy of respect, fulfilling all the requirements demanded by German primordial tribal identity. This, of course, does not mean that anti-Semitism has evaporated in Germany. There is still evidence of anti-Semitism—but because of the small number of Jews in Germany and the proactive policies of the government to promote relations with the Jewish community, it is largely contained.

With the current migration crisis, we are seeing in Germany a dramatic reversal of relationships. The Germans, having first responded to the waves of Muslim refugees with commendable hospitality, began to show signs of compassion fatigue. While there were some cases that confirmed the soft spot for Muslims still existed, it was overwhelmed by a flood of reports from across the land of refugee centers being attacked and the rapid emergence of far-right parties focused entirely on the issue of refugees, which they conflated with a hatred of Islam. From almost nowhere figures like Frauke Petry, dubbed "Adolfina" for espousing brutally extreme measures such as shooting refugees at the borders, emerged to lead the Alternative for Germany party (see chapter 9).

The battered and beleaguered image of Muslims in Germany and the continuing chaos in the Middle East and North Africa contrasted sharply with the German celebration of Muslims in the past—of the Arabs who were seen as honorable in preserving their ancient traditions or the Turks who represented a powerful and vast empire and caused a cultural craze in Vienna and Berlin. Europeans were now seeing a different kind of Muslim, one that for them elicited little but negative emotions. Just as the wheel had turned in favor of the Jewish community with the creation of Israel, it was turning in the opposite direction for the Muslim community as the perception took hold that Muslims were in Europe in overwhelming numbers and threatened primordial identity. The implacable laws of Germanic primordial tribal identity explain the elevation of the Jewish community just as surely as they do the plunging fortunes of the Muslims.

## Jewish Voices from the Field

The fieldwork for this project took place in an atmosphere of high tension between Jews and Muslims in Europe. Yet for large parts of a thousand years Muslims and Jews were able to coexist in Europe with a remarkable degree of mutual acceptance. It is a strange fact of history that we found few in either community who knew about these periods of coexistence and the extent of the interaction.

The roots of the current difficult relationship between Jews and Muslims lie in recent European history—in the intolerable and inexorable rise of anti-Semitism and the desire of Jews to have their own homeland in the Middle East. This movement for a Jewish homeland, which became known as Zionism, was led by Theodor Herzl, an Austrian Jew and journalist who covered the Dreyfus affair in Paris and wrote, "I recognize the emptiness and futility of trying to 'combat' anti-Semitism."[95] He even established contact with leading anti-Semites like Édouard Drumont, who founded the Antisemitic League of France in 1889. In other words, Zionism took as a starting point the tenacity and permanence of European, and particularly

Germanic, primordial and predator identity, with Herzl describing Germany and Austria as the place where anti-Semitism originated.

The ideology of Herzl and the Zionists came out of the ethnic nationalist zeitgeist of the nineteenth century, the work of advocates of Germanic primordial identity like Herder, and concepts such as Volk and Heimat. Even before Herzl, Austrian Jewish thinkers like Nathan Birnbaum, who coined the term Zionism, were arguing for the creation of a Jewish "Heimat" in Palestine.[96] Herzl, who described Palestine as "our unforgettable historical Heimat," declared at the beginning of his landmark 1896 pamphlet *Der Judenstaat* (The Jewish state), "We are a Volk, One Volk!"[97] Herzl and the advocates of Zionism "sought to create and transmit the new *völkisch* nationalist ideology to the fragmented and scattered European Jews," and the contention that the Jews constituted a Volk "stirred the Jewish intellectuals of both Eastern and Western Europe."[98]

In the aftermath of the Holocaust, the dream of the Jewish Heimat recreated on the original soil of the Volk became a reality with the founding of the State of Israel in 1948. The concept of the Jewish Heimat and Volk by definition left no room for the local Arab population, and the contradiction has never been resolved. The precedent of the Sephardic experience of coexistence with Muslims in Andalusia and the Ottoman Empire as a logical model to be remembered and emulated was brushed aside, particularly by the Ashkenazi, the name given to the Jews settled in Northern and Eastern Europe, who had experienced the full and violent brunt of European predator identity. The Holocaust and Zionism, which had their genesis far from the world of Andalusia, would nonetheless lead to a reinterpretation of Andalusia and the place of Jews in it.

There are two distinct perspectives of relations between Jews and Muslims—one from the perspective of the Sephardim and the other the Ashkenazi. To the former, the best possible relations have existed in the past between the faiths, and both the Andalusian and the Ottoman eras have produced, for certain periods, a golden age; to the latter, Muslim rule historically was only marginally better than that of the Christians. Over time, the Ashkenazi view has tended to prevail in the Jewish community. For decades, as a consequence, the idea of a Jewish-Muslim conflict has dominated the perception of relations between Jews and Muslims, and the older history of cooperation and coexistence has gotten short shrift—to the detriment of both peoples. The central problem between Jews and Muslims in contemporary times has been their overwhelming ignorance of each other.

During the course of our fieldwork we were privileged to interview some of the most sagacious Jewish voices whose wisdom needs to be shared and circulated. These are esteemed figures who have spent their lives in their various fields thinking about the issues discussed here, including the relationship of Jews to European identity and the relationship between Jews and Muslims. From England at one end of Europe to Bosnia at the other, the scholars, rabbis, and community leaders threw light on European history, culture, and society from which we, seeking ways to build bridges, may benefit.

## A German-Jewish Historian on the Golden Age

The work of Michael Brenner, a professor of history at Ludwig Maximilian University of Munich and the American University in Washington, D.C., is a good place to begin our discussion of the modern Jewish memory of life under Muslim rule in Andalusia. In 2010 Brenner published the authoritative and comprehensive *A Short History of the Jews*. Writing of the Sephardim in the Iberian Peninsula, Brenner acknowledges that, "A major part of the epoch that later observers would call the Iberian 'Golden Age' took place under Muslim rule in 'al-Andalus.'"[99] But Brenner's section title describing that period comes with a question mark: "A 'Golden Age'?" The time of harmony and prosperity, he argues, came to an end with the fall of the Umayyad dynasty. Brenner's interpretation echoes the widely accepted narrative: civil war and chaos ensued, resulting in the destruction of Madinat al-Zahra and intolerance shown to Jews and Christians including acts such as the expulsion from Cordoba of the great Jewish philosopher Maimonides (see chapter 3). The Umayyads were followed by "more radical Muslim rulers," the Almoravids and then the Almohads. However, Brenner's use of the term *radical*, commonly applied to Muslim "extremists" and "terrorists" in our contemporary times, is sociologically meaningless in explaining tribal societies arriving from North Africa, who practiced what I refer to as tribal Islam. Though their first targets were Muslims who they believed had become "decadent" and "corrupt" through their emphasis on learning and reaching out to other faiths, convivencia survived in many of the *taifas*, or smaller principalities, long after the Almohads, in turn, collapsed.

In an interview with me, Brenner gave evidence of Muslim radicalism by citing the fate of Maimonides. I pointed out that Maimonides was not the only victim of a changed social environment and gave the example of Averroes. Both philosophers had lived in a time when the boundaries of their religious identities were blurred: Maimonides was said to have converted to Islam and Averroes was accused of having Jewish ancestry. That

Maimonides found refuge in Fez and then employment in the court of the most renowned Muslim ruler of his time, Sultan Saladin in Cairo, indicates that his fleeing Cordoba had less to do with Islam than the environment the new rulers had created.

It is precisely because they look back at Andalusia as a Golden Age that so many Jewish intellectuals contemplate it with wistful affection, even referring to Islam with reverence as does Heine, the preeminent Ashkenazi writer in nineteenth-century Germany. Heine, who set his plays in Andalusia, addressed the Prophet of Islam in a letter to a Jewish friend: "you, great Prophet of Mecca, are the greatest Poet and your Qur'an . . . will not easily escape my memory."[100] Many European synagogues, reflecting the nostalgia for Andalusia, mostly found in Germanic societies such as the nineteenth-century Leopoldstädter Tempel in Vienna, were built in the "Moorish style" and evoked the Andalusian Golden Age.

Although Brenner discusses the Jewish community in the Ottoman Empire and Thessaloniki, the largest ethnic group in the city, there is no mention of what the Jewish museum there called a "golden era." Having visited the museum during fieldwork and seen the evidence, we can vouch for that title and the impressive prosperity and success of the Jewish community in that period. Thessaloniki, the museum pointed out, was described as the "Mother of Israel" by a Jewish poet. The city's Jews clothed all Ottoman soldiers in the empire, and it was a "major center of theological studies, attracting students from around the world, and producing excellent rabbis, poets, and doctors, renowned throughout Europe." Jews in the Ottoman lands were owners of large business empires; pashas, or officers of high rank; governors of districts; high-ranking diplomats; and physicians to the most powerful Ottoman sultans like Suleyman the Magnificent—around 1600, for example, there were forty-one Jewish physicians at the sultan's court and only twenty-one Muslim physicians. Jews even ascended to the rank of vizier of the Ottoman Empire, as in the case of Jacopo of Gaeta, also known by his Muslim name Hekim Yakub, who served under Mehmed II, the conqueror of Istanbul, and also held the office of Ottoman minister of finance and attained the Ottoman army's highest military rank.[101]

Also missing from Brenner's account is the story of the impressive interfaith harmony that prevailed in the Balkans (see the interview with Ambassador Jakob Finci, the head of the Jewish community of Bosnia and Herzegovina, below). Examples of pluralism in the empire include an account from a seventeenth-century rabbi and historian in Egypt, who noted that after conquering Istanbul, Mehmed II "reserved three seats in his *divan* (cabinet chamber)—one for the *mufti* of Istanbul . . . one for the

Greek Orthodox Patriarch; and one for the rabbi of the Jews." The sultan made sure that the chair of the chief rabbi, Moses Capsali, who had been the leader of the Jewish community under Byzantine rule, was put "next to that of the *mufti*, and [the sultan] loved him as his own soul."[102]

Brenner's study gives us an idea of the extent of anti-Semitism that existed across Europe and fed into the sense of desperation in the community. Looming over Brenner's study are the vast horrors of the Nazi period. His powerful chapter 19 is called "From Everywhere to Auschwitz: Annihilation." The story is also one of triumph as the community thrives in the United States and is able to contribute to American culture on every level. But it is Andalusia and cities like Thessaloniki under the Ottomans that calls for further research. Perhaps Brenner could pick up the challenge and revisit the subject in a new edition of his otherwise masterly study.

### *A British Jewish Anthropologist*

In London, we interviewed Jonathan Benthall, who for several decades was the director of the Royal Anthropological Institute in Britain and is now at University College London. Benthall discussed the history of Jews in Europe and the persistent anti-Semitism, saying that he believed for Jews "it's difficult to look back on any kind of golden age." "Christian anti-Semitism," observed Benthall, has its roots in theology and "goes back to the fourth Gospel, where the blame is put on the Jews for the crucifixion of Jesus Christ." The theme of anti-Semitism has continued in history, Benthall believed, and "it wasn't only the Nazis but also the Russians in the nineteenth century who caused these people to emigrate to Palestine and the United States and elsewhere."

Benthall offered a sophisticated assessment of modern Jewish identity, which he saw as intrinsically linked to the State of Israel and defined it in terms strikingly reminiscent of Herder. "The Jewish identity," Benthall said, is "like a tripod, you have the Jewish race, the Jewish religion, and the Jewish land." Jews are the only ethnicity, he believed, that also represents a world religion to have such a situation where these three components together constitute identity. Benthall speculated that the Sikhs in South Asia could have been somewhat similar: "If the Sikhs had managed to get their own Sikhistan at the time of partition, you would have had the ethnic tradition with the turbans and the knives and so on, the religion, and their own land, but it's probably a good thing they didn't get it."

"The problem of Israel looms over Muslim and Jewish relations inevitably," said Benthall. Because Benthall has studied Muslim charities, including the needs of orphans and the elderly, he believes that "if people looked at social problems practically . . . then they can come from different disciplines and find how much they agree, how much they have in common."

### A Former Zionist Sociologist

In Dublin, we met with Professor Ronit Lentin of Trinity College in her office. Lentin, a sociologist, has published on Israel and Palestine, the Holocaust, migration in Ireland, race, gender and violence, and the state. Lentin was born to Romanian Jewish parents in 1944 in Haifa, then part of British Palestine, and she became a citizen of Israel upon its creation in 1948. She grew up "as a Jew and Zionist until I realized that Zionism is not the right angle." Lentin wrote that growing up in Israel, she and other "Ashkenazi middle-class Israeli Jews" were "taught to love 'the land' with desperate passion, 'the land' which we were told to 'conquer with our feet' through endless youth movement and family hikes." For her and other Ashkenazim, she noted, Arabs were "shadows": "I remember using words such as *Khirbeh* (ruin) to express contempt for the remains of Palestinian villages which we did, nevertheless, lovingly consider an integral part of 'our' Israel, sparing not a thought for the dispossessed Palestinians."[103] This awareness led Lentin to renounce Zionism and depart Israel, and she has lived in Ireland since 1969.

For Lentin, anti-Semitism is not the concern that it once was in Europe, having been replaced by discrimination "against non-white immigrants and Muslim people." "I don't share this prophecy of doom that another Holocaust is around the corner," she said, "because this is precisely the narrative that Israel is trying to foster. If anything it's constructing or creating or executing communal violence within Israel." She believed that "Jews are acting in the same racist manner as those who exterminated or massacred or fought against the old minority."

In analyzing the causes of the hatred of Jews in European history, Lentin said there was "a very strong church element" in anti-Semitism. Lentin related an experience she had when she arrived in Ireland:

When I came here I was very young and I was meeting someone, and a young girl, younger than me, came to me and asked, "Why did you kill my Lord?" I was a bit stunned and I didn't know how to answer it, because I certainly wasn't there when her Lord was killed. But it's very much a Christian-Catholic notion that the Jews are Christ killers, a people apart.

There is also the "economic element" to anti-Semitism, she believed, explaining that Jewish immigrants tend to work hard and do well, which arouses the anger of the local community.

Lentin argued that there were striking similarities in the way Jews have been historically seen in Europe and Muslims today. Jews "are seen as being everywhere, invisible, no loyalty, can't trust them, don't really become one of us yet compete with us for jobs and such. There is some sort of notion of a conspiracy, that they want to take over the world." "We know now," Lentin said, that there are "these kind of notions of Muslim conspiracy, to turn our states into shariah states and so on. So the discourse used against Muslims is very similar and an equally racist discourse."

### A Jewish Interfaith Pioneer in Britain

In Cambridge, we met Edward Kessler of the University of Cambridge, whom *The Times Higher Education Supplement* described in 2007 as "probably the most prolific interfaith figure in British academia." Kessler is the founder and director of the Woolf Institute, which studies relations between Jews, Christians, and Muslims. In 2006 he founded, along with Amineh Hoti, the Centre for the Study of Muslim-Jewish Relations at the Woolf Institute, which has had a significant impact on relations between Jews and Muslims. Kessler described Judaism and Islam as "incredibly close and intimate religions."

"Muslims are seen as an 'other,'" Kessler said. "Jews understand this because we've been seen as an 'other' for a very long time, and remain so." Addressing the problem of intolerance toward minorities, Kessler recounted, "At football matches as a child I certainly came across a lot of anti-Semitism taunting." For Jews and Muslims to move forward, Kessler believed it was crucial to foster a healthy interfaith dialogue: "You don't start with a discussion of Israel-Palestine, for example. You start with the areas you have in common. You build up understanding. You build up respect. And then you deal with the difficult issues."

### The Former Chief Rabbi of the United Kingdom

Rabbi Lord Jonathan Sacks, the former chief rabbi of the United Kingdom, headed one of the largest congregations in Europe and is widely acknowledged as one of the most prominent and respected religious leaders in the world today. Prince Charles once described him as "a light unto this

*Author and Rabbi Lord Jonathan Sacks embrace after an
event in Washington, D.C., in November 2015*

nation," and, in 2005, Sacks was knighted by Queen Elizabeth. Rabbi
Sacks has been a strong proponent of interfaith dialogue, especially between Jews and Muslims, even though his inclusive approach to faith has
caused controversy among some members of his own community because
of some of his ideas, such as those contained in the following lines from
his popular 2002 book, *The Dignity of Difference*, which reflect the convivencia ethos: "God has spoken to mankind in many languages, through
Judaism to the Jews, Christianity to Christians, Islam to Muslims . . . no
one creed has a monopoly of spiritual truth. In heaven there is truth, on
earth there are truths. God is greater than religion. He is only partially
comprehended by any faith."[104]

In an interview for this project, Sacks emphasized the importance of
Andalusia for Abrahamic interaction:

> This period of al-Andalus and benign Muslim rule was not only one
> of the most benign, convivencia, living together, but one of the most
> intellectually and spiritually creative in all of the Middle Ages.
> These extraordinary Muslim scholars who had recovered the classi-
> cal tradition, the neo-Aristotelians and Platonists—and they were
> the first people in Europe to do so—they lifted Europe out of the
> Dark Ages. They then had an enormous impact on figures like
> Moses Maimonides, the greatest rabbi of the Middle Ages whose,
> not only his philosophy, but almost every aspect of his work was
> influenced by and stimulated by Islam. His creation of this magnificent

legal code was inspired by shariah codes. His formulation of the principles of Jewish faith was inspired by the fact that Muslim thinkers had done this wonderful presentation of Islamic faith. So it spread from Islam to Judaism. It then spread to Christianity through Maimonides and influenced a figure like Aquinas.

Sacks compared the situation for the Jews in Andalusia with that in Northern Europe, explaining, "The Northern Europe experience is an extraordinary negative counterpoint because while Muslims, Christians, and Jews were living in this convivencia in Andalusia, Jews, and for that matter Muslims, were being massacred in Northern Europe by Crusaders." He said he feared we are heading in that direction once again and, comparing the two models, warned, "This may be where we are now, so we'd better quickly shift to the Andalusian model."

When asked to discuss the relationship between Islamophobia and anti-Semitism, Sacks saw similarities in the fear Muslims and Jews aroused in the majority population. In Christian Europe, "Jews were the odd people out. . . . I think that today Europe has become very secular and that's why people don't really understand Muslims because Muslims are for the most part deeply devout and not at all secular. And therefore it's this fear of the person not like me, and fear can very easily mutate into hatred."

Sacks recommended steps we can take to improve relations between Jews and Muslims: "I think what really improves relationships is when we as individuals take the trouble to get to know our Jewish or Muslim neighbors. To my mind friendship is the essence here. We don't always need to engage in high-level interfaith dialogue. Sometimes just being friends is even more powerful." Sacks recalled a major interfaith initiative in which I had participated: "When I occasionally used to make television programs I used to try and show the Muslim community at its best, and if you recall we did a program with you and the father of the murdered journalist Daniel Pearl, Judea Pearl, speaking together and then visiting a Muslim school and a Jewish school. This made a huge impact on the British public."

Sacks felt that Jews and Muslims must have empathy for each other and recognize their own suffering in the other: "Even in modern times Jews are haunted by the Holocaust and many, many terrible events. But I think we have to think also more recently of massacres of Muslims in Srebrenica and so on. So I think just looking at our own tears must make us realize that the other side has had those tears."

*Author and Amineh with the former chief rabbi of
Denmark, Bent Melchior, in Copenhagen*

## The Former Chief Rabbi of Denmark

Like Rabbi Sacks, Rabbi Bent Melchior, the former chief rabbi of Denmark, is a highly respected European moral leader. Melchior, who invited us to his apartment in Copenhagen to interview him, is a pioneer in interfaith relations going back decades in Denmark. He invited a Christian leader to speak in a synagogue in 1972 and more recently co-authored a book with a Danish-Palestinian Muslim member of Parliament. For decades Melchior has publicly supported many causes promoting human rights around the world and was a forceful voice condemning the controversial Danish government proposal, which became law, to confiscate the valuables of refugees arriving in Denmark, comparing it with tactics used by the Nazis to persecute minorities.

Melchior emphasized that he has been fighting hatred and intolerance such as Islamophobia for years and trying to bring different peoples closer together: "For many years I think I was more or less the only speaker who went around talking about the subject of tolerance in present-day Denmark, and trying to tell these people that they were afraid of something that doesn't exist." One of Melchior's sons, Michael Melchior, in addition to holding the title of chief rabbi of Norway, was deputy foreign minister of Israel and works to improve relations between Jews and Muslims.

The Jewish community, said Melchior, had been in Denmark for more than three centuries and was patronized by the monarchy. The close relationship between the monarchy and the Jewish community meant that when the Nazis invaded and occupied Denmark, the fate of the Jews was different from that in other countries. Melchior's father was the chief rabbi during the Nazi period, when the royal family of Denmark opposed the Nazi policy toward the Jews and protected them. He showed us a letter, written by the Danish king in 1942, expressing his solidarity with the Jewish community after an attempted firebombing of a synagogue.

While the Jews were able to remain safe for a while, there reached a point when the Nazis decided to act. Melchior recounted the story of how he, at the age of fourteen, and his family escaped the Nazis after being warned by a German soldier:

> We were staying with a priest who my father had met once. So he could place one here and one there, but he said, "You are all staying with us." We stayed with him and the kitchen was made a kosher kitchen, and only served things we could eat, and people were marvelous, the young people went out and started organizing boats to take the Jews from Denmark to Sweden, which was safe.

The story takes a dramatic turn as the group puts out to sea and almost immediately lands back in Nazi-controlled Denmark after the fisherman got lost. Miraculously, Melchior's group arrived at their destination:

> There was a little boy there who was playing and was seeing our little boat from afar, and his father was also a fisherman, and he went in to get his father, and his father and a colleague came out and took us inland, and I'm still in contact with this little boy, who by now is seventy-seven. I visit him and he lives in the same house where we entered in October 1943.

Melchior summed up the story by talking about the integration of the Jews in Denmark:

> Not only were we integrated, but the Danish Jews have contributed to Danish culture, to Danish business, to Danish political life. Some of the biggest names of Denmark in the various fields were Jews. The name of Niels Bohr, one of the fathers of the atom bomb. Victor Borge was an old Danish Jew. . . . And some of the biggest architects, the first head of the Institution of the Ombudsman was a Jew, a leader in Danish literature was a Jew. You go into any field you find Jews as quite important.

When asked what advice he had for Muslim immigrants in Denmark, Melchior gave tips based on a lifetime's experience:

Number one is to learn the language. We speak Danish better than most Danes, and my father was known as the best-speaking Dane of his time. . . . Number two you have to accept that the law of the country is law. . . . And then you have to understand that you are a minority. A minority in a democratic country has rights, but you have to respect that there is a majority. There are places where the Muslims resist Christmas trees being put up, but the majority has a right there too. There are kindergartens where they insist that all meat should be halal meat. Now it should be halal meat for the Muslims, okay, but you have to accept that the meat for the other children can be other things. I am a minority and I have to respect the majority.

Finally, Melchior spoke about the challenges and inevitability of stereotyping by the majority:

We have to understand that if one Jew is committing a crime, people will say "Aha! That is how the Jews are." That is what they are saying about the Muslims. If a Muslim is a criminal, they would say "Aha! That is how the Muslims are. Muslims are all terrorists." I have learned that from my childhood, we don't say when a member of the Danish Lutheran Church commits a crime, we don't say every Lutheran is. . . . But this is the fate of every minority, justified or not.

### The Senior Rabbi of Munich

While in Munich, we met Rabbi Steven Langnas, the most prominent rabbi in Munich. Originally from the United States, Rabbi Langnas describes himself as a "proud American." He completed his rabbinical training at Yeshiva University in New York before moving to Germany, the land of his ancestry. Langnas gave us a tour of the main synagogue in Munich, which was rebuilt in 2006 after being destroyed under the Nazis in 1938. He told us he was extremely concerned about the current high levels of anti-Semitism in Europe. "In my life, I have never seen it as open, as virulent, as hateful as it is right now. As a rabbi, as a Jew, as a human being I am shocked, more than a little worried to be honest," Langnas stated. "The moment that this open violent hatred is tolerated by the authorities, that's when to pack the bags."

Langnas discussed the various manifestations of anti-Semitism experienced by the Jewish community today. First, there is the threat from people who share Hitler's predator ideology, and he mentioned a foiled plot by neo-Nazis to blow up the synagogue in 2003. Then there is a kind of coded anti-Semitism, he said. "Often it's expressed as anti-Israel senti-ments." In addition to these manifestations of anti-Semitism there was the anti-Semitism coming from Muslims, which was causing fear in the Jewish community and anxiety in the rabbi.

Expressing his concern over the state of relations between Jews and Muslims, Langnas lamented, "There's hardly any contact. If positive con-tact can be established, I think we have a chance. . . . In Europe it works because we are both minorities." For instance, Langnas spoke of his warm relationship with the Penzberg-based imam Benjamin Idriz, who was prominent at the iftar in Munich in July 2014 that we attended with Langnas. He has found that "Idriz is very open to being accepted by and accepting Western culture, yet at the same time remaining a religious Muslim."

Ignorance, Langnas believed, was a central problem in relations be-tween the communities: "I feel that so many of our problems come from ignorance. . . . I think that if you can just explain things to people how they are, that's almost half the battle." In spite of the challenges the Jewish community is facing in Germany and Europe today, Langnas is commit-ted to building interfaith bridges. Langnas said that if Arab countries could officially recognize Israel, "the rest might fall into place." He also felt that Andalusia provided a model of how to proceed. He called con-vivencia there "a reality" and said, "I think that is a very worthy project to try to make that concept come alive again."

### A Visit to the Main Synagogue of Melilla

While the Jewish voices above represent an Ashkenazi perspective, our visit to Spain allowed us to hear from the Sephardic community of Europe. Our team visited the main synagogue of Melilla. Salamund Cohen, who looked after the synagogue, gave us a tour of the premises. Salamund, who had served in the Spanish military, was born in Melilla but is of Moroccan Jewish descent. "I am proud to be Jewish," he said, "and I'm proud to be Spanish."

Christians and Muslims each account for about 48 percent of the popu-lation in Melilla, Salamund told us. "The Jewish community is increasing little by little," he said, "This year eight children have been born." Speak-ing about the relationship between the Jewish and Muslim communities, he observed that "relations are very good. We have a Jewish school here, where we have Christian teachers. We even have had Muslim students in the Jewish school. Many people come with different religions." He contrasted this environment with France. "In France you cannot wear a yarmulke in the streets. It's different."

Salamund sees peace and harmony in Melilla.

> In Melilla we have one example of it. This being a small place, we are all living here together with perfect harmony and peace. . . . I have one Muslim neighbor, below me, I have a Christian neighbor and there is no problem, we all three live in the same block. . . . At the feast of the Muslims we exchange sweets and gifts. When it's Christmas, we give them sweets, we exchange gifts.

And it is the same, Salamund noted, for Jewish holidays.

### The Head of the Jewish Community of Bosnia and Herzegovina

At the main synagogue in Sarajevo, with its intricate designs in the interior, we interviewed Ambassador Jakob Finci, the president of the Jewish Community of Bosnia and Herzegovina and head of the charity organization La Benevolencija. One of Europe's most prominent Sephardic Jewish leaders, Finci, the former Bosnian ambassador to Switzerland and the former director of the national civil service, is descended from members of the community of Jews that fled Andalusia after the Reconquista and eventually settled in the Ottoman Empire. Finci explained that there were five synagogues in Sarajevo, but only the main one was now in use. The oldest synagogue in Sarajevo, he said, was built in 1581. The Jewish community in Bosnia and Herzegovina, Finci explained, consists of about a thousand people, most of whom live in Sarajevo.

When asked if convivencia existed in the Balkans as it did in Spain, Finci replied, "Absolutely, yes—especially in Bosnia. Bosnia was one of the real examples of how you can live together in the mixed society. And this was the best example of tolerance." Living together, he said, is a core part of Bosnian identity. Finci explained that the Jewish community felt secure in Bosnia and had good relations with the Muslim community, the Catholic Church, and the Serbian Orthodox Church. He explained Bosnian society and the position of the Jews by using the metaphor of bread, which reflected the convivencia ethos:

> If Bosnia-Herzegovina is the bread, then three main ethnic groups can be three main ingredients: water, flour, and yeast. Once you've

mixed these three, and you've made the bread, how can you distinguish the water from the yeast or flour from the water? Jews, we are like a little bit of salt between two fingers. And in these 450 years, we gave some taste to this country. But naturally this country easily can exist without Jews, but like a bread without salt, it will be tasteless. But hardly bread can exist without water, without yeast, and without flour.

On the question of anti-Semitism, Finci said with pride,

This country is almost free of anti-Semitism, which is strange because especially these days with the rise of anti-Semitism all over Europe, even in the United States, it's almost strange to have such a country which is free of anti-Semitism. We are very proud of this, and I'm always trying to explain that this is because in the past 450 years, we became very well-incorporated into the Bosnian society, but thank God we are not assimilated.

The Jewish community in Sarajevo, which arrived in 1565, still retains its culture and speaks the Ladino language, although Finci is one of the youngest members of the community who can still speak it. "Language, customs, culture, songs, everything is preserved," he claimed.

Ladino is combination of Old Spanish, it's a combination of Catalan and Castilian. It's a combination with some Portuguese words, and with some additions of the local language. . . . I sing ballads, songs. They are used mainly at home, and some of them became very popular and a lot of local people even don't know that some of the most popular Bosnian songs are originally Spanish Ladino songs.

Foods coming from Spain, Finci explained, are also part of local culture.

When the Ashkenazi Jews arrived in Sarajevo fleeing from kingdoms to the north, Finci recounted with a chuckle, the local Andalusian Jews reacted with some amusement, highlighting the distinction between the two communities:

Prayers have always been in Hebrew—that's a tradition. And when these Ashkenazi Jews arrived here the 100 percent Sephardic community was a little bit astonished to see the people who apparently are Jews but cannot speak the language because the Ashkenazi Jews spoke Yiddish. And if you cannot speak the language, how can you be Jewish? From that time we had a joke that these Ashkenazi, maybe they are Jews, maybe not, but we will accept them as the best friends of the Jews.

When an Ashkenazi man and a Sephardic woman were married for the first time in the early 1920s, Finci told us, a local Jewish newspaper announced it as a "mixed marriage."

Contemplating the synagogue, built in 1902 in the Ashkenazi style, Finci marveled: "What is atypical is while we are praying in an Ashkenazi synagogue, we are using the Sephardic creeds and part of the service is in Ladino." Before the Holocaust, Finci said, Sarajevo was a "small town" with 60,000 residents including 12,000 Jews, meaning one out of five residents was Jewish. The "huge Jewish center" in the region, Finci pointed out, was Thessaloniki. The position of the Jews of Sarajevo, like Thessaloniki, tragically changed during the Holocaust and the rise to power of Croatia's Nazi-backed Ustaše government, when, as Finci noted, "85 percent of our population disappeared, mainly to the Ustaše camps." Finci, who was born in an Italian concentration camp, explained that 50 percent of the population survived, including his parents.

Discussing the devastating war in the 1990s, Finci noted the remarkable role the Jews played as peacemakers caring for people who were suffering, irrespective of their backgrounds. He told us of the activities of his charity organization, La Benevolencija, which means "goodwill," and showed us a short documentary entitled *Survival in Sarajevo: Friendship in a Time of War.* Finci explained that the organization, which dates back to 1892 and endured long bans under the Nazis and Yugoslav socialists, "helped everyone on a strictly non-sectarian basis, providing food, shelter, and the medicines for the citizens of Sarajevo. According to our minister of health, Benevolencija provided almost 40 percent of all the medical needs for the citizens of Sarajevo."

Finci agreed that La Benevolencija reflected the ethos of convivencia in Andalusia. He observed that the activities of La Benevolencija were simply natural. It was the "traditional way we live together.... Living together, working together, helping each other." Despite the horrors of the war, Finci said that he was confident that the pluralistic Bosnian identity would survive. He gave the example of mixed marriages between ethnic groups and religions, which he admitted, although they are not happening as often as they did before the war, continue to occur: "They are something that can prove that this convivencia can exist even today.... So that's the reason why I'm so positive about our future."

*The Jewish Islamic Art Collector and Philanthropist*

In London, we met Nasser David Khalili, a leading European Jewish philanthropist and billionaire businessman who possesses what is said to be the finest collection of Islamic art in the world and is a passionate advocate for interfaith dialogue. Khalili, who is the founder and chairman of the Maimonides Interfaith Foundation, which works to improve relations between Jews, Christians, and Muslims, truly embodies the spirit of convivencia. A UNESCO goodwill ambassador who earned his Ph.D. at the University of London in Islamic art and culture, he is often referred to as a "cultural ambassador of Islam." Khalili was born in Isfahan, raised in Tehran, and has lived in London since 1978.

When asked to name his five greatest role models, Khalili replied, "Moses, Jesus, and Prophet Muhammad and my parents. Simple." Khalili explained the guiding philosophy of his life: "We are all family, one family, one big family." Speaking about his art collection, he said, "I didn't start collecting Islamic art as a Jew because it was Islamic. . . . I collected it because it was the most beautiful and the most diverse art I've ever seen." He described his collection of 500 Qurans as "probably the largest group of holy Qurans that exist anywhere in any museum in the world." However, as he emphasized regarding his "ownership" of items in his collection, "I always believe that every one of us is a temporary custodian of what we own. The real owner of everything is Almighty. We are a guest for sixty years, seventy years, eighty years." Khalili explained how the Quran reflects our deep spiritual connection to God. When someone works on the Quran, Khalili explained, they must be spiritually clean and pure at every step along the way. Completing a Quran took a great deal of time, "because they were writing the word of Almighty. And every single time the calligrapher finished a page . . . he had to go, to wash his hands, do his *namaz*, prayers, and come back and start writing, because he wanted to be 100 percent pure—mentally, physically, and spiritually. . . . What other religion can have a message like this?"

Khalili related one instance in which Muslim dignitaries asked him how he could be working so hard "promoting our culture worldwide and giving us a name that we deserve, and at the end of the day, you are not even one of us. You are Jewish." Khalili replied, "Correction, I am one of you, you are my cousin. Consider what I have done as a gift from one member of the family to another." "The contribution of Islam worldwide, in every field of life, is immense. . . . The West is not ignorant, but oblivious sometimes to this great heritage." "Just to give you an incredible example," he explained, "we have a thirteenth-century globe. . . . There is a star on that globe . . . with a name, and detail, which Galileo claimed to have discovered in the fifteenth century. It was already discovered 250 years earlier by the Islamic scientists."

"Why are we," he asked, "morning and noon and night, through press, through TV, claiming how much is wrong with Islam? My message to the world is, for the sake of sanity: Talk about how much is right with Islam." "Rather than always to go back to talk about the differences," Khalili advised, "talk about what unites people." Khalili summed up his philosophy thus: "The question of the three religions is very simple. There is only one Creator, one God, three names, and we are all his creation. Simple. Simple. The message is simple: every one of us is his creation. There are not three gods, there is only one God."

## *The Head of the Jewish Community in Southeast France*

While visiting southern France, we met another important European Jewish community, the Jews with an Algerian background who immigrated en masse to France when Algeria achieved independence in 1962. Amid terrorist strikes in recent years on Jewish schools and supermarkets, French Jews have grown increasingly concerned for their safety, and there are reports of Jews leaving France in large numbers.

At the Marseille city hall, in the office of Salah Bariki, who handles minority affairs as part of the mayor's cabinet, we met Clement Yana, the president of the Jewish Association of PACA (Provence-Alpes-Côte d'Azur), France's southeast region. Joining them was Aude Eisinger, head of the mayor's cabinet.

There was a "correlation" between rising Islamophobia and rising anti-Semitism in France, Yana believed, which he linked to a general "crisis in European society." "In every period of time in European history," Yana said, "when there is a crisis, the first thing they do is blame those who have immigrated. So this can potentially explain the mounting feeling against Islam."

There was a "new anti-Semitism," Yana contended, emanating from the Muslim community, a counterpart to "Christian anti-Semitism," which has a long history in France. The situation is "manipulated by extremists from abroad, it is a grouping of forces." "The Middle Eastern conflict between Israelis and Palestinians," he explained, "has exacerbated the antagonism toward Jews. The Arab Muslims who think they are obliged to be in solidarity with the Palestinians and the Jews who think they are obliged to be in solidarity with the Israelis. And we find in France there is a conflict between those who support the Palestinians and those who support the Israelis."

When I asked Yana if rabbis and imams were attempting to bridge the gap between Jews and Muslims, he replied that "there is no relationship. There is more dialogue between Christians and Jews, and more dialogue between Christians and Muslims. But not between Jews and Muslims." In the past, Yana stated, "there was never a need for dialogue between Jews and Muslims, because there was a natural understanding" and a "natural coexistence" between the two communities, given their common North African origins. "It's political, this whole situation," he maintained, "not religious." "There needs to be a discourse between Jews and Muslims speaking to one another."

Yana believed that part of the problem was the inability of the French state to absorb Islam:

> I think the French identity is a multicultural identity, there is not just a Judeo-Christian history, that is clear. There is a French saying that France is the eldest daughter of the church. The daughter now has a new religion, Islam. . . . The real political problem is that each time we try to reintegrate this new religion into French identity, officials just say well, we are talking about laws from the beginning of the century, 1905, laïcité. There is a block.

The conversation turned to the topic of Jews becoming sufficiently concerned about anti-Semitism that they are moving away from France. Eisinger said, "Jews in France feel physically threatened by the majority of Muslims that live in France. I guess it's more of a feeling than a real fact. Many Jewish young people leave France for other places like Israel but also Canada, Montreal, or Miami." "Who knows how many will follow eventually." "It's a bit funny," Yana ruminated, "because they leave France for security reasons but then they go to places like Israel where we can say it's not quite stable."

### The Program Director of the Jewish Museum in Berlin

In many European cities there are Jewish museums that serve as important centers of memory and identity for the Jewish community. They capture the culture, traditions, and vitality over the centuries of the local Jews. They are important places of education where Jews and non-Jews alike, often schoolchildren, come to learn about the Jews and their history.

Inevitably the museums are also tragic reminders of Europe's legacy of anti-Semitism and where it led—the decimation of the Jewish community in so many of the cities where these museums exist. The glories of Jewish Cordoba on display in the Jewish museum in Cordoba are viewed in the context of the twenty Jews remaining in the city, and it is the same in Thessaloniki, where around 1,000 Jews remain after 95 percent of the Jewish population here was killed in the Holocaust. In Eastern European countries like Poland and Lithuania it is the same story, with museums telling us of the once thriving nature of the Jewish community, its great scholars and yeshiva schools, and its almost total extermination in the Holocaust. The ever-present anti-Semitism emanating from both the majority society and Muslims means also that the museums are often tense places with tight security.

In Berlin, we visited one of Europe's most prominent Jewish museums and interviewed its program director, Cilly Kugelmann. A native of Frankfurt, Kugelmann spent five years in Israel beginning in 1966 and has lived in Berlin since 2000, when she joined the Jewish Museum to help build its education program. Before joining the museum she worked in the field of immigrant integration, focusing particularly on the Muslim community. While the museum is named the Jewish Museum of Berlin, she explained, it is actually a federal museum designed to focus on the Jewish aspects of German history.

For Kugelmann, German identity today is "a broken identity," and "it is unclear what it is. It is a broken society. . . . You can be overweight and skinny, you can have a scarf, and a burqa, and a kippa, and you can live with a man and a woman. Nobody knows anymore what it means to be German." The lack of a German identity has created a space for the minorities, she believed. She showed us a photo she had taken in a supermarket that she said "is to me postwar Germany." It was of a young Turkish woman with a hijab in the colors of the German flag.

Examining the current state of Jewish-Muslim relations, Kugelmann argued that much of the tension comes from the Israel-Palestine conflict and "has nothing to do with Judaism, it has nothing to do with Islam, but it has a lot to do with the fact that a Jewish state was implemented in a region of Arab states, Arab-Muslim, and Arab-Christian states. Palestine has a very, very big Arab-Christian population, and it had nothing to do with that."

Israel, Kugelmann said, is a very emotional topic in the Jewish community. "Especially after the Holocaust," she explained, "it is an emotional identification with the state of Israel as a kind of a possible future home in the case of anti-Semitism. And so you cannot expect a realistic reading of what is happening there." Expounding on Israel, Kugelmann said that the timing of its founding made it very difficult for it to develop positive relations with the Muslim world:

> I think that maybe if a Jewish state had been founded 100 years earlier, problems may have been much less severe. The historical moment in which the Jewish state was founded was in a time of decolonization, especially in that area we are talking about. And then the creation of a Jewish state, also implementation actually of Western culture in the middle of a group of societies that were in a very different state of their development.

She noted that many Jews gain a sense of security just from the existence of the state of Israel: "A lot of Jews worldwide feel secure wherever they live—that's idiotic, it's a psychological phenomenon, they feel secure because the state exists. The state can do absolutely nothing if there would be anti-Semitic phasing in the United States, Israel can do nothing, nothing at all. I think Jews in the world realize the Israel project is a time-limited project and they are very fearful about that." Israel, she went on to say, is "a foreign, strange little state. . . . And sometimes I think that there's a fear in the Jewish population that this might be true. But nobody would say that." Kugelmann was gloomy about Israel's future: "To tell you the truth I don't see any hope for Israel. I'm afraid this country will disappear from the landscape in, I don't know, twenty or forty years, but I don't see it being there forever. I don't see a chance for this country."

To improve Jewish-Muslim relations, Kugelmann believed, people should talk about matters other than the Middle East because "relations between Muslims and Jews today are really contaminated by the Middle East conflict." One example Kugelmann gave of a successful collaborative project was the West-Eastern Divan Orchestra, conducted by Daniel Barenboim of the Berlin State Opera and inspired by and named after Goethe's collection of lyrical poems: "Barenboim established an orchestra with young musicians from the Middle East—Israelis, Palestinians, Jordanians, Lebanese. . . . And I think such projects are perfect."

### *The Director of the Jewish Museum of London*

In London, we met Abigail Morris, the chief executive of the Jewish Museum of London. Joining her were two young female museum officials, Joanne Rosenthal, the head of exhibitions, and Elizabeth Selby, the curator of social history and collections manager. When we visited the museum there was a prominent exhibition about the 50,000 British Jews who had fought for Britain in the First World War. The museum's displays convey the cultural richness and diversity of the Jewish community in Britain. Like Islamic immigration following the independence of former colonies, Jews also emigrated to the "mother country" from the colonies, and there are exhibitions on Indian, Iraqi, and Yemeni Jews who made a new life for themselves in the United Kingdom and became part of the country's centuries of Jewish history—indeed, one of the oldest items in the museum's collection is a *mikveh,* a Jewish ritual bath from thirteenth-century England.

Discussing Jewish identity in Britain, Morris said the "dominant voice is one of positive integration," that is to be "proud to be both" Jewish and British. British Jews, she said, say a prayer for the Queen and a "prayer for the royal family" at Saturday service, though the ultra-Orthodox do not, she noted. This identification as both Jewish and British, Morris explained, is a new phenomenon. In the past, Jews did not want to be seen as Jewish but as English. In the 1950s, Morris observed, the attitude was to "keep it hidden." Morris recounted that her mother cried once when Morris's brother told her he felt more Jewish than British. In the Reform synagogues Jews introduced an organ and a choir to be more English in their worship. These days, Morris said, Jews are much more assertive, which she sometimes still finds uncomfortable. Jews are more visible, and "people are less nervous about being publicly Jewish." She also believed that Britain's Orthodox community is growing. Yiddish, which had died out, is coming back strongly. The Labour Party in Hackney, Morris told us, distributed leaflets in Yiddish.

Morris herself experienced anti-Semitism at school. It was "terrible at Cambridge," she recalled. She got questions like "You're not English, are you?" Morris believed there was a "left-wing anti-Semitism" and that "anti-Semitism masks as anti-Zionism, especially on the left." Comparing anti-Semitism to Islamophobia, Morris said, "Jews have a better time than the Muslims." In terms of the interaction between Jews and Muslims in the United Kingdom, Morris noted that in the King David School in Birmingham, a Jewish school that receives some state funding, a majority of the students are Muslim. Nevertheless, Rosenthal said, there was a huge amount of "suspicion and mistrust" between Jews and Muslims. This, she believed, is "inherently ridiculous." She has a close Muslim friend and observed that Judaism and Islam are "identical" and "sister religions." But in society today, "Jews have a massive privilege that Muslims don't yet have."

While at the museum, we talked to an elderly man who worked there and complained, "There is still that undercurrent of anti-Semitism, not as much as it used to be." He cited his brother-in-law, who had witnessed fans of the Arsenal football club on a train "singing a song about 'pushing them all into the gas ovens.'" We also asked him whether he believed there had been a golden age in Andalusia for Jews, and he said that he did: "A Jew could live in Muslim Spain without any problem. . . . You could live your whole life and think it is the greatest thing, that's why the Jews call it the Golden Age. Because Jews could own land, become financiers, become advisers at the court of the kings and do any profession they liked. They became the prime minister. That was the Golden Age."

### A Visit to the Jewish Museum in Dublin

In Dublin, we visited the city's nondescript Jewish museum housed in a rather run-down area that had seen better days. Just opposite the door on the other side of the narrow street hung a large banner with an anti-Semitic message: Its authors did not want either Jews or a Jewish museum in the area and warned them to clear out. We were received by Howard Freeman, the museum's manager, and Carol Briscoe, the wife of Ben Briscoe, the former lord mayor of Dublin and a well-known Jewish politician. The museum is located in Dublin's Portobello neighborhood, which was once the center of Jewish life in the city and is housed in what once was a Lithuanian Orthodox synagogue.

Carol, who said she is not Jewish, explained that the neighborhood had been the home of immigrants from other religions for centuries, beginning with French Huguenots in the early seventeenth century, before the arrival of Jews and, more recently, the Muslims. Carol blamed "ignorance" for both anti-Semitism and Islamophobia. Howard added, "Irish people knew very little about any religion other than their own. Even when certain schools come here . . . they have never seen it. They have no knowledge of the Old Testament."

The comparative numbers of the Jewish and Muslim communities affect how the majority population sees them, Carol felt:

We never really had a Jewish problem here because we never really had the numbers to make it a problem. The most the Jewish community ever came to was 5,000. I don't know how many Muslims there are here now but about ten years ago there were 40,000. . . . What's going on around the world is also a problem because people don't know the good Muslims. And I think the majority of Muslims are good Muslims.

## Building Bridges between Jews and Muslims

The concurrent growth in anti-Semitism and Islamophobia was distressing to me, as I had been involved in initiatives that promoted Jewish-Muslim relations in Europe for decades. My education about Jewish history and society began in the United Kingdom in 1992 when I was appointed a commissioner for the Runnymede Trust study of anti-Semitism with other distinguished figures, such as senior Rabbi Baroness Julia Neuberger. We produced the Runnymede report, *A Very Light Sleeper: The Persistence and Dangers of Antisemitism*, in 1994.

As a member of the commission, and along with Rabbi Neuberger, I actively advocated another such commission to examine prejudice and hatred against Muslims. When the commission was formed—the first of its kind—I was asked to join it as commissioner. In 1997 the commission produced an influential report titled *Islamophobia: A Challenge for Us All*. The report selected and popularized the term Islamophobia to mean hatred or fear of things Islamic. Since then, the term has been used globally to describe prejudice against Muslims, especially with regard to the increasing immigration to Europe from the Muslim world.

In the wake of these commissions, I began to undertake other high-profile efforts to build bridges between the Jewish and Muslim communities. In 1999 I was invited to deliver a prestigious annual lecture at a major synagogue in London, accompanied by leaders of the Muslim community. It was our first visit to a Jewish temple. Because of its rarity, the event drew a great deal of media interest, and I have continued to work with many Jewish leaders on both sides of the Atlantic, particularly after 9/11. I have maintained that anti-Semitism and Islamophobia are two sides of the same coin and need to be challenged concurrently. I am fortunate that Amineh joined me in this endeavor after obtaining her Ph.D. at Cambridge in 2004 and has since emerged as an interfaith leader and made major contributions to the field.

### Jewish-Muslim Relations on the Ground in Europe Today

We noted considerable and serious challenges in the relationship between Jews and Muslims during our fieldwork. Incidents of anti-Semitic violence, such as street stabbings and attacks on schools, synagogues, and museums, are commonplace in Europe and are sometimes overshadowed by the sensationalist nature of the terrorist strikes, such as those targeting the kosher grocery store in Paris or the Jewish Museum in Brussels. Even in the United Kingdom, Jews were voicing their fears about anti-Semitism. Among them was Danny Cohen, the head of BBC Television, who in late 2014 said, "I've never felt so uncomfortable being a Jew in the U.K. as I've felt in the last twelve months. . . . I've never felt as I do now about anti-Semitism in Europe." In February 2017 the Community Security Trust, which monitors anti-Semitism in the United Kingdom, announced that anti-Semitic incidents the previous year were at their highest level since the trust began recording data in 1984. In November 2015, the chief rabbi of Brussels stated, "People understand there is no future for Jews in Europe." Following the Barcelona terrorist attack in August 2017, the chief rabbi of Barcelona declared, "Jews are not here permanently. . . . I tell my congregants: Don't think we're here for good. And I encourage them to buy property in Israel. This place is lost. . . . Europe is lost." Commentators were speaking of a Jewish exodus from Europe, with thousands of Jews leaving the continent.

As we traveled through Europe, it was apparent that the Jewish community felt itself under siege. An emphasis on security permeated the synagogues we visited, with visitors to the main synagogues of Berlin and Munich having to go through airport-style security. Yet in these difficult times, we also found many stories of positive and inspiring interactions between Jews and Muslims. In Bradford, Zulfiqar Karim, the senior vice president of the Bradford Council of Mosques, told us that in 2013 Bradford's only synagogue was about to close because the city's small Jewish community was unable to pay for its upkeep. Working with the Council of Mosques and local businesspeople, Karim successfully raised enough money to repair the synagogue and pay for its maintenance.

There was also the case of a synagogue that is actually part of the adjoining East London Mosque, one of the largest and most prominent mosques in Britain. Dilowar Khan, the executive director of the East London Mosque Trust, told us that the synagogue had been there since 1899, long before Muslims arrived. The area, Tower Hamlets, was a predominantly Jewish neighborhood in London with around eighty synagogues, he said, only four of which remain after most of London's Jewish community relocated to the suburbs. The Muslims moved to the site in 1975, and Khan noted, "We've been good neighbors since 1975, and we haven't had any problems being side-by-side, and worshipping our Lord." Today, Khan explained, the synagogue is not used so often, but he maintained that "we have a good relationship with them. We try to help them as much as possible."

We also found a new generation of Muslim activists working with inter-faith organizations who were passionate about and committed to improving relations between Muslims and Jews. Samir Akacha, the Muslim leader of the youth interfaith organization Coexister in France whom we met in chapter 4, told us that he became involved in Coexister "mainly because I never had a Jewish friend, and for me, this culture, this religion, is really close to mine, because I'm Muslim, and so I really wanted to discover the 'other.'" As a result of the experience, Samir said, "I discovered more about my religion. . . . If I discover more about the 'other' and I'm still hungry for knowledge and I'm becoming a better Muslim . . . then it could work for everyone."

Samia Hathroubi, another young French Muslim activist, whom we also met in chapter 4, characterized Jewish-Muslim relations in France as "very complicated, challenging." One reason, she believed, is that France is "completely blind to identities." This attitude served to erase the commonalities between Jews and Muslims because in public they were supposed to be only French. She gave the example of a Muslim student in school seated next to a Jewish student—their teacher will only see them as French and will not acknowledge their shared history. "We have a generation of people who don't even know and understand about their own history as Muslims and Jews and the long history of relations between Jews and Muslims." This is regrettable, Samia stated, because Jews and Muslims, especially in France, have so much in common, coming from a shared culture rooted in North Africa.

When considering the source of anti-Semitism among Muslims, Samia said, "Anti-Semitism is deeply rooted in French history. And in a way, the Muslims being anti-Semitic are just taking over this history of anti-Semitism." Samia traced the rise of anti-Semitism among French Muslims to the time when so many immigrants arrived a generation ago. When the communities first arrived they settled in the same neighborhoods and there were many commonalities related to their shared North African culture. Over time, however, the "Jews and the French" were soon leaving the neighborhoods that had previously been mixed while the Muslims were forced to stay behind in their impoverished banlieues. "Muslims were, and they are still, discriminated against in housing and in employment, while the Jews are not."

Another important element in Muslim anti-Semitism in France is the Israeli-Palestinian conflict. Samia criticized the situation in France where Jews are identified with Israelis and Muslims with Palestinians. She said that young Muslims in the banlieues "go on the Internet and think that what they are seeing, without any context, nothing, is just reality." Samia recommended that the Israeli-Palestinian conflict be incorporated into school curriculums; that way it will "help them to contextualize and have a history of this conflict."

Samia was critical of the leadership of both communities: "We have very terrible leaders among the Muslim and Jewish communities. . . . They have failed and they just played on this division." As an example, Samia mentioned the president of a prominent Jewish organization in France who had gone on the radio the day before "saying Marine Le Pen is just irreproachable, personally, and saying that the violence was coming from young Muslims. I think that those words . . . are damaging the Muslim and Jewish relationship." Meanwhile, she complained,

> you have a lot of Muslim leaders of the Salafi movement using a lot of verses from the Quran without any context, and saying "see in the verse it says you shouldn't take the lies from the Jewish and Christian community." . . . If you don't have any interpretation of what the verse of the Quran means and how it was sent to the Prophet, peace be upon him, those kids know nothing. They don't even speak Arabic.

Samia is currently associated with the Foundation for Ethnic Understanding, an organization based in New York that strives to bring Muslims and Jews closer so they may "work together on fighting against Islamophobia and against anti-Semitism."

I was introduced to another initiative in the summer of 2016. Aycan Demirel and Dervis Hizarci, both Germans of Turkish background working with the Kreuzberg Initiative against Anti-Semitism (KIgA), came to speak with me in my office in Washington, D.C., accompanied by Tad Stahnke of the United States Holocaust Memorial Museum. The KIgA, based in Berlin's famous Kreuzberg district, which has a large Turkish population, was founded just over a decade ago and describes itself as "one of the first German civil society initiatives to develop education-based methods for dealing with anti-Semitism in a multicultural German society." Hizarci told us that the KIgA, which is funded primarily by the German government, focuses on teaching and educating young Muslims in the hope that they will go back to their communities and schools and teach others.

Demirel, who came to Germany from Turkey twenty-five years ago, explained that he started KIgA with friends after observing rising anti-Semitism in the Muslim community. "Jews show a lot of empathy" and understand the situation of Muslims, and it makes sense to create a dialogue, Hizarci believed. The KIgA was first founded as an organization against anti-Semitism, but they now also deal with Islamophobia and radicalization. It has been their experience, Hizarci stated, that people who have a connection to mosques and religious communities do not participate in terrorist activity or attack people. The problem of anti-Semitism is not coming from the imams of Germany, he said, explaining that over the past twelve years he had attended between 400 and 500 Friday prayers without ever encountering anti-Semitism. He noted that while there are around 3,000 mosques or prayer rooms in Germany, a recent report from the Federal Office for the Protection of the Constitution, the German domestic security agency, put the numbers of "problematic" mosques at fewer than fifty, and the authorities were unsure of even those numbers.

In concluding this chapter, we emphasize that to challenge anti-Semitism and Islamophobia, frequent and public dialogue between the Muslim and Jewish communities is essential. In addition, reading and learning about each other furthers understanding and creates empathy. Academic courses on the Abrahamic faiths, such as the online course on Jewish-Muslim relations I teach with Edward Kessler, co-sponsored by the Woolf Institute at Cambridge, England, and the American University, need to be introduced in teaching institutions. Learning together has a profound effect on participants, and there are few thrills as exciting as seeing strangers from different faiths starting a course and, over the period of a few weeks, beginning to engage with one another and soften their initial positions regarding the other. Such dialogue can produce lasting and rich friendships. For example, when I was asked by *The Times Higher Educational Supplement* in 1995 to name the person who had the most impact on my academic life for their Past Masters series, I selected the scholar I called my guru, the Jewish anthropologist and philosopher Ernest Gellner.

Jews and Muslims have many lessons to learn in light of what European predator identity is capable of when it pursues tribal identity to its logical extreme. Jewish and Muslim leaders need to comprehend the central formula that defines their relationship in Europe: What is good for the Muslims is good for the Jews, and what is good for the Jews is good for the Muslims. In Europe, anti-Semitism is on the rise, and Islamophobia grows unchecked. The road of hatred, as history has taught us, is a slippery slope. If Muslims are the main victims today, it could be Jews next; today's Islamophobia is the harbinger of tomorrow's anti-Semitism.

Yet we must acknowledge that to most people the goal of friendship between Jews and Muslims is illusory. It is not an easy journey and not for the faint of heart. It requires both commitment and courage; boondoggle and buncombe will not do. Without building bridges, neither community can fully realize what it is morally required to do: to heal this fractured world in the spirit of the Jewish saying, *tikkun olam.*

# EIGHT

# Terrorism, Immigrants, ISIS, and Islamophobia: A Perfect Storm in Europe

"Fucker," "white man," "fuck you," "gay bastard," "racist twat." The young Muslim boys and girls expressed their anger and contempt in the colorful idiom and characteristic accents of northern England as they streamed out of school. The target of their youthful wrath was my American team parked by a mosque in Bradford as part of our fieldwork.

While Amineh and I were interviewing other people, three American members of my research team, who happened to be white and Christian, were visiting one of the city's major mosques. The team, filming for purposes of our documentary, was driven by a young local British-Pakistani woman who had volunteered to act as guide. As they parked outside the mosque, they found themselves very quickly surrounded by a large number of angry and unfriendly British-Pakistani students who were coming out of a nearby school as classes had just ended for the day. At first playful, the mood rapidly turned ugly. The proximity to the mosque was being seen as an act of provocation. Both the boys, many of whom wore black slacks and a variety of track-style sweatshirts, and the girls, all wearing hijabs, mostly in dark colors, and some dressed in full black abayas, began yelling abuse at the team. They hammered on the vehicle, hit it with force, and opened one of the doors. A member of the team had his hair yanked hard and was shoved and kicked.

The team felt threatened enough to beat a hasty retreat. Not learning from this episode, and with the intrepidity of the innocent, they then proceeded to another mosque. This time, a man with a beard came out screaming abuse and punched the vehicle with full force. There was no misreading the situation anymore, and the team returned to the hotel posthaste to report to me. They were in a state of distress and barely coherent. Even the veteran of my field projects, Frankie Martin, believed that the incident could have developed into a riot like others that had been reported recently in this part of England.

What happened in Bradford reflects the themes of this chapter and captures the current predicament of contemporary European Muslim society: angry and noisy young Muslims, unresolved issues concerning immigration, frequent violence and terrorism, often inspired by ISIS, the rise of the Far Right and its dangerous rhetoric of religious hatred, and rampant Islamophobia. To compound matters, leadership across the different communities is marked by pusillanimity that creates a sense that society is out of control. While each of these themes can be studied on its own, it is only by examining them together, as each one feeds into the other, that we are able to understand the complexity and gravity of the situation in Europe. It is the forming of a perfect storm.

## Terrorism, Immigrants, and Islamophobia

Through Bradford, along with a visit to a mosque in Melilla in southern Spain and one in Brussels in Belgium, with equally excitable results, we enter contemporary Muslim society in Europe. Although each case study is based in fieldwork and set in a different cultural and political context, each one also reflects the lingering impact of history, particularly that of European imperialism (also see chapter 4).

### Case Study 1—Bradford, England

The scene in Bradford that my team described to me was reminiscent of the *Lord of the Flies*, with the social order breaking down and students running amok. As I planned the next move, I did not miss the irony that while Muslims complain constantly about being projected in stereotypes as "terrorists" and "extremists," here they were using stereotypes of the "white man" as racist. To try to understand what had happened, I put myself in the shoes of the students. As they walked by the team's vehicle the students saw a local British-Pakistani woman in Western-style dress, not wearing a veil or hijab, at the wheel of a parked vehicle that was full of young white men, one of whom was outside filming. She was from a Pakistani family that was not part of the dominant Muslim community of Bradford, which was from Azad Kashmir. Their guide was therefore an ethnic outsider. We soon learned that the vehicle in the first instance was outside a mosque that had recently been "invaded" by members of the far-right organization Britain First, and the community felt tense and under siege.

In the meantime, I had contacted the lord mayor of Bradford, Khadim Hussain, a Pakistani from the Azad Kashmir community. He appreciated the gravity of the situation and offered to come round immediately and drive me personally to the same mosque so as to inquire what had happened. He arrived with a prominent Pukhtun member of the community, a man from the old Frontier Province of Pakistan who now had several sons working for the British police. Frankie was with me and able to recount what had occurred. At the mosque, the mayor expressed his concern, and the local junior official in charge, characteristically unaware of what had happened, immediately set about ringing the mosque administration. To drive home the point that what had happened was nothing more than an aberration, the mayor then took us to several other mosques where we were received with cordiality. Later at night, the young woman who had served as the team's guide appeared in the hotel with a female friend and insisted on talking to me. I came down from my room immediately, and we met in the lobby. She appeared in a state of panic. She said that she had a message for me from her father requesting that her name be removed from any association with the project. I suspect they feared backlash from the community. I said that I understood her predicament and would keep her name out of the film and book, a promise that has been honored.

During the drive about Bradford, we heard the background to the tension concerning the mosque. Several people, including the mayor, told us that members of Britain First—white, male, and muscular—had recently barged into the main prayer hall of the same mosque in heavy military boots. Violating the sanctity of the prayer ritual, they aggressively waved copies of the Bible in the faces of the startled Muslims. Later, in an interview for this project, the acting bishop of Bradford, Tom Butler, said that the Bible was not meant to be used as "a weapon" and that this was "outrageous." We also learned of the travails of the mayor himself when members of Britain First decided to force themselves into his house, pushing aside his daughter and demanding to see him. The mayor was not at home, but the incident created further anger and fear in the community. If the mayor's residence was not sacrosanct, what guarantee was there for ordinary Muslims to be safe in their homes? In addition to the bishop and the mayor, we interviewed Mohammed Rafiq Sehgal, the president of the Bradford Council of Mosques, who explained why Muslims were outraged at the behavior of Britain First: by walking into the prayer hall in boots while worshippers knelt in prayer, they had desecrated the act of worship.

The founder of Britain First, Jim Dowson, justified all these acts because, as he put it, the "war" between Islam and Britain had begun. In his interview with Harrison on camera, Dowson brushed aside these incidents, pointing out that Muslims had taken over parts of Britain and had imposed the shariah. Although of Ulster Scottish background, he declared he would rally to his English brethren and fight alongside them against the Muslim "invasion." The future, he said, was nothing but "war," a word he repeated several times, each time with an increasingly Churchillian ring to it.

Given this background, it is imperative to highlight the historical reasons that the Muslim community is in Bradford in the first place. The grandfathers of the students who attacked my team had been invited to come from Pakistan decades before to work in British factories. Britain colonized India and, after independence and the creation of Pakistan, these Muslims naturally saw an opportunity in the United Kingdom for a better livelihood in what was once the omphalos—the "navel," or center—of the British empire. Others were settled in Bradford as compensation when the Mangla Dam was being constructed on the Indus River in the 1960s, which would displace almost 300 villages and two towns consisting of more than 100,000 people in Azad Kashmir. We were told that three-quarters of Bradford's Muslim population traces its roots to Azad Kashmir, and many neighborhoods are almost exclusively populated by Azad Kashmiris. It is not surprising, therefore, that numerous prominent British Muslims in public life—including Lord Nazir Ahmed, the first Muslim in the House of Lords—are from Azad Kashmir. In fact, the majority of Pakistanis and Muslims in England itself are from Azad Kashmir.

It is this concentration of population in Bradford that allows families to speak Punjabi at home, intermarry, and even send their corpses to Pakistan for burial. Shops have signs in Urdu and the shalwar kameez, the traditional Pakistani dress, is frequently seen on the streets. Mostly of middle- or lower-middle-class background, the community is fiercely conservative and has cast itself as the champion of Islam in the United Kingdom. Muslim leaders from Bradford were at the forefront of the campaign in the 1990s to implement Ayatollah Khomeini's fatwa against Salman Rushdie for purported blasphemies in his 1988 novel, *The Satanic Verses*. The local community thus lives in a cultural and social cocoon that has created a strong distaste and antipathy in the majority population, who see it as "taking over" Britain. In the post-9/11 era, Bradford has been widely associated with terrorism. A number of British terrorists, some involved in the London Underground bombing, did indeed come from the Yorkshire area of England, which includes Bradford. There were Bradford Muslim girls who left to join ISIS in 2015.

### Case Study 2—Melilla, Spain

We faced an analogous situation in Melilla, the southern enclave of Spain on the North African coast and the site of our second case study. The local administration had arranged for us to visit the main mosque, but the chatter my team picked up indicated that there was some background tension regarding the Muslim community and the authorities. A local imam's son named Ali Aarrass, a bookseller who lived in the Molenbeek neighborhood of Brussels, was visiting his father in Melilla in December 2010 when he was picked up for "terrorist-related" activity and whisked off without trial to Morocco to be imprisoned and, it was asserted, tortured. There was no further news of him; it was as if he had disappeared from the face of the earth. But the local community would not forsake him; we saw flyers with his photograph plastered in the main entrance of the mosque.

Into this tense situation, we arrived escorted by a Muslim official appointed by the administration to represent the Muslim community. He was half-Turkish and half-Berber, had a Christian wife, and had spent a great deal of time in France, where he had acquired a certain French style in his speech and thinking. He was a well-meaning, well-read, and intelligent man, but his struggle with his own identity was not resolved. It explained his desperation to establish his secular credentials. He boasted to us that he drank alcohol and at meals would brandish his glass and pronounce loudly, "this is haram," "unlawful" in Islam, and then add, with a wink, "I'm in trouble." The irony that he was named after the Prophet of Islam did not escape me. He told us that there were no special problems with the Muslim community in Melilla. He analyzed the past through the lens of contemporary discussions about the war on terror, describing the Berbers who conquered Cordoba as "Salafis." With his language and appearance, bow tie and suit, he appeared to be disconnected from the Muslim community, the very community he had been appointed to represent.

If we conduct a similar exercise in putting ourselves in the shoes of the local community at the mosque, as we did for Bradford, it is clear what they saw when we arrived without notice: a group of Americans with cameras, perhaps snooping around for potential terrorists, and escorted by someone whom they saw as alien to their values and whom they did not acknowledge as their representative. That he was a Muslim did not help his cause with the disgruntled community, which saw him as too Westernized and too unsympathetic.

With our "Muslim" guide we sailed blindly into the crisis. As we entered the mosque, I was somewhat surprised not to see the imam laying out the red carpet for us as had happened on so many of our visits to mosques. Imagine my further surprise when Frankie came up to me alarmed and said that our Muslim guide was not being allowed to enter the mosque and was surrounded by an angry group. I turned to see that an increasingly heated exchange was taking place, voices rising and arms flailing. To make matters worse, more and more people were arriving, and we felt the angry shouting could easily escalate into physical blows. I ordered an immediate withdrawal to our vehicle and then a return to our hotel.

The news of the incident must have traveled swiftly through the community. Within twenty minutes of our ignominious retreat, as my team and I sat in the hotel lobby discussing what to do next, a high-powered delegation from the Muslim community arrived to apologize and invite us formally to re-visit the mosque. They were contrite. Leading the group was the senior imam's son, who held an important official position in the mosque, and Yasin Puertas, a leading political activist in Melilla and a Spanish convert to Islam. Yasin told us that I was known and respected in the community; in fact, he had converted to Islam partly owing to my work. They had wished to welcome me in an appropriate and honorable manner. They explained the matter in terms of simple misunderstanding. There was already tension because of Ali Aarrass's arrest and disappearance. The Muslim youth, mostly Berber and largely unemployed and uneducated, lived in a state of penury, and this kind of predatory action against a member of the community had brought the situation to boiling point. They feared that Spanish security services had riddled the mosque with their agents. It also seemed that there was a clash of personalities involving our official Muslim guide. They requested us humbly to accept their apology and accompany them back to the mosque.

This time round the senior imam himself received us with courtesy and arranged for us to sit on the carpet in the main prayer hall and gave us permission to film the conversation. The Muslim official whose presence had resulted in the disturbance and the imam appeared to harbor resentment against each other from the past. They seemed reluctant even to shake hands, though after my insistence and some hesitation and muttering from both sides, they did. Pushing my luck, I then insisted that they embrace each other so that there was no ill feeling left. This time, they heeded my request without resistance, both men breaking into smiles. The imam's son said jokingly that the men were behaving in a manner typical of their tribal backgrounds. We then sat down with the imam in the main prayer hall and afterward had tea in his office, which, like the rest of the mosque, gave the appearance of being run down and in need of financial assistance.

Our hosts described the problems of the Muslim community, which they told us was 95 percent Berber. They stated that Europeans in Melilla are the "rich class" and Muslims are the "poor class." Over half of the Muslim population, they explained, has no jobs and there is a serious housing problem. "Everyone is worried," about radicalization, which comes from "social media." The communities do not know each other in Melilla, they complained, noting that some schools are 99 percent Muslim and some are 3 percent Muslim. Education was another serious problem, they noted, and said that many young Muslims drop out of school. There was a profound generation gap: while younger Muslims, who identify as "Spanish, European, and Berber," can speak both Spanish and Berber, many elders do not speak Spanish, nor can they read or write their own Berber language, which was described as an "oral language."

The background to the tension in the Melilla mosque and its connection to the war on terror in Europe was explained to us by Yasin through the case of Ali Aarrass:

> They took advantage of him visiting his father here in Melilla, because it's close to the border of Morocco, to be taken from here to Morocco, and that's it, we never knew anything else from him. Even if you're friends with someone that is involved, even if you don't know what he's doing, just becoming a friend of him or going to the mosque together, then you're supposed to be somewhat involved in the business.

Although Ali was born in Melilla, he did not have Spanish citizenship—to the Spanish, therefore, he was a Moroccan. Ali and his sister attended a boarding school run by Spanish nuns in Melilla and when Ali was fifteen, following his parent's divorce, his mother brought him to Belgium looking for work. His mother found a job in a nursing home, and Ali enrolled in night school to learn French. He worked on construction sites in the Flemish region and went on to work in slaughterhouses before finding employment as a bookbinder. As his sister told the French-language periodical *Le courrier du Maghreb et de l'Orient*, "He accepted every job, even poorly paid."

Eventually, Ali opened a bookshop in the Brussels neighborhood of Molenbeek, a rarity in the poor area with its large population of Moroccan Berbers. Ali, according to his sister, regretted not being educated, so he tried to encourage the local youth to be educated themselves and sometimes gave them free notebooks, pens, and pencils. Ali also served in the Belgian military, fulfilling his compulsory military service in 1993, and was granted Belgian citizenship. In 2005 Ali returned to Melilla to attempt to relocate there and opened a restaurant, but it was not successful, and he was forced to close it down.

In November 2006 Ali was arrested by Spanish authorities and accused of arms trafficking. In April 2008 he was arrested again and sent to prison in Madrid, where, as his sister recounted, he was subjected to insulting and degrading treatment and was called "Moro shit" by prison officials. Ali was investigated by Spanish authorities for terrorism.

Ali's sister said that her brother had been implicated, though never in writing, in the terrorist bombings in Casablanca in 2003 as well as with the criminal terrorist network of Abdelkader Belliraj, a Berber from the Moroccan Rif mountains with a shady background, who also lived in Molenbeek. Following a three-year investigation, Ali was freed from Spanish prison after a judge found no evidence of terrorist activity. He returned to Melilla, but in 2010 Spain extradited him to Morocco. In Morocco, Ali was tortured, as described in a 2013 report by Amnesty International. He was forced to sign a document confessing to terrorist activity in Arabic, though he did not speak the language.

The report pointed out that in November 2011 Ali "was convicted of the illegal use of weapons and participation in a group intending to commit acts of terrorism" and was sentenced to fifteen years in prison; the sentence was reduced on appeal to twelve years. But, as his sister told *Le courrier du Maghreb et de l'Orient*, the Belgian "authorities continue to do nothing. . . . There is a form of institutional racism, because Ali is of North African origin."

The day after the visit to the main Melilla mosque, Yasin took us to a small mosque near the fence that separates Melilla from Morocco, where Ali's elderly father, Mustafa Aarrass, is the imam. When I asked him how it felt to have this happen to his son, he began to cry and replied, "It's very hard. Not only me, but for his wife and little daughter. . . . Before I die, the only thing I want is just to see my son. When I see my son, then I can die."

Just as we felt it was important to comment on the historical background of Bradford, we need to do the same for Melilla. Melilla is technically part of Spain, having been conquered in 1497, yet everyone in the enclave is aware that not only is this Africa, but the majority population of Melilla is Muslim of Berber background, and all around the tiny enclave live the Berber tribes. Melilla's hinterland is the Rif mountains, and over one-third of the population of Melilla consists of Rif Berbers.[1] They speak the Berber language rather than Arabic, and they are fiercely tribal in their codes of honor and behavior and in their loyalty to their lineage groups. Melilla and Ceuta, the other Spanish enclave in North Africa, are running sores for the Berbers living outside them, who see their fellow tribesmen being treated as second-class citizens on what is essentially Berber territory; yet because of higher standards of living and economic possibilities, there is a desire among Berbers to migrate there. To complicate matters further, the state of Morocco claims both Melilla and Ceuta as part of Morocco.

The Spanish government too finds itself in a peculiar position. On one hand it maintains a scrupulous and somewhat self-conscious position of promoting convivencia among the four major religions living in the enclaves—Christianity, Islam, Judaism, and Hinduism. The president of Melilla, Juan José Imbroda, told us of his commitment to convivencia and that he wished to keep the balance between the faiths. He has therefore, on these grounds, refused to permit the building of new mosques. On the other hand, Spain ignores the demographic reality that Muslims may well be in the majority in the city and pressing all around the enclave. Certain neighborhoods in both Melilla and Ceuta are almost exclusively Berber. There is also a steady stream of non-Muslims who are emigrating out of Melilla.

Melilla, like Bradford, has been associated with terrorism, as headlines like "Europe's Newest Front Line Against ISIS" by CNN confirm, and there were reports of authorities dismantling "jihadi cells" in both Melilla and Ceuta.[2] Compounding the tension in Melilla and Ceuta is the arrival of asylum-seeking migrants from sub-Saharan Africa, North Africa, the Middle East, and beyond who enter from Morocco. Yasin drove us along the length of the new fence that now separates Melilla from Morocco. In spite of its height and hostile-looking aspect, bristling with barbed wire and generous deployment of pepper spray, there have been frequent attempts by desperate asylum seekers to jump over it and undertake the journey into Spain, then onward to the imagined Utopia of a northern European country. We saw regular police patrols along the fence, but we also saw groups of asylum seekers who had managed to cross it and were living in makeshift and miserable conditions, in one case in ditches outside a migrant facility administered by the government. I felt a shudder of apprehension for them as they had little idea of the trials and tribulations that lay ahead on their journey.

### *Case Study 3—Brussels, Belgium*

"You are European," the Saudi director of the Saudi-funded Grand Mosque of Brussels, the city's largest mosque and situated in an upmarket part of the city, had repeated to young Muslims over and over again to dissuade them from leaving for the Middle East to fight in Syria. It was not your fight, the director told them. Yet over succulent dates flown in from Saudi Arabia and strong coffee, Frankie began to form the impression that this sophisticated and intelligent Muslim leader was not getting through to his own community. The director admitted, paradoxically, though the mosque has good relations with the Belgian government, young Muslims were not paying heed; many of them had left for the Middle East to join ISIS. Young Muslims, especially the Moroccans, opposed both the Belgian government and the Muslim leadership in Brussels.

Frankie was staying in the Anneessens neighborhood of Brussels, far from the Grand Mosque and adjacent to Molenbeek, now notorious for having produced so many of the terrorists who have played havoc across Europe. Frankie noted the blatant Islamophobia that hung over the immigrant community like an ominous cloud:

> Upon arriving in Brussels I was immediately made aware of the controversies and tensions around the city's Muslim population in the conversations I had with several cab drivers. One driver, a middle-aged Portuguese man, said he had been living in Brussels for over a decade. When I asked him about the different populations in the city, he exclaimed, "There are too many Moroccans, too many!" The Moroccans, he stated, live isolated in their own neighborhoods and have a high birthrate. He sounded alarmed: "Each mother has four children!" To make matters worse, the youth unemployment rate in Anneessens, the neighborhood where I stayed with its large North African population, is alarmingly high at 50 percent.

Unemployed, lacking degrees and skills, despised and assailed by the media and administration, and living in socially isolated communities in depressed areas, all the Muslims needed was a spark to provoke them. That spark was provided by ISIS. With the terror strikes in Paris and Brussels, Brussels became the epicenter of some of the deadliest acts of violence in Western Europe since the Second World War. The global media projected the horrifying sequence of massacres in Brussels, which were linked to the heinous episodes in Paris, in real time onto our television screens and created hysteria around the idea of Europe under siege by Muslim terrorists. Belgium ordered a lockdown. Airports and railway stations across the continent were on high alert. A tiny number of men could swiftly terrorize not only a European country but the continent itself.

### Angry Young Muslims

Although groups like ISIS in the Middle East may have provided the catalyst for the attacks, the reality was that they were perpetrated by young Belgian citizens from neighborhoods like Molenbeek. These Belgians, who felt that they were ignored and had no worth in society, now believed they had been empowered. Not only Belgium, but all of Europe was taking notice. It was a perverse and distorted reality; but it was the only reality they understood.

In nonstop and breathless international media coverage, commentators and officials were quick to analyze the series of bloody events as a result of the violent nature of Islam and the deadly hand of ISIS determined to harm Europe. The hundreds of thousands of asylum seekers and refugees entering Europe were also associated with the violence, and aspersions were cast on all migrants as potential terrorists. The Islamophobic commentary, which attacked the Muslim community and depicted it as the potential enemy, skewed and distorted any useful objective analysis. Yet the trope of the terrorists being radicalized by Islam was not supported by the evidence presenting itself. For example, Salah Abdeslam and his older brother Brahim, one of the Paris suicide bombers, "used to run a cafe in Molenbeek that sold alcohol and was closed down for drug offences." A friend of the brothers said that in the café "he would regularly see Brahim Abdeslam 'watching IS videos, with a joint in one hand, and a beer in another.'"[3]

A trainer at a fitness club in Brussels, many of whose members were from Molenbeek, interviewed by the BBC, "argues that the key cause of radicalisation in Molenbeek is a sense, rightly or wrongly, of not having a future. 'Radicalisation doesn't start with a religious ideal,' he says. 'The guys I know [who went to Syria] they have no ideology, they have no big ideas. . . . They are going because they are leaving something. They are fed up with this society.'" A young man in Molenbeek who had been "accused of attempting to travel to Syria" also expressed these sentiments, declaring that the phenomenon of young Muslims in Brussels joining ISIS "was the fault of domestic conditions. He railed against the Belgian government—against white Belgians, who hated those of Arab descent, he said."[4]

In response to the attacks, the Belgian administration opted for a severe assault on the Muslim community, with law enforcement actions that gave the impression of being in a warzone. This was most unfortunate. For the deadly actions of a few, the entire community was being penalized by its own country. Muslims thus felt punished twice over: by the murderous actions of their young men and women and by the unfair categorization as terrorists and terrorist sympathizers. Alienation, fear, and anger permeated the community.

While there was a global outpouring of sympathy for Belgium, it was laced with an undercurrent of criticism. The press was not shy in pointing out that Belgian authorities had taken four months to locate Salah Abdeslam, who had been directly linked to the bombings in Paris in November 2015. The lack of coordination between the agencies and indeed the larger division between the Dutch-speaking Flemish and French-speaking Walloons were highlighted. Reports pointed out the clumsy nature of the administrative structure in Brussels and Belgium. "Brussels," a *New York Times* reporter noted with disbelief, "has 19 municipalities, each with its own council and mayor."[5]

Further exacerbating the linguistic and cultural divisions of the country and challenging the fragile state and immigrants alike was the Far Right. Brussels was still in mourning when, just days after the March 2016 bombings, as many as a thousand black-clad members of Flemish right-wing groups appeared at a memorial vigil to the victims, where they clashed with police, hurled abuse at Muslims, and gave the Nazi salute. Media reports indicated many were from the leading Flemish right-wing party, Vlaams Belang, which saw its Facebook "likes" surge 3,675 percent in the several days following the attacks, according to the media and technology company Vocativ. Vlaams Belang's slogan was "Eigen Volk eerst!" (Our own Volk first), in effect meaning that Walloons and Muslims alike were alien to the country.

Indeed, the terrorist strikes served to increase tension between the French and Dutch-speaking communities. In the aftermath of the Paris terrorist attacks in November 2015, for example, senior lawmakers of the main Flemish nationalist party, the New Flemish Alliance, accused the Francophone socialist party of "years of laxity," resulting in Brussels' becoming "the rear base for Islamic barbarism."

A brief historical comment on Belgium is again appropriate here. Belgium was artificially formed in the nineteenth century by combining the Francophone Wallonia region in the south and Germanic Dutch-speaking Flanders in the north. It was the two world wars and Germany's invasions that helped build Belgium's sympathetic image in Europe. When Germany invaded Belgium the first time, the country was seen in England as the "plucky little nation" standing up to the "big bullying Hun." That is why Agatha Christie's Hercule Poirot plies his trade in the English countryside where he had sought refuge. Belgium soon settled in the public mind as a pleasant, safe, and comfortable land. Not surprisingly, when European nations began to plan for the headquarters of NATO and the European Union, they felt that there could be no safer location than Brussels.

I was struck by the idyllic, picture-postcard quality of the tiny country itself, with its law-abiding, respectable middle-class citizens, neat suburbs, and picturesque towns in the countryside. I also noted that the best-known features associated with Belgium were its famous chocolates and the fictional characters Poirot and Tintin.

Yet something dark and sinister lurked just under the surface. To start with, there is Belgium's own blood-soaked excursion into the sphere of global imperialism. Perhaps not many schoolchildren know that Belgium's Congolese colony was seventy-six times larger than Belgium itself; that at one stage the king, Leopold II, was reportedly the richest man in the world, and he was known as the Butcher of the Congo, directly responsible for the brutal murder and mutilation of some 10 million of his African subjects. His methods were brutally simple: Anyone who failed to produce the daily quota of rubber had his genitals and hands chopped off, and punishments included children being taken hostage, forced starvation, and villages being burnt. Belgian cruelty had reached such a level that even the other European imperial powers, themselves no strangers to genocidal butchery, objected. Sir Arthur Conan Doyle, taking time off from his most famous creation, Sherlock Holmes, wrote a scathing criticism in *The Crime of the Congo* in 1909. Belgium's atrocities were remembered and condemned more recently in *The Legend of Tarzan* (2016), in which the king of the jungle foils the plans of the king of Belgium to take further slaves and steal more diamonds.

The failure of Belgium to integrate its immigrant population has been spectacular. The immigrant community, mainly Moroccans and Turks, arrived as guest workers beginning in the 1960s, on the invitation of the government, to make up for a shortage of manpower and take jobs that Belgians avoided. It was assumed that they would eventually return to their homelands. Not only did they not return, but their next generation was born in Belgium and considered themselves Europeans. The problem was though legally and technically they were Belgian, they were not accepted as such and their economic and political situation forced them into ghetto-like areas. A former senior Belgian police official told the BBC in January 2016 that Belgian society's failure to integrate immigrants had created "a system of apartheid."

Now there is a third generation coming of age in an atmosphere of overt hostility and hopelessness. Members of this generation often find themselves in prison, and once inside they are inevitably introduced to a world of petty crime, gangs, and brutality. Though Muslims make up only around 6 percent of the population, they account for 20 to 30 percent of the prisoners in Belgian jails, a trend reflected in other parts of Europe; for example, 70 percent of prisoners in France are of Muslim origin, while the community forms 7.5 percent of the French population. In addition, a lackluster Muslim leadership ensures that young Muslims look to the Internet for guidance, which often comes from imams and other so-called leaders operating in the Middle East and other parts of the world. Not helping the situation is the fact that out of the 114 imams in Brussels, there are only 8 who speak any local language.

What was missing in both the media commentary about the attacks and the government response was an understanding of the Muslim immigrant community, the source from which the violence emanated. This meant that the very conditions that had produced the violent young men would remain unchanged. There was an alarming lack of knowledge, without which there was no path to making Europe safer. When Frankie went to interview officials at EU headquarters in Brussels, the adviser to the president of the European Commission on outreach to religious groups, after agreeing that it was vital to have contacts in the Muslim community, asked Frankie if he knew any useful names of Muslim leaders in the city or indeed anywhere in Europe. Frankie was beginning to feel less like Poirot and more like Alice in Wonderland, where things were topsy-turvy.

## European Champions of Tribal Identity and an African Asylum Seeker

As the case studies above suggest, multiple dark forces are currently being unleashed in Europe that must be checked and contained if future conflict is to be avoided. One of them is the ascendant European Far Right, which has seized on the current controversies around Islam to argue that Europe is facing an invasion that must be resisted. Dutch politician Geert Wilders summed up the threat in this terse statement: "Masses of young men in their twenties with beards singing Allahu Akbar across Europe. It's an invasion that threatens our prosperity, our security, our culture and identity."

As a matter of strategy, these groups have focused on two highly contentious and interconnected issues, Islam and refugees, while implicitly suggesting that the two are one and the same thing. While setting out to preserve and defend European identity, the Far Right has, in a shrewd strategic move, revived some of the older symbols and signs of primordial tribal identity. Their extreme rhetoric has had the effect of pushing mainstream politicians and society more toward the right than any time since the Second World War. The argument of the Far Right about defending the purity and honor of "their people" against those "invaders" coming from outside Europe, in their minds, is nothing more than the attempt to preserve and champion primordial tribal identity.

Below, we hear the voices of some of these far-right leaders and also that of a newly arrived Muslim asylum seeker, a young Gambian, who represents in their minds the Muslim threat to Europe and is therefore their target. We have interviewed key figures from far-right parties across the continent: Britain First in the United Kingdom, the Danish People's Party in Denmark, and Pegida in Germany.

### The Founder of Britain First

Jim Dowson, the founder of the anti-Islamic Britain First party, was interviewed in Comber, a Protestant Ulster town in Northern Ireland. Dowson, a former activist and financier of the white nationalist British National Party, founded Britain First in 2011. The organization was widely discussed in the global media following the assassination of Labour MP Jo Cox in June 2016 because during the attack, her killer had shouted "Britain First." Britain First, which campaigned for the country's "Brexit" from the EU, had nearly 2 million "likes" on Facebook as of November 2017, the most of any political party in the United Kingdom. Britain First made news in May 2016 when its candidate for mayor turned his back to Sadiq Khan on stage to protest his victory in London's mayoral election. Britain First was put under a global spotlight in November 2017 when President Trump retweeted its Islamophobic videos to his 44 million followers, creating a media frenzy and an international diplomatic row. It is well to remind ourselves of the role of Britain First in staging the invasion of mosques in Bradford and other places shortly before we arrived to do our fieldwork.

Born in Scotland to a Protestant Ulster family from Northern Ireland, Dowson explained that his organization, which he said was based in the south of England, engages in "patrols" of what he called "Islamic-occupied" areas. "We have two different distinct organizations," he expounded.

> We have Britain First, the political party, and we have Britain First Defence, which is an organization that goes out with heavily armored military vehicles to patrol Islamic-occupied areas of Britain. I know that sounds ridiculous but that's what we've got. We have areas now where shariah law is implemented, and people who are even holding hands—you know, English people walking down the street, husband and wife, holding hands—have been beaten up.

Dowson claimed Britain First was "partly responsible" for pushing the "political agenda" in the United Kingdom "over to the right," paving the way for the success of parties like the United Kingdom Independence Party. Britain First, Dowson believed, provides hope and inspiration for the British people to "take their country back."

When asked how he saw the future of Britain, Dowson described a coming war with Islam in "tribal" terms, perfectly capturing the essential elements of European predator identity:

> War. War. That's it. Death. Misery. Thousands of people displaced. . . . That could happen tomorrow. It could happen next week. It certainly will happen in the next few years. . . . It's 100 percent of us against 100 percent of them. That's the way humans are. It's tribal. . . . The Muslims are going to attack. The war's already started. Bus bombing, the tube bombings, Lee Rigby, the attempted bombings in nightclubs and shopping centers. The war has started. People just need to wake up and pick a side.

Those who die in the battle against Islam, announced Dowson, will be "holy martyrs":

> I believe Jesus is guiding the Britain First movement. . . . I get into that church over there most mornings and spend half an hour in

there contemplating what I have to do. And it's the same with our lads in England. We are Christians. We believe God has set us on this path. And that is why we are not frightened when we get 400 death threats. . . . I don't want to be lagging in my duty, and if we die defending our faith and our people, we'll be holy martyrs.

Islam and European identity, he believed, are not compatible: "Islam is not compatible with any situation in the West, whether it's America, whether it's any country in Europe. Western Judeo-Christian-based liberal democracy and Islam, they just don't mix. People need to get this through their head."

Dowson asserted that because of the rising population of Muslims in the United Kingdom and Europe, parliamentary democracy has "no future," and he spoke with alarm about "liberal" Western European countries that have lost their "social cohesion" and are in danger of falling to Islam:

The West is going to have to wake up. But it's too late for us in Europe. The demographics are against us. They're irreversible. Our birthrate is shockingly low. It cannot be reversed. So what we're going to come into is a Balkanization of Europe. Places like Poland and Hungary, where they have a strong nationalist, you know, quite a nasty streak in them to be honest with you. They will survive because they won't put up with it. Places like Germany, Holland, Belgium, England, who are extremely liberal and have lost their faith, have lost their sense of social cohesion. They'll fall to Islam. . . . The Muslims are going to outnumber us in twenty years under the age of forty. And when that happens, you either are subjugated by Islam, keep your mouth shut, go about your business, they probably won't bother you. Or you fight to defend this island that we built over the last 10,000 years. And as far as I'm concerned as long as 100 of us remain alive and freeborn men and Christians, we will never submit to Islam, ever.

He went on to discuss Britain First's campaign involving mosques in "occupied" Muslim areas: "Recently, we've been getting out with armored Land Rovers into these occupied areas and saying to them, we're not putting up with this. If the police can't do it, well, citizens have to do it. We will not sit back and let our people be abused by anyone."

The police, Dowson complained, have refused to take action "because they did not want to upset the Muslim community on two grounds:

frightened to be labeled racist and frightened of the backlash. Because there's been serious riots in these towns. Serious riots, and when the cartoonist in Denmark painted the Muhammad cartoon, 10,000 people were on the streets in Bradford and Rochdale, burning flags and jumping up and down." Hence he believed that the creation of Britain First was necessary: "The only thing a bully with a stick understands is somebody confronting them with a bigger stick. That's it. There's no other way."

The Britain First campaign, Dowson explained, focused on the city of Bradford: "Bradford used to be salt of the earth, hard-working people. . . . It's not multicultural. It's monocultural. And it's Muslim. It's Islamic culture. . . . At 4:30 every morning, the call to prayer, Allah Akbar, the call to prayer goes across the whole city from the minarets. If you try ringing church bells at 4:00 in the morning, you'll be arrested. . . . They've took over. This is not multiculturalism. This is not immigration. This is invasion and colonization."

Britain First's mission in Bradford also included targeting the house of the lord mayor of Bradford. "He refused to meet us," complained Dowson about the lord mayor:

> Now some of our lads live in Bradford. So they're his constituents. We went to his office. We were flung out. So the only course of action, he is a public representative, was we went to his house. We inquired if he was in. We were told he wasn't in. We said thank you very much and left. That man went to the newspapers and said we had invaded his house, searched it top to bottom. Frightened his women, frightened his children. Now he's supposed to be one of the more educated, progressive, liberal Muslims. Yet he resorted to telling such blatant lies.

A key concern of Britain First in these campaigns, explained Dowson, was the "grooming" cases of sexual exploitation of young English girls by Muslims:

> Muslim grooming has been a big thing here. There's a government inquiry into it. Now let's be honest here—most pedophiles in Britain are white Christian English people. That's a fact. But the phenomenon of gangs, organized groups of men targeting young English girls, is predominantly a Muslim problem. But it's worse than that. It is a section of the Muslim community, the Pakistani community. But if we produced a leaflet saying this is a Pakistani community, the laws that the liberals have passed in this country, we would be prosecuted

under racial hatred. We'll get jailed. So we have no choice but to say the Muslim community. . . . So we couldn't say this particular section is the problem.

Dowson said that his Britain First organization is "linked" with other far-right movements in Europe. He explained that in Europe there were "two streams of right-wing movements. . . . There's the American-based counter-Jihad movement, which Spence [Robert Spencer] and [Pamela] Geller is behind. They seem to have a very Zionist, Israeli agenda. They back the EDL [English Defence League]. And they're running all these microgroups all over Europe, anti-Jihad. But they're mainly Facebooks. Three men and a dog and a Facebook. . . . They came to us. We refused their finance. You know, we're British. Whatever happens in Palestine and Israel, that's their pigeon. I'm an evangelical Protestant. I've got sympathies with the Jewish people, of course I have. But am I going to fight their battles on the streets of Britain? No, I'm not. I'm going to fight my own battles."

The other stream Dowson referred to was formed by the European nationalist parties:

> Then there's what I call the real nationalist movement. . . . Most of them are fairly anti-Semitic, which we reject. But they are the real nationalist movements, like Jobbik in Hungary. We are very friendly with them. I go way back with them. They're actually marching about in military uniforms. That could be the first country in Europe that could have, since the war, the first fascist government. . . . I might even move there if things get any worse here.

In March 2015 Dowson attended a conference of European right-wing groups in Saint Petersburg organized by Russia's Rodina (Heimat) Party, described as "a kind of nationalistic branch of Mr. Putin's ruling United Russia party." At the conference, which was also attended by members of Greece's Golden Dawn as well as Jared Taylor, a key figure in the American alt-right movement that helped fuel Donald Trump's presidential campaign, Dowson sang Putin's praises. He displayed a picture of a shirtless Putin riding a bear and declared, "Obama and America, they are like females. They are feminized men. . . . But you have been blessed by a man who is a man, and we envy that."[6]

Video footage surfaced at the end of 2016 showing Dowson in Jungle Jim outfit in a forest with armed masked figures in camouflage carrying flags with a cross on them. Dowson was hunting asylum seekers alongside the right-wing Shipka Bulgarian National Movement on the Bulgarian-Turkish border, which Dowson said must be defended against "invaders." "Remember, the forces of Islam once got as far as Vienna. Now they are as far as John o'Groats in Scotland, and more and more are coming in," he told the Bulgarians. "This is not political, this is a fight between good and evil, black and white, a fight of the cross, a fight of Christ," he exclaimed.

Dowson was also involved in the U.K.-based Knights Templar International, which supported antimigrant militias in places such as Bulgaria and Hungary and established, as did Britain First, a sizable online presence. The Knights Templar International Facebook page garnered over half a million "likes" and featured Islamophobic, pro-Putin, and pro-Trump material and "fake news," such as a December 2016 post with an article purporting to expose the satanic imagery in the Comet Ping Pong pizza restaurant sign, a Washington, D.C. establishment blamed by alt-right conspiracy theorists for hosting a child molestation ring run by Hillary Clinton.[7] It was reported that Dowson was involved in a "constellation" of websites that supported Trump, producing postings that "were viewed and shared hundreds of thousands of times."[8] The Knights Templar International also advertised homes in Ásotthalom, Hungary, a village attempting to create a "white utopia."[9]

### *The Deputy Chairman of the Danish People's Party*

While Jim Dowson was attempting to move society to the right from outside the political system and confronting Muslims on the street level, Søren Espersen, the deputy chairman of the Dansk Folkeparti (Danish People's Party, or DPP), battles Muslims from within the Danish power structure. Espersen, who is also the party spokesman for foreign affairs, represents a far-right ideology that has translated into massive gains at the ballot box. In 2014 the DPP won the European Parliament elections in Denmark with 27 percent of the vote, and in 2015 it won 21 percent of the vote in the Danish general elections, becoming the second-largest party in the nation.

The DPP was founded in 1995 by Pia Kjærsgaard, who now serves as the speaker of the Danish Parliament (the Folketing). Its popularity grew rapidly after 9/11. Kjærsgaard expressed her negative opinion of Muslim civilization in various statements such as this one from 2005: "Not in their wildest imagination would anyone [in 1900] have imagined, that large parts of Copenhagen and other Danish towns would be populated by people who are at a lower stage of civilization, with their own primitive and cruel customs like honor killings, forced marriages, halal slaughtering and blood-feuds."[10]

The party's campaigns have focused squarely on Islam, as seen in the DPP poster for the November 2001 election, which depicted a young blonde girl with the message, "When she retires, Denmark will have a Muslim majority."[11] A 2007 campaign poster for the DPP depicted a hand holding a pen drawing a cartoon of Prophet Muhammad with a message reading, "Freedom of speech is Danish. Censorship is not. We stand our ground in Danish values."[12]

In January 2016, the DPP, with the support of the Social Democrats, passed a law that

> permits police to strip-search asylum-seekers and confiscate their cash and most valuables above 10,000 Danish kroner ($1,460) to pay for their accommodation; delays the opportunity to apply for family reunification by up to three years; forbids asylum-seekers from residing outside refugee centers, some of which are tent encampments; reduces the cash benefits they can receive; and makes it significantly harder to qualify for permanent residence.[13]

Appearing on the BBC program *Hardtalk* to defend the controversial law in February 2016, Espersen disagreed with a comparison made by Bent Melchior, the former chief rabbi of Denmark (see chapter 7), with the policies of the Nazis toward the Jews. Espersen said the Danish law differed from the Nazi policy because when the Nazis seized valuables, there was no welfare state in place, whereas the Danes do have a welfare state:

> These Jews in the Second World War did not come to a welfare state where they were being looked after, they had to look after themselves, and I can understand the outrage over the Nazi regime that stripped them from their assets. They came to countries, they had absolutely nothing. These refugees that come to Denmark now have everything they need, as I said, in housing, in clothing, everything they need. That is a total difference and I think he ought to be ashamed of himself, the ex-chief rabbi, to come with such a comparison.

In July 2016 Espersen, speaking to the Danish newspaper *Berlingske,* called for a ban on all Muslim migrants entering Denmark for up to six years because, he believed, Denmark needs "a respite after recent terrorist attacks in Europe."

In our interview with Espersen, conducted in his office at the Danish Parliament in Copenhagen, he explained that the DPP is both an anti-immigration and anti-European Union party. In describing his political evolution and his personal trajectory toward the DPP, Espersen admitted that he used to be "left wing" until he became alarmed at the immigration situation and its connection to the EU. "I've never been a supporter of the EU, even when I was very young. Originally, I had a left-wing background. I've always had a sort of social interest in maintaining a very good welfare system and looking after our weakest. It's always been my priority."

But when immigrants began to arrive in the early 1980s amid the development of the European Union, Espersen stated, his political views began to change. "1983 was always the year we say that the immigration to Denmark, the modern immigration to Denmark, started after new legislation that came out that gave everyone the right to seek asylum in the country. . . . That was a shock to many, including myself."

The problem of immigration, Espersen explained, was not necessarily immigration as such but Islamic immigration. Espersen said that there had been earlier waves of immigrants who had come to Denmark and were able to fit in right away because they were from the "Judeo-Christian" civilization of Europe, unlike the Muslims.

> Over 400 years ago, the first Jews started coming in from Eastern Europe and Germany and the Poles that would come in great number only a hundred years ago. . . . The Huguenots from France are still here with lots of family, the Dutch would come. . . . They were very easily transformed into Danes. It could take a couple of generations but they were easily, they could easily fit in, even from day one.

Muslim immigrants, Espersen said, were very different: "Islam can be very difficult to integrate into what we call a modern Western civilization. Mainly because the democracy part of it can be very difficult to combine with Islam. Which might also be, I'm not an expert on the Quran and the faith, it could also be the reason that there are hardly any Muslim countries in this world that are democracies." As evidence, Espersen discussed the Christian theology he learned in school, which he felt bore little resemblance to what he saw coming from Islam: "In the Muslim faith, there is no questioning. And if you do, you are a heretic who has to be killed."

Espersen viewed Muslims in Europe as being unable, or unwilling, to become part of Danish society: "We can also see it here in Copenhagen, also in Aarhus, the largest cities, that there are problems, ghettoization and the tendency to move together, to not necessarily always want to keep the laws and making your own jurisdiction. . . . It's a different society. And the question is, do we want that? I don't particularly want that."

In his opinions on Islam and immigration, Espersen emphasized that he was speaking for the mainstream of Danish society: "You're asking me as a representative of the Danish People's Party, but I must say that what I say and the way I put it is very much mainstream in Denmark now." Espersen also expressed his alarm at the threat the Jewish community faced from Muslims in Europe:

> The Jews in Malmö in Sweden have left. They have been there 400 years. They cannot have a synagogue there anymore. Even here, the Jews that go to the synagogue and also the Jewish school up north, they can't wear their kipper anymore. It's dangerous. Go up to the Jewish school, Carolineskolen, named after one of our Queens, and you'll see it's like Fort Knox, with high fences and everything and armed guards out in front of it. . . . I mean, it's not Nazis that do that. It is young Muslims who do these things. You don't see Jews storming Muslim schools and harassing people going to the mosque. That doesn't exist. I see the Jews in Marseille have left. There is an emigration from France. . . . It's not safe to live there anymore. That is an outrageous situation that can only be addressed at one side and that is the Muslims.

Discussing the policies the Danish government has pursued to address the problem of terrorism, Espersen said that there was a consensus across the political spectrum in Denmark not to necessarily imprison those who travel to fight in Syria and Iraq but to attempt to "accommodate" and work with them. Espersen blamed Muslim leaders for allowing young Danish Muslims to go to Syria and Iraq:

> It's very difficult. Not only those young people who go, but you see that their leaders, their imams, their elders are really the problem and understand this comes from the preaching. This comes from the Friday preaching in the mosque whereas we go to the service on Sunday, the result is not necessarily that we come out screaming. But the result after a Friday service in a mosque is often that people come out screaming. So, whereas the priests and the rabbis try to talk peace and understanding and love, then I have the feeling that very many of those imams . . . come out with a completely different mes-

sage. So they are the ones to blame, not necessarily these very young boys who go and who are bewildered.

"I don't think we should work with the leadership of that community," Espersen reiterated, "I don't think we should work with the imams. . . . If we think we can communicate with the imams who have preached hatred and then make them stop this, I think we are wrong. This is what we've done for decades. We've been trying to talk to the elders and it doesn't seem to help."

Instead of working with the leaders of the Muslim community, Espersen believed the solution was secularism:

We don't need religion in our political society. . . . I don't want to be guided by religion. . . . Even if I consider myself a Christian and my wife a Jew, when it comes to the situation for homosexuals, to look up in the Bible and then make up my political decision about that. I think it's ridiculous. . . . I think that religion is the problem.

Espersen stated he wants "these believers in all religions to just calm down for goodness sake and if that could just sort of come down to a reasonable and pragmatic level then I'm sure we could all be here. But otherwise it could be a clash, which I certainly don't hope for and want."

## Pegida's Representative in Bavaria

In Germany, the country that took in the vast majority of the Muslim refugees and asylum seekers entering Europe, far-right forces experienced a rapid resurgence, expressing and promoting a German primordial and predator identity that had been kept underground since the conclusion of the Second World War. Pegida's growth in popularity, for example, was rapid, particularly following the New Year's Eve 2015 sexual assaults in Cologne, and it established a presence across Germany and in other countries such as the Netherlands, the United Kingdom, France, and Ireland. Every week, thousands of Pegida supporters marched through the streets of Dresden to show their opposition to Islam, attracting as many as 25,000 people at one time. The Pegida slogan, "Wir sind das Volk" (We are the Volk), cast Islam and the migrants explicitly outside of the Volk. Other Pegida slogans included "*Lügenpresse*" (Lying press), which was used by German nationalists in the twentieth century and by the Nazis to oppose the "unpatriotic" press. Pegida served to focus German far-right forces against Islam, and there was considerable overlap between Pegida and the emerging Alternative for Germany party (see chapter 9). Pegida also became an umbrella group for those Germans who had been engaged in anti-Islamic activism and wished to work toward the common goal of expelling Islam from Germany.

Michael Stürzenberger of Bavaria was described as "the face of the Munich branch of Pegida" by the Munich newspaper *Süddeutsche Zeitung*. At a January 2015 rally in Munich, the newspaper reported, Stürzenberger led a crowd of 1,500 in chants of the Pegida slogans, "Wir sind das Volk!" and "Lügenpresse! Lügenpresse!" Stürzenberger, a public supporter of the Alternative for Germany party, is also the leader of the anti-Islamic German Freedom Party and had regularly held rallies in the Munich city square long before the establishment of Pegida. In these rallies, Stürzenberger railed against the presence of Islam in Germany—and particularly the efforts of Imam Benjamin Idriz to build an Islamic center in Munich. Stürzenberger had become notorious for publicly maligning people like Imam Idriz—the popular founder of an "open" and "liberal" mosque in Bavaria that our team visited. Stürzenberger was also known for his contributions to the Islamophobic blog *Politically Incorrect*. Stürzenberger had once been the press spokesman for the Christian Social Union, the Bavarian affiliate of Angela Merkel's Christian Democratic Union, and he told us he left the party because of what he thought was its overly accommodating position on Islam and Imam Idriz.

We interviewed Stürzenberger at one of his rallies in the Munich city square. "Islam is incompatible with all Western civilization," he stated.

> Islam is orientated at a civilization that was in the seventh century in Saudi Arabia, and Islam has all the same rules from that time. The Quran is a book full of orders. And Muslims have to fulfill it. . . . Islam is not only a religion; it's a political system. It has its own justice, the shariah, and Islam has the order to rule in every country where Muslims have the majority. So it's a very dangerous threat for freedom, for democracy. And every non-Muslim is considered to be frightened, submissive, and killed if he doesn't want the rule of Islam.

Stürzenberger voiced his alarm at the existence of Muslim "parallel systems" in cities. "We have growing parts of cities that are Islamic and have their shariah already installed, there's violence. There's raping of women—everything is a problem which comes from Islam." The problem facing Germany was not immigration, Stürzenberger argued, but specifically Muslim immigration because Muslims have "the Quran in their head." "It's a book full of hate," he said. "And we have in the history of Islam, since 1,400 years, we have a history of fighting, of conquering countries, of killing people. We have 270 million people killed in the jihad since the seventh century—it's a very dangerous threat."

The solution to the problem of Islam in Europe, Stürzenberger asserted, is for shariah law to be "wiped out" and "deleted":

> We have the problem of people who don't want to integrate, who don't want to live with our Western rules, our free society. . . . We have to tell the Muslims, if you want to live in Europe, you have to accept our culture, our rules, our democratic system. If not, it would be better if you go to your Islamic home countries, there you can live your Islam. But not in Europe.

Sturzenberger spoke of his party's good relations with other European far-right political parties such as the National Front in France, the Swedish Democrats, and the Freedom Party in Austria. Stürzenberger mentioned his admiration for Geert Wilders, whom he sees as a role model. "Wilders says, 'As long as I'm breathing, I will fight against Islam because Islam will destroy Europe.'"

## A Young African Seeking Asylum in Europe

From these European far-right leaders, let us turn to one of those they consider as part of the threatening and barbaric Islamic invasion of Europe. There is a great deal of media coverage of Syrian refugees, but those from Africa—especially the non-Arab parts, who constitute a large part of the migrants coming to Europe—get little attention. We therefore set out to interview people from non-Arab African countries. In Sicily, during a tour of the main mosque in Catania, we met Ahmedu Jalo. Although we had met many recently arrived immigrants on the trip, Ahmedu's story was especially compelling.

A young migrant from Gambia, Ahmedu had only recently arrived by boat. The mosque's imam, a cheerful and welcoming North African, was showing us around the building. He pulled back a curtain to reveal some mattresses where Syrian families were sleeping.

At the entrance of another room I saw Ahmedu. A mop in his hand, he was standing by himself. Something about him struck me. He had an air about him, the way he carried himself. His long journey from home had not diminished his poise and confidence. I went up and talked to him. He seemed distant and defensive and his eyes appeared glazed. When I asked

*Ahmedu and Bahbuka with Frankie in Catania*

him his name, he gave it in a low voice, mechanically, as if answering an official. I then said with a smile that my name was also Ahmed. We were connected, I added. There was the faintest of smiles on his face, but it did not touch his eyes.

Beneath his poise, I felt there was an extraordinary story. He was reluctant to talk. Migrants like Ahmedu know that talking to strangers can land them in trouble, but I was determined to hear his account and interview him for our project. Once he agreed, however, he began to slowly open up. His friend, Bahbuka, another young migrant from Gambia, also joined in the conversation.

Ahmedu, who was seventeen years old, had four siblings. The eldest son, Ahmedu was the pride of his parents. When his mother and father separated, his life changed. He was going to make his fortune in the hope of reuniting his parents and helping his siblings: "I am trying my best to help my family, because I'm the elder. And I want to make something tomorrow, so that my family will be happy about me."

Bidding his father farewell, Ahmedu set out for Europe, without documents or money, on a journey that would take him over a year and two months across the vast expanse of Africa, through Senegal, Mali, Burkina Faso, Niger, Libya, and the Mediterranean Sea. Ahmedu recounted the horrors he encountered on the way, of the times he was jailed by corrupt policemen, of the pain he felt in his body because of the hunger in his stomach. When he could, he found employment helping a barber, hawking water, or serving food, which gave him enough money to get to the next destination. As he spoke, he repeated the phrase "not easy, not easy." When he was attempting to leave Niger he was caught again. "They even sometimes beat me. They don't see nothing, they don't see no documents. No documents. No passport, no documents."

When he arrived in Libya, Ahmedu was given work by a man who was kind to him: "Yes, he take me to his home. I used to go and clean. Clean the whole thing, what he want. I take water to put it in the flower. After, he give me food, I eat. Yes. When I am going home in the evening, he give me money." Ahmedu also spoke of the fear he felt in Libya with the threat of violence always present, "All the time I hear a distant gun."

Another kind Libyan man eventually found Ahmedu a place in a migrant boat bound for Europe, and paid for it. Ahmedu recounted the climax to this nightmare journey when he was crammed into a small open boat with eighty-nine people on the shores of Libya, nearly drowning in the commotion following the outbreak of gunfire in the port. Once the boat departed the shores of North Africa, petroleum leaked into the food, making it inedible. Fortunately, the desperate passengers were rescued in the Mediterranean by the Italian coast guard. "Thank God," Ahmedu said, "everyone survived."

On their arrival in Sicily, Ahmedu and the other migrants were herded into a school hall that served as a migrant center. His problems were just beginning. Ahmedu, who complained that the authorities did not permit him to phone home, left the migrant center and began to sleep on the streets of Catania. It was cold, and he had no warm clothes. He foraged for food in rubbish heaps and drank as much water as he could to stave off hunger. Ahmedu had no one—from the government or anywhere else—to advise him on his options. On one occasion an Italian policeman headbutted him for no apparent reason. Shocked, Ahmedu collapsed in a heap of tears: "One day I came to the police station. One man . . . I don't know whether he was a policeman or what. . . . He looked at me like this, he say, 'Move, move here.' He hit me two times. . . . I cannot do nothing. I just sit and cry. Yes. I just sit and cry." He may have frozen to death on the streets if a kindly Sicilian had not informed him about the central mosque that could provide shelter. Without any documents or money in his pocket, Ahmedu's only concern was that he had no way to speak to his family. It was playing on his mind and kept coming up in our conversation.

When we provided him the means to phone home, his face and body language changed. He began to thaw, and a slow transformation took place. Ahmedu's voice became stronger, his posture straighter and he began to show signs of animation. The thawing—or rehumanizing—of Ahmedu as we got to know one another was a wondrous testament to the power of the human spirit. It was almost as if someone far away began to come into focus, someone who had almost faded began to take on sharp features. As he went deeper and deeper into his story, my research team began to show visible signs of emotion at what they were hearing. Amineh, in particular, sobbed quietly throughout as she was reminded of her own son Ibrahim, who was about the same age as Ahmedu.

I asked Ahmedu what kept him going and he mentioned his faith, but most of all it was the thought of doing something that would help his family and bring his parents back together again: "I have a faith because always I used to pray and I used to thank Him and if you don't forget God, God will save you always. All the time when I used to go and buy a credit and call them and tell them. Yeah, I'm alright, keep on praying."

Ahmedu said he was unsure of his future plans. "I pray that where my success is, God makes me to get there easy. Yes, if it is here, I will do it. If it is France, I will go. . . . Maybe it's in Germany, maybe it's in other place."

When asked if he is happy at the mosque where we met him, Ahmedu replied,

> I cannot say I am happy here, because I'm thinking about to get up and go to school or to get up and go to have work. So, Alhamdulil-lah, praise be to God, these people they are good, yes. Because every day they give us breakfast, they give us lunch. They look after us, yes. But for this also we just wake up and clean everywhere. Yes, because even they don't tell us. . . . Just you wake up, you do it by yourself, by your heart. It's because if somebody nice to you, you have to open to him. So we thank God these people they are good.

At the end Ahmedu seemed a changed man, and when, in a good-natured fatherly way, I said I wanted to see him smiling from now on, he replied with a broad grin, "Thank you very much. Thank you very much. Thank you very much. . . . I will never forget you guys, thank you very much." "You come, join to me, smile together. Smile together. Yeah, thank you very much." Now beaming, Ahmedu reached out and pulled Frankie to hug him. The sight of an African and an American, a black man and a white man, a Muslim and a Christian, embracing in this manner warmed my heart and gave me renewed hope for our common humanity.

Ahmedu's story raises the fundamental issue of the idea of survival. If you were a spirited healthy young African male, deeply conscious of your position as the eldest son of a family that was struggling with poverty, lived in a country where more than half the population existed under the internationally recognized poverty line and were ruled by a president known for his cruelty and tyranny, you would probably be thinking, like Ahmedu, of seeking your fortune elsewhere. If you were desperate enough, nothing would stop you, not even the thought of crossing the Sahara or the dangerous Mediterranean Sea without money or official documents.

Yet to many in the West, a young man like Ahmedu represents an Islamic threat, one based on the erroneous belief that Muslims are hell-bent on conquering parts of Europe to impose an Islamic caliphate. As for the argument that immigrants mean more recruits for terrorists, not once in our two interviews with Ahmedu did he mention words like shariah or jihad. Yet the European Far Right derives its power from the fear of immigrants and Islam.

Here is the paradox of Europe: The comfortable and affluent nations of the north have ceased to look on immigrants as fellow human beings. They are forced into categories that deny them a legal status and effectively the right to even exist. The wrath of the Far Right is focused squarely on them. In contrast, Sicily—viewed in the north as economically and politically backward—still retains the memory of convivencia from its past, and this affects how it treats the constant waves of new migrants. When Sicilians can help them in small ways, they do. If they cannot do very much to alleviate their suffering, Sicilians do not add to the migrants' burdens by deporting them or locking them away. Even the local officials I spoke with hinted that they were not entirely in agreement with the strict policies of the EU. The spirit of Sicilian tolerance has endured despite instances of violence, such as the April 2016 shooting of a Gambian immigrant in the head by a mafioso in an effort to enforce his authority, defend his turf, and demonstrate that migrants were not welcome.

Mayor Leoluca Orlando of Palermo, the champion of convivencia whom we met in chapter 3, while fully aware of the economic crisis that faces his own society and the lingering dangers posed by the mafia, rejected the notion of calling an immigrant illegal and requiring a residency permit. "I will never accept to imagine that a human being can be illegal." "Why," the mayor asked with a rhetorical flourish, "does everybody try to land in Sicily?" "Because," he said, answering his own question with a flash of Sicilian pride, "for Sicilians, no man is illegal."

In August 2015, Orlando described the migration crisis to *The Independent* as a "genocide" for which Europe was culpable. "In the future," he said, "the European Union will be held responsible for this genocide, exactly like we held Nazi fascism responsible for genocide 70 years ago. . . . It's not possible to stop human mobility in the world and if you try to stop it with violence, we are responsible for genocide."

The lack of a moral and coherent European policy on immigration is not sustainable. Too many people are dying, and the lives of many others have become a living hell. Letting people die in the Mediterranean, locking them away in holding facilities, or letting them roam around Europe with no rights—these are all immoral and ineffective policies. We left thinking that the remote and powerful authorities that run immigration policy in the EU—and the United States—have something to learn from the humanity of the people of Sicily.

## Who Is Supporting Terrorism and Why?

I have repeatedly and publicly condemned the heinous acts of ISIS and other groups like it. To defeat terrorism, however, it is imperative that we understand who supports it and why. In this section we rely on anthropological method, fieldwork, research, and case studies to examine the complexity and nuances of those Muslim individuals who support terrorist groups. Our findings confirm that supporters of terrorism are not a monolith, and their paths to terrorism are different. We can divide these Muslims into three categories: those immigrants with a tribal background, those with a modernist Islamic background, and European converts. Muslims from each of these categories have slightly different reasons for becoming involved in terrorism.

### Tribal Muslims of Europe

In my book *The Thistle and the Drone* (2013), I describe Muslim societies that are essentially tribal in organization, leadership, and tradition living in the often-inaccessible peripheries of modern states, where they were usually marginalized and brutalized by central governments dominated by a different ethnic group. Their culture—and indeed their interpretation of Islam itself—was shaped by a defined and ancient culture of honor that prized hospitality, courage, and the taking of revenge. I call this *tribal Islam,* a term that could be applied to the actions and thinking of militants emerging from Muslim tribal societies, such as Osama bin Laden, al-Qaeda, the Taliban, and ISIS. It is to be noted that the tribal notion of revenge, which is so central to the arguments of the militants, is categorically rejected by Islam and in the sayings and actions of the Prophet of

Islam. Indeed, the very notion of tribalism is dismissed by the Prophet in his saying, "There is no Bedouinism in Islam."

In Europe today, it is evident through the actions of young Muslim terrorists with a tribal background that they are comprehending the code of honor in parts only: While they are overactive in emphasizing revenge, they have relegated the need for balance and wisdom to the background. Similarly, when a drone strike takes out a "high-value target" in tribal societies, whether in Waziristan, Yemen, or Somalia, those most closely related to the deceased may well respond according to the tribal laws of revenge.

Our discussion of tribal Islam is necessary because there is a substantial population of Berber Muslims present in Europe. These Berber tribal members, whose ancestors were the leaders in all major wars against North African central governments both during and after the colonial period, lived in mountainous areas that had been colonized by Spain and France. Iconic Berber anticolonial fighters include Abd el-Krim, who led the Rif Berbers against Spain and France. There were small numbers already living in these European countries when the European need for labor after the Second World War brought larger numbers to the continent. While Spain and France had an imperial relationship with the Berbers, countries like Belgium, the Netherlands, and Germany, which invited them as guest workers, did not. In both cases, the Berbers brought with them their identity of tribal Islam. Although we are focusing on the Berbers for purposes of this case study, the arguments apply to other immigrants with a tribal background, for example, the Chechens, the Afghans, the Kurds, and also Arabs from certain parts of the Middle East.

The European guest-worker program after the Second World War provided governments in North Africa another way of dealing with their recalcitrant tribal communities: "Thanks to the escape valve offered by Western Europe, the region's governments had no need to try to satisfy the Berbers' grievances; they simply shipped the 'troublesome' Berbers abroad as guest workers."[14] As Bachir M'Rabet, a youth coordinator at a community center in the Molenbeek neighborhood of Brussels and the son of a Moroccan guest worker, put it to a *New York Times* reporter in April 2016, "When emigration to Europe started, the king was happy to get rid of these people." The migration program was so extensive that by 2000, David Hart, an anthropologist who studied the Rif, reported that "virtually every Rifian family has at least one male member working in Western Europe."[15]

In places like Belgium, France, Germany, and the Netherlands, Berbers were sent to work in mines and factories. But as industrial jobs dried up, the Berbers found themselves high and dry, living as secluded and often disliked minorities in urban ghettos. When the mines in Belgium closed during the economic crisis of the 1970s and 1980s, some Rif Berbers who lost their jobs resorted to trafficking drugs from the Rif, which according to UN estimates provides nearly all European hashish and is the world's top supplier of the drug along with Afghanistan. As the French historian Pierre Vermeren has noted, Rif clans became "the largest exporters and distributors of hashish in Europe." Berber drug traffickers, he said in an April 2016 interview in the French weekly *L'Obs*, "are afraid of nothing, they are used to moving across borders, to having weapons."

For Muslims with a tribal background, involvement in acts of violence and recruitment into terrorist organizations was motivated by the code of honor and revenge: slum-like living conditions, constant cultural humiliation, and lack of education and employment opportunities provide ideal grounds for festering resentment against the system to build up and often push individuals over the brink. These tribesmen would also have heard stories about how their tribes fought against European colonial powers and central governments. In such tribal communities, terrorist recruitment tends to be through kinship and neighborhood links, as in areas like Molenbeek in Brussels. A Belgian security official noted in late 2015 that "entire streets" in some areas have "decamped to Syria."[16]

There is a correlation here with respect to ISIS: the European country that has sent the most fighters to ISIS is France, which has a Berber population of more than 2 million. Many of these are Kabyle Berbers from the mountains named after their ethnic group, the center of resistance during French colonial rule and the war of Algerian independence, in which 10 percent of all Kabyle Berbers were killed.[17] The European country to send the highest number of ISIS fighters per capita is Belgium, in which the majority of Muslims are Berbers from the Rif mountains of Morocco, the center of resistance during colonial rule in Morocco. Both mountainous regions of the Kabyle and Rif Berbers remained restive after independence, breaking out into open warfare against the center at various times.

In each and every one of these cases of tribal groups migrating to Europe, we may note that their asabiyyah, or social cohesion, has, by definition been attenuated in the act of migration. In short, individuals find themselves no longer protected by the carapace of their tribal identity or able to offer guidance to others on how to interact with larger society. If individuals are not able to develop a new identity, they are highly vulnerable to suggestions offered by charismatic figures, which could lead them to acts of violence. This vulnerability is heightened by the fact that when individuals are most susceptible, having lost the asabiyyah of the ancestors, they are, at that very moment, rejected by the new society in which they have chosen to make a home.

The important tribal aspect of the identity of European Muslim terrorists, however, is little understood. When the media examines cases of European Muslim terrorists in Belgium or France, they rarely investigate tribal affiliations. And even if they do identify terrorists as coming from Berber tribes, for example, they do not examine how their tribal identity and background factor in their subsequent behavior.

Take the example of Berber involvement in terrorism—and we must be careful not to condemn the entire community, as in almost all the cases the family has condemned the terrorists and the vast majority of community members have nothing to do with terrorism. In the Madrid train bombings that killed 191 people in March 2004, "five of the seven Madrid conspirators and one of its two leaders, Jamal Ahmidan, hailed from the Jamaa Mezuak neighborhood of Tetouan," a city in the Rif mountain region.[18] Ahmidan, the mastermind of the attacks, followed a life trajectory that would become all too common in future terrorism associated with ISIS. He became a drug dealer in Madrid after illegally emigrating in the early 1990s and "built a lucrative hashish and ecstasy trade that operated from Holland to Morocco."[19] Ahmidan impregnated a teenage Spanish junkie, who gave birth to his son, and was imprisoned by Spanish authorities for drug trafficking. He began to use heroin in prison. In 1993, during a visit home to Tetouan, Ahmidan, while in a drunken stupor, killed a man who tried to rob him. He was later imprisoned in the Netherlands, France, and Switzerland. On a return to Morocco he was imprisoned for the murder he had committed. Ahmidan then, declaring that he was turning over a new leaf, became a prison imam. He was released in 2003 and returned to Spain, angry about the war in Iraq, and resumed selling drugs. He and the other six main suspects blew themselves up when surrounded by Spanish police after the train bombings.

Several months after the bombings in Madrid, a Rif Berber living in Amsterdam, Mohammed Bouyeri, changed the course of the debate about Islam in the Netherlands and Europe when he murdered the filmmaker Theo Van Gogh, who had said incendiary things about Islam and made a film that was seen as highly offensive by Muslims. In May 2014 Mehdi Nemmouche, a French-born Algerian Kabyle Berber who had been imprisoned five times and lived in the Molenbeek neighborhood of Brussels, shot and killed four people in the Jewish museum in Brussels. In August 2015 Ayoub el-Khazzani, a Rif Berber from Tetouan and a Molenbeek resident, who had been convicted in Spain for drug trafficking, opened fire and stabbed passengers on a train from Brussels to Paris before being subdued.

Berbers figured prominently in the wave of terrorism that hit Europe in fall 2015 and spring 2016. The leader of the Brussels network of terrorists was the Molenbeek-based Khalid Zerkani, a Rif Berber described by the Belgian federal prosecutor as "the biggest recruiter of jihadists Belgium has ever known." Ahmed Dahmani, accused of scouting locations for the attacks in Paris that killed 130 people, was a Rif Berber, as was Salah Abdeslam, who provided logistical support for the attacks, and his brother Brahim, one of the terrorists who attacked Parisian bars and restaurants. Additionally, Foued Mohamed-Aggad, one of the terrorists who attacked the Bataclan theater, was also a Rif Berber. Abdelhamid Abaaoud, described as the ringleader of the Paris attacks, was a Berber from the Atlas Mountains in Morocco's south.

Rif Berbers were also heavily involved in the March 2016 attacks in Brussels that killed thirty-two people. All three of the suicide bombers in the attacks at the Brussels airport and metro were Rif Berbers: Najim Laachraoui and Ibrahim El Bakraoui and his brother Khalid El Bakraoui. A cousin of the El Bakraoui brothers, Oussama Ahmad Atar, was named in November 2016 as the Syria-based coordinator of both the Paris and Brussels attacks. All of the eight terrorists directly implicated in the August 2017 Barcelona attacks, young men and teenagers, who either died at the hands of police or in an explosion at their hideout, were Berbers. Seven had origins in the Moroccan Middle Atlas Mountains region and one, an imam, slightly older than the rest, described as the plot mastermind who had been imprisoned for drug smuggling, was from the Rif.

There is, however, a backlash in the Muslim community against those Muslims who reject Europe. The mayor of Rotterdam, Ahmed Aboutaleb, who is himself a Berber from the Rif, had a blunt message for his fellow Muslims in January 2015: "But if you don't like freedom, for heaven's sake pack your bags and leave. . . . And if you do not like it here because humorists you do not like make a newspaper, may I then say you can fuck off."

## Modernist Muslims

If tribal Islam is defined by the heart, with its emphasis on culture, lineage, family, sentiment, and emotion, then modernist Islam is formed by the head, valuing reason, logic, and pragmatism. For those whose profession it is to prevent Muslim terrorism, the understanding of these two different interpretations of Islam is vital to checking and defeating it. Without understanding the difference, our solutions will continue to be inadequate and ineffective.

To discuss modernist Islam in the context of terrorism, we focus on the story of Aqsa Mahmood, a young Muslim woman from Glasgow, Scotland, who left her modernist family in the pursuit of literalist Islam. Aqsa left home for the Middle East and was dubbed "The Bride of ISIS" in the media. Her case came amid a flurry of similar reports of young European women joining ISIS. Coming from a comfortable middle-class family, her posts on social media reveal a sensitive and inquiring personality; we cannot but be moved by the love she expresses for her mother. But equally we cannot but be horrified at her bloody rhetoric of violence and toxic hatred of Jews and Shia alike once she joined the demonic forces of ISIS.

It is tragic to contemplate Aqsa's story because she could have been a successful doctor, journalist, or even a Member of Parliament. She had all the qualities and opportunities for any of these careers. Instead, she chose to throw away her life and cause a blight on her family and community. It was her misfortune that her parents could not provide her spiritual and intellectual guidance; her father in particular refused serious intellectual interaction with her, peremptorily dismissing her as a "Wahhabi." The local imams and community leaders also failed her; they were simply not there. Her story therefore is an indictment of the leadership of the Muslim community. It also reflects a greater tragedy than that of one life and family destroyed. The repercussions of her actions would be felt by the entire community and would add to the general impression that Muslims, even the middle-class and "successful" ones, could not be trusted and harbored terrorists in their midst.

In November 2013 Aqsa Mahmood gave her father a long hug and, saying "Khuda hafiz," or goodbye in Urdu and Persian, departed her family home. The night before, anticipating the journey she was about to undertake, she had asked her sisters to sleep with her in the same bed. When she next contacted her parents four days later, she was crossing the Turkish border into Syria. Her shocked parents pleaded with her to come home, but she refused.

Aqsa's family had emigrated from Pakistan to Scotland in the 1970s. Her father, Muzaffar Mahmood, was the first Pakistani to play for the Scottish national cricket team. Aqsa was raised in an affluent Glasgow neighborhood and attended a prestigious private school before enrolling in university. The impact of Aqsa's disappearance on her family was profound. One of her sisters spiraled into depression. Aqsa's distraught parents addressed her through the media with statements such as, "You are a disgrace to your family and the people of Scotland, your actions are a perverted and evil distortion of Islam. You are killing your family every day with your actions, they are begging you stop if you ever loved them." From her position in Syria, an unrepentant Aqsa used social media to describe her new life and appeal to other Western Muslims, particularly women, to join her.

According to her parents and school friends, Aqsa was a "normal" Western girl, listening to Coldplay, reading Harry Potter, wearing makeup, and discussing boys with her friends. But friends noted that from the age of fifteen, Aqsa, who began to wear the hijab, became more distant, and spent increasing amounts of time alone. Her parents said that Aqsa became concerned about the bloodshed in Syria and began praying and reading the Quran. Her mother described the impact that Syria had on Aqsa to the *Scottish Daily Mail* in February 2016: "She started to talk about Syria. She became very emotional and would cry when she watched the news. I remember after a chemical attack on the news, she burst into tears."

The reasons for Aqsa's decision can be better understood by examining her activity on social media.[20] Of particular interest is her Tumblr blog, titled "Umm layth" (Mother of the lion). The blog began at the start of 2013 and encompassed her time in both Glasgow and Syria. In the fall of 2015 it was shut down, as her Twitter feed had been previously. But before then we had been able to access Aqsa's blog to pick up clues as to why European Muslims followed Aqsa's path.

Aqsa found her voice between the ages of fifteen and nineteen, when she left Scotland for Syria. Much of her development, spanning the Syrian civil war, took place online. In her desire to express herself she used Internet terminology familiar to any young English-speaking Westerner. Through social media, she was able to acquire and disseminate information, which helped shape her ideas. It also put her in touch with like-minded people, allowing her to see what they shared and to comment or share information herself. As her social media profile grew, she began to attract attention and soon gained an online following.

From the time Aqsa started her blog, she filled it with photos of the Syrian war, which was almost two years old at that point. Many of these depicted suffering and bloodied children and women, their haunted faces begging the observer to take action. The videos and GIFs she posted showed intense violence and carnage, including one in which an explosion blew away a Syrian's face. Aqsa attempted to rouse her audience to aid the Syrians. For example, she posted a graphic featuring stills from a video of a young Syrian girl, who was pleading, "We have neither food nor drinks. . . . What is the fault of my siblings and I?" Aqsa wrote in response to these images, "May we be put to shame." She also shared a photo of Syrian children holding a message which read, in full capital letters, "GIVE US A NUMBER! HEY, WORLD, HOW MANY KIDS SHOULD BE KILLED BEFORE YOU DO SOMETHING?"

Through her interest in the Syrian war and the use of social media and the Internet, Aqsa was exposed to the great variety of global Islam. She frequently voiced her delight and awe at the scope of the ummah, sharing romantic photos of ordinary Muslims in traditional dress from across the Islamic world in places like Mali, Morocco, Pakistan, and Afghanistan. The Muslims in the photos conveyed a spiritual calmness and authenticity as they went about their daily lives. These scenes of tranquility, joy, and simple piety, however, were juxtaposed with a multitude of photos and postings of people in these same regions experiencing death, destruction, mayhem, and terror. In addition to her constant posts about Syria, Aqsa voiced outrage about the suffering of Muslims in Afghanistan, Kashmir, Iraq, Palestine, Chechnya, Thailand, and many other places. She spoke particularly of the Rohingya in Burma. In one post, she wrote, "Ya Allah forgive me, forgive us. Let us not stray and forget about our brothers and sisters in Somalia, Burma & Mali. Not let the media decide whom we shall remember in our *du'as* [prayers]." She also often focused on the suffering of people caught up in the U.S. war on terror, posting material on Abu Ghraib and Guantanamo Bay and sharing photos of drone strike victims in Waziristan.

Aqsa featured people whom she considered Muslim champions who fought injustice and oppression, posting photos and quotes associated with them. These included historical figures like Malcolm X, Omar Mukhtar, who fought the Italians in Libya, and Mohammed Abdullah Hassan of Somalia, known as the Mad Mullah, who fought the British. More contemporary figures prominently featured included the Palestinian Abdullah Azzam, who cofounded al-Qaeda in Peshawar; Omar Ibn al-Khattab, the Saudi-born fighter who fought the Russians in Chechnya; al-Qaeda figure Abu Yahya al-Libi of Libya; Abu Musab al-Zarqawi of Iraq; and Anwar al-Awlaki, who was killed by a U.S. drone in Yemen. Aqsa also posted quotes by women associated with these figures, such as al-Zarqawi's wife, who had no regrets for the sacrifices they had made. Additionally, many posts quote and praise the Prophet of Islam and figures such as Caliph Umar as well as Sultan Saladin.

She provided advice and encouragement to her online followers based on her experiences as a European Muslim, writing, for example, "Nothing is more hurtful than your family questioning you why you're wearing the abaya or why you've started growing the beard. But brothers and sisters stay strong. We're all in the same position, some may have it more difficult than others. However never feel like nobody is there to understand or relate to you. *Fa Tuba Lil Ghuaraba* [Glad tidings to the strangers]."

As Aqsa became increasingly drawn into online activism, she expressed acute feelings of loneliness on her blog. She delved into books, many of which she ordered online. Her frustrated parents voiced concern about what she was reading: "My dad asked me if everything is alright, my family think I'm weird because I prefer my own company and being alone. lol. All I need in this life is me and my books." In another post, Aqsa wrote, "LOOOL my mum said she will hit me with a shoe if I order anymore books. I'm so dead. I still have 2 books to come through. . . . DEAD. I tell ya." Two months later, she wrote of her father: "I asked my dad to get me some books while he goes to Pakistan next week. He got angry and said what 'Al Qaeeda' type books. . . . My parents genuinely think I'm extremist." She added in a tag of the post, "just cus i have bin ladens biography." She had written three months earlier: "Nah man cba [can't be arsed] with family members calling me wahabi." Aqsa wrote of the high value Islam places on knowledge, and she would describe her excitement at receiving a new book. She posted one photo, for example, of an unwrapped book she had just received in the mail. The title of the book, which was published in London, was *Book of EMAAN: According to the Classical Works of Shaikhul-Islam Ibn Taymiyah.*

Aqsa's view of Islam seems to have been shaped almost exclusively by social media and through reading books that she learned about online. It was not apparent that Aqsa met with any Muslim leader in Scotland or attended a mosque. A rare example of a reference to the local Muslim leadership was a post Aqsa shared that condemned the Muslim Council of Britain for being "apologetic and defeatist" and "having openly taken sides with the American Government, without shame." These Muslims, the statement claimed, were on "the side of Zionist-controlled America" and "have never expended a drop of sweat or blood in Jihad for the sake of Allah like the Prophet . . . preferring instead to attend 'official' dinners and gatherings standing by the sides of Presidents and Prime Ministers whose hands are still dripping with the blood of Muslims."

She struggled to make changes to her European life in accordance with what she believed were religious obligations. "The more I'm learning the

*Deen* [Islamic religion]," she wrote, "the more and more I'm feeling like a hypocrite. I really need to start implementing a lot more of what I've learnt into my life." Several days later she wrote, "My current-self is constantly at war with my former-self. The two are fighting for control of my future-self. *Jihad al-nafs* [struggle against oneself]." As a European, Aqsa also dealt with practical matters, such as the celebration of holidays, posting a message, for example, by the Saudi scholar Sheikh Muhammad ibn al-Uthaymeen saying that it is not permissible to celebrate Valentine's Day, as well as the question of what constituted appropriate dress. "I just bought my first abaya," Aqsa wrote in February 2013, "actual so excited. Lolz mums gonna freak once she finds out how much money I have spent on online shopping this week." In her posts, Aqsa sometimes noted contradictions or double standards evident in Western countries concerning Muslims, for example, posting a message from another blog, which read, "I LIVE IN A LAND WHERE A COVERED WOMAN HAS TO PAY A FINE FOR BEING COVERED & A NAKED WOMAN GETS PAID FOR BEING NAKED."

On her blog, Aqsa's posts expressed a general worldview of binary and opposed mentalities and geographical regions— that of Islam and non-Islam. Her posts dealing with the Muslim world speak of the need to return to original, authentic Islam and to celebrate those she saw as championing this effort. In the non-Muslim world, the situation was more complex. That Aqsa lived in a non-Muslim country caused her a great deal of anguish and consternation.

As her online education progressed, Aqsa increasingly worried whether she was living an authentic Islamic life and whether this was truly possible at all in a European country. In the words of many of the scholars Aqsa posted, the answer was no. For example, she posted what she described as a legal verdict from "The Permanent Committee of Scholars in Saudi Arabia": "Whoever is not able to call the Adhaan out loud then he has failed to openly perform the rituals of the deen, and it is upon him to make hijrah." We can see Aqsa's dilemma as a Muslim European encapsulated in a single comment from January 2013: "It's funny, I have family members desperately wanting to move to the west and settle down here. And then there's me, who's always trying to convince my Mum to move back to the homeland." She continued in a tag of the post, "that's why I want to marry somebody from back home lolz."

Aqsa came to believe that it was the duty of Muslims in Europe to migrate to the new caliphate announced by ISIS and to fight against its enemies. The terrorist organization was also involved in a war, she believed, that was foretold in prophecy and involved the coming of the Mahdi, the Redeemer. In September 2013, she wrote, "Many scholarly people within the ranks of the Islamic State are preparing for the End time Prophecies concerning Ash Shaam, the Malahim (epic battles) and the arrival of the Mahdi (guided one). This can be seen through titles of the organisations, i.e. Jabhat al Nusra (meaning: the Face of Victory) is mentioned in a Prophetic Hadith."

According to Aqsa, the greatest threat to Islam and the Islamic State was the Shia whom she blamed for the deaths of so many Syrians. For example, in February 2013 she shared a photo of a dead Syrian child with the caption "Shi'ism is killing us. The question is, what are you going to do about it?" In other posts she described the Shia as "filthy," "demons," "dogs," "crazed apes," "crazed animals," and "lying deviants" and wrote that they are "the true enemies of Ahlul Sunnah." "Spilling his [Shia] blood," she wrote in a post quoting Ibn Kathir, "is more lawful than spilling wine." Aqsa frequently criticized Muslims who spoke of ummah unity with the Shia: "I would rather befriend a pig before I go near that lot for unity." In more than one post she suggested that Shiaism is a Jewish sect, and in another she posted a doctored photo of a face that was one-half Israeli prime minister Benjamin Netanyahu and one-half Iranian president Mahmoud Ahmadinejad. The caption read, "DIFFERENT FACE SAME AGENDA."

Before leaving for Syria, Aqsa had frequently posted stories of Muslims who protected Christians, such as the Caliph Umar in Jerusalem, often commenting that the media would never show this side of Islam. She once posted a group of photos of Christian Somali women, for example, writing that "Christian women feel safer and respected under Shariah law and Al-Qaeda rules in Somalia." Aqsa also posted a message from another blog indicating the union of Christians and Muslims in Syria that read, "To anyone that doesn't know Syria. . . . This is just a quick reminder to any non-Syrians who claim muslims or christians in Syria are sectarian. We have co-existed for generations, this revolution will not make it any different."

Yet around the time she departed for Syria, Aqsa seemed to have changed her position. In November 2013 she posted a quote by Sheikh al-Uthaymeen of Saudi Arabia that read, "Expel the Jews and Christians from the Arabian Peninsula." She was sounding increasingly murderous and deranged. She asked her followers in Europe and the United States, for example, to initiate violent attacks. In a series of tweets on June 27, 2014, she urged "Whoever carries out an individual operation (in USA/UK/FRANCE etc) against any country that is openly waging a war against Muslims" to "Follow the example of your Brothers from Woolwich, Texas and Boston etc." She continued, "there's nothing more beautiful than bringing fear into the hearts of the *Kuffar* [non-believers] by attacking them where they think they are safest." "If you cannot make it to the battlefield," she wrote, "then bring the battlefield to yourself. Be sincere and be a Mujahid wherever you may be." In June 2015 she posted a poem that praised as "revenge" a beheading in France, a suicide bombing at a Shia mosque in Kuwait, and the gun attack on tourists in Tunisia that killed thirty-eight people.

Appealing to young Western female Muslims to join ISIS, Aqsa invoked the example of "the 4 greatest women in Islam," Khadija, Aisha, Fatimah, and Maryam. Unlike Muslim women in Europe, she wrote, those in the Islamic State will have the potential to live up to the example of these female role models. Aqsa married an ISIS fighter and posted a series of long pieces in 2014 and 2015 that she called "Diary of a Muhajirah." In one of these posts she wrote, "This is a war against Islam. . . . Either 'you're with them or with us.' So pick a side." She declared, "My allegiance is and will only be to our beloved Ameer, destroyer of the enemies, Abu Bakr al Baghdadi (ha) and to the Islamic State."

Aqsa stressed to her audience that leaving one's family behind was the most difficult aspect of "hijrah." "Everything is always easier said than done," Aqsa wrote, "and leaving my family for the sake of Allah was the biggest sacrifice I've ever made in my selfish life so far." In a lengthy post in April 2014 she addressed her mother:

> The right of a final hug and the last kiss I took away from you, my beloved But there is not a day that goes by where my body does not yearn for your affection For you, ya umee I crossed the seven seas and for you ya umee I beg and cry to Allah I plead and ask him every night to unite us again, to let us be together, forever. . . . Ya umee we will go to a place which the mind cannot comprehend, where no eye has laid upon it yet. A place specially reserved for you my beloved— inshaAllah—a place where the reward for your patience will be presented. So, forgive me, my love. 4 months ago I left without a warning. Forgive me ya Umee I left and I know you've accepted that I'm never coming back.

### Muslim Converts

Just as the case of Aqsa gave us insights into how a modernist Muslim was drawn to militancy, we will rely on the case of Hermann to understand why converts may also be so attracted. Just as Aqsa represented a fairly typical South Asian young immigrant with her quicksilver temperament and intelligence until she went off the rails, Hermann, the tall, blue-eyed, blonde, athletic, serious, and thoughtful young man with a short cropped beard, was the picture of Germanic primordial identity. Hermann came from a comfortable, upper-class, influential German family. Frankie, who had been introduced to the family, arranged a social call for Hermann to meet me and talk about converts.

While the German converts discussed in chapter 6 spoke of their affinity for Sufi Islam and the openness of the religion, Hermann was more attracted to literalist Islam. He had converted to Islam two years earlier, at the age of eighteen, and explained why he became Muslim. It was not a Pauline conversion; he took time to study different religions and eventually settled on Islam: "Basically, a wide range of reasons that had to fit in order to enable me to make this decision. But after all, the most important reason was to have read the Quran, I'd say the most basic element of Islam, and I figured this to be very convincing," he explained, "I think that the idea of tauhid and the unity of God was the argument that I found most reasonable basically and which eventually motivated me." He said he could not find the notion of tauhid in Catholicism, the religion of his upbringing.

Becoming Muslim led Hermann to renegotiate his prior identity as a European teen with his new identity as a Muslim; his pre-Islamic teenage years could be seen in the tattoo on his arm. "It's some poetry saying to fear nobody, it's about fearlessness, about strength." He also had different tattoos on his shoulders and his back, he added, which he got before he converted. After he became a Muslim, Hermann was concerned about his tattoos: "In Europe, there are many brothers and sisters who are tattooed and have this from the past. It's normal, you're raised here and this sort of stuff is popular here. When you're fifteen or sixteen it's so cool." Now he realized that

> to remove it would cost €15,000 and that's only to remove it, then you have sessions afterward to restore the skin because you basically simply burn it, and you've got a big white really weird-looking space. It's very messy, very long, very costly, and we've asked our sheikh what the correct opinion of this issue is, and he said that it's better generally not to remove it because in an authentic hadith, the Prophet, *Salla Allahu 'alayhi wa-sallam*, peace be upon him, says do not harm yourself and others.

Islam, he explained, provided "the information I need to live a fulfilled life with love, with purpose, which is above partying, having fun, stuff like that. . . . It's a perfect description of God that you find in the Quran where God is speaking personally. You don't have that in the Bible." In Christianity, he explained, "You associated Jesus, peace be upon him, with God" and believed "the Holy Spirit to be some part of God, the third part of God." In Catholicism, he said, "you make prayers" to saints, "which is violating Islam, the tauhid, the unity and the worship."

Hermann talked of the widespread Islamophobia and the hostile media: "I typed into Google 'Islam,' 'Muslims,' 'Islamists,' 'Salafists,' stuff like this, and I wanted to see how many positive articles, how many negative, and how many neutral articles there were. And it's basically almost 99 percent negative. And I thought, someone who consumes media, they will be, let's say, suspicious." Hermann felt it his moral duty to defend Islam against those who attacked it. How he acted next would depend on what he understood his Islamic duties to be and how he should carry them out.

Frankie, who was closely observing the conversation between us and taking notes, was interested in the encounter because he saw something more important and bigger than just an ordinary conversation between casual acquaintances. Frankie realized he was witnessing the struggle for the soul of European Islam:

> The discussion was a fascinating one between a young man and an Islamic scholar representing two conceptions of the religion and what it demanded of adherents. While Hermann was coming from a rigid, literalist perspective and had the attitude that what was right was to be followed exactly and what was wrong opposed, Professor Ahmed stressed the need to use core Islamic precepts like compassion and mercy to think for one's self, which, he argued, is precisely what the Quran asks Muslims to do. Muslims need to interpret their own life and make moral decisions based on the life and teachings of the Prophet. This involves thinking critically about how the Prophet would approach different situations and apply them to our own times.

Hermann said that his sheikh, who had been influential in his understanding of Islam, was Syrian and currently fighting in Syria. It seemed Hermann was moving in this direction. He stated that there were "many" people from his area who were fighting in Syria, so he would not be out of place over there. When I questioned the wisdom of fighting in this context, Hermann asked what, then, was to be done about the women and children being killed? He quoted a Quranic verse in Arabic that, he argued, backed up his approach. Hermann had an intense and serious demeanor, and his comments were brief and without elaboration. He did not at first seem to respond to my arguments. It was clear he would not abandon his sheikh.

I replied that these women and children could also be helped by working to assist them in hospitals or by telling their stories. There were options other than resorting to violence, which, I said, in the current context of Islamophobia would not help the ummah but hurt it. I asked Hermann to think about the two greatest attributes of God in the Quran, *rahman* and *rahim*, or compassion and mercy, and that the Prophet is described in the Quran as a "mercy unto mankind." I argued that the example of the Prophet shows that bloodshed and revenge are to be avoided and cited examples that demonstrated that even when it seemed as if violence could be justified, the Prophet showed compassion. These examples included that of the Prophet declaring a general amnesty when he entered Mecca at the head of a victorious army after the Meccans had driven him out with cruelty. I also cited the example of the Prophet forgiving Hind, who had eaten the liver of the Prophet's cherished uncle to insult and provoke him.

To broaden his spiritual and cultural horizons, I also suggested that Hermann listen to Qawwali, the spiritual music of Muslim Sufi mystics that promoted love and compassion. The Qawwali in praise of the Prophet, I said, was the most moving because it emphasized the Prophet's merciful nature that reflected God's own attributes of compassion and mercy. Hermann's immediate response was to ask if these songs had musical accompaniment or only featured the voice, because if they used musical instruments, they were haram, un-Islamic. I replied that some did and some did not, but at any rate the Qawwali songs I was discussing were in praise of God and the Prophet. Hermann had no response. As Frankie observed, "it was clear that he had been told and had understood that music was against Islam but had not considered that music could be in praise of God and the Prophet."

I asked Hermann what scholars he was reading about Islam. He mentioned several authors, including one that he indicated was perhaps most influential, Bilal Philips, author of the book *Fundamentals of Tawheed*. Philips, we later learned, is a Jamaican convert with Canadian citizenship who studied in Saudi Arabia, was banned from entering the United Kingdom, Kenya, and Australia, and was expelled from Germany owing to charges of terrorism and extremism. In April 2014 police in the Czech Republic arrested the local publisher of *Fundamentals of Tawheed* for disseminating hate speech and announced that the book was anti-Semitic and promoted violence against what the book called "inferior races." I asked Hermann whether he read the great Islamic mystics like Ibn Arabi and Rumi, who not only expressed their deep faith but did so in beautiful and universal verses. Hermann looked expressionless.

As the conversation progressed, I could see Hermann thinking about the points I had made. He grew more at ease as he nodded at the religious references. He smiled increasingly, especially when my family came to sit with us. Hermann appreciated Amineh's presence as, in her gentle way, she reached out to him in empathy. When we next met Hermann, he had opened up even more. He said that while his identity was solely Muslim, he found many similarities between Islam and European culture. He also said that he had never thought about the questions I raised.

At our second meeting, Hermann appeared relaxed and friendly, and his answers were more thoughtful and even compassionate. When I asked him how to improve relations between Muslims and non-Muslims, he said that the different communities should meet and get to know one another. "I found in my personal experience, as soon as people get in contact with Muslims, with practicing Muslims is important, then the less they will have those fears. Yeah, they will find them to be unjustified most times."

Frankie noted after the conversation:

> I realized this was a unique interaction. Not only had we obtained an important perspective for our project, but it looked as if Professor Ahmed had got through to Hermann on a theological and emotional level, which had an impact on how he understood how religion was to be interpreted and lived. With the high stakes involved and the difficulty of the current times, it is a lesson in how to counter militants like ISIS and divert those who would join them. Hermann had been exposed to an interpretation of Islam that was fully compatible with his European identity but gave him a new direction in which he could act as a bridge builder. I told Professor Ahmed after the meeting that he may have saved the young man's life by making him see that going off to the Middle East was not necessarily his Islamic duty.

Had Aqsa in Glasgow been similarly guided on theological grounds and convinced that it was possible to live as a good Muslim in Europe, perhaps she would not have left her hometown to join ISIS. In Hermann's case, the potential journey to the Middle East was aborted and a new direction indicated; in Aqsa's case, neither of these happened. Young Muslims who may be inclined to support terrorism, if instructed in the right way, can change their worldview.

*The Reasons Why Muslims Join ISIS*

The question why so many European Muslims have joined ISIS has confounded commentators—and not only in Europe. Between the start of the Syrian war and the end of 2015, roughly 5,000 Europeans left their homes to travel to the Middle East and fight for ISIS, and there has been a succession of terrorist attacks in Europe since then. It is morally and logically incorrect for Europeans to be behaving in this manner, and even one or two cases would be too many. Yet despite blanket coverage in the media, the question of why they go remains a mystery. Let us look at some of the factors that may explain this phenomenon.

## Islam as a "Religion of Violence"

Tracing the violence to Islam as the "usual suspect" is perhaps the most common way of explaining the behavior of Muslim terrorists. However, the vast majority of terrorists are anything but Islamic in their behavior. Thus looking at Islam as the source of the violence, as commentators and security agencies are all too quick to do, is a red herring. If terrorists like Brahim Abdeslam in Brussels, watching ISIS videos with a beer in one hand and a joint in the other, are to be judged by their actions, then they are as far from Islam as is possible. Another example is Mohamed Lahouaiej-Bouhlel, a petty criminal and French citizen of Tunisian origin who killed 86 people and injured 484 when he drove a truck through Bastille Day celebrations in Nice in 2016. Lahouaiej-Bouhlel's father told Agence France-Presse that his son "didn't pray, he didn't fast, he drank alcohol and even used drugs." In addition, Lahouaiej-Bouhlel had a criminal record, ate pork, did not regularly attend a mosque, and was not religious in any way. He was cruel to his wife, who left him. Piecing together the information given by his father, his neighbors, and the officials investigating him, it seems that Lahouaiej-Bouhlel was not a devout Muslim.

We may conclude that associating the word "Islam" with these terrorists is inaccurate in every possible way and can only lead to an inaccurate analysis of how to prevent further similar tragic incidents. The terrorists under discussion have not only rejected the essential pillars of the faith but have also violated the fundamental precepts of Islam by taking innocent lives. While they may be sociologically identified as Muslim because of the background of their parents and family, their actions cannot be associated with Islam by any stretch of the imagination.

Most Western commentators focus on the role of "jihadist" ideology and "radicalization" in motivating these recruits. Such notions tend to simplify and reduce the complex factors that affect the European Muslim communities, internally and externally. They often quote Quranic verses or Islamic scholars in building the argument that terrorism is religiously motivated. These commentators also conflate distinct Muslim societies that speak different languages and have different identities, such as the Arabs and Berbers of North Africa. This is an incorrect understanding that prevents us from finding effective and lasting solutions to the scourge of terrorism.

"Radicalization has nothing to do with Islam but is about psychological issues even though public discourse focuses on Islam," said Marik Fetouh, the deputy mayor of Bordeaux and the Bordeaux municipal officer for equality and citizenship. Fetouh, who was visiting my office in March 2017 as part of an interfaith delegation from France through the U.S. Department of State's International Visitor Leadership Program, unequivocally rejected the notion that radicalization was inherently linked to Islam and attributed it to those who suffer from significant mental health issues and trauma. Fetouh told us that the research he has done through the Center for Action and Prevention of Radicalization of Individuals has confirmed this, though this position gets drowned out in the media, because, he complained, "the media prefers what's selling papers."

The center's study, which analyzed the cases of forty convicted terrorists in France who had been radicalized, found that none of the perpetrators came from practicing Muslim families but rather were either converts to Islam of European descent or Muslims from non-practicing families. They found that 30 percent of the young people who had been radicalized had psychological issues and had been targeted by organizations like ISIS and al-Qaeda to complete simple tasks, as those who are suffering severe psychological issues are unable to take complex action. Unfortunately, the deputy mayor found that rather than tackling these real problems, politicians focus on debates about banning the veil in public spaces. His research and findings confirmed our fieldwork conclusions.

## EUROPE'S NORTH-SOUTH DIVIDE

Nearly all of the European Muslims who have joined ISIS came from countries in Northern Europe. There is a distinct absence of Muslims traveling from places where convivencia existed in the past and where both Muslims and non-Muslims have some memory of this history. Muslims leaving to join ISIS from Andalusia are almost nonexistent; in Sicily, the imam of the main mosque in Catania, a port city that is taking the brunt of the asylum seekers, told us that not one Muslim has left Sicily to join ISIS. In contrast to the northern countries, it is notable how small the numbers are of those leaving from Spain and Italy, although we do not have figures for the northern regions of Spain and Italy, where attitudes toward Muslims are different from the south.

The correlation here is clear. In the northern countries, where Muslim immigrants had either an imperial relationship with the mother country or a guest-worker relationship, facing xenophobia is a reality of life. This is not entirely true for the countries in the south, and particularly the southern regions of these countries, where both Muslims and non-Muslims repeatedly told us that there was little xenophobia and Islamophobia. For example, the deputy chief of police in Syracuse and the imam of the central mosque of Catania emphasized respectively that there was "no xenophobia" and "absolutely no Islamophobia" in Sicily. In the words of Syracuse's deputy chief of police, there was "no sign of it at all."

### THE HEMINGWAY FACTOR

Many Muslim youth who join ISIS are subject to what we could call the Hemingway factor. In the late 1930s, Ernest Hemingway, along with many other Americans, found himself in Spain during the civil war against Franco's fascist government. His novel *For Whom the Bell Tolls*, arguably the most famous literary account of the conflict, tells the story of the American Robert Jordan and his fight alongside guerilla forces in the Sierra de Guadarrama.

To resist Franco, the rebels were involved in some of the activities we are familiar with in the Middle East today—suicide bombings, indiscriminate killing, blowing up of bridges, and random acts of sadism. Americans like Hemingway and Europeans like George Orwell were driven by a sense of championing the underdog, fighting for a cause. Similarly, many Muslims saw what Assad was doing in Syria—with hundreds of thousands of people slaughtered and millions displaced—and the indifference and inaction of the West and decided to act. They had lost faith in their own governments.

This is not the first time the Hemingway factor has been seen among European Muslims. In the 1980s, Europeans traveled to Afghanistan to fight against the Soviets. In the 1990s, youth from places like Britain traveled to Bosnia as they saw the genocide of Muslims and what they perceived to be the deliberate indifference of Europe. Many Muslims went to provide health and social services and some to participate in the fighting in one form or another.

In addition, many immigrants in Europe still harbor negative ideas of colonialism and resentment left over from imperial history that have been passed down from parents to children. For these Muslims, neo-imperial interference in the Muslim world after 9/11 in countries like Iraq, Afghanistan, Yemen, and Libya—in addition to the unresolved Palestinian issue—causes frustration, resentment, and anger and can serve as an additional motivation for supporting groups like ISIS.

### SAMIA HATHROUBI AND THE CALLOUS MOTHER

We have previously met Samia Hathroubi, the French Muslim female activist, who has been studying the question of why so many European Muslims join ISIS and other militant groups. She has come to the conclusion that they feel rejected by society.

"Why do we have people from France going to Daesh, ISIS, fighting and raping and killing Christians and killing any minorities that don't fit in their mindset?" Mentioning the names of prominent French Muslim terrorists, she argued,

> Mohammed Merah, Kouachi, Coulibaly, they are Muslim. Whether we like it or not they are part of us. I am always saying, I wrote years ago when the attacks of Toulouse happened, that I was puzzled to see this Muhammad, who is the name of the Prophet, *Salla Allahu 'alayhi wa-sallam*, peace be upon him, this Muhammad who is the name of my father, the name of my nephew, this guy who could be one of my brothers, killing. I was always wondering how did we reach this. How come? What happened to France? What happened to us, to Muslims in Western countries? To have among our brothers people doing this? . . . France failed to integrate and to make those people feel happy in their own country. When I think about those guys I really think it's like young kids being abandoned by their mother, which is France, and getting very frustrated and finding this ideology that gave them a reason to go to Daesh or to destroy the mother that didn't fully love them.

If the lives of prominent French terrorists are examined, Samia explained, a pattern of marginalization, drug use, and imprisonment is apparent, much akin to the cases discussed above. "If you look at the life of Mohammed Merah, or the Brothers Kouachi, or the guy who went to the supermarket and made the attack against the Jewish grocery in Paris. In a way they have similar paths—dislocated family, being in the very beginning drug dealers, going to jails, and being radicalized in jails."

Samia was right. Take the example from France in February 2017, when a young, black Frenchman, identified only as Theo, found himself in the middle of a police identity check that was meant to target drug dealers. At the check-point, Theo was sodomized, beaten around his genitals, spat at, sprayed with tear gas, and racially abused by four police officers. The neighborhood, on the outskirts of Paris, erupted in response to the incident, with hundreds marching in Aulnay-sous-Bois; riots and arson followed. The former deputy mayor, Abdallah Benjana, reflected that the reaction to this police brutality was inevitable, given the conditions of the neighborhood, "Unemployment, insecurity, high rents. . . . no prospects for future. They do that to a young man, it can only explode."

Considering Samia's and Benjana's thoughtful analysis, we can assert that in the places where the European mother country has rejected her children, in the places where there is high Islamophobia and few opportunities, there is also the potential for violence and support for ISIS. Where there is low Islamophobia, there is low or no support for ISIS. Islamophobia, embodied by the far-right parties, pushes the young, who may already be angry at their social situation, away from society and further feeds into their sense of alienation. Already feeling suspended between several cultures, they can fall prey to those who advocate terrorism or the idea that far from their problems in Europe there is an "Islamic state" promising a better life.

### *The European Countries Losing the Most Muslims to ISIS*

The 5,000 European Muslims traveling to join ISIS up to December 2015, when the flow of fighters reached its climax, raised security and integration concerns across the continent. At one point in October 2014, for example, the commissioner of London's Metropolitan Police Service announced that five British citizens were joining ISIS every week. Upon a closer look at the breakdown by country, some interesting patterns emerge in line with our thesis. We have selected four major countries from which large numbers of Muslims have left to join ISIS: the United Kingdom and France, which represent Europe's major colonial powers, and Germany and Denmark, countries that have invited Muslims in as guest workers. As shown in table 8-1, France has sent the most fighters, in absolute terms, 1,700, followed by the United Kingdom and Germany, at 760 each, with Denmark, at 125, coming in at the bottom of the list. On the surface, it

Table 8-1. *Fighters from Select European Countries Traveling to Syria and Iraq, December 2015*

| | Total population | Muslim population | Total joining ISIS[a] | Per 100,000 | |
| --- | --- | --- | --- | --- | --- |
| | | | | Total population | Muslim population |
| United Kingdom | 65,110,000 | 3,114,992 | 760 | 1.2 | 24.4 |
| France | 63,500,000 | 5,000,000 | 1,700 | 2.7 | 34 |
| Germany | 81,900,000 | 4,700,000 | 760 | 0.9 | 16.2 |
| Denmark | 5,660,000 | 270,000 | 125 | 2.2 | 46.3 |

a. *Source:* Soufan Group, *Foreign Fighters: An Updated Assessment of the Flow of Foreign Fighters into Syria and Iraq*, December 2015.

would appear that France faces the greatest challenge in counteracting the flight of foreign fighters to fight alongside ISIS. However, when the numbers are expressed in per capita terms, the number of fighters per every 100,000 Muslims in the country's population, the picture begins to shift. By this measure, of these four countries, Denmark has the highest rate of individuals joining ISIS, with 46 per 100,000 Muslims leaving the country. Denmark is followed by France, 34 per 100,000 Muslims, the United Kingdom, 24 per 100,000 Muslims, and Germany, 16 per 100,000 Muslims.

What explains these wide variations in the number of Muslims joining ISIS? Before we begin to answer the question, it must be stressed that these numbers are merely estimates. Besides, numbers alone tell us little about the reasons individual Muslims choose to leave their European homes. It could be for a wide range of reasons highlighted throughout the chapter— to fight for a cause, to provide medical and humanitarian assistance, to look for a spouse, or to act on an embittered impulse. There is clearly push and pull involved in the story.

What do the figures tell us? Based on our thesis and fieldwork, the sociological explanations quickly become clear. Earlier in this study, I argued that Britain and France presented two different forms of imperialism—one more benign than the other. It could therefore be safely assumed that immigrants to the former would be better integrated than those to the latter and therefore less inclined to leave for adventures overseas and fight against their adopted country. The statistics confirm this assumption. Some 1,700 Muslims have left from France, almost a thousand more than from Britain. In per capita terms of the Muslim population of the country the picture is similar, with ten more fighters per capita leaving from France than the United Kingdom. But why should the U.K. figures be as high as they are, given the earlier argument in chapter 4? The fact of the matter is that some of the recent harsh policy initiatives taken in the United Kingdom have alienated, marginalized, and even terrorized the Muslim community. Muslims complain that their traditional organizations representing the community are sidelined, and to make matters worse, newly formed and officially backed ones are patronized, thus causing splits and anguish in the community. The British government's anti-terrorism and anti-radicalization initiative called Prevent, for example, is widely seen in the community as Islamophobic. Teachers are asked to report on their students and neighbors on neighbors. During fieldwork we heard Muslims use words like "thought police" and "big brother" to describe Prevent. Stories circulated such as that of the young British Muslim schoolboy who wrote in a school assignment that he lived in a "terrorist house" when he meant "terraced." He was reported to the police by his teachers and as a result was arrested and interrogated. Baroness Sayeeda Warsi publicly called the Prevent strategy "broken" and "toxic," and Amina Yaqin of SOAS, our host and partner in the United Kingdom, criticized the strategy as "clumsy," saying it reduced trust in the community.

The confusion around the subject of Muslims and radicalization is further compounded by the fact that new organizations purporting to speak on behalf of Muslims and combat extremism like the Quilliam Foundation, founded by former "Islamic radicals," while lavishly funded and supported by the British government, are viewed with suspicion by the Muslim community. Quilliam, Imam Hafiz of London explained, uses the same arguments against the community as the Far Right does, for example that the Quran needs to be reformed. They "fundamentally challenge the mainstream position to present a view that 99 percent of Muslims are wrong." Hafiz noted that the same people at Quilliam, when they were "Islamists," also said that 99 percent of Muslims were wrong. "They have a chip on their shoulder." Musharraf Hussain, a community leader in Nottingham, dismissed Quilliam by saying they have "zero" credibility. For Qassim Afzal, a prominent politician and media personality, Quilliam is "Tony Blair's creation." Of its co-founder, he had this to say: "They brought in a terrorist. Maajid Nawaz was in jail in Egypt. He says everything they want him to say." He is a "rent-a-mouth." With exasperation creeping into her voice, Baroness Warsi asked, "What are they offering? What have they done in life? They have been either extremists or former extremists."

The number of Muslims leaving from France, as a share of the Muslim population, is proportionately twice that leaving Germany, and there are eight more per capita leaving from the United Kingdom than Germany. As for Germany and Denmark—nations that invited Muslim immigrants as guest workers—one would assume that because similar conditions prevail in both countries for Muslims they would be likely to join ISIS at a similar rate. This is not, in fact, so. The rate of Muslims leaving Denmark is about three times as high as Germany. In fact, Denmark, with the highest, and Germany, with the lowest, represent the extremes of the four countries examined in this measure.

As Germany and Denmark are both essentially Germanic tribal peoples, why then should there be such a significant difference between the two? We found the answers in our fieldwork.

Germany has tackled the subject of its immigrant population with high earnestness, creating new Islamic chairs in universities, community centers, and employment opportunities. There is also the Merkel factor—the effect of Germany's most prominent politician taking a heroically bold lead to welcome refugees and signal a shift in policy toward immigrants. German guilt from the Second World War perhaps also plays a role, with the country's leaders keen to compensate by showing compassion to minorities. This is not to say that policies will not change in the future or to underestimate the threat from the Far Right and its intense antipathy for Muslim immigrants.

Denmark, on the other hand, appears to be moving in the opposite direction. This was not always the case; Denmark once welcomed immigrants. Who can fail to be moved by Bashy Quraishy's story of the Queen of Denmark who, when he first arrived in the early 1970s, ordered the chief of police to make sure that the young man wrote home to his mother (see chapter 4). Today, after years of facing ever more intense Islamophobia, Bashy is not a happy man. Muslim immigrants in Denmark find it difficult to feel they are fully integrated in a society that describes itself as "tribal." Leading Danish journalists and politicians emphasized the closed tribal nature of their society and the near impossibility of immigrants, especially Muslims, ever being accepted.

### Is There a Connection between Mosque and Terrorism?

There is a widespread perception that the mosque is a nursery for terrorists and a breeding ground for "Salafis," "Wahhabis," and "radical Islamists," terms used in the media interchangeably to imply Muslim groups promoting terrorism. Our fieldwork gave us the opportunity to visit some fifty European mosques across the continent and determine whether this is, in fact, the case.

Even our first cursory introduction to mosques confirmed that there was a dramatic change in the atmosphere in and around mosques in Europe in the last few years. There is a world of difference from the early 1960s, when I first came to Paris. While visiting famous tourist sites such as the Eiffel Tower, Sacré-Cœur, and Les Invalides, I also went to the Grand Mosque of Paris. For me, it rivaled in beauty, concept, and symbolism the other great monuments of Paris. The mosque was built between the wars in the classic North African style, as a tribute to the Muslim soldiers who had fought for the French against the Germans, and had the characteristic tower, tall and imposing, to announce the call to prayer. In the midst of a bustling Paris, it provided a calm and almost otherworldly environment. The calligraphy was dazzling and the foliage complemented it, providing relief from the sun. A fountain gurgled peacefully in the courtyard, and the few other worshippers there were lost in prayer and in thought.

Over the decades, I was able to snatch a few moments of silence and solitude lost in my thoughts of faith and the divine in mosques. I was aware now, however, that tension, anger, and suspicion permeate mosque congregations in Europe who attempt to preserve their dignity and integrity while security agencies, on the lookout for terrorist-related activity, rub up against them. Angry and frustrated Muslim youth, ineffective Muslim and non-Muslim leadership, a Muslim community feeling under siege, and hostile social and media commentators all point to the mosque leadership as the source of the community's problems. These elements create an atmosphere that discourages many of the young from the mosque and therefore prevents them from learning about their faith, understanding about which they then seek from other sources, including online imams who may push them in a radical direction.

To compound the problem, some major European cities—such as Athens, Marseille, and Barcelona—do not have a central mosque. In the case of Barcelona, Mustapha Aoulad Sellam, of the Office of Religious Affairs of the Barcelona City Council, gave us an overview of the Muslim community in Catalonia at the conference organized by Casa Árabe in Cordoba. Although there are 400,000 Muslims in Catalonia, perhaps up to 500,000, mainly Moroccan which form the majority population of Muslims in Spain, there are no mosques or minarets, and the niqab is banned. There is widespread hostility toward Muslims. Mustapha was particularly agitated about the lack of a central mosque and pointed out that without it, the sensible elders of the community did not have a venue where they could offer guidance to the young who were then susceptible to talk of terrorism from other sources.

In such circumstances, the Muslim community is forced to congregate in converted basements, warehouses, garages, or ordinary rooms. European Muslims are also aware that mosques are magnets for Islamophobic attention and the local non-Muslim population commonly believes that permitting their construction is conceding ground to the Muslim "invasion" and that Muslims are "taking over." One of the greatest wholesale destructions of mosques took place in the Balkans in the 1990s when thousands were blown to smithereens by the Serbs. Two states in Austria, Carinthia and Vorarlberg, were the first in Europe to ban minarets in 2008, followed soon after by Switzerland. While many commentators argue that terrorism is connected to mosques, the reality tends to be the opposite. A lack of mosques can itself be a contributing factor to terrorism. France, with a Muslim population of 5 million, the largest Muslim population in Europe, only had five purpose-built mosques in 2002, although a few have been built after overcoming many hurdles, and it has also seen the highest number of Muslims leaving to join ISIS and constantly faces terrorist attacks. We note that the terrorist strikes in Barcelona in August 2017 took place in a city with a large Muslim population and no central mosque.

For the theologian Thomas Lemmen of the Archdiocese of Cologne and advisor to the German Interior Ministry on Islam, the building of mosques is a positive sign of integration, not the reverse, as is so often argued by the Far Right: "When they founded the mosques, they did not have a lot of money, so they took an empty room, a former shop. . . . And now 20, 30 years later, they say we want to construct our own mosques. And I think this is quite natural. And it shows for me integration and not separation, because they are part of this society and they are moving from the backyard to the public."

My experience at the main mosque in Cambridge during our fieldwork confirmed the presence of the different currents and tensions in the community. I was invited to speak after the evening prayer. As we sat on the carpet surrounded by community leaders, I discovered that the former mayor of the city had joined us and sat down beside me. When I finished my speech, which emphasized the need for the community to reach out and build bridges to dispel the anger and frustration against Muslims, I faced an unexpected backlash from several community leaders who were what we have called literalists. They did not appreciate my reference to Christians being persecuted in Muslim countries like Pakistan and Egypt and countered by saying that I should be emphasizing the persecution of Palestinians and Kashmiris. The argument was not new, but what I found disconcerting was the level of the anger, especially considering that there were distinguished non-Muslims like the former mayor present.

Some of the imams who run the mosques are as much part of the problem as they are the solution. Most who belong to the older generation are not familiar with European culture, and many do not speak the local language. The imam in Europe represents the themes of the study: those from the former colonies of France and Britain have gravitated to what once were the "mother countries," and those from Turkey have been contracted to provide their services in places like Germany. We found that many of the Algerian imams in France, Pakistani imams in Britain, and Turkish imams in Germany were strangers to the local culture and were therefore limited in their capacity to advise the congregation. The statistics back up our observations. In the United Kingdom, less than 10 percent of British imams were trained in the country, in France, less than 20 percent of imams have French nationality, and the ones who do were mainly naturalized. And, "In Germany, there was not a single imam of German nationality in a Turkish mosque until 2007."[21]

There were also mosques, however, that had few problems and appeared to be well-adapted to the local environment—such as the central mosques in Dublin, Munich, Penzberg, and Catania. Then there are the Sufi mosques we visited in Dublin, London, Mostar, and Munich, which were islands of spiritual tranquility. Here we heard complaints about the dangers of radicalization among Muslims and the bad name that it is giving Islam. Here were repeated the ninety-nine names of God with the congregants sensing the power in God's great names, especially in the two most frequently used—the Compassionate and the Merciful. Here we glorified the names of Abraham, Moses, Jesus, and Muhammad, blessings be on them all. I was fortunate to be invited to attend these gatherings. The high point on our Sufi tour was, without doubt, the tiny mosque on the outskirts of Mostar, situated in a cave in a mountain by a powerful rushing stream. Nature, the divine, and worshippers met here on earth in unison as we chanted the wondrous names of God.

As for the existence of so-called radical mosques, although we detected hints of sympathy for radical thought and action, the evidence was limited and sporadic. The experts we talked to—from Tim Winter in Cambridge to Margret Spohn in Munich—confirmed that radicalization emanates primarily from the Internet. Winter, whose job it was to deal with mosques and imams, concluded, "We don't have radical mosques in England. . . . Radicalization happens through the Internet, and other private instruments." We were told that an official report issued by the Federal Office for the Protection of the Constitution in Germany concluded that fewer than 50 of the nation's 3,000 mosques were possibly "problematic." Clearly, the mosque per se is neither a breeding ground for terrorists nor a training school for radical thought. That some 500 British imams refused to lead the funeral prayers for the Muslim terrorists who were killed in the London attacks in June 2017 confirms the desire of the mosque-based religious leadership to publicly and actively reject terrorism.

We did find a general backlash against the Saudis. The community harbored the perception that the Saudis are arrogant and too rigid in their interpretation of Islam, which is widely seen as Wahhabi or Salafi. In any case, as most mosques are ethnically based—Turkish mosques in Germany, Pakistani mosques in the United Kingdom, and Algerian mosques in France—there is little chance of having an all-Saudi mosque. While Saudis may in some cases have an imam or board member, they will always have to face the reality of their numbers in the Muslim communities of Europe. Harrison's comment reflects the team's findings in the field:

> What really struck me was the discordance between me being unable to see a great Wahhabi influence within the Muslim community and what people from Islamophobic far-right groups were saying about Wahhabism. During my interviews and conversations with members of Far Right groups for the project, they gave the view that Wahhabism was a specter haunting Europe and converting Muslims en masse to destroy Europe from within and establish a Muslim caliphate, successfully stoking people's fears. Yet I personally saw no evidence of this, especially as an overwhelming trend, from spending time even in more conservative Muslim mosques and communities.

After visiting so many European mosques, often praying with the community and speaking with the imams, we saw that despite all the current tensions and controversies, the mosque still played a critical role in the life of the community, however humble it was and however strong the storms raging around it. Sometimes after the interviews, we would return to a mosque later in the evening. Invariably the congregants would ask us, complete strangers, to join them at their meager meal. Seated on the worn-out carpet, eating couscous and listening to them talk, I saw for those few moments the burden lifted of living as third-class and despised citizens in

Europe. As they talked of families and homes we glimpsed peace and dignity on their haggard faces. It gave me hope. Spending time in the mosques of Sicily was an especially moving experience. To pray behind a North African imam in a mosque recently converted from a disused church, as I did in Palermo, in a land that had driven away Muslims almost a thousand years ago, was to me a miracle of faith; it was also a glimpse into the innate generosity of European humanism.

In this chapter, we have underlined and analyzed the interconnectedness between terrorism, immigration, Islamophobia, and far-right politics. These links need to be recognized if we hope to tackle the grave problems that they engender and to create reassurance and stability in European society. Considering the urgency of the problem of terrorism, this study needs to be read by political leaders, security officials, journalists, media commentators, and interfaith leaders. In the next chapter, we explore how to promote understanding and coexistence in Europe between its cultures and religions.

# NINE

# Europe at the Crossroads: Monsters, Modernity, and the Imperative for Convivencia

IN OCTOBER 1993 I was witness to an event of great historic significance: Prince Charles delivering a widely publicized and much-anticipated lecture on the subject of Islam and the West at Oxford University. As I took my seat in the front row of the Sheldonian Theatre, I noted the high caliber of the audience: the Aga Khan, the Saudi ambassador, and many other dignitaries. The atmosphere was electric as Islam was already, in the early 1990s, a much debated subject; war had just ended in Iraq and was starting in Bosnia, and there were signs of growing Islamophobia in Europe. People were curious to know what the future king of the realm made of the subject.

The prince plunged into his thesis: Muslims, and this he knew would surprise people, had made great contributions to the West and were part of it. Charles ran through a checklist of subjects in which Muslims had contributed—philosophy, astronomy, medicine, literature. He mentioned the Andalusian philosopher Averroes among others. Cordoba, "this great city of cities," he said, then "by far the most civilized city of Europe," had hundreds of thousands of books in its libraries when the biggest European libraries could boast of a scant few hundred. Jews, Christians, and Muslims lived, worked, and created in harmony for long periods of time. Charles passionately argued for the unified vision of life that Islam promoted and criticized the materialism and cynicism of our age. He even cited my favorite saying of the Prophet: "The ink of the scholar is more sacred than the blood of the martyr."

It was a marvelous exposition of what we have called convivencia—and indeed European pluralist identity—at the heart of the Andalusian model

473

in our study. Charles was doing more than paying tribute to the past; he was reconciling it with modernity. As a member of a small group of informal advisers to the prince, I knew firsthand his commitment to this cause. For historians in the audience it would have been easy to spot the similarities between Charles and the great European royals of the past who were accepting of others and passionate about acquiring knowledge, such as Alfonso X of Spain, Roger II of Sicily, and the Holy Roman Emperor Frederick II. After the lecture the audience rose to give the prince a standing ovation.

I felt we were at a special moment in history. If not at the apex of the relationship between Islam and the West, at a time of optimistic possibilities, we were heading in that direction. Charles would go on to give similar lectures elsewhere and even to propose that the monarch, given the multi-religious nature of the nation, adopt the title of "Defender of the Faiths" rather than "Defender of the Faith." In this, he echoed Alfonso X, who called himself the King of the Three Religions in the thirteenth century. Demonstrating his penchant for convivencia, Charles wore a special Jewish kippa with the emblem of the Prince of Wales to events involving the Jewish community and appeared in local dress in various Muslim countries.

He was also glimpsed in an oriental-looking coat, which had the British press flummoxed as to its origin, with tabloids like the *Evening Standard* suggesting he had "borrowed" it from Dumbledore, the eccentric headmaster of Hogwarts. In fact, the garment was from Chitral, in Pakistan, and had been presented to him by me in the late 1990s. An amused Charles had referred to it in a letter he sent me in 2000: "I wear your wonderful coat you gave me on frequent occasions at Highgrove. . . . It causes many comments amongst those who see me in it and most people think it is Tibetan!" In 2005 Charles sent me a photograph in which he is wearing the coat while feeding chickens in the royal back yard, with a note scribbled across it: "Just to prove I wear your coat!"

Charles's spouse, Her Royal Highness Princess Diana, was already showing signs of being a bridge builder between faiths. When I was invited to give her a special lecture on Islam at the Royal Anthropological Institute in London in September 1990, I was impressed by her intelligent questions, curiosity about Islam, and her desire to help improve relations between Islam and the West. Diana exuded a translucent glow that was touched by an undefined spirituality and it embraced and uplifted me. I presented her with my book *Discovering Islam* and an article I had written on Islam in *History Today*. The next morning several British papers dis-

*Author lecturing Princess Diana on Islam. Hastings Donnan and Jonathan Benthall are seated to author's left (photo by Fritz Curzon)*

played a glorious color photograph of a radiant Diana holding the book with its cover facing the cameras featuring headlines such as "The Student Princess" (*Daily Mail*) and "I'm Not Diana's Guru, Says Top Academic" (*Daily Express*).

What author could resist that kind of support? I was won over. So when it was announced that Diana was to make a solo state visit to Pakistan, her first to that country, in 1991, and she invited me to tea at Kensington Palace to ask for advice, I readily consented. To win over Pakistanis, I suggested she quote their beloved poet Allama Iqbal at the state dinner in Islamabad and gave her several beautiful verses that captured the poet's universal humanism. I also suggested she wear the Pakistani shalwar-kameez. She did both—and the Pakistanis loved her for it. The headlines in the Urdu papers the next morning paid her glowing tributes. A few years later, paparazzi photographed Diana on a skiing holiday in Austria reading my book *Living Islam* while sunbathing in a bikini on the balcony of her hotel. The media's fascination with Diana's interest in Islam is also reflected in Kate Snell's *Diana: Her Last Love* (2000), which has an entire chapter on my lecture. The title of Snell's book does refer to a Pakistani, although I

*Author's book launch in the Moses Room of the House of Lords—from left, Lord Melvyn Bragg, author, Lord Nazir Ahmed, and Lord Christopher Smith*

hasten to assure the curious reader it is not your good author. For me, however tawdry the disgusting subsequent attacks on Diana, her luminescent glow would not dim.

The pendulum was moving steadily and visibly toward closing the gap between Islam and the West. It appeared that Western liberal democracy, which embodied the very notion of modernity with its respect for the rule of law and individual rights, had triumphed, causing leading commentators like Francis Fukuyama, the American political scientist, to declare the "end of history." The United States had emerged as the sole superpower, and the United Kingdom and Western Europe were basking in its economic prosperity and supreme military might. It was difficult to escape the conclusion that countries in the future would follow the route of Western liberal democracy with an inclusive approach to minorities.

In the spirit of convivencia, I was able to make a small contribution to building bridges during this period through several initiatives. In 1993 the BBC broadcast *Living Islam*, a six-part TV series, and published the accompanying book; nothing on this scale had been done before on Islam with a Muslim presenter. I became the first Muslim Cambridge don to speak at evensong at a college chapel and the first Muslim to give the annual Rabbi Goldstein Memorial Lecture at London's Liberal Jewish Synagogue in 1999. I was also the Muslim commissioner on the Runnymede

Trust Commissions on anti-Semitism and later on Islamophobia, which would be a catalyst for interfaith initiatives. Also in the 1990s, I completed a quartet of projects I had conceived about Muhammad Ali Jinnah, the founder of Pakistan, who had envisioned a modern, pluralist state: a feature film starring Christopher Lee; a documentary broadcast on Channel 4; an academic book; and a graphic novel. My book, *Islam Today: An Introduction,* was launched in the Moses Room of the House of Lords in front of a packed audience and with several lords present including Bernard Weatherill, Melvyn Bragg, Nazir Ahmed, Christopher Smith, Jeffrey Archer, and Pola Uddin. I appreciated the fact that there were Jewish, Christian, and Muslim lords present. The historic nature of the event was captured in the front page story of *The News* on February 19, 1999, which described the standing ovation given by the overflowing, enthusiastic audience, and in its headline: "Lords book launch marks new point in search for lasting relationship between Islam and the West." As a result of my activities, I was being recognized in both the East and the West: I was awarded the Star of Excellence in Pakistan and the Sir Percy Sykes Memorial Medal by the Royal Society for Asian Affairs in London.

Sitting in the Sheldonian listening to the hopeful message of Prince Charles, I was lulled into dismissing the dire warnings of Muslims who wrote of their communities being prepared for the gas chambers of Europe as the product of a fevered imagination. "The next time there are gas chambers in Europe, there is no doubt concerning who'll be inside them," noted Shabbir Akhtar in *The Guardian* in 1989. Kalim Siddiqui warned of "Hitler-style gas chambers for Muslims" and Mohammed Ajeeb, the former lord mayor of Bradford, received a letter stating, "What you deserve is the gas chambers." Someone in Hanif Kureishi's 1990 novel *The Buddha of Suburbia* remarks that "the whites finally turned on the blacks and Asians and tried to force us into gas chambers." The genocide in the mid-1990s in Bosnia appeared to confirm the worst fears of the Muslims, although its impact was limited because it was happening on the periphery of Europe.

Little could I have guessed that within a decade the pendulum would swing precipitously away from the Andalusian model toward European predator identity. The September 11 attacks were the catalyst, and Islam came to be identified as the main source of Europe's problems; Islamophobia grew exponentially. Inevitably, anti-Semitism also reemerged, with German politicians, for example, talking of the "domestic or internal enemy," meaning the Jews, and the "external enemy," a reference to Muslims. Even American pop stars sounded the alarm, with Madonna in 2015 warning that Europe "feels like Nazi Germany."

In 2016, just as the arrival of the asylum seekers coincided with the recrudescence of the European Far Right, the contentious presidential election in the United States and Donald Trump's victory raised the issue of Islam's place in Europe to another level of controversy. Leaders of far-right movements were jubilant and saw Trump's triumph as a symbol of hope for their own fortunes. The leader of the Dutch Freedom Party, Geert Wilders, gloated, "The people are taking their country back. So will we." Greece's far-right Golden Dawn party hailed Trump's election as a success for forces "in favor of clean ethnic states." Marine Le Pen, president of France's National Front party, celebrated Trump's victory, and her senior adviser, Florian Philippot, proclaimed in a tweet, "Their world is collapsing. Ours is being built."

It was left to Angela Merkel to greet Trump with caution, reminding him that "Germany and America are bound by common values—democracy, freedom, as well as respect for the rule of law and the dignity of each and every person, regardless of their origin, skin color, creed, gender, sexual orientation, or political views." It was good advice, considering that one of Trump's first appointments was to name Steve Bannon, a confirmed promoter of the anti-Semitic and Islamophobic alt-right, as his senior adviser. Bannon was a kindred spirit and inspiration to many of Europe's far-right leaders—some of whom had written for his Breitbart News website. Bannon provided a transatlantic, philosophic motto to galvanize his followers—"Darkness is good"—along with a trinity to worship: "Dick Cheney. Darth Vader. Satan. That's power." Breitbart did not waste time in showing its mettle: early in 2017 the website issued a fake story reporting that a thousand immigrants had set fire to Germany's oldest church on New Year's Eve with cries of "Allah hu Akbar." The story circulated widely until the police investigated the incident and announced it to be incorrect.

On the other hand, there was disbelief and despondency in Europe at the implications of Trump's victory and what it represented, along with Britain's surprising vote in June to leave the European Union. Leading figures warned that the world was changing and we were entering a period of conflict, uncertainty, and dictatorship. In his December 2016 speech at Chatham House, British foreign secretary Boris Johnson sounded the alarm: "We risk reverting to an older and more brutal system where the strong are free to bully or devour the weak, where might is always right, and the rules and institutions we have so painstakingly built fade away into irrelevance." Former archbishop of Canterbury Rowan Williams, in the *New Statesman*, reflected that "mass democracy has failed" and warned,

"The conventional accounts of what is 'right' and 'left' are fast becoming tribal signals, rather than useful moral categories."

European Muslim intellectuals were particularly anxious. A week after Trump's victory was announced, the journalist Mirnes Kovač wrote me from Bosnia to relay the climate of fear throughout Europe: "There is great fear of 'trumpization' in Europe. After Brexit and Trump nothing in politics is impossible, everything is possible!" Professor Tahir Abbas, a senior fellow at the Royal United Services Institute in London, was uninhibited in a post written on his blog the day the results were announced: "It could firmly lead to the end of the West." Muhammad Abdul Bari, a British scholar and secretary of Muslim Aid, noted in an op-ed in the *Middle East Eye*, "Many have started to fear that this 'anti-establishment' politics, some rather call it authoritarian populism, may put an end to the democratic values and inclusiveness of the modern West."

Worried about the implications of the 2016 American presidential election and Brexit, President Barack Obama, in a speech in Greece, voiced concern about the rise of "tribalism" around the world. The prominent Indian writer Pankaj Mishra characterized the time we are living in as the "age of anger" in his 2017 book of the same title. "The world passed the tipping point into a perilous new era," warned Nathan Gardels, editor-in-chief of *The WorldPost*, on the last day of 2016. Prince Charles's customary optimism also seemed to have abandoned him in an end-of-year message: "We are now seeing the rise of many populist groups across the world that are increasingly aggressive to those who adhere to a minority faith. All of this has deeply disturbing echoes of the dark days of the 1930s."

## A Time of Monsters and the Crisis of Modernity

"The old world is dying, and the new world struggles to be born; now is the time of monsters." The quotation famously attributed to Antonio Gramsci, a victim of Mussolini, Il Duce, the fascist leader who was so bloodthirsty that Hitler held him up as a role model, appears to be once again relevant to our times. The process whereby primordial identity adopts an aggressive predatory aspect and monsters take shape is visible in Europe today. If the new far-right leaders are not full-fledged monsters in the category of Hitler and Mussolini, they are goose-stepping their way in that direction.

The Far Right taps the fears of those on the traditional Left and the Right by claiming that the primordial identity of both is under threat and that it will defend the Volk, race, and nation through predatory action.

While doing so, far-right leaders freely and consciously echo the Nazis of the 1930s with displays of the swastika, Nazi salutes, references to Hitler, and ominous slogans that carry the threat of genocide. Their target is mainly the Muslim community, but anti-Semitism and abuse of the Roma are ever present.

Here are some examples of the ugly trends now evident in Europe. Mobs in Rome attacking migrants chanted, "Let's burn them all," "Let's make soap out of them," "The blacks have to go," and "Long live Il Duce." Beppe Grillo, the head of the Five Star Movement, Italy's most popular party, quoted Hitler's *Mein Kampf* extensively on his blog—the country's most popular. Grillo wrote that the infamous manifesto can help us "understand the present" and warned in a tweet that elections should be held soon "before Rome is swamped by rats, rubbish, and illegal immigrants." Matteo Salvini, the head of the far-right Northern League, has been known to slip on a black shirt at rallies, in honor of Il Duce.

The Islamophobic Pegida movement in Germany was founded in Dresden in October 2014 by Lutz Bachmann, the son of a butcher and a former professional football player who has been convicted in the past of assault, drunk driving, drug dealing, and burglary. Bachmann was convicted in 2016 for inciting racial hatred after posting comments on Facebook referring to refugees as "cattle," "filth," and "scum," and his 2015 photograph with Hitler moustache and hairstyle and a crazy glare in his eyes went viral. This was not postmodern irony; it was modern fascism.

Frauke Petry, then the leader of the Alternative for Germany (AfD), which is akin to Pegida, stated that police should have the right to shoot refugees crossing the German border. The German newspaper *Die Welt* quoted party MP Christina Baum as saying that refugees were causing a "creeping genocide against the German population." Wolfgang Gedeon, the notoriously anti-Semitic member of the Baden-Württemberg state parliament, who was also a member of Alternative for Germany, claimed that the fictitious *Protocols of the Elders of Zion* was accurate, argued that Holocaust denial was legitimate in Germany, and described Judaism as the "domestic enemy" of Europe and Islam the "external enemy." Björn Höcke, the party head in the eastern state of Thuringia, warned in a January 2016 speech that the government's immigration policy "will end the history of our Volk" and caused international controversy in early 2017 when he condemned the Holocaust Memorial to the Murdered Jews of Europe in central Berlin, calling it a "memorial of disgrace." He declared in speeches, "One thousand years of Germany!" In Austria, Norbert Hofer, the presidential candidate of the Freedom Party of Austria—which was formed by an SS general—lost the presidential campaign twice but remains a serious contender. He ran on slogans like "Your Heimat needs you now" and "Islam has no place in Austria."

Even before the AfD and Pegida, German intellectuals like Thilo Sarrazin argued in the bestselling *Deutschland schafft sich ab* (Germany abolishes itself, 2010) that Muslims had inferior genetics to Germans. The prominent philosopher Peter Sloterdijk, a decade earlier, in the manner of Schopenhauer, harkened back to Plato in making the case for a human "breeding" project of improvement led by a "Platonic master" as part of a process he called "Anthropotechnology." Sloterdijk's assistant, Marc Jongen, went on to become the leading intellectual of the AfD.

Leading the charge in the Netherlands was Geert Wilders, who drew on the binary distinction between the "autochtoon," or the "native" Dutch of the "soil," and the foreign "allochtoon," a term used for immigrants: *"Autochtonen* reproduce less rapidly than *allochtonen,"* Wilders warned. "In twenty years time they will be everywhere. . . . We sell our country to the devil named Mohammed, and nobody does anything about it."[1] "Fortunately," he said, "the first Islamic invasion of Europe was stopped at Poitiers in 732; the second in Vienna in 1683. . . . Let us ensure that the third Islamic invasion, which is currently in full spate, will be stopped." "We are heading for the end of European and Dutch civilisation as we know it," he declared. "I don't hate Muslims. I hate Islam," he pronounced. "Islam is not a religion, it's an ideology, the ideology of a retarded culture."

In France, Marine Le Pen, whose father Jean-Marie had admitted to torturing prisoners in Algeria and recommended his daughter to the National Front party as a "big healthy blonde girl . . . an ideal physical specimen," compared Muslims praying on the street to the Nazi occupation. Her niece, the MP Marion Maréchal-Le Pen, declared, "Christians must stand up to resist Islam!" and "Either we kill Islamism or it will kill us again and again." In the United Kingdom, Nigel Farage, the leader of the United Kingdom Independence Party and one of the prominent figures behind the Brexit movement, issued dire warnings about Muslims: "People do see a fifth column living within our country, who hate us and want to kill us." Jim Dowson, the founder of the far-right organization Britain First, told us in an interview that "the Roma are the absolute trash of Europe. . . . like a parasite. And now they're coming here."

In Eastern Europe predator identity expressed itself in attacks on minorities, including Muslims, Jews, and Roma. Muslims in particular were targeted with reference to their religion, which was associated with the hated Ottomans. The leaders of the political party Jobbik in Hungary engaged in a steady succession of anti-Semitic actions, including calling for the compilation of official lists of Hungarian Jews and the unveiling of a statue of Hungary's wartime Nazi-backed leader, who deported 437,000 Jews, mostly to their deaths in concentration camps. Senior Jobbik leaders blamed the Jews for the Treaty of Trianon ending World War I, in which Hungary lost two-thirds of its territory. Jobbik's declared candidate for the presidency, EU MP Krisztina Morvai, lashed out at the Jews: "I would be glad if the so-called proud Hungarian Jews would go back to playing with their tiny little circumcised tail rather than vilifying me." Morvai also wrote an open letter to the Israeli ambassador to Hungary during the Gaza war in 2009, saying, "The only way to talk to people like you is by assuming the style of Hamas. I wish all of you lice-infested, dirty murderers will receive Hamas' 'kisses.'" The Roma, who constitute 8 percent of the Hungarian population, were subjected to murder, violence, and terror.[2] In March 2017, the Hungarian Parliament approved a measure, as *The Guardian* described it, "to detain all asylum seekers in container camps."[3]

In November 2015, a Polish MP and supporter of the Law and Justice Party, which swept into power that month, moved a motion that "the good of the nation is above the law," to a standing ovation.[4] The previous month, Jarosław Kaczyński, the leader of the party, warned that letting in large numbers of migrants, who carried "all sorts of parasites and protozoa," "would inevitably lead to the fall of our civilization, the civilization that created liberties and modern technology." A February 2016 issue of the Polish popular current-affairs magazine *wSieci* featured a naked white woman, draped in the European Union flag and screaming in horror, being assaulted by three sets of dark-skinned arms trying to rip the flag from her body with the headline, "Islamic Rape of Europe." The cover article asserted that Islam and the West have been at war "over the last 14 centuries" and that the world was now witnessing a "clash of two civilizations in the countries of old Europe." President Trump reinforced the idea of Western civilization under threat by Islamic radicals in Poland in July 2017. The style and substance of the speech were vintage Bannon. It was music to the ears of the large audience and validated their predatory urges. Unsurprisingly, some 60,000 Poles in Warsaw in November 2017 rallied the nation demanding an Islam-free "white Europe."

The Czech Republic was also staunchly opposed to the migrants and to Islam. *Politico* reported in August 2015 that "the debating fora of major Czech newspapers" and social media regularly contained "statements that all refugees and 'darkies' should be executed, drowned or sent to gas chambers." Activists like Martin Konvička, a lecturer at the University of

South Bohemia who formed the Bloc against Islam party, argued for "concentration camps for Muslims," and threatened, "Muslims, we will grind you into meat and bone meal." The Czech president Miloš Zeman, who publicly voiced agreement with Konvička's positions, described Islam as a "culture of murderers and religious hatred" and argued that Europe was facing an "organized invasion and not a spontaneous movement of refugees."

Similar forces were at work in neighboring Slovakia. Prime Minister Robert Fico declared, "We are monitoring every Muslim in our territory," and "Islam has no place in Slovakia." In 2013 Marian Kotleba, leader of the neo-Nazi Kotleba – People's Party Our Slovakia, won the election for governor of the Banská Bystrica region, the largest of Slovakia's regions. A journalist for one of Slovakia's main newspapers described Kotleba's party to *BBC News* as "skinheads who Sieg Heil in public." Kotleba also accused Slovakia's 100,000 strong Roma community of being "thieves and parasites" and of "raping or killing." In March 2017, Michal Havran, a Slovak television talk-show host and political commentator, noted of current developments in his country, "Something very dark and very troubling from the past is coming back. They feel they are fighting for something very pure, something very old and sacred. A few years ago, they were ashamed to talk about it. Now, they are proud."[5]

In Bulgaria, the European nation with the largest Muslim minority at 13 percent of the population, the Bulgarian Orthodox Church declared that Muslim refugees constituted an "invasion" and that "the Bulgarian people must not pay the price" for the turmoil in the refugees' home countries "by disappearing." In 2011 the church bestowed sainthood on thousands of Bulgarians who were killed in 1876 during the April Uprising against Ottoman rule, an event that began the process that resulted in independence in 1878. There were daily attacks on Muslims and minorities. Instances of mass violence were perpetrated, such as the February 2014 attack on a mosque by hundreds of people in Plovdiv, the country's second-largest city. The poisonous atmosphere led Evgenii Dainov, one of Bulgaria's leading thinkers and a professor of political science and sociology at New Bulgarian University in Sofia, to make a chilling prognosis to the *New Republic* in December 2013: "The situation in Bulgaria now is like that in the Weimar Republic in Germany prior to the rise of Hitler."

Volen Siderov, an MP who leads the far-right Ataka (Attack) party and was the runner-up in the 2006 Bulgarian presidential elections, in his first speech before Parliament, condemned a "genocide" against Bulgaria being directed by foreign powers and declared that "the hour of the Bulgarian revival has come. The Bulgarian nation has woken up from its slumber."[6] Masons and Jews, he argued in books he wrote, were plotting to "destroy Orthodox Christian Slavs in general and Bulgaria in particular." Other enemies included the United States, NATO, globalization, and Turkey, which he said had conducted a "genocide" against Bulgarians "for more than 500 years."[7] Siderov lamented that "Bulgaria is still under Turkish rule." Among Siderov's books are *The Boomerang of Evil* (2002), in which he seeks to reveal the Jewish "worldwide conspiracy" and condemns "the lie of 'the Holocaust,'" and *My Battle for Bulgaria* (2007), which has clear echoes of *Mein Kampf.*[8] Roma were referred to as "cockroaches" on television, and the slogan "Gypsies into soap, Turks under the knife" was spray-painted on mosques and chanted in anti-Roma rallies.

From the sample of ideas expressed above, it is hard to escape the conclusion that the very foundations of European modernity are being challenged. Modernity was Europe's gift to the world. A steady and incorruptible bureaucracy, an impartial judicial system, reliable banks, growing industries, regular elections, a free press, and thriving universities and arts were merely an extension of a functioning modern state and a barometer of its health. At the heart of modernity lay the idea of the worth of the citizen—that all were equal before the law and conversely no one was above the law. That is why justice was depicted with a blindfold over her eyes; she could not see the class, race, or religion of those who stood before her seeking justice. It was what the newly independent states of Africa and Asia aspired to but too often failed in achieving.

Now before our very eyes we are seeing European modernity stumbling and in danger of falling. A citizen stabbing another citizen, attacking a museum, or blowing up people at an airport or café, the state retaliating by suspending its own rules pertaining to human rights, the stories of torture in dark prisons, and the concentrated prejudice against the minority, all these chip away at the foundations of modernity. The very premise of modernity, that all are equal before the law and that the bureaucracy is neutral and fair, appears to be compromised.

The place of modernity at the pinnacle of the cycle of history appears to have reached a point from where the decline is visible, and there is the real danger that once down the steep curve it will be a long and hard struggle to regain lost ground. Just when we are in the most desperate need, there is no Churchill or de Gaulle, Bertrand Russell or Jean-Paul Sartre to provide leadership and remind Europe of the need to maintain its ideals. There are towering figures to be sure—Pope Francis and Angela Merkel—but they appear embattled. The irony is that this time the danger to Europe is not coming from the Turks in the east or Berber warriors from the south but rather is the result of an internal, slow, and agonizing process of a loss of confidence and will. The burden of modernity, it seems, is a cross too heavy to bear, and Europeans are reverting back to primordial identity. The modern world conjured by Weber is being abandoned for the tribal world described by Ibn Khaldun.

Instead of tackling the real global challenges that face mankind like global warming, religious and ethnic conflict, poverty, disease, and hunger, Europe has been distracted by Islam, immigration, "Islamic terrorism," the passionate debates about identity, and the rise of the Far Right movements. In the meantime Stephen Hawking, possibly the most celebrated scientist in the world, warned in 2016 that mankind would have to find another planet to live on, as this one would be uninhabitable within a thousand years. The following year he recalculated his assessment and shortened the life expectancy of the human race to about a century.

## The Gathering Clouds

When I asked Jafer Qureshi, a distinguished British mental health specialist and prominent Muslim community leader, about the state of Muslims in Europe, he replied, "We are in a cosmic depression." As we traveled across Europe for this project, we met Europeans who reflected a similar mood of pessimism and foreboding. Jocelyne Cesari, the French scholar of Islam, replying to my request to estimate on a scale from zero to ten the chances that Muslims would face a Holocaust-like situation, answered, "six." In Copenhagen, we had lunch with a group of younger Muslim activists that included a white Danish Muslim convert married to a Syrian, who said they were buying houses in Lebanon to prepare for what was coming. He issued a warning: "Muslims do not know what they are dealing with. People assume that human rights and civil liberties are deep in society but here they are superficial. Beneath it, all the elements that were in place in the 1930s are still there and the Holocaust will be repeated."

Muslim women talked of facing prejudice in their daily lives. Most had been abused in public and some even assaulted. A young woman in Marseille with an African background related the times when passengers in a bus moved away from her in an overt display of racial prejudice, and she said she planned to leave the country. In Berlin, well-informed and well-educated young Muslim women talked in deeply pessimistic terms and said the majority population did not see them as fully human. In sharp contrast, Samir Akacha, the young French Muslim, was upbeat in spite of the difficult environment. His interfaith work created a glow of optimism in him that was inspiring.

At present, there are ample signs that Europe is implementing a creeping assimilation policy toward the Muslim community that could be a prelude to more dangerous and deadly solutions. There are straws in the wind: construction of mosques is refused permission in one place, and minarets officially banned in another; niqab and hijab are discouraged if not banned in various places across Europe, with people commonly reviling or assaulting women who are covered; Muslim schoolgirls have been denied citizenship if they do not swim in mixed pools and Muslim schoolboys punished if they refuse to shake hands with females. Street vigilante groups across Germanic Northern Europe, for example, the Soldiers of Odin, who are active from Finland and Scandinavia to the Netherlands and beyond, wearing futuristic black masks and black dress, seek out and physically assault terrified asylum seekers. In Denmark, the government authorized the confiscation of cash, jewelry, and other valuables from asylum seekers—a reminder to us that Weberian modernity, with its emphasis on the rights of the individual and the rule of law, is under threat at its most basic level.

The migration crisis produced scenes like the camp in Subotica, Serbia near the Hungarian border, in which hundreds of mainly Syrians and Afghans lived. The camp was on the edge of a landfill and the migrants lived "in huts made of plastic tarps and plywood. They eat food scraps found in the garbage and bathe in a pond."[9] In January 2017, UNHCR called the situation in Greece for migrants "dire" and condemned the sadistic practices of governments in the Balkans including seizing items of clothing from migrants in the harsh cold and confiscating or destroying their phones, preventing them from calling for help. The dehumanization of the refugees, portrayed as an Islamic invasion, prevents us from fully sympathizing with or understanding the implications of the horrors faced by them and particularly the children among them.

There were also ample signs of bizarre sociological and psychological behavior in the immigrant population: Take, for example, David Ali Sonboly, the German-Iranian teenager in Munich, who complained of being bullied for years and in July 2016 went on a killing spree in which he targeted Muslim immigrants and their children. He was said to have converted to Christianity and was inspired by the far-right mass-murderer Anders Breivik. Sonboly declared that he was proud to be "Aryan" and to share a birthday with Adolf Hitler, which he described as a "special honor."

As we wait for the current crisis around Muslims in Europe to resolve itself, we note with alarm the terms that have recently gained currency such as the French *Français de souche*, an "original" French person in contrast to those of Muslim background, a term rooted in late nineteenth-century anti-Semitism and xenophobia. Similar terms with similar implications now circulate in Europe: the German concept of Leitkultur, and *autochtoon/allochtoon* in the Netherlands that effectively separate local from non-local and indigenous from non-indigenous. In normal times these distinctions would be sociological curiosities. In the current atmosphere of high levels of Islamophobia, anti-Semitism, and charged Far Right rhetoric, however, such terms have the potential to act as incendiary time bombs ready to explode into ethnic hatred and violence.

"I believe that you are civilized if you protect weaker groups within your society," mused Haris Silajdžić, reflecting on the fate of his Bosnian community as it faced genocide two decades ago. By that standard, Europe has much work to do in taking care of its minorities before the continent can justifiably consider itself civilized. The situation in Europe today would cast a shadow over the most Panglossian of characters. The dream of a brighter future for Muslims is being rapidly reduced to *tristesse* and tears.

The time is out of joint: the balance between God and man, nature and man, and man and man has been upset. Europe may be heading in a direction where nuance, shades of grey, balance, and compassion are being marginalized for a Manichean view of the world—of good versus evil, us versus them. Demagogues who speak half-truths and spread fake news successfully divert the anger and uncertainty of the community to those who are different. Precisely when the world needs knowledge and compassion, there is a dearth of both. Perhaps Shakespeare's Puck summed it up best: "Lord, what fools these mortals be!"

## Islam's Place in Europe

Keeping in mind the social and political environment sketched above, let us return to the question we raised at the start of this study, which concerns Islam's place in Europe. Europeans see Islam increasingly through the lens of a hyperprimordial identity as, to cite Wilders, a "culture of backwardness, of retardedness, of barbarism." There is a widespread belief that Islam is incompatible with Western civilization and has contributed nothing to it. It is worth our while therefore to check whether this assertion is, in fact, correct. If it is not, the basis of the Islamophobia of Islam's critics like Wilders collapses like a house of cards. They will then have to use some other arguments against Islam or their racial prejudices will stand exposed; they will be naked without benefit of a niqab to cover their modesty.

### *Islam's Contribution to European Civilization*

The impact of Muslims on European culture is deep and extensive. Perhaps Islam's greatest contribution was to introduce the idea of a unified understanding of our spiritual universe, which was reflected in the art, architecture, literature, and society in Andalusia based in religious pluralism and acceptance, one that valued learning and the ilm ethos. It is this society that produced an Ibn Firnas, who attempted flight, and religious philosophers like Maimonides and Averroes, who sought to balance reason and faith. Andalusian society, in turn, sowed the seeds for what would become the European Renaissance, which would lead to the Enlightenment and shape our modern world.

Some of Islam's contributions are familiar in the daily lives of Westerners and yet most people are unaware of their sources. Take, for example, coffee (and café), lemons, oranges, peaches, almonds, eggplant, bananas, rice, dates, pomegranates, sugarcane, dried pasta, spinach, and the croissant is said to be patterned after the Islamic crescent; the guitar, from the Arabic *qitara*, has its origins in the Arabic musical instrument, the *oud*; the names of the notes on the Western musical scale, "do, re, me, fa, sol, la, ti," are believed to derive from the letters the Arabs used to represent the notes, "dal, ra, mim, fa, sad, lam, sin"; the cry "Ole!" so frequently heard at football games derives from "Allah"; silk; muslin, derived from "Mosul," gauze, from "Gaza," and satin after Zayton, the Muslim name for the Chinese port where it was imported from; cotton, from the Arabic *qutn*; financial terms such as tariff, from the Arabic *tarifah*, and check, from *sakk*; the Dutch tulip, deriving "from the Turkish pronunciation of Persian *dulband* or 'turban,'"[10] the marching band, and vaccinations against disease, all of which came from the Ottoman Empire; the development of advanced irrigation systems, including canals, wells, sluices, and waterwheels; the hospital, which was established in accordance with Islamic charity rules and was open to everyone regardless of gender, social status, or religion; Muslim stories like *The Arabian Nights,* which influenced numerous European folktales; the subjects of alchemy and algebra; the concept of zero; chess; the numeral system; and paper.

In the field of architecture, features like the pointed arch, used so often in Gothic cathedrals and much stronger than the rounded arch frequently used in Europe at the time, were derived from Cairo's ninth-century Ibn Tulun Mosque and brought to Europe by southern Italian merchants, who financed their own monastery incorporating the design. In his study of Westminster Abbey, Sir Christopher Wren, arguably England's most celebrated architect, stated, "This we now call the Gothic manner of architecture. . . . I think it should with more reason be called the Saracen style."[11] Wren's crowning achievement, St. Paul's Cathedral in London, displays Islamic influences, including its dome flanked by two towers, which Wren patterned after Ottoman mosques with dome and large minarets. Other iconic European churches were also influenced by Ottoman mosques like Vienna's Karlskirche, or St. Charles's Church, which was inspired by the Hagia Sophia in Istanbul.

European languages and literature were also influenced by Muslims. Dante confirmed that what became known as the Italian language was first used by Sicilians, whose poetry and literary tradition were profoundly influenced by the Arabs. The first literary work in Spanish, commissioned by Alfonso X, was *Calila e Dimna*, a translation of the Arabic book *Kalila wa Dimna*. Less well known is the fact that the legal codes of European monarchs such as Frederick II, Roger II, and Alfonso X, which laid the foundation for jurisprudence in countries across the world, derive in part from Islamic law and the Islamic model of the state, as scholars have demonstrated.

The celebrated European universities, including Oxford, Cambridge, and the Sorbonne, were also influenced by Islamic universities. Islamic universities were the first to grant degrees (*ijazah*), and scholars have argued that the baccalaureate, or bachelor's degree, is derived from the Arabic *bi-haqq al-riwayah*, meaning "the right to teach on the authority of another," a phrase used in ijazah degree certificates for six centuries.[12] A university's faculty "is a direct translation of Arabic *quwwah*, which refers to 'the power inherent in an organ.'"[13] Even the concept of a university chair comes from the Islamic practice of the teacher sitting on an elevated chair, *kursi* in Arabic, so he could be seen and heard by the students. The caliph, aided by a committee of scholars, appointed professors who normally kept their position for life.[14] The first professorships endowed by a Christian European ruler were established by Frederick II when he created the University of Naples in the thirteenth century.

The very foundation of empirical and scientific discovery, the scientific method itself, originated with al-Haytham (Alhazen), who was born in Basra and lived in the tenth and eleventh centuries. In Neil deGrasse Tyson's series *Cosmos*, Alhazen is called "the first person ever to set down the rules of science." Alhazen influenced later scholars, including the thirteenth-century scientist Roger Bacon, often called the father of empiricism, who "adopted Alhazen's theory of vision almost in its entirety."[15] Alhazen was so famous in medieval Europe he was referred to simply as the Physicist. His impact can be seen in his depiction alongside Galileo on the frontispiece of *Selenographia* (1647), a monumental study of the moon by the Polish astronomer Johannes Hevelius, considered the father of lunar topography. Of these two giants representing science itself, Alhazen and Galileo, one has unfortunately been dropped and forgotten in Europe.

Alhazen's contemporary al-Zahrawi (Abulcasis) of Cordoba, considered the father of modern surgery, influenced generations of European physicians. He was the author of the main surgical textbook used in Europe for five centuries and was cited more than 200 times by Guy de Chauliac, the "most eminent authority on surgery during the Middle Ages," in the treatise he published in 1363.[16] Similarly, the main chemistry textbook used in Europe until the seventeenth century was the *Summa perfectionis magisterii*, a Latinized derivation of the work of the eighth- and ninth-century scholar Jabir ibn Hayyan of Persia, known as the father of chemistry.

Indeed, some of the greatest European figures who famously contributed to the creation of Western civilization were influenced directly or indirectly by Muslim thought. The subject merits further research, but let us briefly introduce some of them here. They include Aquinas, Dante, Da Vinci, Dürer, Copernicus, Descartes, Cervantes, Defoe, and Goethe.

## Saint Thomas Aquinas

Averroes's philosophic arguments in balancing faith and reason were of enormous assistance to Christian scholars grappling with this same central dilemma. His translations of and commentaries on Aristotle and Plato were of such high caliber and so impressed Thomas Aquinas and other scholars that they assumed Averroes's name needed no further elaboration and referred to him in their own work as "the Commentator." Declared a saint by the Church, the immense contribution of Aquinas to Christianity and Europe had to do with his efforts to balance and reconcile Aristotle and Christianity in the manner that Averroes did in Islam and Maimonides in Judaism. Pope Leo XIII declared Aquinas, widely considered the Catholic Church's greatest theologian, "patron of all Catholic universities, colleges, and schools throughout the world."[17] In the landmark encyclical *Aeterni Patris* (1879), Leo held up Aquinas as the model for Catholics engaging with "modern" science, capturing the magnitude of the philosopher's achievement concerning reason and faith, which was exactly the project of Averroes: "He joined them together in friendly union, preserving the rights and recognizing the dignity of each; so that reason, reared aloft on the wings of St. Thomas, could scarcely soar higher, and it was almost impossible even for faith to be supported by additional or stronger aids from reason than had already been furnished by the Angelic Doctor."[18]

In his 1998 encyclical, *Fides et Ratio* (Faith and Reason), Pope John Paul II similarly hailed Aquinas, speaking of

> the dialogue which he undertook with the Arab and Jewish thought of his time. . . . Both the light of reason and the light of faith come from God, he argued; hence there can be no contradiction between them. . . . This is why the Church has been justified in consistently proposing Saint Thomas as a master of thought and a model of the right way to do theology.

These popes and Aquinas were following in the footsteps of Pope Sylvester II, née Gerbert of Aurillac, the first French pope, who rose from humble beginnings to the papacy in the tenth century following his studies in Spain, possibly Cordoba, to which he traveled, it was recorded, because he was "thirsty for knowledge." Gerbert, master at the French cathedral school of Reims and tutor to the son of Otto I, the Holy Roman emperor, who would become Otto II, "was the first Christian known to teach math using the nine Arabic numerals and zero," drawing on the work of al-Khwarizmi, known as Algoritmi, the founder of algebra who gave his name to algorithm. This numerical system would later be popularized in Europe by the Italian mathematician Fibonacci, who studied in Almohad North Africa. The abacus that Gerbert devised "has been called the first counting device in Europe to function digitally, even the first computer" and other devices he constructed include an armillary sphere, "a primitive planetarium."[19] Though Gerbert faced many challenges—he was called a devil worshipper and sorcerer, had to flee for his life under excommunication, and was twice accused of treason—he remained steadfast in his love of Islamic and Greek learning, which he felt was fully compatible with Christianity.

## DANTE ALIGHIERI

According to many scholars, including the great Spanish scholar of Arabic Miguel Asín Palacios, Dante's *Divine Comedy* is heavily influenced by Islamic tales of the Prophet's mystical night flight, notably the Andalusian

Arabic work the *Book of the Ladder*. At the time the *Book of the Ladder* was being translated at the court of Alfonso X in Spain, Dante's teacher and guardian after his father's death, Brunetto Latini of Florence, was at Alfonso's court. While in the *Book of the Ladder*, the Prophet ascends through nine circles of heaven guided by the archangel Gabriel, who has been sent by God, *Paradiso*, the third part of the *Comedy*, finds Dante ascending through nine circles of heaven guided by the angelic Beatrice, who has also been sent by God. While Prophet Muhammad meets other prophets in the different circles of heaven, Dante meets various saints. There is also the use of numerous allegories, for example, as Palacios notes, when the Prophet and Dante each meet a woman who uses deception and charm to hide her considerable defects and ravaged body and attempts to seduce them—an encounter presented as a warning to avoid succumbing to the temptations of the world. "The general outlines of the two episodes are clearly identical," concludes Palacios.[20] The *Book of the Ladder* describes the moon as a dazzling precious stone, as does Dante.

In his account of paradise, "Dante makes use of the extraordinary sensuous nature of the Islamic paradise—its begemmed beauty, its overmastering luminescence—in his own depiction of the Christian heaven."[21] There are also many similarities in the depiction of hell in both stories. In the Islamic tale,

> the naked men and women writhing in a furnace inevitably suggest the adulterers in Dante who are incessantly swept on by the gale of hell. Even more striking is Dante's adaption of the Moslem punishment of usurers to those who committed violence and deeds of blood. Submerged in the deep waters of a river of blood, they, like the usurers, strive to gain the shore, only to be forced back by the Centaur archers (who take the place of the simpler stone-throwers in the Moslem legend).[22]

Palacios additionally asserts that there are other important elements in the *Divine Comedy* that have "their precedents in Islamic literature, whether it be in the Koran, in the *hadiths*, in the Moslem legends of the final judgment, or in the doctrine of the theologians, philosophers, and mystics," particularly the towering Andalusian Sufi Ibn Arabi. There is another connection between Dante and Islam. Manuscripts of Brunetto Latini's book *Li Livres dou Tresor* (The Book of the Treasure), which equates treasure to knowledge, feature depictions of Aristotle as an Arab, such was the identification of Aristotle with Islam in Christian Europe at the time.

Aristotle appears "complete with turban, seated upon a mosque floor, reading from a text in Arabic, and teaching it to his students." Brunetto's popular work, the first encyclopedia in a vernacular European language, "transmitted the Islamic literary model of teacher and student" to Christian Europe. It "was to be in turn Dante's model, with Virgil as fatherly schoolmaster and Dante as schoolboy."[23]

### LEONARDO DA VINCI

There is evidence that Leonardo Da Vinci, one of the greatest geniuses in world history, was also influenced by Islamic culture. This could have been owing to his own background, as scholars have increasingly argued that Da Vinci's mother was a baptized slave from Muslim lands, of whom there was a sizable population in Florence at the time. In his extensive studies of the human body Da Vinci used nomenclature that was "for the most part Arabic in origin," and he engaged with the theories of Islamic scholars like Avicenna.[24] Da Vinci also interestingly wrote his Italian right to left in the Arabic fashion.

Drafts of letters in Da Vinci's notebooks are addressed "To the Devatdar of Syria," a senior Mamluk official, whom Da Vinci referred to as "lieutenant of the sacred Sultan of Babylon," which scholars have interpreted as meaning Egypt. Da Vinci notes that he is carrying out "with due love and care the task for which you sent me," which scholars have argued indicates that he was working on projects for the Mamluk sultan. In a first-person account, Da Vinci reports that what appears to be a comet is actually sunlight being reflected off a peak in the Taurus Mountains in Armenia, and he discusses visiting a city that the Da Vinci scholar Jean Paul Richter notes was "probably somewhere in Kurdistan." In another passage, Da Vinci gives an account of a devastating earthquake in the Taurus Mountains, which, he notes, "the new prophet" had "foretold." Da Vinci is referring to the Prophet of Islam, and the reference is to surah 99 of the Quran.[25]

In 1503 Da Vinci wrote to the Ottoman sultan Bayezid II, sending him designs for "a windmill," "a ship's pump," and a 1,200-foot bridge across the Golden Horn in Istanbul, which would have been the longest in the world.[26] The sultan decided that the bridge, like many Da Vinci designs, would be impossible to construct and turned to Michelangelo to propose his own plan, as depicted in the Hollywood film *The Agony and the Ecstasy* (1965).

In Da Vinci's exquisite ceiling frescoes in the *Sala delle Asse*, "room of wooden boards," within the Castello Sforzesco in Milan, we find "'knots' and crosses and stars with eight points, of Islamic derivation."[27] Da Vinci's knot, an "arabesque" design that represented infinity and unity, was particularly important to the artist. It was the emblem for Da Vinci's "Academy," which he recorded in his notebooks, and it is found in many of his works, including the *Mona Lisa* (1503–06), in which the design can be seen on the subject's clothes. Da Vinci's knot set off a craze in Europe, and it soon appeared in clothing, ceramics, book bindings, embroidery, textiles, pottery, fabrics, and works of art, for example in Albrecht Dürer's six works based on Da Vinci's knot.

In Europe the arabesque interlaced pattern would come to be "completely integrated" with Greco-Roman classical Renaissance forms and constitute an important component of Renaissance art and style.[28] Arabesque and the philosophical concepts behind it, particularly infinity and unity, were subsequently adopted in fields such as literature (for example, Karl Wilhelm Friedrich Schlegel's *Lucinde*, 1799; Nikolai Gogol's *Arabesques*, 1835; and Søren Kierkegaard's *Either/Or*, 1843) and music (for example, Robert Schumann's *Arabeske in C*, 1839; and Claude Debussy's *Deux Arabesques*, 1888–91).

### Albrecht Dürer, Copernicus, and European Astronomy

Albrecht Dürer, one of Germany's greatest artists, acknowledged the Islamic contribution to European science and astronomy in his "The Northern Celestial Hemisphere" (1515), which, along with "The Southern Celestial Hemisphere," is possibly the first map of the heavens to appear in print. In each of the four corners of the map, Dürer drew portraits of the four greatest astronomers who had shaped human understanding of the stars. One of them is the tenth-century astronomer Abd al-Rahman al-Sufi, whom Dürer identifies by his Latin name, Azophi Arabus, the Arabic al-Sufi. Al-Sufi was the author of *The Book of Fixed Stars*, which had a profound impact in Europe and in which the Andromeda galaxy, the one closest to the Milky Way, is identified for the first time. *The Book of Fixed Stars* was so influential it "is the source of many of the modern names of stars coming from Latin translations of the Arabic names given by Al-Sufi."[29] Indeed, "the great majority of modern star names in the European languages are corrupt forms of the Arabic names."[30]

Other Muslim astronomers making a profound impact on Europe included the Arab al-Battani, known as Albategnius, who lived in the ninth and tenth centuries and was cited by some of the most illustrious European astronomers, including Nicolaus Copernicus, Galileo Galilei, Tycho Brahe, and Johannes Kepler. The astronomical breakthroughs of Brahe and Kepler were made possible by Brahe's observatories, which "were equipped with instruments of a kind pioneered by the observatory of Samarkand and its successor at Istanbul," as well as the famous Maragha observatory in Persia, which lent its name to a movement in astronomy.[31] Indeed, "it can be said without exaggeration that the observatory as a scientific institution owes its birth to Islamic civilization."[32]

Many scholars have argued that Copernicus's work in particular was deeply indebted to Islamic scholarship, especially the thirteenth-century scholars Nasir al-Din al-Tusi of Persia, the director of the Maragha observatory, and Mu'ayyad al-Din al-Urdi of Syria, both of whose thinking is "organically embedded within [Copernican] astronomy, so much so that it would be inconceivable to extract them and still leave the mathematical edifice of Copernican astronomy intact."[33] Copernicus "has even been called the last and greatest member of the Maragha School."[34] It has been further argued that Copernicus was influenced by the fourteenth-century Arab astronomer Ibn al-Shatir, the religious timekeeper and chief muezzin of the Umayyad Mosque in Damascus, whose models "have a 'heliocentric bias' that made them particularly suitable as a basis for the heliocentric and 'quasi-homocentric' models found in the *Commentariolus*," an early version of Copernicus's seminal work published in 1543, *De revolutionibus orbium coelestium* (On the revolutions of the heavenly spheres).[35]

## RENÉ DESCARTES

The fundamental concept of the "mind/body problem" in Western philosophy associated with Descartes—dealing with the relationship between perception and objects, mind and matter, soul and body, and "how meaning, rationality, and conscious experience are related to a physical world"— can be traced back to the eleventh-century scholar Avicenna.[36] Avicenna was the Latin name of Ibn Sina, who "foreshadowed Francis Bacon and René Descartes by half a millennium when he claimed" that "the universality of our ideas is the result of the activity of the mind itself."[37] This principle was also quoted by Averroes and the scholastics of the medieval universities of Europe, especially the German scholar and saint Albertus Magnus, the teacher of Thomas Aquinas.[38]

The similarity of Avicenna's thinking to that of Descartes—widely regarded as the father of modern philosophy—who posited the primacy of the intellect in his famous dictum *cogito ergo sum*, or "I think, therefore I am," has been noted and explored by many scholars. Avicenna argued that if a man were to have no perception of the external world or his own physical body, "He will not doubt that he affirms the existence of his self."[39] Descartes also wrote of the nature of the self, of what could be known with certainty, the soul, and God. Like Avicenna, he "distinguishes between the intellect and the brain."[40]

The concept of representation, according to which what a person perceives is only representative of external phenomena, has a similar lineage and was "of vital importance for philosophical psychology as it has developed from Descartes onward."[41] Martin Heidegger and Michel Foucault hailed Descartes as initiating the "age of representation" and modernity itself. The concept of "representation" "seems to have its origin in the Latin translation of the works of Avicenna," who was "the initiator of this representational theory of cognition."[42]

### Miguel de Cervantes and Daniel Defoe

*Don Quixote* and *Robinson Crusoe*—routinely cited as among the greatest novels of all time, for example by the *Guardian* in 2003—bear the mark of Islamic culture. Miguel de Cervantes opens *Don Quixote* (1605–15) by disclosing, with tongue in cheek, that it is a manuscript written by an Arab called Cide Hamete Benengeli (Sir Hamid Aubergine) and that his book is a translation into Spanish of the original Arabic. Don Quixote "is born of ideas latent in extinct, condemned texts, whether Arabic or chivalric," the critic Edward Rothstein wrote in the *New York Times*.

Ibn Tufail's twelfth-century novel *Hayy ibn Yaqdhan* is about a man who finds himself on a desert island along with a companion and raises philosophical questions about the relationship between the individual and society, man's capacity to survive in a "natural state," religion and interfaith toleration, and the pursuit of knowledge (English translations were published from a Latin version in 1674 and 1686 and the original Arabic in 1708). The novel bears striking similarities to Daniel Defoe's *Robinson Crusoe* (1719), which is commonly regarded as the first novel in the English language. The protagonists of both novels invent their own tools, make their own weapons, a club, construct a storehouse for food, dress in animal skins, and tame and keep animals. While Hayy has horses, birds of prey, and chickens, Crusoe has a dog, parrot, cats, and goats.

*Hayy ibn Yaqdhan*, which was brought to England from Aleppo in the seventeenth century by Edward Pococke, Oxford's first chair of Arabic and John Locke's favorite professor, caused a sensation among European intellectuals and became the third-most translated Arabic text after the Quran and *The Arabian Nights*. John Locke spoke eagerly of a meeting to discuss *Hayy ibn Yaqdhan*, which was translated by Pococke's son. Baruch Spinoza had it translated into Dutch, and it was twice translated into German and was celebrated by Gottfried Wilhelm Leibniz. Ibn Tufail's book "could be considered one of the most important books that heralded the Scientific Revolution."[43]

### Johann Wolfgang von Goethe

Goethe was profoundly impressed by Islam and was influenced by it in his work. Goethe's *West-Eastern Divan* is inspired by the Persian poet Hafez; major European composers set music to its verses, among them Franz Schubert, Felix Mendelssohn, and Richard Strauss. Johannes Brahms called Schubert's *Suleika I*, adapted from the *Divan* and the name of a figure in the Quran, "the loveliest song that has ever been written." In *West-Eastern Divan*, Goethe made the enigmatic comment that expressed his admiration for Islam: "If 'Islam' signifies 'submitting to God'/In Islam, we all live and die." Goethe also wrote "Mahomet's Song," a powerful poem dedicated to the Prophet of Islam. Most Germans we met during our fieldwork, while aware of Goethe's stature as the Shakespeare of the German language, had no idea of his relationship to Islam.

### Bridges between Europe and the Muslim World

Allama Iqbal, the poet and philosopher from South Asia, synthesized philosophy and religion, engaging with European thinkers like Goethe and Nietzsche as well as Eastern mystics like Rumi. Honored among Muslims, he was given a knighthood by the British government. The presence of Iqbal in contemporary Europe is ubiquitous, as we saw during our fieldwork. As an admirer of his work, and as the former Iqbal chair at Cambridge University, I was delighted to follow the Iqbal trail from one end of the continent to the other—starting from Cambridge University, where he studied at Trinity College, to Sarajevo, where the university has named a lecture room after him. In Cordoba, there is a street named for Iqbal, Poeta Muhammad Iqbal. Iqbal's poem about the mosque of Cordoba hangs in the office of the mayor of Cordoba, and there is a widely known photo of Iqbal praying in the mosque. In Heidelberg, there is a road named after him, a plaque by the river honoring him, and another in the house where he lived. There is also a monument to Iqbal in a city park in Munich.

Iqbal had a considerable influence on both Muslim and non-Muslim Europeans. The German scholar Annemarie Schimmel, for example, spent a lifetime studying and promoting Iqbal. A bored Turkish imam we met in Berlin's main mosque was giving us a rather indifferent interview until I mentioned Iqbal, after which he lit up and said Iqbal was his hero and called him the "prophet-poet"—an understandable emotion, but a strange title from an imam, considering Muslim sensitivity about the exclusivity of prophethood.

Iqbal's role as a bridge builder between Islam and Europe can be seen in *Message from the East*, one of his most famous works of poetry, which is written as a response to Goethe's *West-Eastern Divan*. In it, Iqbal imagines a meeting in heaven between two of his favorite historical figures, Rumi and Goethe. It is an encounter that continues to inspire modern artists and poets. Ahmed Eckhard Krausen, the German photographer and Muslim convert we met in chapter 6, visualizes a meeting in Weimar between Goethe and Iqbal, whom he calls his "icons." Shadab Hashmi, in her poem "Walled City," pays tribute to Rumi, Goethe, and Iqbal and imagines their meeting here on earth in Lahore by the historical Roshnai Gate, The Gate of Lights.

Even before Iqbal, Sir Syed Ahmad Khan acted as a bridge between Europe and the Muslim world in the nineteenth century. He led the Muslims of the subcontinent toward a modern Muslim identity by establishing an institution that would change the course of the subcontinent. Inspired by the universities of Cambridge and Oxford, he established a college for Muslims in Aligarh, India, which would pursue his objective of balancing Islam with science and reason in the manner of Averroes. From this institution came prime ministers, policymakers, historians, and scientists. He argued that we all belong to a common humanity. Today, in London, there is a plaque honoring him in the building in which he lived. The message of Iqbal and Sir Syed is relevant for our times: we need to seek knowledge and better communication with people of other cultures and faiths so that we can overcome the hate and anger expressed through violent extremism that is currently plaguing our lives.

Karol Szymanowski, widely described as Poland's greatest composer after Chopin—Poland declared 2007 the "Year of Karol Szymanowski"—is another figure like Iqbal who acts as a bridge between Europe and the Muslim world. He showed his reverence for Rumi in his third symphony *Song of the Night* (1914–16), which features Rumi's poetry. He also wrote *The Love Songs of Hafiz* (1911–14) in two song cycles, and commented upon encountering the poet, "I am extremely moved by my Hafiz. Allah Himself has thrust him into my hands."[44] Other works include *Songs of an Infatuated Muezzin* (1918), and the opera *King Roger* (1926), which is about Roger II and showcases his close relationship with the sage al-Idrisi.

There are other examples where European and Islamic nations and cultures have met. The French-Ottoman relationship dates back to King

Francis I of France. Francis, seeking assistance against the Hapsburg Holy Roman Empire under Charles V, reached out to Sultan Sulcyman the Magnificent, through Francis's mother, while the king was imprisoned in Spain after a devastating defeat in battle. Suleyman replied to Francis: "It is not unusual for Emperors to be defeated and imprisoned, do not lose your courage."[45] An enduring alliance took shape that proved of crucial value to Francis, who said that the Ottoman Empire was "the only force guaranteeing the continued existence of the states of Europe against Charles V."[46] The French were given permission to trade in all ports in the Ottoman Empire and French Catholics were given custody over the Christian Holy Places in Palestine. Suleyman referred to Francis as his "brother."[47] During the winter of 1543–44 the Ottomans lived in Toulon, France, and Toulon Cathedral was converted into a mosque for 30,000 Turks. During this period, a French artillery unit was also dispatched to fight alongside Suleyman's army in Hungary. An English eyewitness of the aftermath of the failed 1683 Ottoman siege of Vienna mentioned a French engineer who inflicted heavy damage on the city and went on to note, "There was also a great many *French* among the *Junizaries*, and many were found among the Dead with *French* Silver and Gold in their Pockets."[48] There developed in France a craze for all things Turkish and "Oriental." An example is the coffee fashion, which was instigated in 1689 by the Ottoman ambassador to the court of King Louis IV, Suleiman Aga, who introduced it to the Parisian elite.

French intellectuals also lavished praise on the Turks. During a period of vicious sectarian religious warfare in France pitting Catholic against Protestant, the great political philosopher Jean Bodin, the leading thinker of the *politique* movement, which advocated placing the state above all other concerns including differences of religion, saw much to admire in the Ottomans. Bodin wrote glowingly of Ottoman pluralism in his *Six Books of the Republic* (1576), which is hailed by political theorists for introducing the concept of state sovereignty.[49] For Bodin, it was not the Holy Roman Empire which could justifiably claim the mantle of Rome but the Ottomans, arguing, "This fact is obvious to everyone—if there is anywhere in the world any majesty of empire and of true monarchy, it must radiate from the sultan."[50]

The Turkish-French alliance against the Hapsburgs was similar, although longer lasting, to the close relationship forged by Queen Elizabeth with the Turks, also to offset the Hapsburgs, particularly Hapsburg Spain. To counter Spain and reorient the country after breaking with the Catholic Church, Elizabeth built an "impressive network of English residents" in Ottoman lands which facilitated commercial, military, intelligence, and diplomatic relations and interests. By the end of her reign, "thousands of her subjects were to be found in the Islamic world," many of whom converted to Islam and went on to achieve high postings such as Samson Rowlie, or Hassan Aga, who became "chief eunuch and treasurer of Algiers as well as one of the most trusted advisers to its Ottoman governor." Elizabeth had inherited her fascination with Islam from her father Henry VIII, who "often appeared at festivities 'appareled after Turkey fashion,' dressed in silk and velvet and sporting a turban and a scimitar." There were few prosperous homes in Elizabethan England without items like "Turkey carpets."[51] The connections between England and the Muslim world, in fact, stretch back at least to the eighth century, when Offa, the powerful king of the Anglo-Saxon kingdom of Mercia who was crowned in 757, minted coins that read, on one side in Latin, "Offa the King" and on the other in Arabic "There is no God but Allah alone." Offa was apparently attempting to ensure his coins would be accepted abroad as Abbasid gold coins were at that time the accepted global currency. Over 100,000 Islamic silver coins from the Viking age have been found in Scandinavia, and in 2017 Viking burial clothes from Sweden with embroidery reading "Allah" and "Ali" in Arabic script were discovered.

In the siege of Vienna in 1683, "well over half of the 'Turkish' army marching against the Habsburgs were Christians."[52] Among them were troops from Ottoman Balkan vassal states, French soldiers—a reflection of the longstanding French-Ottoman relationship—as well as a sizable Protestant contingent. Imre Thököly, the Protestant Hungarian nobleman who had persuaded the sultan to attempt to take Vienna, led thousands of Hungarian Christians as part of the Ottoman army. As the army marched toward Vienna, Thököly issued a manifesto promising Christians "security of life and property and freedom of religious worship under the Ottoman Sultan" and numerous Christian towns opened their gates for the advancing Turks.[53] Support for Protestants was "one of the fundamental principles of Ottoman policy in Europe."[54] This can be seen in the letter Suleyman the Magnificent wrote to Lutheran princes under Hapsburg rule; he "offered military help and saw them as standing close to him, since they did not worship idols, believed in one God and fought against the Pope and Emperor." In fact, it has been "convincingly argued that Ottoman pressure on the Habsburgs was an important factor in the extension of Protestantism in Europe."[55]

Muslims have also defended European kingdoms and empires against both Muslims and non-Muslims. Tatar cavalry from Poland-Lithuania played a significant role in helping to break the Ottoman siege of Vienna in 1683, and their courage and loyalty fighting against the Russians and Germans in the nineteenth and twentieth centuries, as discussed in chapter 5, have earned them a special place in the hearts of Poles and Lithuanians. The Catholic Church in Poland, acknowledging six centuries of service of the Tatars to the nation, showed their gratitude in 2003 by declaring an annual Day of Prayers Dedicated to Islam, or Day of Islam. We also know that some 4 million Indian Army soldiers fought alongside Britain and its allies in the two world wars and that more than one-third of these were Muslims, whose loyalty and bravery were widely acknowledged by the high command, including Winston Churchill.

Let me end this discussion with the example of the Moorish palace at the heart of the famous Tivoli Gardens in Copenhagen. In the midst of the most celebrated pleasure garden in the land of Hans Christian Andersen, next to pirate ships, roller coasters, and swings, is the jewel of the Tivoli—the imagined Moorish palace with its domes and minarets. As if this were not a startling enough image, there is a crescent on top of the central dome. Late at night, viewing the bulbs that outline the dome's shape and artificial flames that give it a magical glow, the visitor might imagine being taken back in time to Andalusia a thousand years ago. The story is told here that Walt Disney was inspired by his visit and went on to create Disneyland in its image.

### Acts of Omission and Commission

The Muslim contribution to Europe is vast, but it is barely taught in schools, nor is it properly exhibited in museums. A casual glance at the textbook of a high school student in almost any country in Europe or a visit to a central museum will confirm the veracity of my statement. To compound matters, the period of Islam's greatest contributions is inexplicably placed in the Dark Ages period of European history. The reputable Victoria and Albert Museum and the prestigious Science Museum in London, for example, which we visited as part of our field research, have brilliant panels describing the linear progress of "civilization"—from the Greeks to the Romans to the Renaissance to the Enlightenment and, finally, to Modernity. Missing in between the Romans and the Renaissance is the period of Islam and its contributions. The acts of omission involving Islam may also be noted in the media when exploring the history of European civilization and thought. For example, *The Greeks*, an excellent TV mini-series, was broadcast in 2016 by PBS in the United States and produced in association with National Geographic Studios. True to form, the series provided an authoritative overview with historians and other experts on location. But, again, a thousand years of European history—the Muslim part—had been omitted.

This omission is surprising in view of the fact that there are now popular documentaries on the subject such as the award-winning *1001 Inventions and the Library of Secrets,* starring Ben Kingsley as the twelfth-century Arab engineering genius al-Jazari, which was accompanied by a book (2012). Appearing as a mysterious librarian in London, Kingsley rebukes a group of British schoolchildren for using the phrase "Dark Ages" and then goes on to show them some of the scientific discoveries and inventions of the Muslims at that time in history, thus refuting the idea of the Dark Ages and recasting the era as a golden age.

While acts of omission ensure that the positive aspects of Muslim history are not known, acts of commission invent bloodcurdling and distorted stories concerning Muslims, which in time have been accepted as part of local European culture. The cumulative effect is to consolidate the negative image of Islam. Well-known examples of popular acts of commission include the commonly held myth of Muslims burning the famous library in Alexandria, when in fact the incident occurred even before Islam arrived in Egypt, and the role of the Muslims in treacherously attacking the rear of Charlemagne's army in the medieval folk poem epic, *The Song of Roland,* when in fact history informs us it was the Basques. The poem depicts Muslims as evil worshippers of a trinity consisting of Apollo, Muhammad, and Termagant, a violent deity that Europeans invented specially to defame Islam.

Our next European folk hero is famous for mooning the mighty Ottoman armies whose soldiers were so shocked and awed by the sight that they turned and fled. Catherine Ségurane is honored every year on Catherine Ségurane Day—concurrent with Saint Catherine's Day—in Nice for her supposed role in defeating the Ottomans during their siege of the city in 1543. According to the story, Catherine, who led the women of Nice in defending it, at a critical moment turned around and exposed her buttocks to the Turks, who then beat a hasty retreat, their Islamic sense of modesty and propriety offended. Catherine was also said to have seized the Turkish banner from an Ottoman soldier and led a counterattack. There are poems and plays honoring Catherine, and in Nice there are statues of her and streets named after her. On the corner of Catherine Ségurane street is a cannonball lodged into a wall of a building with a plaque reading "Cannonball from the Turkish fleet in 1543 during the siege of Nice, where

Catherine Ségurane, heroine of Nice, distinguished herself." The French Far Right has also appropriated Catherine as an anti-immigration symbol, and she is seen as a reincarnation of Joan of Arc. The fact that historians challenge the very existence of Catherine, that the Turkish siege in question was jointly conducted with the King of France, and that the supposed Turkish sacking of the city was actually carried out by French troops as recorded by contemporary accounts, is conveniently forgotten.

Even Shakespeare is guilty of acts of commission involving Muslims. The "chief architect and plotter of these woes" in *Titus Andronicus*, arguably Shakespeare's bloodiest and most violent play, is the "blackamoor" Aaron, a "barbarous Moor." Aaron, who has a "soul black like his face," is guilty of "murders, rapes, and massacres." To the contemporary audience, Shakespeare's characterization of Aaron suggests the racism and attitudes toward Islam of the Bard's age. But that is somewhat beside the point. Shakespeare sets his play in the late Roman period, probably the fourth century. Islam, as we know, only appears on the scene in the seventh century. Yet by implying that Aaron is a Muslim, Shakespeare is making one of those anachronistic mistakes easily spotted by the audience, such as a character in a medieval play wearing a wristwatch. What is even more confounding is that the learned editors of *The Economist,* in describing Aaron as "Shakespeare's first fully-fleshed out Muslim character," and the play as reflecting "Shakespeare's complex views of the Islamic world," missed the anachronism.

Labeling Aaron a Muslim is not the only example of blaming Muslims for something that they did not, indeed could not, do. In a similar vein, Jan Jambon, the Belgian interior minister, incorrectly accused Belgian Muslims in 2016 of dancing with joy at the terrorist strikes committed by other Muslims in Brussels. In this, he echoed Donald Trump who, during the 2016 presidential election, falsely claimed that he personally saw thousands of American Muslims rejoicing when the World Trade Center towers fell in New York.

Other acts of commission include the repeated propaganda myths about Muslims in Europe, which are a direct consequence of the post-9/11 Islamophobia. Anders Breivik, illustrating his shaky grasp of reality, acknowledged as his inspiration semi-mythical figures like El Cid and Vlad the Impaler, better known as Dracula, who came to symbolize the bitter clashes with the Muslim Moors and Turks respectively. What Breivik did not learn is that El Cid fought for Muslim rulers at one stage in his career, and Vlad's younger brother Radu led elite Ottoman troops against his own brother.

One of the most common propaganda myths is that Muslims breed like rabbits and that Europe will soon become "Eurabia" as the Muslim population overwhelms Western nations. Jean-Luc Marret, a leading French authority on Islam, dismisses this myth: "If the concept of 'Eurabia' implies that the Muslims in Europe will become more and more numerous, and Europe will collapse under the weight of Muslims, I think that's really naïve. . . . This 'Eurabia' thing, I really think that's a stupid concept that tends to polarize people." In fact, while surveys have shown that the French on average think Muslims account for nearly a third of France's population, that figure is closer to 8 percent.

Regarding the myth about the shariah being imposed on Europe—and putting aside the fact that many Muslims believed that it was in any case compatible with European societies—even if every individual Muslim wishes to impose the shariah on their host nation, and this is by no means certain, considering that many have escaped from their homeland precisely because of the fear of religious orthodoxy, their small populations would prevent them from imposing it on the non-Muslim majority.

### A Muslim at Home in Europe

As we explore the place of Islam in Europe today, it may be worthwhile to recount my personal experiences from the time I arrived in the 1960s as a university student. At that time, I had no doubt that Islam and Europe were compatible, as I felt at home there. The continent represented an optimistic modernity and was aware that the monsters that had torn it apart lay dead and buried. Students, including Muslim ones like me, were enthralled by the political and cultural leaders of the time—like John F. Kennedy, Muhammad Ali, and the Beatles. To me it appeared that Europe was slowly rediscovering the idea of convivencia and that it would grow in the future.

Looking through some old and fading personal pictures from that period I am struck by how comfortable I felt in Europe then. The photograph in Greece was taken at a small seaport when my fellow students from England and I visited one of the Greek islands. It was my first visit to Greece, and I was already in love with Greek culture, which I had been introduced to at my school, Burn Hall—from Tennyson's *Ulysses* to Byron's *The Isles of Greece*. In my meager travel bag I always carried one volume of Lawrence Durrell's *Alexandria Quartet* until I finished the set. Durrell's novels were set during the Second World War in Alexandria, Egypt, and presented different perspectives on the same events as seen by different

*From top to bottom: The author in the 1960s . . .*

*. . . with British university students at a port in Greece*

*. . . with Tahir Ayub Khan with King's College, Cambridge, in the background*

*. . . with Sherborne School senior students, Sherborne*

*. . . with his sister Aisha in Paris*

*. . . after receiving his degree from Cambridge*

characters. They confirmed to us, if to no one else, that we were ready for adult themes and esoteric literature that at the same time was erotic. I devoured the novels with my friends that summer on an island, a feat made sweet by the knowledge that Lawrence and his younger brother Gerald, also a famous author, had lived on and been inspired by these very islands. In 2016 PBS broadcast the delightful series *The Durrells in Corfu*, based on Gerald Durrell's books about his life growing up on a Greek island with his family.

My trip to Greece was part of a dare. I impulsively accepted a challenge to hitchhike with a group of English friends from my university in Birmingham to Athens with a limited budget. For me, barely twenty years old, it was an adventure, as I had not done anything like this before. This was before the dangers of hitchhiking long distances were graphically illustrated in the news and in popular films like *The Hitcher* (1986) which, in case we missed the point, was remade in 2007.

It was a hard few weeks on the road—we slept rough, ate little more than baguettes and cheese, and depended heavily on the hospitality of strangers. But it gave me insights into European society. Shortly after this photograph was taken, my Greek friend from my English university came to see me at the youth hostel in Athens, where I was staying with my friends. After a glance at our disheveled and unwashed condition, he asked me to step outside. He was upset with me. He reminded me of my social background and asked what my parents would say if they saw me living like these "dirty" English. After weeks on the road we did look scruffy, but his choice of adjective for my friends interested me. He was reflecting a historic suspicion and dislike of the English in that part of Europe: both the Turks and Greeks, who have little love for each other to this day, blamed the English for their national woes. It also reflected the Southern European antipathy for Northern Europeans more generally. My Greek friend ignored my explanations of having accepted the challenge of hitchhiking as a badge of honor. He insisted on taking me home, and his family, especially his mother and sisters, showed me Greek hospitality at its best. I must confess that I had been missing home-cooked meals, clean clothes, and clean sheets to sleep in, and I was profoundly grateful to my hosts.

In the photograph taken at Sherborne, the English public school in Dorset, I am standing alongside a group of my A-level students, who were not much younger than me. The boys are smartly turned out with ties, jackets, and hats called boaters. I was sent to the school to teach English for a term as part of my diploma in education at Cambridge University. My arrival in the small town was unusual enough to merit a small mention in the local newspaper pointing out the curious fact that a Pakistani would be teaching English at Sherborne. As part of my examination I had to do a "practical," which meant an external examiner would sit in my class at the end of term and observe me teaching and my interactions with the students. To their credit, the boys, who held my fate in their hands, behaved impeccably. The examiner's report mentioned how well the boys had responded to my class and noted their enthusiasm. In the end, I was awarded a "distinction" by the university both in my written and practical examinations.

One picture is with my sister Aisha in Paris and another taken after receiving my degree from Cambridge University. The picture in Cambridge, with the iconic King's College in the background, is with Tahir Ayub Khan, my school-fellow from Burn Hall. I was at Selwyn College and had to cross King's to get to town. As we crossed the college my Pakistani friends and I would often run into Ian Stephens, the former editor of *The Statesman* in India and author of several books on Pakistan. I can still hear his loud greeting as he spotted us and picture his blue eyes and ruddy face lighting up—"Pakistanis! My day is made!" Today, the image of Pakistanis is tarnished with accusations of terrorism. Indeed, the very name Pakistani has been reduced to "paki"—a racially charged term of abuse—which is now applied to all Muslims, for example, as we learned, in Greece. I now wonder if Ian Stephens were alive today and encountered young Pakistanis heading his way across campus, would he greet them as he had me in the 1960s or would he turn around and head the other way? Such is the distance we have traveled over the past half-century.

### Solutions Gleaned from the Field

The solutions to the crisis facing Muslims in Europe presented here are based in our fieldwork findings and the arguments in this book. They are summarized below not only as an effective and practical method to contain the larger social tensions in Europe, but also as a way to alleviate the confusion in the minds of those Muslims who are unsure about their identity. There are ten steps, and the first one evokes the notion of knowledge or ilm:

1. **Acquire knowledge and think for yourself.** The first step for both Muslims and non-Muslims is to acquire knowledge about each other and be encouraged to think for themselves when considering items in the media, as we live in a world of fake news and false information. This suggestion follows the almost universal advice given to us in the field: to use our own common sense. It is based on the assumption that we promote

knowledge, learning, and understanding of the society we find ourselves in. As Kristiane Backer stated, "Islam encourages us to use our reason, to question things. Islam is a religion for people who think." For Backer, "Andalusia was where Europe was at its height of civilization, whereas the rest of Europe was in the Dark Ages, and why?" "Because," she said, "Muslims encouraged the arts and sciences and medicine."

As Lord Rowan Williams told us in Cambridge: "We in Europe and elsewhere simply need to educate ourselves about what Islam really is. And we need to listen very hard to the average Muslim neighbor. Not the extremist voice, but to the real variety that you'll hear outside any mosque on Friday. To listen to the experience of those who are unobtrusively but faithfully living ordinary Muslim lives fully within our society. Listen to them."

But thinking requires a critical and objective approach. Muslims need to appreciate positive and constructive criticism and not to dismiss it as Islamophobia. Muslims need to be more self-reflective and prepared to answer hard questions about their community. Lord Bhikhu Parekh explained in an interview for our study that indigenous Europeans and Muslims need to accept each other's existence before they can coexist. "I think Europeans, sooner or later, have got to come to terms with the presence of Islam, recognize it as an equal interlocutor, equal partner. For their part, I think, Muslims have also got to recognize that they are not a ruling race, they are part of a society which is self-confident, but at the same time a little nervous, and what they have to do is to go slowly in certain respects."

Many Muslims today appear indifferent to the larger local culture and need to work harder and with sensitivity to become part of society. The Muslim lord mayor of Bradford complained of the disinterest of his community to the Brontë sisters, and when I asked a leading British imam to name his favorite Shakespeare play, he looked at me with the stare of a deer in headlights and continued to do so when, as a follow-up question, I asked him to name any sonnet. Similarly, the Bengalis we met in Palermo, near the Palatine Chapel, the jewel of Sicilian architecture, said they had never visited it and had no idea about it; and a smart young French Algerian admitted he had neither visited Les Invalides in Paris, where Napoleon lay buried in state, nor really cared about his significance in French history. I thought to myself that to English, Italian, and French ears this could sound as if Muslims did not care about their culture. On the positive side, a prominent imam in 2016 not only drove Zeenat, Frankie, and me to Sherwood Forest near Nottingham in England to show us the old oak where Robin and his Merry Men gathered but also enthusiastically shared his plans to organize prayers in several mosques for the long life of Queen Elizabeth on the occasion of her ninetieth birthday.

Education leaders across the continent need to introduce a comparative religions curriculum in schools. Islam faces a challenge—many do not know anything about Islam, as they are not taught the subject at school but, nonetheless, encounter incorrect and distorted versions of Islam in the media. Students need to learn early on how to identify and counter negative and distorted portrayals of the faith community. The noted British Channel 4 news anchor, Jon Snow, captured the problem: "People are very wary of the other. They don't really know what goes on in a mosque. Anyone who isn't a Muslim has never even been to a mosque."

There are positive signs. In 1996 one of the most prominent "Orientalist" scholars of Islam, W. Montgomery Watt, wrote an article on my work titled, "A Contemporary Spokesman for Islam." It begins: "In the last decade there has come to the fore, especially in the British world, a Muslim who is attempting to counter the negative images of Islam which keep reappearing in the Western media and to present his own religion more positively." He calls my book *Postmodernism and Islam: Predicament and Promise* (1992) "perhaps the most important book to have been written by a Muslim during the last decade."[56] I am struck by the fact that he could name only one Muslim author in the 1990s, whereas today we have a flood of books and articles on Islam by Muslims. However promising the development, there is still a great deal of work to be done in this field, considering the ever-growing and universally available Islamophobic literature laced with fake news and false information. Germany's funding of five centers and sixteen chairs of Islamic studies at universities around the nation in the past decade is a step in the right direction.[57]

2. **Understand the discussion of identity.** The question of identity is now front and center in Europe, thanks in large part to the far-right leaders who make it a plank of their politics, and it needs to be discussed openly and vigorously. While the far-right focuses on Islam as a threat to Europe, the social and political crisis in Europe is not a result of the presence of Muslims but is rooted in the historical and unresolved debate about European identity, which this study has attempted to illuminate.

In keeping with my anthropological interests, the definition of identity was one of the first questions the research team would put to respondents.

The problem was the lack of unanimity in the responses: in the United Kingdom, some said beer and football, others mentioned the Queen and Shakespeare; and in Germany, while some also spoke of beer and football, many mentioned ethnicity and the land. Some spoke of identity in "pure" terms, tending to discount the massive changes Europe has undergone— the world wars, the European Union and its arrangements for easy internal travel, globalization, mixed marriage, and of course the presence of millions of Asians and Africans and the recent arrival of large numbers of asylum seekers. For others hybridity not purity, ambiguity not certainty is the reality of identity in Europe today. In the face of so much confusion and ambiguity about identity, which identity are we asking the immigrant to assume? Whichever side Europeans may take in the debate about identity, the reality is that the presence of Islam has acted as a catalyst to provoke the discussion. If Europe is not in a discombobulated state, it is not entirely combobulated either.

3. **Focus on youth.** We found on our travels that there were many cases where the administration had little idea about the community and even less about the young and their problems. This left many young immigrants, who had very limited education and few prospects for employment, feeling aggrieved and even hopeless. That is why governments need to urgently create the conditions in which Muslims have equal access to education and employment as the rest of society. The young must be encouraged to divert their energy and imagination to special projects involving, for example, education, filmmaking, and social activity. Youth should be heard and seen in discussions of Islam in the media, as most discussions are conducted by non-Muslim elder males, which is ironic, as the discussion is often about Muslim youth. The youth need to be offered the whole range of education and be integrated into local society while at the same time encouraged to feel pride in their own identities and be given the opportunities to study in their own cultural or religious schools. European governments can fund such programs through mosques and community organizations. But government must reach out to the right leaders in the community, and they will not know who to reach out to unless they understand and learn about the community in the first place.

4. **Support Muslim women.** Women seeking entrepreneurial and cultural opportunities need to be supported by the administration. We saw a noteworthy example in Bradford in May 2016, when our team returned to present our film, *Journey into Europe*, at the Bradford Literature Festival. The Bradford on display was different from the media image of a gritty, angry, "city of Islamic fundamentalists." Bradford was proudly hosting the

festival for the second straight year, and it boasted an impressive collection of some 200 speakers, readings, panels, film screenings, and performances, including those that featured LGBT themes. Some seventy local schools also joined the activities. The festival thrust Bradford into the forefront of Britain's cultural landscape. Every night, our hosts invited the day's speakers and performers to a complimentary meal at the popular Pakistani restaurant, My Lahore. The conversations bustled with energy and ideas as people from different backgrounds exchanged views and email addresses while enjoying the delicious Lahori tikkas and kebabs. Tall young men in shalwar-kameez walked about as if they were in Lahore with something I did not see elsewhere on our journey—a swagger that says I am proud of who I am. The modestly but smartly dressed women of Pakistani descent wearing the most colorful Pakistani dresses in Khaadi, a Pakistani women's clothing store in the glittering new mall in central Bradford, displayed the same confidence.

That the literature festival had been conceived and organized by two British-Pakistani women—Irna Qureshi and Syima Aslam—and supported by women like Baroness Warsi and fully endorsed by the British administration should have alerted the world to dramatic changes taking place in European Muslim society. Naz Shah, the local Bradford MP, and her fellow MP and festival participant Tasmina Ahmed-Sheikh of Glasgow, along with high-profile figures like Amina Yaqin and Zeba Salman of SOAS, suggested changes in the role and status of women in Britain's Muslim community. Indeed, eight of the thirteen Muslims elected to the British Parliament in 2015 were women. Commentators on Islam, as well as those in the government who monitor the Muslim community, need to understand that while the manifestation of "noisy and angry" Bradford is still there, it is this other face of Bradford—one that is inspiring and inclusive—that is clearly emerging. Those seeking role models and future trends will be amply rewarded by looking here.

5. **Facilitate the training of imams.** We found that many imams across Europe were unfamiliar with their cultural environment, and a large number of them had a shaky grasp of the local language or did not speak it at all. This was particularly true of the large numbers of Turkish imams in Germany, who are sent by the Turkish government for fixed periods of time and therefore have little incentive to learn about local culture. There is much that local governments can do to provide the imams and the Muslim community with language and cultural instruction. The mosque we visited in Penzberg, Germany, which provides German language lessons with funding from the German government, is a good example of the

right approach. Tim Winter's Cambridge Muslim College is an excellent model for the training of European imams.

6. **Understand the interconnected nature of society.** Too often we discovered in the field that there is a lack of understanding of how different parts of society are interconnected and therefore there is a lack of coordination that is necessary to check, for example, the repeated acts of terrorism that emanate from the community. Edward Kessler of the Woolf Institute in Cambridge, which promotes interfaith dialogue, explained the crucial role that the government can play, particularly the need for law enforcement to work closely with the Muslim community for the benefit of all: "We work with the foreign service, with the health service, and above all with the police; it's about confidence. Sometimes there's not an ignorance but a fear. If you can understand their faith and their identity as Muslims, for example, you're only better able to build up a relationship in the future."

When we analyze the different case studies of European Muslim terrorists over the past few years, a standard profile emerges: the perpetrators are young, usually unemployed or in low-paying jobs in which they have no interest; many have been to prison; and their families are frustrated with them and they, in turn, have little or no relationship with their families; they have little or no communication with the religious and social leaders of the community and are known not to attend the mosque; they are reputed to indulge in drugs and alcohol; and finally, their marriages have either failed or are in a state of crisis. As for ideological or political influences, these young men and women are not reading either Marx or Guevara, nor Ibn Arabi or Ibn Khaldun. They are simply picking up a mish-mash of ideas that have been rehashed somewhere in the Middle East by semiliterate men claiming to interpret Islam for the modern age, and they have been influenced by these sham leaders to the point that they can justify their violent action in the context of what they imagine is an Islamic cause. The ghosts of imperialism still lurk in their closets. As these countless examples of homegrown terrorists reveal, we must move away from identifying Islam and the putative seventy-two virgins waiting in heaven for martyrs as the cause of terrorism and look elsewhere.

One of the few senior statesmen who pointed away from the standard stereotypical explanation of the causes of terrorism was Labour Party leader Jeremy Corbyn. In May 2017, on the first day of high-level parliamentary election campaigning after a British-Libyan suicide bomber killed twenty-two people at a concert hall in Manchester, Corbyn gave us an important insight into how to interpret, explain, and ultimately diminish European Muslim terrorism. In his speech in Westminster, Corbyn argued that the war on terror has destabilized the Muslim world and has fostered anti-Western attitudes, feeding into the terror threat in the United Kingdom. He called for U.K. foreign policy leaders to rethink the war on terror and consider alternatives to military intervention. Corbyn promised that, if elected, he would change British foreign policy from one of intervention to one of benign interaction.

Instead of gaining the support of this generation of Muslims in Europe, the harsh reactions of the state and the sustained media vitriol have further alienated Muslim youth and therefore supplied the endless stream of disoriented, angry, and desperate young men who commit acts of violence. This has to stop, and it can only stop if there is intelligent, compassionate, and urgent action to coordinate a long-term strategy. The European Muslim terrorists represent a failure not only of the states in which they live for allowing them to become so alienated but also, and in a very direct sense, of their families and their communities. It is time that the state, family, and community, connecting and coordinating, stand up and take responsibility for what is happening and ensure that the scourge of terrorism is effectively challenged in the future.

7. **Understand the nature of the media.** Almost everyone we spoke to during our fieldwork said that media is playing a very important role in promoting a negative image of Islam, which feeds into the general widespread Islamophobia and encourages violence against Muslims. For examples, the stories of "grooming" and the "Trojan horse" education scandal in the United Kingdom implied that the entire Muslim community was somehow implicated and guilty; in fact, Muslim leaders vehemently denounced the former and denied the latter. The media need to be more responsible in informing the public correctly and with accuracy.

Media—and government—should be sensitive to terms that may inadvertently be offensive to the community and can end up causing confusion rather than enlightening or clarifying. As Rowan Williams explained,

> Even at the level of government and educated public discourse, you still hear strange words like "Islamist"—and I'm a bit puzzled by a word like that. You still hear this curious distinction between "moderate" and "radical" Muslims—that is, "nice" and "nasty" Muslims. And I find myself again and again in conversation in recent years saying to people in government and the media, "These categories are meaningless, they don't correspond to what Muslims say about themselves. You just have to be there and listen to how people do describe themselves."

Muslims complained that words such as *Islam, terrorist, extremist, jihadist,* and *Islamist* are used interchangeably and so loosely that people commonly identify Islam with violence. As Mayor Leoluca Orlando of Palermo warned us, "I have to say what I think, the European Union has not understood how dangerous Islamophobia is."

8. **Recognize the importance of interfaith dialogue.** Considering the potential for bridge building among religious leaders, it is vital that interfaith and intercultural exercises are held frequently and publicly. The more people see leaders of different religions, arms linked, in dialogue with the purpose of fostering knowledge, understanding, and coexistence, or are able to read their works on the subject, the greater the chances that the Muslim community enters normal relations with larger society. Such interactions will also provide a direction for those confused younger members of the community who in the absence of mature and compassionate leadership may be inclined to get their religious instructions from imams who have a narrow and exclusivist view of the world. Interfaith dialogue also assists in those societies where Christianity is still an essential and prominent part of identity, as in parts of Eastern Europe. But we need to move beyond traditional interfaith dialogue and more broadly involve scholars and other commentators who would act as genuine bridge builders between different cultures and religions.

An example of the kind of bridge building that needs to occur concerns historical narratives. Leaders should encourage reconciliation between communities whose heroes and villains may be the mirror opposite of each other. Take the role of the Ottomans in Europe. For Muslims in the Balkans, the Ottomans are a source of inspiration and pride. Mirnes Kovač, editor of the Islamic newspaper *Preporod,* wrote to me that Sultan Mehmed II Fatih, "is by far most popular, for he brought Islam here." He explained why he named his son Fatih: "I named him after the Sultan who brought the light of Islam into this land." The mosques and libraries of the region reflect the Ottoman legacy.

The picture regarding the Ottomans is, however, reversed among other populations that have been ruled by them. For the Serbs and non-Muslims of Eastern Europe, there was no greater scourge than the Ottomans. So great was the loathing of the Turks that it transferred to a Hollywood film, *Dracula Untold* (2014), in which the prince of the undead deploys his talents in the dark arts against an invading Ottoman army in the Balkans. Fact and fiction merge in these perceptions, but without understanding where they are coming from we will not be able to gauge the depth of the emotions aroused when dealing with the other. For all the talk of burying the past and looking ahead, memories of the recent genocide in the Balkans, for example, have not faded as there has been little reconciliation in the region.

9. **Create pride in the community.** Muslims are too often depicted in the media and by far-right leaders as worthless, barbaric, unwanted, and failing to contribute to Europe. There are many steps that the government can take to make Muslims feel honored and welcome, such as recognizing Muslim festivals. Muslim representatives could be invited to meet prominent figures and even heads of state, and this could be given wide publicity. Of high symbolic value is the inclusion of prominent Muslims in government, such as the appointment of Baroness Warsi as cabinet minister in the British government in 2012 and in the same year Humza Yousaf as a minister in the Scottish government. The election of Sadiq Khan as the mayor of London in 2016 also gave an undeniable boost to the community.

10. **Recognize that Muslims tend to view the European Union favorably.** The EU remains the best guarantor of a multicultural and multireligious Europe that has the potential to create a peaceful and prosperous populace, but it needs to make a stronger case for itself. In an editorial titled "Can Europe Be Saved?" published in March 2017, *The Economist* reminded its readers that in the sixty years of the EU's existence, its membership has grown from six countries to twenty-eight, peace has been maintained on the continent, and single-market and currency systems have been established. Today, the European Union faces the internal threats of an uncertain economy, questions about the implications of Brexit, and concern about the rise of the Far Right as well as the external threats of influxes in refugees, aggression from Vladimir Putin, and a lack of support from Donald Trump. Indeed, some of its senior leaders began to openly fret about the possibility of the EU disintegrating completely.

Many Muslims we talked to across the continent were supporters of the European Union, believing that it guarantees their political, economic, and human rights. In particular, Muslims in the Balkans, in places like Western Thrace, Greece, were enthusiastic supporters, discussing the marked difference in their treatment by the government before and after the country joined the EU. In the United Kingdom, 70 percent of Muslims voted to remain in the EU. The current uncertainty about the future of the European Union was causing distress among Muslims because it made them vulnerable to increased Islamophobia. It is on precisely this point that Leoluca Orlando expressed his strong support of the EU.

Though the wave of anti-EU European far-right parties was stopped before it reached the presidential palace in the Netherlands and France in

2017, both Geert Wilders and Marine Le Pen prepared to fight another day. The victory of Emmanuel Macron in France, who staunchly supported the EU and talked of humanity, social justice, and equality, was a resounding rebuttal of the European Far Right. Germany's Hamlet-like tendencies aside, developments in Europe's peripheral regions like Scotland and Catalonia and countries like Austria indicate that even with setbacks for the likes of Wilders and Le Pen, there is political tumult ahead.

In our search for solutions, we need to heed the succinct advice of Bram Groen: "The immigrants will not go away," he warned. "The asylum seekers will always be there. Twenty percent of the population in the Netherlands is no longer 'originally Dutch.' That's an important statistic that means that you have to pay serious attention to that proportion of the population, and they need to become part of the process. That is not multiculturalism; that is actual, real integration."

## Re-creating Convivencia

In an editorial published in April 2016, *The Guardian* captured the dominant European narrative in dealing with Islam while discussing the Catholic right and its attitude to the religion: "submission or resistance." Disappointingly, the third option was missing—convivencia. Our fieldwork encouraged us to believe that the spirit of convivencia, with its emphasis on knowledge and pluralism, is not a thing of the past but is alive and well. Those who doubt Europe's capacity to sustain this third choice would do well to contemplate the actions of Pope Francis, washing the feet of immigrants, and Angela Merkel, opening her arms to welcome a million refugees to Germany, actions that embody the courage, compassion, and humility of the best of European humanism.

### Witness to European Humanity

We saw evidence of the spirit of convivencia in numerous spontaneous interactions during the course of our fieldwork. In 2013, at the very start of the project, Alex Salmond invited me for a private lunch in the first minister's residence in Edinburgh. Accompanying me were Harrison Akins and Ibrahim Hoti. When we arrived, I asked the taxi driver whether he was sure this was where the first minister lived because I did not see a single policeman outside the house or anywhere in the square. As we walked toward the door, it opened as if by magic. We were taken upstairs to the living room, which was of modest proportions and had modest furniture. A small table had been arranged for lunch. The menu was simple, and there was no dessert. We were joined by two of Salmond's staff. As Salmond entered the room, instead of grasping the hand I had extended in greeting, he reached out with both arms and embraced me. He was the perfect host—attentive, hospitable, humorous, and full of anecdotes. Proud of his Scottish ancestry, Harrison was thrilled to meet Salmond. My grandson Ibrahim, a teenager not easily impressed by age or high office, was won over by Salmond's humility and humor. In fact, when Salmond took pictures with him, he leaned across with his elbow on Ibrahim's shoulder and his legs crossed in a mock-comic pose as if they were old buddies. All this was remarkable enough; but then, as we were leaving, Salmond said to me, "We will meet again, inshallah."

Lord Parekh hosted the launch of our project in the House of Lords in London as we set out for Europe in 2014; two years later, in late spring 2016, he chaired a discussion of the project at SOAS—both times specially coming down from his home in Hull in the north of England. Sir Nicholas Barrington, my friend of many years, came down from Cambridge to London in 2016 for the screening of the *Journey into Europe* film at SOAS, an occasion also graced by Ibne Abbas, the Pakistan High Commissioner. When I interviewed Barrington as we sat drinking tea by the Cam River in Cambridge, he presented me first with one then the other volume of his memoirs and said with a twinkle in his eye, "I don't normally give books away. I'm giving them to you, because you've given me so many of your books. I was going to give you just this book, but I find you are really mentioned more in this one."

Lord Rowan Williams sitting on a sofa with four-year-old Anah, patiently helping her navigate the intricacies of the Rubik's Cube while we waited to set up cameras in the Master's Lodge at Magdalene College, Cambridge, was the picture of compassionate humanity. Father Cruz-Conde, the vicar general of the Diocese of Cordoba—in spite of defining Spanish identity with one emphatic word, "Catholicism!"—still found it in his heart to say a special prayer to Saint Raphael, the patron saint of Cordoba and of travelers, for our safety and success. The former chief rabbi of Denmark, Bent Melchior, sat unobtrusively in the audience as I lectured at the University of Copenhagen. Later, he spoke haltingly, trying to locate the precise words in English, but affectionately: "That work is so important, that you devote your life, that you put yourself into this hardship of traveling around, and I know what it means. I cannot think of more warm feelings than I have towards your work and . . . I think it's wonderful that you have another generation following up. So you have really my most heartfelt feelings to succeed." Rabbi Lord Jonathan Sacks spontaneously leaned across to me as we conducted an interfaith dialogue in 2015 in front of a packed audience at American University in Washington, D.C., and clasping both my hands addressed me with his customary generosity as his "beloved friend now of many years . . . a great, great, great man."

As we saw above, Nasser Khalili, the celebrated Jewish philanthropist based in London, when asked to name five of the greatest iconic figures of his life, without hesitation replied. "Moses, Jesus, and Prophet Muhammad, and my parents. Simple." He then elaborated: "At the end of the day, the question of the three religions is very simple. There is only one Creator, one God, three names and we are all his creation. Simple. Simple. The message is simple: Every one of us is his creation. There are not three gods, there is only one God."

The human warmth was especially notable in Southern Europe. In Spain and Sicily many local people reminded us of the importance of convivencia and its presence in their respective societies. Here are just a few examples: When José Antonio Nieto Ballesteros, the mayor of Cordoba, heard that little Anah had practiced a bow for our visit, which she executed with spirit, he was delighted and asked about her during the interview. When the interview ended, he gave her a toy, picked her up, and kissed her on the cheeks. In Melilla, we were met at the airport by the interfaith leaders representing its four religions—Christianity, Islam, Judaism, and Hinduism—when we disembarked from the plane. They had been sent by Melilla's president Juan José Imbroda, and they welcomed us with flowers. The group, which included Lachmi Ghanshandas and her Hindu colleagues, was our enthusiastic guide throughout our stay. They took us to the different houses of worship, and all lavished their hospitality on us. On the eve of our departure, Fadela Mohatar, the deputy minister for women in Melilla, hosted an interfaith dinner to wish us farewell, attended by the vice president of Melilla and its prominent interfaith leaders at one of the elegant restaurants of the town. Fadela had overheard that it was my wife Zeenat's birthday and had quietly arranged for a birthday cake with candles to be brought to our table ceremoniously after dinner while the entire party burst into "Happy Birthday." When we were ready to leave for the airport from our hotel, Fadela arrived driving her own car to say goodbye and insisted on dropping off Amineh herself.

There was our chance encounter with a young woman in Granada. She was working as the hotel receptionist when we checked into Casa del Capitel Nazarí, a former palace in the Moorish quarter of Albayzín and located at the base of the Alhambra Palace. We had just arrived from Melilla, dusty and tired after a long and exhausting few days of travel. As we filled in the routine hotel forms and chatted, she told us she was of Jewish descent in the Andalusian past. When I explained our project and showed her some press cuttings from an interview in a Spanish newspaper, she said the world desperately needed this kind of bridge building and applauded its noble intent. She was distressed at the brutality and poverty in the world today. At times, she confessed, she found it difficult to even breathe. She said to me, you are a "man of peace" and "peace is so desperately needed." I could see she was visibly moved and fighting back tears. Then she asked, now crying quite uncontrollably, "May I embrace you?" It was an emotional moment for me too, and, of course, I opened my arms to embrace her. It was as if our mere arrival had reactivated a deep-rooted memory of a time when we could love one another in spite of our differences.

The spirit of convivencia in Sicily was captured by Mayor Leoluca Orlando of Palermo, who described Sicilian society as "a harmonious mosaic." "Please don't ask me the name of God," he had said to us, as related in chapter 3. "When I come inside a mosque, I pray to Allah, when I come inside a synagogue, I pray to Yahweh. At this moment I am Christian."

In Athens, Professor Sotiris Roussos hosted my public events and was always available to answer our questions with Greek wisdom, charm, and humor. I gained an insight into Greek culture when he said Ulysses was his favorite hero from Greek history, while I was half expecting him to say Alexander the Great. Ulysses is not only a man constantly in search of learning and adventure, but he is also human in a way that most of us can relate to. When we first met George Kalantzis, the secretary general for religious affairs of Greece, in his office, the entire team noted that he had the Quran respectfully placed on his table alongside the Bible. A scholarly and thoughtful man, he explained Greeks have no problem with Islam and have long had relations with Muslim lands like Egypt. In the summer of 2016, I received this gracious message from him on the occasion of the Eid festival that marks the end of the month of fasting: "Dear Professor, please accept my warmest greetings for the great celebration of Eid al-Fitr. May Allah always be merciful with our mistakes."

There was also Bishop Gabriel of Diavleia, a charismatic and wise spiritual leader and the second highest-ranking member of the Greek Orthodox Church. He was a supporter of the immigrant community and a mosque for Athens. His attitude to people can be gauged by the story he told us in his office when I asked him what he said to those Christians

who believed all others, including Christians who belonged to other de-
nominations, were destined to burn in hell. With a smile on his face, he
related a story about a man who died and went to heaven where he was
shown around by an angel. The angel pointed to a Muslim community,
then another community, and so on, until they passed a very high wall.
"What is behind that?" asked the man. "Shh!" said the angel. "That is for
those very Christians who believe only they have the right faith. They think
they're alone here."

As for the Bosnians, it was like coming home: Their hospitality, dignity, compassion, scholarly nature, and refusal to talk of revenge in spite of
facing the horrors of genocide and mass rape inspired the entire team,
Muslim and non-Muslim. Several Bosnians, like Husein Kavazović, the
grand mufti of Bosnia and Herzegovina, returned from their summer vacation specially to talk to us. The day before we left Sarajevo, former Bosnian prime minister Haris Silajdžić dropped in at a moment's notice in
short sleeves to the delight of the group. Merima Memić of the Bosniak
Institute wrote after we met, "Come again. There is a famous Bosnian saying: if you drink water in Sarajevo near Gazi Husrev-bey's mosque you
will have to come back, and you will keep coming to Sarajevo over and
over again."

Included in the acts of humanity is the gracious letter Prince Charles
wrote to Amineh in 2017 in which he embraced father and daughter and
moved both of us deeply. He thanked her for the gift of her book and
asked her to, "Please give my kindest regards to your dear father, whose
steadfast support for peace and reconciliation over so many years has been
a constant inspiration. And do tell him not only that it has been *far* too
long since I have seen him and that I do hope I shall see him again before
we all get too old, but that I *still* wear the wonderful Pakistani coat he gave
me whenever I am in the garden at Highgrove during the Winter!"

### Toward a New Andalusia

Europe stands at the crossroads: one path leads to tenebrous forests
where fearsome beasts lurk, waiting to pounce on the weak and the vulnerable; the other to engagement with and fulfillment of modernity and
liberal democracy, promising equality and prosperity for all. The second
path reflects not only convivencia but also the indomitable spirit of scientific enquiry, space exploration, medical breakthroughs, and technological
advancements. There is no denying, however, that if we do not check our
aggressiveness and militaristic impulses, we will find it difficult to over-

come the real existentialist dangers that confront us—global warming and its devastating effects on the planet, overpopulation, poverty, and religious and racial conflict—and their by-product of terrorism.

If unbridled European predator identity is allowed to run amok—and major European commentators like Giorgio Agamben are already pointing out that this was the same path Hitler took in his rise to power in the early 1930s—the minorities will confront the same choices familiar to us from European history: deportation, as desired by the likes of Geert Wilders; concentration camps or gas chambers, as feared by Muslims like Shabbir Akhtar; or a penumbral state of misery at the margins of society, as in the case of the Roma. The convivencia of Andalusia is a European antidote to the European problem of predator identity. This is a critical moment for Europe, and it must decide which path it will take: it is either Andalusia or dystopia.

To move forward toward a New Andalusia, Europe needs to acknowledge both the thesis and the antithesis of our study in order to create a viable synthesis. Primordial identity, which provides stability and continuity in uncertain times and gives pride to the community, needs to be appreciated by Europeans. They also need to accept the fact that the time of convivencia may have gone but its spirit is still alive.

Europe must not forget its legacy of humanism and knowledge, nor should it forget the role played by the Greeks, Muslims, Jews, and Christians working together in the development of these ideals. This is also the time for Europeans to remember the contributions made by Islam to European civilization. Indeed, there would be no European civilization as we know it without Islam. It is the time for Europeans to recognize their own history and talk of not only Judeo-Christian but Judeo-Christian-Islamic civilization. The continent will not fully rediscover its missing parts until Europeans acknowledge Averroes and Ibn Arabi as intellectual forebears, alongside Aquinas and Dante; appreciate that centuries before Da Vinci, Ibn Firnas attempted flight in Cordoba; and recognize the debt to European Muslims for developing the foundations of Greek knowledge and philosophy, the Renaissance, the Enlightenment, and countless other contributions and achievements. When it does so, Europeans will also become better acquainted with the moral and intellectual stature of Christian rulers like Roger II, Frederick II, and Alfonso X, who actively promoted tolerance and acceptance of Muslims and Jews—valuable role models for the leaders of Europe today.

Professor Angeliki Ziaka of the Aristotle University of Thessaloniki linked Islamic to Greek thought through what she called the "circle of light," in which Greek philosophy, especially the ideas of Aristotle, traveled "from Greece to the Middle East, to Damascus and from there to Baghdad, and from the Middle East going to Andalusia with the great Arab philosophers and the great Jewish philosophers like Maimonides. Then the light of scholastic theology and philosophy was understood and interpreted by Thomas Aquinas and entered the Western world, Catholicism, and the Renaissance of course."

Ziaka was right. It is this Greek concept of knowledge that finds an echo in the Islamic notion of ilm, which permeated the civilization of Andalusia. As one of the great sages of Europe, Rabbi Lord Jonathan Sacks, told us,

> When you talk about good relations between faiths at moments of high-intensity conflict, people think you're being Utopian, people just aren't that good. So what brings these aspirations from Utopia to reality is the knowledge that we have been there before. Andalusia showed how it could be done and showed that it could be done. And because of that, for me, Andalusia is the single-most important feature of our current situation.

At the end of the long journey that took me through a quartet of studies, I did not make any earth-shattering discovery of how to live in perpetual spiritual bliss or become a billionaire; but there was the realization that nothing is more precious than the preservation of human life, regardless of color, race, or religion, and there is nothing more sacred than treating it with dignity and kindness. This noble concept is enshrined in European thought; it is also at the core of the Islamic vision of the universe and of the other great cultures of the planet. Its universal implementation is a challenge worthy of our common humanity.

The arc of history turns toward justice and peace, and even though thwarted continues in that direction. It is our hope and prayer that we can begin to create a New Andalusia, one that is not merely a repeat of the past but truly a new world. If that happens, Europe will once again become a beacon of civilization for all of humanity. Perhaps by tilting at the windmills of elevated dreams and high ideals, we confirm that there is a bit of Don Quixote, that universally beloved European character, in all of us.

# ACKNOWLEDGMENTS

I WOULD LIKE to acknowledge those individuals and organizations without whom the film and book project, *Journey into Europe*, would not have been completed as smoothly and efficiently as it was. The project was supported and funded by the Stiftung Mercator Foundation of Germany. In the United Kingdom, Professor Peter Morey and Amina Yaqin deserve warm gratitude for their unstinted support from the very time the project was conceived. In addition, Peter Morey served as executive producer for the film project. They were conducting innovative projects of their own on bridging the gap between Muslims and non-Muslims under the title Muslims, Trust and Cultural Dialogue. The British Council, too, supported us and, with its all-European reach, provided top-notch resources across the continent. I must single out Paul Smith, the U.S. director of the British Council, for his faith in and support of the project from its inception. Casa Árabe, a public consortium headed by the Spanish Foreign Ministry to promote relations between Spain and the Arab and Muslim world, provided support for fieldwork in Spain. Casa Árabe's director, Ambassador Eduardo López Busquets, arranged for our visits to Cordoba, Melilla, and Granada, and staff members such as Javier Rosón Lorente provided us invaluable assistance in multiple areas of our fieldwork. Ambassador López Busquets participated in seminars before and after the fieldwork and even joined us in the field. Professor Hastings Donnan of Queen's University in Belfast hosted us with his usual cheerful hospitality.

I am especially grateful to Carrie Engel, Robert Faherty, William Finan, Kristen Harrison, Valentina Kalk, Yelba Quinn, and Janet Walker of the Brookings Institution Press, and Katherine Kimball, Angela Piliouras, and Richard Walker, for their assistance in the completion of this book; Janet Walker has been a solicitous godmother to all four of my books for Brookings and I am thankful to have had her superbly professional support throughout.

I would additionally like to thank the editorial staffs of the *Huffington Post*, the *Friday Times*, and the *Daily Times* for publishing a number of my articles highlighting a sampling of our findings from the field, which proved invaluable in helping to spread the word about the book before its release.

I owe a special thanks to James Goldgeier, the former dean of the American University School of International Service, who, despite his many duties, was unflagging in his support of our project. I would like to thank the following for providing us support over the course of this project: Leila Adler, Kosar Aftab, Mustafa Aga, Kashif Ahmad, Commodore Adnan Ahmed, Ashfaq Ahmed, Melody Fox Ahmed, Nadeem Ahmed, Tasmina Ahmed-Sheikh, MP, Messaouda Akacha, Samir Akacha, Mustafa Akalay, Mohsin Akhtar, Anastasia Andritsou, Syima Aslam, Ayşe Aydin, Kristiane Backer, Imam Naveed Baig, Khalil Ahmed Bajwa, Pawan Bali, Muhammad Abdul Bari, Salah Bariki, Sir Nicholas Barrington, Annette Bellaoui, Fernando Belmonte, Jonathan Benthall, Gary Berman, Roger Boase, Nuseybe Bosnak, Professor Michael Brenner, Stefan Bress, Stefan Buchwald, Tony Buckby, Grand Mufti Mustafa Cerić, Professor Jocelyne Cesari, Munir Akthar Chaudry, Commander Makhdum Ali Chishty, Lachmi Ghanshandas Choithramani, Congressman Keith Ellison, Imam Sidigullah Fadai, Dr. Susan Fell, Imma Fernandez, Alaya Forte, Sister Francisca, Anisuddin Gabbur, Bishop Gabriel of Diavleia, Professor Ehab Galal, Professor Esmir Ganić, Uffe Gavnholt, Dean Louis Goodman, Adnan Hadrović, Imam Hisam Hafizović, Mia Manan Hameed, Samia Hathroubi, Lord Mayor Khadim Hussain, Musharraf Hussain, Ambassador Ghalib Iqbal, Ambassador Tehmina Janjua, Ambassador Syed Hasan Javed, Sister Maria Jose, Ambassador Masroor Junejo, George Kalantzis, Tahir Kamran, Grand Mufti Husein Kavazović, Professor Edward Kessler, Nasser David Khalili, Mirnes Kovać, Ambassador Heinrich Kreft, Anna Kuchenbecker, Rabbi Steven Langnas, Rachel Launay, Dean Nanette Levinson, Rabbi Bruce Lustig, Madhu Gangaram Manwani, Chief Rabbi Bent Melchior, Munira Mendonça, Fadela Mohatar, Mayor Leoluca Orlando, Lord Bhikhu Parekh, Imam Abdul Wahid Pedersen, Professor Randolph Persaud, Pantelis Christian Poetis, Philomena Poetis, Jan Post, Yasin Puertas, Bashy Quraishy, Aftab Qureshi, Irna Qureshi, Mohammed Jafer Qureshi, Sanila Rana, Julia Rawlins, Stephan Richter, Tim

Rivera, Professor Lawrence Rosen, Professor Sotiris Roussos, Walter Ruby, Rabbi Lord Jonathan Sacks, Ambassador Jauhar Saleem, The Right Honorable Alex Salmond, MP, Captain Abdul Samad, Mohammed Rafiq Sehgal, Brigadier General Asif Adnan Jah Shad, Sana Shah, Haris Silajdžić, Jon Snow, Sananda Solaris, Asmaa Soliman, Professor Tamara Sonn, Riem Spielhaus, Anna Stamou, Julie Taylor, Enes Tuna, Eugenio Vallone, Baroness Sayeeda Warsi, Melissa Wear, Archbishop Lord Rowan Williams, Shaykh Abdal Hakim Murad Winter, Katy Yakoumaki, Humza Yousaf, MSP, and Ambassador Muhammad Yousaf.

Both film and book projects rested on the dedication of the team, and it is to them that I express my deepest gratitude; I can truly say with some pride that it is as much theirs as it is mine. Patrick Burnett proved a virtual dynamo and played a key role in the writing of the book. Anna Brosius, Elisa Frost, Anagha Kadambi, Sushmita Kamboj, and Siriwan Limsakul were important members of the team, which included, at different times, Matthew Agar, Brianna Curran, Frieder Dengler, Alessia de Vitis, Sameena Hakimi, Victoria Hill, Katelyn Lamson, Emily Manna, Joseph Marcus, Lucette Moran, Joshua Rodriguez, Rachael Weiss, and Mehmil Zia. Professor Bram Groen's unfailing involvement and support were exemplary and a source of encouragement for me.

The core field team consisted of Frankie Martin, Harrison Akins, Amineh Hoti, and Zeenat Ahmed. Harrison was a pillar of the project with his consistent intelligence, integrity, and hard work. In addition, and with impressive panache, he took on the burden of filming the documentary. Frankie joined me as a student in my class in 2003 and soon became central to my tetralogy of studies. I can only conjecture with amusement what the students thought of our peregrinations around the campus as, deep in discussion, I expounded on the topic du jour and Frankie, cell phone in hand, typed notes to discuss, debate, and research, a practice we continued even in the gym whether I was on the treadmill or lifting weights. I had the consolation of knowing that we were following the classic pedagogical model of peripatetic ponderings provided to us by none other than the Greeks—Socrates, Plato, and Aristotle. I look forward to the fashion catching on in the academy. With his affection, loyalty, respect, humor, integrity, and above all, passion for the pursuit of knowledge displayed over the years, Frankie became like a favorite son. No father could be prouder of his offspring than I am of Frankie. I owe him far more than he will ever know. Here I simply express my gratitude to him for being who he is and having faith in me and my work over these years.

Various members of my family gave the project valuable assistance on a voluntary basis at its different stages, and I am grateful to each one of them.

Amineh and Zeenat were core members of the team, and in spite of the challenges we faced, they never lost faith in it. Amineh was not only a top-notch and tireless fieldworker but also assisted in the cinematography. In the quartet of studies, wherever I was in the world doing fieldwork, Amineh, overcoming all kinds of hurdles, would join me. The combination of compassion, cheerfulness, and scholarship that she embodied was an inspiration not only to me but the entire team. Zeenat was like a rock with her love and support. When I would finish the day exhausted, she was always there to offer encouragement, useful suggestions, and feedback as I took notes and prepared for a speech or piece-to-camera for the next morning. Amineh and Zeenat provided an excellent gender balance to the project. Amineh had little Anah with us, and her presence not only helped in allowing us to board early on flights, but she was a great icebreaker with other mothers and kept our spirits up. Two of my other grandchildren Mina and Ibrahim joined us as soon as they finished their school exams, and Amineh's husband, Arsallah, and my other daughter, Nafees, came too for fieldwork to cheer us on. My son Babar gave expert guidance to the filming process as the executive producer, and my other son, Umar, came for part of the fieldwork and provided crucial legal services to the project. All of them generously worked gratis. The book is dedicated with love to my grandson Gabriel, Zeenat, and Frankie Martin.

## Chapter One

1. *Ethnography* blog, "Max Weber Was a Funny Guy!," blog entry by Tony Waters, April 28, 2017 (www.ethnography.com/2017/04/max-weber-was-a-funny-guy/).

2. Tacitus, *Germany/Germania*, translated by Herbert W. Benario (Warminster, U.K.: Aris and Phillips, 1999), p. 17.

3. Clifford Geertz, *The Interpretation of Cultures: Selected Essays* (New York: Basic Books, 1973), pp. 351, 354.

## Chapter Two

1. Christopher B. Krebs, *A Most Dangerous Book: Tacitus's* Germania *from the Roman Empire to the Third Reich* (New York: W. W. Norton, 2011).

2. Daniel Chirot and Clark McCauley, *Why Not Kill Them All? The Logic and Prevention of Mass Political Murder* (Princeton University Press, 2006), pp. 27–28.

3. Hans A. Schmitt, "From Sovereign States to Prussian Provinces: Hanover and Hesse-Nassau, 1866–1871," *Journal of Modern History* 57, no. 1 (1985), p. 41.

4. Celia Applegate, *A Nation of Provincials: The German Idea of Heimat* (University of California Press, 1990), p. 244.

5. Robert Reinhold Ergang, *Herder and the Foundations of German Nationalism* (Columbia University Press, 1931), p. 198.

6. Michael D. Kennedy and Ronald Grigor Suny, introduction to *Intellectuals and the Articulation of the Nation*, edited by Ronald Grigor Suny and Michael D. Kennedy (University of Michigan Press, 1999), p. 27.

7. Ergang, *Herder and the Foundations of German Nationalism*, p. 228.

8. Ibid., p. 138.

9. Pierre James, *The Murderous Paradise: German Nationalism and the Holocaust* (Westport, Conn.: Praeger, 2001), p. 89.

10. Ergang, *Herder and the Foundations of German Nationalism*, pp. 115, 119, 151, 244–45, 253.

11. Elie Kedourie, *Nationalism* (New York: Praeger, 1961), p. 59.

12. Ergang, *Herder and the Foundations of German Nationalism*, pp. 127–28, 201, 252–53.

13. Krebs, *A Most Dangerous Book*, pp. 178–79.

14. George L. Mosse, *Toward the Final Solution: A History of European Racism* (New York: Howard Fertig, 1985), p. 37.

15. Lonnie R. Johnson, *Central Europe: Enemies, Neighbors, Friends* (Oxford University Press, 1996), p. 132.

16. Louis L. Snyder, *Roots of German Nationalism* (Indiana University Press, 1978), p. 61.

17. Louis L. Snyder, *German Nationalism: The Tragedy of a People* (Port Washington, N.Y.: Kennikat Press, 1969), p. 130.

18. Krebs, *A Most Dangerous Book*, p. 186.

19. James, *The Murderous Paradise*, pp. 101–02.

20. Krebs, *A Most Dangerous Book*, p. 196.

21. James, *The Murderous Paradise*, p. 120.

22. Snyder, *German Nationalism*, pp. 28, 33.

23. Krebs, *A Most Dangerous Book*, p. 195.

24. Claire E. Nolte, *The Sokol in the Czech Lands to 1914: Training for the Nation* (Basingstoke, U.K.: Palgrave, 2002), p. 13.

25. James, *The Murderous Paradise*, p. 100.

26. Snyder, *Roots of German Nationalism*, p. 42.

27. Louis L. Snyder, "Nationalistic Aspects of the Grimm Brothers' Fairy Tales," *Journal of Social Psychology* 33, no. 2 (1951), p. 211.

28. Richard Wagner, *My Life*, translated by Andrew Gray, edited by Mary Whittall (Cambridge University Press, 1983), p. 260.

29. James, *The Murderous Paradise*, p. 142.

30. Snyder, *German Nationalism*, p. 176.

31. Krebs, *A Most Dangerous Book*, pp. 203–04.

32. Urpo Vento, "The Role of the Kalevala in Finnish Culture and Politics," *Nordic Journal of African Studies* 1, no. 2 (1992), p. 82.

33. Margaret Hayford O'Leary, *Culture and Customs of Norway* (Santa Barbara, Calif.: Greenwood, 2010), p. 108.

34. Benjamin Curtis, *Music Makes the Nation: Nationalist Composers and Nation Building in Nineteenth-Century Europe* (Amherst, N.Y.: Cambria Press, 2008), p. 131.

35. Helene Høyrup, "Grundtvig, Svend (1824–1883)," in *Folktales and Fairy Tales: Traditions and Texts From Around the World*, edited by Anne E. Duggan and Donald Haase, with Helen Callow (Santa Barbara, Calif.: Greenwood, 2016), p. 436.

36. Patrick Kingsley, *How to Be Danish: A Journey to the Cultural Heart of Denmark* (London: Short Books, 2013), p. 24; and Knud J. V. Jespersen, *A History of Denmark*, translated by Ivan Hill and Christopher Wade (New York: Palgrave Macmillan, 2011), p. 119.

37. Julie K. Allen, *Icons of Danish Modernity: Georg Brandes and Asta Nielsen* (University of Washington Press, 2012), p. 54.

38. Hugh Eakin, "Liberal, Harsh Denmark," *New York Review of Books*, March 10, 2016.

39. Lars Lönnroth, "The Vikings in History and Legend," in *The Oxford Illustrated History of the Vikings*, edited by Peter Sawyer (Oxford University Press, 1997), p. 236.

40. Sheri Berman, *The Primacy of Politics: Social Democracy and the Making of Europe's Twentieth Century* (Cambridge University Press, 2006), p. 163.

41. Peter Blickle, *Heimat: A Critical Theory of the German Idea of Homeland* (Rochester, N.Y.: Camden House, 2002), p. 55.

42. Eduard Spranger quoted, ibid., p. 38; and Alfred Polgar quoted in Erhard Schütz, "Berlin: A Jewish *Heimat* at the Turn of the Century?," in *Heimat, Nation, Fatherland: The German Sense of Belonging*, edited by Jost Hermand and James D. Steakley (New York: Peter Lang, 1996), p. 78.

43. David Morley and Kevin Robins, *Spaces of Identity: Global Media, Electronic Landscapes and Cultural Boundaries* (London: Routledge, 1995), p. 85.

44. Karla Schultz, "Todtnauberg and Amorbach: *Heimat* as Name and Orientation," in *Heimat, Nation, Fatherland*, edited by Hermand and Steakley, pp. 163, 168–69.

45. Blickle, *Heimat*, p. 45.

46. Applegate, *A Nation of Provincials*, p. 7.

47. Blickle, *Heimat*, pp. 77–78.

48. Applegate, *A Nation of Provincials*, p. 7.

49. Blickle, *Heimat*, pp. 76, 158.

50. Johannes von Moltke, *No Place Like Home: Locations of Heimat in German Cinema* (University of California Press, 2005), p. 28.

51. Anton Kaes, *From Hitler to Heimat: The Return of History as Film* (Harvard University Press, 1989), p. 15.

52. Ibid., p. 85.

53. Alon Confino, *Germany as a Culture of Remembrance: Promises and Limits of Writing History* (University of North Carolina Press, 2006), pp. 59–60.

54. Applegate, *A Nation of Provincials*, p. 246.

55. Blickle, *Heimat*, p. 154.

56. Maria Björkroth quoted in Peter Davis, *Ecomuseums: A Sense of Place* (London: Continuum, 2011), p. 52.

57. Michelle Facos, *Nationalism and the Nordic Imagination: Swedish Art of the 1890s* (University of California Press, 1998), p. 47.

58. John Sheail, *Nature's Spectacle: The World's First National Parks and Protected Places* (London: Earthscan, 2010), p. 98.

59. Ola Wetterberg, "Conservation and the Professions: The Swedish Context, 1880–1920," in *Towards World Heritage: International Origins of the Preservation Movement 1870–1930*, edited by Melanie Hall (Farnham, Surrey, U.K.: Ashgate, 2011), p. 209.

60. Davis, *Ecomuseums: A Sense of Place*, p. 53.

61. *Heino: Made in Germany*, directed by Oliver Schwabe (rbb/WDR/ARTE, 2013).

62. Kate Connolly, "German Singer Heino Stages Controversial Comeback," *The Guardian*, February 24, 2013.

63. Bruce Baum, *The Rise and Fall of the Caucasian Race: A Political History of Racial Identity* (New York University Press, 2006), p. 98.

64. Ibid., p. 98; and Mosse, *Toward the Final Solution*, p. 41.

65. Shlomo Avineri, "Hegel and Nationalism," in *Hegel's Political Philosophy*, edited by Walter Kaufmann (New York: Atherton Books, 1970), p. 111.

66. Kenneth A. R. Kennedy, "Have Aryans Been Identified in the Prehistoric Skeletal Record from South Asia? Biological Anthropology and Concepts of Ancient Races," in *The Indo-Aryans of Ancient South Asia: Language, Material Culture and Ethnicity*, edited by George Erdosy (Berlin: Walter de Gruyter, 1995), p. 35.

67. Johann Chapoutot, *Greeks, Romans, Germans: How the Nazis Usurped Europe's Classical Past*, translated by Richard R. Nybakken (University of California Press, 2016), p. 33.

68. Theodore Vial, *Modern Religion, Modern Race* (Oxford University Press, 2016), p. 30.

69. Susanne Zantop, *Colonial Fantasies: Conquest, Family, and Nation in Precolonial Germany, 1770–1870* (Duke University Press, 1997), p. 68; and Benjamin Isaac, *The Invention of Racism in Classical Antiquity* (Princeton University Press, 2004), p. 12.

70. Nell Irvin Painter, *The History of White People* (New York: W. W. Norton, 2010), p. 90.

71. Kingsley, *How to Be Danish*, p. 61.

72. Jeppe Trolle Linnet, "Money Can't Buy Me Hygge: Danish Middle-Class Consumption, Egalitarianism, and the Sanctity of Inner Space," *Social Analysis* 55, no. 2 (2011), pp. 26, 29, 30.

73. Richard Jenkins, *Being Danish: Paradoxes of Identity in Everyday Life* (Copenhagen: Museum Tusculanum Press, 2012), pp. 41, 253–54.

74. Linnet, "Money Can't Buy Me Hygge," p. 21.

75. Applegate, *A Nation of Provincials*, p. 67.

76. Jeffrey K. Wilson, *The German Forest: Nature, Identity, and the Contestation of a National Symbol, 1871–1914* (University of Toronto Press, 2012), p. 4.

77. Ibid., p. 3.

78. Von Moltke, *No Place Like Home*, p. 94.

79. Adrian Murdoch, *Rome's Greatest Defeat: Massacre in the Teutoburg Forest* (Gloucestershire, U.K.: History Press, 2008).

80. Christof Mauch, "Nature and Nation in Transatlantic Perspective," introduction to *Nature in German History*, edited by Christof Mauch (New York: Berghahn, 2004), p. 3.

81. Julius Caesar, *The Gallic War*, translated by H. J. Edwards (London: William Heinemann, 1919), p. 351.

82. Mauch, "Nature and Nation in Transatlantic Perspective," p. 3.

83. David Welch, *Propaganda and the German Cinema, 1933–1945* (London: I. B. Tauris, 2001), pp. 87–89.

84. Jeffrey Richards, *Visions of Yesterday* (London: Routledge, 2014), p. 324.

85. Welch, *Propaganda and the German Cinema, 1933–1945*, p. 89.

86. Wilson, *The German Forest*, p. 201.

87. Tim Blanning, *The Romantic Revolution: A History* (New York: Random House, 2012), p. 147.

88. Wilson, *The German Forest*, p. 203.

89. Peter Young, *Oak* (London: Reaktion Books, 2013), pp. 120, 128.

90. George Fenwick Jones, *Honor in German Literature* (University of North Carolina Press, 1959), p. 20.

91. Boria Sax, *Animals in the Third Reich: Pets, Scapegoats, and the Holocaust* (New York: Continuum, 2000), p. 74.

92. Robin Lumsden, *Himmler's SS: Loyal to the Death's Head* (Gloucestershire, U.K.: History Press, 2009), p. 146.

93. Perry Biddiscombe, *Werwolf! The History of the National Socialist Guerrilla Movement, 1944–1946* (University of Toronto Press, 1998), pp. 116, 289–90.

94. Klaus Neumann, *Shifting Memories: The Nazi Past in the New Germany* (University of Michigan Press, 2000), pp. 49–51.

95. Snyder, *German Nationalism*, p. 232.

96. Sax, *Animals in the Third Reich*, pp. 75, 83.

97. Yirmiyahu Yovel, *Dark Riddle: Hegel, Nietzsche, and the Jews* (Pennsylvania State University Press, 1998), p. 30.

98. F. W. Nietzsche, *The Antichrist*, translated by H. L. Mencken (New York: Alfred A. Knopf, 1920), p. 177.

99. C. G. Jung, *The Collected Works of C. G. Jung*, vol. 10: *Civilization in Transition*, translated by R. F. C. Hull (New York: Pantheon, 1964), p. 190.

100. C. G. Jung, *Memories, Dreams, Reflections*, translated by Richard and Clara Winston (New York: Vintage Books, 1989), p. 313.

101. H. G. Baynes, *Germany Possessed* (London: Jonathan Cape, 1941), p. 63.

102. Snyder, *German Nationalism*, p. 153.

103. Charles Osborne, *The Complete Operas of Richard Wagner* (London: Da Capo Press, 1993), p. 270.

104. Susannah Heschel, *The Aryan Jesus: Christian Theologians and the Bible in Nazi Germany* (Princeton University Press, 2008), p. 49.

105. James, *The Murderous Paradise*, p. 121.

106. Harro Segeberg, "Germany," in *Nationalism in the Age of the French Revolution*, edited by Otto Dann and John Dinwiddy (London: Hambledon Press, 1988), p. 155.

107. P. Hume Brown, *Life of Goethe*, vol. 2 (New York: Haskell House, 1971), p. 583.

108. Adolf Hitler, *Mein Kampf*, translated by Ralph Manheim (Boston: Houghton Mifflin, 1971), p. 461.

109. Arthur Schopenhauer, *The World as Will and Representation*, vol. 2, translated by E. F. J. Payne (New York: Dover, 1958), p. 527.

110. Arthur Schopenhauer, *Parerga and Paralipomena: Short Philosophical Essays*, vol. 2, translated by E. F. J. Payne (Oxford, U.K.: Clarendon Press, 1974), p. 158.

111. Heather Pringle, *The Master Plan: Himmler's Scholars and the Holocaust* (New York: Hyperion, 2006), p. 16.

112. Claudia Koonz, *The Nazi Conscience* (Harvard University Press, 2003), p. 137.

113. Robert Gellately, *The Gestapo and German Society: Enforcing Racial Policy, 1933–1945* (Oxford, U.K.: Clarendon Press, 1990), p. 236.

114. Pringle, *The Master Plan*, pp. 7, 194.

115. Richard Breitman, *The Architect of Genocide: Himmler and the Final Solution* (New York: Alfred A. Knopf, 1991), pp. 34–35.

116. Pringle, *The Master Plan*, p. 96.

117. Felix Kersten, *The Kersten Memoirs: 1940–1945*, translated by Constantine Fitzgibbon and James Oliver (New York: Macmillan, 1957), pp. 101–03, 117.

118. Pringle, *The Master Plan*, pp. 56, 80, 228, 282–83.

119. Benjamin Madley quoted in Adam Jones, *Genocide: A Comprehensive Introduction* (London: Routledge, 2011), p. 123.

120. Ibid., p. 261; Breitman, *The Architect of Genocide*, p. 205; and Ian Kershaw, *Hitler, 1936–45: Nemesis* (New York: W. W. Norton, 2000), p. 945, note 70.

121. Pringle, *The Master Plan*, pp. 194, 220.

122. Christopher Hale, *Himmler's Crusade: The Nazi Expedition to Find the Origins of the Aryan Race* (Hoboken, N.J.: Wiley, 2003), p. 315; and Kersten, *The Kersten Memoirs*, p. 252.

123. Kersten, *The Kersten Memoirs*, p. 138.

124. Breitman, *The Architect of Genocide*, p. 177.

125. F. M. Barnard, *Herder on Nationality, Humanity, and History* (McGill-Queen's University Press, 2003), p. 14.

126. Jelena Milojković-Djurić, *Panslavism and National Identity in Russia and in the Balkans, 1830–1880: Images of the Self and Others* (Boulder, Colo.: East European Monographs, 1994), p. 11.

127. Alexander Burry, *Multi-Mediated Dostoevsky: Transposing Novels into Opera, Film, and Drama* (Northwestern University Press, 2011), p. 73.

128. George Barany, *Stephen Széchenyi and the Awakening of Hungarian Nationalism, 1791–1841* (Princeton University Press, 1968), p. 179.

129. Alexander Maxwell and Alexander Campbell, "István Széchenyi, The Casino Movement, and Hungarian Nationalism, 1827–1848," *Nationalities Papers* 42, no. 3 (2014), p. 509; and Alice Freifeld, *Nationalism and the Crowd in Liberal Hungary, 1848–1914* (Washington, D.C.: Woodrow Wilson Center Press, 2000), p. 25.

130. Ulf Brunnbauer, "The Perception of Muslims in Bulgaria and Greece: Between the 'Self' and the 'Other,'" *Journal of Muslim Minority Affairs* 21, no. 1 (2001), p. 41.

131. Francis Dvornik, *The Slavs in European History and Civilization* (Rutgers University Press, 1962), pp. 36–37, note 20.

132. Nick Thorpe, "Visegrad: The Castle Where a Central European Bloc was Born," *BBC News*, February 21, 2016.

133. Jones, *Honor in German Literature*, p. 129.

134. Robert D. Greenberg, *Language and Identity in the Balkans: Serbo-Croatian and Its Disintegration* (Oxford University Press, 2004), p. 163.

135. Ingrid Merchiers, *Cultural Nationalism in the South Slav Habsburg Lands in the Early Nineteenth Century: The Scholarly Network of Jernej Kopitar, 1780–1844* (Munich: Verlag Otto Sagner, 2007), p. 100.

136. R. W. Seton-Watson, *A History of the Roumanians* (Cambridge University Press, 1934), p. 39.

## Chapter Three

1. Stanley Lane-Poole, *The Story of the Moors in Spain*, with the collaboration of Arthur Gilman (New York: G. P. Putnam's Sons, 1896), pp. 76–77.

2. María Rosa Menocal, *The Ornament of the World: How Muslims, Jews, and Christians Created a Culture of Tolerance in Medieval Spain* (New York: Back Bay Books, 2002), p. 33.

3. Michael Hamilton Morgan, *Lost History: The Enduring Legacy of Muslim Scientists, Thinkers, and Artists* (Washington, D.C.: National Geographic, 2007), p. 135.

4. Jack E. McCallum, "Military Medicine, Medieval Islamic," in *Conflict and Conquest in the Islamic World: A Historical Encyclopedia*, edited by Alexander Mikaberidze (Santa Barbara, Calif.: Greenwood, 2011), p. 586.

5. Antony Black, *The History of Islamic Political Thought: From the Prophet to the Present* (Edinburgh University Press, 2011), pp. 120–28.

6. *The Philosophy Book: Big Ideas Simply Explained*, edited by Will Buckingham et al. (New York: Penguin, 2015), p. 82.

7. María Jesús Viguera Molins, "Societies and Cultures of al-Andalus," in *Art and Cultures of al-Andalus: The Power of the Alhambra* (Madrid: TF Editores and Interactiva S. L. V., 2013), p. 42.

8. Menocal, *The Ornament of the World*, p. 109.

9. Molins, "Societies and Cultures of al-Andalus," p. 41.

10. José Miguel Puerta Vílchez, "Written Culture in the Granada of al-Andalus," in *Art and Cultures of al-Andalus: The Power of the Alhambra*, p. 69.

11. Ibid.; and Menocal, *The Ornament of the World*, p. 102.

12. Molins, "Societies and Cultures of al-Andalus," p. 40.

13. Menocal, *The Ornament of the World*, pp. 66, 229–38.

14. Simon R. Doubleday, *The Wise King: A Christian Prince, Muslim Spain, and the Birth of the Renaissance* (New York: Basic Books, 2015), pp. 43, 52.

15. Joseph F. O'Callaghan, *The Learned King: The Reign of Alfonso X of Castile* (University of Pennsylvania Press, 1993), pp. 99, 109, 207; and Doubleday, *The Wise King*, p. 102.

16. O'Callaghan, *The Learned King*, p. 133.

17. Ralph Penny, *A History of the Spanish Language* (Cambridge University Press, 2002), p. 20.

18. Doubleday, *The Wise King*, pp. xx, 139, 167–68.

19. Robert I. Burns, "*Stupor Mundi*: Alfonso X of Castile, the Learned," in *Emperor of Culture: Alfonso X the Learned of Castile and His Thirteenth-Century Renaissance*, edited by Robert I. Burns (University of Pennsylvania Press, 1990), p. 9.

20. Doubleday, *The Wise King*, p. xx.

21. Marcel A. Boisard, "On the Probable Influence of Islam on Western Public and International Law," *International Journal of Middle Eastern Studies* 11, no. 4 (1980), p. 435; and Joseph F. O'Callaghan, "Image and Reality: The King Creates His Kingdom," in *Emperor of Culture*, edited by Burns, p. 30.

22. Boisard, "On the Probable Influence of Islam on Western Public and International Law," pp. 435–36.

23. Maribel Fierro, "Alfonso X 'The Wise': The Last Almohad Caliph?," *Medieval Encounters* 15, no. 2–4 (2009), pp. 175–98.

24. María Elena Martínez, *Genealogical Fictions: Limpieza de Sangre, Religion, and Gender in Colonial Mexico* (Stanford University Press, 2008), p. 80.

25. Richard L. Kagan, *Clio and the Crown: The Politics of History in Medieval and Early Modern Spain* (Johns Hopkins University Press, 2009), p. 19.

26. Ibid.

27. Pidal quoted in Lope De Vega Carpio, *El niño inocente de la Guardia* (London: Tamesis Books, 1985), p. 145, notes 86–89.

28. Susanne Zepp, *An Early Self: Jewish Belonging in Romance Literature, 1499–1627* (Stanford University Press, 2014), pp. 78–79.

29. Andrew Wheatcroft, *Infidels: A History of the Conflict between Christendom and Islam* (New York: Random House, 2005), p. 99.

30. Kagan, *Clio and the Crown*, p. 19.

31. L. P. Harvey, *Muslims in Spain, 1500 to 1614* (University of Chicago Press, 2005), p. 8.

32. Ibid.

33. Roger Collins, *Visigothic Spain, 409–711* (Malden, Mass.: Blackwell, 2004), p. 3.

34. Stanley G. Payne, *Fascism in Spain, 1923–1977* (University of Wisconsin Press, 1999), p. 222.

35. Richard Fletcher, *Moorish Spain* (University of California Press, 1992), p. 3.

36. Akbar S. Ahmed, "Spain's Islamic Legacy," *History Today* 41, no. 10 (1991).

37. Eric Calderwood, "The Reconquista of the Mosque of Córdoba," *Foreign Policy*, April 10, 2015.

38. Rafael Jiménez Pedrajas, *Historia de los mozárabes en Al Ándalus: Mozárabes y musulmanes en Al Ándalus: ¿Relaciones de convivencia?, ¿o de antagonismo y lucha?* (Cordoba: Almuzara, Cabildo Catedral de Córdoba, 2013).

39. Ernst Kantorowicz, *Frederick the Second, 1194–1250,* translated by E. O. Lorimer (New York: Frederick Ungar, 1957), p. 388.

40. David Abulafia, *Frederick II: A Medieval Emperor* (Oxford University Press, 1988), p. 18.

41. Gian Luigi Scarfiotti and Paul Lunde, "Muslim Sicily," *Aramco World*, November–December 1978.

42. Alex Metcalfe, *Muslims and Christians in Norman Sicily: Arabic Speakers and the End of Islam* (London: Routledge, 2003), p. 174.

43. Dirk Booms and Peter Higgs, *Sicily: Culture and Conquest* (London: British Museum Press, 2016), p. 1.

44. Edmund Curtis, *Roger of Sicily and the Normans in Lower Italy, 1016–1154* (New York: G. P. Putnam's Sons, 1912), p. 308.

45. Hubert Houben, *Roger II of Sicily: A Ruler between East and West*, translated by Graham A. Loud and Diane Milburn (Cambridge University Press, 2002), p. 47.

46. Metcalfe, *Muslims and Christians in Norman Sicily*, p. 99.

47. Houben, *Roger II of Sicily*, pp. 108, 121, 153.

48. Harold J. Berman, *Law and Revolution: The Formation of the Western Legal Tradition* (Harvard University Press, 1983), p. 419.

49. Jeremy Johns, *Arabic Administration in Norman Sicily: The Royal Diwan* (Cambridge University Press, 2002), p. 255.

50. Curtis, *Roger of Sicily and the Normans in Lower Italy 1016–1154*, p. 375.

51. Karla Mallette, *The Kingdom of Sicily, 1100–1250: A Literary History* (University of Pennsylvania Press, 2005), p. 149.

52. Metcalfe, *Muslims and Christians in Norman Sicily*, p. 97.

53. Houben, *Roger II of Sicily*, p. 106.

54. S. P. Scott, *History of the Moorish Empire in Europe*, vol. 3 (Philadelphia: J. B. Lippincott, 1904), p. 461.

55. Johns, *Arabic Administration in Norman Sicily*, p. 289.

56. Houben, *Roger II of Sicily*, pp. 83, 104.

57. Abbas Hamdani, "An Islamic Background to the Voyages of Discovery," in *The Legacy of Muslim Spain*, edited by Salma Khadra Jayyusi (Leiden, Neth.: Brill, 1994), p. 276.

58. Scott, *History of the Moorish Empire in Europe*, p. 461.

59. Alessandro Vicenzi, *The Palatine Chapel in Palermo*, translated by Lyn Minty (Modena, Italy: Franco Cosimo Panini, 2011), pp. 40–59, 70, 71, 91.

60. Kantorowicz, *Frederick the Second, 1194–1250*, pp. 343–44.

61. Abulafia, *Frederick II*, p. 2.

62. Matthias Schramm, "Frederick II of Hohenstaufen and Arabic Science," *Science in Context* 14, nos. 1–2 (2001), p. 296.

63. David G. Einstein, *Emperor Frederick II* (New York: Philosophical Library, 1949), p. 183.

64. Thomas Curtis Van Cleve, *The Emperor Frederick II of Hohenstaufen: Immutator Mundi* (Oxford University Press, 1972), pp. 302, 305, 314.

65. Kantorowicz, *Frederick the Second, 1194–1250*, p. 362.

66. Schramm, "Frederick II of Hohenstaufen and Arabic Science," p. 310.

67. Mallette, *The Kingdom of Sicily, 1100–1250*, p. 59.

68. Schramm, "Frederick II of Hohenstaufen and Arabic Science," pp. 302–03, 305.

69. Kantorowicz, *Frederick the Second, 1194–1250*, pp. 348, 356.

70. Schramm, "Frederick II of Hohenstaufen and Arabic Science," p. 307.

71. Kantorowicz, *Frederick the Second, 1194–1250*, p. 349.

72. Ibid., p. 342; and Charles H. Haskins, "Science at the Court of the Emperor Frederick II," *American Historical Review* 27, no. 4 (1922), pp. 678–79.

73. Kantorowicz, *Frederick the Second, 1194–1250*, p. 196.

74. Van Cleve, *The Emperor Frederick II of Hohenstaufen*, pp. 305–06, 316.

75. Schramm, "Frederick II of Hohenstaufen and Arabic Science," p. 301.

76. Haskins, "Science at the Court of the Emperor Frederick II," p. 678.

77. Kantorowicz, *Frederick the Second, 1194–1250*, p. 288.

78. Van Cleve, *The Emperor Frederick II of Hohenstaufen*, p. 332.

79. Kantorowicz, *Frederick the Second, 1194–1250*, p. 411.

80. Mallette, *The Kingdom of Sicily, 1100–1250*, p. 6; and Abulafia, *Frederick II*, pp. 271–72.

81. Mallette, *The Kingdom of Sicily, 1100–1250*, pp. 85, 116–18.

82. Paul Moses, *The Saint and the Sultan: The Crusades, Islam, and Francis of Assisi's Mission of Peace* (New York: Doubleday, 2009), p. 145.

83. Kantorowicz, *Frederick the Second, 1194–1250*, p. 193.

84. Van Cleve, *The Emperor Fredcrick II of Hohenstaufen*, pp. 217, 220.

85. Abulafia, *Frederick II*, p. 185.

86. Van Cleve, *The Emperor Frederick II of Hohenstaufen*, p. 225.

87. P. M. Holt, *The Age of the Crusades: The Near East from the Eleventh Century to 1517* (Abingdon, U.K.: Routledge, 2013), p. 65.

88. Van Cleve, *The Emperor Frederick II of Hohenstaufen*, p. 224.

89. *Arab Historians of the Crusades*, translated by E. J. Costello, edited by Francesco Gabrieli (Abingdon, U.K.: Routledge, 2010), pp. 166–67.

90. Kantorowicz, *Frederick the Second, 1194–1250*, pp. 195, 228, 557.

91. Leonard B. Glick, *Abraham's Heirs: Jews and Christians in Medieval Europe* (Syracuse University Press, 1999), p. 175.

92. David Abulafia, "Ethnic Variety and Its Implications: Frederick II's Relations with Jews and Muslims," *Studies in the History of Art* 44 (1994), p. 219.

93. John P. Dolan, "A Note on Emperor Frederick II and Jewish Tolerance," *Jewish Social Studies* 22, no. 3 (1960), p. 174; and Salo Wittmayer Baron, *A Social and Religious History of the Jews*, vol. 4 (Columbia University Press, 1957), p. 68.

94. Abulafia, *Frederick II*, pp. 43, 85, 144.

95. Kantorowicz, *Frederick the Second, 1194–1250*, p. 131.

96. James Bryce, *The Holy Roman Empire* (London: Macmillan, 1902), p. 209.

97. Van Cleve, *The Emperor Frederick II of Hohenstaufen*, p. 529.

98. Kantorowicz, *Frederick the Second, 1194–1250*, p. 636.

99. Van Cleve, *The Emperor Frederick II of Hohenstaufen*, pp. 528–29.

100. Akbar Ahmed, *Journey into America: The Challenge of Islam* (Brookings Institution Press, 2010).

101. José Antonio Conde, *History of the Dominion of the Arabs in Spain*, vol. 3, cited in Muhammad Abdullah Enan, *Decisive Moments in the History of Islam* (New Delhi: Goodword Books, 2001), p. 235.

102. Menocal, *The Ornament of the World*, pp. 12, 32–33.

103. David Levering Lewis, *God's Crucible: Islam and the Making of Europe, 570–1215* (New York: Norton, 2008), pp. 326–27.

104. Menocal, *The Ornament of the World*, p. 12.

105. Akbar S. Ahmed, *Discovering Islam: Making Sense of Muslim History and Society* (London: Routledge, 1988).

106. Tamara Sonn, *Islam: History, Religion, and Politics* (Malden, Mass.: Wiley-Blackwell, 2016), p. 35.

107. Patricia E. Grieve, *The Eve of Spain: Myths of Origins in the History of Christian, Muslim, and Jewish Conflict* (Johns Hopkins University Press, 2009), p. 30.

108. Glaire D. Anderson and Mariam Rosser-Owen, introduction to *Revisiting al-Andalus: Perspectives on the Material Culture of Islamic Iberia and Beyond*, edited by Glaire D. Anderson and Mariam Rosser-Owen (Leiden, Neth.: Brill, 2007), p. xxii; and Évariste Lévi-Provençal, *Histoire de l'Espagne musulmane*, vol. 1 (Leiden, Neth.: Brill, 1950).

109. Eduardo Manzano Moreno, "Qurtuba: Some Critical Considerations of the Caliphate of Cordoba and the Myth of *Convivencia*," in *Reflections on Qurtuba in the 21st Century*, edited by Javier Rosón (Madrid: Casa Árabe, 2013), pp. 112, 126.

110. Maya Soifer, "Beyond *Convivencia*: Critical Reflections on the Historiography of Interfaith Relations in Christian Spain," *Journal of Medieval Iberian Studies* 1, no. 1 (2009), pp. 27, 29.

111. Kenneth Baxter Wolf. 2007. "Convivencia and the 'Ornament of the World.'" Paper prepared for Annual Meeting of the Southeastern Medieval Association, Wofford College, October 5; and Kenneth Baxter Wolf, "'Convivencia' in Medieval Spain: A Brief History of an Idea," *Religion Compass* 3, no. 1 (2009), pp. 72–85.

112. Ann Christys, *Christians in al-Andalus: 711–1000* (Abingdon, U.K.: Routledge, 2002), p. 94.

113. Wolf, "Convivencia and the Ornament of the World," pp. 3, 17, 18, 26–27.

114. Fletcher, *Moorish Spain*, pp. 172–73.

115. David Nirenberg, *Communities of Violence: Persecution of Minorities in the Middle Ages* (Princeton University Press, 1996), p. 9.

116. Ibid., p. 7.

117. Mark R. Cohen, *Under Crescent and Cross: The Jews in the Middle Ages* (Princeton University Press, 1994), pp. 3, 9.

118. Yitzhak Baer, *A History of the Jews in Christian Spain: From the Age of Reconquest to the Fourteenth Century*, vol. 1 (Philadelphia: Jewish Publication Society of America, 1961), p. 37.

119. Aaron W. Hughes, "The 'Golden Age' of Muslim Spain: Religious Identity and the Invention of a Tradition in Modern Jewish Studies," in *Historicizing 'Tradition' in the Study of Religion,* edited by Steven Engler and Gregory P. Grieve (Berlin: Walter de Gruyter, 2005), pp. 66–67.

120. Baer, *A History of the Jews in Christian Spain*, p. 38.

121. Hughes, "The 'Golden Age' of Muslim Spain," p. 67.

122. Vincent Barletta, editor's introduction to Francisco Núñez Muley, *A Memorandum for the President of the Royal Audiencia and Chancery Court of the City and Kingdom of Granada*, edited and translated by Vincent Barletta (University of Chicago Press, 2007), p. 49; and Giles Tremlett, "Welcome to Moorishland," foreword to *In the Light of Medieval Spain: Islam, the West, and the Relevance of the Past,* edited by Simon R. Doubleday and David Coleman (New York: Palgrave Macmillan, 2008), p. xvii.

123. Charles Hirschkind, "The Contemporary Afterlife of Moorish Spain," in *Islam and Public Controversy in Europe,* edited by Nilüfer Göle (Farnham, Surrey, U.K.: Ashgate, 2013), p. 227.

124. Darío Fernández-Morera, "Shock and Awe, Eighth-Century Style: The Muslim Conquest of Spain," *Modern Age,* Winter 2016, digital edition.

125. Darío Fernández-Morera, *The Myth of the Andalusian Paradise: Muslims, Christians, and Jews under Islamic Rule in Medieval Spain* (Wilmington, Del.: ISI Books, 2016), pp. 81–82.

126. Darío Fernández-Morera, "The Myth of the Andalusian Paradise," *Intercollegiate Review* 41, no. 2 (2006), p. 29.

127. Jacob Burckhardt, *The Civilization of the Renaissance in Italy,* vol. 1 (New York: Harper, 1958), p. 24.

128. Van Cleve, *The Emperor Frederick II of Hohenstaufen*, p. 531.

129. Einstein, *Emperor Frederick II*, p. 182.

130. Van Cleve, *The Emperor Frederick II of Hohenstaufen*, pp. 336, 539.

131. Kantorowicz, *Frederick the Second, 1194–1250*, p. 345.

132. Abulafia, *Frederick II*, p. 439.

133. Abulafia, "Ethnic Variety and Its Implications," p. 213.

134. Abulafia, *Frederick II*, pp. 4, 146, 148, 246, 252, 438.

## Chapter Four

1. David Gilmour, *Curzon: Imperial Statesman* (New York: Farrar, Straus and Giroux, 2003), p. 343.

2. Douglas Porch, *The March to the Marne: The French Army, 1871–1914* (Cambridge University Press, 1981), p. 144.

3. *Encyclopedia of Africa*, vol. 1, edited by Kwame Anthony Appiah and Henry Louis Gates Jr. (Oxford University Press, 2010), p. 90.

4. Eve Darian-Smith, *Religion, Race, Rights: Landmarks in the History of Modern Anglo-American Law* (Oxford, U.K.: Hart Publishing, 2010), p. 42.

5. Andy McSmith, "Khadim Hussain: Former Lord Mayor of Bradford Suspended by Labour Party over Anti-Semitism," *The Independent*, March 23, 2016.

6. Elsa Vigoureux, "Azouz Begag, ex-ministre: 'Il fallait refuser la sémantique guerrière de Sarkozy,'" *L'Obs*, October 26, 2015.

7. Edmond Rostand, *Cyrano de Bergerac*, translated by Brian Hooker (New York: Holt, Rinehart and Winston, 1937), pp. 98–99.

8. Kim Willsher, "French Women's Rights Minister Accused of Racism over Term 'Negro,'" *The Guardian*, March 30, 2016.

9. Sylvain Cypel, "A French Clown's Hateful Gesture," *New York Times*, January 23, 2014.

10. John Lichfield, "Marseille: Europe's Most Dangerous Place to be Young," *The Independent*, September 23, 2012.

11. Madelaine Hron, *Translating Pain: Immigrant Suffering in Literature and Culture* (University of Toronto Press, 2009), p. 99.

## Chapter Five

1. Ulf Brunnbauer, "The Perception of Muslims in Bulgaria and Greece: Between the 'Self' and the 'Other,'" *Journal of Muslim Minority Affairs* 21, no. 1 (2001), p. 53.

2. Adam LeBor, *A Heart Turned East: Among the Muslims of Europe and America* (New York: St. Martin's, 1997), p. 87.

3. Brunnbauer, "The Perception of Muslims in Bulgaria and Greece," p. 54.

4. Ibid., pp. 42–43.

5. Ibid., pp. 44–45.

6. Vemund Aarbakke, "Pomak Language Usage and the Spell of Nationalism: The Case of the Pomaks in Greece," in *Slavia Islamica: Language, Religion and*

*Identity,* edited by Robert D. Greenberg and Motoki Nomachi (Sapporo, Japan: Slavic Research Center, Hokkaido University, 2012), pp. 159, 172.

7. LeBor, *A Heart Turned East,* p. 90.

8. Cecilie Endresen, "Diverging Images of the Ottoman Legacy in Albania," in *Images of Imperial Legacy: Modern Discourses on the Social and Cultural Impact of Ottoman and Habsburg Rule in Southeast Europe,* edited by Tea Sindbaek and Maximilian Hartmuth (Münster, Ger.: LIT Verlag, 2011), p. 43.

9. Ibid., p. 45.

10. Cecilie Endresen, "The Nation and the Nun: Mother Teresa, Albania's Muslim Majority and the Secular State," *Islam and Christian-Muslim Relations* 26, no. 1 (2015), p. 54; and Endresen, "Diverging Images of the Ottoman Legacy in Albania," pp. 45–46.

11. Michael Smith and Sherif Rizq, "Kosovo's Former Finance Minister Announces New Peacebuilding Initiative," Initiatives of Change, August 3, 2015.

12. "The Mosques of Lithuania," *The Economist,* September 14, 2015.

13. Agata S. Nalborczyk, "The Political Participation of Polish Muslim Tatars—The Result of or the Reason for Integration? From Teutonic Wars to the Danish Cartoons Affair," in *Muslim Political Participation in Europe,* edited by Jørgen S. Nielsen (Edinburgh University Press, 2013), p. 240; and Marek M. Dziekan, "History and Culture of Polish Tatars," in *Muslims in Poland and Eastern Europe: Widening the European Discourse on Islam,* edited by Katarzyna Górak-Sosnowska (University of Warsaw, Faculty of Oriental Studies, 2011), p. 28.

14. Harry Norris, *Islam in the Baltic: Europe's Early Muslim Community* (New York: I. B. Tauris, 2009), p. 31.

15. Katarzyna Jerzak, "Defamation in Exile: Witold Gombrowicz and E. M. Cioran," in *Gombrowicz's Grimaces: Modernism, Gender, Nationality,* edited by Ewa Płonowska Ziarek (State University of New York Press, 1998), p. 185.

16. Nalborczyk, "The Political Participation of Polish Muslim Tatars," pp. 243–44.

17. Tharik Hussain, "The Amazing Survival of the Baltic Muslims," *BBC News,* January 1, 2016.

18. Nalborczyk, "The Political Participation of Polish Muslim Tatars," pp. 246–47.

19. Ryan Schuessler, "Poland's Tatars Feel Uncertain as Anti-Muslim Sentiment Grows," *New York Times,* March 16, 2016.

20. Carol Silverman, *Romani Routes: Cultural Politics and Balkan Music in Diaspora* (Oxford University Press, 2012), p. 9.

21. Nikolia Apostolou, "Breaking News No More: Life for Roma in Greece a Year after 'Maria,'" Open Society Foundations, October 17, 2014.

22. Yaron Matras, *The Romani Gypsies* (Harvard University Press, 2015), p. 164; and Becky Taylor, *Another Darkness, Another Dawn: A History of Gypsies, Roma, and Travellers* (London: Reaktion Books, 2014), p. 36.

23. Noel Malcolm, *Bosnia: A Short History* (New York University Press, 1996), pp. 115–16.

24. Zoltan Barany, *The East European Gypsies: Regime Change, Marginality, and Ethnopolitics* (Cambridge University Press, 2002), pp. 85–86, 92.

25. Taylor, *Another Darkness, Another Dawn*, p. 126.

26. "Destroying Ethnic Identity: The Gypsies of Bulgaria," *Human Rights Watch*, June 1991, p. 8.

27. Tatjana Perić and Martin Demirovski, "Unwanted: The Exodus of Kosovo Roma (1998–2000)," *Cambridge Review of International Affairs* 13, no. 2 (2000), pp. 84–85.

28. Lambros Baltsiotis, "The Muslim Chams of Northwestern Greece: The Grounds for the Expulsion of a 'Nonexistent' Minority Community," *European Journal of Turkish Studies* 12 (2011), p. 5.

29. Eleftheria K. Manta, "The Çams of Albania and the Greek State (1923–1945)," *Journal of Muslim Minority Affairs* 29, no. 4 (2009), p. 528.

30. Robert Elsie and Bejtullah Destani, introduction to *The Cham Albanians of Greece: A Documentary History*, edited by Robert Elsie and Bejtullah Destani, in collaboration with Rudina Jasini (London: I. B. Tauris, 2013), p. xxxiv.

31. Manta, "The Çams of Albania and the Greek State (1923–1945)," p. 533.

32. Owen Pearson, *Albania in Occupation and War: From Fascism to Communism, 1940–1945* (London: I. B. Tauris, 2005), p. 430.

33. Quoted in *The Cham Albanians of Greece*, edited by Elsie and Destani, pp. 391–92.

34. Baltsiotis, "The Muslim Chams of Northwestern Greece," pp. 17–19.

## Chapter Six

1. Maïa de la Baume, "More in France Are Turning to Islam, Challenging a Nation's Idea of Itself," *New York Times*, February 3, 2013.

2. Richard Peppiatt, "Women & Islam: The Rise and Rise of the Convert," *The Independent (London)*, November 6, 2011.

3. Kristiane Backer, *From MTV to Mecca: How Islam Inspired My Life* (London: Arcadia, 2012), pp. 48–49.

4. Ibid., p. 123.

5. "Why Danish Abdul Wahid Pedersen Become Muslim," YouTube video, posted by "ask4gain," March 20, 2013.

## Chapter Seven

1. Máttis Kantor, *Codex Judaica: Chronological Index of Jewish History* (New York: Zichron Press, 2005), p. 204.

2. *Readings in Medieval History*, vol. 2, edited by Patrick J. Geary (University of Toronto Press, 2016), pp. 363–65.

3. Lisa Silverman, *Becoming Austrians: Jews and Culture between the World Wars* (Oxford University Press, 2012), p. 248, note 22.

4. Robert Reinhold Ergang, *Herder and the Foundations of German Nationalism* (Columbia University Press, 1931), pp. 91, 182.

5. Sonia Sikka, *Herder on Humanity and Cultural Difference: Enlightened Relativism* (Cambridge University Press, 2011), p. 246.

6. Ergang, *Herder and the Foundations of German Nationalism*, p. 92.

7. Pierre James, *The Murderous Paradise: German Nationalism and the Holocaust* (Westport, Conn.: Praeger, 2001), pp. 94–95.

8. Robert Michael, *Holy Hatred: Christianity, Antisemitism, and the Holocaust* (New York: Palgrave Macmillan, 2006), p. 110.

9. George L. Mosse, *Toward the Final Solution: A History of European Racism* (New York: Howard Fertig 1985), pp. 129, 131–32; and Fritz Stern, *The Politics of Cultural Despair: A Study in the Rise of the Germanic Ideology* (University of California Press, 1961), pp. 40–42.

10. Mosse, *Toward the Final Solution*, p. 131.

11. Robert Irwin, *Dangerous Knowledge: Orientalism and Its Discontents* (Woodstock, N.Y.: Overlook Press, 2006), pp. 153, 169.

12. Michael C. Legaspi, *The Death of Scripture and the Rise of Biblical Studies* (Oxford University Press, 2010), p. 6.

13. Jonathan M. Hess, *Germans, Jews and the Claims of Modernity* (Yale University Press, 2002), p. 70.

14. Ibid., pp. 69–70, 78.

15. Ibid., pp. 59–60.

16. Jonathan M. Hess, "Jewish Emancipation and the Politics of Race," in *The German Invention of Race*, edited by Sara Eigen and Mark Larrimore (State University of New York Press, 2006), p. 206.

17. Martin Luther, *Martin Luther, the Bible, and the Jewish People: A Reader*, edited by Brooks Schramm and Kirsi I. Stjerna (Minneapolis, Minn.: Fortress Press, 2012), p. 165; and James M. Stayer, *Martin Luther, German Saviour: German Evangelical Theological Factions and the Interpretation of Luther, 1917–1933* (McGill-Queen's University Press, 2000), p. 117.

18. Paul Lawrence Rose, *German Question/Jewish Question: Revolutionary Antisemitism in Germany from Kant to Wagner* (Princeton University Press, 1990), p. 7.

19. Hess, *Germans, Jews and the Claims of Modernity*, pp. 53, 173, 174, 177, 197.

20. Louis L. Snyder, *German Nationalism: The Tragedy of a People* (Port Washington, N.Y.: Kennikat Press, 1969), p. 130.

21. Abram Leon Sachar, *A History of the Jews* (New York: Alfred A. Knopf, 1965), p. 276.

22. Hess, *Germans, Jews and the Claims of Modernity*, p. 141.

23. Peter Paret, *Clausewitz and the State: The Man, His Theories, and His Times* (Princeton University Press, 1985), p. 212.

24. Eric Ehrenreich, *The Nazi Ancestral Proof: Genealogy, Racial Science, and the Final Solution* (Indiana University Press, 2007), p. 28.

25. James, *The Murderous Paradise*, p. 142.

26. Snyder, *German Nationalism*, p. 172.

27. James, *The Murderous Paradise*, pp. 139, 141.

28. Ibid., p. 142; and Jonathan Carr, *The Wagner Clan: The Saga of Germany's Most Illustrious and Infamous Family* (New York: Atlantic Monthly Press, 2007), p. 71.

29. R. K. Hudson, "Anti-Semitism Rising," *Jerusalem Post*, February 22, 2016; and James, *The Murderous Paradise*, p. 156.

30. James, *The Murderous Paradise*, pp. 158–59.

31. Stern, *The Politics of Cultural Despair*, pp. 62, 87.

32. James, *The Murderous Paradise*, p. 147.

33. Stern, *The Politics of Cultural Despair*, pp. 62–63.

34. James, *The Murderous Paradise*, p. 146.

35. Mosse, *Toward the Final Solution*, p. 97.

36. Stern, *The Politics of Cultural Despair*, p. 141.

37. James, *The Murderous Paradise*, pp. 150–51.

38. Heather Pringle, *The Master Plan: Himmler's Scholars and the Holocaust* (New York: Hyperion, 2006), p. 4.

39. Felix Kersten, *The Kersten Memoirs: 1940–1945*, translated by Constantine Fitzgibbon and James Oliver (New York: Macmillan, 1957), p. 36.

40. Elisabeth Oxfeldt, *Nordic Orientalism: Paris and the Cosmopolitan Imagination, 1800–1900* (Copenhagen: Museum Tusculanum Press, 2005), pp. 62–63.

41. Martin Schwarz Lausten, *Jews and Christians in Denmark: From the Middle Ages to Recent Times, ca. 1100–1948* (Leiden, Neth.: Brill, 2015), p. 184.

42. Oxfeldt, *Nordic Orientalism*, p. 63.

43. James, *The Murderous Paradise*, pp. 118–19.

44. Heinrich Heine, *Religion and Philosophy in Germany*, translated by John Snodgrass (State University of New York Press, 1986), p. 160.

45. Na'ama Rokem, *Prosaic Conditions: Heinrich Heine and the Spaces of Zionist Literature* (Northwestern University Press, 2013), p. xi.

46. David Levering Lewis, *God's Crucible: Islam and the Making of Europe, 570–1215* (New York: W. W. Norton, 2008), pp. 114–16, 126.

47. *The Visigothic Code*, edited and translated by S. P. Scott (Boston: The Boston Book Company, 1910), p. xv.

48. Sean McMeekin, *The Berlin-Baghdad Express: The Ottoman Empire and Germany's Bid for World Power* (Harvard University Press, 2010), pp. 15–16.

49. Donald M. McKale, *War by Revolution: Germany and Great Britain in the Middle East in the Era of World War I* (Kent State University Press, 1998), p. 9.

50. John C. G. Röhl, *The Kaiser and His Court: Wilhelm II and the Government of Germany*, translated by Terence F. Cole (Cambridge University Press, 1994), pp. 210–11.

51. New York University Center for Dialogues. 2009. "Cultural Awareness in a Time of Crisis." Paper prepared for conference, Bridging the Divide Between the United States and the Muslim World Through Arts and Ideas: Possibilities and Limitations, New York University, June 6–9, p. 9.

52. F. W. Buckler, *Harunu'l-Rashid and Charles the Great* (Cambridge, Mass.: The Mediaeval Academy of America, 1931), p. 35.

53. *Book of Gifts and Rarities*, translated by Ghāda al-Ḥijjāwī al-Qaddūmī (Harvard University Press, 1996), pp. 93–94.

54. Maxime Rodinson, *Europe and the Mystique of Islam*, translated by Roger Veinus (London: I. B. Tauris, 2006), p. 26.

55. Caroline Finkel, *Osman's Dream: The History of the Ottoman Empire, 1300–1923* (New York: Basic Books, 2005), p. 385; and Giles MacDonogh, *Frederick the Great: A Life in Deed and Letters* (New York: St. Martin's Griffin, 1999), p. 305.

56. Joel S. Fetzer and J. Christopher Soper, *Muslims and the State in Britain, France, and Germany* (Cambridge University Press, 2005), p. 99.

57. MacDonogh, *Frederick the Great*, p. 327.

58. Ursula Spuler-Stegemann, "Allah and the Occident: How Islam Came to Germany," *Der Spiegel*, June 16, 2008.

59. Robert Giddings, "Delusive Seduction: Pride, Pomp, Circumstance and Military Music," in *Popular Imperialism and the Military: 1850–1950*, edited by John M. MacKenzie (Manchester University Press, 1992), p. 39.

60. Donald D. Stone, "The Theme of Forgiveness in Western Culture," in *The Concept of Humanity in an Age of Globalization*, edited by Zhang Longxi (National Taiwan University Press, 2012), p. 144.

61. Fred Dallmayr, *Dialogue among Civilizations: Some Exemplary Voices* (New York: Palgrave Macmillan, 2002), pp. 152–54.

62. Katharina Mommsen, "Goethe's Relationship to Islam," *The Muslim* 4, no. 3 (1967), p. 12.

63. Dallmayr, *Dialogue among Civilizations*, p. 152.

64. Nebahat Avcıoğlu, *'Turquerie' and the Politics of Representation, 1728–1876* (Farnham, Surrey, U.K.: Ashgate, 2011), pp. 261–62.

65. Joachim Köhler, *Richard Wagner: The Last of the Titans*, translated by Stewart Spencer (Yale University Press, 2004), p. 248.

66. Richard Wagner, *Richard Wagner's Prose Works*, vol. 8, *Posthumous, Etc.*, translated by William Ashton Ellis (London: Kegan Paul, Trench, Trübner, and Co., 1899), pp. 252, 261.

67. Stefan Ihrig, *Atatürk in the Nazi Imagination* (Harvard University Press, 2014), pp. 22, 33, 46, 48, 154, 155, 172.

68. Ibid., pp. 71, 115–16, 187.

69. David Motadel, *Islam and Nazi Germany's War* (Harvard University Press, 2014), pp. 63, 66, 313.

70. Ibid., p. 65; and Adolf Hitler, *Hitler's Table Talk, 1941–1944: His Private Conversations*, translated by Norman Cameron and R. H. Stevens (London: Enigma Books, 2008), p. 504.

71. Ihrig, *Atatürk in the Nazi Imagination*, p. 104; and Motadel, *Islam and Nazi Germany's War*, pp. 61–62.

72. Motadel, *Islam and Nazi Germany's War*, pp. 61–63.

73. Kersten, *The Kersten Memoirs*, p. 221.

74. Motadel, *Islam and Nazi Germany's War*, pp. 56, 58, 61.

75. Ihrig, *Atatürk in the Nazi Imagination*, p. 128.

76. Motadel, *Islam and Nazi Germany's War*, pp. 58–60, 70.

77. *A History of Jewish-Muslim Relations: From the Origins to the Present Day*, translated by Jane Marie Todd and Michael B. Smith, edited by Abdelwahab Meddeb and Benjamin Stora (Princeton University Press, 2013), p. 352.

78. *The Columbia World Dictionary of Islamism*, edited by Olivier Roy, Antoine Sfeir, and John King (Columbia University Press, 2007), p. 88.

79. Christian Leitz, *Nazi Foreign Policy, 1933–1941: The Road to Global War* (New York: Routledge, 2004), p. 126.

80. Motadel, *Islam and Nazi Germany's War*, pp. 78, 103, 106, 110, 267, 301–02, 303.

81. Meddeb and Stora, *A History of Jewish-Muslim Relations*, p. 352.

82. Motadel, *Islam and Nazi Germany's War*, pp. 124–25, 140, 152.

83. Kersten, *The Kersten Memoirs*, p. 259.

84. Motadel, *Islam and Nazi Germany's War*, pp. 59, 208

85. Ibid., pp. 219, 245.

86. Ibid., pp. 222, 225–26, 313, 319–20.

87. Horst Junginger, "Sigrid Hunke (1913–1999): Europe's New Religion and its Old Stereotypes," in *Antisemitismus, Paganismus, Völkische Religion*, edited by Hubert Cancik and Uwe Puschner (Munich: K. G. Saur, 2004), p. 151.

88. Felix Wiedemann, "The North, the Desert, and the Near East: Ludwig Ferdinand Clauß and the Racial Cartography of the Near East," *Studies in Ethnicity and Nationalism* 12, no. 2 (2012), pp. 329–36.

89. Junginger, "Sigrid Hunke (1913–1999)," p. 155.

90. Karla Poewe, *New Religions and the Nazis* (Abingdon, U.K.: Routledge, 2006), pp. 148–49.

91. Junginger, "Sigrid Hunke (1913–1999), p. 156.

92. Winston S. Churchill, *The Hinge of Fate* (Boston: Houghton Mifflin, 1950), p. 209.

93. Daniel Marston, *The Indian Army and the End of the Raj* (Cambridge University Press, 2014), p. 59.

94. Kenneth M. Lewan, "How West Germany Helped to Build Israel," *Journal of Palestine Studies* 4, no. 4 (1975), pp. 41–43.

95. Kerry Bolton, *Zionism, Islam, and the West* (London: Black House Publishing, 2015), p. 40.

96. Robert S. Wistrich, *Laboratory for World Destruction: Germans and Jews in Central Europe* (University of Nebraska Press, 2007), p. 127.

97. Theodor Herzl, *The Jews' State: A Critical English Translation*, translated by Henk Overberg (Lanham, Md.: Rowman and Littlefield, 1997), p. 88; and Uriel Abulof, *The Mortality and Morality of Nations* (Cambridge University Press, 2015), p. 155.

98. Nur Masalha, *The Zionist Bible: Biblical Precedent, Colonialism and the Erasure of Memory* (Abingdon, U.K.: Routledge, 2014), p. 31; and Joseph Adler, *The Herzl Paradox: Political, Social and Economic Theories of a Realist* (New York: Hadrian Press, 1962), p. 65.

99. Michael Brenner, *A Short History of the Jews*, translated by Jeremiah Riemer (Princeton University Press, 2010), p. 85.

100. Minou Reeves, *Muhammad in Europe*, with a biographical contribution by P. J. Stewart (New York University Press, 2000), p. 228.

101. Avigdor Levy, *The Sephardim in the Ottoman Empire* (Princeton, N.J.: Darwin Press, 1992), p. 76; and Elli Kohen, *History of the Turkish Jews and Sephardim: Memories of a Past Golden Age* (Lanham, Md.: University Press of America, 2007), pp. 18–19.

102. Minna Rozen, *A History of the Jewish Community in Istanbul: The Formative Years, 1453–1566* (Leiden, Neth.: Brill, 2010), pp. 66–67.

103. Ronit Lentin, *Co-memory and Melancholia: Israelis Memorialising the Palestinian Nakba* (Manchester University Press, 2010), pp. 46–47.

104. Sacks quoted in Stephen Bates, "Fresh Attacks on Chief Rabbi's Book: Sacks Fails in Moves to Mollify Orthodox Leaders," *The Guardian*, October 17, 2002.

## Chapter Eight

1. Hastings Donnan and Thomas M. Wilson, *Borders: Frontiers of Identity, Nation and State* (Oxford, U.K.: Berg, 1999), p. 67.

2. Nima Elbagir and Tim Lister, "Europe's Newest Front Line Against ISIS: A Spanish Town in North Africa," *CNN*, September 30, 2014; and Jack Moore, "Spain Dismantles Suspected ISIS Cell in Arrests Across the Country," *Newsweek*, February 8, 2016.

3. Secunder Kermani, "Brussels Attacks: Molenbeek's Gangster Jihadists," *BBC News*, March 24, 2016.

4. Ibid.

5. Chika Unigwe, "The Near-Impossibility of Assimilation in Belgium," *New York Times*, November 25, 2015.

6. Neil MacFarquhar, "Right-Wing Groups Find a Haven, for a Day, in Russia," *New York Times*, March 22, 2015.

7. "Will Trump Use Pizzagate 'Nuke' to Destroy Democrats? VIDEO," Knights Templar International, Facebook, December 11, 2016; shared post from "Patriot News Agency."

8. Mike McIntire, "How a Putin Fan Overseas Pushed Pro-Trump Propaganda to Americans," *New York Times*, December 17, 2016.

9. Erika Benke, "The Village Aiming to Create a White Utopia," *BBC News*, February 7, 2017.

10. Catarina Kinnvall and Paul Nesbitt-Larking, *The Political Psychology of Globalization: Muslims in the West* (Oxford University Press, 2011), p. 140.

11. Sheila L. Croucher, *Globalization and Belonging: The Politics of Identity in a Changing World* (Oxford, U.K.: Rowman and Littlefield, 2004), p. 105.

12. Andrew Brown, "Copenhagen Attacks: Scandinavians Value Free Speech, but Now They Need to Be Practical," *The Guardian*, February 15, 2015.

13. Hugh Eakin, "Liberal, Harsh Denmark," *New York Review of Books*, March 10, 2016.

14. Zeyno Baran with Emmet Tuohy, *Citizen Islam: The Future of Muslim Integration in the West* (New York: Continuum, 2011), p. 86.

15. David M. Hart, *Tribe and Society in Rural Morocco* (London: Routledge, 2014), p. 92.

16. Andrew Rettman, "Belgian Radicals: Bring Me Your Unschooled, Your Jobless," *EU Observer*, November 23, 2015.

17. James Minahan, *Encyclopedia of the Stateless Nations: Ethnic and National Groups Around the World*, vol. 2: *D–K* (Westport, Conn.: Greenwood Press, 2002), p. 866.

18. Manus I. Midlarsky, *Origins of Political Extremism: Mass Violence in the Twentieth Century and Beyond* (Cambridge University Press, 2011), p. 65.

19. Andrea Elliott, "Where Boys Grow Up to Be Jihadis," *New York Times*, November 25, 2007.

20. This section refers to posts that appeared on Aqsa Mahmood's Tumblr blog ("Umm Layth," fa-tubalilghuraba.tumblr.com) and Twitter account (@UmmLayth) between January 2013 and June 2015. Both accounts have been taken offline.

21. Jonathan Laurence, *The Emancipation of Europe's Muslims: The State's Role in Minority Integration* (Princeton University Press, 2012), p. 144; and Jytte Klausen, *The Islamic Challenge: Politics and Religion in Western Europe* (Oxford University Press, 2005), pp. 114, 116.

## Chapter Nine

1. Ineke van der Valk, *Islamofobie en discriminatie* (Utrecht, Neth.: Pallas Publications, 2012), p. 56.

2. "Report by Nils Muižnieks, Commissioner for Human Rights of the Council of Europe Following His Visit to Hungary From 1 to 4 July 2014," Commissioner for Human Rights, December 16, 2014.

3. Patrick Wintour, "Hungary to Detain All Asylum Seekers in Container Camps," *The Guardian*, March 7, 2017.

4. Christian Davies, "The Conspiracy Theorists Who Have Taken Over Poland," *The Guardian*, February 16, 2016.

5. Rick Lyman, "Once in the Shadows, Europe's Neo-Fascists Are Reemerging," *New York Times*, March 19, 2017.

6. Emilian Kavalski, "The Grass Was Always Greener in the Past: Re-Nationalizing Bulgaria's Return to Europe," in *Multiplicity of Nationalism in Contemporary Europe*, edited by Ireneusz Paweł Karolewski and Andrzej Marcin Suszycki (Lanham, Md.: Lexington Books, 2010), p. 219.

7. James Frusetta and Anca Glont, "Interwar Fascism and the Post-1989 Radical Right: Ideology, Opportunism and Historical Legacy in Bulgaria and Romania," in *Historical Legacies and the Radical Right in Post–Cold War Central and Eastern Europe*, edited by Michael Minkenberg (Stuttgart, Ger.: Ibidem-Verlag, 2014), p. 170; and "Bulgaria Genocide Day Idea Gets PM Borisov's Backing," *Sofia News Agency*, August 6, 2009.

8. Krassimir Kanev, "How Should We Think of 'Attack'?" *Obektiv*, May–July 2005.

9. Maximilian Popp, "An Inside Look at EU's Shameful Immigration Policy," *Der Spiegel*, September 11, 2014.

10. Jerry Brotton, *The Sultan and the Queen: The Untold Story of Elizabeth and Islam* (New York: Viking, 2016), p. 5.

11. Stephen Murray, *Plotting Gothic* (University of Chicago Press, 2014), p. 263, note 16.

12. Salim T. S. Al-Hassani, ed., *1001 Inventions: The Enduring Legacy of Muslim Civilization* (Washington, D.C.: National Geographic, 2012), p. 70.

13. Phyllis Ghim-Lian Chew, *Emergent Lingua Francas and World Orders: The Politics and Place of English as a World Language* (New York: Routledge, 2009), p. 88.

14. Al-Hassani, ed., *1001 Inventions*, p. 70.

15. Gary Waldman, *Introduction to Light: The Physics of Light, Vision, and Color* (Mineola, N.Y.: Dover, 2002), p. 5.

16. Logan Clendening, *Source Book of Medical History* (New York: Dover Publications, 1960), p. 88.

17. James C. Livingston, *Modern Christian Thought*, vol. 1: *The Enlightenment and the Nineteenth Century* (Minneapolis, Minn.: Fortress Press, 2006), p. 343.

18. D. J. Kennedy, *St. Thomas Aquinas and Medieval Philosophy* (New York: Encyclopedia Press, 1919), p. 73.

19. Nancy Marie Brown, *The Abacus and the Cross: The Story of the Pope Who Brought the Light of Science to the Dark Ages* (New York: Basic Books, 2010), pp. 5–6, 52.

20. Miguel Asin Palacios, *Islam and the Divine Comedy*, translated by Harold Sutherland (Abingdon, U.K.: Routledge, 2008), pp. 36–37.

21. Suzanne Conklin Akbari, *Idols in the East: European Representations of Islam and the Orient, 1100–1450* (Cornell University Press, 2009), p. 263.

22. Palacios, *Islam and the Divine Comedy*, pp. 8–9, 172.

23. Julia Bolton Holloway, "The Road Through Roncesvalles: Alfonsine Formation of Brunetto Latini and Dante—Diplomacy and Literature" in *Emperor of Culture: Alfonso X the Learned of Castile and His Thirteenth-Century Renaissance*, edited by Robert I. Burns (University of Pennsylvania Press, 1990), pp. 113, 123.

24. Sherwin B. Nuland, *Leonardo Da Vinci* (New York: Lipper/Penguin, 2005), pp. 87, 136.

25. *The Literary Works of Leonardo Da Vinci*, vol. 2, compiled and edited from the original manuscripts, edited by Jean Paul Richter (London: Sampson Low, Marston, Searle & Rivington, 1883), pp. 385–89.

26. Avner Ben-Zaken, *Cross-Cultural Scientific Exchanges in the Eastern Mediterranean, 1560–1660* (Johns Hopkins University Press, 2010), p. 209, note 15.

27. Anna Contadini, "Artistic Contacts: Current Scholarship and Future Tasks," in *Islam and the Italian Renaissance*, edited by Charles Burnett and Anna Contadini (London: Warburg Institute, University of London, 1999), p. 9.

28. Michael Snodin and Maurice Howard, *Ornament: A Social History Since 1450* (Yale University Press, 1996), p. 192.

29. Jerry D. Cavin, *The Amateur Astronomer's Guide to the Deep-Sky Catalogs* (New York: Springer, 2012), p. 43.

30. James Evans, *The History and Practice of Ancient Astronomy* (Oxford University Press, 1998), p. 43.

31. Michael Lessnoff, "Islam, Modernity and Science," in *Ernest Gellner and Contemporary Social Thought*, edited by Siniša Malešević and Mark Haugaard (Cambridge University Press, 2007), pp. 204–05.

32. Seyyed Hossein Nasr, *Islamic Science: An Illustrated Study* (London: World of Islam Festival Trust, 1976), p. 20.

33. George Saliba quoted in Dick Teresi, *Lost Discoveries: The Ancient Roots of Modern Science—from the Babylonians to the Maya* (New York: Simon and Schuster, 2002), p. 4.

34. Lessnoff, "Islam, Modernity, and Science," p. 205.

35. F. Jamil Ragep, "Ibn al-Shāṭir and Copernicus: The Uppsala Notes Revisited," *Journal for the History of Astronomy* 47, no. 4 (2016), p. 395.

36. Henrik Lagerlund, "The Mind/Body Problem and Late Medieval Conceptions of the Soul," introduction to *Forming the Mind: Essays on the Internal Senses and the Mind/Body Problem from Avicenna to the Medical Enlightenment*, edited by Henrik Lagerlund (Dordrecht, Ger.: Springer, 2007), p. 1.

37. Laurel C. Schneider, "Setting the Context: A Brief History of Science by a Sympathetic Theologian," in *Adam, Eve, and the Genome: The Human Genome Project and Theology*, edited by Susan Brooks Thistlethwaite (Minneapolis, Minn.: Fortress Press, 2003), p. 28.

38. William Turner, "Avicenna," in *The Catholic Encyclopedia*, vol. 2, edited by Charles G. Herbermann, et al. (New York: Robert Appleton Company, 1907), p. 157.

39. Lukas Muehlethaler, "Ibn Kammūna (d. 683/1284) on the Argument of the Flying Man in Avicenna's *Ishārāt* and al-Suhrawardī's *Talwīḥāt*," in *Avicenna and His Legacy: A Golden Age of Science and Philosophy*, edited by Y. Tzvi Langermann (Turnhout, Belg.: Brepols, 2009), p. 180.

40. Ahmed Alwishah, "Ibn Sīnā on Floating Man Arguments," *Journal of Islamic Philosophy* 9 (2013), p. 59.

41. Henrik Lagerlund, introduction to *Representation and Objects of Thought in Medieval Philosophy*, edited by Henrik Lagerlund (Hampshire, U.K.: Ashgate, 2007), p. 3.

42. Henrik Lagerlund, "The Terminological and Conceptual Roots of Representation in the Soul in Late Ancient and Medieval Philosophy," in *Representation and Objects of Thought in Medieval Philosophy*, p. 20; and Kimbell Kornu, "'Know Thyself': The Soul of Anatomical Dissection," in *The Resounding Soul: Reflections on the Metaphysics and Vivacity of the Human Person*, edited by Eric Austin Lee and Samuel Kimbriel (Cambridge, U.K.: James Clarke, 2016), p. 103.

43. Samar Attar, *The Vital Roots of European Enlightenment: Ibn Tufayl's Influence on Modern Western Thought* (Lanham, Md.: Lexington Books, 2007), pp. 21–27.

44. Stanislaw Golachowski, *Szymanowski: His Life and Times*, translated from Polish to German by Henryk P. Anders, translated from German to English by Christa Ahrens (Neptune City, N.J.: Paganiniana Publications, 1986), p. 27.

45. Ina Baghdiantz McCabe, *Orientalism in Early Modern France: Eurasian Trade, Exoticism and the Ancien Régime* (Oxford, U.K.: Berg, 2008), p. 37.

46. Halil Inalcik, "The Turkish Impact on the Development of Modern Europe," in *The Ottoman State and Its Place in World History*, edited by Kemal H. Karpat (Leiden, Neth.: E. J. Brill, 1974), p. 52.

47. Roger Bigelow Merriman, *Suleiman the Magnificent 1520–1566* (Harvard University Press, 1944), p. 141.

48. Katharine J. Lualdi, *Sources of the Making of the West: Peoples and Cultures, vol. I, To 1740* (Boston: Bedford/St. Martin's, 2009), p. 322.

49. Richard Bonney, "'God, Fatherland and Freedom': Rethinking Pluralism in Hungary in the Era of Partition and Rebellion, 1526–1711," in *Persecution and Pluralism: Calvinists and Religious Minorities in Early Modern Europe 1550–1700*, edited by Richard Bonney and D. J. B. Trim (Bern: Peter Lang, 2006), p. 95.

50. Noel Malcolm, "Positive Views of Islam and of Ottoman Rule in the Sixteenth Century: The Case of Jean Bodin," in *The Renaissance and the Ottoman World*, edited by Anna Contadini and Claire Norton (Farnham, Surrey, U.K.: Ashgate, 2013), p. 212.

51. Brotton, *The Sultan and the Queen*, pp. 4, 118, 138.

52. Ian Almond, *Two Faiths, One Banner: When Muslims Marched with Christians across Europe's Battlegrounds* (Harvard University Press, 2009), p. 174.

53. Everett Jenkins, Jr., *The Muslim Diaspora: A Comprehensive Chronology of the Spread of Islam in Asia, Africa, Europe and the Americas, vol. 2, 1500–1799* (Jefferson, N.C.: McFarland and Company, 2000), p. 205.

54. Inalcik, "The Turkish Impact on the Development of Modern Europe," p. 53.

55. Ibid.

56. William Montgomery Watt, "A Contemporary Spokesman for Islam," in *Recueil d'articles offert à Maurice Borrmans par ses collègues et amis,* edited by Maurice Borrmans (Rome: PISAI, 1996), pp. 273, 276.

57. "Islamunterricht und Islamische Theologie/Präventionsprojekte gegen Islamismus," WD 8: Umwelt, Naturschutz, Reaktorsicherheit, Bildung und Forschung, Deutscher Bundestag—Wissenschaftliche Dienste, March 16, 2016; and Riem Spielhaus, "Germany," in *The Oxford Handbook of European Islam*, edited by Jocelyne Cesari (Oxford University Press, 2015), pp. 138–39.

# INDEX